T0213052

Communications
in Computer and Information Science 764

Commenced Publication in 2007
Founding and Former Series Editors:
Alfredo Cuzzocrea, Xiaoyong Du, Orhun Kara, Ting Liu, Dominik Ślęzak,
and Xiaokang Yang

Editorial Board

Simone Diniz Junqueira Barbosa
*Pontifical Catholic University of Rio de Janeiro (PUC-Rio),
Rio de Janeiro, Brazil*
Phoebe Chen
La Trobe University, Melbourne, Australia
Joaquim Filipe
Polytechnic Institute of Setúbal, Setúbal, Portugal
Igor Kotenko
*St. Petersburg Institute for Informatics and Automation of the Russian
Academy of Sciences, St. Petersburg, Russia*
Krishna M. Sivalingam
Indian Institute of Technology Madras, Chennai, India
Takashi Washio
Osaka University, Osaka, Japan
Junsong Yuan
Nanyang Technological University, Singapore, Singapore
Lizhu Zhou
Tsinghua University, Beijing, China

More information about this series at http://www.springer.com/series/7899

Mohammad S. Obaidat (Ed.)

E-Business and Telecommunications

13th International Joint Conference, ICETE 2016
Lisbon, Portugal, July 26–28, 2016
Revised Selected Papers

 Springer

Editor
Mohammad S. Obaidat
Department of Computer and Information
  Science
Fordham University
Bronx, NY
USA

ISSN 1865-0929   ISSN 1865-0937 (electronic)
Communications in Computer and Information Science
ISBN 978-3-319-67875-7   ISBN 978-3-319-67876-4 (eBook)
https://doi.org/10.1007/978-3-319-67876-4

Library of Congress Control Number: 2017955725

© Springer International Publishing AG 2017
This work is subject to copyright. All rights are reserved by the Publisher, whether the whole or part of the material is concerned, specifically the rights of translation, reprinting, reuse of illustrations, recitation, broadcasting, reproduction on microfilms or in any other physical way, and transmission or information storage and retrieval, electronic adaptation, computer software, or by similar or dissimilar methodology now known or hereafter developed.
The use of general descriptive names, registered names, trademarks, service marks, etc. in this publication does not imply, even in the absence of a specific statement, that such names are exempt from the relevant protective laws and regulations and therefore free for general use.
The publisher, the authors and the editors are safe to assume that the advice and information in this book are believed to be true and accurate at the date of publication. Neither the publisher nor the authors or the editors give a warranty, express or implied, with respect to the material contained herein or for any errors or omissions that may have been made. The publisher remains neutral with regard to jurisdictional claims in published maps and institutional affiliations.

Printed on acid-free paper

This Springer imprint is published by Springer Nature
The registered company is Springer International Publishing AG
The registered company address is: Gewerbestrasse 11, 6330 Cham, Switzerland

Preface

The present book includes extended and revised versions of a set of selected papers from the 13th International Joint Conference on e-Business and Telecommunications (ICETE 2016), held in Lisbon, Portugal, during July 26–28, 2016.

ICETE 2016 received 241 paper submissions from 51 countries, of which 14% are included in this book. The papers were selected by the event chairs and their selection is based on a number of criteria including the reviews and suggested comments provided by the Program Committee members, the session chairs' assessments, and also the program chairs' global view of all papers included in the technical program. The authors of selected papers were then invited to submit revised and extended versions of their papers having at least 30% new material.

ICETE 2016 was a joint conference aimed at bringing together researchers, engineers, scientists, and practitioners interested in information and communication technologies, including data communication networking, e-business, optical communication systems, security and cryptography, signal processing and multimedia applications, and wireless networks and mobile systems. These are the main knowledge areas that define the six component conferences, namely: DCNET, ICE-B, OPTICS, SECRYPT, SIGMAP, and WINSYS, which together form the ICETE joint international conference.

The papers selected and included in this book contribute to the understanding of relevant trends of current research in the areas of e-business and telecommunications, including wireless networks and technologies, mobile applications, speech recognition and data protection.

We would like to thank all the authors for their contributions and also the reviewers who helped ensure the quality of this publication. We also hope that you will find this collection of papers an excellent source of inspiration as well as a helpful reference for research in the aforementioned areas.

April 2017   Mohammad S. Obaidat

Organization

Conference Chair

Mohammad S. Obaidat   Fordham University, USA

Program Co-chairs

SIGMAP

Enrique Cabello   Universidad Rey Juan Carlos, Spain

WINSYS

Pascal Lorenz   University of Haute Alsace, France

SECRYPT

Pierangela Samarati   Università degli Studi di Milano, Italy

OPTICS

Panagiotis Sarigiannidis   University of Western Macedonia, Greece

ICE-B

Marten van Sinderen   University of Twente, The Netherlands

DCNET

Christian Callegari   RaSS National Laboratory, CNIT, Italy

SIGMAP Program Committee

Harry Agius   Brunel University, UK
Rajeev Agrawal   North Carolina Agricultural and Technical State
                 University, USA
João Ascenso   Instituto Superior de Engenharia de Lisboa, Portugal
Arvind Bansal   Kent State University, USA
Chidansh Amitkumar Bhatt   FX Palo Alto Laboratory, Inc., USA
Adrian Bors   University of York, UK
Christian Breiteneder   Vienna University of Technology, Austria

Wai-Kuen Cham	The Chinese University of Hong Kong, SAR China
Amitava Chatterjee	Jadavpur University, India
Wei Cheng	Garena Online Pte. Ltd., Singapore
Wei-Ta Chu	National Chung Cheng University, Taiwan
Mark Claypool	Worcester Polytechnic Institute, USA
Norishige Fukushima	Nagoya Institute of Technology, Japan
Jakub Galka	University of Science and Technology, Poland
Gheorghita Ghinea	Brunel University, UK
Seiichi Gohshi	Kogakuin University, Japan
Minglun Gong	Memorial University of Newfoundland, Canada
William Grosky	University of Michigan Dearborn, USA
Jing-Ming Guo	National Taiwan University of Science and Technology, Taiwan
Rajarshi Gupta	University of Calcutta, India
Malka Halgamuge	The University of Melbourne, Australia
Emmanuel Ifeachor	Plymouth University, UK
Lazaros S. Iliadis	Democritus University of Thrace, Greece
Razib Iqbal	Missouri State University, USA
Hao Jiang	Boston College, USA
Li-Wei Kang	National Yunlin University of Science and Technology, Taiwan
Sokratis Katsikas	Norwegian University of Science and Technology, Norway
Markus Koskela	University of Helsinki, Finland
Constantine Kotropoulos	Aristotle University of Thessaloniki, Greece
Konrad Kowalczyk	AGH University of Science and Technology, Poland
Sam Kwong	City University of Hong Kong, Hong Kong, SAR China
Adnane Latif	Cadi Ayyad University, Morocco
Choong-Soo Lee	St. Lawrence University, USA
Zitao Liu	University of Pittsburgh, USA
Martin Lopez-Nores	University of Vigo, Spain
Hong Man	Stevens Institute of Technology, USA
Manuel J. Marin-Jimenez	University of Cordoba, Spain
Daniela Moctezuma	Conacyt (CentroGEO), Mexico
Chamin Morikawa	Morpho, Inc., Japan
Alejandro Murua	University of Montreal, Canada
Hiroshi Nagahashi	Tokyo Institute of Technology, Japan
Ioannis Paliokas	Centre for Research and Technology Hellas, Greece
Peter Quax	Hasselt University, Belgium
Maria Paula Queluz	Instituto Superior Técnico, Instituto de Telecomunicações, Portugal
Luis Alberto Morales Rosales	CONACYT-Universidad Michoacana de San Nicolás de Hidalgo, Mexico
Simone Santini	Universidad Autónoma de Madrid, Spain
Massimo De Santo	Università Degli Studi di Salerno, Italy

Wee Ser	Nanyang Technological University, Singapore
Kaushik Das Sharma	University of Calcutta, India
Li Song	Institute of Image Communication and Network Engineering, Shanghai Jiao Tong University, China
Pei-Yun Tsai	National Central University, Taiwan
Aristeidis Tsitiridis	University Rey Juan Carlos, Spain
Andreas Uhl	University of Salzburg, Austria
Iván Vidal	Universidad Carlos III de Madrid, Spain
Sudanthi Wijewickrama	University of Melbourne, Australia
Sanjeewa Witharana	Max Planck Institute for Solar System Research, Germany
Xin-Shun Xu	Shandong University, China
Kim-hui Yap	Nanyang Technological University, Singapore
Hani Camille Yehia	Universidade Federal de Minas Gerais, Brazil
Yongxin Zhang	Qualcomm R&D, USA
Bartosz Ziolko	AGH University of Science and Technology, Poland

SIGMAP Additional Reviewer

Christian Schönauer	IMS, Austria

WINSYS Program Committee

Ali Abedi	University of Maine, USA
Taufik Abrão	Universidade Estadual de Londrina, Brazil
Ramon Aguero	University of Cantabria, Spain
Andreas Ahrens	Hochschule Wismar, University of Technology Business and Design, Germany
Aydin Akan	Istanbul University, Turkey
Vicente Alarcon-Aquino	Universidad de las Americas Puebla, Mexico
Francisco Barcelo Arroyo	Universitat Politècnica de Catalunya, Spain
Jose M. Barcelo-Ordinas	Universitat Politècnica de Catalunya (UPC), Spain
Bert-Jan van Beijnum	University of Twente, The Netherlands
Marko Beko	Universidade Lusófona de Humanidades e Tecnologias, Portugal
Luis Bernardo	Universidade Nova de Lisboa, Portugal
Raffaele Bolla	University of Genoa, Italy
Dajana Cassioli	Universität L'Aquila, Italy
Llorenç Cerdà-Alabern	Universitat Politècnica de Catalunya, Spain
Gerard Chalhoub	Clermont University, France
James M. Conrad	University of North Carolina at Charlotte, USA
Roberto Corvaja	University of Padova, Italy
Orhan Dagdeviren	Ege University, Turkey
Carl Debono	University of Malta, Malta
Bryan Dixon	California State University, USA
Luis Rizo Dominguez	ITESO Jesuit University of Guadalajara, Mexico

Christos Douligeris	University of Piraeus, Greece
Amit Dvir	BME-HIT, Hungary
George Efthymoglou	University of Piraeus, Greece
Mohammed El-Hajjar	University of Southampton, UK
Jocelyne Elias	Paris Descartes University, France
Ozgur Ergul	Cankaya University, Turkey
Panayotis Fouliras	University of Macedonia, Greece
Antonio Grilo	INESC/IST, Portugal
Stefanos Gritzalis	University of the Aegean, Greece
Alexander Guitton	University Blaise Pascal, France
Aaron Gulliver	University of Victoria, Canada
Cynthia Hood	Illinois Institute of Technology, USA
Chih-Lin Hu	National Central University, Taiwan
Ali Abu-el Humos	Jackson State University, USA
Josep Miquel Jornet	University at Buffalo, USA
Georgios Kambourakis	University of the Aegean, Greece
Ala' Khalifeh	German Jordanian University, Jordan
Charalampos Konstantopoulos	University of Piraeus, Greece
Polychronis Koutsakis	Technical University of Crete, Greece
Gurhan Kucuk	Yeditepe University, Turkey
Chong Hyun Lee	Jeju National University, Korea, Republic of
Heejo Lee	Korea University, Korea, Republic of
Wookwon Lee	Gannon University, USA
Wei Li	University of Sydney, Australia
Elsa Macias López	University of Las Palmas de Gran Canaria, Spain
Chung-Horng Lung	Carleton University, Canada
S. Kami Makki	Lamar University, USA
Reza Malekian	University of Pretoria, South Africa
Pietro Manzoni	Universidad Politecnica de Valencia, Spain
Luis Mendes	Escola Superior de Tecnologia e Gestão de Leiria, Portugal
Marek Natkaniec	AGH University of Science and Technology, Poland
Ioanis Nikolaidis	University of Alberta, Canada
Kenjiro Nishikawa	Kagoshima University, Japan
Cristiano Panazio	Escola Politécnica of São Paulo University, Brazil
Grammati Pantziou	Technological Educational Institution of Athens, Greece
Al-Sakib Khan Pathan	IIUM, Malaysia and Islamic University in Madinah, KSA, Bangladesh
Jordi Pérez-Romero	Universitat Politècnica de Catalunya (UPC), Spain
Jorge Portilla	Universidad Politécnica de Madrid, Spain
Nancy El Rachkidy	LIMOS, France
Julian Reichwald	Cooperative State University Mannheim, Germany
Jörg Roth	University of Applied Sciences Nuremberg, Germany
Angelos Rouskas	University of Piraeus, Greece

Farag Sallabi   United Arab Emirates University, United Arab
                                   Emirates
Manuel García Sánchez   Universidade de Vigo, Spain
Altair Olivo Santin   Pontifical Catholic University of Paraná, Brazil
Nicola Santoro   Carleton University, Canada
Christian Schindelhauer   University of Freiburg, Germany
Winston Khoon Guan Seah   Victoria University of Wellington, New Zealand
Kuei-Ping Shih   Tamkang University, Taiwan
Mujdat Soyturk   Marmara University, Turkey
Srinath Srinivasa   International Institute of Information Technology, India
Alvaro Suárez-Sarmiento   University of Las Palmas de Gran Canaria, Spain
Bulent Tavli   TOBB University of Economics and Technology,
                                   Turkey
Cesar Vargas-Rosales   Tecnologico de Monterrey, Campus Monterrey,
                                   Mexico
Sheng-Shih Wang   Minghsin University of Science and Technology,
                                   Taiwan
Hyoung-Sun Youn   HCAC, University of Hawai'i, USA
Magda El Zarki   University of California Irvine, USA
Shibing Zhang   Nantong University, China
Zhenyun Zhuang   LinkedIn Corp., USA
Dimirios Zorbas   Inria Lille, Nord Europe, France

WINSYS Additional Reviewers

Marcelo Pellenz   Pontifical Catholic University of Parana, Brazil
Eduardo Viegas   PUCPR, Brazil
Ian Welch   Victoria University of Wellington, New Zealand

SECRYPT Program Committee

Luís Antunes   Faculdade de Ciências da U. Porto Instituto de
                                   telecomunicações Porto, Portugal
Alessandro Armando   FBK, Italy
Prithvi Bisht   Adobe, USA
Carlo Blundo   Università di Salerno, Italy
Andrey Bogdanov   Technical University of Denmark, Denmark
Francesco Buccafurri   University of Reggio Calabria, Italy
Dario Catalano   Università di Catania, Italy
Sherman S.M. Chow   Chinese University of Hong Kong, Hong Kong,
                                   SAR China
Frederic Cuppens   TELECOM Bretagne, France
Nora Cuppens-Boulahia   Institut Mines Telecom/Telecom Bretagne, France
Jun Dai   California State University, USA
Tassos Dimitriou   Computer Technology Institute, Greece and Kuwait
                                   University, Kuwait

Josep Domingo-Ferrer   Universitat Rovira i Virgili, Spain
Alberto Ferrante   Università della Svizzera Italiana, Switzerland
Josep-Lluis Ferrer-Gomila   Balearic Islands University, Spain
William M. Fitzgerald   Johnson Controls (Tyco), Ireland
Sara Foresti   Università degli Studi di Milano, Italy
Steven Furnell   Plymouth University, UK
Joaquin Garcia-Alfaro   Institut Mines-Telecom, TELECOM SudParis, France
Mark Gondree   Sonoma State University, USA
Dimitris Gritzalis   AUEB, Greece
Waël Kanoun   NOKIA, France
Murat Kantarcioglu   University of Texas at Dallas, USA
Sokratis Katsikas   Norwegian University of Science and Technology,
                            Norway
Florian Kerschbaum   SAP, Germany
Shinsaku Kiyomoto   KDDI Research Inc., Japan
Ruggero Donida Labati   Università degli Studi di Milano, Italy
Costas Lambrinoudakis   University of Piraeus, Greece
Albert Levi   Sabanci University, Turkey
Jiguo Li   Hohai University, China
Peng Liu   Penn State University, USA
Giovanni Livraga   Università degli Studi di Milano, Italy
Javier Lopez   University of Malaga, Spain
Haibing Lu   Santa Clara University, USA
Evangelos Markatos   ICS, Forth, Greece
Olivier Markowitch   Université Libre de Bruxelles, Belgium
Fabio Martinelli   Consiglio Nazionale delle Ricerche, Italy
Vashek Matyas   Masaryk University, Czech Republic
Carlos Maziero   UFPR, Federal University of Paraná, Brazil
Chandrashekhar Meshram   Rani Durgavati University, Jabalpur, India
Atsuko Miyaji   Japan Advanced Institute of Science and Technology,
                            Japan
Refik Molva   Eurecom, France
Eiji Okamoto   University of Tsukuba, Japan
Rolf Oppliger   eSECURITY Technologies, Switzerland
Stefano Paraboschi   University of Bergamo, Italy
Joon Park   Syracuse University, USA
Gerardo Pelosi   Politecnico di Milano, Italy
Günther Pernul   University of Regensburg, Germany
Roberto Di Pietro   Università di Roma Tre, Italy
Joachim Posegga   Institute of IT Security and Security Law, Germany
Silvio Ranise   Fondazione Bruno Kessler, Italy
Indrakshi Ray   Colorado State University, USA
Kui Ren   State University of New York at Buffalo, USA
Nuno Santos   INESC, Portugal
Andreas Schaad   Huawei European Research Center, Germany

Cristina Serban	AT&T, USA
Daniele Sgandurra	Imperial College, London, UK
Juan Tapiador	Universidad Carlos III de Madrid, Spain
Vicenc Torra	University of Skövde, Sweden
Jaideep Vaidya	Rutgers Business School, USA
Luca Viganò	King's College London, UK
Sabrina de Capitani di Vimercati	Università degli Studi di Milano, Italy
Corrado Aaron Visaggio	Università degli Studi del Sannio, Italy
Ivan Visconti	University of Salerno, Italy
Cong Wang	City University of Hong Kong, Hong Kong, SAR China
Haining Wang	The College of William and Mary, USA
Lingyu Wang	Concordia University, Canada
Xinyuan (Frank) Wang	George Mason University, USA
Edgar Weippl	SBA Research, Austria
Qiben Yan	University of Nebraska Lincoln, USA
Alec Yasinsac	University of South Alabama, USA
Meng Yu	Virginia Commonwealth University, USA
Jiawei Yuan	Embry-Riddle Aeronautical University, USA
Lei Zhang	Thomson Reuters, USA

SECRYPT Additional Reviewers

Spiros Antonatos	IBM, Ireland
Ricardo Chaves	INESC-ID, IST, ULisbon, Portugal
Gabriele Costa	University of Genova, Italy
Kaoutar Elkhiyaoui	EURECOM, France
Martianus Frederic Ezerman	Nanyang Technological University, Singapore
Lorena Gonzalez	University Carlos III of Madrid, Spain
Liran Lerman	Université Libre de Bruxelles, Belgium
Alessio Merlo	E-Campus University, Italy
Melek Önen	EURECOM, France
Miguel Pardal	Instituto Superior Técnico, Universidade de Lisboa, Portugal
Sergio Pastrana	Carlos III University of Madrid, Spain
Andrea Paudice	Imperial College London, UK
Pedro Pereira	Center for Research in Advanced Computing Systems, Portugal
Chuangang Ren	Pennsylvania State University, USA
Jennifer Rexford	Princeton University, USA
Cédric Van Rompay	EURECOM, France
Massimiliano Sala	University of Trento, Italy
Vishal Saraswat	CRRao AIMSCS, India
Dimitrios Vasilopoulos	Eurecom, France
Tao Zhang	CUHK, Hong Kong, SAR China

Bin Zhao   Palo Alto Networks, Inc., USA
Yongjun Zhao   The Chinese University of Hong Kong, Hong Kong,
                                    SAR China

OPTICS Program Committee

Tiago Alves   Instituto Superior Técnico/Instituto
                                    de Telecomunicações, Portugal
Siti Barirah Barirah Ahmad   Universiti Putra Malaysia, Malaysia
  Anas
Nicola Andriolli   Scuola Superiore Sant'Anna, Italy
Adolfo Cartaxo   Instituto de Telecomunicações, Instituto Superior
                                    Técnico, Portugal
C.W. Chow   National Chiao Tung University, Taiwan
Giampiero Contestabile   Scuola Superiore Sant'Anna, Italy
Bernard Cousin   University of Rennes 1, France
Brian Culshaw   University of Strathclyde, UK
Anna Manolova Fagertun   Technical University of Denmark, Denmark
Matteo Fiorani   Royal Institute of Technology, Sweden
Marija Furdek   KTH Royal Institute of Technology, Sweden
Sang-Kook Han   Yonsei University, Korea, Republic of
Nicholas Ioannides   London Metropolitan University, UK
Guifang Li   The University of Central Florida, USA
Qi Li   Columbia University, USA
Malamati Louta   University of Western Macedonia, Greece
Guo-Wei Lu   Tokai University, Japan
Barbara Martini   Consorzio Nazionale Interuniversitario per
                                    le Telecomunicazioni (CNIT), Italy
Rainer Martini   Stevens Institute of Technology, USA
Lenin Mehedy   IBM Research Australia, Australia
Tetsuya Miyazaki   National Institute of Information and Communications,
                                    Japan
Maria Morant   Universitat Politècnica de València, Spain
Michela Svaluto Moreolo   Centre Tecnologic de Telecomunicacions de Catalunya
                                    (CTTC), Spain
Thas A Nirmalathas   The University of Melbourne, Australia
Yasutake Ohishi   Research Center for Advanced Photon Technology,
                                    Japan
Satoru Okamoto   Keio University, Japan
Albert Pagès   Universitat Politècnica de Catalunya, Spain
Anirban Pathak   Jaypee Institute of Information Technology, India
Periklis Petropoulos   University of Southampton, UK
João Rebola   Instituto de Telecomunicações, ISCTE-IUL, Portugal
Enrique Rodriguez-Colina   Universidad Autónoma Metropolitana, Mexico
Jitendra Nath Roy   National Institute of Technology, India
Panagiotis Sarigiannidis   University of Western Macedonia, Greece

Mehdi Shadaram	University of Texas at San Antonio, USA
Hamada Al Shaer	University of Edinburgh, Li-Fi Research and Development Centre, UK
Surinder Singh	Sant Longowal Institute of Engineering and Technology, Longowal, India
Georgios Siviloglou	University of Amsterdam, The Netherlands
Salvatore Spadaro	Universitat Politecnica de Catalunya, Spain
Yikai Su	Shanghai Jiao Tong University, China
Ashok Kumar Turuk	National Institute of Technology Rourkela, India
L. Valcarenghi	Scuola Superiore Sant'Anna, Italy
Bal Virdee	London Metropolitan University, UK
Stefan Wabnitz	Università degli Studi di Brescia, Italy
Xingjun Wang	Peking University, China
Yixin Wang	Institute for Infocomm Research, Singapore
Andreas O.J. Wiberg	University of California San Diego, USA
Hui Yang	Beijing University of Posts and Telecommunications, China
Yi Zhu	Hawaii Pacific University, USA
Kyriakos E. Zoiros	Democritus University of Thrace, Greece

ICE-B Program Committee

Andreas Ahrens	Hochschule Wismar, University of Technology Business and Design, Germany
Dimitris Apostolou	University of Piraeus, Greece
Ana Azevedo	CEOS.PP-ISCAP/IPP, Portugal
Elarbi Badidi	United Arab Emirates University, United Arab Emirates
Michael R. Bartolacci	Pennsylvania State University, USA
Morad Benyoucef	University of Ottawa, Canada
Ilia Bider	DSV, Stockholm University, Sweden
Efthimios Bothos	Institute of Communication and Computer Systems, Greece
Rebecca Bulander	Pforzheim University of Applied Science, Germany
Wojciech Cellary	Poznan University of Economics, Poland
Chun-Liang Chen	National Taiwan University of Arts, Taiwan
Dickson Chiu	The University of Hong Kong, Hong Kong, SAR China
Jacek Chmielewski	Poznan University of Economics, Poland
Soon Ae Chun	CUNY-CSI, USA
Lawrence Chung	The University of Texas at Dallas, USA
Michele Colajanni	University of Modena and Reggio Emilia, Italy
Mikael Collan	Lappeenranta University of Technology, Finland
Rafael Corchuelo	University of Seville, Spain
Ioanna Dionysiou	University of Nicosia, Cyprus
Peter Dolog	Aalborg University, Denmark

Yanqing Duan	University of Bedfordshire, UK
Elsa Estevez	United Nations University, Portugal
Marie-Christine Fauvet	Université Grenoble Alpes, France
Erwin Fielt	Queensland University of Technology, Australia
Erwin Folmer	TNO Information and Communication Technology, The Netherlands
Geoffrey Charles Fox	Indiana University, USA
José María García	University of Seville, Spain
Inma Hernández	Universidad de Sevilla, Spain
Marijn Janssen	Delft University of Technology, The Netherlands
Stephan Kassel	University of Applied Sciences Zwikau, Germany
Kin Keung Lai	City University of Hong Kong, Hong Kong, SAR China
Winfried Lamersdorf	University of Hamburg, Germany
Olga Levina	FZI Research Center for Information Technology, Germany
Yung-Ming Li	National Chiao Tung University, Taiwan
Ben van Lier	Centric, The Netherlands
Rungtai Lin	National Taiwan University of Arts, Taiwan
Peter Loos	German Research Center for Artificial Intelligence, Germany
Gavin McArdle	University College Dublin, Ireland
Brian Mennecke	Iowa State University, USA
Gianluca Carlo Misuraca	European Commission, Joint Research Centre, Spain
Wai Yin Mok	The University of Alabama in Huntsville, USA
Ali Reza Montazemi	McMaster University, Canada
Maurice Mulvenna	Ulster University, UK
Paulo Novais	Universidade do Minho, Portugal
Wilma Penzo	University of Bologna, Italy
Krassie Petrova	Auckland University of Technology, New Zealand
Willy Picard	Poznan University of Economics, Poland
Charmaine Du Plessis	University of South Africa, South Africa
Pak-Lok Poon	RMIT University, Australia
Ela Pustulka-Hunt	FHNW Olten, Switzerland
Arkalgud Ramaprasad	University of Illinois at Chicago, USA
Wolfgang Reinhardt	University of the Bundeswehr, Germany
Manuel Resinas	Universidad de Sevilla, Spain
Carlos Rivero	Universidad de Sevilla, Spain
Gustavo Rossi	University of La Plata, Argentina
Jarogniew Rykowski	The Poznan University of Economics (PUE), Poland
Ahm Shamsuzzoha	Sultan Qaboos University, Oman
Boris Shishkov	Bulgarian Academy of Sciences/IICREST, Bulgaria
Marten van Sinderen	University of Twente, The Netherlands
Hassan A. Sleiman	Commissariat à l'énergie atomique et aux énergies alternatives (CEA), France
Riccardo Spinelli	Università degli Studi di Genova, Italy

Zhaohao Sun   PNG University of Technology;
                               Federation University Australia, Papua New Guinea
James Y.L. Thong   Hong Kong University of Science and Technology,
                               Hong Kong, SAR China
Anthony Townsend   Iowa State University, USA
Alfredo Vellido   Universitat Politècnica de Catalunya, Spain
Yiannis Verginadis   ICCS, National Technical University of Athens, Greece
Wlodek Zadrozny   University of North Carolina, Charlotte, USA
Edzus Zeiris   ZZ Dats Ltd., Latvia
Lina Zhou   University of Maryland, Baltimore County, USA

ICE-B Additional Reviewers

Nick Russell   QUT, Australia
Nagarajan Venkatachalam   Science and Engineering Faculty, Queensland
                               University of Technology, Australia

DCNET Program Committee

Ilija Basicevic   University of Novi Sad, Serbia
Marco Beccuti   University of Turin, Italy
Pablo Belzarena   UdelaR, Uruguay
Chiara Buratti   Università di Bologna, Italy
Valentín Carela-Español   TALAIA.io, Spain
Maurizio Casoni   University of Modena and Reggio Emilia, Italy
Fernando Cerdan   Polytechnic University of Cartagena, Spain
Paskorn Champrasert   Chiang Mai University, Thailand
Kang Chen   Southern Illinois University, USA
Min-Xiou Chen   National Dong Hwa University, Taiwan
Zesheng Chen   Indiana University, Purdue University Fort Wayne,
                               USA
Rolf Clauberg   IBM Research, Switzerland
Jitender Deogun   University of Nebraska-Lincoln, USA
Josep Domenech   Universitat Politècnica de València, Spain
Ziqian Dong   New York Institute of Technology, USA
Mahmood Fathi   Iranian University of Science and Technology, Iran,
                               Islamic Republic of
Carlos Fernandez-Llatas   ITACA -TSB Universidad Politécnica de Valencia,
                               Spain
Hiroaki Fukuda   Shibaura Institute of Technology, Japan
François Gagnon   Cégep Sainte-Foy, Canada
Pawel Gburzynski   Vistula University, Poland
Katja Gilly   Miguel Hernandez University, Spain
Francesco Gringoli   University of Brescia, Italy
Carlos Guerrero   Universitat de les Illes Balears, Spain

Antonio Izquierdo-Manzanares	National Institute of Standards and Technology (NIST), USA
Brigitte Jaumard	Concordia University, Canada
Dimitris Kanellopoulos	University of Patras, Greece
Randi Karlsen	University of Tromso, Norway
Randy Katz	University of California Berkeley, USA
Peng-Yong Kong	Khalifa University of Science, Technology and Research (KUSTAR), United Arab Emirates
Michael Kounavis	Intel Corporation, USA
Matthieu Latapy	LIP6, CNRS and UPMC, France
Changhyun Lee	Electronics and Telecommunications Research Institute (ETRI), Korea, Republic of
Isaac Lera	Universitat de les Illes Balears, Spain
Hai Lin	Victoria University of Welling, New Zealand
Yaoqing Liu	Clarkson University, USA
Ziping Liu	Southeast Missouri State University, USA
Pascal Lorenz	University of Haute Alsace, France
Stéphane Maag	TELECOM SudParis, France
Olaf Maennel	Tallinn University of Technology, Estonia
S. Kami Makki	Lamar University, USA
Marco Milanesio	Eurecom, France
Carlos León de Mora	University of Seville, Spain
Liam Murphy	University College Dublin, Ireland
Ibrahim Onyuksel	Northern Illinois University, USA
Maurizio Patrignani	Roma Tre University, Italy
José Pelegri-Sebastia	Universidad Politécnica de Valencia, Spain
Adrian Popescu	Blekinge Institute of Technology, Sweden
Gianluca Reali	Università degli Studi di Perugia, Italy
Nasser-Eddine Rikli	King Saud University, Saudi Arabia
Guanying Ru	AT&T Lab, USA
Matteo Sereno	University of Turin, Italy
Adel Soudani	King Saud University, Saudi Arabia
Maciej Stasiak	Poznan University of Technology, Poland
Giovanni Stea	University of Pisa, Italy
Tatsuya Suda	University Netgroup Inc., USA
Krzysztof Szczypiorski	Warsaw University of Technology (WUT), Poland
Sebastien Tixeuil	Université Pierre et Marie Curie, Paris 6, France
Kurt Tutschku	Blekinge Institute of Technology, Sweden
Thierry Val	Toulouse University, France
Adriano Valenzano	National Research Council of Italy, Italy
Luis Javier García Villalba	Universidad Complutense de Madrid, Spain
Bernd E. Wolfinger	University of Hamburg, Germany
Józef Wozniak	Gdansk University of Technology, Poland
Christos Xenakis	University of Piraeus, Greece
Gaoxi Xiao	Nanyang Technological University, Singapore

Jianbin Xiong	Guangdong University of Petrochemical Technology, China
Bo Zhang	Concurrent Computer Corporation, USA
Cliff C. Zou	University of Central Florida, USA

DCNET Additional Reviewers

Gabriele Lospoto	Roma Tre University, Italy
Massimo Rimondini	Roma Tre University, Italy
Piotr Sapiecha	Warsaw University of Technology, Poland

Invited Speakers

Hamid Aghvami	King's College London, UK
Giuseppe Bianchi	University of Roma Tor Vergata, Italy
Anastasios Economides	University of Macedonia, Greece
Mateo Valero	Universidad Politecnica de Catalunya, Spain
Indrakshi Ray	Colorado State University, USA

Contents

Optical Communication Systems

Security and Cryptography

Signal Processing and Multimedia Applications

Wireless Networks and Mobile Systems

Invited Paper

User Perceptions of Internet of Things (IoT) Systems

Anastasios A. Economides[(⊠)]

University of Macedonia, Thessaloniki, Greece
economid@uom.gr
http://conta.uom.gr

Abstract. This chapter proposes a user perceptions model regarding an IoT system that is based on the user's beliefs about important factors of this IoT system. Initially, the chapter classifies the IoT applications and services in twelve (12) sectors across the personal, business and public domains. It also outlines the technological, societal, business and human challenges. Then, it defines the IoT User Perceptions Model (IoT-UPM) which is composed from thirty-three (33) fundamental factors. Also, it formally defines these thirty-three (33) factors in order to establish a universally accepted model regarding user perceptions of a particular IoT system.

Keywords: Easy-of-use · Effectiveness · Efficiency · Internet of Things · Interoperability · IoT · IoT-UPM · Personalization · Satisfaction · Security · Technology Acceptance Model · Ubiquity · Usefulness · User control · User experience · User perceptions · Value-for-money

1 Introduction

IoT is the worldwide digital infrastructure that supports ubiquitous services among interacting humans, things, data and applications. A thing carries sensors which sense, measure and collect data. It may process and analyze these data either locally or transmit them to other systems. Subsequently, these systems make recommendations to people or order actuators to act appropriately. Thus, a thing may carry one or more sensors and/or actuators and be able to communicate with other things. It is forecasted that there will exist around 30 billion connected devices by 2021 [21, 23, 24]. Correspondingly, the IoT economic impact is expected to be around $1 trillion by 2022 [36]. Major IoT applications sectors include smart cities, smart transportation and logistics, smart industry, and smart home. It is expected that the market in emerging sectors will exceed $100 billion per sector by 2021 [2, 25, 36, 45, 46].

IoT has the potential to transform not only businesses but also society and everyday life [3, 5, 19, 47, 48, 53]. It will bring together people, things, data, applications and services. It will empower people to achieve their objectives (regarding health, education, enjoyment, family, work etc.), companies to accomplish their purpose and governments to serve their citizen. It will change the ways people, businesses, and governments interact among themselves. All the following interaction types would co-exist in IoT: Person-to-Person (P2P), Person-to-System (P2S), Person-to-Business

© Springer International Publishing AG 2017
M.S. Obaidat (Ed): ICETE 2016, CCIS 764, pp. 3–20, 2017.
https://doi.org/10.1007/978-3-319-67876-4_1

(P2B), Person-to-Government (P2G), Person-to-Environment (P2E), Business-to-Person (B2P), Business-to-System (B2S), Business-to-Business (B2B), Business-to-Government (B2G), Business-to-Environment (B2E), Government-to-Person (G2P), Government-to-System (G2S), Government-to-Business (G2B), Government-to-Government (G2G), Government-to-Environment (G2E). Each actor (Person, Business, or Government) could be a single or a group of actors.

The proliferation of connected things, connected people, connected devices, connected networks, connected data and connected processes would create revolutionary opportunities in economy, society, business, and personal life. For example, an IoT system might continuously monitor elderly health and instantaneously alert emergency services in case of abnormal conditions. A carry-on IoT system might interact with Facebook and inform the user when someone of his friend is close to him. Food would be continuously monitored to guarantee that its ingredients, cooking, storage, and transportation adhere to hygiene standards. City officials would control traffic, parking, lighting, park irrigation and waste management. Government would monitor and maintain bridges, tunnels and other infrastructure conditions.

Currently, there are available sensors to collect temperature, location, motion, velocity, acceleration, force, pressure, flow, humidity, light, acoustic, magnetic, seismic, imaging, luminosity, chemical, radiation and body measurements. These measurements would be used by connected applications and services to better serve people, society and businesses.

Various organizations and international projects are actively developing the IoT ecosystem. Major players include European Smart Anything Everywhere (SAE) Initiative, Alliance for the Internet of Things Innovation (AIOTI), Internet of Things (IoT) Global Standards Initiative (GSI), W3C - Web of Things Community, ISO/IEC JTC 1/SWG 5 IoT; INCITS 5G on IoT, One M2M, AllSeen Alliance, Open Interconnect Consortium, Industrial Internet Consortium (IIC), Eclipse IoT, among others. Also, major companies (Intel, Qualcomm, IBM, MS, Cisco, Samsung, Amazon, Google, Apple, HP, SAP, Huawei, etc.) are intensively participating in this evolution.

However, while much attention has been given to the technology needed to develop IoT; little attention has been given to the end user. Even if the technology and the applications are available, it is not guaranteed that the users will accept and use them. In this chapter, we propose a model that considers the major factors that affect the IoT acceptance by users. These concepts have been presented initially in two keynote speeches given by the author [16, 17].

In the next Sect. 2, we outline the IoT services and applications across the various sectors. Then in Sect. 3, we describe the challenges. In Sect. 4 we describe the proposed model and that factors that compose it. Finally, we conclude in Sect. 5 and suggest directions for future research.

2   IoT Services and Applications

The increasing connectivity among people, things and data enable great opportunities for developing applications in almost any sector of society, economy or personal life (e.g. [38]). After classifying the various sectors in three main domains (i.e. personal domain, business domain, and public domain), we outline various services and applications in every sector (Diagram 1).

Personal Domain

In this domain, we consider IoT applications sectors that would improve the quality of personal life using IoT. The Personal domain includes the following sectors: Smart Healthcare and Wellbeing, Smart Education, and Smart Home.

Smart Healthcare and Wellbeing

A user would wear smart clothes and carry wearable devices (e.g. smart clothes, glass, watch, telephone) while he is exercising, eating, working, studying, having fun, sleeping. An IoT system would monitor a person's health (physical, mental, emotional), analyze health state (e.g. diagnostics), notify appropriate agencies (e.g. doctors, family, emergency units), make recommendations (e.g. a special diet) or even take appropriate actions (e.g. in case of user's inability). For example, it would encourage exercising or alert him when it is time to take his medicine. Special assistance would be given to infant, elderly, patient, or persons with special needs (e.g. [1, 11, 26]). Also, doctors would study the effect of a therapy or medication. Hospitals would use IoT systems to monitor connected devices, instruments, equipment, pharmaceuticals, drugs, etc.

Smart Education

An IoT system continuously monitors the learner and encourages him (e.g. [15, 37]), recommends to him educational material to study or next appropriate question during exams according to his progress and his emotional state (e.g. [12, 14, 42]).

Correspondingly, it may notify the teacher, the school administration and other interested parties about the learner's progress. For example, an adviser gets an alert when a student is at risk of dropping out. Also, group of students and teachers may interact and collaborate among themselves using IoT systems to monitor the environment (i.e. plants, water, and air) and accomplish an educational activity.

Smart Home

An IoT system would continuously monitor home's safety (e.g. smoke, gas, motion detection), environment (e.g. heat, air, light), appliances, equipment, consumption (e.g. electricity, gas, water), security and surveillance, make recommendations, adjust systems to prescribed state (e.g. adjust temperature) or take appropriate actions (e.g. extinguish fire) (e.g. [20, 49]). A user would monitor infant, elderly and patients. Also, a user would control and manage home appliances, entertainment devices, and eventually the whole home.

Business Domain

In this domain, we consider IoT applications sectors that enable business to accomplish their purpose and benefit from IoT. The Business domain includes the following sectors: Smart Building, Smart Industry, Smart Services, Smart Retailing and Logistics, and Smart Transportation and Smart Vehicle, Smart Agriculture and Livestock (Animal Farming).

Smart Building

IoT systems would monitor and control the building's (e.g. offices, hotel, museum) access, lighting, heating/air-conditioning, equipment and resources' usage etc. (e.g. [40]). IoT systems would be used for smart metering to control energy consumption in order to reduce cost. Also, IoT systems would be used for security and surveillance, alarm in case of emergency (e.g. fire, intruders) or take appropriate actions (e.g. improve air quality, close lights if no one is around).

Smart Industry

Connected machines and robots would be used in smart factory, manufacturing, mining, construction to improve production (e.g. customized, on-time, on-demand production) (e.g. [31, 34, 43]).

Smart Services

IoT systems would be used in the financial, banking, insurance (health, building, car, etc.) services to monitor people, data and resources in order to improve their offered services (e.g. [10]). For example in tourism, IoT systems would track visitors and recommend destinations, sites, tours, hotels, driving routes, hiking paths, and other activities based on the tourists' characteristics.

Smart Retailing and Logistics

IoT systems would be used to track products, monitor cargo and warehouses in order to optimize inventory and stock levels, reduce theft, and maintain product quality (e.g. [4]). An IoT system would monitor the state of products in storage and during transport, make recommendation and alert when the products are not stored according to requirements, when the product's expiration date approaches or when unauthorized access happens.

Smart Transportation and Smart Vehicle

IoT systems would be used to monitor passengers (e.g. mobile tickets), luggage's, vehicles (e.g. cars, buses, airplanes, ships), containers, infrastructure conditions (e.g. roads, airports, railways, harbors, bridges, tunnels, tolls) to optimize transportation via land, air, or water, or schedule predictive maintenance. For example, sensors could monitor the traffic and appropriately control the lighting in tunnels [41].

Connected cars and smart vehicles would interact to avoid accidents, enhance infotainment, and reduce traffic congestion, power consumption, pollution, and time waste. Smart fleet management would reduce cost, delivery time, wasted empty space in tracks etc. (e.g. [22, 32]). Finally, transportation of hazardous material (e.g. corrosives, flammables, toxic, explosives) would be improved.

Smart Agriculture and Livestock

IoT systems would monitor a farm, crop, vineyard, green house, livestock, animals, farm equipment and machinery (tractors, fertilizer distribution), make recommendations or take appropriate actions (e.g. irrigation, feeding) to enhance the production quality and quantity (e.g. [33]).

Public Domain

In this domain, we consider IoT applications sectors that enable the public sector to better serve the citizens using IoT. The Public domain includes the following sectors: Smart City/Community, Smart Utilities, and Smart Environment.

Smart City and Community

IoT systems would monitor streets for security reasons and alarm police in case of crime or violence. Similarly, they would monitor the city's environment and alarm

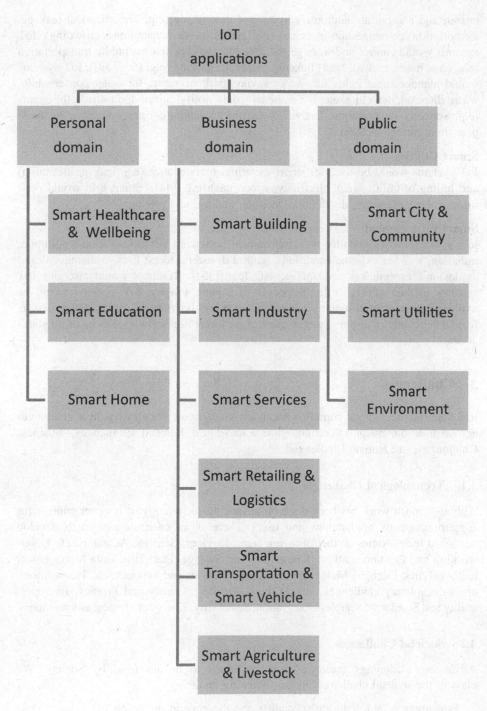

Diagram 1. IoT applications.

citizen and appropriate authorities in case of emergency (e.g. fire, chemical leakage, air-pollution) or congestion instances (e.g. accidents, demonstrations, crowding). IoT systems would control and manage traffic lights, parking spaces, public transportation (e.g. cars, buses, metro), smart ticketing, and bike sharing (e.g. [6, 7, 54]). IoT systems would manage street lights for energy saving, park irrigation for water conservation, waste disposal, recycling, etc. IoT systems would notify citizen and tourists for events (e.g. concerts, celebrations, festivities, artistic happenings, open education lectures) near their current location.

Smart Utilities

IoT systems would be used for smart metering, maintenance (e.g. leakage detection) and billing of utilities (e.g. electricity, water, gas) (e.g. [44]). Smart grid would optimize power generation, distribution, storage, trading, and pricing.

Smart Environment

IoT systems would monitor the environment and warn people regarding pollution, radiation, weather extreme conditions, natural disasters, forest fires, tsunami, volcano explosions, earthquakes, avalanches, etc. (e.g. [35]). Rescuers would also use IoT systems in their efforts to rescue people in danger. Finally, IoT systems would be exploited for territorial monitoring, surveillance and boarder guard. Dropping sensors from a helicopter or airplane would monitor for forest fire, snow avalanche or oil slicks at sea.

3   Challenges

IoT opportunities are not coming without any challenges. We classify these challenges across four dimensions: Technological Challenges, Societal Challenges, Business Challenges, and Human Challenges.

3.1   Technological Challenges

Although much work has been done on advancing technology, it is never enough for supporting greedy applications and users. There is an everlasting need to develop advanced technologies on the following areas: Devices (Sensors, Actuators, etc.), Networking and Communications, Computing and Storage, Platforms, Data Management and Analytics, Decision Making Systems, Applications and Services, etc. Furthermore, cross-disciplinary challenges include the following: Security and Privacy, Interoperability and Standards, Seamless Integration, Scalability, Energy efficiency, among others.

3.2   Societal Challenges

Advancing technology creates various questions to be answered by Society. We classify the societal challenges in the following areas:

Education: how to educate specialists and the general public on IoT? How to use IoT to enhance education?

Democracy and Participation: how democracy and citizen participation will be affected by IoT? How to use IoT to enhance democracy and citizen participation?
Legislation: what legislation is needed in the IoT era? How to use IoT to enhance legislation?
Economics: how the global economy will affect IoT? How to use IoT to develop the economy?
Security and Privacy: how security and privacy will be affected by IoT? How to use IoT to enhance security and privacy?
Universal Access, Inclusion and Non- Discrimination, etc.: how Universal Access, Inclusion and Non- Discrimination will be affected by IoT? How to use IoT to enhance Universal Access, Inclusion and Non- Discrimination?

Finally, other major societal challenges include Ethics, Sustainability, and Environmental Protection, among others.

3.3 Business Challenges

Businesses that develop and sell IoT systems or businesses that buy and use IoT systems should be adapted to these new advances and changes. They should change not only their working practices but also their thinking and limits. For example, to cope with these radical and rapid changes companies should cooperate and collaborate with other private and public organizations, even with competing companies.
They should adapt their Strategies, Alliances, Partnerships, as well as Business Models, Marketing, Products and Services taking into consideration the evolving technology, laws, regulations, taxation, customer requirements, worldwide economy and competition among others.

3.4 Human Challenges

In order this new revolution happens, users should accept the offered IoT systems. So, it is extremely important to understand what users need, want, and expect? What drives them to buy and use the offered IoT systems? What prevents them of using the offered IoT systems? How much are they willing to pay? etc.
In the next section, we identify the factors that would affect the users' acceptance of IoT systems. Companies that built IoT systems should seriously take into consideration the users perceptions regarding these IoT systems.

4 IoT User Perceptions Model (IoT- UPM)

The acceptance of a particular IoT system by the user as well the intention to use it and the actual usage of it depend on a variety of factors. We would classify these factors to factors related to the characteristics (features, attributes) of the User, of this IoT System itself, of this IoT system Producer, and of the Environment where these stakeholders act (Diagram 2). Actually, all these characteristics describe the context [13, 14]. For example, User's characteristics include age, gender, education, experience (with computers, mobiles, specific devices etc.), personality, emotions, preferences, interests, abilities, competencies, etc. IoT System's characteristics include usability, functionalities, performance, reliability, security, interoperability etc. IoT system Producer's characteristics include brand name, industry sector, size, customer support, etc. Environment's characteristics include other users, other IoT systems, other producers, society state, economy state, market, companies, competition, public policies, ethics, etc.

The characteristics of the User interact among themselves as well with the characteristics of the IoT System, of the IoT system Producer, and of the Environment. Similarly, the characteristics of the IoT System interact among themselves as well with the characteristics of the User, of the IoT system Producer, and of the Environment. The characteristics of the IoT system Producer interact among themselves as well with the characteristics of the User, of the IoT System, and of the Environment. The characteristics of the Environment interact among themselves as well with the characteristics of the User, of the IoT System, and of the IoT system Producer. Finally, all these characteristics interact with the user's attitude, acceptance, adoption, intention to use, actual use, and continuance intention to use the IoT System (Diagram 3).

Although it is desirable to be able to measure these characteristics, it is not always easy or even possible to quantify and accurately measure them. In other words, we want like to have accurate and current measurements of the actual characteristics of the User, of the IoT System itself, of the IoT system Producer and of the Environment. However, we may content to perceptions about the User, the IoT System itself, the IoT system Producer and the Environment. So, there is the "Real Context" and the "Perceived Context".

In this chapter, we are further investigating the factors that are related to the IoT System. In a future paper, we will describe the factors associated with the User, the Producer and the Environment. The IoT System has some characteristics that can be either measurable or not. However, even if some IoT System characteristics could be measured it would be difficult for the User to really measure them with accuracy and reliability. Furthermore, it may not be easy, convenient, and comfortable for him to measure these characteristics. So, eventually what it matters to him is his perceptions about these IoT System characteristics. So, in this chapter we explicitly define the important IoT System factors from the User's perspective to decide if he will accept and use a particular IoT System. A User needs some features to be offered by an IoT System in order to achieve his objectives and goals. He expects that using the particular IoT System he would fully achieve his desired outcomes and results. The IoT system Producer would promote the corresponding IoT System's characteristics (features, attributes) to influence the User's attitude towards his IoT System. For example, a User would like to be able to use an IoT System (e.g. an e-health equipment) anytime, anywhere, via any device and any network. Thus, the Producer would try to provide this ability to the IoT System.

In this section, we propose the IoT User Perceptions Model (IoT- UPM) that was inspired by previous models such as the Technology Acceptance Model (TAM) (e.g. [8, 9, 50–52]), ISO Quality models (e.g. [27–30]) as well quality frameworks for evaluating mobile devices (e.g. [18]) or websites (e.g. [39, 55]) that were proposed in different from IoT contexts.

The IoT-UPM is composed from thirty-three (33) factors categorized in 3 dimensions: (i) User- IoT System Interaction, (ii) IoT System Operation, and (iii) IoT System Results (Diagram 4). These factors affect the attitude of a user towards using, the intention to use, the acceptance, the actual use, and the continuance intention to use a particular IoT system. The producer of a particular IoT system could try to improve the IoT system's characteristics that correspond to these factors in order to develop favorable user perceptions towards his IoT system.

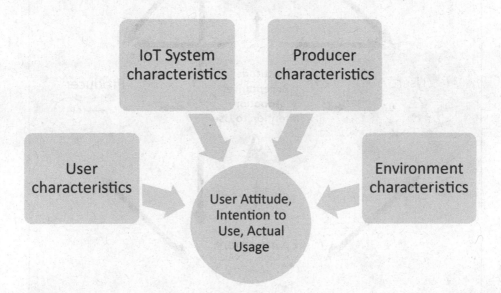

Diagram 2. Factors that influence the User's Attitude toward Using, Intention to Use, Actual Use, and Continuance Intention to Use the IoT System.

Next, we define "resource" to be any of the following: space, energy, money, processing and computations, storage and memory, communications and bandwidth, software, etc.

4.1 User - IoT System Interaction

- Perceived Ease-of-Use is defined as the degree to which a user believes that using a particular IoT system would be easy (simple, clear, intuitive, comfortable) and without much effort (mental, emotional and/or physical effort, time spent) to carry it, to install it, to initiate it, to understand its usage, to learn its usage, to remember its usage, as well as to actually access, use (operate), control (manage, manipulate), maintain, pay and terminate (shut down, retire, withdraw) it. It includes Simplicity, Clarity, Convenience, Comfort, Manageable size, weight, noise, etc.
- Perceived Accessibility (Universality and Non-discrimination) is defined as the degree to which a user of a particular IoT system believes that it could efficiently be

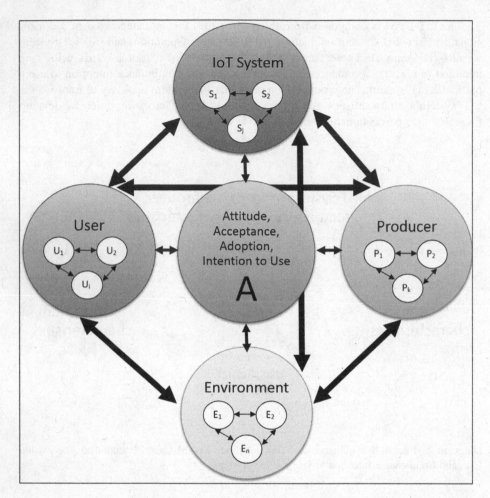

Diagram 3. Interaction among all factors, where U_i: User's characteristics #i, S_j: IoT System's characteristic # j, P_k: IoT system Producer's characteristic #k, E_n: Environment's characteristics #n, A: user's attitude, acceptance, adoption, intention to use, actual use, and continuance intention to use the IoT system.

used by various users with diverse characteristics (e.g. language, gender, age, education, religion), skills, capabilities and disabilities (e.g. vision or hearing impairments) to achieve a specified goal.

- Perceived Awareness (Visibility and Observability) is defined as the degree to which a user believes that using a particular IoT system he would know with accuracy, clarity and real time the system's resources usage, billing costs, actions and communications with other systems to accomplish his objective. For example, he might know who is monitoring the user, what operations are being executed, what information is processed, stored and communicated, when, how long, why (for what purpose), where, to whom (which entities are informed), what cost is charged for every activity every moment, what is the response time of an activity, to what networks it is connected, etc.

- Perceived Aesthetics (Appeal) is defined as the degree to which a user of a particular IoT system believes that it would be attractive and beautiful with respect to visual, auditory, haptic, olfactory senses.
- Perceived Support (Help and Assistance) is defined as the degree to which a user of a particular IoT system believes that he would be supported by the system itself and/or by the providing company (e.g. helpdesk, documentation, interactive tutorials, troubleshooting) continuously, real-time, anytime, anywhere, on-time accurately, completely on how to install, use, maintain, recover from failure, adapt, extend the system.
- Perceived Ubiquity (Seamlessness, Invisibility, Unobtrusiveness) is defined as the degree to which a user of a particular IoT system believes that he would be able to access and use the system continuously, without any interruption or disturbance anytime and anywhere as he moves from one environment (hardware, software, network) to another.
- Perceived Personalization is defined as the degree to which a user of a particular IoT system believes that its interface, appearance, functionalities and operations could be tailored to his personal characteristics such as preferences, interests, abilities, competencies, gender, age, language, measurement units, currency, culture, etc.
- Perceived Control is defined as the degree to which a user of a particular IoT system believes that he could control its resources, data and operations during usage in order to achieve his objective. It includes the ability of the user to also control and correct any information about himself.

4.2   IoT System Operation

- Perceived Efficiency is defined as the degree to which a user believes that using a particular IoT system he would achieve a specified level of performance and outcomes utilizing the minimum amount of resources (time, effort, cost, processing, storage, energy, bandwidth, etc.).
- Perceived Functionality is defined as the degree to which a user of a particular IoT system believes that the system would provide the necessary functions to achieve his objective.
- Perceived Performance is defined as the degree to which a user of a particular IoT system believes that the speed, response times, task completion times and throughput rates of the IoT system would meet his requirements.
- Perceived Reliability is defined as the degree to which a user of a particular IoT system believes that using the system there will be no interruptions since the system will prevent, reduce, handle (deal with) and recover from failures, faults, errors, downtime or breaks for a specified period of time usage.
- Availability is defined as the degree to which a user of a particular IoT system believes that he would be able to continue using it even in case of external factors failure (e.g. electricity shutdown/interruption/pause, network disconnection) or internal factors failure (e.g. not enough memory).

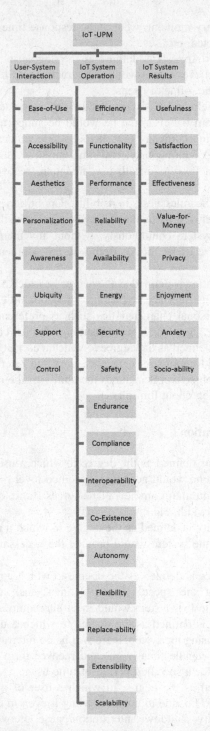

Diagram 4. IoT user perceptions model

- Perceived Energy Efficiency is defined as the degree to which a user of a particular IoT system believes that the system would efficiently operate powered by its energy sources for the specified time duration exploiting any energy conserving techniques (e.g. sleeping mode, solar panels).
- Perceived Security is defined as the degree to which a user of a particular IoT system believes that he would be protected from unauthorized access to, use, modification, destruction, or disclosure of either its resources or the user's personal information during processing, storage and transmission of data.
- Perceived Safety is defined as the degree to which a user believes that using a particular IoT system he would be free from possible dangers (health, physical, mental, financial, social, environmental, etc.), risks, losses, negative outcomes that can be caused from its usage.
- Perceived Endurance (Sustainability) is defined as the degree to which a user of a particular IoT system believes that he would use it for long time and it would not become obsolete soon.
- Perceived Flexibility (Versatility, Portability, Transferability, Modifiability, Reusability) is defined as the degree to which a user of a particular IoT system believes that he could efficiently use it (as it is or by easily and/or slightly modifying it) in many diverse environments or in building other systems or for achieving different objectives beyond those initially specified in the requirements. The least effort needed the most flexible it is. The more environments can be used in the more portable it is.
- Perceived Compliance (Conformance, Openness) is defined as the degree to which a user of a particular IoT system believes that it would follow/adhere to standards, laws, regulations etc.
- Perceived Interoperability (Compatibility) is defined as the degree to which a user of a particular IoT system believes that it could efficiently interact, communicate and collaborate with various other systems.
- Perceived Co-existence (Smooth Integration) is defined as the degree to which a user of a particular IoT system believes that it could perform its required functions efficiently while sharing a common environment, infrastructure and resources with other systems, without damaging impact on any other system.
- Perceived Autonomy is defined as the degree to which a user of a particular IoT system believes that he would use it with minimum extra (additional) required resources (e.g. additives, complements, accessories, extra hardware, extra software, extra networking, extra energy).
- Perceived Replace-ability is defined as the degree to which a user of a particular IoT system believes that he would replace this system with (switch to) another one without substantial switching costs (e.g. financial, time, learning, cognitive and emotional costs).
- Perceived Extensibility (Expandability) is defined as the degree to which a user of a particular IoT system believes that he could easily extend (upgrade) it with new functionalities and abilities to address new requirements.

- Perceived Scalability is defined as the degree to which a user of a particular IoT system believes that he could increase his performance and outcomes (in quantity) or accommodate extra demands by adding extra resources to the system.

4.3 IoT System Results

- Perceived Usefulness is defined as the degree to which a user believes that using a particular IoT system he would achieve results and outcomes that he considers useful, such as solving a problem, achieving an objective, producing a desired outcome (result, accomplishment), enhancing his performance (productivity, abilities, skills, etc.), decreasing his weaknesses (disabilities, shortcomings, deficiencies, risks, etc.).
- Perceived Satisfaction is defined as the degree to which a user believes that using a particular IoT system he would satisfy (fulfill, meet) his requirements, needs, expectations, desires, goals, and objectives.
- Perceived Effectiveness is defined as the degree to which a user believes that using a particular IoT system he could fully and accurately achieve the expected results and outcomes.
- Perceived Value for Money is defined as the degree to which a user believes that using a particular IoT system he would receive benefits (positive results, outcomes, accomplishments) in comparison to the cost for buying, learning, using, operating, maintaining and retiring it cost efficiency. The benefits would be financial, educational, health (physical, mental, emotional), amusement, time-saving etc.
- Perceived Privacy is defined as the degree to which a user believes that using a particular IoT system he could control (or give his consensus) when, how and what information related to him (private information, e.g. financial, health, gender, age, religion, geo-location, etc.) may be accessed, collected, stored, used, manipulated (altered) and communicated by whom, and to whom that information may be disclosed.
- Perceived Enjoyment is defined as the degree to which a user believes that using a particular IoT system would be enjoyable, fun and pleasant.
- Perceived Anxiety (Stress) is defined as the degree to which a user believes that using a particular IoT system would cause him anxiety and stress.
- Perceived Sociability is defined as the degree to which a user believes that using a particular IoT system he would be able to connect, relate, communicate, collaborate, interact and play with many other people using corresponding systems, as well as he would enhance his reputation (fame, prestige, esteem, "image") since others find it smart, worthy, remarkable and trendy.

5 Conclusions and Future Research

In this chapter we classified the IoT systems, applications and services in twelve (12) sectors across the personal, business and public domains. We also outlined the technological, societal, business and human challenges regarding the IoT revolution.

Then, we argued that there are various important factors that affect the user' attitude towards using, acceptance, intention to use, actual use, and the continuance intention to use such IoT systems. We classified these factors to those related to the IoT system itself, to the user, to the producer as well to the environment. It would be desirable that the user knows with accuracy and reliability the real characteristics of a particular IoT system. However, this is not the usual case. Usually, the user has only perceptions about the IoT system characteristics. So, we defined the IoT User Perceptions Model (IoT-UPM) which is composed from 33 fundamental factors that describe the user's perceptions about the IoT system. Also, we formally defined these 33 factors in order to establish a universally accepted model regarding user perceptions about IoT systems. Thus, an IoT system producer would try to enhance the IoT system parameters that correspond to these factors in order to influence the users' attitude towards using, intention to use, actual use, and the continuance intention to use this particular IoT system.

In a future paper, we will examine the interrelationships among these IoT-UPM factors as well the factors that are related to the User's characteristics, the Producer's characteristics and the Environment's characteristics.

References

1. Ahmed, M.U., Bjorkman, M., Causevic, A., Fotouhi, H., Linden, M.: An overview on the Internet of Things for health monitoring systems. In: 2nd EAI International Conference on IoT Technologies for HealthCare (HealthyIoT2015) (2015)
2. Allied Market Research. Internet of Things (IoT) Healthcare Market- Global Opportunity Analysis and Industry Forecast, 2014–2021 (2016). https://www.alliedmarketresearch.com/iot-healthcare-market
3. Atzori, L., Iera, A., Morabito, G.: The Internet of Things: a survey. Comput. Netw. **54**, 2787–2805 (2010)
4. Balaji, M.S., Roy, S.K.: Value co-creation with Internet of things technology in the retail industry. J. Mark. Manag. **33**, 7–31 (2016)
5. Borgia, E.: The Internet of Things vision: key features, applications and open issues. Comput. Commun. **54**, 1–31 (2014)
6. Chourabi, H., Nam, T., Walker, S., Gil-Garcia, J.R., Mellouli, S., Nahon, K., Pardo, T.A., Scholl, H.J.: Understanding smart cities: an integrative framework. In: Proceedings 45th Hawaii International Conference on System Sciences, pp. 2289–2297 (2012). doi10.1109/HICSS.2012.615
7. Cocchia, A.: Smart and digital city: a systematic literature review. In: Dameri, R.P., Rosenthal-Sabroux, C. (eds.) Smart City, Progress in IS, pp. 13–43 (2014). doi:10.1007/978-3-319-06160-3_2
8. Davis, F.D.: Perceived usefulness, perceived ease of use, and user acceptance of information technology. MIS Q. **13**(3), 319–340 (1989). doi:10.2307/249008
9. Davis, F.D., Bagozzi, R.P., Warshaw, P.R.: User acceptance of computer technology: a comparison of two theoretical models. Manag. Sci. **35**, 982–1003 (1989). doi:10.1287/mnsc.35.8.982
10. Dineshreddy, V., Gangadharan, G.R.: Towards an "Internet of Things" framework for financial services sector. In: 3rd International Conference on Recent Advances in Information Technology (RAIT-2016) (2016)

11. Domingo, M.C.: An overview of the Internet of Things for people with disabilities. J. Netw. Comput. Appl. **35**, 584–596 (2012)
12. Economides, A.A.: Emotional feedback in CAT (Computer Adaptive Testing). Int. J. Instr. Technol. Distance Learn. **3**(2), 11–20 (2006)
13. Economides, A.A.: Context-aware mobile learning. In: Lytras, M.D., Carroll, J.M., Damiani, E., Tennyson, R.D., Avison, D., Vossen, G., Ordonez De Pablos, P. (eds.) WSKS 2008. CCIS, vol. 19, pp. 213–220. Springer, Heidelberg (2008). doi:10.1007/978-3-540-87783-7_27
14. Economides, A.A.: Adaptive context-aware pervasive and ubiquitous learning. Int. J. Technol. Enhanced Learn. **1**(3), 169–192 (2009)
15. Economides, A.A.: Conative feedback in computer-based assessment. Comput. Sch. **26**(3), 207–223 (2009)
16. Economides, A.A.: Internet of Things (IoT) and sensor networks security. In: Keynote Speech at International Conference on Advances in Computing, Communication and Information Technology (CCIT 2014) (2014). http://www.slideshare.net/economides/internet-of-thingsbyeconomideskeynotespeechatccit2014final
17. Economides, A.A.: User acceptance of Internet of Things (IoT) services and applications. In: Invited Speech/Keynote Lecture, at 13rd International Joint Conference on e-Business and Telecommunications (ICETE 2016) and 3rd International Conference on Physiological Computing Systems (PhyCS 2016) (2016). https://player.vimeo.com/video/178591064?title=0&portrait=0
18. Economides, A.A., Nikolaou, N.: Evaluation of handheld devices for mobile learning. Int. J. Eng. Educ. (IJEE) **24**(1), 3–13 (2008)
19. Guo, B., Zhang, D., Wang, Z., Yu, Z., Zhou, X.: Opportunistic IoT: exploring the harmonious interaction between human and the internet of things. J. Netw. Comput. Appl. **36**, 1531–1539 (2013)
20. Hui, T.K.L., Sherratt, R.S., Sánchez, D.D.: Major requirements for building smart homes in smart cities based on Internet of Things technologies. Future Gener. Comput. Syst. **76**, 358–369 (2017)
21. Ericsson: Ericsson Mobility Report (2015). http://www.ericsson.com/res/docs/2015/mobility-report/ericsson-mobility-report-nov-2015.pdf
22. Ibáñez, J.A.G., Zeadally, S., Contreras-Castillo, J.: Integration challenges of intelligent transportation systems with connected vehicle, cloud computing, and internet of things technologies. IEEE Wirel. Commun. **22**(6), 122–128 (2015)
23. IDC: Worldwide and regional Internet of Things (IoT) 2014–2020 forecast: a virtuous circle of proven value and demand (2015). http://www.idc.com/downloads/idc_market_in_a_minute_iot_infographic.pdf
24. IHS: IoT Platforms - Enabling the Internet of Things (2016). https://www.ihs.com/Info/0416/internet-of-things.html
25. Industry ARC: Industrial Internet of Things Forecast 2016–2021 (2016). http://industryarc.com/Report/7385/industrial-internet-of-things-(IIoT)-market-report.html
26. Islam, S.M.R., Kwak, D., Kabir, H., Hossain, M., Kwak, K.-S.: The Internet of Things for health care: a comprehensive survey. IEEE Access **3**, 678–708 (2015). doi:10.1109/ACCESS.2015.2437951
27. ISO/IEC 24765: Systems and Software Engineering Vocabulary (2008)
28. ISO/IEC 25000: Software Engineering - Software product Quality Requirements and Evaluation (SQuaRE) - Guide to SQuaRE (2005)
29. ISO/IEC 25010: Systems and software engineering - Systems and software Quality Requirements and Evaluation (SQuaRE) - System and software quality models (2011)
30. ISO/IEC 9001: Quality Management Systems

31. Jeschke, S., Brecher, C., Meisen, T., Özdemir, D., Eschert, T.: Industrial internet of things and cyber manufacturing systems. In: Jeschke, S., Brecher, C., Song, H., Rawat, D.B. (eds.) Industrial Internet of Things. SSWT, pp. 3–19. Springer, Cham (2017). doi:10.1007/978-3-319-42559-7_1

32. Juan, A.A., Mendez, C.A., Faulin, J., Armas, J., Grasman, S.E.: Electric vehicles in logistics and transportation: a survey on emerging environmental, strategic, and operational challenges. Energies 9(2), 1–21 (2016). doi:10.3390/en9020086

33. Karapistoli, E., Mpampentzidou, I., Economides, A.A.: Environmental monitoring based on the wireless sensor networking technology: a survey of real-world applications. Int. J. Agric. Environ. Inf. Syst. 5(4), 1–39 (2014). doi:10.4018/ijaeis.2014100101

34. Lerche, C., Hartke, K., Kovatsch, M.: Industry adoption of the Internet of Things: a constrained application protocol survey. In: Proceedings IEEE 17th Conference on Technologies and Factory Automation (ETFA) (2012). doi:10.1109/ETFA.2012.6489787

35. Laplante, P.A., Voas, J., Laplante, N.: Standards for the Internet of Things: a case study in disaster response. IEEE Comput. 49(5), 87–90 (2016). doi:10.1109/MC.2016.137

36. Markets and Markets: Internet of Things Technology Market by Hardware, Platform, Software Solutions, and Services, Application, and Geography - Forecast to 2022 (2016). http://www.marketsandmarkets.com/Market-Reports/iot-application-technology-market-258239167.html

37. Moridis, C.N., Economides, A.A.: Affective learning: empathetic agents with emotional facial and tone of voice expressions. IEEE Trans. Affect. Comput. 3(3), 260–272 (2012)

38. Nunes, D., Zhang, P., Silva, J.S.: A survey on Human-in-the-Loop applications towards an Internet of All. IEEE Commun. Surv. Tutor. 17(2), 944–965 (2015)

39. Pallas, J., Economides, A.A.: Evaluation of art museums' web sites worldwide. Inf. Serv. Use 28(1), 45–57 (2008)

40. Pan, J., Jain, R., Paul, S., Vu, T., Saifullah, A., Sha, M.: An Internet of Things framework for smart energy in buildings: designs, prototype, and experiments. IEEE Internet Things J. 2(6), 527–537 (2015). doi:10.1109/JIOT.2015.2413397

41. Papagiannis, G., Economides, A.A., Syleos, C., Protogeros, N.: Developing a near-optimal lowest-consumption tunnel lighting system using software agents through power line communications. J. Comput. Inf. Technol. (CIT) 15(2), 1–8 (2007)

42. Papamitsiou, Z., Economides, A.A.: Temporal learning analytics for adaptive assessment. J. Learn. Anal. 1(3), 165–168 (2014)

43. Perera, C., Liu, C.H., Jayawardena, S., Chen, M.: A survey on Internet of Things from industrial market perspective. IEEE Access 2, 1660–1679 (2014)

44. Ramakrishnan, R., Gaur, L.: Smart electricity distribution in residential areas: Internet of Things (IoT) based advanced metering infrastructure and cloud analytics. In: International Conference on Internet of Things and Applications (IOTA), (2016). doi:10.1109/IOTA.2016.7562693

45. Research and Markets: Internet of Things (IoT) Global Forecast to 2021 (2016a). http://www.researchandmarkets.com/research/gsjxb5/internet_of

46. Research and Markets: Connected Home and IoT: Market Opportunities and Forecasts 2016–2021 (2016b). https://www.compassintelligence.com/connected-home-and-iot-market-opportunities-and-forecasts-2016-ndash-2021.html

47. Rose, K., Eldridge, S., Chapin, L.: The Internet of Things - An overview - Understanding the issues and challenges of a more connected world. ISOC (2015). http://www.internetsociety.org

48. Shin, D.: A socio-technical framework for Internet-of-Things design: a human-centered design for the Internet of Things. Telematics Inform. 31, 519–531 (2014)

49. Stojkoska, B.L.R., Trivodaliev, K.V.: A review of Internet of Things for smart home: challenges and solutions. J. Clean. Prod. Part 3 **140**, 1454–1464 (2017)
50. Terzis, V., Economides, A.A.: The acceptance and use of computer based assessment. Comput. Educ. **56**(4), 1032–1044 (2011)
51. Venkatesh, V., Morris, M.G., Davis, G.B., Davis, F.D.: User acceptance of information technology: toward a unified view. MIS Q. **27**(3), 425–478 (2003)
52. Venkatesh, V., Thong, J.L., Xu, X.: Consumer acceptance and use of information technology: extending the unified theory of acceptance and use of technology. MIS Q. **36**(1), 157–178 (2012)
53. Whitmore, A., Agarwal, A., Xu, L.D.: The Internet of Things—a survey of topics and trends. Inf. Syst. Front. **17**, 261–274 (2015). doi:10.1007/s10796-014-9489-2
54. Zanella, A., Bui, N., Castellani, A., Vangelista, L., Zorzi, M.: Internet of Things for smart cities. IEEE Internet Things J. **1**(1), 22–32 (2014)
55. Zarifopoulos, M., Economides, A.A.: Evaluating mobile banking portals. Int. J. Mob. Commun. **7**(1), 66–90 (2009)

Data Communication Networking

Multipath Forwarding in Named Data Networking: Flow, Fairness, and Context-Awareness

Abdelkader Bouacherine$^{(\boxtimes)}$, Mustapha Reda Senouci, and Billal Merabti

Department of Computer Science, Ecole Militaire Polytechnique, Algiers, Algeria
bouacherine.abdelkader@gmail.com, mrsenouci@gmail.com,
billalmerabti@gmail.com

Abstract. Being a rising architecture for the future Internet, Named Data Networking (NDN) needs adaptive, effective, and efficient forwarding strategies. In this paper, we elicit essential requirements for forwarding strategies and show that existing strategies struggle to fully fulfill these requirements. After that, we investigate how to unlock the full capabilities of NDN by enabling the consideration of context information in the forwarding plane. In this scope, we provide new definitions of NDN sub- and micro-flow. Afterward, we propose a Context-aware Parallel MultiPath forwarding strategy (*CPMP-FS*). The *CPMP-FS* strategy wisely splits NDN flows by determining how the faces will be used while taking into consideration several requirements such as in-network caching, fairness, Interest aggregation, context-awareness, and scalability. We expect *CPMP-FS* to be a step closer to adaptive, effective and efficient forwarding that satisfies both NDN consumers and providers.

1 Introduction

Nowadays Internet is mainly used to distribute and manipulate named information. As a reaction to this shift in Internet usage model from *host-centric* to *data-centric*, a new approach known as Information-Centric Networking (ICN) has emerged. This latter also known as content-aware, or data-oriented networking seeks an Internet architecture with an operation model matching the Internet current and the future usage model by evolving the Internet infrastructure to directly support named data rather than numerically addressed hosts. This approach is being concretized under different projects including but not limited to: Network of Information (NetInf) [13], Content-Centric Networking (CCN) [16], and Named Data Networking (NDN) [42,43]. The focus of this paper is on this latter approach.

NDN [16,42,43] is a future Internet architecture proposal rolling under the ICN paradigm. NDN comes with a new communication model based on four main characteristics:

1. *Receiver-driven data retrieval model*: the user expresses an Interest with a uniquely identified name. The routers use this latter to retrieve the data whose name matches the requested one, and return it to the user;

© Springer International Publishing AG 2017
M.S. Obaidat (Ed): ICETE 2016, CCIS 764, pp. 23–47, 2017.
https://doi.org/10.1007/978-3-319-67876-4_2

2. *Local state information decisions*: they are based on the kept local state information. No global knowledge exists;
3. *Loop free forwarding plane*: a built-in loop prevention mechanism in the forwarding process (maintaining local-state information at each NDN router along with the use of nonces). Thus, neither the Interests nor the data objects can loop for a sufficient period of time;
4. *One-to-one flow balance*: one Interest brings back at most one data object.

The above communication model led to an adaptive forwarding plane. The latter combined with the NDN in-network caching constitute a platform for multipath support called "NDN native multipath support". In this context and in order to benefit of NDN native multipath support, in a previous work [1], we have explained and clarified ambiguities of the inherited definitions of flow and fairness, and we have proposed new definitions in the context of NDN. Furthermore, we have formulated the parallel multipath forwarding packets as an optimization problem and described the initial design of a localized parallel multipath forwarding strategy (*PMP-FS*). Although, this latter shows promising results, serious issues remain open, which is also the case of prominent forwarding strategies as it will be discussed in Sect. 2. Before discussing these issues, it is important to elicit essential requirements for forwarding strategies. Accordingly, we have identified six requirements, namely: flow identification, parallel multipath exploitation, fairness enforcement, flexibility in open networks, and scalability.

Existing forwarding strategies are unable to fully fulfill the aforementioned requirements. This is due, among others, to unrealistic assumptions. For instance, in contrary to existing works, we believe that it is not practical to assume that a requested data packet, with a given name serving different end-users, is related to similar applications. Indeed, a fresh produced data packet of a picture from a disaster scene may be requested by the first-responders application and at the same time by a Facebook application. These requests should not be treated the same way by NDN nodes. In other words, the problem here is how to retrieve the same data with different service classes while ensuring the other requirements.

To tackle this problem, this paper investigates how to unlock the full capabilities of NDN by enabling the consideration of context information in the forwarding plane by building upon our previous work [1]. More specifically, this paper makes the following additional contributions:

- We introduce new definitions of NDN sub- and micro-flow;
- We elicit essential requirements for forwarding strategies and discuss the current NDN literature in regards to these requirements;
- We investigate the enhancement of context-awareness of *PMP-FS*, and propose an advanced context-aware multipath forwarding strategy (*CPMP-FS*). This latter takes into consideration a set of requirements to achieve weighted alpha fairness among different flows.

The remainder of this paper is organized as follows. Section 2 reviews background information and relevant related work. The necessary definitions are grouped in Sect. 3. Section 4 presents an overview of the *PMP-FS* forwarding strategy, while Sect. 5 is devoted to introduce the proposed forwarding strategy *CPMP-FS*. Section 6 concludes the paper and discusses future work.

2   Forwarding in NDN: Requirements *vs.* Reality

In this section, we first present background information on forwarding in NDN. After that, we examine essential requirements for effective forwarding strategies and we sketch our solution for fulfilling these requirements. Finally, we discuss related work and provide a comprehensive qualitative comparison between existing forwarding strategies.

2.1   Background

Forwarding is the process or the action of sending a packet to the preferred next-hop(s) toward a destination based on costs or rankings of faces. In the current Internet based on TCP/IP paradigm, routing plane also referred to as the *control plane* diminished to null the role of forwarding. Indeed, at TCP/IP routers, the forwarding plane also referred to as the *data plane*, has no adaptability. It strictly follows the one choice defined by the routing plane (i.e. the FIB usually has only one next-hop interface to pick). Instead of a native/built-in mechanism for loop prevention in the current network's architecture design, the routing has taken over the responsibilities of loop prevention and the robust data delivery plane solely [38].

By contrast to TCP/IP, NDN loop free forwarding plane is a result of a built-in loop prevention mechanism in the forwarding process (maintaining local-state information at each NDN router). This latter, allows the routing mechanisms to populate each FIB entry with multiple output faces. It also provides the forwarding plane with the flexibility of selecting face(s) for forwarding from multiple eligible available faces [16].

Besides maintaining local-state information at each NDN router, NDN allows the forwarding plane to measure the performance (e.g. Round Trip Time (RTT)) while retrieving data. When multiple next hops exist in a FIB entry, a layer called the *Forwarding Strategy* decides which next hop(s) will be used in forwarding Interests based on routing cost, forwarding plane measurements, and local policies [37]. NDN forwarding decisions are made based first on the route cost corresponding to a *name-prefix* made available by the routing protocol in order to bootstrap the delivery of packets, then utilize the collected local data-plane performance measurements (e.g. RTT, Delay, ...) of each next hop in retrieving data corresponding to *a name-prefix or to the desired granularity* to dynamically update face rankings[1]. Furthermore, the *Forwarding Strategy* based on the latter measurements can detect and recover from packet delivery problems and link

---

[1] Setting the performance metrics to use and how to use them is the responsibility of each forwarding strategy.

failures locally at the opposite of TCP/IP paradigm were the global convergence of the routing protocol is necessary [37]. In addition, the *Forwarding Strategy* also decides about the unsatisfied Interest retransmission within a specific amount of time. It is responsible of congestion control prevention mechanism, load balance, and fairness policies.

2.2   Forwarding in NDN: Requirements

We believe that for a successful deployment of NDN, the forwarding plane should be able to satisfy several requirements. In the sequel, we enumerate the most important ones and as we go along with the requirements, we present the challenges facing the forwarding strategy developer, and we sketch our solution for fulfilling these requirements.

Flow Identification. TCP/IP paradigm was built on end-to-end communication model. In this model, the source and the destination are known. Packets in the network are tagged by this information. With this legacy, we inherited most of the definitions that we use in nowadays communications and networking community. On the other hand, identifying the end-user's packets in NDN (Interests and data) is meant to be impossible in-between within the network. This is the main difference between NDN and the TCP/IP paradigm caused by the disappearance of end-to-end communication model. The NDN architecture is location-independent. Therefore, the NDN Interests can be forwarded individually and independently and data can be duplicated anywhere and so many times in the network (NDN in-network caching feature). This made the definitions and the rich literature about multipath forwarding strategies, fairness, and congestion control for the TCP/IP architecture no longer appropriate.

From the above discussion, it is clear that the NDN flow should be defined independently of the source and destination of Interests and data. This is still an open issue in the NDN community.

Parallel Multipath Exploitation. This feature can be used to take advantage of the Internet multiplicity in a parallel (simultaneously) or in a sequence manner (serial) as a backup configuration (detect failure and retry alternative paths). NDN native multipath support is used to optimize the efficiency (throughput) on the one hand, and ensures that end-users get a fair share (fairness) on the other hand.

To design a multipath forwarding strategy, besides the definition of the NDN flow, it is mandatory to maintain end-user's fairness and to adopt approaches without relying on *RTT* measurements.

Fairness. Fairness is a crucial concept in networking that needs complementary information to be understood, since it varies from equality to equity and can be defined in many ways. It has therefore already been the subject of intensive research. Many definitions were given such as Weighted Proportional Fairness [17], Proportional Fairness [21], and the Max-Min Fairness [14]. A unifying mathematical model to fair throughput was first introduced in [22]. The so-called alpha-fair utility functions $U_s(x_s)$ (Eq. 1), which defines the different notions of fairness depending on the choice of a parameter α. This latter is a kind of degree of fairness that controls the trade-off between efficiency and fairness. Please refer to Table 1 for notations.

$$U_s(x_s) = \begin{cases} w_s^\alpha \; \frac{x_s^{1-\alpha}}{1-\alpha} \, , & \text{if } \alpha \neq 1 \\ w_s \log(x_s) \, , & \text{if } \alpha = 1 \end{cases} \tag{1}$$

for $w > 0$, $\alpha \geq 0$, and $s \in S$

For example, $\alpha = 0$ with $w = 1$ corresponds to the system maximum efficiency or throughput, $\alpha \to \infty$ with $w = 1$ corresponds to the Max-Min fairness, and $\alpha = 2$ with $w = \frac{1}{RTT^2}$ corresponds to the TCP fair [20].

Table 1. Notations.

Notation	Meaning
S	Set of flows
s	Individual flow (session)
w_s	Weight of flow (session) s
x_s	Rate of flow (session) s
$U_s(x_s)$	Alpha-fair utility functions
α	A parameter reflecting the fairness

Serving end-users in a fair manner while maximizing network throughput is fundamental and a challenging task in designing a forwarding plane. The TCP/IP paradigm was built on end-to-end communication model where Packets in the network are tagged by the source and destination information. As a consequence, the fairness between end-users is directly related to the fairness between the flows. This is possible thanks to the sharp definition of the flow, which is not the case of NDN.

Flexibility in Open Networks. Ben Abraham and Crowley [7] studied the existing bindings between the application design and the basic or primitive forwarding strategy (as implemented in NFD[2] [3]) and the effect of the assigned

---

[2] NDN Forwarding Daemon (NFD) is a network forwarder that implements and evolves together with the NDN protocol.

forwarding strategy for a name-space on the application's performance or correctness. Indeed, in a closed environment, the network operator can control the assignment of forwarding strategies to name-spaces but in open networks the local choices could not be guaranteed to be saved.

The flexibility of a forwarding strategy in open networks is primordial for application's performance or correctness. In fact, a forwarding strategy should encapsulate different and as many as possible primitive or basic behaviors to serve the same type applications. Thus, the network operator's choice and the assignment of forwarding strategy in the out-of-control networks will not deeply affect the local application's performance.

Context-Awareness. NDN is designed as a common or universal platform for all types of applications (elasticity principal). The requirements of applications are different and they are addressed by the assignment of a strategy to a name-space and by the behavior of the forwarding strategy which includes the decisions about the used next-hop(s), the used performance metrics, and its behavior regarding the unsatisfied Interest (retransmission).

Existing forwarding strategies are unable to fully fulfill the application requirements. The data immutability imposes that the data name does not change in time and in space (storage locations). For instance, a data packet of a critical live stream (e.g. tele-surgery assistance) should not be treated the same way by NDN nodes in time (e.g. stocked for teaching purposes).

Content centricity offered by NDN can address all the application requirements by simply adding the finest possible context to data-names at the time of creation of data. Indeed, NDN imposes no restrictions on names except the hierarchy component structure. The first component for instance can serve as a context component. A byte can be used to define the service-class for the data and time of creation can be used to define the freshness of data. The security certificates can be used to control the announcements of certain service-classes by the eligible producers. We can suffix a context component to the delegation names (a component at the end of the name) indicating the desired treatments and requirements to the core routers.

Scalability. NDN names are composed of multiple components (any string of arbitrary length) arranged in a hierarchy, where the slash symbol is the delimiter of components (Fig. 1a and b). Routing scalability was addressed by hierarchical distributed routing through aggregation of routing information. Indeed, NDN FIBs entry contain a name-prefix instead of a complete object name. In addition, NDN FIBs does not and has no need to store two separate FIB entries for example, the name-prefixes /Algeria.dz and /Algeria.dz/emp if they have the same outbound face(s). The latter solution for NDN routing scalability was not satisfactory. Furthermore, it does not resolve producer mobility and (identifier, locator) decoupling.

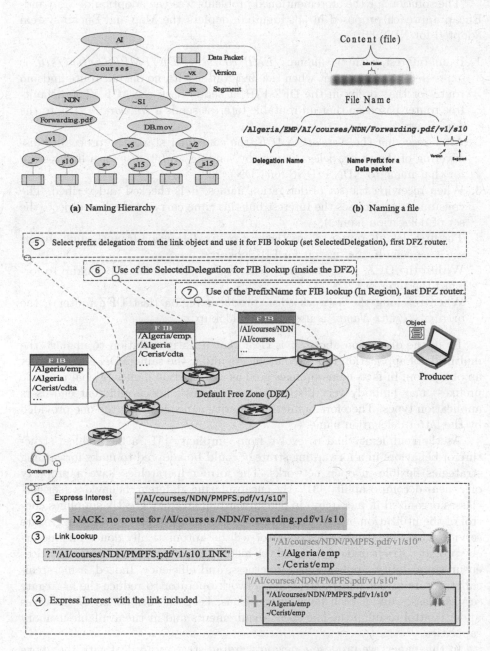

(a) Naming Hierarchy

(b) Naming a file

(c) Map-and-Encap Mechanism in Action

Fig. 1. Naming in the NDN architecture.

The solution for the aforementioned problems was the adoption of Map-and-Encap approach proposed in [4]. Figure 1c depicts the Map-and-Encap system adopted for NDN [4]:

1. If an Interest with the name: */EMP/courses/NDN/PMPFS.pdf/v1/s10*, is expressed by a consumer, when the first router with no default route finds no route for that prefix in the DFZ FIB, it sends back a NACK. The default-free router based on that un-routable Interest sends a *Network NACK* to the consumer;
2. After receiving the *Network NACK*, the consumer starts the process of discovering of the prefix delegation set by sending an Interest for a link lookup for that name to NDNS (DNS for NDN) [2];
3. When receiving the set of delegation names, it is checked and verified. The consumer re-expresses the Interest but this time carrying the link object (the set of delegation names);
4. The first-default-router selects the best prefix delegation from the link object, set it as default, and uses it for FIB lookup;
5. Within the DFZ, nodes use the *"SelectedDelegation"* for FIB lookup to forward the Interest;
6. When reaching the network edge (producer region (last DFZ router)), the original *"Prefix-Name"* is used for FIB lookup.

From the discussion above, it is clear that a native solution to manage the multitude of application types requirements under the same NDN flow becomes an obligation. In fact, name-prefixes used as a delegation names (global routable prefixes) may embody very distinct name-prefixes[3], hence, different end-users application types. Therefore, a finer granularity is needed than the one provided by the latter delegation name.

As the complexity had to evolve from simplicity [31], a hierarchical structure of behaviors in a forwarding strategy could be adopted to make forwarding strategies flexible in open networks. The former hierarchies have a property of a near-decomposability [31]. By encapsulating different behaviors (service-classes organized in hierarchy) in one forwarding strategy greatly simplifies control of the utilization of resources and the assignment to pre-set finite aggregate service-classes by the network operator will be automatically done. The hierarchy provides structured context and the hierarchical aggregation of class-services ensures scalability, applications correctness, and efficiency. Indeed, a hierarchical structure of behaviors allows the network operator to reduce the aggregate service-classes under each name-space. Thus, keep the utilization of resources under control to fulfill the line speed requirements and fit the available memory capacities.

In this paper, we propose a new forwarding strategy to deal with the above requirements. Before discussing our new strategy, the next subsection reviews existing literature on NDN forwarding strategies in regards to the aforementioned requirements.

---

[3] Names of Interests forwarded under the same delegation-name are very distinct.

2.3   Related Work

BroadcastStrategy [3] (renamed recently to MulticastStrategy) is the simplest forwarding approach. In this latter, each incoming Interest is forwarded to all available interfaces in FIB entry for the Interest's prefix except the Interest's incoming interface. Another basic strategy is the BestRoute strategy [3] that sends the Interest to the lowest cost face (e.g. RTT, hop count, ...) using the routing protocol assigned cost (e.g. NLSR [15]). As long as that face has the cheapest cost, the strategy keeps sending Interests on it, whether it return the data or not, until the routing protocol deletes the face from the FIB. The authors in [39], proposed a similar strategy dubbed GreenYellowRed. It is an adaptive forwarding that ranks the faces according to their status using a color-coding (Green, Yellow, and Red). Green faces are those returning data, when an interface may or may not return data its marked Yellow, whereas, Red identifies interfaces that do not work.

The NCC strategy [3] (CCN in backward) sends the Interest on one face and waits for a specific prediction time, set by the strategy, for a data packet to be returned. This face is denoted as the "best face" and it is used to forward future Interests with the same name-prefix. The prediction timer is adjusted down upon the reception of requested data on best face and adjusted up whenever the Interest is not satisfied within the predicted time while trying another face. Authors in [10] formulated the problem of joint multipath congestion control and request forwarding as an optimization problem. They proposed the Request Forwarding Algorithm (RFA) strategy as a solution. RFA monitors and extracts the number of corresponding pending Interests of each name-prefix per face. The records are used as weights (a moving average over the reciprocal count of the PIT entries) for the resolution of the optimization problem. The solution is used as the forwarding probabilities of the Interest with a name-prefix over output faces.

In [18], the authors tackled the problem of forwarding with Quality of Service (QoS) in NDN. The main idea of their proposal, *QoS-FS*, is to monitor and estimate, in real-time, bandwidth and RTT of interfaces and use them to determine when and which interface to use to forward an Interest. Chiocchetti et al. [12] proposed *INFORM*, a distributed forwarding strategy based on the Q-routing algorithm. *INFORM* discovers temporary copies of content not addressed in routing tables and forwards requests over the best performing interface at every hop. The best interface was defined as the one with the smallest delivery time.

Authors in [33], proposed an On-demand Multi-Path Interest Forwarding (OMP-IF) strategy. OMP-IF uses only the node disjoint paths to forward Interests simultaneously over multiple paths. The consumer first router uses a weighted round-robin mechanism based on path delays to distribute Interests over multiple faces. In [30], the authors proposed a Multiple Attribute Decision Making (MADM) strategy that supports QoS requirements through the simultaneous use of multiple access networks. MADM extends two existing strategies, the Lowest Cost Strategy (LCS) and Selective Parallel Strategy (SPS). LCS uses three parameters to determine the lowest cost face that satisfies all of the three requirements of an application, which are: (i) a maximum packet loss threshold not to be exceeded, (ii) a maximum delay accepted, and (iii) a minimum bandwidth guaranteed. SPS uses the same parameters as LCS but if one of the requirements is not met, it sends the Interest over multiple faces simultaneously in order to satisfy the specified requirements.

The authors in [26], proposed a Stochastic Adaptive Forwarding (SAF) strategy. SAF sends Interests probabilistically over multiple paths. It uses a feedback mechanism to decrease the traffic over congested links. SAF introduces a virtual face enabling content and context-aware adaptation. A Virtual Interest Packets (VIP) strategy was proposed in [35]. VIP is a framework for joint dynamic forwarding and caching in NDN. It employs a virtual control plane to measure the demand for data. Distributed control algorithms are used to guide caching and forwarding strategies.

As mentioned previously, in a recent work [1], we have proposed a localized parallel multipath forwarding strategy (*PMP-FS*). As we will build upon our previous work, *PMP-FS* will be discussed with more details in Sect. 4.

Table 2 depicts a comprehensive comparison between the aforementioned forwarding strategies. This comparison considers all the above-discussed requirements.

2.4 Motivation

Native context-aware in the forwarding plane enhances QoS/QoE and fulfill the applications requirements as discussed in Sect. 2.2. Despite that, there has been little effort in the area of context-aware forwarding in NDN. Two recent works worth mentioning are Posch et al. [27] and Kim et al. [19].

Posch et al. [27] discussed how to introduce context information in SAF [26]. They proposed to order content classes as follows: VoIP > Video > Data, and introduce a weighting mechanism that enforces this ordering by dropping low-priority content in favor of high-priority content. As discussed above, such an approach is unable to handle important issues such as delegation names (Map-and-Encap adoption) and competition among flows (fairness).

Kim et al. [19] proposed a differentiated services (DiffServ) model for NDN. By following the DiffServ model of the current Internet, the authors propose two differentiated models one at the forwarding plane and the other at the caching plane. The former proposed Differentiated forwarding suffers from several limitations such as flow identification and computation scalability at the edge routers, security risks, and PIT scalability at the core routers. In fact, the proposed control of Interest marking rate algorithm (Algorithm 1 in [19]) suffers from three major limitations:

1. The assumption that a stable RTT can be computed by the NDN routers that monitor the Interests in the PIT does not hold. In fact, the RTT oscillations is the main reason behind the lack of an effective NDN congestion control mechanism as mentioned in [28, 29];

Table 2. Comparison between existing forwarding strategies.

Forwarding Strategy	Granularity	Parallel multipath	Fairness	Considered context information	Flexibility in open networks	Target applications	Scalability
Broadcast [3]	Name-space	Yes	No	—	Depend on the sharp choice of the network operators (name-space and strategy)	Loss-sensitive	Yes
BestRoute [3]	Name-space	No	No	Cost of the upstream face (e.g. in terms of hop count)	Depend on the sharp choice of the network operators (name-space and strategy)	Delay-sensitive	Yes
GreenYellow Red [39]	Name-space	No	No	Status of the upstream face	Depend on the sharp choice of the network operators (name-space and strategy)	Loss-sensitive	Yes
NCC [3]	Name-space	Yes	No	Face latency (the time it takes to satisfy an Interest)	Depend on the sharp choice of the network operators (name-space and strategy)	Delay-sensitive	Yes
RFA [10]	Name-space	Yes	No	Current load of a face as indicated by the PIT	Yes	Bandwidth-sensitive	No
INFORM [12]	File	No	No	Delivery times toward other nodes	Depend on the sharp choice of the network operators	Delay-sensitive	Yes
QoS-FS [18]	Name-space	Yes	No	Bandwidth and RTT	Depend on the sharp choice of the network operators (name-space and strategy)	Delay-sensitive Bandwidth-sensitive	Yes
OMP-IF [33]	Name-space	Yes	No	-Path delays -Packet loss	Depend on the sharp choice of the network operators (name-space and strategy)	Delay-sensitive Loss-sensitive	No
MADM [30]	Name-space	Yes	No	Generic (one combination of metrics)	Depend on the sharp choice of the network operators (name-space and strategy)	Many (application require-ments trade-off)	No
SAF [26]	Name-space	Yes	No	Generic, considers all available information	Depend on the sharp choice of the network operators (name-space and strategy)	Loss-sensitive	Yes
VIP [35]	Packets	Yes	Yes	Generic, considers all available information	A general framework	All	No
PMP-FS [1]	NDN-flow	Yes	Yes	-Requested throughput (based on the number of Interests and sub-Interests under each name-space) or the desired granularity (Name tree node)) -Cost of every name-space separately -Current load of faces as indicated by the PIT	A general framework	All	Yes

2. In complex scenarios (the presence of cross-traffic with network-intensive workloads) where the flows are competing for the limited resources, the algorithm marks more and more Interests packets, which may lead to:
   - Computation scalability, and thus causing more delay at the edge routers;
   - PITs scalability at core routers. The existing PIT schemes are already a source of scalability concerns [11].
3. Security concerns arise from the marking of Interest packets. In fact, there are two options for marking:
   - Put the marks inside the security envelope, which implies more delay due to the process of embedding self-certification[4] in the Interest packets, or in other words rebuilding the Interest packet;
   - Put the marks outside the security envelope which could be used for a distributed denial-of-service (DDoS) attack.

In this context, we propose to extend our previous work [1] by enabling the consideration of context information natively in the forwarding plane. For this reason, we will follow our recommendations as described in Sect. 2.2.

3 Definitions

To define an NDN flow two questions should be answered:

1. How NDN routers treat names?
2. How NDN routers treat different types of data?

To answer the first question, let us examine the NDN Forwarding Information Base (NDN FIB) functionalities. The NDN FIB entry contains a list of ranked next-hop for specific name prefix. Due to scalability issues [6,23], consensus has not yet been reached on how and what prefix names to populate the FIB. They are a subject of intensive research [4,5,32,41]. All mentioned proposals advocate that NDN packet is forwarded by performing a look-up of its content name using the Longest Prefix Matching (LPM) or the Longest Prefix Classification (LPC). The different Interests with the same routable prefix name issued by different end-users are forwarded under the same FIB name-prefix. Furthermore, the Interests forwarded under the same FIB entry at one router might be forwarded under different FIB entries at another router, and therefore could be forwarded separately.

To answer the second question, we examined the NDN Pending Interest Table (NDN PIT) functionalities. As a core component, PIT is responsible for keeping track of the awaiting Interest packets [39,40]. An Interest is issued by one end-user but it could be aggregated (becoming subsequent Interest) once or many times at the downstream routers. Therefore, for a given router within the network, a pending Interest could be issued by one or many end-users. A returned data object could satisfy one or multiple end-users. The Interest aggregation

---

[4] Cryptographic mechanism ensuring integrity by binding the prefix-name and data packet content.

feature combined with other features (NDN in-network caching, adaptive forwarding plane, ...) make the power of the NDN architecture. It is important to notice that Interests to be aggregated should have the exact same prefix name and generally this concerns the static content or a Content Delivery Networks (CDN) content. Another aspect to consider is the fact that under the same routable name (prefix-name), we can find a big number of different distinct Interests issued by one or more than one end-user.

From the above discussion, it is clear that defining a flow should be local to the router and for a specific period of time (FIB update). In order to have a clear idea, we model a Router R and its links with its neighbor routers by a weighted directed graph G.

3.1   Router Model

A router R is connected to its K^{ith} neighbor router by a link L_k with capacity C_k, through the corresponding face F_k. The faces of the router R are completely connected to each other with infinite capacity links (Fig. 2a).

We model the router and its direct links as a directed graph $G = (F, L, C)$ (Fig. 2b) where:

- F is a set of vertices (Router faces and a virtual central node R);
- L is the set of edges (Router links);
- C is a function whose domain is L, it is an assignment of capacities to the edges (Router links in terms of inputs and outputs bandwidth);
- The order of graph is $k + 1$ and the size of G is $|L(G)| = 2k$;
- L_{ki} denotes the arc going from F_k to R, represents the downstream through the K^{ith} face F_k, with a capacity C_{ki};
- L_{ko} denote the arc going from R to F_k, represents the upstream through the K^{ith} face F_k, with a capacity C_{ko};

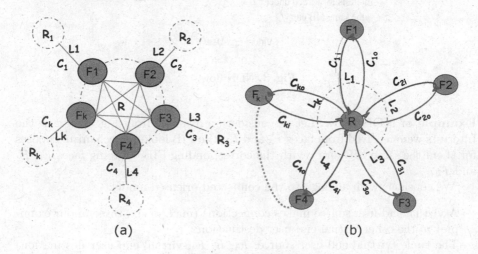

(a)   (b)

Fig. 2. Router model.

– $C_{ki} + C_{ko} <= C_k$, is the capacity of bidirectional link k connecting the router R and the K^{ith} neighbor router, through the face F_k (Fig. 2).

Definition 1. *A Flow in NDN context is a set of Interests and their corresponding returned data objects forwarded under the same FIB entry proper to a router during a given period. These Interests may have been requested from one or multiple faces and forwarded through one or multiple faces (Fig. 3).*

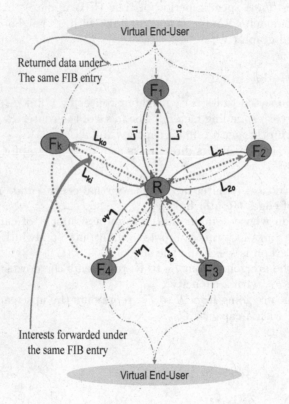

Fig. 3. NDN flow.

Example of NDN Flow. Let us consider an example from Fig. 3. In case the Interests were received from faces F_3 and F_4, the FIB lookup mechanism chooses for them the same FIB entry with the corresponding FIB outgoing faces F_1, F_2 and F_k.

We consider, with analogy to the connected oriented model:

– A virtual end-user source makes connections (max. of six, three in our example) to the other virtual end-user destination;
– The tuple (virtual end-user source, F_3, R, F_2, virtual end-user destination) is a connection;

- If an Interest is forwarded through face F_2 and it is received from face F_3, the Interest will use the resources l_{3i} through R and l_{2o};
- The returned data will follow the reverse path l_{2i} through R and l_{3o}.

This set of Interests and their corresponding returned data objects, are considered for this router as one NDN flow.

Definition 2. *In the presence of competing elastic flows, a Flow Assignment is fair in NDN context if the assignment is weighted alpha-fair, where:*

- *Weights represent the normalized number of distinct awaiting sub-Interests and the answered Interests from the Content Store (CS) as a function of time.*
- *Distinct data object packets sizes and heterogeneous round-trip times (RTTs) are taken into consideration.*

3.2 Discussion

The fairness must be addressed across flows, across network and across time [9]. The proposed definition of NDN flow and the fairness criteria does not specify whether many flows can serve a common end-user. We claim in this paper a realistic user-centric conception of fairness. The weighted α-proportional fairness imposed between virtual end-users flows at each node ensures fairness between the real end-users. The notion of friendliness imposed by the emergence of the peer-to-peer networks in the context of TCP/IP paradigm does not need to be addressed in the context of NDN. Taking the definitions above, all the applications and sessions are friendly to each other if the flows are fairly tackled.

In [36], the authors present Fair Interest Limiting (FIL). An NDN version of the fair queuing mechanism used in the TCP/IP paradigm that suffers from the same limitations in terms of fairness [9]. Besides, it does neither take the unpredictable effect of content in-network caching and the Interest aggregation feature nor the distinct data object packets sizes and heterogeneous round-trip times (RTTs) into consideration on the fairness evaluation. At the opposite, weights presented in the above definition come as an answer. The weights must be a function of time to deal with the dynamic nature and unpredictable changes in the network caused by the effect of in-network caching and the Interest aggregation features.

4 PMP-FS Overview

The Parallel Multi-Path Forwarding Strategy (PMP-FS) is a localized strategy that takes advantage of NDN native support of parallel multipath forwarding. In PMP-FS, we formulated the parallel multipath forwarding packets as an optimization problem for Coordinated Multipath Flow Control. The PMP-FS proactively splits traffic by determining how the multiple routes will be used. It takes into consideration the NDN in-network caching and the NDN Interest aggregation features to achieve local weighted alpha fairness among different NDN flows and serves end-users in a fair manner without the need of identifying them while maximizing network throughput. Here, it is significant to mention:

- The requested data objects in NDN may be cached in different locations and in different periods of time by the multi-homing mechanism and/or the NDN in-caching mechanism. The whole data objects may be in one place or dispersed in different places;
- The order of data packets arrival constitutes another difference in forwarding packets between NDN and TCP/IP paradigm. The order of data packets arrival is very important in TCP/IP, which is not the case in NDN. The returned data will be recomposed for application use by end-users;
- Each flow (session) aims at maximizing its throughput;
- Resources are limited: the competition between flows as to be better served by forwarding them to the set of the best possible face(s) is unavoidable;
- Preserving not only fairness between end-users but also efficiency and scalability are a requirement;
- PMP-FS is executed at every NDN router;
- PMP-FS respects the real time (line-speed) constraint;
- PMP-FS takes the effect of content in-network caching mechanism and the subsequent awaiting Interests on the evaluation of fairness;
- Hop-by-hop Interest shaping mechanism to ensure the whole network stability is used;
- We assumed that the flows are elastic, the routing plane is responsible for populating the FIB and we make no assumptions about whether the paths are disjoint.

The PMP-FS splits traffic and achieves fairness in NDN context of the active flows over multiple different faces at each time slot. This increases reliability, robustness, and fault tolerance. The PMP-FS works as follows:

- A hop-by-hop Interest shaping module proposed in [34] is used as a congestion control mechanism. It is executed at every NDN router to ensure the whole network stability. The result of this module is the links input and output capacities between the router at hand and its neighbor routers;
- At every new FIB entry picked: when a router receives an Interest and in case the checking of the CS and the PIT results in a negative response, the FIB is checked and a FIB entry is picked. If the FIB entry has no local measurements (picked for the first time), the PMP-FS qualifies this entry as new.
  - New flow queue is created and set as inactive and the "*after receive Interest*" action is triggered.
  - The first group of Interests (f Interests) of a newly created flow is forwarded immediately. The variation in data object sizes is taken into consideration by the per-flow queuing (counters per flow) and the flow will be considered by the Flow Assignment module only when it is active (the flow queue becomes active when the forwarded Interests bring back data). In this case, we have the estimated size of the data object packets. The latter is smoothly updated at each received data object ("*the before satisfy Interest*" action is triggered).

- Forwarding the first group of Interests of a newly created flow over a set f of faces gives us an opportunity to measure the performance and rank the faces both dynamically and locally (f best faces ranked by the routing plane).
- As an acceptance mechanism the Proportional Integral Controller Enhanced (PIE) is used to drop incoming Interests and send back NACKs based on a probability. Departure rate and the flow queue length are used [25]. When sending NACKs the *"before expire Interest"* action is triggered to update the counters in measurements table.

– At every time slot: this is done in parallel of the receipt of packets and forwarding of Interests.
  1. The PMP-FS collects:
     - The information about the pending and the awaiting Interests with their corresponding FIB entries for each active NDN flow and the Interests that hit the cache. These will be used as weights;
     - The links input and output capacities: the result of the capacities of the hop-by-hop shaping minus the reserved space for the ending sessions (empty flows queues);
  2. The flow assignment module is executed for the active flows. The result is a matrix A of Flow Assignment over the faces. The objective of this module is to perform a controlled splitting of the active flows over the faces while satisfying the limited bandwidth constraints of the outgoing and ingoing router links.
  3. The forwarding decision module: the one-to-one interdependence between Interests and data objects called NDN flow balance propriety gives us the opportunity to carry out a controlled splitting of the flows over the faces by only deciding where and how many Interests of the active flows to forward. Taking as inputs the matrix of Flow Assignment of the last step and the vector of estimated sizes of the active flows data objects, we get the matrix D of the maximum number of Interests to be forwarded for each flow over each face. The matrix D is used to forward the incoming Interests, the next time slot and for every Interest answered another one from the same flow is sent.

– The matrix D is used to forward the incoming Interests and for every Interest answered another one from the same flow is sent.

The time slot must be chosen in a manner that enable us to integrate the new flows softly and eliminate the RTT variations effect on fairness. We take 25 $msec$ as the time slot which is about the third of mean Internet RTT.

Regarding the performance of PMP-FS, preliminary results are reported and discussed in [1].

5   Best Effort Context-Aware Adaptation: The *CPMP-FS* Strategy

NDN is designed as a common or universal platform for all types of applications (elasticity principle). The requirements of applications are different, some are delay- and loss-tolerant but aim at maximizing the bandwidth, and others are delay-sensitive and require relatively small bandwidth. NDN elasticity must be reflected in the forwarding plane. The latter should aim at achieving the most possible optimal performance for the wide range of application types.

In this section, we investigate the enhancement of context awareness in the PMP-FS forwarding strategy in order to support various types of traffic and their QoS requirements.

5.1 Diagnosis: The Nature of the Challenge

In TCP/IP paradigm, packets of the same flow are implicitly used by the same application. Hence, application requirements have been tackled to a certain point using Intserv and Diffserv approaches [8]. On the other hand, in ICN, the only consistent information that we can use to categorize and classify the packets is the name carried by both Interests and data packets.

In this context, authors in [24] tried to define the CCN flow as "the packets bearing the same object name". This is an ideal definition, if only we do not have unlimited name-space and only if we know the components allocated to object name in the name-prefix. For the sake of clarity, let us assume that we have a limited name-space (very big to support the existing data but limited) and we know the component of each object name (the use of a field in each prefix indicating where the name starts and ends). The resulting over-load from comparing the prefix-name of an incoming Interest, component by component (each component composed of any character type), with the existing prefix-names of the pending Interests will be very high in terms of computation.

Authors in [35] clearly defined the flow through the use of labeling. However, the utilization of labeling constitutes a scalability handicap as mentioned in [29].

In general, the assumption that requested data packets, with a given name serving different end-users, are related to similar type of applications[5] is not realistic. For instance, a produced data packet of a picture from a disaster scene may be requested by the first responder's application and at the same time requested by a Facebook application. These requests should not be treated the same way by NDN nodes. In this work, we do not aim at resolving such a problem, we will tackle it in a future work by considering additive modules while taking into consideration computation scalability and preserving the NDN basis, especially the data immutability and the embedded self-certification. In this paper, we discuss how to enable a native best effort context-awareness at the forwarding plane while considering the aforementioned recommendations sketched in Sect. 2.2.

As a consequence of the adoption of Map-and-Encap [4] approach, with the purpose of scaling NDN routing and resolving producer mobility, a native solution to manage the multitude of application needs under the same NDN flow becomes an obligation. Indeed, name-prefixes used as delegation names (global

---

[5] Application with the same requirements.

routable prefixes) may embody very distinct name-prefixes, hence, different end-users application types. Therefore, a finer granularity is needed than the one provided by the latter delegation name.

Definition 3. *An NDN sub-flow is a sub-set of Interests and their corresponding returned data of a given NDN flow that need particular forwarding treatment (see Fig. 4). The forwarding strategy specifies the outgoing face(s) ranking (associated measurements (delay, packet loss,...)) and their usage, i.e., how many faces to use and how to send Interests over the chosen faces (multi-cast, send to the best and probe others, ...).*

In this paper, we assume that Interests of the same NDN sub-flow are serving end-users applications with the same requirements. We assume that at the time of creation of data, the first component of the name is a code (a field of one byte) representing a service-class or in other words represents the desired forwarding treatment of the data packet as desired by the producer. The name of data containing the service-class code is inside the security envelope and never changes (immutable name).

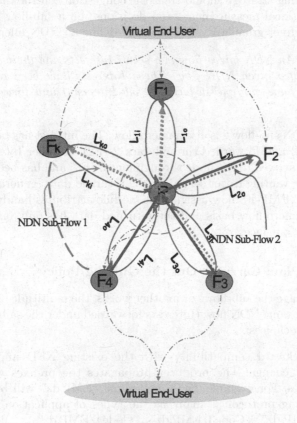

Fig. 4. NDN sub-flow.

5.2   Guiding Policy: Dealing with the Challenge

In this work, we propose a native best effort context-aware scheme providing the best possible QoS/QoE to the end-users. By allowing per-hop management and a simple packet classification in order to control the processing time and storing space according to the computation and storage capabilities of each node. Consequently, the service-class code of each data does not change, it is the assignment to an aggregated service-class at each node that changes. The method used to define equivalent classes and the corresponding code that can be used by the nodes forwarders is outside the scope of this paper and needs more exploration. The six-bit code used by the IP Diffserv can serve as a start point.

The choice of the first name component to carry the service-class code is justified. Indeed, NDN naming schemes can *evolve independently* from the network (NDN imposes no restrictions on names except the component structure). It is worth mentioning that NDN names are opaque to the network and applications may choose the naming scheme that fit their needs. In addition, names are suffixed by components for versions and segmentation of the data (Fig. 1b).

The forwarding strategy should treat the congestion control and the Interest retransmission (local measurements and decisions) on a sub-flow basis. Therefore, we need a finer granularity. For that, we define an NDN micro-flow as:

Definition 4. *An NDN micro-flow is a set of Interests and their corresponding returned data of a given NDN flow. These Interests have been requested from one face (may have multiple in-faces as sub-Interests) and forwarded through one face.*

In Fig. 4, NDN sub-flow 2 is also a micro-flow. The Interest has been requested from face 4 (F4) and forwarded through face 2 (F2). Another Interest with the same name has arrived to the node through face 3 (F3) and has been aggregated in the PIT table waiting to get served by the returned data (general multi-cast). Notice that, the PMP-FS flow assignment module attributes bandwidth at each time slot on a micro-flow basis and the returned data has only one in-face and may have many out-faces.

5.3   Action Plan: Carrying Out the Guiding Policy

In order to manage the sub-flows or in other words, the multitude of applications needs under the same NDN flow (Interests forwarded under the same FIB entry), one has got two choices:

1. Preserve backward compatibility with the existing NFD implementations without any change. The producer propagates the prefixes with different service-classes. For example, the prefix-name "EMP.dz" will be propagated by the routing protocol as many as the types of application requirements ("Code1/EMP.dz", "Code3/EMP.dz", "Code4/EMP.dz", ...). This will be reflected in the FIB table by many FIB-entries (many NDN flows). All the Interests under an NDN flow will be treated by the forwarding strategy in

the same way. In fact, the NDN flow comprises one sub-flow. This solution could raise FIB scalability problems.

2. Change the Longest Prefix Matching (LPM) procedure so that it ignores the first component when performing the matching. In this case, a table called Aggregate Service contains the aggregate services defined by the operator (to reduce the per-sub-flow status managed by each router in order to control processing time and storing space) for each name-prefix (see Fig. 5). Each aggregate service-class represent an NDN sub-flow.

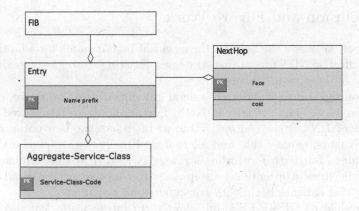

Fig. 5. Aggregate service-class table.

Multipath Utilization. The forwarding strategies implemented in the NFD are in fact special cases of the proposed *CPMP-FS* strategy:

- Best Route Strategy: CPMP-FS with one best link;
- Multi-cast Strategy: CPMP-FS with all upstreams indicated by a FIB entry;
- Client Control Strategy: CPMP-FS testing specific Interests and allowing them to be forwarded to pre-configured outgoing faces.

It is worth pointing out that each one of the mentioned strategies can be considered as a service-class. Therefore, for a name-space, the operator can choose to associate with it one or many sub-service classes.

The flow assignment module performs a controlled splitting of the active flows over the eligible outgoing faces while satisfying the limited bandwidth constraints of the outgoing and ingoing router links. The module defines the share for each micro-flow. The bandwidth of the service-classes under each flow must respect this share.

Congestion Control and Retransmission. The explicit signaling mechanism (NACKs) is used. There is different type of NACKs, representing the reason behind the non-satisfaction of the Interest (congestion, an empty or no forwarding entry at all, upstream face(s) down). The NACK concerns a specific micro-flow unless it is an extreme congestion (upstream face is fully utilized), in this case, the hop-by-hop shaping module is active. Otherwise, NACK may trigger the forwarding strategy to adjust the rate of the micro-flow and to select alternative micro-flow(s) to re-transmit the Interest or *send a NACK only for that micro-flow* (one downstream face).

6 Conclusion and Future Work

In this paper, we shade the light on the essential requirements for adaptive, efficient, and effective NDN forwarding strategies. Existing strategies were discussed in the light of these requirements.

Based on the above, we inferred general guidelines for an adaptive, efficient, and effective forwarding strategy in NDN. Furthermore, we introduced a novel definition for NDN fairness concept. Then, we introduce two new notions related to the NDN flows, namely sub- and micro-flow. Finally, we sketched a Context-aware Parallel MultiPath forwarding strategy (CPMP-FS) that implement the proposed guidelines in order to get a step closer to adaptive, effective and efficient forwarding that satisfies both NDN consumers and providers.

Fully evaluating CPMP-FS is our short-term future work. We also plan to introduce guaranteed QoS based on CPMP-FS (NDiffserv).

References

1. Abdelkader, B., Senouci, M.R., Merabti, B.: Parallel multi-path forwarding strategy for named data networking. In: Proceedings of the 13th International Joint Conference on e-Business and Telecommunications, pp. 36–46. SCITEPRESS - Science and Technology Publications, 0005964600360046 (2016). http://www.scitepress.org/DigitalLibrary/Link.aspx?doi=10.5220/
2. Afanasyev, A.: Addressing operational challenges in named data networking through NDNS distributed database. Ph.D. thesis, Citeseer (2013). http://lasr.cs.ucla.edu/afanasyev/data/files/Afanasyev/afanasyev-phd-thesis.pdf
3. Afanasyev, A., Shi, J., Zhang, B., Zhang, L., Moiseenko, I., Yu, Y., Shang, W., Huang, Y., Abraham, J.P., Dibenedetto, S., Fan, C., Pesavento, D., Grassi, G., Pau, G., Zhang, H., Song, T., Abraham, H.B., Crowley, P., Amin, S.O., Lehman, V., Wang, L.: NFD developer's guide. NDN Proj. **4**, 1–52 (2015). http://named-data.net/wp-content/uploads/2016/03/ndn-0021-6-nfd-developer-guide.pdf
4. Afanasyev, A., Yi, C., Wang, L., Zhang, B., Zhang, L.: Map-and-Encap for scaling NDN routing. Technical report, NDN-0004 (2015). http://named-data.net/techreports/
5. Afanasyev, A., Yi, C., Wang, L., Zhang, B., Zhang, L.: SNAMP: secure namespace mapping to scale NDN forwarding. In: Proceedings - IEEE INFOCOM, vol. 2015-August, pp. 281–286. IEEE. http://ieeexplore.ieee.org/lpdocs/epic03/wrapper.htm?arnumber=7179398

6. Baid, A., Vu, T., Raychaudhuri, D.: Comparing alternative approaches for networking of named objects in the future internet. In: Proceedings - IEEE INFOCOM, pp. 298–303. IEEE (2012). http://ieeexplore.ieee.org/lpdocs/epic03/wrapper.htm?arnumber=6193509

7. Ben Abraham, H., Crowley, P.: Forwarding strategies for applications in named data networking. In: Proceedings of the 2016 Symposium on Architectures for Networking and Communications Systems - ANCS 2016, New York, USA, pp. 111–112 (2016). http://dl.acm.org/citation.cfm?doid=2881025.2889475

8. Blake, S., Black, D., Carlson, M., Davies, E., Wang, Z., Weiss, W.: RFC-2475: an architecture for differentiated services. IETF -Network Working Group, December 1998. https://tools.ietf.org/html/rfc2475

9. Briscoe, B.: Flow rate fairness: dismantling a religion. CCR **37**(2), 63–74 (2007). http://portal.acm.org/citation.cfm?id=1232926

10. Carofiglio, G., Gallo, M., Muscariello, L., Papalini, M., Wang, S.: Optimal multipath congestion control and request forwarding in information-centric networks. In: 2013 21st IEEE International Conference on Network Protocols (ICNP), pp. 1–10. IEEE (2013). http://ieeexplore.ieee.org/document/6733576/

11. Carofiglio, G., Gallo, M., Muscariello, L., Perino, D.: Pending interest table sizing in named data networking. In: Proceedings of the 2nd International Conference on Information-Centric Networking - ICN 2015, New York, USA, pp. 49–58 (2015). http://dl.acm.org/citation.cfm?doid=2810156.2810167

12. Chiocchetti, R., Perino, D., Rossi, D., Rossini, G.: INFORM: a dynamic INterest FORwarding mechanism for information centric networking. In: Proceedings of the 3rd ACM SIGCOMM Workshop on Information-Centric Networking - ICN 2013, pp. 9–14 (2013). http://doi.acm.org/10.1145/2491224.2491227

13. Dannewitz, C., Kutscher, D., Ohlman, B., Farrell, S., Ahlgren, B., Karl, H.: Network of Information (NetInf) -an information-centric networking architecture. Comput. Commun. **36**(7), 721–735 (2013). http://linkinghub.elsevier.com/retrieve/pii/S0140366413000364

14. Hahne, E.: Round-robin scheduling for max-min fairness in data networks. IEEE J. Sel. Areas Commun. **9**(7), 1024–1039 (1991). http://ieeexplore.ieee.org/lpdocs/epic03/wrapper.htm?arnumber=103550

15. Hoque, A., Amin, S.O., Alyyan, A., Zhang, B., Zhang, L., Wang, L.: NLSR: named-data link state routing protocol. In: Proceedings of the 3rd ACM SIGCOMM Workshop on Information-Centric Networking - ICN 2013, New York, USA, p. 15 (2013). http://dl.acm.org/citation.cfm?doid=2491224.2491231

16. Jacobson, V., Smetters, D.K., Thornton, J.D., Plass, M.F., Briggs, N.H., Braynard, R.L.: Networking named content. In: Proceedings of the 5th International Conference on Emerging Networking Experiments and Technologies - CoNEXT 2009, New York, USA, p. 1 (2009). http://doi.acm.org/10.1145/1658939.1658941

17. Kelly, F.: Charging and rate control for elastic traffic. Eur. Trans. Telecommun. **8**(1), 33–37 (1997). http://dx.doi.org/10.1002/ett.4460080106

18. Kerrouche, A., Senouci, M.R., Mellouk, A.: QoS-FS: A new forwarding strategy with QoS for routing in named data networking. In: 2016 IEEE International Conference on Communications (ICC), pp. 1–7. IEEE, May 2016. http://ieeexplore.ieee.org/lpdocs/epic03/wrapper.htm?arnumber=7511378

19. Kim, Y., Kim, Y., Bi, J., Yeom, I.: Differentiated forwarding and caching in named-data networking. J. Netw. Comput. Appl. **60**, 155–169 (2016). http://dx.doi.org/10.1016/j.jnca.2015.09.011

20. Low, S.: A duality model of TCP and queue management algorithms. IEEE/ACM Trans. Netw. **11**(4), 525–536 (2003). http://ieeexplore.ieee.org/lpdocs/epic03/ wrapper.htm?arnumber=1224453

21. Mazumdar, R., Mason, L., Douligeris, C.: Fairness in network optimal flow control: optimality of product forms. IEEE Trans. Commun. **39**(5), 775–782 (1991). http://ieeexplore.ieee.org/lpdocs/epic03/wrapper.htm?arnumber=87140

22. Mo, J., Walrand, J.: Fair end-to-end window-based congestion control. IEEE/ACM Trans. Netw. **8**(5), 556–567 (2000). doi:10.1109/90.879343

23. Narayanan, A., Oran, D.: NDN and IP routing can it scale? In: Proposed Information-Centric Networking Research Group (ICNRG), Side meeting at IETF-82, Taipei (2015). http://named-data.net/techreports/

24. Oueslati, S., Roberts, J., Sbihi, N.: Flow-aware traffic control for a content-centric network. In: 2012 Proceedings IEEE INFOCOM, pp. 2417–2425. IEEE, March 2012. http://ieeexplore.ieee.org/document/6195631/

25. Pan, R., Natarajan, P., Piglione, C., Prabhu, M.S., Subramanian, V., Baker, F., VerSteeg, B.: PIE: a lightweight control scheme to address the bufferbloat problem. In: 2013 IEEE 14th International Conference on High Performance Switching and Routing (HPSR), Taipei, Taiwan, pp. 148–155. IEEE, July 2013. http://ieeexplore. ieee.org/lpdocs/epic03/wrapper.htm?arnumber=6602305

26. Posch, D., Rainer, B., Hellwagner, H.: SAF: stochastic adaptive forwarding in named data networking, pp. 1–14, May 2015. arXiv preprint arXiv:1505.05259

27. Posch, D., Rainer, B., Hellwagner, H.: Towards a context-aware forwarding plane in named data networking supporting qos. Computer Communication Review, 9 January 2017, to appear

28. Ren, Y., Li, J., Shi, S., Li, L., Wang, G., Zhang, B.: Congestion control in named data networking-a survey. Comput. Commun. **86**(3), 1–11 (2016). http:// linkinghub.elsevier.com/retrieve/pii/S0140366416301566

29. Schneider, K., Yi, C., Zhang, B., Zhang, L.: A practical congestion control scheme for named data networking. In: Proceedings of the 2016 3rd ACM Conference on Information-Centric Networking - ACM-ICN 2016, pp. 21–30. ACM Press, New York (2016). http://dl.acm.org/citation.cfm?doid=2984356.2984369

30. Schneider, K.M., Krieger, U.R.: Beyond network selection. In: Proceedings of the 2nd International Conference on Information-Centric Networking - ICN 2015, pp. 137–146 (2015). http://dl.acm.org/citation.cfm?doid=2810156.2810164

31. Simon, H.A.: The architecture of complexity. In: Klir, G.J. (ed.) Facets of Systems Science, vol. 106, pp. 457–476. Springer, Heidelberg (1991). doi:10.1007/ 978-1-4899-0718-9_31

32. Song, T., Yuan, H., Crowley, P., Zhang, B.: Scalable name-based packet forwarding. In: Proceedings of the 2nd International Conference on Information-Centric Networking - ICN 2015, USA, pp. 19–28 (2015). http://dl.acm.org/citation.cfm? doid=2810156.2810166

33. Udugama, A., Zhang, X., Kuladinithi, K., Goerg, C.: An on-demand multi-path interest forwarding strategy for content retrievals in CCN. In: 2014 IEEE Network Operations and Management Symposium (NOMS), pp. 1–6. IEEE, May 2014. http://ieeexplore.ieee.org/document/6838389/

34. Wang, Y., Rozhnova, N., Narayanan, A., Oran, D., Rhee, I.: An improved hop-by-hop interest shaper for congestion control in named data networking. ACM SIG-COMM Comput. Commun. Rev. **43**(4), 55–60 (2013). http://dl.acm.org/citation. cfm?doid=2534169.2491233

35. Yeh, E., Ho, T., Cui, Y., Burd, M., Liu, R., Leong, D.: VIP: joint traffic engineering and caching in named data networks. In: 2015 International Conference on Computing, Networking and Communications (ICNC), pp. 695–699. IEEE, February 2015. http://ieeexplore.ieee.org/document/7069430/
36. Yi, C.: Adaptive forwarding in named data networking. Ph.D. thesis, The University Of Arizona (2014). http://www.cs.arizona.edu/~yic/paper/dissertation.pdf
37. Yi, C., Abraham, J., Afanasyev, A., Wang, L., Zhang, B., Zhang, L.: On the role of routing in named data networking. In: Proceedings of the 1st International Conference on Information-Centric Networking - INC 2014, New York, USA, pp. 27–36 (2014). http://dl.acm.org/citation.cfm?doid=2660129.2660140
38. Yi, C., Afanasyev, A., Moiseenko, I., Wang, L., Zhang, B., Zhang, L.: A case for stateful forwarding plane. Comput. Commun. **36**(7), 779–791 (2013). http://dx.doi.org/10.1016/j.comcom.2013.01.005
39. Yi, C., Afanasyev, A., Wang, L., Zhang, B., Zhang, L.: Adaptive forwarding in named data networking. ACM SIGCOMM Comput. Commun. Rev. **42**(3), 62 (2012). http://dl.acm.org/citation.cfm?doid=2317307.2317319
40. Yuan, H., Crowley, P.: Scalable pending interest table design: from principles to practice. In: IEEE INFOCOM 2014 - IEEE Conference on Computer Communications, pp. 2049–2057. IEEE, April 2014. http://ieeexplore.ieee.org/lpdocs/epic03/wrapper.htm?arnumber=6848146
41. Yuan, H., Song, T., Crowley, P.: Scalable NDN forwarding: concepts, issues and principles. In: 2012 21st International Conference on Computer Communications and Networks (ICCCN), pp. 1–9. IEEE, July 2012. http://ieeexplore.ieee.org/lpdocs/epic03/wrapper.htm?arnumber=6289305
42. Zhang, L., Estrin, D., Burke, J., Jacobson, V., Thorton, J.D., Smetters, D.K., Zhang, B., Tsudik, G., Claffy, K., Krioukov, D., Massey, D., Papadopoulos, C., Abdelzaher, T., Wang, L., Crowley, P., Yeh, E.: Named Data Networking. Technical report, NDN-0001 (2010). http://named-data.net/techreports/
43. Zhang, L., Afanasyev, A., Burke, J., Jacobson, V., Claffy, K., Crowley, P., Papadopoulos, C., Wang, L., Zhang, B.: Named data networking. ACM SIGCOMM Comput. Commun. Rev. **44**(3), 66–73 (2014). http://dl.acm.org/citation.cfm?doid=2656877.2656887

Towards Understanding the Role of Execution Context for Observing Malicious Behavior in Android Malware

Catherine Boileau[1], François Gagnon[2(✉)], Jérémie Poisson[2], Simon Frenette[2], and Mohammed Mejri[1]

[1] Université Laval, Québec, Canada
catherine.boileau.1@ulaval.ca, mohamed.mejri@ift.ulaval.ca
[2] CybersecLab at Cégep de Sainte-Foy, Québec, Canada
cybersecurity@cegep-ste-foy.qc.ca

Abstract. Favorite target of mobile malware, Android operating system can now rely on numerous tools, instrumentations and sandbox environments to fight back the malware threat. Sandboxing is a popular dynamic approach to detect malware, where an application is submitted to a plethora of tests in order to determine the presence of malicious behavior. Such existing sandboxes usually performed analysis on a malware sample once, given the tremendous amount of applications to analyze. In order to further study what trigger malware behavior, we decided to submit a malware sample multiple times to our sandbox, each time with slightly different experiment parameters, such as level of user simulation, the number of user actions performed, and the network configuration. Our results show that a proper configuration of these parameters will yield more information about the sample under study.

1 Introduction

Android was the most popular platform in 2015 for mobile devices and malware designers alike, as 97% of malware were designed for Android, who holds 85% of the market share in the mobile world. Besides its popularity, the burgeoning of many third-party app stores is helping to distribute malware around the world, as some of them may contain up to 8% of malicious applications [1].

In order to countenance this threat and protect the Android operating system, tools and systems are developed to study and detect malicious behavior in applications. In recent years, sandboxing, defined as the execution of malware in a closed and virtual environment [2], has been used to analyze Android applications and monitor malicious behavior.

Most of the systems are focusing on detecting malicious applications, by submitting an application to a sandbox. Once the experiment is completed, the results are saved in a report and the application is not analyzed again, as analysis is time-consuming and new applications hit markets at an ever faster rate.

Since the literature is currently bent on detecting malware by a one-time submission to a sandbox, we explored a different approach, studying the same

© Springer International Publishing AG 2017
M.S. Obaidat (Ed): ICETE 2016, CCIS 764, pp. 48–71, 2017.
https://doi.org/10.1007/978-3-319-67876-4_3

malware repeatedly in slightly different environments. These variations would allow us to determine the optimal environment to discover malicious behavior and possibly help to detect more malware on their first submission to a sandbox. For example, applications depending on specific events or parameters (e.g. time-bombs or location-specific apps) to expose their malicious behavior could be detected in repeated experiments where a parameter (e.g. the location, the time) is changed to different values.

In our preliminary group of experiments, we started with 3 variations in application usage: only installing the application, installing and starting the application and finally, installing, starting and simulating the application [3]. In this paper, we repeat our preliminary paper experiment, and add 3 new groups of experiments where the variation is the number of actions performed in user simulation, the rest period after simulation and the network configuration. Other parameters are still on our to-do list, such as using a different Android version of the emulator and different types of emulators.

Therefore, we will first present, in Sect. 2, related work about publicly available sandboxes performing dynamic analysis and then, a brief description will follow of our sandbox environment and its possible configurations in Sect. 3. Afterwards, a description of the experiment will be presented in Sect. 4 as well as the scenarios used. Finally, results will be discussed in Sect. 5, together with future work in Sect. 6, and concluding remarks in Sect. 7.

2 Related Work

Before the first Android malware was discovered in August 2010 [4], sandboxing techniques were already useful to fight PC-based digital threats [5–7]. Malware then started to spread to the mobile world, and static [8–11] and dynamic [12–14] analysis tools were adapted to face the new challenge. Afterwards, hybrid systems using both static and dynamic analysis [15,16] sprang to life and matured into the following public sandboxes analyzing Android malwares.

First among them is ANDRUBIS [17], a system performing both static and dynamic analysis on a large scale. Using similar tools as our sandbox, and keeping tracks of numerous metrics, ANDRUBIS analyzes an app once, and if submitted again, the report from the first run is presented to the user. Mobile-sandbox [18] is another hybrid analysis system tracking native API calls. As their goal is to detect malware via a new metric, they process their apps once.

CopperDroid [19] is also part of the dynamic analysis sandbox family and their approach is closer to our own, as they compare applications behaviour with and without user simulation. They are thus able to demonstrate the usefulness of simulation during an experiment, whereas we pushed this logic to multiple scenarios and are interested in putting results into perspective. Tracedroid [20] is also a hybrid analysis service, based on method traces as an extension on the virtual machine. As the other tools, they aim at processing a quantity of apps, to then label and sort out malware. To our knowledge, Android sandboxing is mostly used to detect malware from good applications and not to observe behaviour in different contexts. Moreover, once a malware is processed, it is not analyzed again.

As our approach implies multiple runs with variations in parameters, environments and network configurations, we find that fuzzing is somehow related to our work. Per definition, fuzzing is an automated technique that provides boundary test cases and massive inputs of data in order to find vulnerabilities [21]. In the Android world, the framework AndroidFuzzer was developed in the cloud to that intent. Some tools focused on a particular area of testing, such as permissions [21], activities or intents [22,23]. However, to the best of our knowledge, fuzzing has not been extended to the analysis or detection of malwares.

3 Methodology

In order to observe variations in application behaviour, we use a client-server sandbox [24,25] that executes an experiment in a particular context. An experiment is defined as the execution of a scenario (a series of actions to configure, install, test, and collect data on apps) applied to all samples of our dataset. The server side of the sandbox is responsible for the management of the experiment (i.e., managing the clients pool, the distribution to clients, etc.), whereas clients manage runs (i.e., the execution of the selected scenario for one particular app of the pool). The client-server architecture was selected for its scalability, for it is as simple as adding a client to process more applications in the same time. A server-controlled experiment also ensures that all runs in an experiment will execute the same scenario with the same parameters (network configuration, android version, etc.), since the configuration of the experiment is done on the server and then forwarded to each available client. All machines, server and clients are connected to the same dedicated subnet, policied by our fake server to provide the same network context to all clients. Thus, the sandbox architecture lowers the variability in an experiment to allow a sound comparison between runs of a same experiments and between experiments on the same malware.

3.1 Client-Server Architecture

First, our sandbox server works as a controller over the whole experiment. To begin with, all parameters are defined in the configuration file, to prepare the environment (network configuration and android version) and the parameters (scenario to use, dataset to analyze, etc.) needed for the experiment. Once configured, the server will start and monitor the pool of clients. Each new client will register itself to the server pool of clients, thus notifying the server of its availability to perform a part of the experiment. As soon as the server detects that a client is ready to execute a run, it will give that client the scenario to execute and the application to analyze.

At that moment, the client starts its run by loading the scenario and the application to install. The scenario is parsed by the client, to extract its parameters and actions to perform (see following Sect. 3.2 for more details). Following that, the analysis phase starts with the sequence of actions to execute. Once the client concludes the action phase, data collected (see following Sect. 3.4) by multiple tools is bundled into a result file and the server is notified that results are ready to be stored. Finally, the client changes its status back to available, thus letting the server know it is ready to execute another run.

Thus, the server pushes runs to available clients until all the applications in the dataset are processed, completing the experiment. Gathered data is then stored into our results database, where it is available for post-processing and analysis.

3.2   Experiment Scenario

The scenario, an XML document, contains two parts: the environment configuration and the action sequence to execute. The environment configuration indicates which Android virtual device (AVD) must be used, thus specifying the version of Android to use, and what network services should be provided (e.g. DNS and HTTP proxies). The action sequence is an ordered list of commands that is launched by the client to successfully perform a credible simulation of the application. Each scenario starts with the same set of instructions, to prepare the environment for the experiment. For example, starting the AVD, waiting for the boot sequence to complete and starting the monitoring of metrics are parts of the initialization sequence.

Once this preparation phase is over, the second phase, the installation of the app to test and user simulation, starts. When a scenario includes user simulation steps, the Application Exerciser Monkey[1] tool is used to perform the number of actions contained in the simulation step. Its capacity to generate pseudo-random and system-level events to navigate the application under scrutiny makes for a basic simulation. The final user simulation action is a rest period, where no simulation is done, but the application continues to run. Finally, once all actions have been executed, the data collection phase is launched and a report with all the metrics is sent back to the sandbox server.

Finally, in order to simulate a basic network connectivity, our sandbox, server and clients, can run a DNS proxy (relaying DNS queries/responses to a real server) as well as a gateway to redirect all outgoing network traffic generated by the mobile applications to our own fake server, who can complete TCP handshake, to let apps perform requests (i.e. HTTP GET requests).

3.3   Applications Datasets

We performed our preliminary experiments [3], which are presented in Sect. 4, on a different dataset than the new experiments presented in this paper. The first dataset, labelled D1, was composed of 5519 applications, both legitimate and malicious, as shown in Table 1. Of these applications, 3519 were tagged as

---

[1] http://developer.android.com/tools/help/monkey.html.

malware, coming from 2 different sources: the Malware Genome project[2] provided 1260 apps while DroidAnalytics [11] provided the remaining 2259 malware. The rest of the dataset comprehend 2000 legitimate applications, where the first thousand were collected on the Google Play Store[3] and the remaining were pulled from the application store AppsAPK[4]. In all figures, application sources were labelled as follows: GooglePlay, for the Google Play Store, and MalGenome, for the Malware Genome Project, while AppsAPK and DroidAnalytics remained the same.

Table 1. Composition of datasets D1 and D2.

Source	Dataset1 (D1)	Dataset2 (D2)	Type
MalGenome	1260	100	Malware
DroidAnalytics	2259	100	Malware
Contagio	0	100	Malware
Source-2013	0	100	Malware
Source-2014	0	100	Malware
GooglePlay	1000	100	Legitimate
AppsAPK	1000	100	Legitimate
Total	5519	700	Both

Our second dataset (referred to as D2) was composed of 700 applications (see Table 1), coming from 7 different sources. We randomly selected 100 applications from each source in D1, dividing applications into 200 malware and 200 legitimate applications. Furthermore, we added 3 other sources of malware, that provided 100 applications each: Contagio[5], and a private source with malware from 2013 and 2014, which were named Source-2013 and Source-2014. These 3 new sources brought the number of malware to 500, creating a bias toward malware in Dataset2. In all figures, these 3 sources are labelled with their respective names.

We created a second dataset following the first experiments, in order to confirm trends from our first observations but also to increase the number of experiments performed in the same amount of time. On a smaller number of applications, more experiments were possible and, therefore, we were able to study a wider range of parameters in our experiments.

3.4 Data Collection

This client-server sandbox relies on different tools to collect static and dynamic information during the experiments. A processing of the Android manifest for

[2] http://www.malgenomeproject.org/.
[3] https://play.google.com/store.
[4] http://www.appsapk.com/.
[5] http://contagiodump.blogspot.ca/.

permissions used, broadcast receivers and intents is performed. Of the dynamic analysis tools used, Taintdroid [13] monitors the sensitive data leakages to public channels. Equally, outgoing SMS and phone calls are recorded, through an instrumented version of the Google Emulator. Finally, the rest of the network traffic is recorded for post-experiment analysis of protocols and requests used.

4   Experiment

For this paper, we performed 13 experiments that are listed in Table 2. For each experiment, we specify the context by showing the value of each of the 4 variable parameters, namely the application usage, the number of actions in user simulation, the rest period after simulation and the network configuration of the sandbox. We regroup experiments with the same variation in context in five different groups, presented below.

Table 2. List of experiments.

Experiment label	Dataset	Application usage	Number of actions in user simulation	Rest period	Network context
E1	D1	Install	0	5 min	Full network
E2	D1	Start	0	5 min	Full network
E3	D1	Simulation	5000	5 min	Full network
E4	D2	Install	0	5 min	Full network
E5	D2	Start	0	5 min	Full network
E6	D2	Simulation	5000	5 min	Full network
E7	D2	Simulation	5	5 min	Full network
E8	D2	Simulation	50	5 min	Full network
E9	D2	Simulation	500	5 min	Full network
E10	D2	Simulation	5000	1 min	Full network
E11	D2	Simulation	5000	5 min	No network
E12	D2	Simulation	5000	5 min	DNS
E13	D2	Simulation	5000	5 min	DNS + TCP

Representing a preliminary study [3], group G1 comprises experiments E1, E2 and E3, with application usage as a variation parameter, as shown on Table 3. In this group, an application was only installed in experiment E1, was installed and launched with no other interaction in experiment E2 and finally, was installed, started and simulated with 5000 random actions. These experiments E1, E2 and E3 are all configured with a 5-min rest period, a full network configuration and performed with dataset D1.

Table 3. Context of G1.

Experiment label	Application usage	Number of actions	Rest period	Network context	Dataset
E1	Install	0	5 min	Full network	D1
E2	Start	0			
E3	Simulation	5000			

In the beginning, experiments in G1 were selected to constitute a proof-of-concept that variations of parameters would lead to a means of comparing malware behaviour. Since most of the aforementioned dynamic analysis tools are researching ways to expand their simulation engine, a difference in the level of simulation appeared as a natural starting point for our first experiments.

In second place, as displayed on Table 4, a second group G2 with experiments E4, E5 and E6 aims at confirming results from group G1. Therefore, group G2 is identical to group G1 (where E1 ≡ E4, E2 ≡ E5 and E3 ≡ E6) for all variation parameters but a different dataset, D2.

Table 4. Context of G2.

Experiment label	Application usage	Number of actions	Rest period	Network context	Dataset
E4	Install	0	5 min	Full network	D2
E5	Start	0			
E6	Simulation	5000			

As a logical next step, group G3 variable parameter is the number of actions performed in user simulation. As shown on Table 5, G3 regroups experiments E7, E8, E9 and E6, where all perform user simulation, but with a number of actions respectively set to 5, 50, 500 and 5000 actions. Again, for all experiments in G3, there is a 5-min rest period after user simulation, a full network configuration and samples are from dataset D2.

Table 5. Context of G3.

Experiment label	Application usage	Number of actions	Rest period	Network context	Dataset
E7	Simulation	5	5 min	Full network	D2
E8		50			
E9		500			
E6		5000			

Next, as displayed in Table 6, group G4 is composed of E10 and E6, with the length of the rest period as a variation parameter. Experiment E10 configuration is a 1-min rest period, while E6 has a 5-min rest period. The rest of the context is the same for both experiments, namely both perform user simulation with 5000 actions in a full network configuration on dataset D2.

Table 6. Context of G4.

Experiment label	Application usage	Number of actions	Rest period	Network context	Dataset
E10	Simulation	5000	1 min	Full network	D2
E6			5 min		

Finally, the last group, G5, tests applications in a different network context. As shown on Table 7, G5 includes experiments E11, E12, E13 and E6, where E11 has no network access, E12 evolves in a network where there is only a DNS active[6], E13 has not only a DNS server active, but also completes TCP handshake connections[7] and finally, where E13 has a full network configuration. The rest of the variation parameters are equals for all experiments: user simulation with 5000 actions is performed, a 5-min rest period occurs after simulation and all applications are from dataset D2.

Table 7. Context of G5.

Experiment label	Application usage	Number of actions	Rest period	Network context	Dataset
E11	Simulation	5000	5 min	No network	D2
E12				DNS Only	
E13				DNS + TCP	
E6				Full network	

5   Results

Results from each experiment are compared using metrics presented in this section. Failure rate of experiment in Sect. 5.1, SMS activity in Sect. 5.2, data

---

[6] All IP traffic other than DNS queries is sinkholed to an IP not on the network.

[7] All IP traffic other than DNS queries is sinkholed to an IP for which no ports are open but fake TCP SynAck packets are sent back in response to any TPC Syn (thus properly completing the 3-way handshake).

leaks in Sect. 5.3 and network traffic (DNS and HTTP requests) in Sect. 5.4, help to give a picture of different application behaviour in different contexts.

All results that have a graphic figure associated display the metric calculated on each source of the dataset used, except for the last column, labelled 'Total'. This column represents the metric on all samples as a whole, often qualified as the overall metric.

5.1 Failure Rate

The first metric we use is the failure rate of an experiments, which is defined by the number of runs that do not successfully complete a scenario. To qualify as a success, all scenario steps of a run must be completed, otherwise, the run is considered a failure (a step may not be completed, may stop or fail to execute in the allotted time).

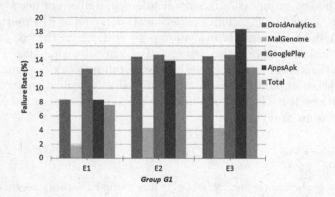

Fig. 1. Failure rate for group G1 (application usage on D1) [3].

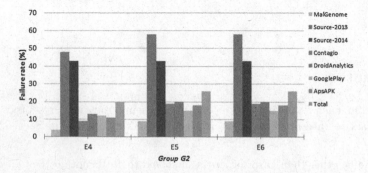

Fig. 2. Failure rate for group G2 (application usage on D2).

For group G1, overall failure rate is at 7.7% for experiment E1, while E2 is at 11.8% and experiment E3 fails in 12.9% of the cases, as it is shown on Fig. 1. The interesting point is that simulation do not raise the failure rate significantly, as only a small percentage (1.1%) of applications are launched successfully, but are not able to pass through the user simulation phase.

Within group G2, with which we sought to confirm our results, overall failure rate for experiment E4 is at 20%, and is slightly higher, at 26% for both experiments E5 and E6, as is shown on Fig. 2. Failure rates recorded for experiments in group G2 confirm observations from experiments in G1, for all sources. User simulation do not modify the failure rate when compared to starting the application, as experiments E5 and E6 show a similar failure rate, while the number recorded for experiment E4 is significantly lower.

As experiments in group G3, G4 and G5 all have the same usage application (simulation), failure rates are almost identical to numbers presented for experiment E6.

Therefore, in all experiments, simulation of user actions does not significantly increase failure rate when compared to starting an app, but launching an application does when compared to only installing it. Moreover, varying the other parameters (number of action, rest period and network configuration) does not affect failure rate.

5.2 Sending SMS

First, for experiments in group G1, we observe that only malicious applications send unauthorized SMS, and that text activity increases with application usage, as displayed on Fig. 3. Indeed, not even one application sent an SMS in experiment E1. However, in experiment E2, the overall percentage of applications sending SMS is at 0.74% and is up to 1.2% for some sources. Then, in experiment E3, the overall percentage is 4.60% and for some sources, the percentage is as high as 8.8% [3].

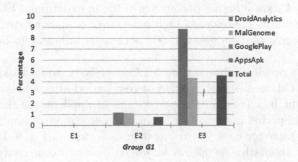

Fig. 3. Percentage of apps sending SMS for Group G1 (application usage on D1) [3].

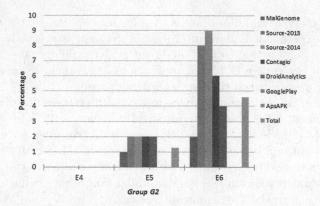

Fig. 4. Percentage of apps sending SMS for Group G2 (application usage on D2).

With group G2, we again seek confirmation of what is observed in experiments from group G1. As displayed on Fig. 4, only malicious applications send unauthorized SMS. Also, when application usage is installation only, in experiment E4, text activity is null. Only in experiment E5 can we see a beginning of text activity, as 1.3% of all applications send SMS. With experiment E6, the percentage climbs to 4.6% of all applications and reaches up to 11% of applications for some sources. Therefore, our preliminary observations for experiments in group G1 are confirmed. Only malware send unauthorized SMS and text activity is most often triggered by user simulation.

Following is group G3, to verify how the number of actions in user simulation would influence the percentage of applications sending SMS. As is shown on Fig. 5, the percentage of applications sending SMS with 5 actions (that is, experiment E7) is no higher than 1.4%, but climbs at 2.9% in experiment E8 (with 50 actions) and 3.9% with 500 actions, in experiment E9. Although experiment E6, with 5000 actions, has a percentage of 4.6%, if we look at percentages per source, for all sources but Source-2014, the percentage are identical. Malware from Source-2014 show a higher percentage of 9% in experiment E6 compared to 7% in experiment E9. Therefore, a high number of actions reveals text activity better, and it seems that, in general, 500 actions is sufficient to detect most of activity.

Based on the previous observations for text activity, when looking at experiments in group G4, we see that a different rest period after simulation does not have a significant incidence on the percentage of applications that send SMS. Whether the rest period is set to 1 or 5 min, the percentage of applications sending SMS is the same for each source, as demonstrated on Fig. 6. It is expected, given that user simulation is such a factor to detect text activity, that a rest period of any length of time do not raise the percentage of applications sending SMS. As part of our future work, we intend to confirm this conclusion with new experiments with longer rest periods.

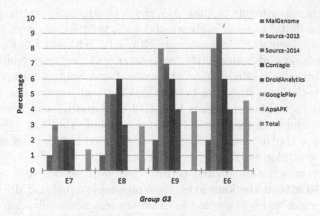

Fig. 5. Percentage of apps sending SMS for Group G3 (number of actions).

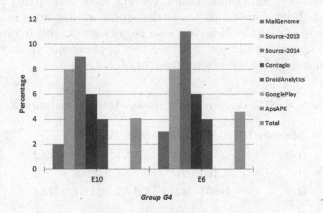

Fig. 6. Percentage of apps sending SMS for Group G4 (rest period).

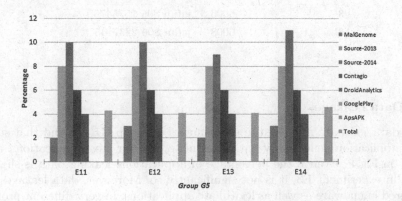

Fig. 7. Percentage of apps sending SMS for Group G5 (network configuration).

Moreover, in experiments of group G5, the network configuration has no incidence on text activity. Indeed, as shown on Fig. 7, the percentage of applications sending SMS are identical in experiments E11, E12, E13 and E6, for all sources except MalGenome and Source-2014, no matter what network configuration is selected and varies only slightly for Malgenome and Source-2014. As for both sources with variations, since the percentages for MalGenome are respectively 2%, 3%, 2% and 3% for experiments E11, E12, E13 and E6 and are respectively 10%, 10%, 9% and 11% for Source-2104, we conclude that the randomness of actions, and not the network configuration, changed the percentages slightly. The problem of randomness is discussed in Sect. 5.5.

Also, other information related to SMS has been recorded in experiments of group G1, to extend the knowledge base on malware using SMS. When text activity is detected, we estimate that 2.5 SMS are sent per application on average. Convergence about SMS numbers and text content could also be observed, as only 23 different numbers and 50 different texts were found in 254 text messages. As shown in Table 8, SMS numbers and content show a recurring pattern. No comparison has been done on these metrics so far, as few apps in our sample turn out to be sending SMS. However, on a larger sample, this information may further help to compare and sort SMS-sending applications. It may also prove valuable when comparing metrics for families of malware.

Table 8. SMS numbers and texts sent by some malware [3].

Malware ID	SMS Number	SMS Text
1	10621900	YXX1, YXX4, YXX2
1	10626213	C * X1, C * X2
1	1066185829	921X1, 921X2, 921X4
2	3353	70 + 224761
2	3354	70 + 224761
3	6005	jafun 806 1656764
3	6006	jafun 806 1575475
3	6008	jafan 806 2237145

5.3 Data Leakages

When data leaks are measured in experiments of group G1, we find that starting an application is necessary but sufficient to discover most applications, as is shown on Fig. 8. Even if the percentage of applications leaking data is slightly higher in experiment E3, it is not significantly so. Moreover, data leakages are registered in malware as well as legitimate applications, in very different proportions. Of all applications leaking data, 91% were malware while only 9% were legitimate applications.

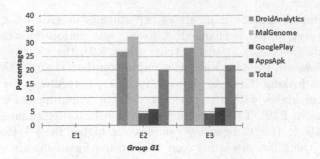

Fig. 8. Percentage of apps leaking sensitive data for Group G1 (application usage on D1) [3].

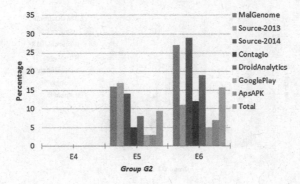

Fig. 9. Percentage of apps leaking sensitive data for Group G2 (application usage on D2).

First looking at experiments in group G2 for confirmation, we are able to confirm partially our observations. Indeed, as shown on Fig. 9, malware are far more prone to leak data (89% of all leakages are registered on malicious applications). Experiments in group G2 also confirm that it is necessary to launch the application to register leakages, but contrary to experiments in G1, comparison between experiment E5 and E6 shows that user simulation helps to find more data leaks. For all sources but two, percentages are higher by at least 4% in experiment E6. For source GooglePlay, the percentage is also higher in E6, but only by 2%. Contrary to what was observed for group G1, we conclude that, although a large part of the data leakages are caught when starting the application, user simulation is in order for a better result. We discuss the odd result in E2 for Source-2013 (more leaks are observed without user simulation, E5 vs E6) in Sect. 5.5.

With this new observation, it is interesting to look at experiments in group G3, where the number of actions in user simulation is the variation parameter. Number of actions starts at 5 actions in experiment E7 and increases to 50, 500 and 5000 actions in experiments E8, E9 and E6. As displayed on Fig. 10, the higher percentages are reached in experiment E6, for all sources.

Also interesting are the numbers of experiments in group G4, where the length of the rest period is changed. A longer rest period does not influence the failure rate (Sect. 5.1) or text activity (Sect. 5.2), the first two metrics in this article. However, for data leaks, this parameter does change the percentage of applications leaking data. As shown on Fig. 11, percentages for all sources are equals to or higher with a rest period of 5 min (experiment E6) instead of 1 min (experiment E10). The percentage of data leaks for legitimate application is either equals to (for GooglePlay samples) or higher by 1% (for AppsApk samples), but the difference is between 1% and 6% for malicious applications. Therefore, a longer rest period after user simulation is susceptible to help discover more leaky applications.

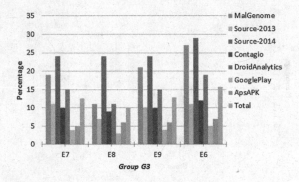

Fig. 10. Percentage of apps leaking sensitive data for Group G3 (number of actions).

Finally, data leakages is measured in experiments of group G5, to show the effects of network configuration on this metric. In Fig. 12, leaks of sensitive information are higher when a full network configuration is active (experiment E6), for all sources of applications except one. For that source, Source-2013, the percentage is higher in experiment E13 (17% instead of 11% in E6), which will be discussed in Sect. 5.5. For some other sources (GooglePlay, AppsAPK, Droid-Analytics and Contagio), the percentage of leaky applications are only slightly different (2% or less) between the experiment E13 and E6. However, for applications from MalGenome and Source-2014, there is respectively a 9% and 12% difference between E13 and E6, that allows us to conclude that a full network configuration is best to find data leaks.

5.4   Network Traffic

During an experiment, network traffic is closely monitored, to gather information about malware servers, addresses they may contact, etc. For all experiments, we analyze DNS and HTTP requests that are presented in the following sections.

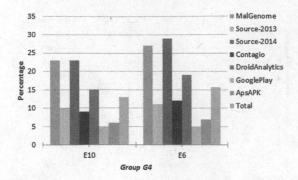

Fig. 11. Percentage of apps leaking sensitive data for Group G4 (rest period).

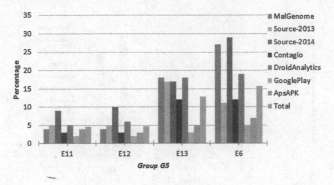

Fig. 12. Percentage of apps leaking sensitive data for Group G5 (network configuration).

DNS Requests. The metric considered for DNS requests is the average number of requests made by an app. We first look for confirmation of results observed in experiments of group G1, in which an overall average of 0.002 request is made in experiment E1, of 2.62 requests in E2 and of 4.86 requests in E3, as displayed on Fig. 13. These results show that the average number of DNS requests is higher in experiment E3, that is when user simulation is used. As is shown on Fig. 14, results from experiments in group G2 show that the same conclusions can be reached. In experiment E4, the average number of DNS requests is 0.01 request, number that climbs to an average of 0.4 request in experiment E5 and reaches a high mark of 1.3 request per application in experiment E6.

Also, we observe in experiments of group G1 that malware from all sources have a higher average of DNS requests than legitimate applications. However, in experiments of group G2, legitimate applications from both sources have a higher average than applications from malware sources, except for Source-2014. Average number of DNS requests for applications of Source-2014 are at 2.33 requests per application, while applications from GooglePlay are at 2.06 requests per application and apps from AppsAPK are at 1.38 request per application. Malware from all other sources are showing an average below 1.2 DNS request per application,

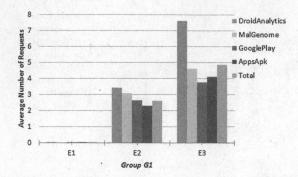

Fig. 13. Average number of DNS requests per application, for Group G1 (application usage on D1) [3].

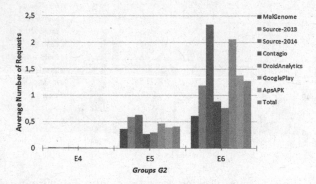

Fig. 14. Average number of DNS requests per application, for Group G2 (application usage on D2).

making their averages lower than the average of legitimate applications. Hence, our previous observation is not confirmed by the new experiment.

Moreover, when looking at results from experiments in group G3, displayed on Fig. 15, where the number of actions in user simulation is the variation parameter, the highest average is always obtained in experiment E9 or E6, respectively configured with 500 and 5000 actions. Therefore, we can say that a high number of actions is required to get a significant average for DNS requests, but the number of actions, when sufficiently high, reaches a critical point where more actions will not significantly increase the average number of DNS requests made by an application.

Now, for experiments of group G4, where the rest period after user simulation was changed, the longer rest period of 5 min in experiment E6 yielded the highest average in general. As shown on Fig. 16, the overall average of DNS requests for experiment E10 is 1.1 request while experiment E6 has an overall average of 1.3 request.

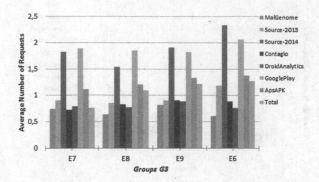

Fig. 15. Average number of DNS requests per application, for Group G3 (number of actions).

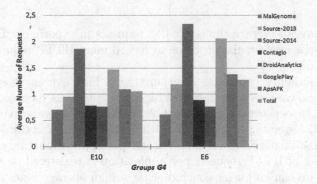

Fig. 16. Average number of DNS requests per application, for Group G4 (rest period).

Finally, in experiments of group G5, the variation parameter is the network configuration. Unsurprisingly, experiment E11 has the lowest average number of DNS requests, as shown on Fig. 17. Experiment E12 is comparable to experiment E11, with slightly, but not significantly, higher averages for all sources. With experiment E6, however, the highest average of DNS requests was reached for all sources, by a large margin for some sources. Therefore, we can conclude that a full network configuration is best to gather the maximum number of DNS requests. Lower results from experiment E13 will be discussed in Sect. 5.5.

HTTP Requests. In this section, the metric is similar than for DNS requests, namely the average number of HTTP requests per application. In experiments of group G1, shown on Fig. 18, experience E3, with user simulation, shows an average of 12.2 requests per application, while experiment E2 (starting the application) displays an average of 6.11 requests. No HTTP requests are recorded in experiment E1, where an application is installed only. As a confirmation of our results, experiments in group G2 do not show any HTTP requests in experiment E4 and the average number of HTTP requests for experiment E5 is 0.63

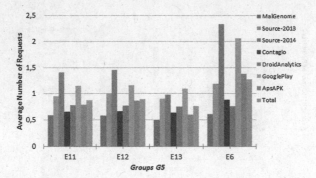

Fig. 17. Average number of DNS requests per application, for Group G5 (network configuration).

request. The overall average climbs to 4.18 requests in experiment E6, confirming that a proper user simulation helps to record more HTTP requests. Results are presented in Fig. 19.

In our preliminary paper, we mention that a high average may be symptomatic of a malware, as a significantly higher average was recorded for a malware dataset. In experiment of group G2, the highest average recorded for a dataset is 11.72 requests per application, while the second- and third-highest are respectively standing at 8.23 and 5.48 requests per application. Since the highest average number of HTTP requests per application is registered on the Google-Play dataset, we can no longer conclude that a high average hints at malicious applications.

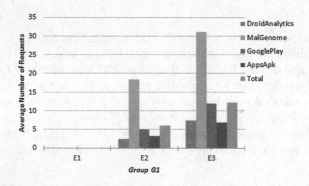

Fig. 18. Average number of HTTP requests per application, for Group G1 (application usage on D1) [3].

Furthermore, when looking at the number of actions in user simulation (group G3) in Fig. 20, the average number of requests for experiment E7, E8 and E9 is respectively 2.3, 2.2 and 2.6 requests per application. Therefore, whether we

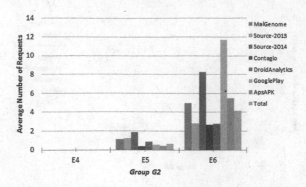

Fig. 19. Average number of HTTP requests per application, for Group G2 (application usage on D2).

perform 5, 50 or 500 actions, the variation does not have a significant effect on the results. However, the average number of requests in experiment E6 reaches 4.18 requests per application, a significantly higher average than the other 3 experiments in group G3. So, not only is user simulation essential, but also a high number of actions helps to trigger more HTTP requests. Also, in experiments of group G4, displayed in Fig. 21, an overall average of 2.39 HTTP requests are sent, per application, when using a rest period of 1 min. That average climbs to 4.18 requests per application when using a rest period of 5 min, allowing us to conclude that a longer rest period increases the average number of HTTP requests per application.

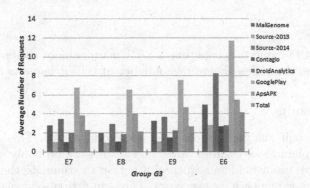

Fig. 20. Average number of HTTP requests per application, for Group G3 (number of actions).

Finally, when network configuration is changed in experiments of group G5 (shown on Fig. 22), no HTTP request is recorded with scenario in experiments E11 and E12, as expected. When enabling TCP handshake completion, in experiment E13, an average of 1.41 HTTP request per application is recorded, while

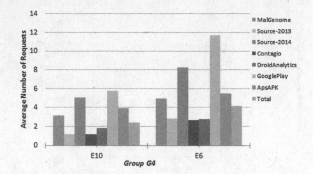

Fig. 21. Average number of HTTP requests per application, for Group G4 (rest period).

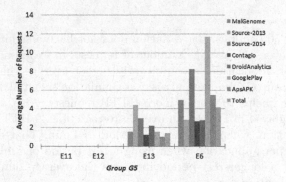

Fig. 22. Average number of HTTP requests per application, for Group G5 (network configuration).

the average is 4.18 requests in experiment E6. Unsurprisingly, the better network configuration is, the higher the average number of HTTP requests is.

5.5   Odd Results

Through the result analysis, we observed some odd results. This section tries to partially explain those oddities. Most odd results are probably explained by the fact that we use a random sequence of action to stimulate the application and there is a new sequence for every run. Thus, an action sequence may fail to trigger the malicious behavior in a rich execution context while another action sequence will have succeeded in more limited context (e.g., Fig. 6 indicates in E13 vs E12 for MalGenome dataset that some apps sent SMS with only a DNS on the network but they did not with a DNS+ a fake TCP server). Section 6 will provide insight regarding how we plan to address these shortcomings.

Another explanation may apply to a subset of those odd results and is worth considering. Figure 10 (E13 vs E6) indicates that for the source-2013 dataset, some apps leaked information with a network config consisting of a DNS server and a Fake TCP handshake server (E13) but not with a full Internet access (E6). This could be explained by the different random action sequences as above, but the discrepancy is important (6% difference) so we consider a second explanation. Let's assume that the server the malware tries to contact on the Internet is unavailable (e.g., C&C has been taken down), the malware would not leak the information (connection cannot be established with destination). On the other hand, with a fake internal server the communication can be established (fake TCP handshake) and the malware could leak the information as the first packet sent to the fake server (before noticing that the server is not responding past the TCP handshake) and we would see it in our simulated network. Further investigation is required, but, although running malware in a live network is usually considered better for dynamic analysis, it might be a good idea for a sandbox to integrate a fake server that take over whenever the online server does not respond.

6   Future Work

Following the discussion in Sect. 5.5, we will work towards a repeatable sequences of user actions and perform our current set of experiments with this change. We will also look into testing a longer rest period, to confirm observations on text activity in Sect. 5.2.

Moreover, as stated in our preliminary paper [3], we would like to introduce new variation parameters, like the Android OS version and types of emulators. It would also be interesting to look at other parameters, like location. Equally, it is our intention to refine our current metrics and add others, to get a clearer picture of analyzed applications.

Finally, increasing our application dataset with more samples is still in our to-do list, as is the classification of malware per families.

7   Conclusion

In this paper, we compare experiments with different contexts, in order to study the influence of such contexts on the behavior of applications from multiples sources. To achieve this goal, we designed 13 experiments, separated in 5 different groups, where each group was assigned a variation parameter and a dataset. These parameters currently are application usage, number of actions in simulation, rest period after simulation and network configuration.

Then, experiments were executed in a virtual sandbox with dynamic analysis revolving around different metrics like failure rate, SMS activity, data leakages, DNS and HTTP activity. With these metrics, we compare each experiment and its variation parameters, to help increase our knowledge of application behavior.

In general, variation in application usage will influence all metrics, as shown in Table 9. A different number of actions will influence SMS, DNS and HTTP activity, but will have no incidence on failure rate and the percentage of applications leaking sensitive data. Finally, both network configuration and rest period

Table 9. Influence of variations on metrics.

	Application usage	Number of actions	Network configuration	Rest period
Failure rate	✔			
SMS activity	✔	✔		
Data leaks	✔		✔	✔
DNS activity	✔	✔	✔	✔
HTTP activity	✔	✔	✔	✔

will modify DNS and HTTP activity, as well as the percentage of application leaking data, but will not influence the failure rate or SMS activity.

Results also demonstrate that simulation with a high number of actions, a full network configuration and a longer rest period will yield best results on metrics they have incidence on, with leaks of sensitive data being an exception. We intend to continue on this path, refining our current work to precise our global comprehension of Android application behavior.

References

1. PulseSecure: 2015 Mobile Threat Report. Technical report, Pulse Secure Mobile Threat Center (2015)
2. Blasing, T., Batyuk, L., Schmidt, A.D., Camtepe, S.A., Albayrak, S.: An android application sandbox system for suspicious software detection. In: Proceedings of the 5th International Conference of Malicious and Unwanted Software, pp. 56–62 (2010)
3. Boileau, C., Gagnon, F., Poisson, J., Frenette, S., Mejri, M.: A comparative study of android malware behavior in different contexts. In: Proceedings of the 13th International Joint Conference on e-Business and Telecommunications, vol. 1, pp. 47–54. DCNET (2016)
4. Dunham, K., Hartman, S., Morales, J.A., Quintans, M., Strazzere, T.: Android Malware and Analysis. Auerbach Publications, Boston (2014)
5. Bayer, U., Habibi, I., Balzarotti, D., Kirda, E., Kruegel, C.: A view on current malware behaviors. In: LEET (2009)
6. Bayer, U., Kruegel, C., Kirda, E.: TTAnalyze: a tool for analyzing malware (2006)
7. Willems, C., Holz, T., Freiling, F.: Toward automated dynamic malware analysis using CWSandbox. IEEE Secur. Priv. **5**, 32–39 (2007)
8. Arp, D., Spreitzenbarth, M., Hubner, M., Gascon, H., Rieck, K.: DREBIN: effective and explainable detection of android malware in your pocket. In: Proceedings of the 2013 Network and Distributed System Security (NDSS) Symposium (2014)
9. Arzt, S., Rasthofer, S., Christian Fritz, E.B., Bartel, A., Klein, J., Traon, Y.L., Octeau, D., McDaniel, P.: FlowDroid: precise context, flow, field, object-sensitive and lifecyle-aware taint analysis for android apps. In: Proceedings of the 35th ACM SIGPLAN Conference on Programming Language Design and Implementation, pp. 259–269 (2014)

10. Gonzalez, H., Stakhanova, N., Ghorbani, A.A.: DroidKin: lightweight detection of android apps similarity. In: Tian, J., Jing, J., Srivatsa, M. (eds.) SecureComm 2014. LNICST, vol. 152, pp. 436–453. Springer, Cham (2015). doi:10.1007/978-3-319-23829-6_30

11. Zheng, M., Sun, M.: DroidAnalytics: a signature based analytic system to collect, extract, analyze and associate android malware. In: Proceedings of 12th IEEE International Conference on Trust, Security and Privacy in Computing and Communications (TrustCom), pp. 163–171 (2013)

12. Burguera, I., Zurutuza, U., Nadjm-Tehrani, S.: CrowDroid: behavior-based malware detection system for android. In: Proceedings of the 1st ACM Workshop on Security and Privacy in Smartphones and Mobile Devices, pp. 15–26 (2011)

13. Enck, W., Gilbert, P., Chun, B.G., Cox, L.P., Jung, J., McDaniel, P., Sheth, A.N.: TaintDroid: an information-flow tracking system for realtime privacy monitoring on smartphones. ACM Trans. Comput. Syst. (TOCS) 32 (2014)

14. Rastogi, V., Chen, Y., Enck, W.: AppsPlayground: automatic security analysis of smartphone applications. In: Proceedings of the ACM SIGSAC Conference on Computer and Communications Security, pp. 209–220 (2013)

15. Zhou, Y., Wang, Z., Zhou, W., Jiang, X.: Hey, you, get off of my market: detecting malicious apps in official and alternative android markets. In: NDSS (2012)

16. Eder, T., Rodler, M., Vymazal, D., Zeilinger, M.: Ananas-a framework for analyzing android applications. In: 2013 Eighth International Conference on Availability, Reliability and Security (ARES), pp. 711–719. IEEE (2013)

17. Neugschwandtner, M., Lindorder, M., Fratantonio, Y., van der Veen, V., Platzer, C.: ANDRUBIS - 1,000,000 apps later: a view on current android malware behaviors. In: Proceedings of the 3rd International Workshop on Building Analysis Datasets and Gathering Experience Returns for Security, pp. 161–190 (2014)

18. Spreitzenbarth, M., Freiling, F., Echtler, F., Schreck, T., Hoffmann, J.: Mobile-sandbox: having a deeper look into android applications. In: Proceedings of the 28th Symposium on Applied Computing, pp. 1808–1815 (2013)

19. Reina, A., Fattori, A., Cavallaro, L.: A system call-centric analysis and stimulation technique to automatically reconstruct android malware behaviors. In: Proceedings of 6th European Workshop on Systems Security (2013)

20. van der Veen, V., Bos, H., Rossow, C.: Dynamic analysis of android malware. Internet & Web Technology Master thesis, VU University Amsterdam (2013)

21. Au, K.W.Y., Zhou, Y.F., Huang, Z., Lie, D.: PScout: analyzing the android permission specification. In: Proceedings of the 2012 ACM conference on Computer and communications security, pp. 217–228. ACM (2012)

22. Sasnauskas, R., Regehr, J.: Intent fuzzer: crafting intents of death. In: Proceedings of the 2014 Joint International Workshop on Dynamic Analysis (WODA) and Software and System Performance Testing, Debugging, and Analytics (PERTEA), pp. 1–5. ACM (2014)

23. Ye, H., Cheng, S., Zhang, L., Jiang, F.: Droidfuzzer: fuzzing the android apps with intent-filter tag. In: Proceedings of International Conference on Advances in Mobile Computing & Multimedia, p. 68. ACM (2013)

24. Gagnon, F., Lafrance, F., Frenette, S., Hall, S.: AVP-an android virtual playground. In: DCNET, pp. 13–20 (2014)

25. Gagnon, F., Poisson, J., Frenette, S., Lafrance, F., Hallé, S., Michaud, F.: Blueprints of an automated android test-bed. In: Obaidat, M.S., Holzinger, A., Filipe, J. (eds.) ICETE 2014. CCIS, vol. 554, pp. 3–25. Springer, Cham (2015). doi:10.1007/978-3-319-25915-4_1

e-Business

Security Framework for Adopting Mobile Applications in Small and Medium Enterprises

Basel Hasan[✉] and Jorge Marx Gómez

Department of Computing Science, Oldenburg University, Oldenburg, Germany
{basel.hasan,jorge.marx.gomez}@uni-oldenburg.de

Abstract. Nowadays, people increasingly rely on mobile devices (namely, smartphones and tablets) in their daily life. Beside their private use, mobile devices are also used for work. Hence, companies are motivated to integrate mobile devices into their business processes, and they demand mobility and flexibility of their employees. However, in spite of the advances in mobile technologies, security is still the primary concern that slows down the adoption of mobile applications within Small and Medium Enterprises (SMEs). Companies should first know the potential threats in the mobile environments and then the requirements and measures to mitigate the potential risks. Typically, the existing security tools such as frameworks, guidelines and threat catalogues target IT-professionals, but not business users who mostly lack the technical knowledge to navigate through these tools. This chapter presents a mobile security framework that mainly supports SMEs by adopting mobile applications. Potential threats have been included in a risk catalogue, which forms a main component of the presented framework. This catalogue will help business users in extending their awareness of possible mobile security risks. Moreover, this framework guides business users and helps them by mapping between security requirements, threats and measures when adopting mobile enterprise applications.

Keywords: Enterprise mobility · Mobile enterprise applications · Mobile security · Mobile threats · Risk catalogues

1 Introduction

This article presents an extended version of our previous publication [21]. This extended version represents a security framework that utilizes the risk catalogue presented in our previous publication [21]. This framework recommends mobile security requirements and measures that are needed to mitigate the potential risk when enterprises adopt Mobile Enterprise Applications (MEAs).

As by the definition from NIST SP 800-124 [53], mobile devices have the following main characteristics: (1) small size, (2) at least one wireless network interface, (3) local non-removable data storage, (4) an Operating System (OS) that is not a full-fledged desktop or laptop OS, (5) applications available through multiple methods. Taking this definition into account, smartphones and tablets are the main target in the scope of this article.

© Springer International Publishing AG 2017
M.S. Obaidat (Ed): ICETE 2016, CCIS 764, pp. 75–98, 2017.
https://doi.org/10.1007/978-3-319-67876-4_4

Increasingly, mobile devices have become a usual part of people's everyday life. As reported by Gartner, global sales of smartphones to end users totaled 403 million units in the fourth quarter of 2015, a 9.7% increase over the same period in 2014 [14]. Furthermore, global mobile data traffic is predicted to reach 173 million terabytes (TB) through 2018, an increase of over 300% from 2014 [13].

Increasing advance in mobile technologies and their usages, not only in private but in business sectors as well, triggered the enterprises to consider the mobility as a key success factor in their business. Enterprise mobility represents the next logical transition in mobile technology evolution which will continue to gain more prominence in enterprises not just to improve the return on investment, but also to improve operational efficiency of the mobile worker [37].

As predicted by the market research company IDC (International Data Corporation), the number of enterprise applications optimized for mobility will quadruple by year 2016 compared to year 2014, and IT organizations will dedicate at least 25% of their software budget to mobile applications by year 2017 [24]. The key enablers of Enterprise Mobility are mobile devices that run MEAs, which enable quick access to corporate data. Companies gain many advantages when integrating mobile devices into their IT infrastructure. This integration enables business users to access critical business information while they are out of their offices. Consequently, they can make decisions in shorter time and meet their customers' needs.

The usage of MEAs can lead to higher productivity, higher employee satisfaction, and ubiquitous information access [22]. However, despite the many advantages of mobility, the adoption of MEAs is often slowed down not only because of classical factors like development costs and complexity of the systems, but also because of security concerns. According to a trend study by Luenendonk in year 2014, more than three-quarters of the interviewed companies rate security and privacy as the biggest hurdle when adopting MEAs [36]. Furthermore, as mobile devices become ubiquitous, new risks and challenges rise from this. They are increasingly dealing with personal and business data, and they are roaming in public networks with limited security and cryptographic protocols to protect the data [31].

The rest of this Section is divided into two parts. The first part presents an overview of mobile business applications and the second part defines the security problems the companies face when they plan to adopt MEAs. Section 2 presents the related work. A risk catalogue for MEAs along with mobile business scenario that describes an example of MEAs in use are presented in Sect. 3. The security framework for MEAs is explained in Sect. 4 including the framework structure and its main components. Section 5 presents the framework implementation and evaluation. Finally, this article comes to the end with a conclusion and outlook in Sect. 6.

1.1 Mobile Business Applications

Nowadays, there are a huge variety of possible mobile applications, which can be used in every department or field of functions in the enterprise, e.g. Customer Relationship Management (CRM), Business Intelligence (BI) or Human Resource (HR). Typically, mobile business applications are focused on the Business-to-Customer (B2C) and Business-to-Employee (B2E) domains.

Three main types of mobile business applications are differentiated according to the target group of users [18]. These are depicted in Fig. 1. In this article, "apps" stands for mobile applications that run on smartphones and tablets. The first type of mobile business applications is mobile applications for costumers, e.g. apps for buying tickets. The second type is mobile applications for employees, e.g. mobile CRM (see Sect. 3.1). The third type is mobile applications for business partners, which support inter-organizational interaction, e.g. in supply chains.

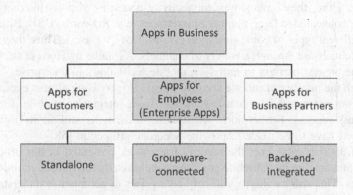

Fig. 1. Classification of apps in business (Source: [18] as cited in [21]).

Mobile applications for employee are further classified into three categories [18]: (a) standalone mobile applications that are not integrated with a server-side and data storage, (b) groupware-connected mobile applications that are linked with standard enterprise groupware systems, e.g., Microsoft Exchange, (c) back-end-integrated mobile applications are tightly integrated with the company's back-end, e.g. mobile ERP and mobile CRM.

In this article, we focus on mobile applications for employees, which are also called MEAs. The scenario we defined in Sect. 3 belongs to the category "back-end-integrated" mobile applications.

Employees may use either corporate devices that are offered by the company or their own mobile devices for work purposes. Beside corporate mobile devices, the mobile technology Bring Your Own Device (BYOD) also offers advantages and opportunities for companies by reducing technology costs and increasing employees' productivity [3]. However, the companies need to know the potential risk associated with both cases, corporate devices or BYOD. The following Section defines the research problem behind this work.

1.2 Security Risk in Mobile Enterprise Applications

IT security gains an increased importance for MEAs, due to the large number of interfaces the mobile devices have and the associated security threats [6]. However, many organizations seem to procrastinate on adopting mobile solutions due to security concerns. In other words, they doubt that the possible gain from using mobile business solutions will be greater than the harm that could be done. According to CISCO 2016 annual security report, the enterprises believe that mobility is at a high risk for security breach [7].

Compared to traditional computing domains like Personal Computers (PCs), mobile devices have very different security principles. He et al. distinguished mobile security from traditional computer security according to three major factors [10]. First, mobile devices have high mobility. Therefore, they can easily get stolen or lost. Second, mobile devices are strongly personalized, and they are normally operated by a unique user. Third, they have strong connectivity accessing various Internet services, and they are connected to large number of interfaces (e.g. SD-cards, USB, Bluetooth … etc.), and different types of communication (Wi-Fi, UMTS …etc.). Thus, they are more vulnerable to malware through a variety of channels. As stated by Hoos et al., "Security is one of the biggest barriers to introduce mobile technology in enterprises" [22].

Although the number of mobile security threats is increasing almost exponentially, enterprises are not aware of threats which rise from integrating mobile devices into their business process, furthermore, smartphone security is still in its infancy and improvements have to be made to provide adequate protection [58].

Through its risk catalogue, the security framework presented in this article determines the potential threats in mobile environments based on the needed mobile security requirements. This risk catalogue will help enterprises to get a better understanding of the potential risks. The idea behind the risk catalogue is to make the potential mobile threats and their accompanying risk more transparent to the enterprises. Knowing the potential mobile threats will help enterprises by defining the security requirements when adopting mobile business applications. This complies with the following statement: "Safe use of mobile devices arises from knowing the threats" [39]. The existing risk catalogues found in literature need a technical background in security. This make such catalogues very complex and therefore note easily understood by business users. Such catalogues are included in the following Section.

2 Related Work

A very recent work that addresses the inherent threats of mobile devices has been presented by NIST in form of mobile threat catalogue [4]. It was published in September 2016. Whereas the catalogue from NIST targets mobile security engineers, information system security professionals, mobile application developers and other technical staff like mobile OS developers and Mobile Network Operators (MNOs); the security framework presented in this article targets business users, who are mostly not security experts. In this regard, the security framework will support business users like managers through its decision model namely. However, MEAs developers and security professionals may also benefit from utilizing our security framework, where the information about mobile security can be maintained in a well-structured way.

A framework to develop MEAs has been presented in [57]. That framework offers a systematic and comprehensive solution to mobile application development and maintenance. It introduced security as a major concern for the enterprise when adopting and developing mobile applications. However, it does not provide a detailed overview on security issues in mobile environments. The security framework presented in this article gives a detailed overview on mobile security issues in mobile environments. One of the main components of this framework is a threat catalogue.

When it comes to threats catalogues, the STRIDE Model and IT-Grundschutz Catalogue are often mentioned. The STRIDE model is a threat modelling approach provided by Microsoft [23]. It defines six categories of threats depending on the kind of attack that might be performed. Those categories are: Spoofing identities, Tampering with data, Repudiation, Information disclosure, Denial of services and Elevation of privileges. This approach is a classification scheme for characterizing known threats when conducting risk analysis, however it does not provide a detailed listing of potential threats. Moreover, it lacks a business context like the possible malicious impact on business, and it does not focus on mobile business applications. In the second example, the IT-Grundschutz Catalogue [5] is also used when conducting risk analysis. However, it is very generic and does not focus on mobile business applications.

In general, risk catalogues are often classified by size and specialization into domain-general and domain-specific catalogues [17]. In addition to IT-Grundschutz, ISO/IEC 27002 [26] and NIST 800-53 [46] are domain-general catalogues. Such catalogues are very complex for business users. On the other hand, Domain-specific catalogues like PCI DSS [47] for banking domains will help business users in such domains to better understand the potential risks. Furthermore, a threat catalogue specific for a Mobile Device Management (MDM) system has been presented by [51]. That catalogue focuses on mobile users, administrators, unauthorized entities and nature as threats sources. However, it is specific to MDM and not for mobile business applications in general. Moreover, it does not cover further threat sources, like mobile OS, mobile networks and third-party mobile applications.

The risk catalogue, that presented in this article as a component of the security framework, provides a business view of the potential threats to mobile business applications along with an estimation of the risks to business. An interesting empirical study was conducted to investigate whether existing threat catalogues facilitate the risk assessment process [17]. The qualitative analysis in that study revealed that people who aren't security experts are mostly worried about the difficulty of navigating through the catalogue (the larger and less specific the worse it was). Obviously, that result supports the idea behind our risk catalogue since it is specific for mobile business applications and targets business users, who are mostly not security experts. Specific risk catalogues for mobile business applications have not been presented so far.

Furthermore, Enterprise Mobility Management (EMM) enables organizations to integrate and manage mobile devices in their IT infrastructures. According to Gartner, AirWatch is recognized as a leading EMM suite [15]. EMM encapsulates security mechanisms in one mobile security solution. For business users, this solution is seen a black box, but the mobile security requirements and the related possible threats still are unclear for business users. However, our security framework will also guide the business users in answering the question: Why does a particular mobile security mechanism need to be applied when adopting MEAs?

3   Risk Catalogue

This Section presents the risk catalogue for MEAs (refer to [21]). To determine the threats in mobile environments and to estimate their accompanying potential risks on business, mobile business scenarios are first defined and a set of assets have been extracted from those scenarios. These assets will help to estimate the risk on business.

3.1   Mobile Business Scenario

In this Section, mobile business scenarios will be described to show the typical usage of mobile applications for working purposes. These scenarios will help later on to determine the potential threats to mobile business applications. They have been derived from practice through discussion with business users from different enterprises who use mobile devices for work purposes. Then, a set of possible business assets related to mobile business applications have been derived (see Sect. 3.1). Those assets help to estimate the possible impact on business when enabling mobile devices for work purposes.

Figure 2 shows a general infrastructure of mobile enterprise. Enterprises have business applications like Customer Relationship Management (CRM) and Microsoft SharePoint. They also have Personal Information Manager (PIM) services like email, contacts and calendar, which are mostly the starting point and a key requirement for mobile enterprise [11]. On the left side of Fig. 2, are the mobile devices with different mobile OSes, like iPhone OS (iOS) and android. For MEAs, the communications between these devices and the application server take place over internet and mobile communications (these include Wi-Fi, cellular networks, Bluetooth, GPS, and others) through mobile middleware, which encapsulate the access to different backend systems

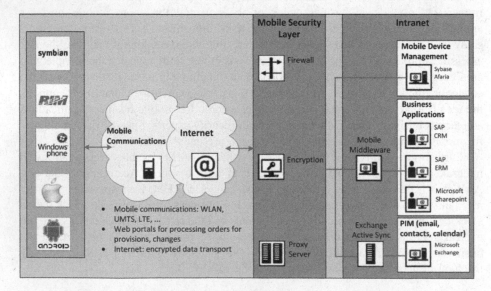

Fig. 2. Mobile enterprise infrastructure (Source: Adapted from [11]).

and prepares and send data to different mobile platforms per push or synchronization. Moreover, mobile devices can be enrolled and managed by Mobile Device Management (MDM) system, like Sybase Afaria.

The defined business scenarios focus on the mobile devices and mobile communications. Possible threats in company's server-side (mobile security Layer and intranet) are not in focus of this work. The remainder of this Section describes an excerpt of a scenario on mobile CRM.

A sales representative (sales rep) is on a duty visit to a customer and uses a mobile CRM application on his mobile device to access important financial information about the customer. The sales rep is also able to gain insight into present and past sales and returns belonging to the customer, and can access the needed sales data from his enterprise database server through the Internet. There are two options: (a) a Wireless Local Area Network (WLAN) connection, which is available in the customer's company, or (b) mobile internet, which is provided by Mobile Service Provider (MSP) of sales rep's company.

The sales rep is also able to present new products and marketing campaigns to the customer. The information about products and marketing campaigns can be stored locally on the hard drive of the representative's tablet, so access to it does not need an internet connection, but, such data should be synchronized from time to time.

During the duty visit, the sales rep connects his tablet with his enterprise's Virtual Private Network (VPN). Now he can use a reporting tool to get some personal information about his customer. Here, personal data are seen as information that the customer gives about himself, his family, his coworkers or his business that are not directly related to some kind of monetary or service-related transactions. Such data are stored on an enterprise database server and can be accessed via mobile devices.

During the sales negotiations with the customer some difficulties appear. The customer did a supplier evaluation and concluded that there is a cheaper supplier than the sales rep's company. The sales rep now has to act quickly to retain the customer. He uses his tablet to get access to a reporting tool in order to get some information about the customer's possible frequency of orders, and the customer's willingness to pay. Such information helps the sales rep to estimates the customer's value to give him some kind of discount on the offered transaction conditions. After this meeting, the sales rep heads home. Once there, he uses his smartphone to connect to the internet via his own WLAN in order to create a report about his working time, and give feedback about extra hours and travelling distances using a mobile application adopted by his HR department.

Assets. After mobile business scenarios are defined, a set of assets are extracted from those scenarios. An asset represents an entity with a financial value for the enterprise [51]. It does not only represent a physical object and data, but also business processes. For example, if a MEA uses customer data to analyze the buying behavior of the customers and the process of analyzing is threatened, the company gets distorted results, which can lead to an adverse impact on the business.

Table 1 includes the extracted assets classified into three categories. The first category is business data (B) that contains customer business data (e.g. name, address, company), customer personal data (e.g. notes about customers' behavior, like notes about hobbies from personal conversations), data about new products (product data), text messages, calls and business contacts. This category also includes campaign data (e.g. marketing campaign). Moreover, corporate data, which should only be accessed by employees, can possibly be threatened. If these kinds of data are altered, deleted, or tracked by an attacker, it can cause severe damage to the business (e.g. misplaced or forgotten orders, deleted customer profiles). Therefore, an attack on these data can cause an enormous direct or indirect negative financial impact on the company. Financial data, orders and returns are summarized as customer business data or corporate data.

Table 1. Assets associated to the usage of MEAs (Source: [21]).

Business data (B)	• Campaign data (B1) • Contacts (B2) • Corporate data (B3) • Customer business data (B4) • Customer personal data (B5) • Potential customer business data (B6) • Messages (B7) • Product data (B8) • Production data (B9)
Personal data (P)	• Authentication data (P1) • Contacts (P2) • Documents (P3) • Messages (P4) • Media (P5)
Technical-related (T)	• Battery (T1) • Billing (T2) • Configuration data (T3) • Hardware (T4) • OS (T5) • Services (T6) • Software (T7)

The second category, personal data (P), contains personal documents, videos, pictures, private authentication data, text messages, calls and contacts, which are stored on mobile devices. These data are typically stored on every smartphone or tablet.

The third category includes the technical-related (T) assets like battery, hardware, software and OS of the mobile device. Also for large companies, an attack on these assets could be worse, because the device itself just costs about a few hundred euros, while an attack on transactional or other business data can costs up to hundreds of thousands of euros. The configuration data of the mobile device, applications and the billing of used services are classified under this category.

3.2   Risk Catalogue Overview

This Section presents the potential threats and their accompanying risks that enterprises may face when they adopt mobile business applications. These potential threats have been summarized in a risk catalogue and classified into five categories based on the source of the potential threats. The structure of this catalogue is shown in Table 2 and an excerpt of this catalogue was presented in [21].

Table 2. Risk catalogue structure (Source: [21]).

Threats	Description and risk estimation	
Threat name	Threats short description	
	Likelihood of occurrence	Low, medium or high
	Short argumentation about the likelihood of occurrence	
	Possible impact	Low, medium or high
	Short argumentation about the possible adverse impact on business Assets: list of possible affected assets (see Sect. 3.1)	
	Risk level	Low, medium or high

Two factors are taken into consideration when estimating the risk level of a threat, namely likelihood of occurrence and adverse impact on business. The estimation of the likelihood of occurrence has been done based on the literature review and available reports taking into consideration two criteria: (a) the estimated frequency of threat appearance and (b) the motivation and the capability of attacker.

In this work, the potential impact on business is estimated based on the potential assets (see Sect. 3.1) that can be affected by a threat. For instance, the impact is considered high if the threat may enable access to personal customer data; publishing this information can damage the reputation of the enterprise severely, and lead to a huge loss of monetary resources. On the other hand, the potential impact is considered medium if business user cannot carry out a business process for a short time because the service needed is unavailable. Table 3 describes how the risk is estimated based on the both aforementioned factors.

Table 3. Risk levels estimation matrix (Source: [21]).

Threat		Adverse impact		
		Low	Medium	High
Likelihood of occurrence	High	Medium risk	High risk	High risk
	Medium	Medium risk	Medium risk	High risk
	Low	Low risk	Medium risk	Medium risk

The following subsections describe the potential threats in mobile environments. Such description will help business users to understand the potential risks when using mobile devices for work, without needing high technical knowledge in security.

Mobile Device. This category covers the physical threats that are related to the mobile device itself. Mobile devices themselves can be attacked in several ways. They can be harmed physically, but also the data stored locally on the them and thus business processes can be threatened as well.

The first threat in this category is the physical damage of mobile devices. Every piece of the hardware (e.g. battery, network adapter, hard drive...etc.) can break at any time, because of defects in the production process or because of mishandling through the user. If we take the business scenario, the sales rep can unintentionally drop his mobile device due to its small size. The direct financial loss is the mobile device itself, however, the sale rep now cannot look up or place a customer's order because of the broken mobile device. This can result in an indirect financial loss. Moreover, the productivity of the sales rep will consequently decrease. If the mobile device's hard drive is broken, important data can be lost. However, most business data are not only stored on the device, but they are synchronized with the company system. The impact on business is therefore low. The likelihood of occurrence of such threats is also estimated as low, because the physical damage of mobile devices is unintentional and the motivation and capability to threaten the business through broken mobile devices is very low.

The second threat in this category is the loss of mobile devices. Back to the business scenario: the sales rep may lose his tablet, while in a hurry on the way to the customer. Consequently, he would not be able to perform business processes, such as placing orders for the customer. In addition, if business data are stored locally on the mobile device, the impact on business can be high, since corporate or customer data can be exposed and sold to competitors or other potential buyers. On the other hand, if the business data is not directly stored on the mobile device, the confidentiality and integrity of these data are not affected. However, the device could still be used to access business data or perform business processes through mobile business applications installed on it, which are not secured enough or if login data is stored on the device. This leads to a loss of authenticity of certain performed actions and processes. Therefore, potential impact on business through the loss of a mobile device is rated as medium. According to the Kaspersky survey in 2013, one in every six users has experienced a loss, theft, or catastrophic damage to a mobile device (such as laptop, smartphone or tablet) in the last 12 months [29]. The same survey revealed that 32% of smartphones and 28% of tablets had work emails, 20% of smartphones and 29% of tablets had business documents. Furthermore, Srinivasan and Wu differentiated between device theft and data theft [54]. According to them, the theft of a mobile device is random in nature and the adversary is not interested in the data stored on the device, but motivated by the financial gains from reselling the stolen mobile device. However, the third-party who buys the device may be interested in the data on the device.

Further threat in this category is unattended mobile devices, that are left temporary unsupervised and picked up later by the user. In the business scenario for example the sales rep leaves his tablet unattended in order to make a call. A device left unattended for a short time is not such a great threat, because of the limited time and probable lack of intention of the unauthorized user to cause severe damage to the business. In addition, the capability of accessing the smartphone or tablet of such a person is often not good enough to use critical applications or access essential data. Therefore, the potential risk to business from temporary loss of mobile devices is estimated as low.

Third Party Mobile Applications. Mobile applications can be threatened through other mobile applications that unintentionally exploit errors or use unnecessary access rights to perform their tasks. Malicious software or so called malware can threaten mobile applications. Malware come in many different forms. Viruses contain every type of malicious code that is mostly unintentionally downloaded by the user of the mobile device. This can happen, for example, through drive-by-downloads. The first malware aimed at smartphones hit in 2004 and the first virus for mobile phones was written by a group known as 29A in June 2004 [49]. Malware (e.g. Trojans, worms, spyware, Ransomware and Grayware) can be distributed through different channels, like peer-to-peer networks or through mobile applications stores from the OS vendor.

Trojans typically come with applications that look useful, and then deliberately perform harmful actions once installed, their real intention is a malicious action targeting mobile device and its data [58]. For instance, ZitMo is a mobile version of the Trojan Zeus, which works in conjunction with the Zeus banking Trojan to steal login information or money from user's bank account [48].

Worms can self-reproduce and propagate themselves to mobile devices via mobile technologies like SMS, MMs or Bluetooth. For instance, a Symbian OS worm that targets mobile phones through Bluetooth, so that the infected mobile becomes a portal for further propagation of this malware to all its Bluetooth neighbors. This can cause massive consequences, like increased network throughput, battery depletion, and causing mobile failure by corruption of system binaries [2].

Spyware typically focuses on collecting data from the user's mobile device without the user's knowledge or approval, and sending it to an attacking entity [34]. The collected data can range from personal data like locations, contacts and messages to critical business data used by mobile business applications.

Another type of threats in this category is grayware that is often downloaded and installed with free software or applications, for example adware. What makes adware dangerous is that the proposed advertisements can lead to scamming websites or websites with more downloadable malware, which can carry out many unintended activities without the user being even aware of them [50].

This category also includes malware that prevents the user from accessing some functionalities or files, requiring a payment in order to unblock the access to them, is ransomware [32]. For instance, Lockdroid.E is a Trojan that targets Android devices and it functions like typical ransomware that locks the victim's screen; the victim may then be asked to pay a ransom to unlock their mobile device [59].

To sum up, malware can have a severe impact on business. They can hinder the normal usage of mobile devices and applications, bother the user with unwanted advertisements, or destroy all data stored locally on mobile device (e.g. sensitive customer data). Moreover, spying on data can provide critical business data to an unauthorized third party.

Mobile OS. The mobile OS (mOS) can serve as a source for possible threats to mobile business applications. Two main misconfigurations are considered as threat sources under this category. The first threat source is the rooting of mOS. Rooting itself is not a threat. However, it compromises the integrity of the OS and therefore makes security technologies that depend on the OS, such as containers, vulnerable to attack [35]. Rooting describes an action from the user to gain root permissions of the respective device and OS. This process is generally referred to as root on Android OS and jailbreak on iPhone OS (iOS) [9]. Rooting of mOS is usually used to remove prein-stalled, unwanted applications, customize the theme and functions of the mOS or so that the user can install unofficial applications. However, not only the user of the rooted mobile device is able to use these gained permissions, but malware or attackers can also use them to perform even more severe adverse actions. Consequently, this makes the mobile OS more vulnerable.

As predicted by Gartner, 75% of mobile security breaches by year 2017 will be the result of mobile application misconfigurations like jailbreaking or rooting [12]. According to the same report, Gartner recommends that IT security leaders enforce "no jailbreaking/no rooting" rule, and devices in violation should be disconnected from sources of business data, and potentially wiped, depending on policy choices. If an attacker gains root access to the mOS, the attacker may also get access to the MEAs intercepting data streams to prohibit remote IT commands, or access to data stored locally on a mobile device [42]. Usually enterprises apply a mandatory enterprise device management with jailbreak & rooting detection [42]. This will decrease the chance of having a rooted mobile device enrolled into an enterprise device management. Therefore, the possible malicious impact on business is estimated as medium.

The second threat source in this category is that of missing updates of the mOS. Missing updates can cause risk because they always include patches and security updates. However, the impact depends on how critical the missing updates are.

Mobile Networks. This category includes threats that can be launched against mobile devices using mobile networks. These threats can have severe consequences and differ in their likelihood of occurrence and possible adverse impacts on business.

The first type of threats in this category is Denial of Service (DoS), that denies performing a certain service or running a certain software or application. DoS-attacks do not only focus on the denial of services, they can reduce the ability of valid users to access resources [44] or they can induce incorrect operation [51]. Most commonly known are Distributed Denial of Service (DDoS) attack, which uses a huge number of malware-infected devices and PCs to disrupt the correct working of a server. Denial of Service-attacks can be launched through wired and wireless network connections like Wi-Fi or internet connections from mobile service providers. Typically, such networks are attacked via a DDoS attack, which is launched using botnets. A botnet is a network of internet-connected devices, which are infected with malicious software without the knowledge of their users. It is capable of executing computationally demanding tasks in feasible time [58]. DDoS is one of the adverse actions that can be performed by using botnets, although their users are unaware of that. Moreover, an attack on the cellular internet of a MSP can have adverse consequences for businesses. If such an attack is launched, the use of services like Long Term Evolution (LTE) can be limited or completely denied [28].

Referring back to the business scenario (see Sect. 3.1), MEAs often need a functioning Internet connection to company's server. If the sales rep wants to place an order, he needs an Internet connection to the server. If the server or the mobile internet connection of the MSP is attacked through a Denial of Service-attack, he cannot place the orders. This might cause an indirect financial loss. Therefore, the impact level is estimated as medium. Furthermore, DoS-attacks can also target Mobile Ad-hoc Networks (MANETs) like direct Peer-to-Peer Wi-Fi or Bluetooth-connections.

Another kind of denial of service, which particularly targets mobile devices, is the sleep deprivation or battery exhaustion. Such threats are used to drain the battery of a mobile device by preventing the mobile device from saving battery in sleep modes or similar through constant service requests [40]. In addition, sleep deprivation can also be applied in form of flooding attack in MANETs, where either a specific node or a group of nodes is targeted by forcing them to use their vital resources (e.g. Battery) [27]. However, the impact level of this type of DoS is estimated as low.

The second type of threats in this category is Man-in-the-Middle attack (MitM), that intercepts communications in networks to eavesdrop, alter, or delete the exchanged data. The attacker is placed in the middle between the client/server communication flows. [43] described three popular MitM attacks (SSL Hijacking, SSL Stripping, DNS Spoofing) targeted at smartphone applications. Two scenarios of MitM attacks were simulated in [30]. The first scenario is an unencrypted Wi-Fi networks, that do not provide encryption of network traffic. A type of such networks is captive portals, that typically use encryption to secure user's credentials when authenticating to the network, but the network traffic is not encrypted and can be sniffed over the air [16]. In the second scenario, an active malicious actor can control the wireless access points and can launch attacks against mobile applications. For instance, the evil twin attack can be used to deceive users into connecting to a rogue access point [45]. Back to the business scenario, the sales rep may use an available open WLAN when meeting with customer, unaware that this network is unsecured. This open WLAN may be provided by an adverse entity, not from the customer' company.

Mobile User. This category deals with potential threats that can be caused by the mobile user as a potential threat source, through unintentional actions without being aware of the security risks while using the mobile device. The major problem is the use of or access to untrusted content in the form of websites, which are accessed by users. This is often used for phishing activities or the distribution of malware through hostile entities. Business users are mostly unaware of such risks and threats, which they are exposed to by simply browsing the internet and looking up things like shops, online travel agencies, etc. [38].

Phishing websites try to steal login and personal data from the user, e.g. using mails, SMS, or advertisements as phishing channels. These are used to trick the user into entering private information and login data in replica websites of commonly known websites or through the offering free downloads or low price shopping. Phishing is a serious threat for business in areas like auction sites, payment services, retail, and social networking sites [56]. In addition to the direct costs of phishing, company can also lose trust of customers if the customer data is compromised. Furthermore, if the attacker succeeds in obtaining the login credentials (username, password und PIN, etc.), then the attacker can perform all actions authorized to the mobile device's owner. As result, the impact of risk to business is considered as high.

McAfee Labs Threats Report in 2014 revealed that phishing continues to be an effective tactic for infiltrating enterprise networks [41]. According to the same report, 80% of test takers in a McAfee phishing quiz have fallen for at least one in seven phishing emails. Furthermore, results showed that finance and HR departments, those holding the most sensitive corporate data, performed the worst at detecting fraud, falling behind other departments by a margin of 4% to 9%. Attackers are motivated to target mobile devices due to several different reasons, one of which is the mobile device's display constraints that could be used to hide the URL bar [1].

The second type of threats under this category is downloading untrusted mobile applications, which might take place due to the fact that the user is unaware of the associated risks of such applications. The most known form of threat is called drive-by download, that works by exploiting vulnerabilities in web browsers, plug-ins, or other components that work within browsers [33]. This kind of threats try to prompt users through advertisements or adverse websites to take an action that downloads malware on their mobile devices. An area of concern for mobile devices is also the Quick Response (QR) codes; They can be scanned with a mobile device' camera as input into QR reader's app, then malicious attackers can use these codes to redirect users to malicious websites to download malicious apps [38]. As the drive-by download can install and launch a malware, the impact to business is estimated as high. Another threat under this category is social engineering, which is based on human behavior. For instance, phishing is solely based on social engineering by exploiting human vulnerability in order to trick the victim into providing sensitive credentials [1].

Finally, unaware privilege granting to the third-party mobile applications can be done without the knowledge of the mobile user. For example, Android and iOS inform the user about the access rights required while installing a mobile application. Although users are warned or informed about that, they tend to overlook this information and just grant the access privileges to the mobile application. Potential risk to business can arise if the installed third-party application gets the privilege to access contacts list that might include business contacts.

4 Security Framework for MEAs

The functional specification of the security framework for MEAs has been developed in [19]. Afterwards, the framework has been further refined and implemented as a web-based tool in [52].

For designing the security framework and for identifying its contents (e.g. threats and measures), ISO 31000:2009 risk management process [25] is considered. The standard ISO 31000:2009 has been developed on the basis of the world's first formal standard for managing risk, the Australian/New Zealand Standard AS/NZS 4360 that published in 1999 and revised in 2004. The following Sections represent the framework structure and describe its models.

4.1   Framework Structure

The security framework presented in this chapter is a role-based software tool which provides recommendations that help users to create security concepts for MEAs. Two roles are provided within this framework, namely, business user and expert users. Business users are the standard users of the framework and they use it to create security concepts for individual projects in the context of MEAs. Expert users are privileged users in the framework and they have the specialized know-how in the context of the mobile security.

In general, the framework consists essentially of two models, namely, guidance model and decision model. Figure 3 shows the structure of the framework.

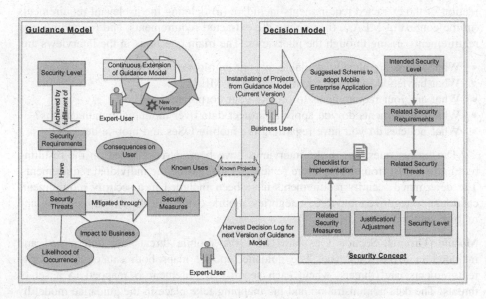

Fig. 3. The structure of the security framework for MEAs.

4.2   Guidance Model

This model includes four main profiles for security levels, requirements, threats and measures. These three profiles are mapped to each other. A security level of MEA is achieved by the fulfillment of a set of security requirements, that have potential security threats. Each threat in this framework is described along with its likelihood of occurrence and the possible impact on business. The framework maps these threats to security measures to mitigate the potential risks caused by said threats.

The maintenance of the content and the mapping of these four profiles are made by the role "expert user". In addition, expert users can also manage the versioning of the guidance model.

Security Levels. The framework's guidance model defines three security levels (high, medium, low). However, additional security levels can also be handled in this model. Each security level is achieved by the fulfillment of a set of security requirements. In other words, each security level in the guidance model is mapped to a set of security requirements. This mapping is based on current literature and discussions with experts within enterprises. However, enterprises can define their own security levels and requirements and administrate these in the framework.

Mobile Security Requirements. The security requirements for MEAs have been determined in two steps. In first step, a list of current requirements was extracted from the existing literature and standards, especially BSI [5], NIST [46] and Common Criteria [8]. The resulting list has been validated through expert interviews. This validation of the extracted requirements included: (a) deleting the irrelevant requirements (in the context of MEAs), (b) refining the extracted requirements, and (c) adding new requirements arising through the interviews. The main questions in the interviews are:

- What MEAs are already available to your employees today?
- What barriers do you see when adopting of MEAs?
- What are your requirements to protect your corporate data?
- What requirements do you apply to protect data over mobile communications?
- What policies do you have regarding the mobile OSes and mobile devices?

The further questions in the interviews have been derived based on the resulting requirements list from the literature review, by discussing the individual requirements. The determined security requirements have been included in a security requirements catalogue, categorized into three categories: mobile communications, mobile OSes, and mobile applications.

Mobile Threats. Section 3 explains how the mobile threats are determined and included in a risk catalogue. The guidance model maps both catalogues, security requirements, and threats, where each security requirement is mapped to a set of threats. The data administration and the mapping take place in the guidance model by expert users, who also map each threat to a security solution, which is a set of security measures needed to fulfill the related security requirements and to mitigate the risk can be caused by potential threats.

Mobile Security Measures. Mobile devices have limited resources (CPU power, memory, battery life) compared to PCs [10]. Moreover, limited resources such as storage space and computational capability form an intrinsic characteristic of mobile device [55]. Due to these limitation, traditional security measures for PCs seem to be ineffective for mobile devices, e.g. complex intrusion detection algorithms are not suitable for mobile devices, because they require excessive CPU power [10]. In addition, a balance between security and usability is of crucial importance when applying security measures, due to usability barriers of mobile devices (e.g., screen size, keypad size). As security measures, restrictions can also be applied on mobile device, like restricting user and mobile application access to hardware, like digital camera, GPS, and removable storage. However, mobile security measures and restrictions can have consequences on the user (e.g. high chance of error when entering a complex alphanumeric password).

In our previous work, existing mobile security measures and restrictions along with their consequences for mobile users have been presented based on literature review and best practices within companies [20]. That work also proposed a model for user acceptance of mobile security measures and restrictions in business context.

In its guidance model, the framework maps each threat from the risk catalogue to one or more security solutions (A security solution is a combination of one or more mobile security measures, e.g. Authentication through password and fingerprint). Hence, the framework suggests security measures along with their possible consequences on user and their known uses in previous MEAs.

4.3 Decision Model

The decision model represents an instantiation of the guidance model in form of projects, which in turn represent security concepts of MEAs. Within the framework, security concept includes the security requirements, threats, and measures that should be taken into consideration when adopting a MEA. The decision model is available for business users and expert users as well. However, expert users are responsible for the content administration of the guidance model and the framework content is made available to the business users through the decision model.

In the first step, the business user creates a new project and then selects the needed security requirements. Alternatively, the business user can directly select a security level and the framework will automatically show the security requirements that are needed to achieve the selected security level.

In the second step, after the business user selects the needed security requirements (intended security level), the framework will present, based on the selected requirements, the related threats that have to be taken into consideration. Those related threats are presented along with their likelihood of occurrence and their impact on business. The framework also shows an estimation of the potential risk that might be caused by a threat. This estimation of risk is done based on a risk estimation matrix shown in Table 3. In addition, the business user will still have the ability to add new threats that are not included into the guidance model. These added threats are associated with an individual security concept and will first be shown only in the related project. However, the added threats will be submitted to the guidance model, to be administrated by expert users, who will accept or reject those threats. If accepted, they will be included in the next version of the guidance model and they will be available for business users in the new version of guidance model.

In the third step, the framework will suggest one or more security solutions for each threat and business users can select one security solution for each threat based on the solution's potential consequences on the user. At this step, the balance between security and usability can take place.

In the last step, business users can close their own projects and they can export the closed projects as PDF files, which include a summary report of the selected security requirements, the related security threats, and the needed security measures.

5   Framework Implementation and Evaluation

The security framework has been implemented as a prototype in form of a web-based tool. The main goal behind this implementation is to demonstrate the framework's main functions, which in turn will enable a practical use of this framework in business sectors.

Figure 4 shows a screenshot of the prototype where an expert user is logged in and navigated to security requirements tab. Four areas are shown: (1) main menu for login and framework's models, (2) field set to administrate the framework's versions and possible justifications submitted by decision model, (3) a field set to navigate through the main components of the guidance model, (4) main area to show and administrate the content of the guidance model.

Fig. 4. Screenshot of the implemented framework as web-based tool.

Essentially, the prototype fulfills the following main functional requirements:

- User and role management
- Administration of content in the guidance model
- Administration of versions of the guidance model
- Administration of projects in the decision model
- Administration of the adjustments that were provided in the decision model to the guidance model
- Exporting project(s) as a PDF

The framework has been implemented in C# programing language under Microsoft Visual Studio Community 2015 Edition as IDE (Integrated Development Environment). ASP.NET MVC5, as a software design pattern, has been used for building the framework as a web-based tool. Microsoft SQL Server 2016 Express has been used as a database management system. SQL Server Management Studio has been used to access the SQL server for configuring, managing, and administering its components. Moreover, the following main technologies have been used: entity framework, JQuery and AJAX, DataTables, Rotativa.

The evaluation of the resulting prototype has been performed in two ways. First, it was tested against its functional requirements through function tests. Second, the prototype was evaluated through expert interviews with different roles, namely, IT security officer, IT operation manager, IT manager, and managing director within four German SMEs. Four intensive interviews were done; each interview took about 120 min. This includes, (1) about 10 min for a short presentation explaining the idea behind this work, (2) about 20 min for a live demonstration of the framework based on two prepared scenarios, (3) conducting an interview based on a prepared questionnaire.

As evaluation results, all interviewees have evaluated the framework as a very useful tool. Such a framework is ideally suited for deriving the necessary security measures needed to achieve a security level. This derivation is nowadays not an easy task, even in companies with a good IT. The interviewees also found that the use of the framework can significantly accelerate the adoption of new MEAs by supporting business users with their decision-making process. They said that operational issues are often excluded from the decision-making process, however these can be easily included in that process using this framework. Moreover, the administration of the guidance model's versions and the adjustments, that may be provided by business users, support the continuous extension of the guidance model by including new content. In addition, as the security requirements can be different for each enterprise, depending on its size and domain, each enterprise can generate and administrate its own versions of guidance model.

For enterprises that outsource their mobile technologies, the framework can serve as an interface between the enterprise and its external service provider.

Besides business users, expert users like IT security officers, who have a good IT security expertise, can benefit from the framework, since it enables a sustainable and structured documentation of the decisions made.

6 Conclusion and Outlook

This book chapter presented a security framework that supports SMEs when adopting MEAs. This framework consists of two models: the guidance model, in which the framework's content is administrated by expert users, and the decision model, that enables business users to instantiate decision models into projects, where each project represents the security concept of the MEAs the enterprise wants to adopt.

First, the mobile security requirements were determined based on literature review and have been validated through expert interviews.

Second, the resulted list of requirements was mapped to a risk catalogue, which includes a list of potential mobile threats classified in five categories. To determine the potential mobile threats, mobile business scenarios were defined to get insight in the typical usage of MEAs. Then, a set of business assets were determined, considering the defined scenarios. An estimation of the potential impact on business were made by mapping between potential threats and assets. This catalogue gives a business view on the mobile threats. Generally, there are existing risk catalogues, but they show a generic and not business-context view, which makes them too complex for business users. Separated from the framework, the resulted risk catalogue was evaluated through discussion with experts from the business domain. They found that the threats overview in the risk catalogue is detailed enough and would allow a reader to access important information quickly. Moreover, they found that mapping the assets with potential threats is meaningful for business users especially for those who do not know which assets can be threatened when using mobile devices for work purposes. Based on their feedback, a good improvement can be made by assigning a value for each asset and considering that value in the risk estimation.

Third, in our previous work, existing mobile security measures and restrictions along with their consequences for mobile users were presented based on literature review and best practices within companies. Through its guidance model, the framework maps the threats from risk catalogue to these security measures and restrictions are needed to mitigate the potential risk on business and to achieve the intended security level.

Finally, the framework was implemented as prototype in form of web-based tool, and it has been evaluated through discussion with experts within German companies. Results from those interviews are presented in Sect. 5. In addition, the interviewees suggested wide improvements that can be implemented in the future. The most important suggestions are: (1) supporting further application types (not only MEAs), in addition to that, the association of projects to each other would be also conceivable, because mobile applications often communicate with backend applications. (2) as the framework suggests security measures without providing information about their implementation or if they are implemented, the framework can be extended to enable business users to assign a flag for the implemented security measures within a specific project. (3) the framework does not support the reevaluation of closed projects against a new version of guidance model, e.g. for new arising threats, the framework might check if these new threats affect the closed projects.

Last but not least, the framework is being refined and improved based on the feedback and suggestions from interviewers.

References

1. Abura'ed, N., Otrok, H., Mizouni, R., Bentahar, J.: Mobile phishing attack for Android platform. In: 10th International Conference on Innovations in Information Technology, Al Ain, United Arab Emirates, pp. 18–23 (2014)
2. Adeel, M., Tokarchuk, L.N.: Analysis of mobile P2P malware detection framework through cabir & commwarrior families. In: IEEE Third International Conference on Privacy, Security, Risk and Trust, Boston, MA, USA, pp. 1335–1343 (2011)
3. Andriole, S.J., Bojanova, I.: Optimizing operational and strategic IT. IT Prof. **16**(5), 12–15 (2014). doi:10.1109/MITP.2014.74
4. Brown, C., Spike, D., Joshua, M.F., Neil, M., Sharon, V.-N., Michael, P., Bart, S.: Assessing threats to mobile devices & infrastructure. The Mobile Threat Catalogue. Draft NISTIR 8144. NIST (2016). http://csrc.nist.gov/publications/drafts/nistir-8144/nistir8144_draft.pdf
5. BSI: IT-Grundschutz-Catalogues (2013). https://www.bsi.bund.de/EN/Topics/ITGrundschutz/ITGrundschutzCatalogues/itgrundschutzcatalogues_node.html
6. Bundesministerium für Wirtschaft und Energie: Ergebnisse des SimoBIT-Arbeitsforums IT-Sicherheit in mobilen Geschäftsprozessen. Leitfaden IT-Sicherheit (2010). http://www.digitale-technologien.de/DT/Redaktion/DE/Downloads/leitfaden-it-sicherheit.pdf
7. CISCO: Cisco 2016 Annual Security Report (2016). http://www.cisco.com/c/en/us/products/security/annual_security_report.html
8. Common Criteria: Common Criteria for Information Technology Security Evaluation (2009). http://www.commoncriteriaportal.org/cc/
9. Damopoulos, D., Kambourakis, G., Anagnostopoulos, M., Gritzalis, S., Park, J.H.: User privacy and modern mobile services. Are they on the same path. Pers. Ubiquit. Comput. **17** (7), 1437–1448 (2013). doi:10.1007/s00779-012-0579-1
10. He, D., Chan, S., Guizani, M.: Mobile application security: malware threats and defenses. IEEE Wireless Commun. **22**(1), 138–144 (2015). doi:10.1109/MWC.2015.7054729
11. Euler, M., Hacke, M., Hartherz, C., Steiner, S., Verclas, S.: Herausforderungen bei der Mobilisierung von Business Applikationen und erste Lösungsansätze. In: Verclas, S., Linnhoff-Popien, C. (eds.) Smart Mobile Apps, pp. 107–121. Springer, Heidelberg (2012). doi:10.1007/978-3-642-22259-7_8
12. Gartner: Gartner Says 75 Percent of Mobile Security Breaches Will Be the Result of Mobile Application Misconfiguration (2014). http://www.gartner.com/newsroom/id/2753017
13. Gartner: Gartner Forecasts 59% Mobile Data Growth Worldwide in 2015 (2015). http://www.gartner.com/newsroom/id/3098617
14. Gartner: Gartner Says Worldwide Smartphone Sales Grew 9.7% in Fourth Quarter of 2015 (2016). http://www.gartner.com/newsroom/id/3215217
15. Gartner: Magic Quadrant for Enterprise Mobility Management Suites (2016). https://www.gartner.com/doc/reprints?id=1-390IMNG&ct=160608&st=sb
16. Godber, A., Dasgupta, P.:Secure wireless gateway. In: Maughan, D., Vaidya, N.H. (eds.) The ACM Workshop, Atlanta, GA, USA, pp. 41–46 (2002)
17. de Gramatica, M., Labunets, K., Massacci, F., Paci, F., Tedeschi, A.: The role of catalogues of threats and security controls in security risk assessment: an empirical study with ATM professionals. In: Fricker, S.A., Schneider, K. (eds.) REFSQ 2015. LNCS, vol. 9013, pp. 98–114. Springer, Cham (2015). doi:10.1007/978-3-319-16101-3_7

18. Gröger, C., Silcher, S., Westkämper, E., Mitschang, B.: Leveraging apps in manufacturing. A framework for app technology in the enterprise. Procedia CIRP **7**, 664–669 (2013). doi:10. 1016/j.procir.2013.06.050

19. Hasan, B., Dmitriyev, V., Marx Gómez, J., Kurzhöfer, J.: A framework along with guidelines for designing secure mobile enterprise applications. In: International Carnahan Conference on Security Technology (ICCST), pp. 1–6. IEEE, Rome (2014)

20. Hasan, B., Rajski, E., Gómez, J.M., Kurzhöfer, J.: A proposed model for user acceptance of mobile security measures – business context. In: Kim, K.J., Wattanapongsakorn, N., Joukov, N. (eds.) Mobile and Wireless Technologies 2016. LNEE, vol. 391, pp. 97–108. Springer, Singapore (2016). doi:10.1007/978-981-10-1409-3_11

21. Hasan, B., Schäfer, P., Marx Gómez, J., Kurzhöfer, J.: Risk catalogue for mobile business applications. In: Proceedings of the 13th International Joint Conference on e-Business and Telecommunications, pp. 43–53 (2016)

22. Hoos, E., Gröger, C., Kramer, S., Mitschang, B.: ValueApping: an analysis method to identify value-adding mobile enterprise apps in business processes. In: Cordeiro, J., Hammoudi, S., Maciaszek, L., Camp, O., Filipe, J. (eds.) ICEIS 2014. LNBIP, vol. 227, pp. 222–243. Springer, Cham (2015). doi:10.1007/978-3-319-22348-3_13

23. Howard, M., Lipner, S.: The Security Development Lifecycle. SDL: A Process for Developing Demonstrably More Secure Software. Microsoft Press, Redmond (2006)

24. IDC: IDC Reveals Worldwide Mobile Enterprise Applications and Solutions Predictions for 2015 (2014). http://www.businesswire.com/news/home/20141218006258/en/IDC-Reveals-Worldwide-Mobile-Enterprise-Applications-Solutions

25. ISO 31000:2009: Risk Management—Principles and Guidelines. Geneva: International Standards Organisation (2009)

26. ISO/IEC: ISO/IEC 27002: Information technology – Security techniques – Code of practice for information security controls (2013)

27. Jain, S.: Security threats in manets. A review. IJIT **3**(2), 37–50 (2014). doi:10.5121/ijit.2014. 3204

28. Jermyn, J., Salles-Loustau, G., Zonouz, S.: An analysis of DoS attack strategies against the LTE RAN. J. Cyber Secur. Mob. (JCSM) **3**(2), 159–180 (2014). doi:10.13052/jcsm2245-1439.323

29. Kaspersky: One in Every Six users suffer loss or theft of mobile devices (2013). http://www. kaspersky.com/au/about/news/press/2013/one-in-every-six-users-suffer-loss-or-theft-of-mobile-devices

30. Kennedy, M., Sulaiman, R.: Following the Wi-Fi breadcrumbs: network based mobile application privacy threats. In: 2015 International Conference on Electrical Engineering and Informatics (ICEEI), Denpasar, Bali, Indonesia, pp 265–270 (2015)

31. Kizza, J.M.: Mobile Systems and Corresponding Intractable Security Issues. In: Kizza, J.M. (ed.) Guide to Computer Network Security, pp. 491–507. Springer, London (2015)

32. Lacerda, A., Queiroz, R., Barbosa, M.: A systematic mapping on security threats in mobile devices. In: 2015 Internet Technologies and Applications (ITA), Wrexham, UK, pp. 286–291 (2015)

33. Levinson, M.: 6 ways to defend against drive-by downloads (2012). http://www.cio.com/ article/2448967/security0/6-ways-to-defend-against-drive-by-downloads.html

34. Lookout: Enterprise Mobile Threat report. The State of iOS and Android Security Threats to Enterprise Mobility [Whitepaper] (2015). https://info.lookout.com/rs/051-ESQ-475/images/Enterprise_MTR.pdf

35. Lookout: Lookout Mobile Threat report (2011). https://www.lookout.com/img/images/lookout-mobile-threat-report-2011.pdf

36. Luenendonk: Mobile Enterprise Review. Mehr Strategie wagen (2014). http://www.luenen donk-shop.de/out/pictures/0/mc_mobileenterprisereview_studie_f210214_fl.pdf

37. Maan, J.: Enterprise mobility – a future transformation strategy for organizations. In: Wyld, D.C., Zizka, J., Nagamalai, D. (eds.) Advances in Computer Science, Engineering & Applications, vol. 167, pp. 559–567. Springer, Heidelberg (2012)

38. Marble, J.L., Lawless, W.F., Mittu, R., Sibley, C.: The human factor in cybersecurity: robust & intelligent defense. In: Jajodia, S., Shakarian, P., Subrahmanian, V., Swarup, V., Wang, C. (eds.) Cyber Warfare, vol. 56, pp. 173–206. Springer, Cham (2015). doi:10.1007/978-3-319-14039-1_9

39. Markelj, B., Bernik, I.: Safe use of mobile devices arises from knowing the threats. J. Inf. Secur. Appl. **20**, 84–89 (2015). doi:10.1016/j.jisa.2014.11.001

40. Martin, T., Hsiao, M., Ha, D., Krishnaswami, J.: Denial-of-service attacks on battery-powered mobile computers. In: Proceedings of the Second IEEE International Conference on Pervasive Computing and Communications (PerCom 2004), pp. 309–318. IEEE Computer Society, Washington, DC (2004)

41. McAfee Labs: McAfee Labs Threats report (2014). http://www.mcafee.com/us/resources/reports/rp-quarterly-threat-q2-2014.pdf

42. Michaelis, P.: Enterprise mobility – a balancing act between security and usability. In: Reimer, H., Pohlmann, N., Schneider, W. (eds.) ISSE 2012 Securing Electronic Business Processes, pp. 75–79. Springer Fachmedien Wiesbaden, Wiesbaden (2012)

43. Moonsamy, V., Batten, L.: Mitigating man-in-the-middle attacks on smartphones - a discussion of SSL pinning and DNSSec. In: The 12th Australian Information Security Management Conference, pp. 5–13. Edith Cowan University, Perth (2014)

44. Myagmar, S., Lee, A.J., Yurcik, W.: Threat modeling as a basis for security requirements. In: Symposium on Requirements Engineering for Information Security (SREIS) (2005)

45. Nikbakhsh, S., Manaf, A.B.A., Zamani, M., Janbeglou, M.: A novel approach for rogue access point detection on the client-side. In: 2012 IEEE Workshops of International Conference on Advanced Information Networking and Applications (WAINA), pp. 684–687. IEEE, Fukuoka (2012)

46. NIST: Security and Privacy Controls for Federal Information Systems and Organizations (2013). http://nvlpubs.nist.gov/nistpubs/SpecialPublications/NIST.SP.800-53r4.pdf

47. PCI DSS: PCI DSS Risk Assessment Guidelines (2012)

48. Pu, S., Chen, Z., Huang, C., Liu, Y., Zen, B.: Threat analysis of smart mobile device. In: URSI General Assembly and Scientific Symposium (URSI GASS), pp. 1–3. IEEE, Beijing (2014)

49. Ramu, S.: Mobile Malware Evolution, Detection and Defense. EECE 571B, Term Survey Paper (2012)

50. Rao, U.H., Nayak, U.: Malicious software and anti-virus software. In: Rao, U.H., Nayak, U. (eds.) The InfoSec Handbook, pp. 141–161. Apress, Berkeley (2014)

51. Rhee, K., Won, D., Jang, S.W., Chae, S., Park, S.: Threat modeling of a mobile device management system for secure smart work. Electron. Commer. Res. **13**(3), 243–256 (2013). doi:10.1007/s10660-013-9121-4

52. Eilts, S.: Technische Konzeption und prototypische Umsetzung eines Sicherheitsframeworks für mobile Unternehmensapplikationen. Master thesis, Carl von Ossietzky University of Oldenburg (2016)

53. Souppaya, M., Scarfone, K.: Guidelines for managing the security of mobile devices in the enterprise. NIST SP- 800-124 (2013). http://dx.doi.org/10.6028/NIST.SP.800-124r1

54. Srinivasan, A., Wu, J.: SafeCode – safeguarding security and privacy of user data on stolen iOS devices. In: Xiang, Y., Lopez, J., Kuo, C.-C.J., Zhou, W. (eds.) CSS 2012. LNCS, vol. 7672, pp. 11–20. Springer, Heidelberg (2012). doi:10.1007/978-3-642-35362-8_2

55. Sun, Z., Yang, Y., Zhou, Y., Cruickshank, H.: Agent-based resource management for mobile cloud. In: Rodrigues, J.J., Lin, K., Lloret, J. (eds.) Mobile Networks and Cloud Computing Convergence for Progressive Services and Applications, pp. 118–134. IGI Global (2014)
56. Symantec: Fraud Alert: Phishing — The Latest Fraud Alert: Phishing — The Latest Tactics and Potential Business Impacts – Phishing [White Paper] (2014). http://www.symantec.com/content/en/μs/enterprise/white_papers/b-fraud-alert-phishing-wp.pdf
57. Unhelkar, B., Murugesan, S.: The enterprise mobile applications development framework. IT Prof. **12**(3), 33–39 (2010). doi:10.1109/MITP.2010.45
58. v Do, T., Lyche, F.B., Lytskjold, J.H., van Thuan, D.: Threat assessment model for mobile malware. In: Kim, K.J. (ed.) Information Science and Applications. LNEE, vol. 339, pp. 467–474. Springer, Heidelberg (2015). doi:10.1007/978-3-662-46578-3_55
59. Venkatesan, D.: Android ransomware variants created directly on mobile devices (2016). http://www.symantec.com/connect/blogs/android-ransomware-variants-created-directly-mobile-devices

BPMN4V for Modeling and Handling Versions of BPMN Collaborations and Choreographies

Imen Ben Said[1,2(✉)], Mohamed Amine Chaâbane[1], Eric Andonoff[2], and Rafik Bouaziz[1]

[1] MIRACL, University of Sfax, Route de L'aéroport,
BP 1088, 3018 Sfax, Tunisia
{Imen.Bensaid, ma.chaabane, raf.bouaziz}@fsegs.rnu.tn
[2] IRIT, University of Toulouse 1, 2 rue du Doyen Gabriel Marty,
31042 Toulouse Cedex, France
andonoff@univ-tlse1.fr

Abstract. This paper presents BPMN4V, an extension of BPMN with versions to address business process flexibility, which is an important issue that Business Process Management (BPM) systems must face before their definitive acceptance and use in companies. This issue has mainly been investigated in the context of intra-organizational processes but it received little attention in the context of Inter-organizational Processes (IoP), which correspond to processes crossing the boundaries of companies. This paper deals with IoP flexibility modeled as collaborations and choreographies in BPMN, advocating a version-based approach. Firstly, the paper introduces the provided extensions to BPMN 2.0 meta-model to take into account the notion of version considering both static and dynamic aspects of collaboration versions. Secondly, it presents a mapping approach for deducing version of choreography from version of collaboration. Thirdly, it introduces the BPMN4V-Modeler, which is an implementation of BPMN4V on top of the well-known BPMN-Modeler Eclipse plug-in.

Keywords: Process flexibility · BPMN · Collaboration · Choreography · Version

1 Introduction

Over the two last decades, there has been a shift from Data-aware Information Systems to Process-aware Information Systems (PaISs) [1]. Processes play now a fundamental role in companies: they are considered as first class citizen and they are the support of the alignment between IS of companies and their business strategies [2, 3]. This shift is mainly due to the maturity of the Business Process Management (BPM) area, which is a well-established research area, defining concepts, methods and systems supporting the whole process life cycle [4]. However, BPM systems fail to become widely adopted by companies as they still have important challenges to address. Process flexibility is one of these challenges. It is a fundamental challenge as the economic environment in which companies are involved is more and more dynamic, competitive, and open: companies

© Springer International Publishing AG 2017
M.S. Obaidat (Ed): ICETE 2016, CCIS 764, pp. 99–123, 2017.
https://doi.org/10.1007/978-3-319-67876-4_5

frequently change their processes in order to meet, as quickly and efficiently as possible, new customer requirements or to benefit from new collaboration opportunities [5].

Flexibility has been deeply investigated, mainly in the context of intra-organizational (or internal) processes. Several taxonomies to feature process flexibility and to evaluate the ability of BPM systems and process models to support process flexibility have been proposed in literature. The more suitable one is given in [3]. This taxonomy differentiates between two times for process flexibility: flexibility at design-time, which refers to foreseeable changes which can be taken into account in modeled process schemas, and flexibility at run time, which refers to unforeseeable changes occurring during process execution. In addition, this taxonomy identifies four needs of flexibility [3]: (i) *variability*, for representing a process differently, depending on the context of its execution, (ii) *adaptation*, for handling occasional situations or exceptions which have not been necessarily foreseen in process schemas, (iii) *evolution*, for handling changes in processes which require occasional or permanent modifications in their schemas, and finally (iv) *looseness*, for handling knowledge intensive processes whose schemas are not known a priori and which correspond to non-repeatable, unpredictable and emergent processes. Such processes require loose specifications. Note that flexibility at run-time requires migration techniques to support the propagation of changes from a given process instance towards its other running instances [3]. However, process flexibility is still an open issue in the context of Inter-organizational Processes (IoP). In this context, IoP flexibility may be related to the availability of involved processes or to the IoP schema.

On the other hand, BPMN (Business Process Model and Notation) [6] is considered as the de-facto standard for process modeling, and it is easily understood by BPM practitioners: analysts designing processes, developers implementing them, process owners supervising them, and finally actors involved in their enactment. BPMN considers not only intra-organizational processes (modeled as private processes) but also IoPs modeled as Collaborative Processes (CPs) that can be collaborations or choreographies. Moreover BPMN has been extended in various ways: for instance, for improving the modeling of the organizational dimension of processes (e.g., [7]), for business activity or business process monitoring (e.g., [8]), for time modeling in processes (e.g., [9]), for goal modeling (e.g., [10]), and also for addressing process flexibility (e.g., [11–13]).

This paper addresses the following research question: how to deal with IoP flexibility modeled as BPMN collaborations or choreographies? We deal with this research question advocating a version-based approach. The reasons justifying such an approach are the following. Firstly, handling versions of processes facilitates the migration of instances from an initial schema to a final one allowing, if the migration is not possible, two different instances of the same process to run according to two different schemas [14]. Secondly, the notion version has been recognized as a key notion to deal with process flexibility and more marticularly with process variability, process evolution and process adaptation (when adaptation can be defined a priori, at design-time) [15].

More precisely, the paper extends our contribution presented in [12] in which we have introduced collaboration versioning and a recommended mapping approach for deducing versions of choreographies from corresponding versions of collaborations. With respect to [12], this paper gives more details about collaboration versioning by defining both static and dynamic aspects of versions. It also gives implementation details about the BPMN4V-Modeler, a tool dedicated to modeling and handling versions of collaborations and choreographies.

Accordingly this paper is organised as follows. Section 2 is an overview of related works, considering process flexibility both in an intra-organizational and in an inter-organizational context. Section 3 gives the background of the paper. It also introduces the radiological examination process, which motivates the need for flexibility of processes crossing the boundaries of companies. Section 4 addresses the modeling of versions of collaborations: it introduces BPMN4V, an extension of BPMN to support version of collaboration modeling, focusing on both static and dynamic aspects of version modeling. Section 5 describes our approach supporting the mapping from version of collaborations into corresponding versions of choreographies. Section 5 presents BPMN4V-Modeler, a specific tool dedicated to the modeling and handling of versions of collaborations and choreographies. Finally, Sect. 6 concludes the paper and gives some directions for future works.

2 Related Works

Process flexibility has been highly investigated in the context of intra-organizational processes since the end of the 1990s. Different contributions have been made to deal with this issue, and they follow several approaches: activity-driven approach [14, 15], constraint-driven approach [16], data-driven approach [17], case-driven approach (case handling) [18], and more recently social-driven approach [19]. In this paper, we rather focus on activity-driven process flexibility as activity-oriented models are used in the majority of (service-oriented) PaIS.

Regarding flexibility of activity-driven intra-organizational processes, we can mention works supporting the modeling of process variants [20, 21]. These contributions address process flexibility and more precisely process variability, according to the typology of [3]. A variant is an adjustment at run-time of a base process schema according to the context. We differentiate between behavioral approaches, which define the base process schema as a superset of variants and derive a specific process variant by hiding and blocking process components of the base process schema, and structural approaches, which derive a process variant by applying a set of changes to a base process schema [22]. Specific notations and systems such as for instance C-EPC [20] or Provop [21] support process variants.

We can also mention works supporting the modeling of process versions for capturing process changes over time. In the version-based approach, the significant changes on process schema results in the definition of new process versions. Several contributions advocate this approach to deal with process flexibility [14, 15, 23–25]. ADEPT [25] is probably the most comprehensive BPM system supporting version management. [23, 24] have proposed versioning models to keep track of process changes. The versioning model proposed by [23] allows to model versions of processes as directed graphs named VPG (Version Preserving Graph). The nodes of VPG are activities of the process while the arcs of VPG define coordination between these activities. [23] has also proposed operations to modify the VPG: Add node, Delete node, etc.... Moreover, the versioning model proposed by [24] represents each version of process as an RPST (Refined Process Structure Tree). The RPST is a linear-time method to decompose a process model into a tree of hierarchical SESE fragments. A SESE fragment is a sub-graph of a process model with a single entry and a single exit node. However, these works have two main drawbacks. Firstly, they mainly focus on the behavioral dimension of processes, leaving aside their organizational and informational dimensions. Secondly, each of these contributions introduces specific notations, which are not standards and are unlikely to be used by process designers who are in charge of modeling flexibility of processes. Therefore, we have introduced an extension of BPMN to support intra-organizational process version modeling, considering both behavioral (what, how), organizational (who) and informational (when) dimensions of processes [11]. More precisely we have extended the BPMN meta-model for private processes with version notion to support flexibility of intra-organizational processes. In addition, in [13] we have proposed another extension to BPMN to consider the contextual dimension of private processes. This dimension allows capturing the situations in which process versions are executed, thus allowing to define why some versions have to be used instead others according to the context.

BPM community has paid less attention to IoP flexibility, and it is still an open issue. More precisely, IoP flexibility may be related to the availability of involved processes or to the change of collaboration schemas. Research in IoP flexibility mainly addresses process availability in the context of dynamic inter-organizational processes [26]. Dynamic inter-organizational processes refer to IoPs where the different partners involved are not necessarily known at design-time, or can evolve at run-time (e.g., they become unavailable or their quality of service decreases significantly) [27]. The provided solutions support finding new partners offering requested services, along with negotiation, contracting and service execution, in separate or comprehensive frameworks.

On the other side, collaboration schema change has been rather neglected. However, we have found some contributions in the SOA context [28]. Firstly, [28] mainly considers chained execution and subcontracting collaborative processes, and they provide high level patterns for service adaptation (adding, removing, substituting services) called LC-IOWF. These contributions address IoPs variability and adaption but they do not address IoPs looseness and evolution. Secondly, [29] recommends an extension of the WS-BPEL language to deal with exceptions in collaborative processes. However, the proposed solution is specific since it depends on a particular execution language and it only deals with IoPs adaptation. We also have found some contributions focusing on the propagation of private process changes towards processes of the other partners involved in CPs represented as BPMN choreographies [30]. More precisely, they provide a set of algorithms to deal with changes of process schema by adding, deleting, replacing or updating process fragments. However, they only focus on variability of CP schema and they do not consider changes that can affect activities and messages (i.e., information) exchanged between collaborative process partners. Finally, [31, 32] have proposed a meta-model called VP2M (Version of Process Meta-model) that supports the modeling of flexible IoP using versions. This work deals with static and dynamic aspect of versions of processes that are modeled as instances of the VP2M. Despite this work considers all process dimensions to deal with IoP flexibility, the proposed solution is not based on existing standards for modeling IoPs.

3 Background

This section introduces the background of the paper, namely collaboration and choreography modeling in BPMN. It also presents the radiological examination example, which will be used through the paper to illustrate collaboration and choreography versioning.

3.1 Concepts for BPMN Collaboration and Choreography

BPMN 2.0 allows the creation of three basic types of diagrams within an end-to-end process [6]: *private process*, *collaboration* and *choreography*. Firstly, a Private Process is internal to a specific company. It describes a sequence of activities performed within the company in order to carry out an objective. It is depicted as a directed graph. Secondly, a Collaboration depicts the interactions between two or more business entities (each one being represented as a process) in order to carry out a common business target. These interactions specify the orchestration between the partners involved as message flows, i.e. messages exchanged between partners. Thirdly, a Choreography is another way to model interactions between partners. Unlike collaborations, the focus is not on orchestration of the work performed within partners, but rather on the exchange of information (messages) between them. Note that BPMN collaborations describe both orchestration of partners activities and messages exchanged. Thus BPMN choreographies can be deduced from BPMN collaborations.

As this paper deal with BPMN collaboration and choreography flexibility, we present below the necessary concepts for collaborations and choreographies modeling. These concepts are visualized in white in Fig. 3.

Regarding collaborations, each involved partner is seen as a participant that represents a *PartnerEntity* (*e.g.*, a company) or a *PartnerRole* (*e.g.*, a buyer, a seller, or a manufacturer). A participant is often responsible for the execution of a *Process*. A process involved in a collaboration is a *FlowElementContainer* that may contain *SequenceFlow* and *FlowNode* (*Gateway*, *Event* and *Task*). More precisely, processes of collaboration are provided within tasks, events and the way these tasks and events are synchronised using sequence flow and gateways. Furthermore, within a collaboration, participants are prepared to send and receive *Messages* within *Message flows*. A message flow illustrates the flow of messages between two interaction nodes. An *Interaction node* is used to provide a single element as the source (*send* relationship) or the target (*receive* relationship) of a message flow, and therefore of a message. An interaction node can be a participant, a task or an event. Note that within a collaboration, tasks (and events) are considered as the "touch point" between participants. Only those tasks (or events) that are used to communicate with the other participants are included. They define the public part of the process. As a consequence, all other internal (*i.e.*, private) tasks or events of the process are not shown in a collaboration diagram [6].

A *Choreography* is a FlowElementContainer that may contain sequence flow and *FlowNode* (Gateway, Event and Choreography activity). A *Choreography activity* represents a point in a choreography flow where an interaction occurs between two or more participants. A choreography activity can be a choreography task or a sub choreography. A *ChoreographyTask* is an atomic activity in a choreography that represents an interaction in which one or two messages are exchanged between two participants. A *SubChoreography* is a compound activity in a choreography that contains the flow of other choreography activities.

3.2 The Radiological Examination Collaboration

The radiological examination collaboration, inspired from [3], describes how a clinic interacts with a radiology center for X-ray examination towards clinic patients. Note that these two companies are independent.

Three cases are possible, each one corresponding to a version of the collaboration. Figure 1 shows these versions, in which each participant process is represented in a specific pool. The first version starts when a clinic's patient needs a radiological examination. Thus the clinic sends a request for an X-ray examination to the radiology center. After checking the request, either the center sends back a reject notification to the clinic, or it notifies the clinic of the chosen X-ray appointment. On the appointment day, the clinic drives the patient to the radiology center. After the X-ray examination, the radiologist interprets the examination and sends the result of this interpretation to the clinic. Note that in this first version of collaboration, messages exchanged (*e.g.*, result of the interpretation) are paper documents transmitted manually.

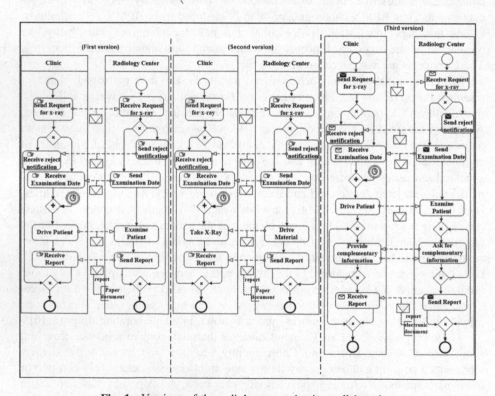

Fig. 1. Versions of the radiology examination collaboration.

The second version of the collaboration is suitable when the patient cannot be driven to the radiology center. In this case, a radiologist from the radiology center takes specific portable X-ray material from the radiology center to the clinic to perform the requested X-ray in the patient's room.

In order to improve the quality of their services, both the clinic and the radiology center implement a specific application supporting the automation of their interaction. Thus a new version of the collaboration is defined. In this version, exchanged messages are electronically transmitted within application. In addition, before interpreting the examination, the radiologist can interact with the patient's doctor for additional information.

According to the taxonomy of Reichert and Weber, this example highlights two flexibility needs: variability and evolution. Indeed the second version of the process is a variant of the first version, as it is suitable when the patient cannot move to the radiology center. The third version is rather an evolution of the first version of the process as the interactions between the clinic and the radiology center are no longer manual interactions but they are directly encoded in a specific application.

4   BPMN4V for Modeling and Handling Versions of Collaboration

This section introduces the notion of version and presents the versioning pattern we recommend to model both entities and their corresponding versions. Then the section describes the provided extensions to BPMN for modeling versions of collaboration. Finally, this section illustrates the modeling of the first version of the radiological examination collaboration.

4.1   Version Concept

A version corresponds to one of the significant states (*i.e.*, values) an entity (*e.g.*, collaboration, process) may have during its life cycle. So, it is possible to describe changes occurring to entities through their different versions. These versions are linked by a derivation link: they form a derivation hierarchy.

When created, an entity is described by only one version. The definition of every new version is done by derivation from a previous one: such versions are called derived versions. Of course, several versions may be derived from the same previous one: these are called alternatives. They capture the variability of the corresponding entity (*e.g.*, process) and they correspond to their various variants. Thus using the notion of version, it becomes possible to model collaborative process (*i.e.*, IoP) flexibility and more precisely, collaborative process schema variability (through the notion of alternative or variant), collaborative process schema adaptation that can be modeled a priori in the schema, and collaborative process schema evolution [11].

We introduce a versioning pattern to support version modeling. The underlying idea is to model, for each versionable class (a versionable class is a class for which we handle versions) of the BPMN meta-model, both entities and their corresponding versions. The versioning pattern is given in Fig. 2. Each versionable class is described as a class, called *Versionable*. We associate to each versionable class a new class, called *Version of Versionable*, whose instances are versions of Versionable, and two links: (i) the *is_version_of* composition, which links each instance of the Versionable class with its corresponding instances of the Version of Versionable class and (ii) the *derived_from* relationship, which supports version derivation hierarchy modeling. This latter relationship is reflexive and the semantics of both relationship sides is: (i) a version (SV) succeeds another one in the derivation hierarchy and, (ii) a version (PV) precedes another one in the derivation hierarchy. Regarding versions, we also introduce attributes such as version number, creator name, creation date and state in the Version_of_Versionable class.

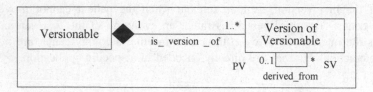

Fig. 2. Versioning pattern [12].

4.2 Modeling Versions of Collaborations: The BPMN4V Meta-model

BPMN4V Meta-model: Extension of BPMN for Collaboration Version Modeling. We model versions of collaborative processes providing extensions to the BPMN 2.0 collaboration meta-model previously presented. More precisely, we use the previous versioning pattern to make some classes of BPMN 2.0 collaboration meta-model versionable. Figure 3 presents the resulting meta-model, namely BPMN4V (BPMN for Versions), focusing on collaboration and choreography versioning. BPMN 2.0 classes are visualized in white while BPMN4V classes are visualized in grey.

In order to keep track of collaboration flexibility, we recommend handling versions for the following BPMN 2.0 classes: Collaboration, Message, Process, Task and Event. In fact, each of these classes represents key concepts for collaborations and plays a strong role in the definition of collaboration. The idea is to keep track of changes occurring to components which play a part in the description of how the collaboration is carried out.

Generally speaking, a new version of an element (*e.g.*, collaboration) is defined according to changes occurring to it: these changes may correspond to the addition of information (property or relationship) or to the modification or the deletion of existing ones. More precisely, regarding messages, we consider that a modification of their property *ItemDefinition* results in the creation of a new version of message. For instance, if *Report* is a message referring to a paper document (*Itemkind* value is physical), and as a result of technical changes, if it becomes an electronic document (Itemkind value is information) then a new version of Report has to be created. However we do not necessarily create a new version of message if there is change in the interaction in which the message is involved. Indeed an interaction (*i.e.*, a message

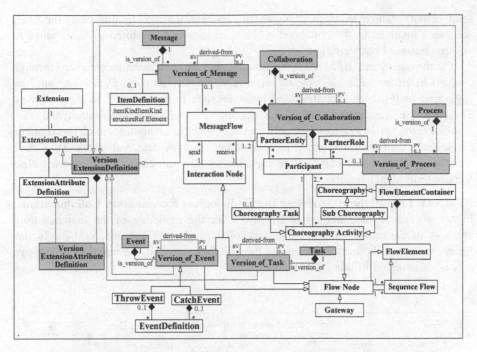

Fig. 3. BPMN4V: extension of BPMN for version of collaboration modeling [12].

flow) being defined as the triplet (message, send node, receive node), where send and receive nodes are interaction nodes involved in the message exchange that either correspond to versions of task or versions of event, changing the interaction does not necessarily lead to the creation of a new message. For instance, if message M is sent from task A to task B, and if a new task C is defined after an organizational change and the message is no longer sent from A to B but rather from C to B, then we do not create a new version of the message M if it carries the same information. Thus we manage M.v1 as a message exchanged between A and B, and M.v1 and we also manage M.v1 as a message exchanged between C and B.

Regarding processes, we create new versions when there are changes to the involved tasks and/or events or in the way they are linked together using sequence flows and gateways. In the same way, changes to tasks and events may result in the creation of new task and event versions. In addition, we create new versions of tasks or events involved in message exchange, when there are changes to the exchanged messages.

Finally, regarding collaborations, new versions may result from changes to participants involved. Thus when we add or delete a participant, it is necessary to adapt the current collaboration to this change: we have to incorporate the added participant or to possibly replace the deleted one. New versions of collaborations may also result from changes to involved processes or exchanged messages. Exchanged messages have an important impact in collaboration flow. Thus any change in a sent or a received message affects the involved tasks or events, and consequently the involved process. So, when we add (or delete) a message, we have to add (or to delete) a received and a send activity, which leads to changing the process schema. In this case, the other processes involved in the collaboration have in turn to be adapted to this change to ensure continued collaboration.

On the other hand, BPMN 2.0 meta-model provides extension mechanisms through classes *Extension*, *ExtensionDefinition* and *Extension AttributeDefinition*, and, as suggested in [6], each recommended extension has to be assigned to these classes. Therefore we recommend adding the classes *VersionExtensionDefinition* and *VersionExtensionAttributeDefinition* to model the specific attributes which versionable classes include (version number, creator name, creation date and state). Thus each Version of Versionable class of the meta-model is a sub-class of the abstract class VersionExtensionDefinition.

BPMN4V Instantiation: Modeling the Radiological Examination Collaboration.
Figure 4 gives an instantiation of BPMN4V for the modeling of the first and third versions of the radiological examination collaboration (VC1-1 and VC1-3). In this figure, we model both the versions of the collaboration and the versions of the two processes involved in this collaboration.

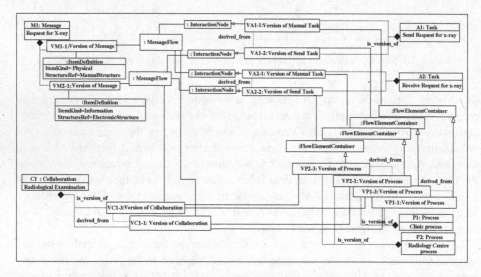

Fig. 4. Instantiation of BPMN4V meta-model [12].

VC1-1 and VC1-3 differ from one another in their partner processes, tasks type and message flows. Thus we have defined two versions of the clinic process, namely VP1-1 and VP1-3, each one defining the behavior of the clinic partner in each version of the collaboration. We have also defined two versions of the radiology center process, namely VP2-1 and VP2-3, each one defining the behavior of the radiological center partner in each version of the collaboration. VP1-1 and VP2-1 hold for the first version of the collaboration VC1-1 whereas VP1-3 and VP2-3 hold for the third version VC1-3.

Versions of processes involved in versions of the radiology examination collaboration also differ from one another in their component tasks and their coordination. For instance, we have defined two versions of the send task *Send Request for X-ray*. The first one VA1-1 participates in VP1-1 whereas the second one VA1-2 participates in VP1-3. VA1-1 has been created first and VA1-2 has been derived from VA1-1 since there is change in the task type.

Finally Fig. 4 defines the versions of messages involved in the collaboration. For instance, we have defined two versions of the message *Request for X-Ray*. The first one VM1-1 holds for VC1-1 and refers to a paper document whereas the second one, VM1-2, holds for VC1-3 and refers to an electronic document.

4.3   Handling Versions of Collaborations

In this section, we first give an overview of the operations available for collaboration version management within a state chart, before detailing them.

State Chart. In order to handle versions of collaborations modeled as instances of BPMN4V, we propose a taxonomy of operations which allows to create, derive, update, validate and delete collaboration versions.

The UML state chart given in Fig. 5 indicates when these operations are available with respect to the version state. Some of them are available whatever the state of the version on which they are performed, while others are available only in some cases. In the state chart, each operation is described using the notation Event/Operation whose meaning is "if Event appears then Operation is triggered".

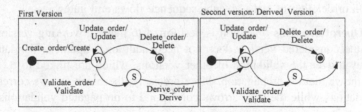

Fig. 5. UML state chart for versions.

When the create order event appears, the create operation is carried out to create both a collaboration and its corresponding first version. The state of the created version is working (W state). In this state, a version is not yet a final one and it can be updated using the Update operation. Create and update operations can be specified using a set of primitives. These primitives change according to the classes in which they are defined. However, they share the same general idea that is to give values to properties and relationships of the considered classes. A working version can be deleted (Delete operation) or validated (Validate operation). When the Validate operation is performed, the corresponding version becomes stable (S state). This state indicates that a version is a final one, on which no additional updates can be performed. Finally, a stable version can be deleted or can serve as a basis for the creation of a new version using the Derive operation. The created version is a working version. Before being updated, it has the same value as the derived one.

Update Operation. Table 1 below gives the definition of Update operation, indicating the low-level primitives this operation includes.

Table 1. Primitives of the update operation.

BPMN4V concepts	Primitives
Collaboration	± Participant/Process
	± Interaction
Interaction	± Message
	± Message flow
Participant/Process	± Task
	± Event
	± Sequence flow
	± Gateway

For instance, the update of collaboration includes low-level primitives supporting the addition (+) or deletion (−) of participants (*i.e.*, their process) involved in the collaboration along with their interactions (*i.e.*, message flows between their processes). In the same way, the update of an interaction includes low-level primitives supporting the addition or deletion of messages, and the addition and deletion of message flows which are triplet gathering a message sent from a send node to a receive node. Finally, the update of collaboration also includes low-level primitives supporting the addition or deletion of tasks, events, sequence flows and gateways.

Validate Operation. This operation is performed to make a working version stable, i.e. when the considered version does not need additional updates. Validation of a version may trigger the validation of other versions, which are linked to it. Figure 6 illustrates the validation propagation. More precisely, the black arrows correspond to initial validations while the grey arrows correspond to propagated validations.

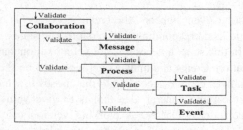

Fig. 6. Validation propagation.

According to Fig. 6, the validation of a collaboration version triggers the validation of processes and messages within this collaboration. In the same way, the validation of a process version triggers the validation of its versioned components, i.e. versions of its tasks and versions of its events.

Derive Operation. This operation allows the creation of a new version from an existing stable one. The created version is a working version. Before being updated, it has the same value as the derived one. Moreover, derivation of a version may trigger the derivation of other versions, which are linked to the derived one. Figure 7 illustrates this derivation propagation. Again, the black arrows correspond to initial derivations, while the grey ones correspond to propagated derivations.

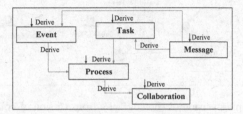

Fig. 7. Derivation propagation.

This propagation is due to the composition relationships existing between collaboration, message, process, task and event. Therefore, the derivation of a task or event triggers the derivation of its corresponding process. In the same way, the derivation of a process triggers the derivation of the corresponding collaboration. In addition the derivation of a message triggers the derivation of its corresponding events or tasks (*i.e.*, the events or tasks involved with the message in a message flow).

5   Mapping Versions of Choreographies

As indicated before, BPMN collaboration describes both orchestration of partners activities and messages exchanged. Thus BPMN choreography can be deduced from BPMN collaboration. For this reason, we recommend an approach for mapping versions of collaborations into versions of choreographies instead of directly model versions of choreographies.

Figure 8 below illustrates the proposed approach for deducing version of choreography from version of collaboration. This approach includes the following four steps:

- Step 1 builds a VP-Tree for each version of process involved in the considered version of collaboration. Building a VP-Tree requires breaking down each version of process into canonical single-entry single-exit (SESE) fragments [33].

- Step 2 links the VP-Trees built in the previous step. More precisely, a Linked-VP-Tree is composed of the VP-Trees of the considered version of collaboration along with links corresponding to messages exchanged.
- Step 3 deduces the corresponding VC-Tree *i.e.*, the corresponding version of choreography represented as a tree.
- Finally, step 4 deduces the corresponding choreography, represented according to the BPMN meta-model, from the VC-Tree.

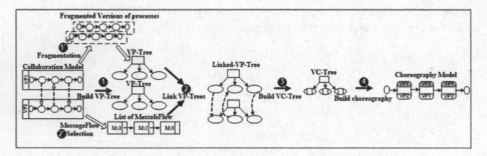

Fig. 8. Mapping version of choreography from version of collaboration.

The recommended algorithm, namely *generateChoreography*, supporting the generation approach is given below. It includes a single parameter which corresponds to the version of collaboration to be mapped and it uses the following set of functions to consider the different steps of the approach. The interested reader can consult [12] to have details about algorithms implementing these functions.

- getVersionsofProcesses(vc) returns the list of process versions that compose the version of collaboration *vc*.
- getMessageFlows(vc) returns the list of MessageFlows of the version of collaboration *vc*.
- fragmentation(vp) decomposes a version of process *vp* into fragments and returns the resulting fragments.
- BuildVP-Tree(f) builds the corresponding VP-Tree from a fragment *f*.
- add(vpt, list-vpt) adds the VP-Tree *vpt* to the list of VP-Trees list-*vpt*.
- Build-Linked-VP-Trees(listvpt, listmg) builds the corresponding Linked-VP-Trees from the list of VP-Tree *listvpt* and the list of MessageFlow *listmg*.
- Build-VC-Tree(n) builds the corresponding VC-Tree from a Linked-VP-Trees. The parameter *n* corresponds to the root of the VP-Tree that initiates the Linked-VP-Trees.
- Build-Choreography(vct) builds the corresponding choreography from the VC-Tree *vct*.

```
generateChoreography(VersionofCollaboration vc): Choreog-
raphy
local setof-VP: {Version_of_Process}
  vp: Version_of_Process
  vpt: VP-Tree
  l-vpt: Linked-VP-Trees
  setof-VPT: {VP-Tree}
  f: Fragment setof-VPT: {VP-Tree}
  setof-MF: {MessageFlow}
  vct: VC-Tree
  ch: Choreography
Begin
  setof-VPT= getVersionsOfProcesses(vc)
  setof-MF= getMessageFlow(vc)
  /* step1 building VP-Trees */
  For each vp in setof-VP
    f=fragmentation(vp)
    vpt= BuildVP-Tree(f)
    add(vpt,setof-VPT)
  End For
  /* step2 building Linked-VP-Trees */
  l-vpt=Build-Linked-VP-Trees(setof-VPT, setof-MF)
  /* step3 building VC-Tree */
  vct= Build-VC-Tree(root(initial(l-vpt)))
  /* step4 building Choreography */
  ch=Build-Choreography(vct)
  Return ch
End
```

6 BPMN4V-Modeler

BPMN4V-Modeler is a tool dedicated to versions of collaboration and choreography modeling. This section addresses the modeler presentation, mainly focusing on collaboration and choreography flexibility support. More precisely, BPMN4V-Modeler allows for creating and handling of versions of collaborations taking into account the recommended extensions of BPMN 2.0 and the dynamic aspect of versions. It also allows for generating versions of choreographies from version of collaboration. We provide open access to the source code of this modeler via GitHub[1]. We also provide online demonstration videos[2] illustrating the editor functionalities.

6.1 BPMN4V-Modeler Architecture

The tool architecture is given in Fig. 9. As illustrated in this figure, BPMN4V-Modeler is an extension of the already existing Eclipse plug-in called BPMN-Modeler.

---

[1] See https://github.com/BPMN4V/BPMN4V-Modeler.

[2] See https://www.youtube.com/watch?v=jPXhydHK9Kw.

This extension is done by using the Eclipse extension mechanism (extensions and extension points). More precisely, the Eclipse BPMN-Modeler plug-in defines a set of extension points which declare a contract (typically a combination of XML markup and Java interfaces) to which extensions must conform to. Thus the BPMN4V-Modeler plugin provides a set of extensions based on this contract. For example, we define an extension as instances of the extension point org.eclipse.ui.views for creating new Eclipse views. Furthermore, BPMN4V-Modeler interacts with an XML database called BPMN4V-DB. This database stores versions modeled with the editor. More precisely, when creating or updating a version of collaboration, queries are executed to insert or to replace the new values of the version in the database. Moreover, stored versions can be selected in order to be used in the definition of new versions. To support interactions between the editor and the database, we consider new contextual menu providing a set of commands used to handle versions.

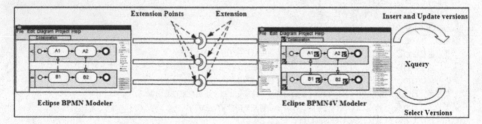

Fig. 9. Architecture of BPMN4V Modeler.

We detail in the following (i) how we can use org.eclipse.ui.views extension point to create new Eclipse views showing versions detail, (ii) how we can revisit existing code of Eclipse BPMN-Modeler plug-in to create new contextual menu supporting collaboration and choreography version management and (iii) how we can use these functionalities to model and handle versions of the Radiology Examination Collaboration.

6.2   Eclipse View Extension

The BPMN4V-Modeler extends the Eclipse BPMN-Modeler plug-in by integrating new Eclipse views to show version details. Figure 10 below gives an overview of BPMN4V Modeler.

The central part of the screenshot (part ❶) is the drawing canvas which provides multiple tabs, each one being used to model and display a separate BPMN diagram (that represents a particular version of collaboration). The right part of the figure (part ❷) represents the Tool Palette which contains tools that can be dragged onto the drawing canvas to create BPMN elements. The left part of the figure (part ❸, ❹, and ❺) corresponds to the added Eclipse views. Actually, we have defined tree Eclipse views which are Version Data view, Hierarchy view and List of Activities view.

- Versions Data view indicates for the active versionable concept the corresponding properties: name, version id, version state and version details. For example, the Versions Data view presented in Fig. 10 part ❸ indicates that the active version of collaboration identified by VC1-1 is a stable version and corresponds to the first version of the radiology examination collaboration. In addition, this view details each process, task and event that makes up the considered version. More precisely, this view illustrates (i) that this version of collaboration is an interaction between the first version the center process (VP1-1) and the first version of the clinic process (VP2-1), (ii) that each version of these two processes is composed of a set of versions of tasks and events and (iii) that all these versions are in the stable state.
- Hierarchy view is intended to provide a hierarchical tree oriented view representing the derivation hierarchy of the active versionable concept (*e.g.*, Collaboration or Process) of the drawing canvas. In Fig. 10 part ❺, the Hierarchy view shows the derivation hierarchy of the radiology examination collaboration since the active versionable concept is this collaboration.
- List of Activities view, presented in Fig. 10 part ❹, displays all the previously modeled tasks and their corresponding versions. This view allows designers for reusing previously modeled versions by dragging and dropping them into the drawing canvas.

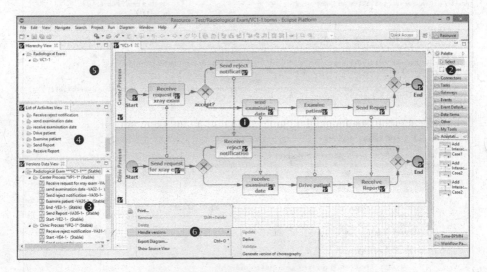

Fig. 10. BPMN4V-Modeler overview.

We detail in the following how we use the extension point org.eclipse.ui.views to define the Versions Data view in the BPMN4V-Modeler. The left part of Fig. 11 is a definition of the extension point presented as a DTD (Document Type Definition) description. This definition indicates that an extension may have several views, each one containing/having an id, a name, a class and eventually an icon and a description.

The right part of Fig. 11 is an instance of the extension point org.eclipse.ui.views that supports the definition of the Version Data view. The attribute "class", with the value org.eclipse.bpmn2.modeler.ui.views.VersionsDataView, specifies a fully qualified name of the class that allows the creation of a new TreeViewer and invokes an instance of the VersionsDataContentProvider class to consider the content of this TreeViewer. This class selects version details of versionnable components of the active diagram and fills the TreeViewer. Figure 12 is an extract of VersionsDataView and VersionsDataContentProvider classes.

Extension Point Definition	Extension Definition

`<!ELEMENT extension (view)*>`
`<!ATTLIST extension point CDATA #REQUIRED>`
`<!ELEMENT view (description?)>`
`<!ATTLIST view`
`id CDATA #REQUIRED`
`name CDATA #REQUIRED`
`class CDATA #REQUIRED`
`icon CDATA #IMPLIED>`
`<!ELEMENT description (#PCDATA)>`
	`<extension point="org.eclipse.ui.views">`
	`<view id="org.eclipse.bpmn2.modeler.ui.views.VersionsDataView"`
	`name="Versions Data View"`
	`class="org.eclipse.bpmn2.modeler.ui.views.VersionsDataView"`
	`icon="icons/SMALL/version.png"/>`
	`</extension>`

Fig. 11. Extension point and extension definitions for the Versions Data view.

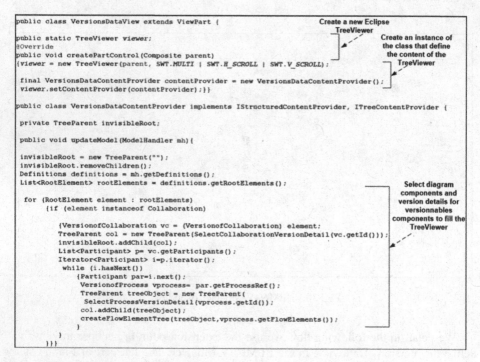

Fig. 12. Extract of VersionDataView and VersionDataContentProvider classes.

6.3   Contextual Menu for Handling Versions of Collaborations and Choreographies

In order to support dynamic aspects of versions, we have added a new contextual menu called "Handle versions". This menu holds for each versionale element in collaboration diagram (*i.e.*, Task, Event, Process and Collaboration). For instance, Fig. 10 part ❻ shows the contextual menu "Handle versions" available for versions of collaboration. Of course this menu implements operations of the state chart (*i.e.*, Update, Derive and Validate) but it also supports the automatic generation of versions of choreographies from versions of collaborations.

To do so, we have extended functionalities of the BPMNToolBehaviorProvider class of the Eclipse BPMN Modeler plug-in. Basically, this class provides several tools (such as ContextButtons, ToolTips and ContextMenu) that define behavior of BPMN diagrams and their elements. In addition, we have implemented the method getContextMenu shown in Fig. 13. This method identifies the active element in the diagram and creates the corresponding contextual menu. For instance, if the active element is a version of collaboration, then the menu "Handel versions" is created with their different commands (*i.e.*, Update, Derive, Validate and Generate Choreography Version). Furthermore, commands of the "Handle versions" contextual menu are in line with the state of the selected version (working or stable). For instance, operations "Update" and

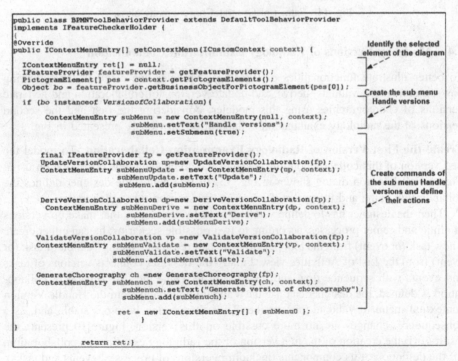

Fig. 13. Extract of BPMNToolBehaviorProvider class.

"Validate" of versions of collaborations are available when the state of the considered version is "working" whereas operations "Derive" and "Generate Choreography Version" are available when the state of the considered is "Stable".

To do so, we have implemented classes that define behavior of each command of the contextual menu. For example, Fig. 14 illustrates the GenerateChoreography class that defines the action to be executed when the command "Generate Choreography Version" is fired and specifies that this action is executed when the version state is "Stable".

```
public class GenerateChoreography extends AbstractCustomFeature {

public GenerateChoreography (IFeatureProvider fp) {        Define the behavior to execute
            super(fp);}                                     when the command Generate
                                                            Version of choreography is
@Override                                                   selected
public void execute(ICustomContext context) {
            generateChoreography(getDiagram()); }
                                                            Define that the command Generate
@Override                                                   Version of choreography can be
public boolean canExecute(ICustomContext context) {        executed when the state of version
                                                            of collaboration is Stable
boolean ret = false;
PictogramElement[] pes = context.getPictogramElements();
Object bo = getBusinessObjectForPictogramElement(pes[0]);

if (bo instanceof VersionofCollaboration && bo.state.compareTo("Stable")==0
ret = true;
return ret;}
}
```

Fig. 14. Extract of GenerateChoreography class.

6.4   Modeling Versions of Radiology Examination Collaboration

To better illustrate functionalities of BPMN4V-Modeler, we detail in the following how we can create, validate, derive, and update versions of collaboration and generate versions of choreographies using this modeler, considering the first and the second versions of the radiology examination collaboration previously presented in Fig. 1.

Create the First Version of Radiology Examination Collaboration. To model the first version of this collaboration, the designer has to create a new collaboration using Create Collaboration dialog shown in Fig. 15. In this dialog the designer defines the collaboration name and the name of processes making up this collaboration.

Then the designer has to define versions of tasks and events that make up versions of clinic and center processes, according to two possible scenarios: he can either create a new task (or event) from the tool palette or he can reuse an existing version of task (or event) from the List of Activities view. Finally the designer connects versions of tasks and events with sequence flow and message flow. Once the first version of collaboration is defined, the designer can use the Validate command from the Handle Version contextual menu to validate this version. Thus the version becomes stable and, as a consequence, changes are no more possible on this version. Figure 10 presents the result of (i) the creation of the first version of the radiology examination collaboration, (ii) the definition of its components (including versions of processes, events and tasks), and (iii) its validation (the version state moves from working to stable).

Fig. 15. Create Collaboration dialog.

Definition of the Second Version of the Radiology Examination Collaboration. In order to design the second version of the collaboration the designer has first to derive the first version of this collaboration (*i.e.*, VC1-1), and then to perform the necessary operations to update this version. To do so, the designer triggers the Derive command from the Handle Version contextual menu. The derivation results in the creation of a new tab that contains a copy of the derived version. More precisely, when the designer derives VC1-1, a new tab named VC1-2 appears in the drawing canvas. VC1-2 is a working version that corresponds to the second version of the radiology examination Collaboration and it has the same definition as VC1-1. Figure 16 part ❶ is a screenshot illustrating the handle versions contextual menu used to derive VC1-1, and Fig. 16 part ❷ shows the result of the derivation of this version.

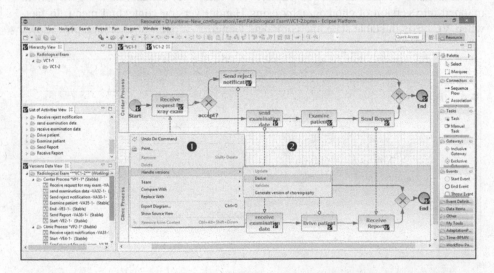

Fig. 16. Derivation of the first version of the radiology examination collaboration.

Actually VC1-2 has to be updated to be consistent with the definition presented in Fig. 1. More precisely in this version the first version of Drive Patient task and the first version of Examine Patient have to be replaced respectively with the first version Take X-Ray task and the first version of Drive Materiel task. To do so, first we have to delete the corresponding versions of tasks. This deletion triggers derivation of the corresponded versions of processes since their schemas are modified. Then the new versions of tasks are added in the corresponding versions of processes. Finally the version of collaboration has to be validated to be in a stable state. Figure 17 illustrates the result of derivation, update and validation of VC1-2.

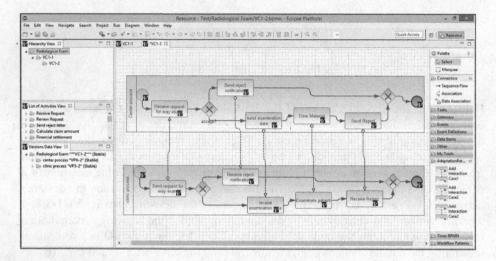

Fig. 17. The second version of the radiology examination collaboration.

Generation of Version of Choreography. The version of collaboration VC1-2 can be mapped into version of choreography using Handel version contextual menu. In fact, when VC1-2 is in stable state, the command Generate version of choreography allows

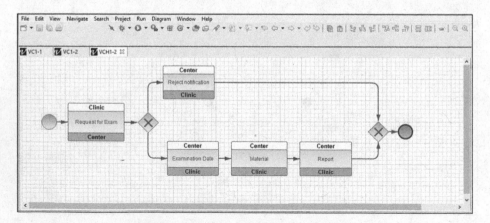

Fig. 18. Generated version of choreography.

the creation of the corresponding choreography diagram. Figure 18 gives the version of choreography resulting from the mapping of VC1-2.

7 Conclusion

This paper has addressed an important issue in the BPM area which is Inter-organizational Process (IoP) flexibility. It has presented BPMN4V, an extension of BPMN using versions to deal with this issue focusing on BPMN collaborations and choreographies versioning. We believe that versioning is an interesting solution to deal with process flexibility issues since it makes the migration of processes running according to an old schema to a new one easier to perform and it supports process variability, process evolution and process adaptation (when adaptation can be defined at design-time), which are three fundamental process flexibility needs according to Reichert and Weber's taxonomy [3].

More precisely, the paper contributions are the following. Firstly, the paper has extended the BPMN2.0 meta-model to incorporate version modeling capabilities considering versioning, and thus flexibility, at different granularity levels: task, event, message, information exchanged, process and collaboration. The paper has also addressed the dynamic aspects of collaboration version management, defining state charts for versions and corresponding operations (create, update, delete, validate and derive operations).

Secondly, the paper has introduced a four step approach for mapping versions of collaborations into corresponding versions of choreographies. More precisely it has presented the main algorithm supporting this mapping. This choice is mainly due to BPMN collaborations, which subsume choreographies, highlighting both the orchestration of involved partners activities and messages exchanged. However the recommended algorithm is based on the following assumption: the mapped versions of collaboration have to be well structured and consistent in that they can be decomposed into SESE fragments and they do not include any dead-lock, cycle and so on.

Finally, this paper has presented the BPMN4V-Modeler that is a tool dedicated to the modeling and the handling of versions of collaborations and choreographies.

Our future works will take three directions. Firstly, regarding future works in relation to the notion of version, we will incorporate the notion of context in BPMN4V in order to take the explicit definition of situations in which versions of collaborations have to be used, as we did for intra-organizational processes [13].

Secondly regarding future works in relation with versions management, we plan to specify in a formal way a set of adaptation pattern used to update versions of collaborations schemas. These patterns will represent high-level primitives that are well-suited for coping with the evolving nature of IoP [34].

Thirdly, regarding future works in relation to choreographies, BPMN practitioners can directly model choreographies without modeling corresponding collaborations. Thus we also have to extend BPMN to directly model versions of choreographies.

References

1. Dumas, M., van der Aalst, W., ter Hofstede, A.: Process-Aware Information Systems: Bridging People and Software through Process Technology. Wiley, Hoboken (2005)
2. Rolland C.: Fitting system functionality to business needs: alignment issues and challenges. In: International Conference on Software Methodologies, Tools and Techniques, Japan, pp. 137–147 (2010)
3. Reichert, M., Weber, B.: Enabling Flexibility in Process-Aware Information Systems: Challenges, Methods, Technologies. Springer, Heidelberg (2012)
4. Weske, M.: Business Process Management: Concepts, Languages, Architectures. Springer, Heidelberg (2007)
5. Nurcan, S.: A survey on the flexibility requirements related to business process and modelling artifacts. In: International Conference on System Sciences, USA, pp. 378–387 (2008)
6. OMG Business Process Model and Notation (BPMN) Version 2.0. OMG Document Number: formal/2011-01-03 (2011). http://www.omg.org/spec/BPMN/2.0
7. Stroppi, L., Chiotti, O., Villarreal, P.: Extended resource perspective support for BPMN and BPEL. In: Iberoamerican Conference on Software Engineering, Argentina, pp. 56–69 (2012)
8. Baumgrass, A., Herzberg, N., Meyer, A., Weske, M.: BPMN extension for business process monitoring. In: International Conference on Enterprise Modelling and Information Systems Architectures, Luxembourg, pp. 85–98 (2014)
9. Gagné, D., Trudel, A.: Time-BPMN. In: International Conference on Commerce and Enterprise Computing, Austria, pp. 361–367 (2009)
10. Korherr, B., List, B.: Extending the EPC and the BPMN with business process goals and performance measures. In: International Conference on Enterprise Information Systems, Portugal, pp. 287–294 (2007)
11. Ben Said, I., Chaâbane, MA., Andonoff, E., Bouaziz, R.: BPMN4V-an extension of BPMN for modelling adaptive processes using versions. In: 17th International Conference on Enterprise Information Systems, Spain, pp. 258–267 (2014)
12. Ben Said, I., Chaâbane, M.A., Bouaziz, R., Andonoff, E.: A version-based approach to address flexibility of BPMN collaborations and choreographies. In: International Joint Conference on e-Business and Telecommunications, Portugal, pp. 31–42 (2016)
13. Ben Said, I., Chaâbane, MA., Andonoff, E., Bouaziz, R.: Context-aware adaptive process information systems: the context-BPMN4V meta-model. In: International Conference on Advances in Databases and Information Systems, Macedonia, pp. 366–382 (2014)
14. Kradolfer, M., and Geppert, A.: Dynamic workflow schema evolution based on workflow type versioning and workflow migration. In: International Conference on Cooperative Information Systems, Scotland, pp. 104–114 (1999)
15. Chaâbane, M.A., Andonoff, E., Bouzguenda, L., Bouaziz, R.: Versions to address business process flexibility issue. In: International Conference on Advances in Databases and Information Systems, Latvia, pp. 2–14 (2009)
16. Pesic, M., Schonenberg, H., Sidorova, N., van der Aalst, W.: DECLARE: full support for loosely-structured processes. In: International Conference on Enterprise Distributed Object Computing, USA, pp. 287–300 (2007)
17. Müller, D., Reichert, M., Herbst, J.: A new paradigm for the enactment and dynamic adaptation of data-driven process structures. In: Bellahsène, Z., Léonard, M. (eds.) CAiSE 2008. LNCS, vol. 5074, pp. 48–63. Springer, Heidelberg (2008). doi:10.1007/978-3-540-69534-9_4

18. van der Aalst, W., Weske, M., Grünbaur, D.: Case handling: a new paradigm for business process support. Int. J. Data Knowl. Eng. **53**(2), 129–162 (2005)
19. Bruno, G., Dengler, F., Jennings, B., Khalaf, R., Nurcan, S., Prilla, M., Sarini, M., Schmidt, R., Silva, R.: Key challenges for enabling agile BPM with social software. Softw. Maint. Evol.: Res. Pract. **23**(4), 297–326 (2011)
20. Rosemann, M., van der Aalst, W.: A configurable reference modeling language. Inf. Syst. **32**(1), 1–23 (2007)
21. Hallerbach, A., Bauer, T., Reichert, M.: Capturing variability in business process models: the provop approach. Softw. Maint. **22**(6–7), 519–546 (2010)
22. La Rosa, M., van der Aalst, W., Dumas, M., Milani, F.: Business process variability: a survey. Technical report, QUT ePrints (2013)
23. Zhao, X., Liu, C.: Version management for business process schema evolution. Inf. Syst. **38**(8), 1046–1069 (2013)
24. Ekanayake, C., La Rosa, M., ter Hofstede, A., Fauvet, MC.: Fragment-based version management for repositories of business process models. In: International Conference on Cooperative Information Systems, Greece, pp. 20–37 (2011)
25. Dadam, P., Reichert, M.: The ADEPT project: a decade of research and development for robust and flexible process support. Comput. Sci. Res. Dev. **23**, 81–97 (2009)
26. Aalst, W.: Loosely coupled inter-organizational workflows: modelling and analysing workflows crossing organizational boundaries. Inf. Manag. **37**(2), 67–75 (2000)
27. Andonoff, E., Bouaziz, W., Hanachi, C., Bouzguenda, L.: An agent-based model for autonomic coordination of inter-organizational business processes. Informatica **20**(3), 323–342 (2009)
28. Boukhedouma, S., Oussalah, M., Alimazighi, Z., Tamzalit, D.: Adaptation patterns for service-based inter-organizational workflows. In: 7th International Conference on Research Challenges in Information Systems, France, pp. 1–10 (2013)
29. Domingosa, D., Martinhoa, R., Cândidoa, C.: Flexibility in cross-organizational WS-BPEL business processes. Proc. Technol. **9**, 584–595 (2013)
30. Fdhila, W., Indiono, C., Rinderle-Ma, S., Reichert, M.: Dealing with change in process choreographies: design and implementation of propagation algorithms. Inf. Syst. **49**, 1–24 (2015)
31. Ellouze, F., Chaâbane MA., Andonoff, E., Bouaziz R.: Modelling flexible collaborative process: the VCP2M approach. In: International Conference on E-Business, France, pp. 56–63 (2015)
32. Ellouze, F., Chaâbane, MA., Bouaziz, R., Andonoff E.: Addressing inter-organisational process flexibility using versions: the VP2M approach. In: 10th International Conference on Research and Challenges in Information Science, France, pp. 1–12 (2016)
33. Polyvyanyy, A., Garcia-Banuelos, L., Dumas, M.: Structuring acyclic process models. Inf. Syst. **37**(6), 518–538 (2012)
34. Ben Said, I., Chaâbane, M.A., Bouaziz, R., Andonoff, E.: Flexibility of collaborative processes using versions and adaptation patterns. In: 9th International Conference on Research Challenges in Information Science, Athens, pp. 400–411 (2015)

Content Protection Scheme to Realize Edit Control Including Diversion Control and Composition Control

Tatsuya Fujimoto[1(✉)], Keiichi Iwamura[1], and Masaki Inamura[2]

[1] Department of Electrical Engineering, Tokyo University of Science,
6-3-1Niijuku, Katsushika-Ku, Tokyo 125-8585, Japan
`fujimoto@sec.ee.kagu.tus.ac.jp`,
`iwamura@ee.kagu.tus.ac.jp`
[2] School of Science and Engineering, Tokyo Denki University, Ishizaka,
Hatoyama-Machi, Saitama 350-0394, Japan
`minamura@rd.dendai.ac.jp`

Abstract. We have proposed a copyright protection technology suitable for editable contents, which can control the change, deletion, and addition of partial contents. In this paper, we propose a new scheme that can control the diversion of partial contents to other contents and composition of contents, in addition to control of the change, deletion, and addition of partial contents using digital signatures based on the author's intention. This scheme realizes edit control between two or more contents, and is effective with Internet contents such as consumer generated media represented by YouTube. We also evaluate the security of our proposed scheme against various attacks.

Keywords: Edit control · Diversion control · Composition control · Digital · Signature · Aggregate signature

1 Introduction

Please note that the first paragraph of a section or subsection is not indented. The first paragraphs that follows a table, figure, equation etc. does not have an indent, either.

Subsequent paragraphs, however, are indented. With the advances in network connectivity, there has been a rapid increase in the distribution of online content. In recent years, a concept of consumer generated media (CGM) is prevalent, as per which anyone can be a content provider and can distribute contents on the Internet. YouTube [1] and CLIP [2] are typical examples of CGM-services. In CGM, the creation of secondary content is called mashup, which is a process of creating new content using existing content on the Internet. Mashup is performed frequently.

Typical conventional copyright protection technology [3] provides viewing control and copy control which is not suitable for the CGM-service. This is because viewing control is meaningless for authors who have created the content, and want it to be seen widely, and copy control interferes only with the secondary usage of content. In contrast, copyright protection technology recommended for CGM-services presupposes

© Springer International Publishing AG 2017
M.S. Obaidat (Ed): ICETE 2016, CCIS 764, pp. 124–138, 2017.
https://doi.org/10.1007/978-3-319-67876-4_6

the content editing, and can protect the author's copyright when the content is exhibited secondarily.

Previously, we proposed a copyright protection technology [4, 8], that divided content into partial contents, controlled edits with respect to the change, deletion, and addition of the partial contents using digital signatures. However, the technology could not control the diversion of partial contents and the composition of contents. This means that the technology reported in [4, 8] considers only the edit control in a content. Therefore, the edit control between two or more contents became unrealizable, and the partial contents could be used contrary to the author's intention in other contents.

Therefore, in this paper, we extend the range of the edit control from the change, deletion, and addition of partial content to the diversion of partial contents and the composition of contents only using digital signatures. This means that our proposed scheme can ensure edit control between two or more contents.

The rest of this paper is organized as follows: In Sect. 2, we describe the digital signature used in this paper and the conventional edit control scheme. In Sect. 3, we propose a new edit control scheme for realizing diversion control and composition control between contents in addition to the edit control within a content. In Sect. 4, the security of our scheme are discussed. Finally, Sect. 5 concludes the paper.

2 Related Works

2.1 Aggregate Signature Scheme Based on BLS Signature

Boneh, et al. have proposed an aggregate signature scheme [6] based on the Boneh-Lynn-Shacham (BLS) signature [5] using the operation on an elliptic curve and pairing. This scheme aggregates two or more different signatures for every message into one signature of steady length without relying on the number of signers.

We denote

$$L = \{u_{i\_1}, \cdots, u_{i\_t}\} \tag{1}$$

as a set of signer's group who participate in generating aggregate signature, and

$$J = \{i\_1, \cdots, i\_t\} \tag{2}$$

as a set of symbol of signer's who participate in generating aggregate signature. Then, the scheme of construction of aggregate signature is as follows:

Key Generation
Key Generation center calculates

$$v_i = x_i g \tag{3}$$

where g is a generator of $\mathbb{G}_1$, x_i is value of Z_p (x_i means a private key of $u_i \in L$), and v_i means a public key of u_i.

Signing

We denote $H : \{0,1\}^* \to \mathbb{G}_2$ is one-way hash function. m_j is a message of a signer u_j. Then, signer u_j calculates

$$h_j = H(m_j) \tag{4}$$

and set

$$\sigma_j = x_j h_j \tag{5}$$

as the own signature corresponding to m_j. After signing, we collect all signatures and calculate an aggregate signature σ.

$$\sigma = \sum \sigma_j (j \in J) \tag{6}$$

Verification

Verifier collects $m_{i\_1}, \cdots, m_{i\_t}, \sigma, g$ and the verification keys $v_j (j \in J)$. Then, verifier calculates

$$h_j = H(m_j) \tag{7}$$

from all m_j and judges whether the following is realized using pairing:

$$e(g, \sigma) = \prod e(v_j, h_j)(j \in J) \tag{8}$$

If the aggregate signature is created correctly, the upper equation is realized.

2.2 Edit Control

In [4], an edit control scheme of that is responsible for the change, deletion, and addition of partial content within a single content has been proposed. This scheme extends the sanitizable signature [7] which can control only deletion. In this scheme, an author divides his/her content into partial contents, sets signatures of each partial content, and aggregates those signatures to one signature for the content. Hereafter, we call the signature of partial content the edit control signature. If an author permits editing of the partial content, he/she exhibits the edit control signature. When an editor changes the partial content, the edit control signature is deleted from the aggregate signature and a new signature of the editor's partial content is added to the aggregate signature. If the author does not permit editing of the partial contents, he/she keeps the edit control signature secret. In this case, the editor cannot edit the partial content since he/she cannot change the edit control signature in the aggregate signature.

In [4], edit control for the change, deletion, and addition is realized by three kinds of signatures, namely change control signature, deletion control signature and addition control signature, respectively. The operation of deletion is performed by actually deleting the partial content. Therefore, when edit is performed repeatedly, the composition of content may change and control may become impossible. Therefore, the technique reported in [4] targets only one-time edit, and can control the edit only in one content as mentioned before.

The scheme proposed in [8] simultaneously realizes edit control and right succession and. The right succession shows the hierarchical relation between authors. However, it cannot also control the diversion of partial contents to other contents and the composition of contents. Therefore, this scheme has the same drawback as [4] with respect to edit control.

3 Our Proposed Scheme

3.1 Entity

Since our scheme treats two or more contents produced by two or more authors, we introduce the i-th author without using the word "editor". Therefore, we define two entities called the i-th author and a verifier, as follows.

The I-th Author
He/she is concerned with a work, can set up edit control signatures to the partial contents, and update the aggregate signatures. For simplicity, we express the work using a tree structure, as shown in Fig. 1. We refer to the author who is in the deepest portion of the tree as the 1-st author, and the author who is in the portion of the tree route as the n-th author, when the tree height is n − 1. When an original content of an author is used by the i-th author, he/she is called the (i − 1)-th author. Therefore, i is defined as the position in the work.

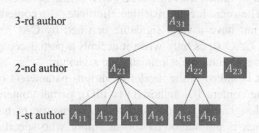

3-rd author

2-nd author

1-st author

Fig. 1. Examples of entities in a work with the tree structure.

The i-th author can set the edit control signature to the partial contents that he/she has produced or edited, only when edit is permitted by the edit control signatures defined by the (i − 1)-th authors. In Fig. 1, A_{11} to A_{16} are the primary contents made by two or more 1-st authors, and the 2-nd authors create the secondary contents A_{21} and A_{22} using the primary contents of 1-st authors. Finally, the 3-rd author produces the final content A_{31}. Here, the 2-nd authors can edit according to the setting of the edit control signature by each 1-st author, and the 3-rd author follows the setting of the entire edit control signature by the 1-st and 2-nd authors. The author of A_{23} with the original content is called the 2-nd author, because it is utilized by the 3-rd author.

Verifier

The verifier verifies whether a given content has a valid signature. If this function is available in a reproduction machine, we can construct a system such that the content cannot be reproduced if it does not have a valid signature.

3.2   Contents and Partial Contents

In our proposed scheme, the partial contents consist of two kinds of data: empty data and real data. The empty data are placed on the portion, that is due to be added or eliminated, and the real data constitutes the displayed contents. The empty data are treated as control data for controlling addition and deletion, and control data are not carried as contents displayed.

An author produces one or more partial contents and makes it available to the public as a form. Content comprises start data, one or more partial contents, and last data. The start data and the last data are the control data. Each data is identified by an identifier.

Each author has an author ID, each content has a content ID, and each partial content has a partial content ID. For example, A_{11} in Fig. 1 is a content made by author ID_{11}. Its content ID is IC_{11}. If it is assumed that A_{11} is composed of m partial contents A_{111}–A_{11m}, A_{11} has the start data before A_{111} as A_{110} and the last data after A_{11m} as A_{11m} $_{+1}$. We set I_{110}–I_{11m+1} as the partial content ID of A_{110}–A_{11m+1}. Among A_{111}–A_{11m}, empty data are set to the portion, that can be added or the deleted portion of partial contents.

We call the author ID of a partial content aID, and each partial content is linked to its corresponding aID. This link is guaranteed for the trusted content administration center (CAC) to sign to linked data (the hash value of the connection with the partial contents and aID). The reproduction machine eliminates the contents with the partial contents, which do not have a valid signature certified by CAC, and are treated as invalid content. The CAC signs only when it accepts a partial content as the original content. We call this signature the administration signature.

A partial content is linked in the header to various parameters required for verification. These include content ID, author ID (= aID), partial content ID, identifier of data, change control signature and deletion control signature or hash values for the signatures, bID, which is the author ID for an author who specified that no edit is permitted, diversion control signature, composite control signature, administration signature, and others, as shown in Fig. 2. In Fig. 2, the message expresses the content of partial content. These parameters can be overwritten and changed. However, if an attacker changes these data maliciously, the equation by pairing does not realize in the algorithm shown in 3.6. Thus, we can detect illegal edit.

Our scheme detects edit contrary to an author's intention, but does not prevent legitimate content from becoming unjust content by violating processing such as overwrites or changes in the parameters. Since edit of contents is performed to just copied contents, the original contents are not influenced by violation processing.

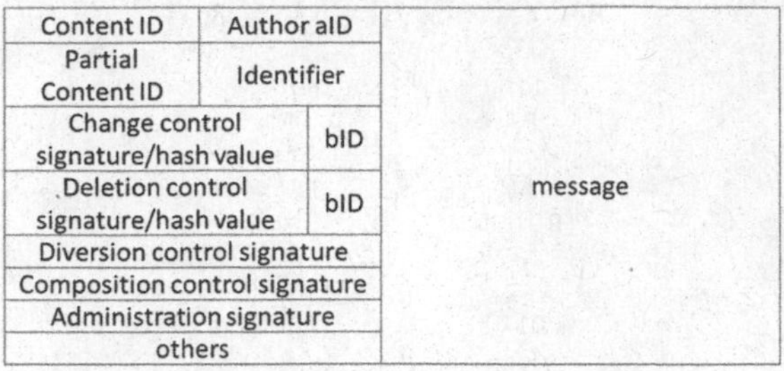

Content ID	Author aID	
Partial Content ID	Identifier	
Change control signature/hash value	bID	
Deletion control signature/hash value	bID	message
Diversion control signature		
Composition control signature		
Administration signature		
others		

Fig. 2. Example of structure of partial content.

Therefore, even if an attacker performs violation processing, the attacker gains no merit by changing only the edited contents to unjust contents.

3.3 Edit Control in One Contents

We set the following two types of signature to control the change, deletion, and addition of partial content: change control signature and deletion control signature. Addition control is realized by change control as the addition of content is performed by changing empty data to real data. Deletion refers to changing real data to empty data. However, the deletion needs to be controlled independent of change. For example, contents of a fixed form such as a four-frame cartoon allow each frame to be changed but does not allow the deletion of frames to prevent breaks in the fixed form. More specifically, in a movie credit title deletion is allowed but change is not. Each signature is exhibited when permitting the edit, and when editing is not allowed, the signature is kept secret and the hash value used for the signature and bID are exhibited as shown in Fig. 2.

If the change of empty data is allowed, then the empty data can be changed to real data. If the change of empty data is not allowed, then the deletion of the partial contents is considered as fixed. On the other hand, the deletion control to empty data is meaningless as the deletion of empty data replaces empty data. Therefore, we set empty data allows either change and deletion to be permitted or change and deletion to be prohibited.

An aggregate signature is generated for each change control signature and deletion control signature. Each aggregate signature is composed of a start signature, the group of edit control signatures of partial contents, and a last signature. The public cannot open or view the start signature and the last signature. The aggregate signatures are linked to the contents and opened to the public. We treat the content published without the aggregate signature as unauthorized content.

Figure 3 shows the four states that are used to control partial content. State {11} allows the change and deletion of partial content. State {10} allows change, but deletion is not allowed. State {01} does not allow change, but allows deletion. State {00} allows neither change nor deletion. In Fig. 3, P means partial content including real data and empty data, R means real data, and E means empty data. Figure 3 shows the transition states between each state of the partial content.

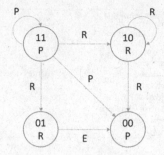

Fig. 3. Control state transition of the partial contents.

The proposed scheme achieves continuous edit, which cannot be realized in [4], since the four state transitions are controlled according to each edit control signature and the form of the contents does not change.

3.4 Diversion Control of Partial Contents

When the change and deletion of the partial content is permitted, it can be used in other contents using each edit control signature. To control the diversion of partial contents, we introduce a diversion control signature. The diversion control signature is opened to the public only when allowing diversion of the partial contents.

Basically, content has only one content ID, therefore the diversion control signatures of each partial content includes the same content ID. We can detect diversion only by examining the consistency of the content ID. However, when content has many partial contents with different content ID, we must identify the original content ID. To identify the original content ID, the primary author who creates the content sets specific values, such as 0, as the content ID of the partial content which permits diversion. Therefore, a content consists of the original partial contents with the original content ID, which do not allow divert, and the partial contents with a specific value as content ID, which allow diversion or are diverted.

The diversion control signature is always verified by the key of aID. Therefore, only the author of aID can set up the diversion control signature and the author who diverts the partial contents cannot change the signature, unlike the edit control signatures mentioned in Sect. 3.3. On the other hand, the edit control of the diverted partial contents is possible as mentioned in the previous session, since each edit control signature is processed independently. However, when a partial content does not be allowed the change and/or deletion, the edit control signatures need to be recreated by the author who diverts. In addition, a partial content, which is changed or added as new partial content, is necessary to be set the content ID of the diverted content in the signature to match the contents ID.

3.5 Composition Control of Contents

The content composition is to line up some contents in a specific order and compose them as one content. We refer to the contents generated by the composition processing as the composite content. A composite content has structural data as a control data which describes the composition of contents in addition to the contents group that comprises the composite contents.

We introduce the composition control signature to all of the partial contents, and generate the aggregate signature. All the composition control signatures in a content are opened to the public only when allowing composition of the contents.

In cases where the composition of both content A and content B were permitted, both the contents are compounded, and we can prohibit the compounding of any other contents between content A and content B. In this case, at least one of the partial contents of each A and B must be edited, the composition control signatures are exchanged, and the composition, change and deletion control signatures of the partial contents must be hidden, to avoid reuse of the edit control signatures. The edit of partial contents in the composite contents can be done as mentioned in Sect. 3.3, since each control signature is set independently. However, the composition control signature is recreated when the partial content is edited.

On the other hand, it is necessary to change only the structural data, if the author compounds the contents without making them compoundable to uncompoundable. In this case, authors can be freely re-compounded. However, it does not infringe the primary author's intention to allow composition.

3.6 Algorithm

In this section, we explain the concrete algorithm of the proposed scheme. In this algorithm, it is assumed that the binding between the signers and the verification keys is guaranteed by a Certification Authority, and information that is being prepared is not obtained by a third party.

Key Generation
ID_{ij} is the author ID defined according to the location of a work. ID_{ij} has a private key s_{ij} to sign and exhibits verification key

$$v_{ij} = s_{ij}g \tag{9}$$

to it. All of the signing keys differ.

Signing
The author always performs the signature generation process before publishing the original content that has obtained an administration signature. The definition of each ID is as shown in Sect. 3.2. To prevent duplication, the content ID of each content is different, and the author can be identified from the content ID (here, the first half of IC_{ij} is equal to ID_{ij}). We refer to the main contents of a partial content with the exception of header, message as shown in Fig. 2.

(1) Author ID_{ij} determines the control permissions of change, deletion, addition and diversion for each partial content and the composition for the content. For empty data, only {00} and {11} are permitted for change and deletion. Author ID_{ij}

determines the content ID, where IC_{ij} is set to zero for partial contents that are allowed to be diverted.

(2) Author ID_{ij} makes the start data A_{ij0}^* and the last data A_{ijm+1}^*. Here, d is the message of control data. Then, author ID_{ij} generates the start signature α_{ij} and the last signature β_{ij}, Here, each start and last signature is different for every edit as r is a different constant. The constant r varies according to the edit with respect to change, deletion, diversion and composition.

$$A_{ij0}^* = IC_{ij} \parallel I_{ij0} \parallel d \tag{10}$$

$$A_{ijm+1}^* = IC_{ij} \parallel I_{ijm+1} \parallel d \tag{11}$$

$$\alpha_{ij} = s_{ij}H\left(IC_{ij} \parallel I_{ij0} \parallel H\left(A_{ij0}^*\right) \parallel r\right) \tag{12}$$

$$\beta_{ij} = s_{ij}H\left(IC_{ij} \parallel I_{ijm+1} \parallel H\left(A_{ijm+1}^*\right) \parallel r\right) \tag{13}$$

(3) Author ID_{ij} makes data A_{ijk}^* for the message of each partial content A_{ijk} (the message of empty data is d), where

$$A_{ijk}^* = IC_{ij} \parallel I_{ijk} \parallel A_{ijk} \tag{14a}$$

(4) Author ID_{ij} uses p and r properly according to the edit and permission, and generates a hash value for each edit. Here, $p = 1$ when an edit is allowed, and $p = 0$ when no edit is allowed.

$$h_{ijk} = H\left(IC_{ij} \parallel I_{ijk} \parallel H\left(A_{ijk}^*\right) \parallel p \parallel r\right) \tag{14b}$$

(5) Author ID_{ij} makes each edit control signature for each of the partial contents as follows (h_{ijk} differs in every edit):

Change control signature:

$$\sigma_{ijk} = s_{ij}h_{ijk} \tag{15}$$

Deletion control signature:

$$\tau_{ijk} = s_{ij}h_{ijk} \tag{16}$$

Diversion control signature:

$$\chi_{ijk} = s_{ij}h_{ijk} \tag{17}$$

Composition control signature:

$$\delta_{ijk} = s_{ij} h_{ijk} \tag{18}$$

(6) Author ID_{ij} makes each aggregate signature (α_{ij}, β_{ij} differs in every edit) as follows:

Change aggregate signature:

$$\sigma_{ij} = \alpha_{ij} + \sum \sigma_{ijk} + \beta_{ij} \tag{19}$$

Deletion aggregate signature:

$$\tau_{ij} = \alpha_{ij} + \sum \tau_{ijk} + \beta_{ij} \tag{20}$$

Diversion aggregate signature:

$$\chi_{ij} = \alpha_{ij} + \sum \chi_{ijk} + \beta_{ij} \tag{21}$$

Composition aggregate signature:

$$\delta_{ij} = \alpha_{ij} + \sum \delta_{ijk} + \beta_{ij} \tag{22}$$

(7) A partial content attaches parameters required for signature verification, as shown in Fig. 2. Here, it attaches edit control signatures if it permits an edit, and it attaches hash values in Step (4), and bID = aID if editing is not allowed. The aggregate signatures are attached to the contents.

Edit

Let us consider the case where Author ID_{ab} changes the partial content A_{ijk} in the content A_{ij} which is created by Author ID_{ij} to A_{abk}, which he/she created, and deletes, adds, and diverts the partial content A_{ijk}.

(1) Author ID_{ab} confirms whether editing of contents A_{ij} is allowed by signature verification. If it is not allowed, the edit is stopped.

(2) When a diversion is permitted, author ID_{ab} can divert the partial content.

(3) When a change, deletion or addition is permitted, author ID_{ab} can substitute A_{ijk} to A_{abk}, and decide the edit permission of A_{abk} according to Fig. 3. Here, A_{ijk} is a real data in change and deletion, and A_{ijk} is an empty data in addition. A_{ab} is a real data in change and addition, and A_{ab} is an empty data in deletion.

(4) Author ID_{ab} generates the data A^*_{abk} and the hash value to the substituted partial contents according to the edit (r differs in every edit). IC_{ij} is not changed when diversion is not permitted, but when diversion is permitted, IC_{ij} is set to 0.

$$A'_{abk}{}^* = IC_{ij} \parallel I_{ijk} \parallel A'_{abk} \tag{23}$$

$$h'_{abk} = H\left(IC_{ij} \parallel I_{ijk} \parallel H\left(A^*_{abk}\right) \parallel p \parallel r\right) \tag{24}$$

(5) Author ID_{ab} generates edit control signatures $\sigma_{abk}, \tau_{abk}, \chi_{abk}$ and δ_{abk} of A_{abk} as same as Step (5) during Signing process.

(6) Author ID_{ab} updates each aggregate signature as follows.
     Change aggregate signature:

$$\sigma_{ij} = \sigma_{ij} - \sigma_{ijk} + \sigma_{abk} \tag{25}$$

Deletion aggregate signature:

$$\tau_{ij} = \tau_{ij} - \tau_{ijk} + \tau_{abk} \tag{26}$$

Diversion aggregate signature:

$$\chi_{ij} = \chi_{ij} - \chi_{ijk} + \chi_{abk} \tag{27}$$

Composition aggregate signature:

$$\delta_{ij} = \delta_{ij} - \delta_{ijk} + \delta_{abk} \tag{28}$$

(7) The edited partial content includes parameters required for signature verification as shown in Fig. 2.

Composition

Edit and composition can be repeated arbitrarily.

(1) When Author ID_{i+1j} composes content A_{ia} and content A_{ib}, he/she verifies whether the composition of A_{ia} and A_{ib} is allowed.

(2) If the composition is allowed, he/she marks the composition order of A_{ia} and A_{ib} in the structural data.

(3) If Author ID_{i+1j} fixes the relation of A_{ia} and A_{ib}, he/she recreates the aggregate signatures of A_{ia} and A_{ib} as follows. However, a partial content in both A_{ia} and A_{ib} needs the edit and hiding of the composition, change and deletion control signatures. Here, $\delta_{iat}, \delta_{ibq}$ and $\delta'_{iat}, \delta'_{ibq}$ are the signature of the partial content before and after the edit, respectively.

$$\delta_{ia} = \delta_{ia} - \delta_{iat} + \delta'_{ibt} + \delta'_{ibq} \tag{29}$$

$$\delta_{ib} = \delta_{ib} - \delta_{ibq} + \delta'_{ibq} + \delta'_{iat} \tag{30}$$

Verification

$p = 0$ when each edit control signature is hidden, and $p = 1$ when each edit control signature is visible.

(1) The administration signature of the entire partial content is verified.

(2) If the entire administration signature is valid, the verifier decomposes the composite content into specific contents using structural data. The following processing is performed for each content.

(3) The verifier verifies whether the partial contents of each content have proper content ID. The content IDs are unified except for specific contents ID such as 0.

(4) If the above verification does not fail, the verifier checks the correctness of the composition aggregate signature as follows. In the case where the composition is fixed, h_{ijk} includes the hash value of the edited partial content of other contents and v_{ij} is the verification key of aID of the partial contents. The start and last signatures are verified using the key of the author decided from content ID.

$$e(g, \delta_{ij}) = \prod e(v_{ij}, h_{ijk}) \tag{31}$$

(5) If the content is proper in composition, the verifier checks if each content is proper in diversion using the key of aID as follows:

$$e(g, \chi_{ij}) = \prod e(v_{ij}, h_{ijk}) \tag{32}$$

(6) If the content is proper in diversion, the verifier checks if the content is proper in the edit about change, deletion, and addition. First, he/she checks if the empty data has the permission {00} or {11} with respect to change and deletion. Next, the verifier generates the hash value of each partial content for each edit. If the real data does not have a change control signature, the verifier checks by matching the generated hash value and the attached hash value for change. If an empty data does not have a change control signature, the verifier checks by matching the generated hash value and the attached hash value for deletion. The verifier prepares the key of aID and the generated hash value for each partial content with the signature, and the key of bID and the attached hash value for each partial contents with no signature. He/she verifies the following equations for change and deletion. If all checks are proper, the content is accepted as being valid.

$$e(g, \sigma_{ij}) = \prod e(v_{ij}, h_{ijk}) \tag{33}$$

$$e(g, \tau_{ij}) = \prod e(v_{ij}, h_{ijk}) \tag{34}$$

4 Security Analysis and Practicality

The practicality of our scheme is guaranteed by the trusted CAC and trusted verifying machine. If the CAC and verifying machine are trusted, the security of our scheme can be shown as follows:

Our proposal is not of a new signature scheme. The security of the signature used in our proposed scheme is based on the security of the aggregate signature using the BLS signature shown in 2.1.

Our proposal is the edit control scheme using the above-mentioned signature. Namely, the security of our scheme is determined by whether a violation of the edit is detectable by our scheme. Therefore, under the premise that the signature scheme is secure and forgery of the signature is impossible, we consider the security of our scheme against following attacks.

(1) An attack that falsifies the author of partial content

The author of partial content is guaranteed by the administration signature from the CAC. CAC generates the signature only if it accepts the original content. The originality of the partial content is given by another means. For example, image similarity searches for a still image. Even if an attacker claims that the author of a partial content is himself, when the partial content does not have an administration signature including his ID and the hash value of the partial content, he is not accepted as author of the partial content. Therefore, in the proposed scheme the attacker cannot falsify the author of the partial content, if the CAC is trusted. CAC and the administration signature are not proposed in [4, 8]. In other words, [4, 8] have the premise that the key for every partial content has is known for some means. This paper shows the means and the structure of partial content required to verify concretely.

(2) An attack that fakes the content ID of contents

The diversion control signature of partial content for which diversion is not permitted includes the content ID of the content. If the partial contents allow change or deletion, the attacker can change or delete them, add new partial contents with a different content ID, and make different content with an aggregate signature corresponding to the new content ID. However, it is not violation processing, since it is equivalent to having created different contents combining new partial contents and the partial contents that allow diversion. On the other hand, if there remains partial content that does not permit diversion to another content, the new partial contents that are changed or added must be set the same content ID or special content ID for diversion in the signature. Therefore, the attacker cannot fake the content ID of content with partial content with no permission of diversion.

(3) An attack that divert partial contents with no permission on diversion

Since the diversion control signature is inspected with the verification key of aID which is the author ID of the partial content guaranteed by the administration signature, the attacker cannot be changed into a signature that can be diverted. (2) and (3) realize diversion control unrealizable in [4, 8].

(4) An attack that improperly changes real data1 into real data2

During the verification of change, malicious edit is detected by the consistency of the hash value of the real data2 and that of real data1 attached in the partial contents. In the case where the attached hash value of real data1 is rewritten to that of real data2, malicious change is detected by signature verification of change.

(5) An attack that improperly deletes real data1.

During the verification for deletion, malicious edit is detected by the consistency of the hash value of the empty data and that of real data1 attached in the partial contents. In the case where the attached hash value of real data1 is rewritten to that of the empty data, malicious deletion is detected by signature verification for deletion.

(6) An attack that improper changes real data1 into empty data.
In attack (4), if real data1 is used as empty data, malicious change will be detected for the same reason. The measures against attacks (4), (5), and (6) and state control according to Fig. 3 realize repeated change, deletion, and addition control, which unrealizable in [4, 8].

(7) An attack that changes the hidden edit control signature of one partial content in a content
Even if a content has only one partial content that hides the edit control signature, the edit control signature cannot be specified since the aggregate signature has the hidden start and last signatures. However, in the case where only one partial content is changed to a new partial content, the edit control signature of new partial content can be determined from the difference in Eq. (25–28) in [4, 8], since they assume the simultaneous edit of two or more partial contents. In our scheme, the hidden edit control signature is set to $p = 0$. The signature with $p = 1$ can be generated by only the author of the partial content. Therefore, the attacker cannot change the signature even if the hidden signature is known from the edit of only one partial content.

(8) An attack that compounds uncompoundable contents
Uncompoundable content includes an unknown hidden composition control signature. Therefore, the attacker cannot change the aggregate signature. (8) realizes composition control that is unrealizable in [4, 8].

5 Conclusions

In this paper, we propose an improved content protection scheme. Our new scheme can control edit such as diversion of partial contents to other contents, and it can also control the composition of contents. In other words, our proposed scheme enables the control of not only the edit in one content but the edit between two or more contents. In addition, we solve the problem about a repetition of edits on change, deletion, and addition which remains a problem in the conventional scheme. This scheme is a next generation content protection scheme suitable for CGM on the Internet.

In future, we aim to apply signatures using Identity-Based Encryption [13] in our scheme.

References

1. YouTube Homepage. https://www.youtube.com/. Accessed 1 May 2017
2. CLIP Homepage. http://www.clip-studio.com/clip_site/. Accessed 1 May 2017
3. Association of Radio Industries and Businesses, Conditional Access System Specifications for Digital Broadcasting (ARIB STD-B25 ver6.0., 3rd edn.). Association of Radio Industries and Businesses, Tokyo (2013)

4. Inamura, M., Saito, A., Iwamura, K.: A pre-control system to edit contents with an extended sanitizable signature. IEEJ Trans. Electron. Inf. Syst. **133**(4), 802–815 (2013). Japan
5. Boneh, D., Lynn, B., Shacham, H.: Short signatures from the weil pairing. In: Boyd, C. (ed.) ASIACRYPT 2001. LNCS, vol. 2248, pp. 514–532. Springer, Heidelberg (2001). doi:10. 1007/3-540-45682-1_30
6. Boneh, D., Gentry, C., Lynn, B., Shacham, H.: Aggregate and verifiably encrypted signatures from bilinear maps. In: Biham, E. (ed.) EUROCRYPT 2003. LNCS, vol. 2656, pp. 416–432. Springer, Heidelberg (2003). doi:10.1007/3-540-39200-9_26
7. Miyazaki, K., Susaki, S., Iwamura, M., Matsumoto, T., Sasaki, R., Yoshiura, H.: Digital document sanitizing problem. ISEC **103**(195), 61–67 (2003). Japan
8. Koga, K., Inamura, M., Kaneda, K., Iwamura, K.: Content control scheme to realize right succession and edit control. In: 12th International Joint Conference on e-Business and Telecommunications (ICE-B2015), pp. 249–257. Colmar (2015)

Product Service System Design and Implementation in a Customer Centric World

An Approach to a User Oriented PSS Framework

Alexander Richter[✉], Rebecca Bulander, Bernhard Kölmel,
and Johanna Schoblik

IoS3 - Institute of Smart Systems and Services, Pforzheim University,
Tiefenbronner Str. 65, Pforzheim, Germany
{alexander.richter, rebecca.bulander, bernhard.koelmel,
johanna.schoblik}@hs-pforzheim.de

Abstract. By offering of Product Service Systems (PSS) traditional product-oriented companies get an excellent opportunity to create new value by delivering customers a unique utility. This comes along with the improvement of the companies' competitive position on both, the domestic and the international marketplaces. A PSS is a combination of tangible or intangible products and services. Current available PSS approaches in literature as a set of guided methodologies how to implement a PSS out of a traditional product are manly focussed on the needs of large companies. Small and medium-sized enterprises (SMEs) habitually tend to block such approaches due to much complexity of the frameworks and missing usability and adaptability. However, PSS can also provide many opportunities for SMEs to generate new and innovative business models. In addition, the concept of customer centricity is currently not present at SMEs as well as the PSS research. To attract interest of SMEs in PSS a framework that is suitable to fit their needs is required. Hence, a first step is presented in this paper as the interaction based approach will help to make complex PSS frameworks applicable for SMEs.

Keywords: Product Service System · Customer centricity · PSS frameworks · Usability

1 Introduction

Traditional goods manufactured by production oriented companies are more and more considered as commodities. Through globalization and the application of information systems as well as other new technologies nowadays it is possible to produce quite complex and know-how intensive products. These used to be the showcases of western industries, at a very low price and a remarkably similar quality anywhere in the world. Furthermore, today's speed of imitation and copying is enormous and is getting faster since the introduction of technologies like 3D Scanners and 3D Printers. These devices allow rapid analysis and prototyping at a comparably low price. Even the produced

© Springer International Publishing AG 2017
M.S. Obaidat (Ed): ICETE 2016, CCIS 764, pp. 139–157, 2017.
https://doi.org/10.1007/978-3-319-67876-4_7

quality is not the main argument to convince buyers any more. Hence customers are unlikely to be attracted by the usual arguments such like quality, performance or the reputation of the brand. The transformation towards service orientation of a product-oriented company and the focus on individual customer needs seem to be possible ways out of the described dilemma. In order to cope with these changes and challenges, it is not enough to just expand the company's portfolio to some customer oriented services. The adoption of the concept of service orientation and customer centricity requires a transformation of the corporate culture, the leadership, and management, the employee's mindset as well as the company's internal processes right from the beginning. For this transformation companies are forced to put themselves into their customer's situation. They have to try to experience their own products and services and therefore become a part of the feedback cycle. Furthermore, the increasing integration into the customer's processes not only means a new field of action for traditional business, but also a remarkable opportunity to improve the development of new products towards an offering that solves customer problems and fulfils their jobs. The experiences gained by the usage of its own products can be used to provide customers even more value out of the existing relationship. In turn this will strengthen the existing relationship and thereby put cost arguments of the global competition clearly into perspective. A further argument for intense and close customer relationships is the possible integration with the customer's processes. The objective is to establish change barriers for the customer to prevent a switch to the offer of a competitor.

The design and implementation of such a service approach through Product Service Systems (PSS), which consists by definition out of a service and a product component [1], has already often been discussed in literature since the late 1990s [2]. However, this business model concept still lacks detailed comprehensible procedures for the introduction and the implementation of a Product Service System to an average small and medium-sized enterprise (SME) [3] and is therefore elusive for this important target group which is traditionally quite practice oriented. Practitioners of the target group are result biased. This means they are focused on pragmatic and applicable tools. Therefore, this research has the aim to highlight the importance of customer centricity for PSS and to determine the essential interactions for the preparation, development, introduction and the operation of such a system. Interactions are easy to understand for practitioners who are not familiar with academic approaches. Furthermore, a literature review comprising books, scientific magazines and articles as well as the web provided evidence that there are currently no frameworks in this area which use interactions (see examples in Table 1). Hereby a PSS framework is defined as a set of actions to build and implement a PSS in a company.

The current PSS approaches which are discussed in literature are complex and quite academic methods. Therefore, they are rather suitable for large organizations, which usually possess a research and development department as well as the qualified workforce to research and apply these methods in order to create new offerings. In particular the stakeholders of SMEs block these approaches [4] because of their limited capabilities or other set of priorities. An average SME has a tight organization, lean structures and a practice-oriented staff. Based on the lean resource structure and the priority on the business operation their employees do not have the time to familiarize themselves with these methods. The interaction based approach should take all

Table 1. Examples of the current PSS approaches [5].

PSS-approach	Description
Aurich et al. [6]	Control loop model of life cycle management of capital intensive PSS: The authors designed a product life cycle for PSS based on the manufacturers and customers perspective spanning from "organizational design" to "PSS Realization"
Lindahl et al. [7]	Integrated Product and Service Engineering: Lindahl [7] created a development method with focus on environment-oriented business models and sustainable influence of consumption patterns with phases from "Need & requirement analysis" to "Take back"
Spath and Demuß [8]	Model for hybrid product development: The model of the authors aims at the development of customized products and services. By means of a requirement model and requirement management the different engineering disciplines should coordinate their activities

stakeholders into account and facilitate the usage of current PSS frameworks. The approach is adapted to the structures of SMEs, i.e. kept simple and understandable. Therefore, it is especially applicable for this kind of companies.

Product Service Systems also provide a great opportunity for SMEs. In order to convince the target audience of the PSS concept by also considering the goals of usability this paper presents a PSS framework translation tool. This tool includes all important steps towards the implementation of a PSS approach; therefore, all activities and interactions between all relevant roles are documented and visualized in Interaction Maps. As the interaction approach focuses towards the usability of PSS Frameworks, usability is defined as: "The extent to which a product can be used by specified users to achieve specified goals with effectiveness, efficiency, and satisfaction in a specified context of use." [9].

Although this definition aims at products the scope could be extended to include Product Service Systems.

The usage of an Interaction Map was necessary, because the implementation process of a PSS is primarily based on interaction and communication but low in actions on a higher level. In a deeper level of the framework a process modelling language, e.g. BPMN 2.0, can be used to document business processes on a lower level.

Having formulated the objectives and benefits of the interaction based approach as well as the importance of customer centricity; Sect. 2 outlines the basic principles of customer centricity. Section 3 provides the foundations of Product Service Systems. Section 4 elaborates how the approach was developed and discusses the main aspects of the approach. The paper concludes with a summary and an outlook in Sect. 5.

2 Customer Centricity

Even though this paper focuses on Product Service Systems and especially on the implementation of PSS Design approaches, our literature research provided evidence of a lack of intense customer centricity approaches within current PSS Frameworks.

Therefore this chapter will give a motivation for the subject and an overview of the term and its main aspects.

The development of new technologies, especially the latest innovations in information technology, changed traditional markets and led to an unprecedented transparency. Today companies are facing much more competitive factors which have to be considered, then ever before. Especially the possibility for customers to check and compare all available offerings on local and worldwide markets in nearly real time can result in a tough competition for the respective providers. At the same time, companies have new opportunities to interact with customers, get in direct contact with them and even to integrate their business operation with their customer's processes.

Even though there are a lot of chances for companies which apply this strategy, customer centricity can still be a fuzzy concept and is hard to measure. Therefore, management often doubts the profitability of customer centricity [10]. The named fuzziness of the subject is why it's quite difficult to state a definition for the subject of customer centricity. Therefore in the following two explanations for this term are presented. The first is originated by Loshin and Reifer [11] who state that customer centricity is "(…) the ability to augment every customer interaction to provide the perception of increased value exchange for both the company and the customer." Another explanation for the term is delivered by Womack and Daniel [12] who present six customer-oriented principles which are (1) solve the customer's problem completely by ensuring that all the goods and services work, and work together. (2) Don't waste the customer's time. (3) Provide exactly what the customer wants. (4) Provide what's wanted exactly where it's wanted. (5) Provide what's wanted where it's wanted exactly when it's wanted, (6) Continually aggregate solutions to reduce the customer's time and hassle. As Gummerson [10] commented those principles, they seem to be common sense, but often the obvious is the most difficult to implement in complex organizations and in the market. Therefore, the next chapter will broach the issue of barriers and hurdles for the implementation of customer centricity in a firm.

2.1   Comparison of Two Fundamental Approaches and Transformation Barriers for Product Oriented Companies

Comparing the product-centric versus customer-centric approach Shah et al. [13] identified nine categories, by which fundamental differences for those two approaches can be compared. Those categories are (1) basic philosophy, (2) business orientation, (3) product positioning, (4) organizational structure, (5) organizational focus, (6) performance metric, (7) management criteria, (8) selling approach and (9) customer knowledge (Table 2).

Focusing on those categories four potential organizational barriers on a company's path towards a customer centric organization can be identified. The named barriers are (1) cultural, (2) organizational, (3) processes and (4) financial metrics-barriers (see Fig. 1) [13].

Overcoming these four barriers on the path towards a customer centric company is a though challenge that was also experienced by a German Insurance company which faced similar challenges by changing their corporate company strategy from 2009 until 2012 towards a customer centric organization and becoming an insurance company

Table 2. Comparison of a product- and customer-centric approach [13].

	Product-centric approach	Customer-centric approach
Basic philosophy	Sell products; we'll sell to whoever will buy	Serve customers; all decisions start with the customer and opportunities for advantage
Business orientation	Transaction-oriented	Relationship-oriented
Product positioning	Highlight product features and advantages.	Highlight product's benefits in terms of meeting individual customer needs
Organizational structure	Product profit centers, product managers, product sales team	Customer segment centers, customer relationship managers, customer segment sales team
Organizational focus	Internally focused, new product development, new account development, market share growth; customer relations are issues for the marketing department	Externally focused, customer relationship development, profitability through customer loyalty; employees are customer advocates
Performance metric	Number of new products, profitability per product, market share by product/subbrands	Share of wallet of customers, customer satisfaction, customer lifetime value, customer equity
Management criteria	Portfolio of products	Portfolio of customers
Selling approach	How many customers can we sell this product to?	How many products can we sell this customer?
Customer knowledge	Customer data are a control mechanism	Customer knowledge is valuable asset

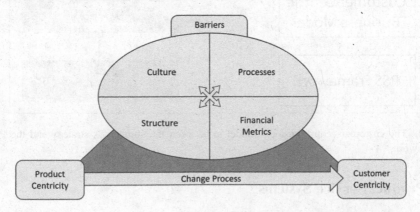

Fig. 1. Barriers within the change process to a customer centric organization [based on 13].

which has the aim to solve the customers problems. Thereby the company set a major focus on its employees as a strategic factor for the implementation of the customer centric change process; especially these employees who are immediately in contact with the customers [14]. In this case the four organizational barriers described by Shah et al. [13] were also considered. The mayor results of this customer centricity change process were significant improvements of the customer and service orientation of the employees and processes. These improvements were measured in a survey. The main indicators that could be significant improved where: the availability of employees for customers, the attention of employees with customer contact and the liability of all statements given to customers [14].

2.2   Customer Centricity for the Concept of PSS

The three layer model in Fig. 2 shows the way customer centricity is integrated into the PSS and interaction concept. At the top layer of the model is the companies' overall business strategy serving as general guide. Every action which is executed on the second layer which is the customer centric business model is aligned with the business strategy on the top layer. Thereby the business model contains the main ideas and value propositions that should be delivered to the customer. The intended Product Service System can be developed by the usage of a PSS Framework which builds the foundational layer.

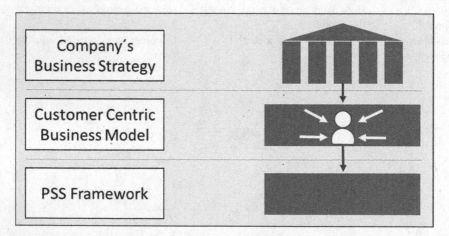

Fig. 2. The customer centric business model in-between the company's strategy and the PSS Framework.

3   Product Service Systems

By focusing the research of this paper on interactions and usability, the main emphasis was not on developing new Product Service System frameworks yet. However, comprehensive literature research on the subject was conducted. Numerous publications about currently discussed taxonomies, PSS design frameworks and past as well as current research projects on this topic were accessed and analysed.

To provide the reader an overview of the PSS subject, two definitions and one common classification of PSSs will be introduced in the following chapter. Subsequently the "Product-Service-System Life Cycle" [15], which is a compelling and well thought-out PSS framework, will be presented and explained.

3.1 Definitions

To provide an elementary understanding of the Product Service System topic two common PSS definitions are stated in the following: "A PSS consists of tangible products and intangible services, designed and combined so that they are jointly capable of fulfilling specific customer needs. Additionally, PSS tries to reach the goals of sustainable development." [16].

"Product Service-Systems (PSS) may be defined as a solution offered for sale that involves both a product and a service element, to deliver the required functionality." [17].

Those two definitions show as others, too, that a PSS mandatorily consists of a product and a service component. In addition many common definitions also focus on a specific customer need or a specific utility which has to be delivered by the system. Numerous definitions, mainly European and especially the ones of the Nordic School, also include a focus on sustainability as a key element of PSSs. The work of this paper is based on the definition of Wong [17].

3.2 Eight Types of Product Service Systems

The Dutch researcher Arnold Tukker classified Product Service Systems into eight types which range from product-oriented over use-oriented to completely result-oriented offerings. The insights which led to the development of his taxonomy are based on the results of a European Union founded research project named SusProNet (Sustainable Product Development Network) [18].

The following figure depicts the three main and eight subcategories of a PSS according to Tukker [19]. The subsequent section describes the graph in full detail (Fig. 3).

A Product-Service System is always in between a pure product and a pure service. The PSS has a material product part and an immaterial service part.

Depending on the composition of the shares, the PSS can have three forms, it can be product-oriented, use-oriented or result-oriented. As a product-oriented PSS, it has a high proportion of product and can either (1) contain a product-related service component or have a product-related consulting (2). Here both types offer added value for the customer by for example causing a more efficient use of material and human resources. At the same time this service is reflected in additional material or labor related costs for the provider. A product-oriented company, which wants to offer these types of PSS must usually invest in capital- and organization-related changes. Thereby advantages in terms of lower customer barriers (in the case of financial services), higher customer loyalty and faster innovation cycles through closer customer contact arise for

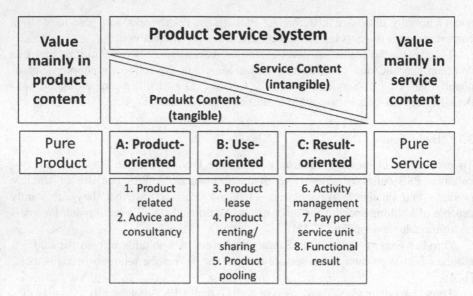

Fig. 3. Main and subcategories of PSS [19].

these companies. The Product Leasing (3) has tangible value for the customer, since operating costs and maintenance are offered and performed by the provider. The provider usually has to take precautions, as a more thoughtless usage by the customer can be expected caused by the lack of ownership of the product. The barriers of the acquisition of new customers are low because less investment (compared to the traditional purchasing) is needed by the customer. On the other hand, in this case now the PSS provider must raise the capital for the leased products due to the remaining ownership. In terms of customer loyalty it can be said that this loyalty may evolve to an all-round carefree package through the service offerings. The lower the service amount is, the easier it is for the customer to switch to another provider at any time. If the manufacturer occurs in this scenario, as the lessor, a positive effect on the business model can be expected due to the customer proximity and the customer feedback. In the case of product rental and product sharing (4) a customer doesn't own the product anymore. This means the product is not in the property of the customer. The customer only uses the product if he immediately needs it. Hereby the customer has to invest time and efforts in order to get the product and to be able to use the product whenever he needs it. Also a contribution to the personal satisfaction, such as the self-confidence through possession cannot be expected here. However, through the share of usage the total cost of capital in the system are to be set lower and the barrier of participation for new customers is very low due to the reduced offer purchase costs. The provider on the other hand also has to reckon with high capital costs for the provision of the offer including higher labor expenses and the remaining ownership of the product. At the product pooling (5) the analysis is almost the same as for the renting and sharing. The activity management (6) transfers staff and material costs from the user to the provider, which then can generate profits through specific expertise and the efficient reorganization of the outsourced activity. Here it is important to define performance and quality criteria from the outset in order to prevent a deviation from expectation and delivery of the service. Since the activity management is typically designed for long contract durations, high customer loyalty can be expected. In addition, the specialization of the provider can lead to a high degree of innovative potential. The concept of payment per service unit (7) of one or more activities provides a perceivable value for the customer. Furthermore, the barrier to entry for the user is considered to be low in this concept. The position of the provider is located in the customer's value chain and is clearly better for the provider with respect to direct customer contact, customer processes and customer loyalty. In order to offer this service at an attractive price, the provider must be able to predict the customer needs, since by facing inaccurate need forecasts a risk premium must be included. In addition, the provider must raise additional capital due to the remaining ownership of the tangible product. Another positive effect is that through intensive contact with customers a high potential for innovation can be expected. The functional result (8) provides the same result as an activity which is carried out by the customer and thus brings the same benefit. In principle, the provider can try to offer a solution that requires a comparatively lower input. Here the expected level of performance must be constantly observed and complied with. Capital costs should be relatively small in this concept, while replacement costs are classified as high. This model provides the highest degree of freedom in terms of innovation [18, 19].

3.3 Product Service System Life Cycle

As a framework which the research can be based on, the Product Service System Life Cycle approach of Aurich and Clement [15] was chosen. The PSS Life Cycle describes how to plan, build and realize a Product Service System for capital intensive products.

Aurich and Clement's [15] framework was analysed in order to apply the Inter-action Map tool afterwards to the five life cycle phases described. Those are (1) Organizational Design, (2) PSS Planning, (3) PSS Development, (4) PSS Configuration and (5) PSS Realization. Since this framework is a cycle, it starts with PSS Planning and ends with PSS Realization. The step of Organizational Design has usually to be conducted once for every use case. The following figure shows the PSS Life Cycle (Fig. 4):

Organizational Design. The application of Product Service Systems provides traditionally oriented companies with special organizational but also corporate cultural challenges. In order to put the company on the path of development of a PSS, a one-time implementation phase of an organizational design is recommended. This usually begins with the decision of the company's management of the intention to introduce a PSS. At this time, there is no existing PSS expertise within the company available. The knowledge must be acquired from outside the firm. This can be done by means of tendering, head hunters or business consultants. It is of advantage to be able to attract an expert who not only has PSS expertise, but also leadership skills for the implementation of such a project. Experience with change projects is also advantageous, since the fundamental change of a business model can mean new implications for the corporate culture. In the next step the business processes must be considered,

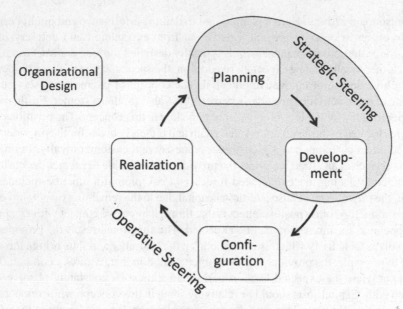

Fig. 4. PSS Life Cycle [15].

and business models must be developed (if not already happened) so that the PSS can be aligned to them. To ensure the acceptance of employees for the coming changes, they must be extensively trained and convinced of the benefits of PSS. Organizational and operational structure changes can only be made with the acceptance of the employees. This is done using a proposed resolution, which will be presented to the board. It is also important to ensure that all levels of management share the new decisions. If some people are still not on board, they must be trained and instructed again. Furthermore their concerns and fears must be addressed and those employees must be convinced of the benefits which come along with a PSS. After that the implementation of the organizational design phase can begin on the team level [15].

The application of Product Service Systems provides traditionally oriented companies with special organizational but also corporate cultural challenges. In order to put the company on the right path of development of a PSS, a one-time implementation phase of an organizational design is recommended. This usually begins with the decision of the company's management of the intention to introduce a PSS. At this stage, there is no PSS expertise existing within the company. The knowledge must be acquired from outside the firm. This can be done by means of tendering, head hunters or business consultants. It is of advantage to be able to attract an expert who not only has PSS expertise, but also leadership skills for the implementation of such a project. Experience with change projects is also advantageous, since the fundamental change of a business model can mean new implications for the corporate culture. In the next step the business processes must be considered, and business models must be developed (if not already happened) so that the PSS can be aligned to them. To ensure the acceptance of the coming changes by the employees, they must be extensively trained and convinced of the benefits of PSS by effectively communicating what's in for them.

Organizational and operational structure changes can only be made with the acceptance by the employees. This is done using a proposed resolution, which will be presented to the board. It is also important to ensure that all levels of management share and buy-in to the new decisions. If some people are still not on board, their individual reasons of reluctance have to be understood thoroughly and addressed in an appropriate manner. Their concerns and fears must be addressed and those employees must be convinced of the benefits which come along with a PSS. After that the implementation of the organizational design phase can begin on the team level [15].

PSS Planning. The objective of PSS Planning is to define all planning related activities. Those include tasks like the definition of the product, its utility and the definition of the goals for the development project. This phase is finalized with the PSS development assignment and the preparation of a PSS development request for the management. The PSS planning phase gives companies the opportunity to generate and also to rate possible PSS development projects [15].

PSS Development Project. The development phase has the goal to develop a market-ready Product Service System. By building on the preliminary work of the planning phase, the development process starts at this point. An essential requirement is the systematization of the integrated product and service development for a harmonized result that delivers true utility for the customer. At the end of this phase, a PSS which consists of products and services is developed. The last steps of PSS development are the creation of market specific offerings for different markets, the documentation of the development process and other formal internal procedures [15].

PSS Configuration. The phase of PSS Configuration aims to offer a customer individual Product Service System which also meets the provider's objectives. Therefore, the technical configuration of the physical product, the configuration of suitable and individual customer centric service products, the generation of different offering combinations as well as their evaluation and selection are required. The configuration phase is essential, because in order to exploit the strengths of Product Service Systems a customer individual fit of the offering is fundamental [15].

PSS Realization. In addition of providing the configured PSS and generating customer utility, a core responsibility of the PSS realization phase is the retention of a high quality offer and the ensuring of high-quality standards throughout the whole PSS Life Cycle. To be able to assure this, a continuous improvement process, performance measurement indicators, further improvement and monitoring measures are applied [15].

3.4   PSS for Targeting Barriers of Customer Acceptance

The customer acceptance of an offered Product Service System is quite essential for its success and must therefore be taken into account at an early stage in the development process. For being able to avoid wrong tendencies in the PSS development process, it is important to have knowledge of potential barriers for customer acceptance of offered goods. In their paper, Schmidt et al. [20] conducted a literature research with the aim to identify customer barriers of product acceptance for being able to give suggestions, how PSS offerings could target those barriers and to be able to offer a higher value offering to the potential customer.

The identified barriers can be divided into two categories, which are (1) products' attributes and (2) customer behaviour. The category of products' attributes contains the complexity, interoperability, costs as well as the reliability and availability of products. The identified barriers of customer behaviour were irrationalities, trust and unawareness of need. Furthermore values and beliefs were identified as a barrier for both categories [20].

The identification of the named barriers can be important for future development of customer centric PSS offers, by targeting the listed hurdles and offering as well as communicating a unique, valuable and attractive value proposition.

3.5   Importance of Usability for a Theoretical Framework

The common PSS design frameworks are well reasoned, but quite academic and also often not user centered. By mentioning the user of a PSS design framework those people are meant, who are responsible for generating business models and business model ideas within a firm. Within the context of the research project "Use-PSS" many interactions with German SMEs proved that the companies are interested in new approaches but have great difficulties to cope with academic research approaches and results as well as with the usage of academic literature. These insights could be acquired during workshops with SMEs and discussions with participants of public presentations. This means, that the real life usability and applicability of these approaches often lacks a detailed description and guidance for SMEs which also uses a more practical oriented wording. This paper's research has the aim to combine the existing academic frameworks with a tool, that helps to translate the academic research into real life action and interaction plans for SMEs which cannot afford a R&D department which brings complex research results to life.

4   Interaction Based Approach for PSS Implementation

This chapter introduces a method for higher PSS-Framework-Usability; the method is based on the Product Service System Life Cycle framework of Aurich and Clement [15]. The following concept can be applied to many other frameworks to provide a better understanding of the detailed interactions required for the implementation of a PSS development framework.

4.1   Overview

Figure 5 depicts the integration of the interaction based approach in-between a PSS framework (layer 1) and the detailed business processes (layer 4) of a company.

The interaction based approach helps to translate the often rather abstract and roughly described frameworks into a detailed business process model. Thus, the interaction based approach contains two steps. In the first step several interaction matrices for each PSS Life Cycle phase depicted as Interaction Tables in layer 2 of

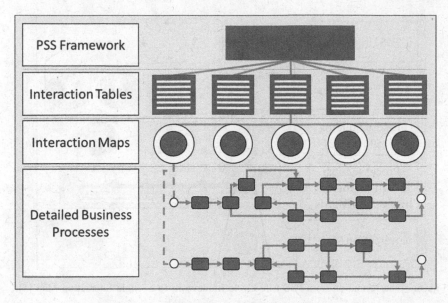

Fig. 5. Integration of the interaction based approach in-between a PSS framework and a company's detailed business processes [5].

Fig. 5 are created. The interaction matrices contain the main process steps and the required information about interactions within these steps. In the second step of the interaction concept the matrices are separated into various Interaction Maps (layer 3 in Fig. 5). Those are created for each process step within the interaction matrix.

4.2 Interaction Description

This section describes the interactions within the company and also in-between the company and the external partners which are involved. Therefore, the term "interaction" is defined for the research as follows: Interactions are based on two or more-directional relationships between two or more actors, which can get in contact through synchronous or asynchronous communication. All processes of a company are affected by interactions. Interactions concentrate on the existing roles within a company and their actions and communication within the Product Service System Lifecycle.

To define a scope for the approach, the procedure of describing the interactions is elaborated. Furthermore, the single roles within a company are defined. The proposed roles do not always fit to every company and therefore have to be adjusted.

The subject of interaction description for PSS is new and could not be found in the existing literature before; therefore a literature was conducted prior to the development of this concept. Thus the development of the approach started from draft. The PSS Life Cycle framework [15] which was already introduced provides a solid base for the interaction concept.

Figure 6 shows the transformation of the PSS Life Cycle framework down to a single Interaction Map. In a first step in layer 2 the framework was split into the five Life

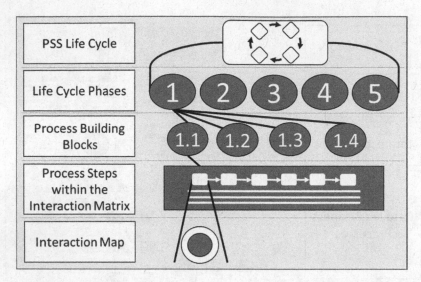

Fig. 6. Transformation from PSS Life Cycle framework to a single Interaction Map [5].

Cycle phases (e.g. Planning) which were divided into many process building blocks (layer 3; e.g. Planning Preparation). Afterwards each building block was converted into an Interaction Matrix (layer 4). Each Interaction Matrix consists of several process steps (e.g. Define Physical Product Core) which were separately analysed for their occurring interaction. Finally, an Interaction Map (layer 5) for each process step was created.

4.3 Interaction Matrix

The Interaction Matrix analyses each of the process building blocks and divides them into single process steps. A matrix contains the process steps on the x-axis and the actors on the y-axis. Within the matrix, methods which can be applied to the steps as well as internal and external actors and their interaction status are shown. The status is visualized using the assigned symbols. Additionally, for a better understanding, there is a possibility to add a short description to each process step at the bottom of the table.

During the interaction analysis phase the following interaction states can be assigned:

- **Active Actor; Symbol: +**
  The actor is actively involved in this phase and indispensable. He/she interacts with other participants and is always located in the inner circle of the Interaction Map.
- **Passive Actor; Symbol: −**
  The passive actor is not directly involved in an interaction but has a supporting function. He/she can have an indirect interest in a certain process part or may have an interest in getting certain information. The passive actor only delivers information for the main interaction process by request.
- **Doesn't play a role; Symbol: 0**
  The actor doesn't have any activity in this phase and is also not indirectly involved.

- **Role is non-existent at this time; Symbol: /**
  The actor in this phase is irrelevant and doesn't have any reference concerning the presented interaction or process part. This actor might change its status at a later point in time.

Figure 7 shows an extract from the "Planning Preparation" Interaction Matrix.

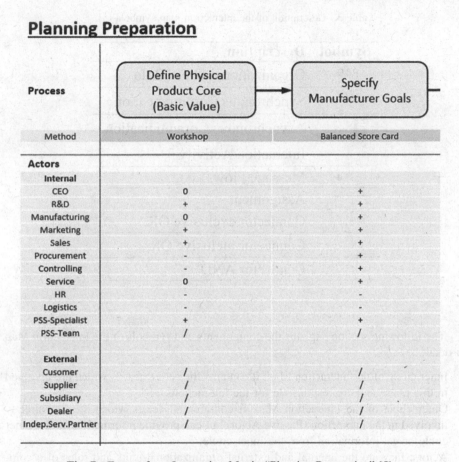

Planning Preparation

Process	Define Physical Product Core (Basic Value)	Specify Manufacturer Goals
Method	Workshop	Balanced Score Card
Actors		
Internal		
CEO	0	+
R&D	+	+
Manufacturing	0	+
Marketing	+	+
Sales	+	+
Procurement	-	+
Controlling	-	+
Service	0	+
HR	-	-
Logistics	-	-
PSS-Specialist	+	+
PSS-Team	/	/
External		
Cusomer	/	/
Supplier	/	/
Subsidiary	/	/
Dealer	/	/
Indep.Serv.Partner	/	/

Fig. 7. Extract from Interaction Matrix "Planning Preparation" [5].

4.4 Interaction Map

The next step after creating the Interaction Matrix was a detailed analysis of the single process steps and their contained interactions. The main aim of the Interaction Map, which was inspired by Stickdorn and Schneider's [21] "Stakeholder Map", is to give the PSS framework user a tool which allows the presentation and explanation of an implementation process in easy to understand interactions which are displayed graphically. The Interaction Map does not aim to replace established process modelling languages; it rather gives the practitioners a tool, which helps to translate a rough framework through interactions into detailed business processes. At this point of research, it is recommended using the maps with a short explanatory text of a few sentences.

For the purpose of keeping the interactions within the Interaction Map simple and informative, the number of symbols used is limited. In the following table the symbols for modelling an interaction map are shown (Table 3).

Table 3. Description of the interaction map symbols [5].

Symbol	Description
R&D	Organizational Unit / Role
	Synchronous Communication
	Asynchronous Communication
	Interaction Activity
------▶	Message Flow
———	Assignment
XOR	Connector exclusive OR
OR	Connector inclusive OR
AND	Connector AND

The following section explains the components and symbols of the Interaction Map in detail.

- Inner circle of the Interaction Map: it contains the active actors, which are involved in this phase and are responsible for the interactions.
- Outer circle of the Interaction Map: it contains all actors which are not directly involved in the interaction (Passive Actor) but can provide information for the inner circle or get information from the inner circle.
- Actors: they are the internal and external organizational units and roles of a company, e.g. CEO or supplier.
- Synchronous communication symbol: it stands for e.g. telephone call, video conference, live meeting or chat.
- Asynchronous communication symbol: it represents e.g. letter, telefax, email, internal social media or automatic communication via database.
- Activity symbol: it stands for the interaction between several actors. An interaction activity is always a synchronous communication and could be for example a meeting or a workshop.
- Data or information: they can be transferred via message flow. It is used for example to communicate the output of a meeting to actors in the inner or outer circle.

- Assignment: it shows the connection between an organizational unit or role and the interaction activity.

Connectors (AND/exclusive OR/inclusive OR): The AND signals that several interactions could be executed in parallel. The fact that only one out of several interactions could be executed is shown by the exclusive OR. The inclusive OR represents the fact that one or more interactions could be executed.

Figure 8 shows the Interaction Map of the first process step "Define Physical Product Core" of the "Planning Preparation" Interaction Matrix. It represents a workshop for defining the physical product core of a PSS. The organizational units R&D, Marketing and Sales as well as the PSS-Specialist are active actors in this process step. The output of the workshop is asynchronously reported to passive actors, CEO, Manufacturing and Service.

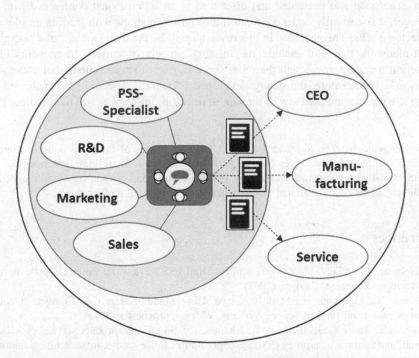

Fig. 8. Interaction Map for the process step "Define Physical Product Core" [5].

5 Summary and Outlook

This paper highlighted Product Service Systems as an important way of developing new offerings, generating more value for the customer and to ensure a sustainable business and strong competitive position for the offering company. Furthermore a PSS can be advantageous for both, the offering firm and the customer as well. The benefits of this concept are clear, but the application of PSS theories is not easy and can lead to a refusal of the PSS idea. A literature review provided evidence of a lack of usability of the current PSS design frameworks, which are quite academic, not user oriented and therefore not applicable for SMEs which are in need for new business models in today's fast changing, highly competitive markets. A further missing aspect is the explicit and unconditional customer centricity of PSS. This customer centricity aspect is important for both, the PSS framework itself and developed PSS that are offered to the customer. Hence, putting the customer in the middle of all actions must be implemented into future PSS developments and customer barriers must be addressed appropriately.

In a further chapter a new methodology considering the requirements of SMEs was introduced as a first step towards PSS framework usability. The presented method is an interaction based approach which uses Interaction Maps as a key element for the implementation and acceptance of PSS frameworks within a company.

The current state of the interaction based approach is, that it was reviewed in an expert discussion and presented and discussed at an international conference [see 5]. Moreover, it is currently under evaluation through workshops with leading employees of selected SMEs. The next step in this research will be the development of a complete PSS framework that will include the missing aspects of current frameworks. The interaction based approach will therefore serve as one of several methods for the new framework. Furthermore, the newly developed PSS framework will be evaluated by testing it with selected SMEs with the aim to develop, implement and market new PSS ideas.

Acknowledgements. The Research Project "Use-PSS" is part of the focal point of support "Middle Class Digital – Strategies for a Digital Transformation of Business Processes" of the German Ministry of Economics and Energy (BMWi). This support campaign was assigned to push the digitalization of small and medium sized enterprises and craft businesses.

References

1. Tischner, U., Verkuijl, M., Tukker, A.: First Draft PSS Review. SusProNet Report, draft 15 December. Econcept, Cologne (2002)
2. Baines, T., Lightford, H.: Made to Serve: How Manufacturers Can Compete Through Servitization and Product Service Systems. Wiley, Chistchester (2013)
3. Hernández Pardo, R.J., Bhamra, T., Bhamra, R.: Sustainable product service systems in small and medium enterprises (SMEs): opportunities in the leather manufacturing industry. Sustainability **4**, 175–192 (2012)
4. Hsin, C., Ching-Fang, W.: A comparative analysis between SMEs and large companies in relation to integration technologies adoption. In: Proceedings of ICEB 2005, 5th International Conference on Electronic Business, Hong Kong, 5–9 December 2005, pp. 839–848 (2005)
5. Richter, A., Schoblik, J., Kölmel, B., Bulander, R.: Development of an interaction based approach for product service system implementation - an approach towards PSS usability. In: Proceedings of the 13th International Joint Conference on e-Business and Telecommunications (ICETE 2016), INSTICC, Lisbon, Portugal, 26–28 July 2016, vol. 2, pp. 132–139. ICE-B (2016)

6. Aurich, J.C., Schweitzer, E., Mannweiler, C.: Integrated design of industrial product-service systems. In: Mitsuishi, M., Ueda, K., Kimura, F. (eds.) Manufacturing Systems and Technologies for the New Frontier, pp. 543–546. Springer, London (2008). doi:10.1007/978-1-84800-267-8_111

7. Lindahl, M., Sundin, E., Sakao, T., Shimomura, Y.: Integrated product and service engineering versus design for environment – a comparison and evaluation of advantages and disadvantages. In: Takata, S., Umeda, Y. (eds.) Advances in Life Cycle Engineering for Sustainable Manufacturing Businesses, pp. 137–142. Springer, London (2007). doi:10.1007/978-1-84628-935-4_24

8. Spath, D., Demuß, L.: Entwicklung hybrider Produkte – Gestaltung materieller und immaterieller Leistungsbündel. In: Bullinger, H.-J., Scheer, A.-W. (eds.) Service Engineering – Entwicklung und Gestaltung innovativer Dienstleistungen, pp. 463–502. Springer, Berlin (2003). doi:10.1007/3-540-29473-2_20

9. DIN EN ISO 9241-1, 2002-02-00: Ergonomische Anforderungen für Bürotätigkeiten mit Bildschirmgeräten - Teil 1: Allgemeine Einführung (ISO 9241-1:1997)

10. Gummerson, E.: Customer centricity: reality or a wild goose chase? Eur. Bus. Rev. 20(4), 315–330 (2008)

11. Loshin, D., Reifer, A.: Using Information to Develop a Culture of Customer Centricity. Customer Centricity, Analytics, and Information Utilization. Morgan Kaufmann, Burlington (2013)

12. Womack, J.P., Daniel, T.J.: Lean consumption. Harv. Bus. Rev. 83, 58–68 (2005)

13. Shah, D., Rust, R.T., Parasuraman, A., Staelin, R., Day, G.S.: The path to customer centricity. J. Serv. Res. 2006(9), 113 (2006)

14. Schwarz, S.: Kulturwandel bei AXA: „Kundenzentrierung" als Erfolgsfaktor bei der Strategieumsetzung. In: Zimmermann, G. (ed.) Change Management in Versicherungsunternehmen, pp. 153–163. Springer Fachmedien Wiesbaden, Wiesbaden (2015). doi:10.1007/978-3-658-05974-3_8

15. Aurich, J.C., Clement, M.H.: Produkt-Service Systeme. Springer, Heidelberg (2010). doi:10.1007/978-3-642-01407-9

16. Brandstotter, M., Haberl, M., Knoth, R., Kopacek, B., Kopacek, P.: IT on Demand – Towards an Environmental Conscious Service System for Vienna (AT). In: Proceedings of EcoDesign 2003, 3rd International Symposium on Environmentally Conscious Design and Inverse Manufacturing, pp. 799–802. IEEE (2003)

17. Wong, M.: Implementation of innovative product-service systems in the consumer goods industry. Ph.D. thesis, Cambridge University (2004)

18. Tukker, A., Tischner, U.: New Business for Old Europe. Greenleaf Publishing, Sheffield (2006)

19. Tukker, A.: Eight types of product-service system: eight ways to sustainability? Experiences from SusProNet. Bus. Strategy Environ. 13, 246–260 (2004)

20. Schmidt, D.M., Bauer, P., Mörtl, M.: PSS for influencing customer barriers and acceptance. J. Econ. Bus. Manag. 3(10), 990–993 (2015)

21. Stickdorn, M., Schneider, J.: This is Service Design Thinking. BIS Publishers, Amsterdam (2011)

Optical Communication Systems

Mode Excitation and Multiplexing for MIMO Systems Focusing on Digital Mirror Devices

André Sandmann, Andreas Ahrens$^{(\boxtimes)}$, Steffen Lochmann, and Peter Bartmann

Department of Electrical Engineering and Computer Science,
Communications Signal Processing Group, Hochschule Wismar,
University of Applied Sciences: Technology, Business and Design,
Philipp-Müller-Straße 14, 23966 Wismar, Germany
{andre.sandmann,andreas.ahrens,steffen.lochmann}@hs-wismar.de
http://www.hs-wismar.de

Abstract. In the fiber-optic telecommunication community space division multiplex, synonymously referred to as optical multiple-input multiple-output (MIMO), is a potential candidate to overcome the imminent capacity crunch. The concept of transmitting parallel data streams on different optical modes of a few-mode or multi-mode fiber is in the focus of this work. Thus, different approaches for mode-selective excitation, mode multiplexing and demultiplexing are presented. This includes a completely new approach in this field based on digital mirror devices (DMDs) which benefits from its high flexibility when it comes to pattern generation and its theoretical low insertion loss of around −1.27 dB. However, the blazed grated structure of the micromirror array (MMA) makes it complex to find the optimal coupling conditions. This work shows an intuitive solution for that problem. In addition to the DMDs, photonic lanterns and optical fusion couplers combined with offset splices are studied with respect to their optical MIMO suitability.

Keywords: Optical MIMO · Space division multiplexing · Digital Mirror Devices (DMDs) · Digital Light Processor (DLP) · Photonic lantern · Mode combining

1 Introduction

Time division, wavelength and polarization multiplexing as well as high order modulation schemes have been developed coping with the exponential grow of data traffic in optical networks and have reached a state of maturity. Therefore, there exists an increasing interest in optical space division multiplexing (SDM). Adapting well-known wireless communications multiple-input multiple-output (MIMO) techniques to optical multiple-input multiple-output (OMIMO) transmission has been discussed in several papers like [8,9]. In analogy to wireless communications, where spatial diversity gained by separated antennas is sufficient for a MIMO channel, OMIMO exploits mode diversity in multi-mode fibers (MMFs) among others. However, the first experiment for modal multiplexing dates back to 1982, where it was demonstrated in a 10-m long MMF [3].

© Springer International Publishing AG 2017
M.S. Obaidat (Ed): ICETE 2016, CCIS 764, pp. 161–176, 2017.
https://doi.org/10.1007/978-3-319-67876-4_8

Newer publications show the feasibility of 2×2 up to 12×12 OMIMO systems in longer optical links of km-domain [12,16]. However, efficient excitation of specific modes in a MMF and their respective coupling and splitting is an open question.

This paper tackles the problem of mode-selective excitation into conventional MMFs. Conventional approaches use centric and eccentric splices of a single-mode fiber (SMF) to a MMF [15]. Due to the offset launching condition different modegroups are excited within the MMF depending on the eccentricity of the splice. Afterwards two or more modegroups in different MMFs are combined using fusion or other couplers [13]. The crucial reproducibility as well as the low flexibility are two drawbacks of this method. Another approach is to utilize spatial light modulators (SLMs). With SLMs as described in [5], for instance, individual modes can be excited with high contrast. Nevertheless, the attenuation due to the serial mode combining with semi-permeable mirror couplers, which has to be used for a concatenation of SLMs, leads to an exponentially growing power loss of 3 dB in each step.

Addressing these problems this paper shows a new approach utilizing Digital Light Processor® (DLP) chips as coupling devices [1,2]. The use of digital mirror devices (DMDs) in optical networks has been described in [19], where the DMD has been used as a signal level controlling or network switching device. However, this paper extends its usability for SDM. The micromirror array (MMA) of a DMD has to be considered as a diffraction grating with blazed condition. Hence, the reflection of an inciting laser beam produces multiple diffraction maximums. Finding the global maximum in a mechanical setup becomes a complex task. In order to reduce the complexity this paper concentrates on a 2×2 MIMO configuration. This work compares the DLP-based concept to the approach utilizing SMF to MMF offset splices and fusion couplers as well as to the concept based on photonic lanterns.

This contribution is structured as follows: Sect. 2 introduces the general concept of optical MIMO. The use of photonic lanterns for optical MIMO purposes is described in Sect. 3. Section 4 shows the concept of mode-selective excitation with SMF to MMF offset splices and mode multiplexing and demultiplexing with fusion couplers. A novel approach of using DMDs for optical MIMO is presented in detail in Sect. 5. This includes the mathematical description, derivation of optimal coupling conditions and measurement results. Finally, Sect. 6 provides the concluding remarks.

2   Optical MIMO Overview

The idealized concept of a multi-mode MIMO transmission is shown in Fig. 1. Herein, a transmitter (Tx) emits multiple modulated optical signals which are then carried on the LP_{01} modes through multiple SMFs in parallel. Mode-selective excitation transforms the LP_{01} modes of the SMFs into orthogonal optical modes carried in a few-mode or multi-mode fiber (FMF/MMF). Subsequently these modes are multiplexed (MUX) into a FMF/MMF where they

appear as superimposed modes. It should be noted that the mode-selective excitation and the mode MUX can be conducted by a device in a single step, e.g.
by a photonic lantern. Subsequent to the transmission of the modes through the
FMF/MMF they are demultiplexed (DEMUX) and the parallel signals are then
processed with a MIMO receiver (Rx).

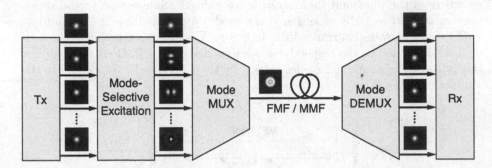

Fig. 1. Ideal multi-mode MIMO system model showing the electrical field distributions
in the fiber cores (Activated modes in the FMF: LP_{01}, LP_{11}^a, LP_{11}^b, LP_{21}^a, LP_{21}^b, LP_{02}).

Compared to conventional single-mode systems, multi-mode systems have to
cope with the additional modal dispersion by reducing the differential mode
group delays (DMGD), which can be taken care of with the technological
advances in the fiber manufacturing process, or the cancellation of the modal
dispersion in the receiver at an increased signal processing cost. In addition,
mode mixing during the transmission needs to be considered. This mixing can
be interpreted as cross-talk and removed with appropriate MIMO signal processing. Further challenges for the implementation of such an OMIMO system are
to select and optimize components that are able to conduct the MIMO tasks
described above and to come as close as possible to these ideal conditions. Moreover, multi-mode amplifiers and switching devices for optical MIMO networks
are also of significant interest in the research community [18].

In this work three concepts for mode-selective excitation and mode MUX
are presented. The first concept implements the frequently referenced photonic
lantern. Secondly, a concept, comprising SMF to MMF splices for mode-selective
excitation and multi-mode fusion couplers for mode MUX and DEMUX, is presented. However, the main focus in this work is on the third concept which uses
a digital mirror device to conduct both tasks. In inverse operation the MUX
components can be utilized for the DEMUX task as well.

3   Photonic Lantern Based Optical MIMO Systems

One method for manufacturing photonic lanterns (PLs) is to insert a bundle
of SMFs into a capillary tube having a lower refractive index than the SMF's

cladding. This array is then fused and tapered such that the SMF cladding forms the FMF core and the capillary forms the new cladding [11]. In such a PL the binary information carried on the LP_{01} mode in different single-mode fibers (SMFs) is transfered to discrete modes in a FMF and vice versa. The corresponding physical transmission model is depicted in Fig. 2. The number of modes carried by the FMF depends on the geometric as well as the physical structure of the fiber and the operating wavelength. Subsequent to the transmission through a FMF of length ℓ, the modes are demultiplexed to multiple SMFs with an inversely arranged PL. In theory, lossless transitioning of the incident SMF modes to the respective modes carried in the FMF is feasible. For this purpose the number of modes carried by the FMF needs to be equal to the number of SMFs [11].

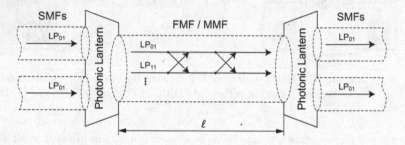

Fig. 2. Multi-mode MIMO transmission model using photonic lanterns for mode combining and splitting.

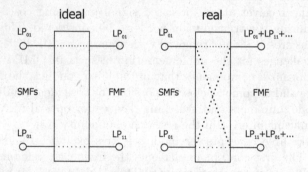

Fig. 3. Comparing the spatial mode transformation characteristic of a real PL with an ideal PL.

Considering the modal behavior, under ideal conditions the PL transfers the signals from each SMF to a discrete mode in the FMF, see Fig. 3. In contrast, the spatial intensity patterns measured at the output of a 6-port PL, compare Fig. 4, show that a real PL excites a combination of modes. This leads to crosstalk which is noticeable by the correlation of the six patterns. However, the measured patterns still differ to a certain extent and are therefore able to be used for an optical MIMO transmission.

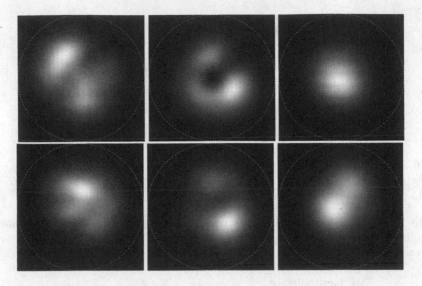

Fig. 4. Measured spatial intensity patterns at the output of the fusion type PL using different input SMFs at an operating wavelength of $\lambda = 1550$ nm; the dotted line represents the 30 μm FMF core diameter.

4   SMF to MMF Splices and Fusion Couplers for Optical MIMO

The use of SMF to MMF splices with a radial offset for mode-selective excitation and optical fusion couplers for mode MUX and DEMUX is a different concept which stands out due to its passive nature and simple manufacturing process. Figure 5 depicts the alignment of a SMF to a MMF with a radial offset δ. Since the physical dimensions do not allow simultaneous alignment of two SMFs to a MMF, the modal excitation is carried out in parallel and a fusion coupler subsequently combines the excited modes. For this concept the spatial intensity patterns are measured for a centric launch condition, i.e. $\delta = 0$ μm, and for a launch eccentricity of $\delta = 15$ μm. The measurements depicted in Fig. 6 show that the resulting dot and ring pattern are well-separated.

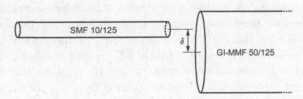

Fig. 5. Fiber core alignment of a SMF to MMF splice with a certain offset δ for mode-group-selective excitation.

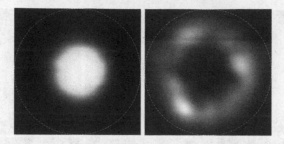

Fig. 6. Measured spatial intensity patterns as a function of the light launch position at an operating wavelength of $\lambda = 1550$ nm (left: eccentricity $\delta = 0$ μm, right: eccentricity $\delta = 15$ μm); the dotted line represents the 50 μm MMF core diameter.

Table 1. Insertion loss measurements when launching from different SMF inputs through a fusion type and photonic integrated circuit (PIC) type 6-port photonic lantern compared to a 2-port fusion coupler based system.

SMF input number	1	2	3	4	5	6
Fusion type PL insert. loss [dB]	6.7	6.7	4.2	4.1	7.0	4.1
PIC type PL insert. loss [dB]	1.7	2.2	1.5	2.2	2.0	1.7
Fusion coupler insert. loss [dB]	0.1	8.1	–	–	–	–

In addition to the intensity patterns, insertion losses are compared for the two optical MIMO concepts. The measured insertion losses for two types of 6-port PLs and a system consisting of offset splices and a fusion coupler are listed in Table 1. Contrary to expectations, the photonic integrated circuit (PIC) type 6-port photonic lantern outperforms the fusion type PL in terms of insertion loss. The fusion type 6-port PL shows quite a noticeable insertion loss and slight asymmetries between the different SMF inputs. Still, these asymmetries are relatively small when comparing to the insertion loss differences of an optical 2-port MIMO system based on offset SMF to MMF splices and fusion couplers. In such a system, choosing the centric launch condition mainly excites low order modes which do not couple into the opposing path in the fusion coupler since their electrical field is guided in the center of the fiber core, explaining the very low insertion loss at SMF input 1. In contrast, launching with $\delta = 15$ μm excites mainly higher order mode groups which have a broader electrical field distribution and therefore they couple partly into the opposing path of the fusion coupler. The other portion, which is at least 50% of the optical power, is not used. This explains the high insertion loss at SMF input number 2. Furthermore, extending a fusion coupler based system to 6-ports requires the concatenation of multiple 2-port systems which is accompanied by a significant insertion loss increase [14]. Therefore, in terms of insertion loss specifically for higher order optical MIMO systems the PL-based system is superior to the coupler based system.

5   Utilizing DMDs in Optical MIMO

The breakthrough of the DLP technology can be traced back to efforts made by Texas Instruments (TI) at the beginning of the eighties, more precisely to Larry J. Hornbeck. The heart of a DLP projector is the DMD, which was patented by TI in 1986. The DMD consists of thousand of small mirrors having sizes in micrometer domain. The micromirrors are synonymously referred as pixels. The principle of a DMD is quite simple: each mirror can be tilted such that a light source is reflected to either an optical output system or an absorber. Hence, each pixel can be switched into so called 'on'- and 'off'-states. This principle is adapted for OMIMO as depicted in Fig. 7.

Utilizing the property that each single mirror can be addressed to two opposite states, two independent sources can be arranged in front of the DLP such that the main output direction of both reflected laser beam patterns is equal for both sources. The light sources are simply two SMFs with collimating lenses attached to their end faces to widen the light into collimated laser beams. These beams are reflected by the MMA where mirrors in 'on'-state reflect only one source to the output direction, for the other source mirrors in 'off'-state do. In this output direction an optic focuses the reflected laser beams onto a MMF. Thus, the tilt pattern on the MMA performs SDM. A flexible solution for a parallel excitation of low and high order modes can be designed.

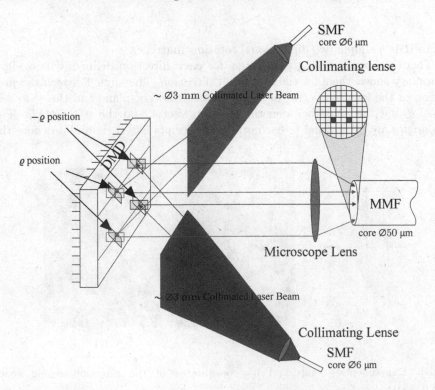

Fig. 7. DMD supported optical space division multiplexing (Source: [1]).

5.1   Definitions

This section defines in a first step two different coordinate systems: one aligned with the DLP, the other one with the setup as well as their mathematical connectedness. In a second step the coupling parameters are defined in the second space volume.

The whole mathematical description is made in the direction cosine space (DCS) [17] whose axes are orientated with the micromirror vertices. Figure 8 illustrates its orientation. The origin lies in the MMAs center. The tilt axes of each micromirror is parallel to $\alpha = -\beta$. This means in other words that the normal of each mirror lies parallel to the plane spanned by the γ-axis and the line $\alpha = \beta$. In the 'on'- or 'off'-state of a pixel the angle between the normal of the mirror and the γ-axis is either $+\varrho$ or $-\varrho$, respectively. The second DCS is motivated by the aim that the experimental setup is symmetrically related to the vertical plane on an optical breadboard as defined and depicted in Fig. 8(b) and (c). The DMD is rotated in the $\alpha'\beta'$-plane by ε such that each normal of a micromirror is parallel to the $\alpha'\gamma'$-plane. Hence, mirrors in 'on'-state can be used by one source, mirrors in 'off'-state by the other source. The two DCSs are connected by

$$\begin{pmatrix} \alpha' \\ \beta' \end{pmatrix} = \mathbf{R} \begin{pmatrix} \alpha \\ \beta \end{pmatrix} \tag{1}$$

and

$$\gamma' = \gamma, \tag{2}$$

where $\mathbf{R}$ is a simple two dimensional rotation matrix.

There are two coupling parameters for each direction defined, where Fig. 8 exemplary shows them for the first input direction. The angle between the projection of the location vector of a source onto the $\alpha'\gamma'$-plane and the γ'-axis is called θ and the angle between the location vector and the β'-axis is φ. The two angles are orthogonal to each other. Subscripts like i1, i2 and o denote the

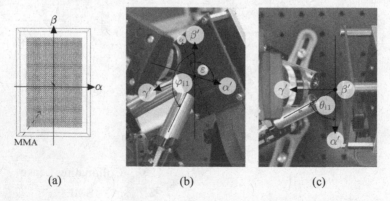

(a)   (b)   (c)

Fig. 8. Experimental setup and its coordinates of the direction cosine space (Source: [1]).

connection of a parameter to the first or second input or the output direction. By applying simple vector calculation as well as the connection between a Cartesian space and the DCS one can easily derive the association between coupling parameters and the DCS

$$\alpha' = \cos(\theta)\sin(\varphi) \tag{3}$$

$$\beta' = \cos(\varphi). \tag{4}$$

5.2 Diffraction Behaviour of the MMA

Due to the physical structure of the MMA, the DMD has to be considered as a two dimensional blazed grating. If the mirrors are not tilted, the MMA reacts as a common diffraction grating with the difference that the light is reflected instead of passing a two dimensional lattice. In the case of one dimension the macroscopic equation of diffraction is given by

$$\sin \xi_i \pm \sin \xi_o = m\frac{\lambda}{g}, \tag{5}$$

where ξ_i is the incident angle, ξ_o the output angle, λ the used wavelength and g the grating constant [4]. Note that the angles ξ are measured to the array normal, which is different to the definition of θ. The variable m gives the order of the grating which is an integer limited by physical possible directions. In the setup corresponding angles of zeroth order are given by

$$\theta_o = \pi - \theta_i \tag{6}$$

and

$$\varphi_o = \pi - \varphi_i. \tag{7}$$

In [6] the derivation of (5) to the appropriate DCS representation is presented. By extending these equations to the two dimensional case the grating behaviour can be described by

$$\alpha_o + \alpha_i = \left(m\frac{\lambda}{g}\right) \tag{8}$$

and

$$\beta_o + \beta_i = \left(n\frac{\lambda}{g}\right). \tag{9}$$

The transition from the macroscopic equation to the real intensity distribution of the reflected light has to be taken in order to find optimal coupling parameters. By neglecting the faceted profile of the MMA [7], i.e., the blazed structure, and by utilizing the same mathematical tools as in [6], the full intensity distribution is defined by

$$I_D(\alpha, \beta) = I_0 \left(\frac{\sin\left(P_\alpha \pi(g/\lambda)\,(\alpha - \alpha_o)\right)}{P_\alpha \sin\left(\pi(g/\lambda)\,(\alpha - \alpha_o)\right)} \right)^2$$

$$\left(\frac{\sin\left(P_\beta \pi(g/\lambda)\,(\beta - \beta_o)\right)}{P_\beta \sin\left(\pi(g/\lambda)\,(\beta - \beta_o)\right)} \right)^2. \tag{10}$$

The number of micromirrors (pixels) in α- and β-direction is denoted by P_α and P_β. Under the condition that (8) and (9) hold, (10) becomes the normalization constant I_D which are multiple global maxima.

By considering the profile of the MMA the blazed grated structure needs to be taken into account. Due to the symmetric setup the blazed behaviour influences the output parameter θ_o whereas the φ_o stays unchanged compared to (7). Due to the tilt of the mirror ϱ the angle $\theta_{o,b}$ becomes

$$\theta_{o,b} = \begin{cases} \pi - 2\varrho - \theta_i & \text{for } \varepsilon = -\pi/4 \\ \pi + 2\varrho - \theta_i & \text{for } \varepsilon = +3\pi/4 \,, \end{cases} \tag{11}$$

where the subscript o,b denotes the blazed output direction. From [10] it is known that the faceted profile creates a $\text{sinc}^2(\cdot)$-envelope on the intensity distribution (10) in each direction. By considering the rotation (1) and applying (3) to (11) to get the blazed parameters $\alpha_{o,b}$ and $\beta_{o,b}$ one ends up with

$$I(\alpha, \beta) = I_D(\alpha, \beta) \text{sinc}^2\left(\frac{s}{\lambda}(\alpha - \alpha_{o,b})\right)$$
$$\text{sinc}^2\left(\frac{s}{\lambda}(\beta - \beta_{o,b})\right) , \tag{12}$$

being the complete description of the intensity distribution of the MMA reflected laser beam, where s is the length of an edge of a micromirror.

5.3   Optimal Conditions for Optical MIMO Coupling

Using this equation one can define an optimization program whose result gives the coupling parameters one has to apply in the experimental setup. A simplified program is evaluated as follows:

$$(\theta_{i1}, \varphi_{i1}) = \underset{\substack{0 < \theta_{i1} < \pi/2 \\ \pi/2 < \varphi_{i1} < \pi}}{\arg\max} \ \underset{\substack{\alpha = 0 \\ \beta \\ \varrho = +\pi/15 \\ \varepsilon = -\pi/4}}{\max} \ I(\alpha, \beta). \tag{13}$$

This program considers the symmetric setup achieved by the DMD rotation by ε. The optimization returns the coupling parameters of the first source i1. Note that $\alpha = 0$ assumes $\theta_o = \pi$. The missing parameters of the second source i2 as well as for the output o are defined by the symmetry

$$\theta_{i2} = \pi - \theta_{i1} \tag{14}$$
$$\varphi_{i2} = \varphi_{i1} \tag{15}$$
$$\varphi_o = \pi - \varphi_{i1} \,. \tag{16}$$

However, the program (13) is of highly non-convex structure. For a few selected wavelengths the found results were obtained by exhaustive searches over a predefined subset of optimization parameters. The subset is chosen to $61/180 \cdot \pi \leq \theta_{i1} \leq 71/180 \cdot \pi$ and $0/180 \cdot \pi \leq \varphi_{i1} \leq 90/180 \cdot \pi$ with steps of

Table 2. Optimal coupling parameters of two sources arranged in front of the DLP (Source: [1]).

λ	$\varphi_{i1/i2} \cdot 180/\pi$	$\theta_{i1} \cdot 180/\pi$	$\theta_{i2} \cdot 180/\pi$
675 nm	36.025	66.025	113.975
778 nm	44.600	65.650	114.350
1326 nm	38.000	66.375	113.625
1576 nm	46.125	66.000	114.000

$0.025/180 \cdot \pi$ in each direction. The results are given in Table 2. The coupling loss at this point, which is defined by the ratio between the energy located within output direction and its -3 dB cut-off and the overall energy, for the selected wavelength is $L_{DMD} \approx -1.27$ dB. This loss neglects the window attached in front of the MMA, which has to be passed twice, as well as the reflectivity of the mirrors. However, by intuition the angles θ_{i1} and θ_{i2} are around $\pi \pm 2\varrho$ which is expected by (11) because the output direction is required to be $\theta_o = \pi$. By applying this condition to the program (13) an evaluation was made using a wider range of wavelengths. To these results regressions on the previously sorted sets were made assuming analytic functions of quadratic form

$$
\begin{aligned}
\lambda &= f_j(\theta_{i1} = 11/30 \cdot \pi, \varphi_i) \\
&= \left[\lambda_m \left(\varphi_{i1} - \pi/2 \right)^2 + \lambda_o \right] \cdot 10^{-9} .
\end{aligned}
\tag{17}
$$

The results for the regression parameters λ_m and λ_o are given in Table 3. The family of curves is given in Fig. 9.

With this result one can directly determine optimal coupling parameters for an operating wavelength. The choice, which curve has to be chosen, is a trade off between stability around this operating wavelength, e.g., for wavelength division multiplexing systems, and the mechanical stability of the setup. The more flat the slope of the curve in a chosen working point, the higher is the robustness of the

Table 3. Analytic functions of shape (17) to obtain optimal coupling parameters using the DLP (Source: [1]).

j	λ_m[nm]	λ_o[nm]
1	-311.0	624.5
2	-354.9	728.1
3	-415.1	872.3
4	-507.5	1088.0
5	-666.7	1448.0
6	-994.0	2167.0
7	-1604.0	3886.0

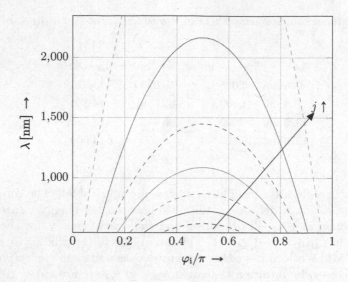

Fig. 9. Illustration of Table 3 (Source: [1]).

mechanical setup against variations of the positioning. In contrast, the steeper the curve the higher is the stability against wavelength variations around this point.

5.4   Realization and Results

Figure 10 shows the first version of the experimental setup. Two collimating lenses ① widen the signal carrying light at the end of two SMFs to two collimated laser beams. These two beams are reflected at the DLP ②, where a previously assigned bit map determines the tilt pattern of the underlying MMA. This consequently decides which source later activates low and which source high

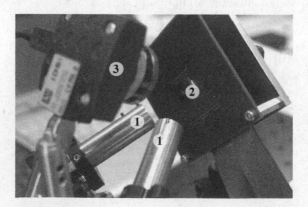

Fig. 10. Experimental setup (Source: [1]).

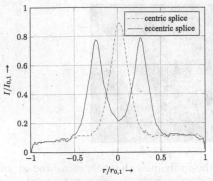 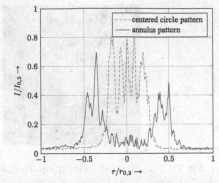

(a) Mode field pattern realized by a fusion coupler with center and offset launch condition

(b) Measured DLP-controlled mode field pattern

Fig. 11. Cut through light intensity measurements (Source: [1]).

order modes, respectively. The camera UI-1240LE ③ measures the reflected laser beam pattern in the main output direction, which will be later replaced by an optic focusing the light pattern onto an attached MMF.

The first proof of concept has been made using visible light with wavelength $\lambda = 675$ nm. Therefore, the camera gives a more detailed and intuitive insight into the mechanical structure and its optimization parameters. The setup has two orthogonal degrees of freedom for each source as previously mentioned: $\theta_{i1/i2}$ and $\varphi_{i1/i2}$. As the experiment is realized using standard optical adjustment components, the parameters, which can be varied, are not orthogonalized to each other. The adjustment becomes an iterative process, which is easier achievable for visible light. The optimized parameters are $\varphi_{i1} = \varphi_{i2} \approx 0.62\pi$, $\theta_{i1} \approx 0.37\pi$ and $\theta_{i2} \approx 0.63\pi$ which are chosen from Table 3 curve $j = 2$.

The DLP was programmed with a bitmap with an inner circle of ones and zeros around this circle. Hence, one source is seen as a circle on the MMA from the camera, the other one as the corresponding annulus. For the evaluation process the camera took pictures from each source while the parallel source was switched off. Through these pictures a vertical cut was taken to look at the light intensity as a function of the radius. By looking at the orthogonality of the curves generated by the different sources the capability of the SDM setup is demonstrated. To have a better reference, these curves are compared to light intensity distributions measured at the end surface of a 1.4 km MMF. The different distributions are obtained by splices of SMFs to MMFs with centered and offset launching conditions and a subsequent fusion coupler for the mode combining process into that MMF as used in the OMIMO testbed in [13]. Figure 11(a) and (b) show the field pattern of the measurements. Figure 11(a) shows the intensity distribution over a vertical cut through a surface of a MMF. The dashed curve is the distribution produced by a centric splice as described and the solid curve produced by an 18 μm eccentric splice. The graph shows

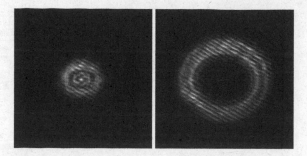

Fig. 12. DLP-controlled intensity patterns of the individual channels measured at an operating wavelength of 675 nm (left: centered circle pattern, right: annulus pattern); measured at Fraunhofer IZM Berlin.

well separated low and high order modes as expected. In contrast to Fig. 11(a), Fig. 11(b) represents vertical cut through pictures acquired by the camera. For the dashed curve a centered circle pattern is set to the DLP, for the solid curve the corresponding annulus. Note that the parameters $I_{0,1/0,2}$ as well as $r_{0,1/0,2}$ are normalizing constants taken from the measured bit map acquired by different sensors, which only allows a conclusion about relative power distribution within one graph rather than absolute power distribution or a comparison between both graphs with respect to the measured power.

The measured DLP intensity distributions are depicted in Fig. 12, which show disturbance by fringes. They originate from a non-optimal anti-reflection coating of the protection window attached to the DLP. An additional difficulty appears if one compares the left and right maximum of the annulus which are different in their intensities. The differences are related to the mechanical setup which was not able to match the optimal coupling conditions as described in Sect. 5.3, perfectly. Nevertheless, a clear separation of both curves can be seen as good as in Fig. 11(a). This meets the requirement such that the inner source excites low order modes and the outer source high order modes when both sources are concurrently stimulated and the reflected pattern is focused onto a MMF. An advantage of the mode coupling technique utilizing the DLP compared to the splices concatenated with a fusion coupler is that the ratio between the inner circle and the outer one can be freely chosen by the tilt pattern of the MMA and is not fixed. Moreover, the achievable theoretical power loss of $L_{DLP} \approx -1.27$ dB of our setup is far less than $L_{SLM} \approx -3$ dB for a two step serial concatenation of SLMs.

6   Conclusion

In this work different components have been analyzed with respect to their optical MIMO suitability. SMF to MMF splices with radial offsets have shown to be a simple method for mode-selective excitation. However, the necessity for an extra fusion coupler or multiple concatenated couplers so as to combine the excited modes into a MMF significantly attenuates the higher order mode path. As an alternative photonic lanterns as passive components offer low insertion losses and are able to conduct the mode-selective excitation and multiplexing task in a single step. The focus of this work is on the use of DMD for mode-selective excitation and multiplexing. This includes the derivation of the optimal coupling conditions and its practical implementation. The intensity patterns measured with visible light show the potential of DMDs for optical MIMO applications.

Acknowledgements. This work has been funded by the German Ministry of Education and Research (No. 03FH016PX3).

References

1. Ahrens, A., Lochmann, S., Bartmann, P.: Digital mirror devices for mode selective excitation in multimode fibers. In: Proceedings of the 13th International Joint Conference on e-Business and Telecommunications - Volume 3: OPTICS, pp. 19–24 (2016)
2. Bartmann, P., Lochmann, S., Ahrens, A.: Utilizing the DLP1700 as a coupling device for optical MIMO transmission. In: ITG-Fachbericht 257: Photonische Netze, pp. 122–127. VDE VERLAG GmbH, Leipzig, Germany, 07–08 May 2015
3. Berdagué, S., Facq, P.: Mode division multiplexing in optical fibers. Appl. Opt. **21**(11), 1950–1955 (1982)
4. Goodman, J.W.: Introduction to Fourier Optics, 2nd edn. The McGraw-Hill Companies Inc., New York City (2005)
5. Gu, R.Y., Ip, E., Li, M.J., Huang, Y.K., Kahn, J.M.: Experimental demonstration of a spatial light modulator few-mode fiber switch for space-division multiplexing. In: Frontiers in Optics 2013 Postdeadline. Optical Society of America (2013)
6. Harvey, J.E., Vernold, C.L.: Description of diffraction grating behavior in direction cosine space. Appl. Opt. **37**(34), 8158–8159 (1998)
7. Hayat, G.S.: Handbook of Diffraction Gratings - Ruled and Holographic. JOBIN-YVON S.A
8. Hsu, R., Tarighat, A., Shah, A., Sayed, A., Jalali, B.: Capacity enhancement in coherent optical MIMO (COMIMO) multimode fiber links. IEEE Commun. Lett. **10**(3), 195–197 (2006)
9. Hsu, R.C.J., Shah, A., Jalali, B.: Coherent optical multiple-input multiple-output communication. IEICE Electron. Expr. **1**(13), 392–397 (2004)
10. Texas Instruments: Using lasers with DLP DMD technology. Technical report, Texas Instruments, September 2008
11. Leon-Saval, S.G., Argyros, A., Bland-Hawthorn, J.: Photonic lanterns. Nanophotonics **2**, 429–440 (2013)
12. Ryf, R., Fontaine, N.K., Mestre, M.A., Randel, S., Palou, X., Bolle, C., Gnauck, A.H., Chandrasekhar, S., Liu, X., Guan, B., Essiambre, R.J., Winzer, P.J., Leon-Saval, S., Bland-Hawthorn, J., Delbue, R., Pupalaikis, P., Sureka, A., Sun, Y., Grüner-Nielsen, L., Jensen, R.V., Lingle, R.: 12 × 12 MIMO transmission over 130-km few-mode fiber. In: Frontiers in Optics 2012/Laser Science XXVIII, p. FW6C.4. Optical Society of America (2012)
13. Sandmann, A., Ahrens, A., Lochmann, S.: Experimental description of multimode MIMO channels utilizing optical couplers. In: ITG-Fachbericht 248: Photonische Netze, pp. 125–130. VDE VERLAG GmbH, Leipzig, Germany, 05–06 May 2014

14. Sandmann, A., Ahrens, A., Lochmann, S.: Experimental evaluation of a (4 x 4) multi-mode MIMO system utilizing customized optical fusion couplers. In: ITG-Fachbericht 264: Photonische Netze, pp. 101–105. VDE VERLAG GmbH, Leipzig, Germany, 12–13 May 2016

15. Schollmann, S., Schrammar, N., Rosenkranz, W.: Experimental realisation of 3 × 3 MIMO system with mode group diversity multiplexing limited by modal noise. In: Conference on Optical Fiber communication/National Fiber Optic Engineers Conference, 2008. OFC/NFOEC 2008, pp. 1–3, February 2008

16. Shah, A., Hsu, R., Tarighat, A., Sayed, A., Jalali, B.: Coherent optical MIMO (COMIMO). J. Lightwave Technol. **23**(8), 2410–2419 (2005)

17. Tang, K.T.: Mathematical Methods for Engineers and Scientists 2. Springer, Berlin (2007)

18. Winzer, P.J., Foschini, G.J.: Optical MIMO-SDM system capacities. Opt. Fiber Commun. Conf. Exhib. (OFC) **2014**, 1–3 (2014)

19. Yoder, L.A., Duncan, W.M., Koontz, E.M., So, J., Bartlett, T.A., Lee, B.L., Sawyers, B.D., Powell, D., Rancuret, P.: DLP technolgy: applications in optical networking. SPI Proc. **4457**, 54–61 (2001)

Security and Cryptography

Hardware Implementation of HS1-SIV

Sergei Volokitin$^{(\boxtimes)}$ and Gerben Geltink

Institute for Computing and Information Sciences, Radboud University,
Nijmegen, The Netherlands
volokitinss@gmail.com, g.geltink@gmail.com

Abstract. Design of the hardware implementation of the CAESAR competition second round candidate, HS1-SIV, with regular cipher parameter settings is described in this paper. Given implementation of HS1-SIV cipher was developed in such a way to be conforming to the specification of the authenticated cipher as well as a hardware API. The implemented API is conforming to the specifications of the GMU Hardware API for authenticated ciphers. The VHDL implementation was synthesized using Xilinx XST High Level Synthesis for the target device Xilinx Virtex-7. We achieved a throughput over 120 Mbit/s utilizing area of 103,214 LUTs for the cipher implementation with the data length of the message and the associated data set at 64 bytes and the length of the key set at 32 bytes. Based on the performance results obtained hardware API overhead was calculated which is equal to 8% for 8-byte data length and 15% for 2048-byte data length when compared to the cipher-core.

Keywords: HS1-SIV · CAESAR · Authenticated encryption · FPGA · VHDL

1 Introduction

Due to the reason that encryption algorithms only provide confidentiality of the encrypted data, real life applications of encryption require the use of additional mechanisms to provide integrity and authenticity of messages. Although it is possible to build an authenticated encryption scheme using an encryption algorithm and a message authentication code (MAC), such an approach is often less computationally efficient. Authenticated encryption schemes are designed to perform encryption of the message and provide a message authentication code. Additionally, Authenticated encryption with associated data (AEAD) not only provides an authentication code of the secret message but also authenticates the associated data which is often a header.

As part of the second round of the Competition for Authenticated Encryption: Security, Applicability, and Robustness (CAESAR), candidates have to submit a hardware implementation of their authenticated cipher [1]. The competition was announced in 2013 at the Early Symmetric Crypto workshop in Mondorf-les-Bains, Luxembourg. Similarly to AES [2], eSTREAM [3], SHA-3

© Springer International Publishing AG 2017
M.S. Obaidat (Ed): ICETE 2016, CCIS 764, pp. 179–194, 2017.
https://doi.org/10.1007/978-3-319-67876-4_9

(Keccak [4]) and PHC (Argon2 [5]), CAESAR seeks to select a portfolio of algorithms which most likely will include a number of encryption algorithms. With this portfolio, the confidence in the security, applicability and robustness of authenticated encryption ciphers will be improved.

Although functional software requirements have been set for the CAESAR candidates, details of the hardware Application Programming Interface (API) have not yet been specified. However, the GMU Hardware API, which was introduced to provide a basis for benchmarking the hardware implementations of the CAESAR candidates, is considered as a standard amongst the hardware implementers of the CAESAR candidates [6]. This API provides specifications for the interface (AEAD-core) of the authenticated cipher-core as well as the communication protocol needed.

Implementing HS1-SIV is not trivial due to a number of reasons. First, HS1-SIV is designed to be efficient on 32-bit architectures, which means that the numerous amount of multiplications and modulo operations have to be implemented thoughtfully. Second, the computation of the hashes require the entire input message, which means that the architecture needs to be implemented such that these continuous computations are supported.

We describe the first effort to implement HS1-SIV [7] with regular security parameter settings (hereafter called HS1-SIV-MED) on a Field Programmable Gate Array (FPGA). Regular security settings of the cipher include:

- the number of bytes used by the hashing algorithm, which is equal to 64 bytes;
- the collision level of the hashing algorithm, which is equal to 4 bytes;
- the number of internal rounds of the steam cipher, which is equal to 12 bytes;
- the byte length of synthetic IV, which is equal to 16 bytes.

The structure of the paper is as follows. In Sect. 2, we describe the authenticated encryption cipher HS1-SIV-MED and its subroutines. Section 4 describes the related work. Section 5 describes our contributions. In Sect. 6, we describe the hardware design of the HS1-SIV-MED cipher-core. In Sect. 7, we present the performance results of the implementation. Section 8 describes some topics for future research. And finally, Sect. 9 concludes the paper.

2   HS1-SIV

HS1-SIV is an abbreviation for "Hash-Stream 1 - Synthetic Initialization Vector". As the name suggests the algorithm of HS1-SIV uses HS1 as a Pseudo-Random Function (PRF) to provide deterministic authenticated encryption with Rogaway and Shrimpton's SIV mode [8]. Specifically, HS1-SIV is composed of six subroutines: HS1-SIV-Encrypt, HS1-SIV-Decrypt, HS1, HS1-Hash, HS1-Subkeygen and ChaCha. This section describes these subroutines for HS1-SIV-MED using Python pseudocode. The subroutines in the pseudocode contain comments about the required inputs and provided outputs.

2.1   HS1-SIV-Encrypt

HS1-SIV-Encrypt is the main algorithm which encrypts a message using a key, an initialization vector and associated data. The algorithm uses the HS1 and HS1-Subkeygen subroutines [9].

```
def HS1_SIV_ENCRYPT(K, M, A, N):
# K, a list containing up to 32 bytes
# M, A, a list containing up to 2**64 bytes
# N, a list containing 12 bytes
# T, a list of 16 bytes
# C, a list of len(M) bytes
    k = HS1_SUBKEYGEN(K)
    A_ = pad(64,A)
    M_ = pad(16,M)
    A_len = pad(8,[len(A)])
    M_len = pad(8,[len(M)])
    M_prime = (A_ + M_ + A_len + M_len)
    T = HS1(k, M_prime, N, 16)
    C_ = HS1(k,T,N,64+len(M))[64:64+len(M)]
    C = map(xor, M, C_)
    return (T,C)
```

2.2   HS1-SIV-Decrypt

HS1-SIV-Decrypt is the main algorithm which can decrypt a cipher-text using a key, an initialization vector, an authenticator for the associated data and the associated data itself. The algorithm uses the HS1 and the HS1-Subkeygen subroutines [9].

```
def HS1_SIV_DECRYPT(K, (T,C), A, N):
# K, a list containing up to 32 bytes
# T, a list of 16 bytes
# C, A, a list containing up to 2**64 bytes
# N, a list containing 12 bytes
# M, a list of len(C) bytes
    k = HS1_SUBKEYGEN(K)
    M_ = HS1(k,T,N,64+len(C))[64:64+len(C)]
    M = map(xor, C, M_)
    A_ = pad(64, A)
    M_ = pad(16, M)
    A_len = pad(8, [len(A)])
    M_len = pad(8, [len(M)])
    M_prime = A_ + M_ + A_len + M_len
    T_prime = HS1(k, M_prime, N, 16)
    if T == T_prime:
        return M
    else:
        return []
```

2.3 HS1

HS1 is the algorithm for HS1-SIV's PRF [9], it uses four results from HS1-Hash to supply as a key for ChaCha [10].

```
def HS1(k, M, N, y):
# k, a list [K_S, k_N, k_P] containing
#   K_S, a list of 32 bytes
#   k_N, is a list of 28 integers
#   k_N, is a list of 4 integers
# M, a list containing any number of bytes
# N, a list containing 12 bytes
# y, an integer
    K_S = k[0]
    k_N = k[1]
    k_P = k[2]
    a = []
    s = [0x00]*y
    for i in range(4):
        a += HS1_HASH(k_N[4*i:4*i+16],k_P[i],M)
    a = pad(32, a)
    key = map(xor, a, K_S)
    Y = CHACHA(12, key, 0, N, s)
    return Y
```

2.4 HS1-Hash

HS1-Hash is the subroutine to produce the hash of a message using several sub-keys produced by HS1-Subkeygen. It also uses the NH-function in order to produce NH hashes [9].

```
def HS1_HASH(k_N, k_P, M):
# k_N, a list of 16 integers
# k_P, an integer
# M, a list containing any number of bytes
# Y, a list of 8 bytes
    n = int(max(math.ceil(len(M)/(64.0)),1))
    h = k_P**n
    for i in range(n):
        M_i = M[i*64:i*64 + 64]
        m_i = toInts(4, pad(16,M_i))
        a_i =(NH(k_N,m_i)+(len(M_i)%16))%2**60
        h += (a_i * k_P ** (n - i - 1))
        h %= (2**61-1)
        Y = toStr(8,h)
    return Y

def NH(v1, v2):
# v1, v2 a list of a multiple of 4 integers
    n = min(len(v1), len(v2))
```

```
res = 0
for i in range(1, n/4+1):
    res += (
          ((v1[4*i-4]+v2[4*i-4]) % 2**32) *
          ((v1[4*i-2]+v2[4*i-2]) % 2**32) +
          ((v1[4*i-3]+v2[4*i-3]) % 2**32) *
          ((v1[4*i-1]+v2[4*i-1]) % 2**32)
          )
return res % 2**64
```

2.5   HS1-Subkeygen

HS1-Subkeygen is the subroutine to produce the sub-keys, it uses the ChaCha subroutine [9].

```
def HS1_SUBKEYGEN(K):
# K, a list containing up to 32 bytes
# k, a list [K_S, k_N, k_P] containing
#   K_S, a list of 32 bytes
#   k_N, is a list of 28 integers
#   k_N, is a list of 4 integers
    K_ = K
    while len(K_) < 32:
        K_ += K_
    K_prime = K_[:32]
    N = (
        [len(K), 0x00, 0x10, 0x00] +
        [0x0c, 0x04, 0x40] + [0x00] * 5
        )
    T = CHACHA(12, K_prime, 0, N, [0x00]*152)
    K_S = T[:32]
    k_N = toInts(4,T[32:128])
    k_P_ = toInts(8,T[128:152]
    m = 2**60
    k_P = map(mod, k_P_, [m, m, m, m])
    k = (K_S, k_N, k_P)
    return k
```

2.6   ChaCha

ChaCha is HS1-SIV's stream cipher to encrypt intermediate results [9]. For details on the setState, round and addStates we encourage the reader to consult [11].

```
def CHACHA(r, K, b, N, M):
# r, b, an integer
# K, a list of 32 bytes
# N, a list of 12 bytes
# M, a list containing any number of bytes
```

```
Y = []
n = int(max(math.ceil(len(M)/64.0),1))
for j in range(n):
    s = setState(K, N, b)
    b += 1
    ws = s[:]
    for i in range(r/2):
        ws = round(ws)
    state = addStates(s, ws)
    Y += serialize(s)
Y = map(xor,Y[0:len(M)],M)
return Y
```

3 API

The hardware API consists of the interface of the cipher-core (AEAD) as well as the communication protocol. Both of them will be described in this section.

The 64-bit AEAD implemented uses the HS1-SIV-MED cipher-core component and a FIFO component for storing the associated data (apart from several intermediate signals and registers). The communication protocol of the AEAD is realized using a finite state machine.

Figure 1 illustrates the 64-bit data format of the public data input and data output for encryption. Although it is not specified in the API, we set the TAG at the end of the cipher-text of the decryption data format. Also note that because we implemented a 64-bit AEAD, the NPUB occupies two segments (12 bytes) and the TAG occupies two segments (16 bytes). Here, the AD and MESSAGE (and thus also the cipher-text) are of maximum 8 bytes. It is possible to load larger AD and MESSAGE, simply cut these in chucks of 8 bytes and load them sequentially. Because of the cipher, larger MESSAGE will result in more segments for the cipher-text at the data output.

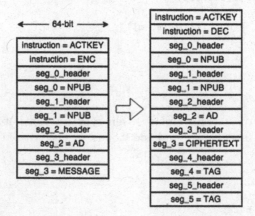

Fig. 1. 64-bit data format of public data input (pdi, left) and data output (do, right) for encryption.

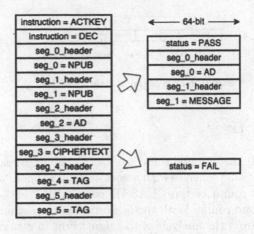

Fig. 2. 64-bit data format of public data input (`pdi`, left) and data output (`do`, right) for decryption.

Fig. 3. 64-bit data format of secret data input (`sdi`).

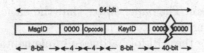

Fig. 4. 64-bit instruction/status format.

Figure 2 illustrates the data format of the public data input and data output for decryption. Also here, the `TAG` is set at the end of the `cipher-text` and the `NPUB` and `TAG` both occupy both segments. The result of the decryption can either pass or fail. In case of a pass, the `AD` and `MESSAGE` are being unloaded.

Figure 3 illustrates the secret data input of the key used when the instruction `ACTKEY` is set in the encryption or decryption. Once the key has been loaded, the encryption or decryption can continue to load data.

Figure 4 illustrates the 64-bit instruction format and status format. Our AEAD does not do checks on the `MsgID` and `KeyID`, but these can be used by testers to trace segments. Hence, only the `Opcode` (or the `Status` for the status format) is being checked.

Figure 5 illustrates the 64-bit segment header format. Also here, the `MsgID` is not being used. As specified in the GMU Hardware API, the first four bits of the `Info` contain the `SegType`, the penultimate bit contains the `EOI` bit and the last bit contains the `EOT` bit. Also, because our AEAD is 64-bit (8-byte), the `SegLen` only needs to be 4-bits.

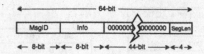

Fig. 5. 64-bit segment header format.

4   Related Work

As mentioned in the introduction there is a lot of ongoing research in the area of authenticated encryption schemes with associated data. There were 57 submitted ciphers in the first round of the CEASAR competition and 29 of them were selected for the second round. With the beginning of the second round the focus of research shifted from the analysis of the algorithms in general to the study of hardware and software implementations and their optimizations.

In a recent paper [12] a number of hardware implementations of CAESAR candidate ciphers were optimized and their performance was analyzed. The paper focuses on implementation and optimization of four CAESAR candidates, namely AES-OTR, SILC, AES-COPA and POET. In the results section we compare the performance of these ciphers with our performance.

One paper [13] presents ICEPOLE, a high-speed hardware-oriented authenticated encryption algorithm which also made it to the second round of the CAESAR competition. The algorithm was designed initially to be efficient when implemented on hardware. The paper states that the basic iterative architecture reaches 41 Gbit/s throughput.

The paper describing the API for hardware implementations [6] also presents the performance results and API overhead for eight CAESAR candidates. This presented data will be discussed in details in the results section.

Although there is a lot of research in the area of hardware implementations of authenticated encryption algorithms there are no published results on HS1-SIV implementations and its optimizations.

5   Contribution

The main contribution of this paper is presenting the first effort to implement HS1-SIV with regular parameter settings including an API on a FPGA such that it can be used as a reference implementation in further research. To our best knowledge, there are no other hardware implementations of HS1-SIV yet.

6   Design

This section describes the hardware design of HS1-SIV-MED. All hardware descriptions are written in VHSIC Hardware Description Language (VHDL) and synthesized using Xilinx ISE 14.7.

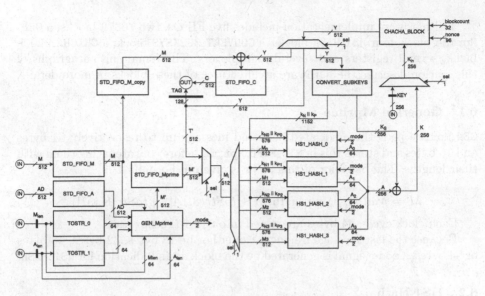

Fig. 6. Hardware architecture of HS1-HS1-MED. $\oplus$ denotes a bitwise XOR [9].

We implemented HS1-SIV-MED using the hardware architecture illustrated in Fig. 6 and a state-machine. For clarification purposes of this paper, the figure only illustrates the general outline of the architecture. That means that the selection signals (`sel`), `blockcount`, `nonce` and `mode` signals are controlled by the state-machine. Also, in the architecture, `IN` and `OUT` denotes that signals communicate through the `IO` buffers of HS1-SIV-MED. Apart from these signals and the standard clock and reset signal, the implementation acts on an input instruction signal indicating the kind of data that is on the input, an input signal indicating encryption or decryption and an output signal indicating that the encryption or decryption is finished. The block also contains a generic which specifies the `MAX_DATA_SIZE` of either the message/cipher-text or the associated data which is needed to reserve memory for the FIFOs.

Upon encryption the state-machine first loads the message, the associated data, the nonce and the key, before computing the sub-keys. Then, using `GEN_Mprime`, the algorithm pads and stores the associated data, the message and both their lengths in the `Mprime` FIFO. `GEN_Mprime` also produces a `mode` signal which indicates the amount of data of the last 64 byte block in `Mprime` (this is needed for `HS1_HASH`). Following, the algorithm computes the tag using `Mprime` and stores it in a register. When the tag is computed, the cipher-text is produced using this tag and stored in the `C` FIFO. Finally, the cipher-text and the tag are ready to be unloaded.

Upon decryption, all previously mentioned inputs and the tag are loaded before the sub-keys are computed. Then, the cipher-text is being decrypted and stored in the `C` FIFO. Following, the tag is being computed using the resulting decrypted cipher-text and compared to the loaded tag. If the computed tag is equal to the loaded tag, the resulting decrypted cipher-text is ready to be unloaded.

The hardware implementation includes five FIFOs, two TOSTR blocks, a GEN_Mprime block, four HS1_HASH blocks, a CONVERT_SUBKEYS block, a CHACHA_BLOCK block, several registers and several multiplexers. The remaining paragraphs of this section describe the hardware architectures of these blocks in more detail.

6.1 Generate Mprime

GEN_Mprime pads the associated data and message up to respectively 64 bytes and 16 bytes and stores this in STD_FIFO_Mprime before concatenating them with their lengths. The behavior of this block is given in Formula 1 [9].

$$M' = pad(64, A) \parallel pad(16, M) \parallel toStr(8, |A|) \parallel toStr(8, |M|) \tag{1}$$

Each clock cycle, 64 bytes are stored into STD_FIFO_Mprime.

Because the last message fragment can either be 16 bytes, 32 bytes, 48 bytes or 64 bytes, a mode signal is generated by the block as an indication for HS1_HASH.

6.2 HS1 Hash

Figure 7 illustrates the hardware architecture of HS1_HASH. The HS1 hash block implements the hashing functionality of the cipher. With regular parameter settings for HS1-SIV, HS1 hash acts on message fragments of 64 bytes up to the last message fragment. Hence, our input message length for the HS1 hash block is 64 bytes. The last message fragment can either be 16 bytes, 32 bytes, 48 bytes or 64 bytes. Depending on which of these four modes the HS1 hash block operates, the results of the NH function blocks are added up.

Also note that the HS1 hash block modifies the intermediate result **h** on each clock/input until the block is being reset again.

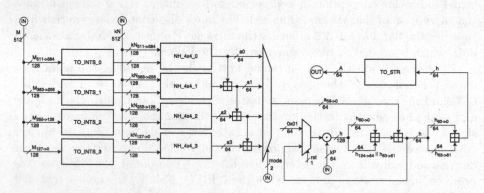

Fig. 7. Hardware architecture of HS1_HASH. $v_{n->m}$ denotes bits n (MSB) to m (LSB) of v where $n > m$ and $0 \leq n, m < |v|$ (if $n + m < |v| - 1$ then v is padded with zeros at the MSB), $\boxplus$ denotes an addition in $GF(2^{64})$ and $\odot$ denotes a multiplication in $GF(2^{128})$ [9].

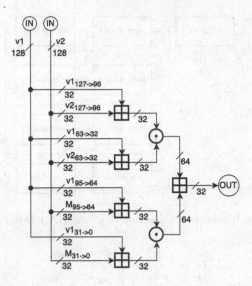

Fig. 8. Hardware architecture of the NH (4×4) function. $v_{n->m}$ denotes bits n (MSB) to m (LSB) of v where $n > m$ and $0 \leq n, m < n_{max}, m_{max}$, ⊞ denotes an addition in $GF(2^{32})$ and ⊙ denotes a multiplication in $GF(2^{64})$ [9].

NH Function. Figure 8 shows the hardware architecture of NH_4x4. Because there are four different message fragment lengths, it is convenient to split the NH function block into four blocks that each act on two vectors of four 4-byte integers (NH_4x4). Depending on the mode of HS1 hash, the result of all four, the first three or the first two NH function blocks are added up and returned or the result of the first NH function block is returned.

6.3   Convert Subkeys

The convert sub-keys block is needed to convert the ChaCha output into usable sub-keys. For this, the implementation uses a block to convert the streams into 4-byte little-endian integers (for kN) and 8-byte little-endian integers (for kP).

6.4   ChaCha Block

The hardware architecture of the ChaCha block is illustrated in Fig. 9. CHACHA_BLOCK has four different sub-blocks, SET_STATE, INNERBLOCK, ADD_STATES and SERIALIZE.

Setstate. CHACHA_SETSTATE rewires the key, block-count and nonce into a signal of 512 bits that represents the ChaCha state. This 512-bit state is composed of 16 words of 32 bit long. The ChaCha state is initialized as follows:

- The first four words (indexed 0–3) are constants: 0x61707865, 0x3320646e, 0x79622d32, 0x6b206574.

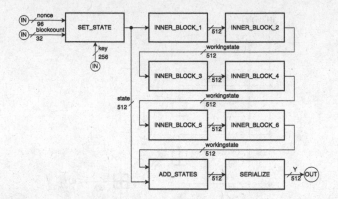

Fig. 9. Hardware architecture of CHACHA_BLOCK [9].

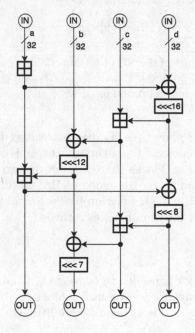

Fig. 10. Hardware architecture of the ChaCha quarter-round. $\oplus$ denotes a bitwise XOR, $\boxplus$ denotes an addition in $GF(2^{64})$ $\boxed{<<<n}$ denotes a left-rotation over n bits [9].

- The next eight words (indexed 4–11) are taken from the 256-bit key by reading the bytes in little-endian order, in 4-byte chunks.
- Word 12 is a block counter.
- Words 13–15 are a nonce. The 13th word is the first 32 bits of the input nonce taken as a little-endian integer, while the 15th word is the last 32 bits.

Innerblock. CHACHA_INNERBLOCK contains the logic for two ChaCha rounds. As a result, the ChaCha block contains six of these blocks (HS1-SIV-MED has 12

ChaCha rounds). The inner block contains four quarter-round blocks that represent the 'column' ChaCha round and four quarter-round blocks that represent the 'diagonal' ChaCha round. The architecture of the quarter-round is depicted in Fig. 10. Here, depending on the round, a, b, c and d are 32-bit words drawn from the ChaCha state.

Addstates. CHACHA_ADDSTATES contains the logic to add the working state to the current state. For this, the input words are added up with the output words from the working state.

Serialize. CHACHA_SERIALIZE contains the logic to return the serialized output of the ChaCha block. For this, the words are sequenced one-by-one in little-endian order.

7   Results

This section describes the analysis of the performance of HS1-SIV-MED's AEAD-core. Table 1 shows the performance results of HS1-SIV-MED's AEAD-core using Xilinx XST High Level Synthesis (HLS) on a Virtex-7 device. These results have been achieved by restricting the use of Block RAM and DSP. Moreover, the optimization goal is set on Area and the optimization effort on Normal. The key length was fixed to 32 bytes. We found out that the area overhead of the AEAD-core is between 8% (8-byte data length) and 15% (2048-byte data length) in comparison to the cipher-core.

Table 1. Performance results of HS1-SIV-MED's AEAD-core using Xilinx XST HLS on a Virtex-7 device [9].

Data length [bytes]	Area [LUT]	Throughput [Mbit/s]	Throughput/Area [(Kbit/s)/LUT]
8	100,397	28.039	0.279
16	100,925	50.539	0.501
32	101,004	84.406	0.836
64	103,214	122.200	1.184
128	103,967	156.697	1.507
256	107,325	182.449	1.700
512	111,919	198.784	1.776
1024	122,813	208.100	1.694
2048	155,666	213.093	1.369

In the table, **Data length** corresponds to both the length of the associated data as well as the length of the message. The difference in area is mainly because of the memory that needs to be reserved for the FIFOs.

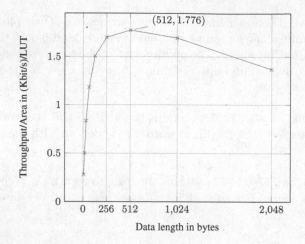

Fig. 11. Performance results of the throughput-to-area ratio of HS1-SIV-MED's AEAD-core using Xilinx XST HLS on a Virtex-7 device [9].

The performance results of the throughput-to-area ratio is also given in Fig. 11. This figure shows that the optimal data length is at 512 bits. At 512 bits, the AEAD-core has a throughput of 198.784 Mbit/s, an area of 111,919 LUTs and an throughput-to-area ratio of 1.776 (Kbit/s)/LUT. In comparison to the ATHENa Database of Results [14], the performance of this hardware implementation of HS1-SIV-MED is not as good as some other ciphers. For example, the area required by the HS1-SIV-MED implementation takes over 8 times more than the AES-COPA implementation.

The performance results of AES-OTR, SILC, AES-COPA and POET high level synthesis is presented in the paper [12] with optimization goal on **Area** are 122 Mbit/s, 126 Mbit/s, 117 Mbit/s and 124 Mbit/s respectively. It is clear to see that our implementation of HS1-SIV outperforms all of those implementation in throughput. Unfortunately, direct comparison of the area that is being used by the ciphers to the area that is being used by HS1-SIV is not possible because the paper presents the area of the ciphers in logic slices whereas the HS1-SIV area is measured in LUTs.

The ICEPOLE cipher [13] basic iterative implementation achieved 41 Gbit/s throughput on FPGA Virtex-6 without usage of any dedicated resources such as Block RAM or DSP. The presented performance results are much higher than other published results on hardware implementation performances of CAESAR candidates. It is not possible to compare performance results of ICEPOLE and HS1-SIV because the ICEPOLE implementation presented in the paper does not include an API which highly likely will cause some overhead. Despite the fact it is obvious that ICEPOLE cipher has higher throughput by a few orders of magnitude. One of the reasons only moderate performance results of HS1-SIV are achieved in comparison to the ICEPOLE cipher is that the design of HS1-SIV was optimized to be efficient running on x86 architecture and other

32-bit platforms, whereas ICEPOLE was initially designed to provide a high throughput on hardware. A larger area required for the implementation of HS1-SIV can be explained by the bigger input sizes of the message and the nonce. For instance, the ICEPOLE cipher takes 128-bit inputs whereas HS1-SIV operates on 64-byte long blocks.

8   Future Work

We have seen that the cipher uses quite a lot of FPGA resources. Although we have not focused on optimizing the implementation, we think that this is also an unfortunate characteristic of HS1-SIV. Future improvements that focus on optimizing the operations and the number of instructions should confirm this prediction. The paper proposed by At et al. [15] provides a good basis for optimizing ChaCha.

Also, our paper only describes the hardware implementation of HS1-SIV with regular parameter settings, different parameter settings will have different results. For HS1-SIV on high parameter settings, in general, the intermediate keys get larger and more ChaCha rounds need to be executed. On the other hand, HS1-SIV on low parameter settings requires less ChaCha rounds and uses smaller intermediate keys.

Another possible future improvement is to simplify the implemented architecture. Now, the AEAD-core does not contain a pre- and post-processor, meaning that upon unloading the results, no new data can be loaded. Also, the HS1-HASH function includes four blocks which in our implementation are executed in parallel. Each HS1_HASH block requires approximately 1500 LUTs, thus a serial computation of these blocks might decrease the area by up to 4500 LUTs. The same holds for the NH_4x4 blocks in HS1_HASH, the INNER_BLOCK blocks in ChaCha and the quarter-rounds in ChaCha's INNER_BLOCK.

Finally, the state-machines in both the AEAD-core as well as the cipher-core are very large, a future study towards a new hardware architecture with a reduced number of states could reveal whether the overall performance can be optimized.

9   Conclusions

The first effort to implement HS1-SIV with regular parameters settings which includes hardware API was introduced in the paper. HS1-SIV hardware implementation is an subject of the study of the second round of the CAESAR competition and future improvements, analysis and study will reveal if HS1-SIV is a good candidate to be used as a cipher for authenticated encryption with associated data.

Acknowledgements. We would like to thank Ted Krovetz for answering our questions regarding HS1-SIV. Also, our thanks go out to Antonio de la Piedra and Kostas Papagiannopoulos for their support and technical expertise.

References

1. Bernstein, D.J.: CAESAR: Competition for authenticated encryption: security, applicability, and robustness (2016). http://competitions.cr.yp.to/caesar.html
2. Daemen, J., Rijmen, V.: AES proposal: Rijndael (1999)
3. Babbage, S., Canniere, C., Canteaut, A., Cid, C., Gilbert, H., Johansson, T., Parker, M., Preneel, B., Rijmen, V., Robshaw, M.: The eSTREAM portfolio. eSTREAM ECRYPT Stream Cipher Project (2008)
4. Bertoni, G., Daemen, J., Peeters, M., Van Assche, G.: The keccak sha-3 submission. Submission NIST (Round 3) **6**, 16 (2011)
5. Biryukov, A., Dinu, D.D., Khovratovich, D.: Argon and Argon2 (2015)
6. Homsirikamol, E., Diehl, W., Ferozpuri, A., Farahmand, F., Sharif, M.U., Gaj, K.: GMU hardware API for authenticated ciphers. Cryptology ePrint Archive Report 2015 669 (2015). http://eprint.iacr.org/
7. Krovetz, T.: HS1-SIV (v2). CAESAR 2nd Round, competitions.cr.yp.to/round2/ hs1sivv2.pdf (2014). competitions.cr.yp.to/round2/ hs1sivv2.pdf
8. Rogaway, P., Shrimpton, T.: Deterministic Authenticated-Encryption A Provable-Security Treatment of the Key-Wrap Problem (2007)
9. Geltink, G., Volokitin, S.: FPGA implementation of HS1-SIV. In: Proceedings of the 13th International Joint Conference on e-Business and Telecommunications, pp. 41–48 (2016)
10. Bernstein, D.J.: ChaCha, a variant of Salsa20. In: Workshop Record of SASC: The State of the Art of Stream Ciphers, vol. 8 (2008)
11. Nir, Y., Langley, A.: ChaCha20 and Poly1305 for IETF Protocols. Technical report, RFC 7539, DOI 10.17487/RFC7539, May 2015 (2015). http://www.rfc-editor.org/ info/rfc7539
12. Kotegawa, M., Iwai, K., Tanaka, H., Kurokawa, T.: Optimization of hardware implementations with high-level synthesis of authenticated encryption. Bull. Networking Comput. Syst. Softw. **5**, 26–33 (2016)
13. Morawiecki, P., Gaj, K., Homsirikamol, E., Matusiewicz, K., Pieprzyk, J., Rogawski, M., Srebrny, M., Wójcik, M.: ICEPOLE: high-speed, hardware-oriented authenticated encryption. In: Batina, L., Robshaw, M. (eds.) CHES 2014. LNCS, vol. 8731, pp. 392–413. Springer, Heidelberg (2014). doi:10.1007/ 978-3-662-44709-3_22
14. Cryptographic Engineering Research Group (CERG) at GMU: ATHENa Database of Results (2016). https://cryptography.gmu.edu/athenadb/fpga_auth_cipher/ rankings_view
15. At, N., Beuchat, J.L., Okamoto, E., San, I., Yamazaki, T.: Compact Hardware Implementations of ChaCha, BLAKE, Threefish, and Skein on FPGA. Circuits and Systems I: Regular Papers, IEEE Transactions on **61**, 485–498 (2014)

Runtime Classification of Mobile Malware for Resource-Constrained Devices

Jelena Milosevic, Miroslaw Malek, and Alberto Ferrante$^{(\boxtimes)}$

ALaRI, Faculty of Informatics, Università Della Svizzera Italiana,
Via G. Buffi, 13, 6904 Lugano, Switzerland
{jelena.milosevic,miroslaw.malek,alberto.ferrante}@usi.ch

Abstract. In the resource-constrained and battery-operated environment of mobile devices accurate detection of malware and discrimination between diverse types of existing malware are challenging tasks and most of the currently proposed solutions are focused on only one of the mentioned aspects.

In this work, we propose a solution that is able to detect malware that appears at runtime and, at the same time, provides useful information to discriminate between diverse types of malware while taking into account limited resources of mobile devices. On device we monitor a set of the most representative features for presence of malware and use a detection algorithm of low complexity that provides an alarm if malware infection is observed. When the malware detection module raises an alarm, we analyse a set of previously stored information relevant for malware classification, in order to understand what type of malware is being executed. In order to achieve low consumption, we minimize the set of observed system parameters to only the most informative ones for both detection and classification and we offload part of the calculations related to discrimination between diverse types of malware to an external server. Our results show that dynamic features that we take into account (memory, CPU, and network) reflect well the behavior of the observed system and can be used to detect malware executions on a mobile device and to perform its classification.

1 Introduction

Mobile devices have conquered all fields in personal and in professional life. With widespread usage of these devices, the focus of Internet security is shifting from the desktop and the data centers to mobile and IoT devices. It is already estimated that the number of connected devices will continue to grow both in volume and variety, and that by 2020 it may reach 200 billion [1]. Together with the increased number and volume of connected devices, security threads are increasing as well.

Currently, malicious software, commonly called *malware*, is the most severe threat to mobile devices. Malware can leak private and sensitive information, make the device unavailable for its intended purpose, damage or even completely disable the operating system of a device. In order to enable secure usage

© Springer International Publishing AG 2017
M.S. Obaidat (Ed): ICETE 2016, CCIS 764, pp. 195–215, 2017.
https://doi.org/10.1007/978-3-319-67876-4_10

of mobile devices, protection methods able to detect presence of malware are needed. Additionally, identification of what type of malware could be running on a mobile device is important, in order to understand better the goal of the attack and put in place suitable countermeasures. However, having in mind the constrained computational environment of mobile devices, detection of malware and, particularly, identification of type of malware being executed (malware classification) are challenging tasks, and most of the existing works fail to provide optimised solutions that balances well between high malware detection accuracy, malware classification, and low resource consumption.

The approach we propose contributes to this research direction and has as the goal of finding an optimized solution considering a tradeoff between low resource consumption and suitability for battery-operated devices on one side, and on the other, accurate identification of malware at runtime and its accurate classification. We propose to identify and monitor on the mobile device the most informative features that reflect well the nature of running processes (malicious or benign) and then, by monitoring only these features to perform execution records classification in order to understand if infection is happening and what kind of infection it is. The features we use are dynamic features related to the applications consumption of memory, CPU, and network behavior. In order to understand if the executing code on the device is malicious we use detection algorithms of low complexity suitable for limited resources of mobile devices, and when these algorithms detect suspicious activities, the identification of malware type is triggered. At that time, a set of the most informative features, representing the behavior of the application under analysis, is sent to external servers for further analysis. In a nutshell, we perform malware detection on device and, only when a potential attack is detected, we send information about it to a remote server that performs malware classification.

In the remaining parts of this paper we first discuss related work in Sect. 2. Then, in Sect. 3, we outline the methodology we propose in order to achieve accurate malware detection and classification at low computational cost. Following, in Sect. 4, we describe the experiments we perform in order to validate the proposed approach, and in Sect. 5 we discuss the results obtained using those experiments. Finally, Sect. 6 concludes the paper.

2   Related Work

Existing mobile malware detection methods can be divided based on different metrics: type of features considered (static or dynamic), detection technique (anomaly detection or machine learning), detection side (device or cloud detection), or considered operating system (e.g., Android and iOS) [2]. In this work, we discuss both static and dynamic based detection methods together with the different detection techniques that they use. We focus on providing a detection method suitable for devices with limited resources and, due to this, we discuss on device solutions. Finally, since most of the existing works propose detection solutions for Android that, as an open-source operating system enables researchers to contribute to its development, we discuss only these Android-based solutions.

The methods based on static detection are the ones that use static features, like requested permissions, that can be collected without executing applications. One static approach to malware detection is proposed in [3] where high detection quality is achieved by using features from the manifest file (hardware components, requested permissions, app components, filtered intents) and feature sets from disassembled code. Using these features, detection is performed with Support Vector Machines. Also, the mechanism presented in [4] uses static features including permissions, Intent messages passing and API calls to detect malicious Android applications, with K-means being the best performing clustering algorithm.

Another static approach is presented in [5] where the authors propose to identify malware based on sets of permissions. In [6], as a static feature for detecting susceptibility of a device to malware infection, a set of identifiers representing the applications on a device is used. The assumption is that the set of applications used on a device may predict the likelihood of the device being classified as infected in the future.

Although reported detection performance of static detection methods is high, it has been shown that static methods cannot cope well with increased number of malware samples and their variations, they are prone to obfuscation, and that alone may no longer be sufficient to identify malware [7]. Promising candidates to overcome these difficulties are approaches based on dynamic detection. These approaches observe dynamic features, that change during the program execution, and based on them identify if the running code is malicious or benign.

Some dynamic approaches focus on the investigation of battery power, that as a dynamic feature, appears as a promising candidate for detection of malware. One of the proposed solutions, VirusMeter [8] monitors and audits power consumption on mobile devices with a power model that accurately characterizes power consumption of normal user behaviors. Also in [9] the authors use power monitoring to detect malware. They first extract characteristic power consumption signatures of malicious and benign applications and then, while using the system, detect if its power consumption is more similar to benign or malicious sample. However, although it appears as a promising feature, to what extent malware can be detected on phones by monitoring just battery power remains an open research question [10].

In [11], Andromaly, a framework for detecting malware, is proposed. It uses a variety of dynamic features related to: touch screen, keyboard, scheduler, CPU load, messaging, power, memory, calls, operating system, network, hardware, binder, and leds. The authors compared False Positive Rate, True Positive Rate, and accuracy of different detection algorithms and concluded that the algorithms that outperformed the others were Logistic Regression and Naive Bayes. The results were obtained using 40 benign applications and four malicious samples, developed by the authors, since real malicious samples did not exist at that time.

In [12], feature selection was performed on a set of runtime features related to network, SMS, CPU, power, process information, memory, and virtual memory. Four different classification algorithms were evaluated and as a measure of features usefulness Information Gain was used. Random Forest was the one that provided the best performance. Random Forest is a combination of different tree classifiers [13]. Results have been obtained by only considering 30 benign and five malicious applications, with a limited coverage of the high variety of malware available to date.

Our recent work extends state-of-the-art methods, taking into account new dynamic features, related to memory, CPU, and network aspects, that were previously not observed, so as taking into account bigger dataset consisting of more than 1000 malicious applications that better cover a variety of existing malware behavior. The features we consider, according to our experiments, reflect well the behavior of the system, while, at the same time, are easy to collect in terms of resource consumption, enabling a possibility to have both effective and efficient detection on mobile devices. More in detail, in [14], we take into account memory and CPU features, analyze them and their significance within the malware families they belong to, and take into account the most indicative ones for each family. By using Principal Component Analysis to analyse importance of features, we conclude that some features are good candidates for malware detection in general, some features are good candidates for detection of specific malware families, and some others are simply irrelevant. Further investigation of the features of interest for effective malware detection is presented in [15], where we present an approach that using only six features related to memory behavior and one feature related to behavior of CPU, is able to detect malicious executions records running on devices. The proposed detection technique is Logistic Regression, that due to its low complexity, is suitable for on device detection. While the approach proposed in [15] detects malicious execution records, in [16] we present an approach that is able to discriminate between complete malicious and benign applications, using a sliding window technique of low complexity and notifying the user about the infection taking place within, in average, the first three minutes of applications execution. Both approaches presented in [15] and [16] deal with malware detection on a device. In [17], in order to be able to further increase detection accuracy while keeping the resource consumption low, we propose a malware detection architecture in which more computationally demanding components are offloaded in the could infrastructure. In [18], we introduce an approach to efficient malware classification that identifies for each considered family a set of the most indicative features and, using them at runtime, discriminates between different types of malware.

Due to the resource-constrained environment of mobile devices most of the existing detection methods focus only on malware detection. However, with constantly increasing variety of mobile malware behavior existing on the market, there is also need for malware classification, that up to date was not well investigated in the state of the art. In this paper, we extend the existing state-of-the-art methods by providing a methodology for both methods, that is also designed to take into account limited resources of mobile devices, in a way that previously was not considered. Namely, it identifies only the reduced set of informative features to be monitored for effective malware detection, and, at the same time, stores the indicative ones for effective malware classification, that are, when a detection module rises an alarm sent over a network for more detailed analysis.

3 Methodology

The goal of this work is to provide a framework and specific methods for malware detection and malware classification at low computational cost. These two mechanisms are based on monitoring of selected system features at runtime and on using these features to perform detection and classification. As shown in Fig. 1, where the outline of the envisioned detection system is given, at runtime on the mobile device we monitor the set of the most indicative features for the presence of malware and, simultaneously, we record a set of the most representative features for malware classification task. Then, if malware is detected, we raise an alarm and send to a remote server a set of recorded indicative features for further analysis and classification. Based on the outcome of classification, possible countermeasures are decided and the device is notified about them.

One of the main characteristics of our approach is that it is designed to take into account limited resources of mobile devices from its early beginning. Namely, we reduce the number of observed features to only the most indicative ones for effective malware detection. Then, we perform detection on execution records using algorithms of low complexity. At the same time, we store information needed to perform malware classification, that has to be sent into the network when an alarm is raised. Also collection of this information is designed so that it records a set of only the most indicative features for observed families presence, and not all available information. In the remaining part of this section we discuss more in detail the proposed architecture of detection and classification parts.

3.1 Malware Detection

As it can be seen in Fig. 1, in our approach to malware detection, in order to detect potentially malicious records, a set of the most indicative features are monitored and analyzed by using detection algorithms suitable for resource-constrained devices [15]. In order to detect malicious applications, which is the successive step, we consider the history of execution records (marked as malicious or not) [16]. The features that are observed in this module are related to memory and CPU usage of running applications. These features are easy to collect in terms of computational resources and at the same time they are informative about the device behavior. Out of all features related to memory and CPU that can be monitored on Android mobile devices, we select a set of the most indicative ones; this selection process is performed offline and it is depicted in Fig. 2. Namely, after the execution of both malicious and benign applications, we extract all the features of interest, and then, using feature selection methods, identify the most indicative ones. Using only this reduced set of features, we train a set of classifiers, and at runtime we use the most suitable one in terms of detection accuracy and computational complexity.

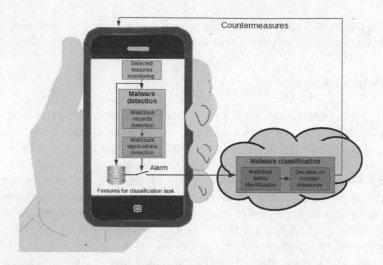

Fig. 1. Architecture of the malware detection and malware classification system.

Fig. 2. Offline development of the malware detection mechanism.

Intuitively, a better classification result can be achieved if we add more features to the dataset, however this is not always the case, and it can happen that irrelevant and redundant features confuse classifiers and decrease detection performance. Due to this fact, we perform feature selection as a separate step. The feature selection methods that we used, due to their different approach to selection of the most indicative features, are: Correlation Attribute Evaluator, CFS Subset Evaluator and Information Gain Attribute Evaluator [19]. Correlation Attribute Evaluator calculates the worth of an attribute by measuring the correlation between it and the class. CFS Subset Evaluator calculates the worth of a subset of attributes by considering the individual predictive ability of each feature along with the degree of redundancy between them. Information Gain Attribute Evaluator calculates the worth of an attribute by measuring the information gain with respect to the class.

In order to validate usefulness of the selected features, we use the following detection algorithms having different approaches to detection: Naive Bayes, Logistic Regression, and J48 Decision Tree, since they are, for their low computational complexity, good candidates for on device detection. A brief description of the aforementioned classification algorithms follows:

- *Naive Bayes* is a probabilistic classifier. It applies Bayes theorem making an assumption that the features are independent. Under this assumption it calculates probability of an unknown instance belonging to each class and selects the one with the highest probability as an output [20].
- *Logistic Regression* is a linear classifier that calculates the conditional probabilities of possible outcomes and chooses the one with the maximum likelihood.
- *A decision tree-based J48 classifier* is a classifier that for each node of the tree, chooses the attribute of the data that the most effectively splits its samples into subsets; the splitting criterion being maximum information gain [21].

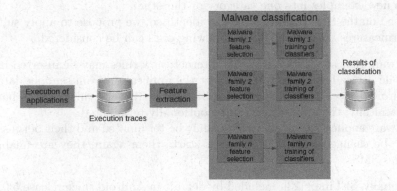

Fig. 3. Offline development of the malware classification mechanism.

3.2 Malware Classification

As shown in Fig. 1, at runtime we store a set of features related to malware classification and when an alarm is raised we send it to a remote server for further analysis. The offline development of the classification module is depicted in Fig. 3, where it can be seen that, after the execution of applications and collection of their traces, we derive the set of most indicative features for each observed family and validate their importance using a suitable classifier. Then, at runtime on the mobile device, we store a set of all the features identified as the most indicative for observed families and, when an alarm is raised, we send it to the network. In the offline phase different classifiers are tested and the most suitable ones for observed families can be identified to be used for their later detection.

For this purpose, we observe features related to memory and CPU, and we also take into account network behavior of the considered applications. Network observation is included having in mind how different malware families interact with network in different ways (some connect to an external server to obtain further instructions, some send users sensitive data, etc.) and assuming that this information might be significant in discriminating them.

Also in this scenario, in order to remove irrelevant features, to decrease complexity of monitoring infrastructure and required memory, we use feature selection as a separate step. As feature selection method we use CFS Subset Evaluator. In order to evaluate the importance of selected features and find out whether they contain enough information to discriminate between different families, we validate the ones selected as the most indicative by using the Support Vector Machines model, that is a supervised learning model proven to be successful in many real world problems, that given a set of training examples, each marked for belonging to one of two categories (malicious or benign), builds a model that assigns new examples into one category or the other.

Based on the type of malware being identified, we propose to apply suitable countermeasures. For example, the following ones can be considered:

- Malware that sends data over the Internet: new rules may be inserted in the mobile device local firewall to prevent the application from sending data; on Android devices, firewall is provided by Iptables [22] and rules can be changed dynamically; the application can be optionally terminated.
- Malware applications sending SMSs may be terminated and their permissions may be changed so that, if the user starts them again, they are unable to access SMS.

Additionally, SELinux [23], included by default in Android since release 5.0, can be used to sandbox applications [24]. While it might not be possible to do it while the applications are running, malicious applications can be terminated and the new SELinux policy can be applied when they are restarted.

4   Evaluation

The methodology, that we propose in Sect. 3, is not dependent on any operating system in particular. However, we propose its usage for Android OS, since it is, at this point, the most prevalent operating system for mobile devices. At the same time Android OS is frequently attacked with malware and, according to [25], the number of malware families and malware variants is constantly on the rise.

In this section, we describe the experiments that we have performed for validating the proposed approach in Android OS. In both cases of malware detection and malware classification, we have considered an execution environment that could allow us to efficiently and effectively record the features necessary to develop and validate our approaches. Features were recorded by running the applications, one at a time, on the Android emulator. For each application, a maximum of 2,000 stimuli were applied with a maximum execution time of 10 min. For most of the applications, all the stimuli could be applied in this timeframe. In some of the traces none of the two limits is reached due to emulator hiccups. Although it could be the case that a longer execution period would provide us more significant results, we believe that the duration that we have chosen is a good trade-off between time when most of the malware samples expose their malicious intents and duration of the overall experimentation. Monitoring of the aforementioned features is performed with a period of two seconds.

The Android emulator of the Android Software Development Kit [26] for Android 4.0 (release 20140702) was used. While a real device could provide results closer to reality, it would require an enormous amount of time to execute all the considered applications. The Android emulator was identified as the best solution to guarantee good-quality results as well as an acceptable execution time of the whole set of samples. To guarantee that the system is always in a mint condition when a new sample is started, thus avoiding possible interferences (e.g., changed settings, running processes, and modifications of the operating system files) from previously run samples, the Android operating system was each time re-initialized before running each application.

The application execution process was automated by means of a shell script that made use of Android Debug Bridge (adb) [27] and that was run on a Linux PC. adb is a command line tool that lets the PC communicate with an emulator instance or with an Android device. The Monkey application exerciser [28] was also used in the script. The Monkey is a command-line tool that can be run on any emulator instance or on a device; it sends a pseudo-random stream of user events (i.e., the aforementioned stimuli) into the system, which acts as a stress test on the application software. In our script, Monkey was used to exercise the applications, thus activating malware, and adb was used to monitor application features of interest, as well as to install the applications.

4.1 Malware Detection

We have executed 2,199 applications, 1,247 malicious and the rest benign, by using the Android SDK emulator and we have observed 53 features representing phone state. In the following, we describe the dataset that we have used in more detail, the experiments that we have performed, as well as how we trained our malware detection algorithm.

Dataset. The malware dataset is composed of 1,247 malicious applications taken from the Malware Genome project [29] and belonging to 49 families. These malware families represent different malicious behaviors, containing samples that use different installation methods (repackaging, update, drive-by download, standalone), activation mechanisms (Boot Completed, Phone Events, SMS, Calls, USB, Battery, Package, Network, System Events) and different malicious payloads (privilege escalation, remote control, financial charges, and personal information stealing). Details on each of these families are provided in [29].

The benign dataset is composed of 952 benign applications downloaded from the Google Play Store [30] that were among the most downloaded in different categories (travel, education, entertainment, etc.). In order to make sure that the considered benign applications do not contain any malware, they were analysed by means of VirusTotal [31], a service that checks submitted apps by using 57 different antimalwares, and in none malware was found.

Collected Features. We have taken into account all the features related to memory and CPU that we could access in Android. These features, 53 in total, are listed in Table 1. Out of considered features, 48 are related to different aspects of memory usage; the other five are related to CPU: three related to CPU usage, and two to virtual memory exceptions (major and minor faults). All features are referred to single applications resource consumption.

Algorithms and Settings. In Sect. 3.2, three considered feature selection methods are introduced. More precisely, CFS subset evaluation is performed by using Greedy forward search through the space of attribute subsets [32]. Correlation Attribute Evaluator and Information Gain Attribute Evaluator are used together with Ranker method that ranks attributes by their individual performance.

As discussed in Sect. 3, the classifiers of choice are: Naive Bayes, Logistic Regression, and J48 Decision Tree. Naive Bayes has been set assuming normality and modelling each conditional distribution with a single Gaussian; Logistic Regression has been used with ridge estimator, since it has been shown that it can improve attribute estimation and decrease the error made in further predictions [33]. J48 has been used with pruning, setting the confidence factor used for pruning to 0.25 and the minimum number of instances per leaf to 5,000. These values represent a trade-off between number of instances in the dataset, speed of execution and the quality of classification. For the mentioned feature selection methods and classification algorithms, their implementations in Weka data mining tool [19] have been used.

To validate our approach we used ten-fold cross validation, a widely used model validation technique that can estimate how accurately observed models perform in practice [34]. In this technique, the dataset is divided into ten parts, where at each round one part, consisting of nine folds, is used as a training set and the remaining part is used as a test set. This procedure is repeated ten times, each time using a different training and a test set, and after ten rounds the results are averaged.

4.2 Malware Classification

To validate our approach to classification of malware into families, we have observed a set of different families and from them identified the set of the most indicative features to be sent to a remote server for classification and decision on countermeasures. We now discuss these families, observed features, so as used algorithms and settings. For the observed malware families we have selected a set of Trojan families, that due to their similarity with legitimate applications

Table 1. List of all the considered features; totals are related only to single applications [15].

Features category	Features name
CPU Usage	Total CPU Usage
	User CPU Usage
	Kernel CPU Usage
Virtual memory	Page Minor Faults
	Page Major Faults
Native memory	Native PSS
	Native Shared Dirty
	Native Private Dirty
	Native Heap Size
	Native Heap Alloc
	Native Heap Free
Dalvik memory	Dalvik PSS
	Dalvik Shared Dirty
	Dalvik Private Dirty
	Dalvik Heap Size
	Dalvik Heap Alloc
	Dalvik Heap Free
	Dalvik Cursor PSS
Cursor memory	Cursor Shared Dirty
	Cursor Private Dirty
Android shared memory	Ashmem PSS
	Ashmem Shared Dirty
	Ashmem Private Dirty
Memory-mapped native code	.so mmap PSS
	.so mmap Shared Dirty
	.so mmap Private Dirty
Memory mapped Dalvik code	.dex mmap PSS
	.dex mmap Shared Dirty
	.dex mmap Private Dirty
Memory-mapped fonts	.ttf mmap PSS
	.ttf mmap Shared Dirty
	.ttf mmap Private Dirty
Other memory-mapped files and devices	.jar mmap PSS
	.jar mmap Shared Dirty
	.jar mmap Private Dirty
	.apk mmap PSS
	.apk mmap Shared Dirty
	.apk mmap Private Dirty
	Other mmap PSS
	Other mmap Shared Dirty
	Other mmap Private Dirty
Non-classified memory allocations	Unknown PSS
	Unknown Shared Dirty
	Unknown Private Dirty
	Other dev PSS
	Other dev Shared Dirty
	Other dev Private Dirty
Memory totals	Total PSS
	Total Shared Dirty
	Total Private Dirty
	Total Heap Size
	Total Heap Alloc
	Total Heap Free

are more difficult to identify than regular malware families. The intention behind such selection is that if the collected information in behavior of memory, CPU and network is enough to discriminate different kinds of Trojans-like behaviors, it will more likely be also able to discriminate between other more aggressive malware families, once they are included. An additional motivation was that, as opposed to the aggressive malware of the past, in these days we observe more subtle malware that tries to hide its presence and, as such, it resembles a Trojans-like behavior.

Dataset. The used malware and trusted applications, together with their number are shown in Table 2. The five Trojan families, taken from Drebin [3,35] and Malware Genome project [29] datasets, that were considered as a proof-of-concept, are following:

- **DroidKungFu:** Once installed, Trojans in this family attempt to gain control of the system by using exploits that are stored in the malware package and encrypted with a key. It collects the following pieces of information from the phone: International Mobile Equipment Identity (IMEI), mobile device model, network operator and type, OS APIs and type, and information stored in phone and SD card memory.
- **Fake Player:** Trojans belonging to this family pretend to be a movie player, but instead send SMS messages.
- **Geinimi:** Trojans belonging to this family send personal data (location coordinates, device identifiers, the list of installed apps) to remote servers.
- **GinMaster:** If triggered, Trojans in this family harvest confidential information from devices without users knowledge nor consent. Phone identification numbers (IMEI and IMSI, SIM number, telephone number), network type, current version of applications, and serial number are stolen by this malware in this family.
- **Kmin:** Trojans in this family collect user and device data (Device ID, Subscriber ID, current time) and send it to a remote server.

The benign subset has been obtained by running benign applications belonging to a variety of categories and downloaded from the Google Play Store [30].

Table 2. Dataset description.

Category	Name	Number of samples
Malware	DroidKungFu	667
	Fake Player	6
	Geinimi	92
	Ginger Master	339
	Kmin	147
Benign Apps	–	300

Collected Features. In total, 68 features were analysed. The collected features are all the ones used for malware detection, listed in Table 1, with the addition of network statistics at transport and Internet layer, that are given in Table 3.

Table 3. List of the considered network features.

Features category	Features name
Network load	AVG. PKT Size bytes
	bps
	Size in byte standard deviation
	Network load over last minute
	Maximum packet size in bytes
	Minimum packet size in bytes
	Number of bytes
	Number of packets
	Number of packets per second
Control protocols	Number of ARP packets
	Number of ICMP packets
Data protocols	Number of IPv4 packets
	Number of IPv6 packets
	Number of TCP packets
	Number of UDP packet

Algorithms and Settings. Collected features are analysed by using CFS Subset Evaluator, that is described in more detail in Sect. 3.2, and its implementation that uses Greedy forward search is used in Weka tool [19].

The SVM implementation suggested in [36] and available in Weka was used; this implementation includes sequential minimal optimization. The selected kernel is the commonly used polynomial one, that allows learning of non-linear models.

In order to investigate if there are behavioural differences among different malware families, in the performed experiments we marked as *malware* only the samples belonging to the considered Trojan family and all the others as *benign*. As in malware detection scenario, we used ten fold cross-validation for validating the obtained results.

5   Results

The obtained results show that memory and CPU contain enough information to discriminate malicious from benign executions, and that memory, network and CPU contain enough information to perform malware classification. In the remaining part of this section, we discuss these results in more detail.

5.1 Malware Detection

Results show that, by observing a limited number of features related to memory and CPU (only seven in case of Naive Bayes and Logistic Regression, and six in case of J48 Decision Tree), the execution traces belonging to malicious applications can be identified with precision and recall of more than 84% [15].

Using Information Gain Attribute Evaluator we have obtained significance of the observed features, out of which the first fifteen highest ranked ones are shown in Fig. 4. Similarly, the first fifteen highest ranked features obtained by using Correlation Attribute Evaluation are shown in Fig. 5. Following, instead, the features selected by the CFS Subset Evaluator method: *.so mmap Shared Dirty, .jar mmap PSS, .ttf mmap PSS, .dex mmap PSS, .dex mmap Private Dirty, Other mmap, Private Dirty, CPU Total.* Although the three considered feature selection methods follow different approaches, we can notice that there are some features that are selected as the most significant ones by all the three methods. For example, a number of features related to memory mapping, such as *.ttf mmap PSS*, are among the highest ranked ones for all methods. While in this paper we discuss only results obtained by considering the three aforementioned feature selection methods, results obtained by considering also other methods can be found in [15].

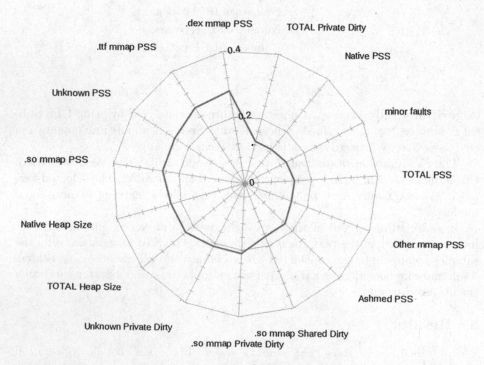

Fig. 4. 15 most significant features obtained by using the Information Gain Attribute Evaluator feature selection method.

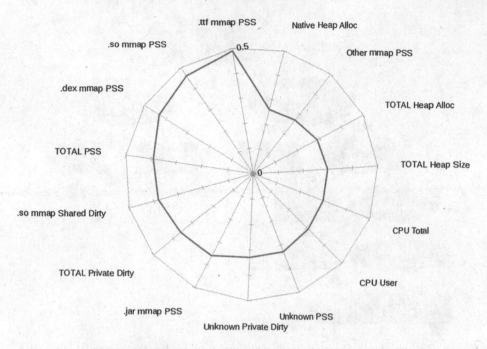

Fig. 5. 15 most significant features obtained by using the Correlation Attribute Evaluator feature selection method.

Table 4. Performance of the classifiers when different number of features are considered [15].

Classifier	Performance	Initial	Model Max. F-measure	Optimized
Naive Bayes	Precision	0.79	0.84	0.84
	Recall	0.76	0.83	0.83
	F-measure	0.77	0.83	0.83
	No. of features	53	7	7
Logistic Regression	Precision	0.84	0.86	0.84
	Recall	0.84	0.86	0.84
	F-measure	0.83	0.86	0.84
	No. of features	53	38	7
J48 Decision Tree	Precision	–	–	0.83
	Recall	–	–	0.83
	F-measure	–	–	0.82
	No. of features	–	–	6

Table 4 summarizes the results obtained using three different classifiers with the settings described in Sect. 4.1. The initial model includes all the 53 features available. The second model, instead, is the one providing maximum F-measure; the last one provides the best ratio between F-measure and the number of features considered. We use F-measure as a quantitative description of the quality of detection models, since it takes into account both precision and recall as it is their harmonic mean.

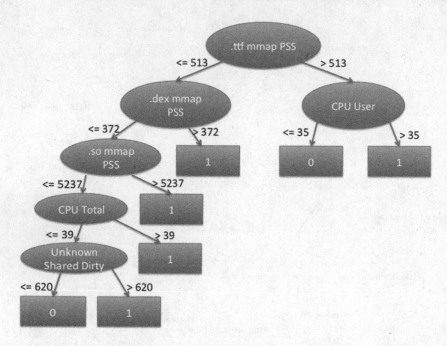

Fig. 6. Optimized J48 Decision Tree; malicious and benign traces are labelled with *0* and *1*, respectively [15].

In case of Naive Bayes, with the dataset containing all 53 features, an F-measure of 0.77 is obtained. We identified an optimized set of features, both with respect to their number and to F-measure, as the one computed with the CFS Subset Evaluator. As it can be seen in Table 4, the F-measure obtained in this case is 0.83, with a set of only seven features.

With Logistic Regression and by considering all features, we obtained an F-measure equal to 0.83. However, decreasing the number of features and observing system performance, we could find a reduced set of features that maximized F-measure, bringing it to 0.86. The reduced set, composed of 38 features, was determined by using Correlation Attributes and by considering features ranked more than 0.03. The optimal model with respect to both number of features and quality of detection is again achieved by using features selected by CFS Subset Evaluator. This model provides an F-measure equal to 0.84.

For J48 Decision Tree, in the training phase we were changing the maximum number of instances that a node could have by observing, at the same time, its quality of detection. The obtained decision tree model, that uses six features and has an F-measure of 0.82, is shown in Fig. 6.

A brief description of the most indicative features used in the best performing models is provided in Table 5. The best detection performance with respect to the ratio between F-measure and the number of features considered, is achieved by the Logistic Regression algorithm. Also the other two detection algorithms considered, namely, Naive Bayes and J48 Decision Tree, perform well, showing similarly good detection performance.

Table 5. Brief description of the most indicative features [15,37].

Feature name	Feature description
.so mmap Shared Dirty	Shared memory, in the *Dirty* state, being used for mapped native code. The *Dirty* state is due to fix-ups to the native code when it is loaded into its final address
.so mmap PSS	Memory used for native code, including platform code shared across applications
.jar mmap PSS	Memory usage for Java archives, including pages shared among processes
.ttf mmap PSS	Memory usage for true type fonts, including pages shared among processes
.so mmap PSS	Memory used for Dalvik, including platform code shared across applications
.so mmap Private Dirty	Private memory, in the *Dirty* state, being used for mapped Dalvik. The *Dirty* state is due to fix-ups to the native code when it is loaded into its final address
Other mmap Private Dirty	Private memory used by unclassified contents that is in the *dirty* state
Unknown Shared Dirty	Shared memory that in the *dirty* state that cannot be classified into one of the other more specific items
CPU User	Userspace CPU usage by the considered application
CPU Total	Total (User + System) CPU usage by the considered application

5.2 Malware Classification

According to our experiments, information contained in the observed features can be used to discriminate different types of malware families, once the analysis of the features is performed in the cloud. For the validation of the proposed approach we have used the malware Trojan families described in Sect. 3.2 as the initial dataset. Then, from these families we have identified the sets of most indicative features representing their behavior and we have validated their usefulness in malicious execution record classification by using Support Vector Machines (SVM) classifier.

Out of the selected sets of the most indicative features per family, we create a superset that is formed by the union of the sets of features identified as the most significant ones for each family. This superset is the one that is monitored and stored on device and sent for remote analysis in case of malware detected. The features in this superset are listed in Table 6, where they are also described.

The most informative features for the Droid Kung Fu family, as shown in Table 6, are three; by considering these three features and the SVM classifier, we are able to achieve a detection accuracy equal to 74.2% on detection of malicious records. Also in the case of the Fake Player family, three features are selected

Table 6. Selected features for each Trojan family.

Feature name	Description	Droid Kung Fu	Fake Player	Geinimi	Ginger Master	Kmin
		Trojan family				
.ttf mmap PSS	Memory usage for true type fonts, including pages shared with other processes	×			×	×
Network load over last minute	Network load in bits/second registered in the last minute	×	×		×	
Maximum packet size in bytes	Maximum network packets size in bytes observed in the 2 s monitoring period	×				
.dex mmap Pss	Memory usage for Dalvik, including pages shared with other processes		×			
Number of ARP packets	Number of ARP network packets received and transmitted in the 2 s monitoring period		×			
.jar mmap Pss	Memory usage for Java code, including pages shared among processes			×		
Other mmap Pss	Memory usage for non-classified purposes, including pages shared among processes			×		
Other mmap Shared Dirty	Memory shared among processes, in the *Dirty* state, being used for non-classified purposes			×		
Number of TCP packets	Number of TCP network packets received and transmitted in the 2 s monitoring period			×		
Unknown Pss	Memory usage for unknown purposes, including pages shared among processes			×		
TOTAL Heap Size	Total heap size allocated for the process			×		×
CPU User	User-space CPU usage of the process			×		
CPU kernel	Kernel-space CPU usage of the process			×		
minor faults	Virtual memory minor page faults caused by the process			×	×	×
bps	Network load in bits/second registered in the 2 s monitoring period			×	×	×
Number of ICMP packets	Number of ICMP network packets received and transmitted in the 2 s monitoring period			×		
Size in byte standard deviation	Standard deviation of the network packet size in bytes in the 2 s monitoring period			×		
Number of bytes	Number of bytes transmitted and received in the 2 s monitoring period			×		
.so mmap Private Dirty	Private memory of the process, in the *Dirty* state, being used for mapped native code				×	×
Number of UDP packets	Number of UDP network packets received and transmitted in the 2 s monitoring period				×	×
Ashmem Private Dirty	Private memory of the process, in the *Dirty* state, being allocated as Android shared memory					×
.so mmap Pss	Memory usage for mapped native code, including pages shared with other processes					×
.so mmap Shared Dirty	Memory shared with other processes, in the *Dirty* state, being used for mapped native code					×
.apk mmap Pss	Memory usage for Android application package files, including pages shared with other processes					×
TOTAL Shared Dirty	Total memory of the process that is shared and it is marked as dirty					×

as the most indicative ones and malware in this family can be detected with an accuracy of 99.7%. Also the Geinimi family can be detected accurately by using SVM. The most indicative features that have been selected are 13 (5 related to memory usage, 3 related to CPU consumption, and 8 related to network traffic). Considering only these features we have achieved an accuracy equal to 97%. Six features have been selected for the Ginger Master Trojan family. By using these features, the obtained detection accuracy is 78.7%. For the Kmin Trojan family, eight memory-related, one CPU-related, and two network-related features have been selected as the most significant ones, and using them the detection accuracy of 95.4% is achieved [18].

From the performed experiments and by comparing the selected features per each malware family, we can observe that different behaviors of different Trojan families are reflected in different usage patterns of memory, CPU, and network. The behavior of some families (Kmin) is better reflected in memory related features; the behavior of some other families (Droid Kung Fu, Fake Player) is, instead, better reflected through network-related features; for some other families (Geinimi), features from all categories are important for detection. The differences are significant enough to allow us to identify these families with good accuracy. We validated this observation by using SVM and showed that high detection accuracy can be achieved using only a reduced set of features.

6   Conclusions

We propose and validate an approach to malware detection and classification that is suitable for resource-constrained environments and operates at runtime. Our current solution monitors on the device the most representative features for discovering a potential malware infection and, in case it happens, it sends to the cloud the crucial features needed for malware classification; these features are the ones previously stored during the applications execution. Our results show that memory and CPU related information can be used to detect malicious executions on a mobile device by using only seven features and with F-measure equal to 0.84. Additionally, memory, CPU and network behavior can be used to identify the malicious family to which the execution records belong, with an accuracy that varies from 74.2% to 99.7% using from three to thirteen features depending on the type of considered family.

References

1. Labs, M.: McAfee Labs Threats Report. Technical report, McAfee Labs (2015)
2. Milosevic, J., Regazzoni, F., Malek, M.: Malware threats and solutions for trustworthy mobile systems design. Springer (2017, to appear)
3. Arp, D., Spreitzenbarth, M., Hubner, M., Gascon, H., Rieck, K.: DREBIN: effective and explainable detection of android malware in your pocket. In: NDSS (2014)
4. Wu, D.J., Mao, C.H., Wei, T.E., Lee, H.M., Wu, K.P.: DroidMat: android malware detection through manifest and API calls tracing. In: 2012 Seventh Asia Joint Conference on Information Security (Asia JCIS), pp. 62–69 (2012)

5. Enck, W., Ongtang, M., McDaniel, P.: On lightweight mobile phone application certification. In: 16th ACM conference on Computer and communications security (CCS), pp. 235–245. ACM (2009)
6. Truong, H.T.T., Lagerspetz, E., Nurmi, P., Oliner, A.J., Tarkoma, S., Asokan, N., Bhattacharya, S.: The company you keep: mobile malware infection rates and inexpensive risk indicators. In: Proceedings of the 23rd International Conference on World Wide Web (WWW 2014), pp. 39–50. ACM, New York (2014). doi:10.1145/2566486.2568046
7. Moser, A., Kruegel, C., Kirda, E.: Limits of static analysis for malware detection. In: Twenty-Third Annual Computer Security Applications Conference, pp. 421–430 (2007)
8. Liu, L., Yan, G., Zhang, X., Chen, S.: VirusMeter: preventing your cellphone from spies. In: Kirda, E., Jha, S., Balzarotti, D. (eds.) RAID 2009. LNCS, vol. 5758, pp. 244–264. Springer, Heidelberg (2009). doi:10.1007/978-3-642-04342-0_13
9. Kim, H., Smith, J., Shin, K.G.: Detecting energy-greedy anomalies and mobile malware variants. In: Proceedings of the 6th International Conference on Mobile Systems, Applications, and Services. MobiSys 2008, pp. 239–252. ACM, New York (2008)
10. Becher, M., Freiling, F.C., Hoffmann, J., Holz, T., Uellenbeck, S., Wolf, C.: Mobile security catching up? Revealing the nuts and bolts of the security of mobile devices. In: Symposium on Security and Privacy, SP 2011, pp. 96–111. IEEE Computer Society (2011)
11. Shabtai, A., Kanonov, U., Elovici, Y., Glezer, C., Weiss, Y.: "Andromaly": a behavioral malware detection framework for android devices. J. Intell. Inf. Syst. **38**, 161–190 (2012)
12. Ham, H.S., Choi, M.J.: Analysis of android malware detection performance using machine learning classifiers. In: 2013 International Conference on ICT Convergence (ICTC), pp. 490–495 (2013)
13. Breiman, L.: Random forests. Mach. Learn. **45**, 5–32 (2001)
14. Milosevic, J., Ferrante, A., Malek, M.: What does the memory say? Towards the most indicative features for efficient malware detection. In: The 13th Annual IEEE Consumer Communications & Networking Conference, CCNC 2016, Las Vegas, NV, USA. IEEE Communication Society (2016)
15. Milosevic, J., Malek, M., Ferrante, A.: A friend or a foe? Detecting malware using memory and CPU features. In: Proceedings of the 13th International Joint Conference on e-Business and Telecommunications, SECRYPT, vol. 4, pp. 73–84 (2016)
16. Milosevic, J., Ferrante, A., Malek, M.: Malaware: Effective and efficient run-time mobile malware detector. In: The 14th IEEE International Conference on Dependable, Autonomic and Secure Computing (DASC 2016), Auckland, New Zealand. IEEE Computer Society Press (2016)
17. Milosevic, J., Dittrich, A., Ferrante, A., Malek, M.: A resource-optimized approach to efficient early detection of mobile malware. In: 2014 Ninth International Conference on Availability, Reliability and Security (ARES), pp. 333–340 (2014)
18. Milosevic, J., Ferrante, A., Malek, M.: Trojan families identification using dynamic features and low complexity classifiers. In: 24th EICAR Annual Conference 2016 "Trustworthiness in IT Security Products", Nuremberg, Germany, EICAR, EICAR (2016)
19. Hall, M., Frank, E., Holmes, G., Pfahringer, B., Reutemann, P., Witten, I.H.: The WEKA data mining software: an update. SIGKDD Explor. Newsl. **11**, 10–18 (2009)

20. John, G., Langley, P.: Estimating continuous distributions in Bayesian classifiers. In: Proceedings of the Eleventh Conference on Uncertainty in Artificial Intelligence, pp. 338–345. Morgan Kaufmann (1995)

21. Quinlan, J.R.: C4.5: Programs for Machine Learning. Morgan Kaufmann Publishers Inc., San Francisco (1993)

22. Netfilter - firewalling, NAT, and packet mangling for Linux. https://www.netfilter.org

23. Smalley, S., Vance, C., Salamon, W.: Implementing SELinux as a linux security module. Technical report, US National Security Agency (2001). http://www.nsa.gov/research/files/publications/implementing_selinux.pdf

24. Shabtai, A., Fledel, Y., Elovici, Y.: Securing android-powered mobile devices using SELinux. IEEE Secur. Priv. **8**, 36–44 (2010)

25. Symantec Corporation: Internet security threat report, vol. 21. Technical report (2016). https://www.symantec.com/content/dam/symantec/docs/reports/istr-21-2016-en.pdf

26. Android Open Source project: Android Software Development Kit (2015). https://developer.android.com/sdk/index.html

27. Android Open Source project: Android Debug Bridge (2015). http://developer.android.com/tools/help/adb.html

28. Android Open Source project: UI/Application Exerciser Monkey (2015). http://developer.android.com/tools/help/monkey.html

29. Zhou, Y., Jiang, X.: Dissecting android malware: characterization and evolution. In: Proceedings of the 2012 IEEE Symposium on Security and Privacy, SP 2012, pp. 95–109. IEEE Computer Society, Washington, D.C. (2012)

30. Google Inc.: Google Play (2015). https://play.google.com

31. Virus Total: (Suspicious Files Analyser). https://www.virustotal.com

32. Hall, M.A.: Correlation-based feature subset selection for machine learning. PhD thesis, University of Waikato, Hamilton, New Zealand (1998)

33. Le Cessie, S., Van Houwelingen, J.C.: Ridge estimators in logistic regression. Appl. Stat. **41**, 191–201 (1992)

34. Kohavi, R.: A study of cross-validation and bootstrap for accuracy estimation and model selection, pp. 1137–1143. Morgan Kaufmann (1995)

35. Spreitzenbarth, M., Freiling, F., Echtler, F., Schreck, T., Hoffmann, J.: Mobile-sandbox: having a deeper look into android applications. In: Proceedings of the 28th Annual ACM Symposium on Applied Computing, SAC 2013, pp. 1808–1815. ACM, New York (2013)

36. Platt, J.C.: Advances in Kernel Methods. MIT Press, Cambridge (1999)

37. Google Inc.: Android Developers - Investigating Your RAM Usage (2015). http://developer.android.com/tools/debugging/debugging-memory.html

Towards Realising Oblivious Voting

Dirk Achenbach[2(✉)], Anne Borcherding[1], Bernhard Löwe[1],
Jörn Müller-Quade[1], and Jochen Rill[2]

[1] Karlsruhe Institute of Technology, Karlsruhe, Germany
`anne.borcherding@student.kit.edu`, {`loewe,mueller-quade`}`@kit.edu`
[2] Research Center for Information Technology, Karlsruhe, Germany
{`achenbach,rill`}`@fzi.de`

Abstract. Electronic voting machines promise to determine election results more efficiently without sacrificing reliability. Two desirable security properties seem to contradict each other however: First, the voter's choice is to be kept secret at all costs, even from election officers who set up and administrate the election machine. On the other hand, ballot secrecy should not compromise the correctness of the tally.

We present a construction that conceals the voter's choice even from the voting machine while producing a provably-correct tally. Our scheme is an improvement of Bingo Voting [1]. To hide the voter's choice from the voting machine, we conceive of an electro-mechanical physical oblivious transfer (pOT) device. We further use blind commitments, an extension of cryptographic commitments. Blind commitments can jointly be created by a group of entities, while no single entity is aware of the hidden secret. They can later be unveiled in another multi-party computation.

This work is an extended version of a conference paper [2]. In this version, we work out the details of our construction. Our results corroborate the feasibility of an electronic voting machine that is oblivious to the voters' choices.

Keywords: Electronic voting · Ballot secrecy · Bingo Voting

1 Introduction

The widespread use of electronic voting systems increases convenience, but imperils the foundation of democracy.

There is a strong tendency to migrate formerly "analogue" systems to digital systems to increase effectiveness and reduce costs. Elections are no exception. Indeed, counting votes by hand is error-prone and does not scale well. By contrast, machines do not suffer from oversights and never tire. However, as their performance scales well, their damage potential does also. For a malicious adversary bent on rigging an election, voting machines are a prime target.

Research in cryptographic voting schemes addresses this issue. Indeed, a number of schemes have been proposed that produce a provably-correct tally even if the voting machine is compromised, e.g. [1,3]. On the other hand, they do

© Springer International Publishing AG 2017
M.S. Obaidat (Ed): ICETE 2016, CCIS 764, pp. 216–240, 2017.
https://doi.org/10.1007/978-3-319-67876-4_11

not hide the voter's choice from a potentially corrupted voting machine. This neglect seems unreasonable as voting machines are often made from general-purpose memory-programmable computers and thus pose an easy target for an adversary [4]. Such a weakness is deemed unavoidable, as the device that receives the voter's input naturally is aware of it. But for a voter to resist coercion, the secrecy of her vote is essential. Many security notions for coercion resistance in presence elections consequently assume that the machine that handles the user's input is trusted.

Further, to achieve coercion resistance one must design electronic voting schemes such that no adversary can discern information about any voter's behaviour, even in the long run. Thus, all data that is published must have everlasting privacy, i.e. be statistically or even perfectly secret.

Another concern when designing electronic voting schemes is usability. Voting schemes that require the voter to calculate some integer or to navigate an intricate user interface may be of academic interest, but are not well-suited for real-world elections where people are bound to make mistakes [5]. Only a simple point-and-push interface guarantees that the voter actually votes as intended. We limit the scope of this work to schemes that allow for such interfaces.

We address the above-mentioned concerns by introducing an architecture where the trust is distributed among several components with very limited functionality—they do not have to be capable of general-purpose computation—and where an honest-but-curious voting machine can not glean any knowledge about the voter's choice. To cast a vote, the voter pushes the mechanical button that is associated with her choice. An electro-mechanical principle then ensures that the rest of the machine is unaware of *which* data it processes. To the best of our knowledge, we are the first to address the privacy of the voter's choice in light of a passively corrupted voting machine in this setting. Our work is an improvement over the Bingo Voting [1] scheme.

This paper is an extended and improved version of a paper presented at the SECRYPT conference in 2016 [2].

Bingo Voting in a Nutshell. Bingo Voting is a protocol for presence elections. Before the actual election, for each candidate a number of *dummy votes* is prepared. A dummy vote is a number drawn uniformly at random. To cast a vote, the voter marks her choice on a designated voting machine. The machine then generates a receipt for the voter with the name of all candidates and a random number next to it: a dummy vote next to each candidate the voter did *not* vote for and a fresh random number for the candidate of choice. For the chosen candidate a *fresh number* is generated from a trusted and observable random number generator, e.g. a bingo cage (hence the name). All receipts generated in this manner are published after the election. The final tally is obtained by counting the number of dummy votes *not* used and thus inferring the number of *fresh votes* a candidate received. The trick behind the scheme is that *during the casting process* the voter can observe that the candidate she voted for is assigned a fresh random number. As *dummy votes* and *fresh randomness* are indistinguishable *after the fact*, the receipt is of no use to an outside adversary

Voting Receipt	P_1 1234523134
	P_2 7634875451
	P_3 3422335718

Fig. 1. A Bingo Voting receipt [2]. The numbers printed next to the candidates are chosen uniformly at random. Yet, only one of them has been drawn in the presence of the voter.

and hence Bingo Voting is receipt-free (see Fig. 1). The voting machine learns the voter's choice, however, and must be trusted not to leak that information.

Oblivious Bingo Voting. We propose a remedy for this weakness by employing a second device: *physical oblivious transfer* (physical oblivious transfer (pOT)). The central idea is that the voter selects between "fresh" and "dummy" randomness using the pOT device and thus leaves the voting machine oblivious as to which kind of "randomness" was selected. Hence, the voting machine cannot tell which candidate was voted for. We believe this idea of using a mechanical device to shield information from a potentially untrusted machine is of independent interest for the design of cryptographic schemes.

1.1 Our Contribution

At the SECRYPT conference in 2016 we presented a novel protocol for a "point and push" type electronic voting machine [2]. In addition to producing a provably-correct tally, our scheme ensures that no single component of the voting machine can learn the voter's choice. Our construction is an extension of Bohli et al.'s Bingo Voting [1]. We use a physical principle to conceal the voter's input from the voting machine. This paper is an extended and improved version of a conference paper, presented at the SECRYPT conference in 2016 [2]. We improved upon our original work in the following areas: First, we optimised the internal communication between components of the voting machine. Particularly, data is exchanged more efficiently between the random number generator and the storage device. Second, we elaborated the creation of blind commitments to the candidates during precomputation, thereby improving transparency compared to our initial idea. We added Sect. 5 where we work out the details of our construction. There we also provide detailed algorithms in pseudocode.

This work is structured as follows. After reviewing related work in this section, we discuss preliminaries in Sect. 2. Namely, we introduce two major building blocks, blind commitments and physical oblivious transfer. In Sect. 3 we give a short introduction to Bingo Voting. We present our construction in Sect. 4 and work out the details of our scheme in Sect. 5. Section 6 concludes.

1.2 Related Work

Related work on electronic voting can roughly be divided into two categories: protocols which are executed offline in a voting booth on dedicated machines, and protocols which are run on general-purpose machines in a decentralised manner (e.g. over the Internet). In an online setting, coercion resistance is generally much harder to achieve than offline (one reason is that a coercer can literally look over the voter's shoulder). It requires very different mechanisms to achieve the same level of coercion resistance or correctness in an online setting. As our scheme is offline, we only address related work on offline voting. Also, there are numerous voting schemes used in practice (both online and offline) whose main design goals do not include security. These schemes are not cryptographic and can often trivially be broken. We only address cryptographic voting protocols.

- In PEVS [6], Based et al. ensure coercion resistance by allowing the voter to generate an unbounded number of key pairs. They get signed by the voting authority using a blind signature. The adversary cannot know which key pair was actually used to vote. The scheme requires the voting machine to be trusted however, since it can collude with the adversary and use a specific key to cast the vote (e.g. always the first). Also, the scheme is not robust against a passively-corrupted voting machine, as the voting machine can simply observe the keys the voter used.
- Split-ballot voting [7] addresses the requirement to trust one single voting authority. The basic scheme does not involve a voting machine, however. It requires the voter to perform a modular addition on paper to split her vote. It seems a strong assumption that every voter is capable of such a feat. However, implementing the operation on a voting machine to simplify the voting process, again requires trust in the voting machine, since it will know how the voter split his vote among the ballots. Similar to our scheme, in order to achieve everlasting security, they also jointly compute commitments and encryptions of their reveal information.
- BeleniosRF [8] is an extension to Helios [9] to achieve strong receipt-freeness (even a malicious voter cannot prove how she voted). To achieve that, Cortier et al. use "signatures on randomisable ciphertexts", a cryptographic primitive introduced by Blazy et al. [10]. It makes possible that the voting machine can re-randomise the encrypted and signed vote of the voter, as well as its signature, before publishing the vote. This way, a voter cannot identify her published vote. However, a passively corrupted voting machine can learn the individual votes since it must encrypt them. Also the scheme also does not offer everlasting security.
- Selene [11] aims to simplify the interface for the voter to allow her to easily verify that her vote was counted correctly. To achieve that, Selene publishes the vote in the clear and assigns each voter a tracking number which she can use to verify that her vote was counted correctly. Ryan et al. argue that a voter can mitigate coercion by lying to an adversary about her tracking number. However, as with other voting schemes, the voting machine learns the individual votes, since it has to encrypt them.
- Scantegrity II [3,5] is a coercion resistant voting scheme which has been used for a municipal election at Takoma Park. It is based on a scanner and uses verification codes for end-to-end verifiability. The coercion resistance has been proven. However, the polling station, the server which creates the verification codes, and the printing service, have to be honest.

2   Preliminaries

In this section, we give an overview of our notation. We also introduce *blind commitments* as well as physical oblivious transfer, which are the main building blocks of our construction.

2.1   Notation

In this paper, we use the following notation. We consider an election with n_P parties (candidates) p_i and n_E electors (voters) e_j. We use the index variable i to denote one voter's choice and j to differentiate between different voters. We rely on the trustworthiness of a majority of k out of n_A members of a voting authority. k is also used as the treshhold of the treshhold encryption scheme we use in the following chapters. To enumerate authority members, we use l as the index variable. Each authority member a_l has a key pair $(s_l^{(\text{ver})}, s_l^{(\text{sig})})$ for an EUF-CMA secure signature scheme $(\text{gen}(\cdot), \text{sig}_{s_l^{(\text{sig})}}(\cdot), \text{ver}_{s_l^{(\text{ver})}}(\cdot))$.

Further, c is a commitment, u and v are ciphertexts, and N and R are random numbers. C, C', D, and D' are 3-tuples containing a commitment c and two ciphertexts u and v.

See Table 1 for an overview of other variables we use.

Table 1. Overview of some of the variables used in this paper.

Variable	Description
i, j	index variable for voter and candidate
n_A	Number of authority members, k of them are trustworthy
a_l	Authority member l
sk_l	Secret key of authority l
n_P	Number of candidates/parties
p_i	Candidate/party i
n_E	Number of voters/electors
e_j	Voter/elector j
$b_{i,j}$	$\in 0,1$, represents the choice of the voter
$B_{i,j}$	$\text{enc}(b_{i,j})$
$N_{i,j}$	Dummy vote for candidate i used for voter j
R_j	Random number generated for voter j
Variable	Blind commitment to
$C_{i,j} = (c_{i,j}^{(C)}, u_{i,j}^{(C)}, v_{i,j}^{(C)})$	candidate i for voter j
$D_{i,j} = (c_{i,j}^{(D)}, u_{i,j}^{(D)}, v_{i,j}^{(D)})$	candidate i for voter j
$C_{i,j}' = (c_{i,j}^{(C')}, u_{i,j}^{(C')}, v_{i,j}^{(C')})$	fresh random number used for candidate i voter j voted for
$D_{i,j}' = (c_{i,j}^{(D')}, u_{i,j}^{(D')}, v_{i,j}^{(D')})$	dummy vote for candidate i used for voter j

2.2 Blind Commitments

For protecting the privacy of the votes in the presence of a corrupted voting machine, we introduce a new primitive: *blind commitments*. Cryptographic commitments allow a sender to commit to a value without revealing it to the receiver of the commitment. He can then later send unveil information to unveil the value. Commitments are required to be *hiding* as well as *binding*—a commitment may not reveal its contents before it is unveiled by the sender, while also only allowing the sender to unveil to the value he committed to. We extend this standard notion of commitments to *blind* commitments whose content and unveil information are both encrypted and not known to a single entity. The unveil information is kept in encrypted form so that the voting machine cannot unveil on its own. Moran et al. [7] use the same idea in their voting protocol. By using perfectly-hiding commitments, one can then achieve everlasting security for the public data. Our intent is to create the blind commitments in a distributed computation. We require the following properties from a blind commitment:

Definition 1 (Homomorphic Encryption, Homomorphic Commitment). *Let* $\mathsf{enc}(m, r)$ *be an* IND-CPA *secure homomorphic encryption scheme, encrypting message* m *with randomness* r. *Let* $\mathsf{enc}(m)$ *be the same scheme without explicit mention of the randomness.*

Let $\mathsf{com}(m, r)$ *be a perfectly hiding and computationally binding homomorphic commitment scheme, committing on message* m *with randomness* r. *Let* $\mathsf{com}(m)$ *be the same scheme without explicit mention of the randomness.*

For messages m, m' *with randomness* r, r', *we require that there exist operations* $+, \cdot, \circ, \star$ *such that*

- $\mathsf{enc}(m_1, r_1) \cdot \mathsf{enc}(m_2, r_2) = \mathsf{enc}(m_1 + m_2, r_1 \star r_2)$.
- $\mathsf{com}(m_1, r_1) \cdot \mathsf{com}(m_2, r_2) = \mathsf{com}(m_1 + m_2, r_1 + r_2)$.
- $\mathsf{com}(m, r) \circ r' = \mathsf{com}(m, r + r')$.

Definition 2 (Blind Commitment). *We call* $C := \mathsf{bCom}(m, r_1, r_2, r_3) = (c, u, v)$ *a blind commitment on a message* m *with randomness* r_1, r_2, r_3, *where*

- $c := \mathsf{com}(m, r_1)$ *is a perfectly hiding and computationally binding commitment on message* m *using randomness* r_1,
- $u := \mathsf{enc}(m, r_2)$ *is an encryption of the message* m *using randomness* r_2, *and*
- $v := \mathsf{enc}(r_1, r_3)$ *is an encryption of randomness* r_1 *using randomness* r_3.

We use $\mathsf{bCom}(m)$ when we do not mention the randomness explicitly.

We call a pair of blind commitments $(C, \ C') := (\mathsf{bCom}(p_i), \mathsf{bCom}(N_{i,j}))$ a *commitment pair* on a candidate p_i and a dummy vote $N_{i,j}$.

During the tallying, the blind commitments have to be shuffled. To this end, all three parts c, u, and v of each commitment have to be re-randomisable. We achieve this using the homomorphic properties of both the encryption and the commitment scheme.

Definition 3 (Re-randomisation of Blind Commitments).
Let $\mathsf{bCom}(m, r_1, r_2, r_3)$ be a blind commitment to message m with randomness r_1, r_2, r_3. Let r_4, r_5, r_6 be fresh random values. We define

$$\mathsf{re\text{-}rand}(\mathsf{bCom}(m, r_1, r_2, r_3), r_4, r_5, r_6) := \mathsf{bCom}(m, r_1 + r_4, r_2 \star r_5, r_3 \star r_6)$$

Further, we require a re-randomisation of a blind commitment to be indistinguishable. That is, $\mathsf{re\text{-}rand}(C, r_4, r_5, r_6)$ is indistinguishable from a blind commitment to any different value. For any messages m, m' and randomness $r_1, r_2, r_3, r_4, r_5, r_6$ there exists randomness r_7, r_8, r_9 such that $\mathsf{re\text{-}rand}(\mathsf{bCom}(m, r_1, r_2, r_3), r_4, r_5, r_6)$ is indistinguishable to $\mathsf{bCom}(m', r_7, r_8, r_9)$.

We prove the correctness of the shuffle by using shadow mixes [9], which is a standard procedure in cryptographic voting.

As already mentioned, we need to create the encryptions and commitments in a distributed way. During the pre-voting phase the authorities generate n_E blind commitments on random numbers $N_{i,j}$ for every candidate p_i. We achieve this by combining the Pedersen scheme [12] with a compatible threshold encryption. We then exploit the homomorphic property of those schemes. See Sect. 5 for details.

2.3 Physical Oblivious Transfer

In traditional elections, the trust in the integrity and confidentiality of ballots relies on sealed ballot boxes. Cryptographically speaking, an intact mechanical seal serves as a trust anchor for the voting protocol. Indeed, many cryptographic schemes also use *tamper-proof hardware* as their setup assumption [13,14]. The idea is to exploit a physical property of a device that no adversary can violate. We propose such a device—*physical oblivious transfer* (pOT)—with two inputs and one output. The pOT outputs exactly one of its two inputs and also obscures which input was selected. The decision which of the two inputs to take is made by the voter who operates a physical button to indicate her decision.

The name for the device is inspired by the *oblivious transfer* (OT) cryptographic primitive [15]. Here, the receiver selects which of the inputs to receive, without learning the other input, while the sender never learns which of the inputs was delivered.

We imagine the pOT device to be realised in a electromechanical fashion. On the electrical side, it is constructed like an optocoupler, but with two sending diodes (see Fig. 2). One of the diodes is covered by a screen. By pushing a button, the voter moves the screen from one diode to the other. Constructed this way, the pOT acts as a galvanic isolation between the input and the output pins. As both diodes are connected and consume power, the sender cannot gain any knowledge on which input is delivered.

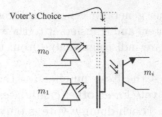

Fig. 2. pOT device [2]: The device functions similarly to an optocoupler. On the left, two diodes (continuously) send messages m_0 and m_1. On the right, there is a photo-transistor. One of the diodes is screened. When the voter selects a vote, she moves the screen from one diode to the other.

3 Bingo Voting

We first describe the original Bingo Voting scheme as it is outlined by Bohli et al. [1]. Bingo Voting aims to provide both a secure and verifiable voting mechanism as well as coercion resistance to the voters. The main idea is that each voter is given a receipt for her elected candidate as well as a receipt *for every other candidate* (so called "dummy votes"). This ensures that the voter can, on the one hand, verify that her vote was counted correctly, and on the other hand, present a receipt for any candidate. The number to represent the voter's actual vote is generated in the voting booth, where the voter can witness its "freshness". To get the number of votes per candidate, the scheme will determine the number of *unused* dummy votes, since when a candidate receives a vote, a dummy vote is left unused. For correctness, Bingo Voting relies only on the trustworthiness of the random number generator. However, since the voting machine learns the voters inputs, ballot secrecy requires that the voting machine is fully trusted.

In the following we describe the scheme in more detail. We assume a poll with n_P candidates and n_E voters.

3.1 Pre-voting Phase

Before the election, the voting machine generates n_E random numbers $N_{i,j}$ for every candidate p_i resulting in $n_P \cdot n_E$ pairs $(N_{i,j}, p_i)$ of random numbers and candidates (dummy votes). Unconditionally hiding commitments $c_{1,1}, \ldots, c_{n_P, n_E}$ to these pairs are computed with $c_{i,j} = \mathsf{com}((N_{i,j}, p_i), r_{i,j})$ where $r_{i,j}$ denotes a fresh random coin. The commitments are shuffled and published on a public bulletin board. Further, it is proven that the dummy votes are equally distributed among the candidates.

3.2 Voting Phase

In order to cast a vote, the following steps are performed.

- The voter enters her choice into the voting machine.

- A trusted random number generator generates a fresh random number R_j (it must be visible to the voter) and transfers it to the voting machine. Note that these random numbers are indistinguishable from the precalculated dummy votes.
- The voting machine uses the fresh number for the selected candidate and draws a random dummy vote for all other candidates from the pool of dummy votes for that candidate. (Each dummy vote is only used once.)
- The voting machine prints a receipt containing the dummy votes as well as the fresh number.
- The voter verifies that the fresh number is assigned to the candidate she voted for.

Even though the voter receives a receipt for her vote, an outside person (e.g. a coercer) can not distinguish the fresh number from the dummy votes and thus can not tell which candidate the vote was cast for. Since the voter knows which one of the numbers on the receipt was generated freshly, she can check if that number also appears on the public bulletin board afterwards.

3.3   Post-voting Phase

After the election, the voting machine publishes the results together with a proof of correctness on a public bulletin board. The published data consists of

- the final outcome of the poll,
- a lexicographically sorted list of all receipts issued to voters,
- a list of all unused dummy votes with the respective reveal information, and
- non-interactive zero-knowledge proofs that each unopened dummy vote was indeed used on one receipt.

The voters can verify the correctness of the election by checking if their individual receipt is included in the list of all receipts and by checking whether the number of unopened commitments is as expected (that is, for every vote cast, one dummy vote will be left unused).

4   Our Construction

In this section we introduce our construction. It is based on a modularisation of the original Bingo Voting protocol. First we give a brief summary of the protocol and our goal. We then describe the components of our construction in detail. The public output of our scheme is identical to that of the original protocol. Thus, we inherit the correctness and security properties of the original Bingo Voting construction.

4.1   Basic Idea

In the original Bingo Voting construction the voting machine itself is trusted to keep the secrecy of the ballot. It is aware of the dummy votes $N_{i,j}$ and the fresh random number R_j, and it thus learns the choice of the voter. With this information, the voting machine can not only reconstruct the voter's choice, but it also has the ability to determine interim election results.

The general idea behind our construction is to shield the voter's choice from the voting machine. In particular, we deal with an untrusted voting machine by letting it only handle encrypted information. Any public data is—like in the original scheme—unconditionally hidden. Private data is protected by a computationally hiding (encryption) scheme. The voting authorities only take part in the process during the pre- and post-voting phases. We mainly use three techniques:

1. During the pre-voting phase the commitments to the pairs of candidate and dummy vote are computed jointly and blindly by the authorities a_l.
2. The encrypted unveil information for these commitments is also jointly and blindly generated using a homomorphic threshold encryption scheme.
3. The voter chooses her vote using a mechanism that hides the actual choice from the rest of the machine.

As the unveil information for all commitments is encrypted and has never been revealed, the voting machine cannot unveil the precomputed commitments and thus cannot calculate intermediate results of the election by the commitments alone.

Our construction keeps the choice of the voter hidden from all components of the voting machine. We achieve this by using an electro-mechanical pOT device to select between an encrypted dummy vote and an encrypted fresh random number. We describe a possible realisation of pOT in Sect. 2.3.

For the receipt to be printed, we envision a printing device to which each of the voting authorities can input their keys for the threshold encryption scheme in form of a security token. The printing device will then use these tokens to jointly decrypt the dummy votes and the fresh random number. Note that no component of the voting machine learns the choice of the voter since the dummy votes are indistinguishable from the fresh random numbers of the random number generator. During the tallying we publish the same information as in the Bingo Voting scheme. When a commitment has to be revealed (i.e. as it is the case with dummy votes), the voting authorities will decrypt the corresponding reveal information jointly. Note that, because we use a threshold encryption scheme, no single voting authority can unveil commitments by itself.

4.2   A Modular Voting Protocol

The original Bingo Voting protocol introduced a separation between the random number generator and the voting machine to ensure correctness of the result in spite of a corrupted voting machine. We build upon this idea and further separate the protocol (see Fig. 3). In particular, we introduce a separate storage device, an input device, and a printing device. The storage device stores the precomputed encrypted dummy votes, while the input device is used to select a vote (using our novel pOT mechanism). The printing device eliminates the need for the storage device and input device to decrypt votes. Further, we define several small components for very specific tasks: an *append box*, a *split box*, and a *re-randomisation box*. All these components are assumed to be dedicated hardware devices with a very distinct functionality. They are thus easy to build and verify. We assume them to be trusted, thus removing the trust assumption from the entire machine and distributing it among the components. This is not only a reduction in scope, but also in complexity. The assumption is reminiscent of standard tamper-proof hardware assumptions [13, 14].

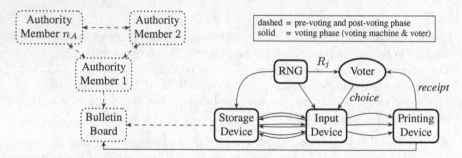

Fig. 3. We separate the voting machine into four main components [2]: a storage device, used to store the encryptions computed during the pre-voting phase; an input device (Figs. 6 and 7), used to perform the actual voting based on an oblivious transfer mechanism; a printing device (Fig. 8); and a random number generator (Fig. 5). See Fig. 4 for the data interchanged between the authority members, the bulletin board, and stored in the storage device.

Authority Members. We rely on a group of n_A authority members. We assume that at least k of them are trustworthy. The members of this group jointly perform the pre-computation and the tallying. They prove the correctness of their computation to each other. If the verification of a proof fails, the verifying member is to stop the process and to protest immediately. How to resolve such a situation is outside the scope of this work. Further, the authority members need a communication channel to exchange information. We assume an authenticated and secret broadcast channel for the authority members.

The Bulletin Board. For the proof of correctness we need to publish data. We put all required data on a public bulletin board. The concept of a bulletin board is used by many voting schemes.

In Fig. 4 we show which data is published on the bulletin board (•). The index (i,j) as well as the commitments of the blind commitments $D_{i,j}$, $D'_{i,j}$, and $C_{i,j}$ are published in the pre-voting phase. The other elements marked with • are published in the post-voting phase.

$$\bullet \bullet \mid \circ \mid \bullet \circ \circ \mid \bullet \circ \circ \mid \bullet \circ \circ \mid \bullet \circ \circ \mid \bullet$$

$$i \; j \mid B_{i,j} \mid (\, c,\, u,\, v\,)=C_{i,j} \mid (\, c,\, u,\, v\,)=C'_{i,j} \mid (\, c,\, u,\, v\,)=D_{i,j} \mid (\, c,\, u,\, v\,)=D'_{i,j} \mid \text{ballot}$$

$$\downarrow \downarrow \mid \uparrow \mid \qquad \uparrow \uparrow \uparrow \mid \qquad \qquad \mid \qquad \downarrow$$

Fig. 4. The table shows a subset of the elements published in the pre- and post-voting phase. The ID (i,j) of each row, the commitments (c), and the ballot are published on the bulletin board ($\bullet$). The ciphers ($B_{i,j}$, u, and v) are only communicated among the authority members ($\circ$). $C_{i,j}$ and $D_{i,j}$ are blind commitments on candidate i. $D'_{i,j}$ is a blind commitment on a dummy vote. $C'_{i,j}$ is a commitment on the fresh random number. The cipher $B_{i,j}$ contains a bit whether voter j voted for candidate i. The ciphers u of $D'_{i,j}$ are stored on the storage device before the voting phase starts ($\downarrow$). During the voting phase, $B_{i,j}$ and $C'_{i,j}$ are stored on the storage device ($\uparrow$).

Summarising the above, the encryption part of the blind commitments and its corresponding data—like mixes including proofs—as well as intermediate results of the creation of the blind commitments, are broadcast in secret between the authority members. The commitment part of the blind commitments and its corresponding data are published on the bulletin board.

The Storage Device. The central element of our modular voting machine is the storage device. Only this part stores data permanently. All other parts need not keep state.

Figure 4 is a symbolic representation of all data: Data stored on the storage device in the pre-voting phase is marked with $\downarrow$. Data stored on the storage device in the voting phase is marked with $\uparrow$.

The Random Number Generator. The random number generator (RNG) has a similar functionality as in the Bingo Voting scheme. During each voting process, it creates a fresh random number R_j and displays it to the voter. In contrast to the Bingo Voting scheme, the RNG sends an *encryption* of R_j to each pOT of the input device and $C'_{1,j} := \mathsf{bCom}(R_j)$ to the storage device. We envision a dedicated channel from the RNG to each pOT instance. We point out that, since the RNG generated the fresh random number (and thus can distinguish it from dummy votes) it can break the security of the protocol. Thus, similar to the original Bingo Voting scheme, we require the RNG to be trusted.

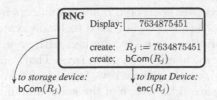

Fig. 5. The random number generator has two outputs [2]: first, it outputs an encryption of the fresh random number to the pOTs of the input device, second it outputs a blind commitment to the random number to the storage device. See Fig. 3 for an overview of the system.

Append-x Box, Re-randomisation Box, and Split Box. In order to control the flow of information between the main components of the voting machine, we use small, state-less devices (see Fig. 7).

One device (*append-x box*) appends an encryption of $x \in \{0,1\}$ to each message it receives. We call the plaintext $b_{i,j} := x$ and the cipher $B_{i,j} := \mathsf{enc}(b_{i,j})$. Note that the device does not necessarily need to encrypt these two values every time, since encryptions can be precomputed and encoded into the device as a fixed string (which will be re-randomized later on).

The second device (*split box*) splits an input tuple into its parts and sends each part to a dedicated component.

The third device (*re-randomisation box*) re-randomises ciphertexts. On input $(\mathsf{enc}(m_1, r_1),\ \mathsf{enc}(m_2, r_2))$ it chooses uniformly at random $\bar{r}_1$ and $\bar{r}_2$ and outputs a tuple of ciphertexts containing the same plaintext: $(\mathsf{enc}(m_1, r_1) \cdot \mathsf{enc}(0, \bar{r}_1),\ \mathsf{enc}(m_2, r_2) \cdot \mathsf{enc}(0, \bar{r}_2)) = (\mathsf{enc}(m_1, r_1'),\ \mathsf{enc}(m_2, r_2'))$.

Such devices have a very limited and fixed functionality. Thus, we assume them to be easy to build and to verify and therefore trustworthy.

Input Device with Physical Oblivious Transfer. The input device consists of one physical oblivious transfer (pOT) module for each candidate. We describe a possible realisation of a pOT in Sect. 2.3. Each of these modules takes two inputs: the first input is an encryption of the fresh random number generated by the RNG. The second input (the standard selection) is an encryption of the dummy vote as it is stored in the storage device (see Fig. 6). Both of these values are marked (by appending an encrypted 0 or a 1, respectively). Afterwards, the tuples are re-randomised. When voting for a specific candidate, the voter advises the corresponding pOT module for that candidate to select the fresh random number instead of the encrypted dummy vote. As per the construction of the pOT module, the storage device cannot learn whether the dummy vote or the fresh randomness was selected, and thus will not know for which candidate the vote was cast. The outputs of all these pOT modules are processed by split boxes. The first part is sent to the printing device, where it is used to print out the receipt. The second part is sent to the storage device, where it is used to produce the tally (see Fig. 6).

Printing Device. The printing device's task is to create a receipt identical to the receipt used in the original Bingo Voting scheme. It has the list of candidates stored internally and receives encrypted random numbers from the input device. They arrive on dedicated channels, but need to be decrypted prior to printing.

To this end, the printing device is supplied with security tokens that hold copies of the authority member's decryption keys. They jointly decrypt the random numbers without revealing their keys (see Fig. 8). We point out that the printing device is unaware of the origin of the random numbers and thus cannot break the confidentiality of the vote *even given access to the decryption tokens*. Further, for each voting machine, different keys are to be generated and used in the security tokens. This way, a potential theft of the security tokens has a

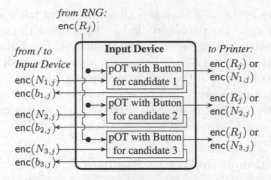

Fig. 6. Our input device consists of one pOT module per candidate [2]. Each module receives two inputs: and encrypted dummy vote and encrypted fresh random number. See Fig. 7 for details.

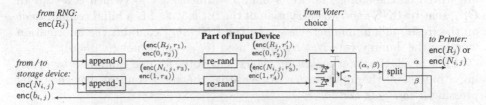

Fig. 7. Physical oblivious transfer (pOT) module [2]: both inputs are amended with an encryption of a 0 or a 1, respectively and re-randomised. See Figs. 6 and 3 for an overview.

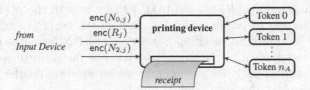

Fig. 8. The printing device uses security tokens to decrypt the encrypted random numbers, obtained by the input device through the pOT mechanism [2]. The security tokens store the key securely and are able to decrypt jointly.

limited effect (similar to that of a broken ballot box). The printing device publishes each receipt on the bulletin board. To secure this connection one could use a commercially available data diode hardware appliance.

4.3 Pre-voting Phase

In the pre-voting phase the keys of the threshold encryption scheme are created and distributed. Every authority member publishes the public key of her signing key $s_l^{(ver)}$ with $1 \leq l \leq n_A$. After this step $n_P \cdot n_E$ blind commitment pairs to the dummy votes $(D_{i,j},\ D'_{i,j})$ with $1 \leq i \leq n_P$ and $1 \leq j \leq n_E$ are created in a distributed manner (see Sect. 2.2). When all commitment pairs are created, each authority member signs the published data and publishes the signature as well. (Recall that only the commitments are published on the bulletin board—the encrypted unveil information is only broadcast among the authority members.)

After the pre-computation the voting machine is prepared and the encryptions of the dummy votes are stored on the storage device. Furthermore, each authority member provides the printing device with a secure hardware module that contains her secret decryption key.

4.4   The Execution of the Voting Protocol

Recall that during the pre-voting phase, we store a set of encrypted dummy votes for each expected vote $1 \leq j \leq n_E$ on the storage device. During each individual voting process by voter j, for each candidate i two additional data components are stored on the storage device: a blind commitment $C'_{i,j}$ (which is a copy of $C'_{1,j}$, sent by RNG) and an encryption of the bit $b_{i,j}$. $C'_{i,j}$ is a blind commitment on the fresh random number, chosen by the RNG. $b_{i,j}$ contains the information whether the dummy vote $N_{i,j}$ has been used ($b_{i,j} = 1$) or not ($b_{i,j} = 0$).

First of all, the voter makes her choice and votes for one candidate by pressing a button on the input device. Afterwards, the voter confirms her choice by pressing a *cast vote button.*

Now, the storage device sends one element of an unused set to each pOT instance of the input device via its n_P dedicated channels (one dummy vote per candidate). On their way, these encrypted values are fed through an append-1 box and are re-randomised. At the same time the RNG sends an encryption of the fresh random number R_j to each pOT. On its way to the pOT an encryption of 0 is attached by an append-0 box and—both $\mathsf{enc}(R_j)$ and $\mathsf{enc}(0)$—are re-randomised by a re-randomisation box. Also, the RNG creates a blind commitment $C'_{1,j}$ and sends it to the storage device. For the voter to verify that the fresh random number matches the number which appears on the receipt later on, the RNG displays the fresh random number.

Because an encryption of a 0 is appended to all fresh random numbers and an encryption of 1 appended to all dummy votes, the authority members (which possess the decryption keys) can distinguish which dummy votes were used and which were not.

All of the pOT instances are evaluated. For the candidate of the voter's choice, the fresh random number is selected by the pOT module. For all other candidates, the dummy vote is used. The selected tuples (either $(\mathsf{enc}(R_j), \mathsf{enc}(b_{i,j} := 0))$ or $(\mathsf{enc}(N_{i,j}), \mathsf{enc}(b_{i,j} := 1)))$ are sent to a split box. There, the first part is sent to the printing device and the second part is sent back to the storage device to mark which dummy votes were used and which were not.

The printing device then uses the authority members' security tokens to decrypt the values and prints the results next to the corresponding candidate name p_i. The voter verifies that the number displayed on the RNG is assigned to the party she intended to vote for. If this is not the case, the voter has to protest immediately [1]. When the voter is satisfied with the receipt, it is published on the bulletin board.

4.5   Tally and Verification

To compute the tally, data from the storage device is published on the bulletin board as shown in Fig. 4. Afterwards, the authority members process the entries of the bulletin board. In the following we do not consider the sets of dummy votes that were prepared for voters who never voted. They can be unveiled to show they have never been used.

Publishing. For each $1 \leq j \leq n_E$, the storage device has received one blind commitment $C'_{1,j}$ and n_P ciphers $\{B_{i,j}\}^{n_P}_{i=1}$. $D_{i,j}$ and $D'_{i,j}$ have been published in the pre-voting phase. We complete these entries as follows (see Fig. 4):

- A copy of each element in $\{C'_{1,j}\}^{n_E}_{j=1}$ is stored in the cells labelled with $C'_{i,j}$ where $1 \leq i \leq n_P$.
- The cells $C_{i,j}$ are filled with a copy of the corresponding cell $D_{i,j}$.
- All ciphers in $\{B_{i,j}\}^{n_P}_{i=1}$ are stored in the cell with the corresponding name.

Verification. For the verification of the ballots and the tally, the authority members create an empty list U ("unused"). We now describe the verification process for $1 \leq j \leq n_E$. It shows that the set with the rows (i,j) $(1 \leq i \leq n_P)$ fits to the published ballot. All ballots are processed in the same way. After that procedure, the tally can be computed.

The rows of the set are shuffled by the authority members—the columns i and j are ignored, though. Afterwards the authority members jointly decrypt the bit $b_{i,j}$ of each entry. The authority members create an empty list P_j ("print"), which stores the dummy votes and blind commitments to the candidates which have been used the voting process.

$$
\begin{aligned}
\text{if } b_{i,j} = 0: \quad U &:= U \cup \{(D_{i,j},\ D'_{i,j})\} \\
P_j &:= P_j \cup \{(C_{i,j},\ C'_{i,j})\} \\
\text{if } b_{i,j} = 1: \quad P_j &:= P_j \cup \{(D_{i,j},\ D'_{i,j})\} \\
\text{delete} & \quad (C_{i,j},\ C'_{i,j})
\end{aligned}
$$

The authority members shuffle the list P_j and unveil the commitments by decrypting the ciphers. Recall that only the commitment part of the blind commitment as well as its unveil information are stored on bulletin board. The ciphers—also part of the blind commitment—are only known to the authority members. Except for its order, the unveiled data should fit to the corresponding ballot. This proves the correctness of the ballots.

Tally. When the correctness of all ballots is proven, U contains the commitment pairs of the unused dummy votes. U serves to figure out the final tally and to prove its correctness: after shuffling U, the commitment pairs are unveiled. Each pair contains an unused dummy vote and the according candidate name. This list of unveiled candidate names constitutes the tally.

4.6   Authority

Trust assumptions are a fundamental aspect of cryptographic election schemes. It is our belief that such trust is best placed in an independently constituted group who forms the voting authority. The size of the group and the tasks of the group members should not depend on the design of the voting scheme. In our case all authority members have the same task: Create a share for each dummy vote and ensure that her share is part of the according dummy vote. During the tallying the authority members jointly decrypt the tally as described above. The size of the group can be chosen as necessary. Thus, coercion resistance can not be undermined without the collusion of at least k authority members.

4.7   Security

We claim that a passively corrupted voting machine does not receive any information about the voter's choice. We hide the voters choice from the storage device by using our pOT mechanism. We prove that the storage device can not learn anything from the information it observes using an adaptive game-based indistinguishability proof. In this game, the attacker first votes on behalf of a number of voters and observes all communication inside the storage device. Then, he outputs two candidates and receives the transfered data for one of them. We prove that he can not tell which vote he received the communication for by giving a reduction to IND-CPA. Concluding, the adversary cannot learn a single bit of the voter's choice.

Definition 4 (View). *We define* $\mathsf{view}(j, x) := \{\forall i \leq n_p : (\mathsf{enc}(b_{i,j}), \mathsf{enc}(N_{i,j}), \mathsf{com}(p_i, r), \mathsf{enc}(p_i), \mathsf{enc}(r), \mathsf{com}(R_j, r'), \mathsf{enc}(R_j), \mathsf{enc}(r'))\}$ $(b_{i,j} = 0$ *if* $i = x)$ *as the set of all messages the voting machine can observe when voter e_j has voted for p_x.*

Security Game 1 $(\mathsf{IND\text{-}CV}^{\mathcal{A}}_{(\mathsf{enc},\mathsf{com})}(k))$

1. The experiment performs the setup for enc, receives (pk, sk) and chooses a random bit $b \leftarrow \{0, 1\}$.
2. The adversary outputs n_p and n_E to the experiment. The experiment performs the precomputation for the voting scheme according to these parameters. It gives the precomputed values to the adversary.
3. The adversary chooses a voter $1 \leq j \leq n_E$ and a choice $1 \leq x \leq n_p$ for the voter, and outputs (j, x) to the experiment. The experiment executes the voting protocol for voter j choosing candidate x, and outputs $\mathsf{view}(j, x)$ to the adversary. (The adversary is only allowed to choose a voter j that has yet to vote.)
4. The adversary can repeat this step as often as he wishes (bounded by his running time). Afterwards, he outputs "end" to the experiment.
5. The adversary then again chooses a (yet-undecided) voter $1 \leq j_c \leq n_E$ and *two* votes for candidates x_0, x_1 with $x_0 \neq x_1$ and submits (j_c, x_0, x_1) to the experiment. The adversary receives $\mathsf{view}(j_c, x_b)$.
6. The adversary outputs b' as a guess for b.

Definition 5 (Indistinguishability under Chosen Votes). *A voting process has* indistinguishability under chosen votes (IND-CV), *if*

$$\forall \mathcal{A}, c \in \mathbb{N} \exists k_0 \forall k > k_0 : |\Pr[\text{IND-CV}_{(\text{enc,com})}^{\mathcal{A}} = 1]| \leq \frac{1}{2} + k^{-c}$$

Theorem 1. *Oblivious Bingo Voting exhibits indistinguishability under chosen votes if* enc *is an* IND-CPA *secure encryption scheme and* com *is a perfectly hiding commitment scheme.*

Proof. We prove the claim in two steps. First, we modify the security game: we omit the commitments from the view. By assumption the commitments are perfectly hiding, and thus information-theoretically indistinguishable from randomness. The adversary cannot gain information from them. The remaining view is $\text{view}(j, x) := \{\forall i \leq n_p : (\text{enc}(b_{i,j}), \text{enc}(N_{i,j}), \text{enc}(p_i), \text{enc}(r), \text{enc}(R_j), \text{enc}(r'))\}$.

Second, towards a contradiction assume a successful adversary on IND-CV. We will use this adversary to break IND-CPA. To this end, the reduction has to simulate IND-CV to the adversary, using only the IND-CPA experiment. The reduction is as follows:

- When receiving n_p and n_E from the adversary, use (pk) (received from the IND-CPA experiment) to generate all hidden commitments on dummy votes and give them to the adversary.
- Receive a voter $1 \leq j \leq n_E$ and a choice $1 \leq x \leq n_p$ from the adversary. Generate the encryptions in the view using enc with pk as key.
- When receiving the "end" message from the adversary, also receive a voter j_c and candidates x_0, x_1 from the adversary.
- Generate two views $\text{view}(j_c, x_0) =: m_0$ and $\text{view}(j_c, x_1) =: m_1$ and pass them as the challenge to the IND-CV experiment.
- Upon receiving m_b from the experiment, pass it to the adversary running in IND-CV and forward its guess b' to the IND-CPA experiment.

The reduction perfectly simulates the IND-CV experiment to the adversary. Thus, we inherit the adversary's success probability. As we assumed that the encryption scheme has IND-CPA security, this is a contradiction, which concludes the argument.

5 Realisation

In this section we give a more detailed description of the protocols and algorithms involved. Our aim is to facilitate an implementation of our voting protocol. In particular we show how we realise blind commitments and how we generate them in a distributed way.

5.1   Blind Commitments

Blind commitments, as introduced in Sect. 2, are based upon a perfectly hiding and computationally binding commitment scheme ($\mathsf{com}(m, r)$) and an IND-CPA encryption scheme ($\mathsf{enc}(m, r)$). We require them to be *homomorphic* (according to Definition 1) and *re-randomisable* (according to Definition 3).

We instantiate them with the Pedersen commitment scheme [12] and a compatible threshold encryption scheme by Cramer et al. [16] (which in turn, is based on Paillier's encryption scheme [17]). In the following, we present both schemes in detail and show how they need to be combined for the blind commitments to work.

Pedersen Commitment Scheme. The Pedersen commitment scheme requires two large primes p_c and q_c, such that q_c divides $p_c - 1$. In addition, let g_c and h_c be elements of G_{q_c} where G_{q_c} is the unique subgroup of $\mathbb{Z}_p^*$ of order q_c. For the security of the scheme, it is essential that $log_{g_c} h_c$ is hard to compute. Committing to a message $m \in \mathbb{Z}_q$ with randomness $r \in \mathbb{Z}_q$ is defined as

$$\mathsf{com}(m, r) := g_c^m h_c^r \bmod p_c$$

Using this equation we can see the homomorphic property of the scheme as follows:

$$
\begin{aligned}
\big(\mathsf{com}(m_1, r_1) \cdot \mathsf{com}(m_2, r_2)\big) \bmod p_c &= \big((g_c^{m_1} h_c^{r_1}) \cdot (g_c^{m_2} h_c^{r_2})\big) \bmod p_c \\
&= (g_c^{m_1 + m_2} h_c^{r_1 + r_2}) \bmod p_c \\
&= \mathsf{com}(m_1 + m_2 \bmod q_c, r_1 + r_2 \bmod q_c)
\end{aligned}
$$

The re-randomisation of a Pedersen commitment can be done as follows.

$$
\begin{aligned}
\mathsf{re\text{-}rand}(\mathsf{com}(m, r), \bar{r}) &:= \mathsf{com}(m, r) \cdot h_c^{\bar{r}} \bmod p_c \\
&= (g_c^m h_c^r) \cdot h_c^{\bar{r}} \bmod p_c \\
&= (g_c^m h_c^{r + \bar{r}}) \bmod p_c \\
&= \mathsf{com}(m, r + \bar{r})
\end{aligned}
$$

Threshold Encryption Scheme. The encryption scheme presented by Paillier has been used by Damgård and Jurik to create a (k, n_A)-threshold encryption scheme [17, 18]. Cramer et al. [16] first proposed to combine this scheme with the Pedersen commitment scheme. Their goal is to base multiparty computation on homomorphic threshold systems.

The threshold encryption system is based on two strong primes p_e and q_e with $p_e = 2p_e' + 1$ and $q_e = 2q_e' + 1$.

Let $n_e = p_e q_e$, $m_e = p_e' q_e'$, and $g_e = n_e + 1$[1]. The coefficients b_i, $i \in [1, .., k-1]$, are chosen randomly. Additionally, the secret key d is chosen such that

---

[1] In addition, Damgård and Jurik introduce the parameter s which has an influence on the size of plaintext space and chipertext space. This parameter can be changed without changing the other parameters of the scheme. In this paper we set $s = 1$.

$d = 0 \bmod m_e$ and $d = 1 \bmod n_e$. The value b_0 is set to d. Afterwards, the polynomial $f(X) = \sum_{i=0}^{k-1} b_i X^i \bmod m_e n_e$ of degree $k - 1$ is constructed. The secret share sk_l of authority a_l corresponds to the lth support point of the polynomial f: $sk_l := f(l)$. The scheme uses n_e as the public key. Note that g_e can be calculated from this value.

Encryption. Encrypting a message m using randomness $r \in \mathbb{Z}_{n_e}^*$ is defined as

$$\text{enc}(m, r) := g_e^m r^{n_e} \bmod n_e^2$$

Similar to the Pedersen commitment scheme, the homomorphic property of the encryption scheme can be shown as follows:

$$\begin{aligned}
\text{enc}(m_1, r_1) \cdot \text{enc}(m_2, r_2) \bmod n_e^2 &= \left((g_e^{m_1} r_1^{n_e}) \cdot (g_e^{m_2} r_2^{n_e})\right) \bmod n_e^2 \\
&= \left((g_e^{m_1 + m_2}(r_1 \cdot r_2)^{n_e})\right) \bmod n_e^2 \\
&= \text{enc}(m_1 + m_2 \bmod n_e, r_1 \cdot r_2 \bmod n_e)
\end{aligned}$$

To re-randomise an encryption, one calculates:

$$\begin{aligned}
\text{re-rand}(\text{enc}(m, r), \bar{r}) &:= \text{enc}(m, r) \cdot \bar{r}^{n_e} \bmod n_e^2 \\
&= (g_e^m \bar{r}^{n_e}) \cdot \bar{r}^{n_e} \bmod n_e^2 \\
&= (g_e^m (r \cdot \bar{r})^{n_e}) \bmod n_e^2 \\
&= \text{enc}(m, r \cdot \bar{r})
\end{aligned}$$

Decryption. To decrypt, we use the characteristics of the Lagrange interpolation. The lth authority uses her secret share sk_l to compute $c_l = c^{2(n_A!)sk_l}$. Then, k of these results (which we define as set S) are combined by calculating:

$$\hat{c} := \prod_{l \in S} c_l^{2\lambda_{0,i}} \bmod n_e^2, \text{ where } \lambda_{0,i} =: n_A! \prod_{l' \in S \setminus l} \frac{-l'}{l - l'} \in \mathbb{Z}.$$

Since we use Lagrange interpolation, $\hat{c}$ is of the form $c^{4(n_A!)^2 d}$. Taking into account the form of the secret key d, it follows that $\hat{c} = (1 + n_e)^{4(n_A!)^2 m}$ where m is the plaintext (see the work of Damgård and Jurik [18] for more details). Algorithm 1 [17] shows how to extract the plaintext m from this equation. Note that, using this procedure, the authorities are not required to reveal their secret keys.

Algorithm 1. Calculating m out of $\hat{c}$ for $s = 1$—derived from Paillier [17].

1: **procedure** CALCULATEPLAINTEXT($\hat{c}$)
2:     $e \leftarrow L(\hat{c} \bmod n^2)$ ▷ calculating log of $\hat{c}$, exploiting the form of $\hat{c}$
3:     $m \leftarrow e \cdot (4(n_A!)^2)^{-1}$
4: **end procedure**
5: **procedure** L(x)   ▷ $x \in \mathbb{Z}$
6:     return $\frac{x-1}{n} \in \mathbb{Z}$
7: **end procedure**

Proof of Correctness. To ensure that each authority calculated c_l correctly, one can use a zero-knowledge proof. Let H be a hash function, ν a general verification key, and $\tilde{c} := c^{4(n_A!)}$.

Each authority chooses a $r \in \{0, ..., 2^{k+2k'} - 1\}$ at random and calculates $\nu_l = \nu^{(n_A!)sk_l} \mod n^2$, $\nu' = \nu^r$, $c' = \tilde{c}^r$, $\eta = H(\nu, \tilde{c}, \nu_l, c_l^2, \nu^{(n_A!)r}, c')$, and $z = sk_l \cdot \eta + r$. The proof then consists of the values (z, η). Alternatively, each authority broadcasts $(z, \eta, c, c_l, \nu, \nu_l)$ internally to simplify the communication between the authorities. The verifying authority calculates $\eta' = H(\nu, \tilde{c}, \nu_l, c_l^2, \nu^{z(n_A!)}\nu_l^{-h}, \tilde{c}^z c_l^{-2\eta})$ and checks whether $\eta' \overset{?}{=} \eta$. This will convince each proving authority that the verifying authority a_l indeed calculated c_l correctly.

5.2 Combining the Two Primitives

The definition of blind commitments (Definitions 1 and 2) requires the commitment scheme and the encryption scheme to be compatible regarding the $+$ operation. We achieve this by setting $q_c := n_e = p_e q_e$. Note that this construction results in a composite value for q_c (with two prime factors). It is essential for the security of the commitment scheme to choose q_e and p_e large enough to make finding the discrete logarithm hard in the corresponding groups.

Re-randomisation. With the presented tools, it is possible to re-randomise a blind commitment $C = (c, u, v) = \mathsf{bCom}(m, r_1, r_2, r_3)$ as follows. We define the re-randomisation
$\mathsf{re\text{-}rand}(C, r_4, r_5, r_6) := (c', u', v')$ with

$$c' := c \cdot h_c^{r_4} = \mathsf{com}(m, r_1 + r_4)$$
$$u' := u \cdot \mathsf{enc}(0, r_5) = \mathsf{enc}(m, r_2 \cdot r_5)$$
$$v' := v \cdot \mathsf{enc}(r_4, r_6) = \mathsf{enc}(r_1 + r_4, r_3 \cdot r_6)$$

5.3 Pre-voting Phase

During the pre-voting phase the blind commitments are created and the parameters for the threshold encryption as well as the Pedersen commitment scheme are calculated. It is necessary to create $n_P \cdot n_E$ blind commitments to the dummy votes (see Algorithm 3) and n_P blind commitments to the eligible candidates (see Algorithm 4). Each blind commitment to the candidates is assigned to n_E blind commitments to the dummy votes. This assignment is necessary for the tally. Also, this allows for an open verification that each candidate has the same amount of dummy votes at the begin of the election.

Algorithm 3 shows how to create blind commitments to dummy votes. Similar to the coin toss algorithm suggested by Blum [19], each authority member commits herself to her share. To avoid problems caused by malleable commitment schemes, we invert the unveil order (see Line 17 of Algorithm 3). Now, it can be shown that the binding and hiding properties ensure that the authority members chose their shares independently from each other. Creating the distributed commitments to the candidates differs from this since the authorities need to commit themselves to a fixed value instead of a random value. The procedure is shown in Algorithm 4. Using this procedure, everyone can convince herself that the commitment to the candidate has been created correctly. In addition, each authority member can convince herself that the encryptions have been calculated properly by authority a_1.

Merging the described tools, we can substantiate the procedure of the pre-vote phase (see Algorithm 2). The correlation between the different blind commitments is disguised by the mix nets we use during the tallying.

Algorithm 2. Pre-Vote Phase—algorithm for each authority member.

```
1: static 1 ≤ l ≤ n_A                                          ▷ ID of authority member a_l
2: procedure PreVotePhase(n_P, n_E, {p_i}_{i=1}^{n_P})
3:     publish: s_l^{(ver)}                               ▷ publish verification key for sig (·)
4:     CreateBlindCommitmentsOnDummyVotes(n_P, n_E)
5:     if l equals 1 then
6:         CreateBlindCommitmentsOnCandidates(n_P, {p_i}_{i=1}^{n_P})
7:         copy: {{C_{i,j}}_{i=1}^{n_P}}_{j=1}^{n_E} = {{D_{i,j}}_{i=1}^{n_P}}_{j=1}^{n_E}     ▷ copy bCom(p_i)
8:     end if
9: end procedure
```

---

6 Conclusion and Future Work

We present a voting scheme that, to the best of our knowledge, is the first to achieve ballot secrecy as well as correctness without relying on a fully trusted voting machine.

This paper is an extended and improved version of a conference paper [2]. Assuming a passive adversary, no single component of our voting machine can break the coercion resistance on its own. This extended version improves upon the original publication in terms of efficiency and transparency. We also added a section which elaborates on the details of our construction. More concretely, we discuss which techniques to select and how to combine them. We also give algorithms in pseudocode to demonstrate how to carry out particular procedures. These details are a step towards an implementation of our scheme, which we leave open for future work.

In our construction we substitute complete trust in the voting machine with trust in simpler components which are easier to comprehend and to verify. In particular, we use a pOT to hide the selection of the vote from the voting machine. Future work in this area should focus on investigating the feasibility of the pOT device and implementing it.

We assume security tokens which can securely store the authorities' keys in order to decrypt and print a receipt for the voter, without even the printer being

Algorithm 3. Create blind commitments—algorithm for each authority member.

1: static $1 \leq l \leq n_A$ ▷ ID of authority member a_l
2: **procedure** CREATEBLINDCOMMITMENTSONDUMMYVOTES(n_P, n_E)
3:     **for** $1 \leq i \leq n_P$ **do**   ▷ for each Candidate and...
4:        **for** $1 \leq j \leq n_E$ **do**   ▷ ...for each voter...
5:           $r_1, r_2, r_3, r_4 \leftarrow$ random value   ▷ ...choose 4 random values and:
6:           $c_{i,j}^{(a_l)} \leftarrow \mathsf{com}(r_1, r_2)$ ▷ create commitment
7:           $u_{i,j}^{(a_l)} \leftarrow \mathsf{enc}(r_1, r_3)$ ▷ create unveil information
8:           $v_{i,j}^{(a_l)} \leftarrow \mathsf{enc}(r_2, r_4)$ ▷ create unveil information
9:        **end for**
10:     **end for**
11:           ▷ commit to own shares without knowledge of the other shares:
12:     $\zeta^{(a_l)} \leftarrow \mathsf{com}(\{\{c_{i,j}^{(a_l)}, u_{i,j}^{(a_l)}, v_{i,j}^{(a_l)}\}_{i=1}^{n_P}\}_{j=1}^{n_E})$
13:     **if** $l \neq 1$ **then**   ▷ publish commitment in ascending order
14:        wait until $\zeta^{(a_{l-1})}$ is broadcast internally
15:     **end if**
16:     broadcast internally: $\zeta^{(a_l)}$
17:     **if** $l \neq n_A$ **then**   ▷ unveil commitment in reverse order
18:        wait until $\zeta^{(a_{l+1})}$ is unveiled
19:     **end if**
20:     broadcast internally: unveil information of $\zeta^{(a_l)}$
21:     **if** unveil information of $\zeta^{(a_1)}, \zeta^{(a_2)}, \ldots,$ or $\zeta^{(a_{n_A})}$ does not fit **then**
22:        throw error and abort
23:     **end if**
24:     ▷ Recall, $\{\{c_{i,j}^{(a_l)}, u_{i,j}^{(a_l)}, v_{i,j}^{(a_l)}\}_{i=1}^{n_P}\}_{j=1}^{n_E}$ is part of the unveil information of $\zeta^{(a_l)}$
25:     **for** $1 \leq i \leq n_P$ **do**   ▷ for each Candidate and...
26:        **for** $1 \leq j \leq n_E$ **do**   ▷ ...for each voter:
27:           $c_{i,j}^{(D')} \leftarrow \prod_{k=1}^{n_A} c_{i,j}^{(a_k)}$ ▷ create commitment of blind commitment
28:           $u_{i,j}^{(D')} \leftarrow \prod_{k=1}^{n_A} u_{i,j}^{(a_k)}$ ▷ create unveil information of blind commitment
29:           $v_{i,j}^{(D')} \leftarrow \prod_{k=1}^{n_A} v_{i,j}^{(a_k)}$ ▷ create unveil information of blind commitment
30:        **end for**
31:     **end for**
32:     $\sigma_{\mathrm{pub}}^{(a_l)} \leftarrow \mathsf{sig}_{s_l^{(\mathrm{sig})}}\left(\left\{\{c_{i,j}^{(D')}\}_{i=1}^{n_P}\right\}_{j=1}^{n_E}\right)$ ▷ confirm correct result
33:     $\sigma_{\mathrm{int}}^{(a_l)} \leftarrow \mathsf{sig}_{s_l^{(\mathrm{sig})}}\left(\left\{\{(u_{i,j}^{(D')}, v_{i,j}^{(D')})\}_{i=1}^{n_P}\right\}_{j=1}^{n_E}\right)$ ▷ confirm correct result
34:     **if** $l = 1$ **then**   ▷ first authority member a_1 publishes data
35:        publish: $\{\{c_{i,j}^{(D')}\}_{i=1}^{n_P}\}_{j=1}^{n_E}$ ▷ publish commitments
36:        broadcast internally: $\{\{u_{i,j}^{(D')}, v_{i,j}^{(D')}\}_{i=1}^{n_P}\}_{j=1}^{n_E}$ ▷ send unveil information
37:     **end if**
38:     publish: $\sigma_{\mathrm{pub}}^{(a_l)}$ ▷ publish confirmation
39:     broadcast internally: $\sigma_{\mathrm{int}}^{(a_l)}$ ▷ send confirmation
40:     **for** $1 \leq l \leq n_A$ **do**
41:        verify $\sigma_{\mathrm{pub}}^{(a_l)}$ and $\sigma_{\mathrm{int}}^{(a_l)}$ ▷ if not, throw error and abort
42:     **end for**
43:     sign and publish "everything is ok"
44: **end procedure**

Algorithm 4. Create blind commitments on each p_i—algorithm only for a_1.

1: **procedure** CREATEBLINDCOMMITMENTSONCANDIDATES($n_P, \{p_i\}_{i=1}^{n_P}$)
2:     **for** $1 \leq i \leq n_P$ authority member a_1 **do**   ▷ for each Candidate...
3:        $r_1, r_2, r_3 \leftarrow$ random value   ▷ ...choose 3 random values and create:
4:        $c_{i,1}^{(D)} \leftarrow \mathsf{com}(p_i, r_1)$ ▷ create commitment
5:        $u_{i,1}^{(D)} \leftarrow \mathsf{enc}(p_i, r_2)$ ▷ create unveil information
6:        $v_{i,1}^{(D)} \leftarrow \mathsf{enc}(r_1, r_3)$ ▷ create unveil information
7:        publish: $c_{i,1}^{(D)}, p_i, r_1$ ▷ publish commitment and unveil information
8:        broadcast internally: $u_{i,1}^{(D)}, v_{i,1}^{(D)}, r_2, r_3$
9:     **end for**
10: **end procedure**

---

able to break coercion resistance. An interesting area of future investigation is achieving coercion resistance even when some of these devices are actively malicious.

References

1. Bohli, J.-M., Müller-Quade, J., Röhrich, S.: Bingo voting: secure and coercion-free voting using a trusted random number generator. In: Alkassar, A., Volkamer, M. (eds.) Vote-ID 2007. LNCS, vol. 4896, pp. 111–124. Springer, Heidelberg (2007). doi:10.1007/978-3-540-77493-8_10
2. Achenbach, D., Löwe, B., Müller-Quade, J., Rill, J.: Oblivious voting–hiding votes from the voting machine in bingo voting. In: Proceedings of the 13th International Joint Conference on e-Business and Telecommunications, SECRYPT, vol. 4, pp. 85–96 (2016)
3. Chaum, D., Carback, R.T., Clark, J., Essex, A., Popoveniuc, S., Rivest, R.L., Ryan, P.Y., Shen, E., Sherman, A.T., Vora, P.L.: Scantegrity II: end-to-end verifiability by voters of optical scan elections through confirmation codes. IEEE Trans. Inf. Forensics Secur. **4**, 611–627 (2009)
4. Feldman, A.J., Halderman, J.A., Felten, E.W.: Security analysis of the diebold accuvote-ts voting machine (2006)
5. Chaum, D., Carback, R.T., Clark, J., Conway, J., Essex, A., Herrnson, P.S., Mayberry, T., Popoveniuc, S., Rivest, R.L., Shen, E., Sherman, A.T., Vora, P.L.: Scantegrity II municipal election at takoma park: the first E2E binding governmental election with ballot privacy. In: 19th USENIX Security Symposium (2010)
6. Based, M.A., Tsay, J.-K., Mjølsnes, S.F.: PEVS: a secure electronic voting scheme using polling booths. In: Xiang, Y., Pathan, M., Tao, X., Wang, H. (eds.) ICDKE 2012. LNCS, vol. 7696, pp. 189–205. Springer, Heidelberg (2012). doi:10.1007/978-3-642-34679-8_18
7. Moran, T., Naor, M.: Split-ballot voting: everlasting privacy with distributed trust. ACM Trans. Inf. Syst. Secur. (TISSEC) **13**, 16 (2010)
8. Cortier, V., Fuchsbauer, G., Galindo, D.: Beleniosrf: a strongly receipt-free electronic voting scheme. Cryptology ePrint Archive, Report 2015/629 (2015). http://eprint.iacr.org/2015/629
9. Adida, B.: Helios: web-based open-audit voting. In: USENIX Security Symposium, vol. 17, pp. 335–348 (2008)

10. Blazy, O., Fuchsbauer, G., Pointcheval, D., Vergnaud, D.: Signatures on random-izable ciphertexts. In: Catalano, D., Fazio, N., Gennaro, R., Nicolosi, A. (eds.) PKC 2011. LNCS, vol. 6571, pp. 403–422. Springer, Heidelberg (2011). doi:10.1007/978-3-642-19379-8_25

11. Ryan, P.Y.A., Roenne, P.B., Iovino, V.: Selene: voting with transparent verifiabil-ity and coercion-mitigation. Cryptology ePrint Archive, Report 2015/1105 (2015). http://eprint.iacr.org/2015/1105

12. Pedersen, T.P.: Non-interactive and information-theoretic secure verifiable secret sharing. In: Feigenbaum, J. (ed.) CRYPTO 1991. LNCS, vol. 576, pp. 129–140. Springer, Heidelberg (1992). doi:10.1007/3-540-46766-1_9

13. Katz, J.: Universally composable multi-party computation using tamper-proof hardware. In: Naor, M. (ed.) EUROCRYPT 2007. LNCS, vol. 4515, pp. 115–128. Springer, Heidelberg (2007). doi:10.1007/978-3-540-72540-4_7

14. Moran, T., Segev, G.: David and Goliath commitments: UC computation for asym-metric parties using tamper-proof hardware. In: Smart, N. (ed.) EUROCRYPT 2008. LNCS, vol. 4965, pp. 527–544. Springer, Heidelberg (2008). doi:10.1007/978-3-540-78967-3_30

15. Kilian, J.: Founding crytpography on oblivious transfer. In: Proceedings of the Twentieth Annual ACM Symposium on Theory of Computing, pp. 20–31. ACM (1988)

16. Cramer, R., Damgård, I., Nielsen, J.B.: Multiparty computation from threshold homomorphic encryption. In: Pfitzmann, B. (ed.) EUROCRYPT 2001. LNCS, vol. 2045, pp. 280–300. Springer, Heidelberg (2001). doi:10.1007/3-540-44987-6_18

17. Paillier, P.: Public-key cryptosystems based on composite degree residuosity classes. In: Stern, J. (ed.) EUROCRYPT 1999. LNCS, vol. 1592, pp. 223–238. Springer, Heidelberg (1999). doi:10.1007/3-540-48910-X_16

18. Damgård, I., Jurik, M.: A generalisation, a simpli.cation and some applications of paillier's probabilistic public-key system. In: Kim, K. (ed.) PKC 2001. LNCS, vol. 1992, pp. 119–136. Springer, Heidelberg (2001). doi:10.1007/3-540-44586-2_9

19. Blum, M.: Coin flipping by telephone a protocol for solving impossible problems. SIGACT News **15**, 23–27 (1983)

A Methodology for Silent and Continuous Authentication in Mobile Environment

Gerardo Canfora[1], Paolo di Notte[2], Francesco Mercaldo[3],
and Corrado Aaron Visaggio[1(✉)]

[1] Department of Engineering, University of Sannio, Benevento, Italy
{canfora,visaggio}@unisannio.it
[2] Koine srl, Benevento, Italy
dinotte.paolo@gmail.com
[3] Institute for Informatics and Telematics,
National Research Council of Italy (CNR), Pisa, Italy
francesco.mercaldo@iit.cnr.it

Abstract. Since the pervasiveness of mobile technologies has been increasing, sensitive user information is often stored on mobile devices. Currently, mobile devices do not verify the identity of the user after the login. This enables attackers full access to sensitive data and applications on the device, if they obtain the password or grab the device after login. In order to mitigate this risk, we propose a continuous and silent monitoring process based on a set of features: orientation, touch and cell tower. The assumption is that the features are representative of smartphone owner interaction with the device and this is the reason why the features can be useful to distinguish the owner from an impostor. Results show that our system, modeling the user behavior of 21 volunteer participants, obtains encouraging results, since we measured a precision in distinguishing an impostor from the owner between 99% and 100%.

1 Introduction

Smartphones have become ubiquitous computing platforms, allowing users to access the Internet and many online services anytime and anywhere. As a personal device, a smartphone contains important private information, such as text messages, always-logged-in emails, and contact list. As a portable device, a smartphone is much easier to get lost or stolen than conventional computing platforms. In order to prevent the private information stored on smartphones from falling into the hands of adversaries, the authentication of mobile devices has become an important issue. Most of the methods for authenticating users on mobile devices define an entry point into the system. Login-time pins and textual and graphical passwords [1–3] are the most popular mechanisms for authenticating smartphone users. With the growing popularity of touch interface based mobile devices, the touch-surface has become the dominant human-computer interface. This has led to the need for authentication techniques better suited to a touch interface, such as Sae-Bae and Memon [4]. These mechanisms suffer

© Springer International Publishing AG 2017
M.S. Obaidat (Ed): ICETE 2016, CCIS 764, pp. 241–265, 2017.
https://doi.org/10.1007/978-3-319-67876-4_12

from two drawbacks: (i) they are static, that means they authenticate the user only at the beginning of the session and does not offer any protection against illicit access after the login, i.e. in the case of abandoned device or when a remotely controlled program runs on the device, (ii) passwords and pins require user's attention to their entry and therefore they are not suitable for continuous authentication, and finally (iii) passwords can be stolen or forgotten. In order to overcome this one-step authentication, the *continuous authentication*, also called *active authentication*, was introduced, where the identity of the user is verified during all the usage of the device. Continuous authentication methods complement the entry point methods by monitoring the user after a successful login.

Research on continuous authentication started in 1995 when Shepherd [5] and Monrose et al. [6] showed some impressive results on continuous authentication using keystroke dynamics. Continuous authentication is prevalently realized by checking two subsets of biometric authentication, physiological and behavioral. These authentication methods identify the user through measurable physical or behavioral characteristics.

Physiological biometric authentication measures physical characteristics of users body that make them unique. Physiological methods include fingerprint scanning, facial recognition, hand geometry recognition or retinal scans [7]. One drawback of physical biometrics is that they need specific hardware to collect the biometric data. This hardware entails additional costs and a layer to the login process. Another drawback is that all of the physical biometric methods still produce an error rate which is not acceptable for real applications [8].

Behavioral biometric authentication makes use of behavioral profiles of a user resulting from both psychological and physiological differences from person to person. Behavioral methods include keystroke dynamics [9,10], mouse dynamics [11,12], voice recognition [7], signature verification [7] and Graphical User Interface (GUI) usage analysis [13]. Due to the variability of the human body and mind, the adoption of this type of biometrics has lagged behind physiological biometrics.

In this paper we propose a method to silently and continuously verify the identity of a mobile user. Our method, presented in [14] defines the user profile by merging together information about:

– how the user handles the device;
– how the user touches the keyboards;
– daily habits of the user.

Using well-known machine learning algorithms we classify the features set obtained from real devices employed in real environment to test the effectiveness of the features extracted.

We evaluate the features set in two experiments:

– the first one is aimed to verify whether the feature set is able to discriminate mobile owner from impostors;

– the second one is aimed to verify whether considering the feature set values obtained jointly with the usage of a specific application it is possible to discriminate the mobile owner from the impostors.

The first experiment demonstrated that the fusion of these three classes of features is able to detect impostors with a precision of 0.995, a false acceptance rate of 0.7% and a false rejection rate of 0.3%, which are values largely better than the values gathered with the antagonist methods for the continuous authentication that can be found in literature.

The second one confirms that the fusion of the three classes of features is able to discriminate between owner and impostors even considering the events sent by users to a single application.

The main advantages of our method are:

– these biometrics can be captured by using the device built-in sensors without additional hardware;
– the features can be gathered with a good degree of precision and are not influenced by external factors (noises, air impurity);
– they can be collected while the user is using the mobile phone: the user is not required to enter any image or voice (this is the reason why our method is called *silent*);
– the performances obtained are significantly better than those reported in literature.

The paper proceeds as follows: Sect. 2 describes and motivates our detection method; Sect. 3 illustrates the results of experiments; Sect. 4 discusses the related work; finally, conclusions are drawn in Sect. 5.

2   The Method

In this section we discuss the approach we propose. Basically, we extract a set of features, captured directly on the device, representing the user behavior.

We consider the following elements of the human behavior in order to characterize mobile users:

– *How users hold the devices*: each user is inherently characterized by the way she holds the device. The inclination is determined by the user's arm and eyes, in order to make the experience of device use comfortable. Indeed the way in which the device is held depends on both the anatomic aspects and the personal habits, including the confidence degree with the device;
– *How users write on the device keyboard*: in addition to the combination of eyes and arm position, an user is also characterized by the way she types. It is a consequence of the first aspect we expose, e.g. an user that keeps the device with one hand will have a different typing style from an user that keeps the device with two hands;

– *User daily habits*: this feature captures the frequency a user is located in a certain place. For instance, people usually work in the same place, and this is the reason why the device is connected for many hours a day with the same cell tower.

Starting from these considerations we define the information we need to collect to characterize mobile users: information about orientation (*How users hold the devices*), about touch (*How users write on the device keyboard*) and about cell (*User daily habits*).

In order to obtain *Orientation information* we use the orientation sensor, which uses a device's geomagnetic field sensor in combination with a device's accelerometer. Using these two hardware sensors, an orientation sensor provides data for the following three dimensions (i.e., the orientation features):

– *Azimuth*, i.e. the degrees of rotation around the z axis. This is the angle between the magnetic north and the device's y axis. For example, if the device's y axis is aligned with the magnetic north this value is 0, and if the device's y axis is pointing south this value is 180. Likewise, when the y axis is pointing east this value is 90 and when it is pointing west this value is 270.
– *Pitch*, i.e. the degrees of rotation around the x axis. This value is positive when the positive z axis rotates toward the positive y axis, and it is negative when the positive z axis rotates toward the negative y axis. The range of values is 180° to −180°.
– *Roll*, i.e. the degrees of rotation around the y axis. This value is positive when the positive z axis rotates toward the positive x axis, and it is negative when the positive z axis rotates toward the negative x axis. The range of values is 90° to −90°.

The orientation sensor derives its data by processing the raw sensor data from the accelerometer and the geomagnetic field sensor. Because of the heavy processing that is involved, the accuracy and precision of the orientation sensor is diminished (specifically, this sensor is only reliable when the roll component is 0). As a result, the orientation sensor was deprecated in Android 2.2 (API level 8).

The *Touch information* is retrieved using a 1 pixel per 1 pixel size window, placed at the top left corner of the touch-screen. When a touch event occurs, the hardware layer sends a signal to a component called dispatcher, that is able to perform a check using the User Identifier. The check verifies who generated the information: if the check fails, the information is lost. The check was introduced in 2012 from API 17. We want to gather information everywhere in uncontrolled environment, and we used the WATCH_OUTSIDE_TOUCH parameter. Android documentation says "Note that you will not receive the full down/move/up gesture, only the location of the first down"[1]. We obtain the timestamp for each

---

[1] https://android.googlesource.com/platform/frameworks/native/+/master/include/android/window.h.

touch event and by a difference with the last touch event we retrieve the *Touch Gap*, i.e. the *Touch information*.

The *Cell information* is retrieved by using getCid() and getLac() methods provided by the GsmCellLocation class.

The getCid() method returns the GSM Cell ID (CID), an unique number used to identify each Base transceiver station (BST), while the getLac() method returns the location area code. A location area is a set of base stations that are grouped together to optimize the signaling. To each location area, a unique number called location area code (LAC) is assigned. The LAC is broadcast by each base station, known as a BST in GSM, or a Node B in UMTS, at regular intervals.

Regarding the *Cell information* we consider as features the *CID* and the *LAC*.

In order to collect the features we implemented three components:

- *an Android application*: the application is able to retrieve the user-oriented features we previously described; it works at user-level and it does not require root privileges. The application was developed to retrieve the full feature set: (i) *Orientation information*, (ii) *Touch information* and (iii) *Cell information*;
- *Drop Server*: we deployed a server to collect all the information retrieved by various devices with the Android application installed;
- *NoSQL database*: once the information is retrieved, it is stored in a non-relational database (namely, MongoDB) for facilitating the analysis. We chose this type of database because of the great amount of data accumulated from the devices, but also for its schema-less feature. We developed a script to read JSON files obtained from the devices and to insert them into the database. Using MongoDB we created one collection for each device and we stored every received features in a heterogeneous collection associated to it; it stores JSON files using an own format called BSON.

We use the Accessibility Service that must be enabled by the users in order to collect the sensitive information we need.

3   The Evaluation

We designed an experiment in order to evaluate the effectiveness of the proposed technique.

More specifically, the experiment is aimed at verifying whether the features are able to classify a behavioral trace that distinguishes the owner by an impostor. The classification is carried out by using a classifier built with the features discussed in the previous section. The evaluation consists of two stages: (i) a comparison of descriptive statistics of the populations of traces; and (ii) a classification analysis aimed at assessing whether the features are able to correctly classify the owner's and the impostor's behavioral traces.

We observed 21 users for 10 days: the evaluation time window began on *September 1, 2015* and finished on *September 11, 2015*. At the end of the observation window we gathered approximately 1 GB of raw data. Unfortunately two devices presented issues with the sensors and we were forced to conduct analysis on the remaining 18 users. Another user was not considered in the final results because the device suffered of incompatibility.

Table 1 shows the observed devices used to evaluate our method.

Table 1. Devices involved in the evaluation with owner characterization.

#	Device	OS	API	Age	Sex	Used
1	*Samsung Galaxy S3*	KitKat	19	19	Female	Y
2	*LGE Nexus 5*	Marshmallow	23	22	Male	Y
3	*Samsung Galaxy S5*	Lollipop	21	26	Male	Y
4	*Samsung Galaxy S3*	KitKat	19	27	Male	Y
5	*Samsung Mini 2*	Gingerbread	10	33	Male	Y
6	*Samsung Note 3*	Lollipop	21	26	Male	Y
7	*Samsung S5 Dual*	Lollipop 5.1	22	28	Male	Y
8	*Samsung S4*	Jelly Bean	18	56	Male	Y
9	*Samsung Galaxy S4*	Jelly Bean	17	24	Male	Y
10	*LGE Nexus 5*	Lollipop	22	23	Female	Y
11	*Samsung Galaxy A5*	Jelly Bean	21	27	Male	N
12	*LGE G2*	Jelly Bean	17	29	Male	Y
13	*Samsung Galaxy S2*	Jelly Bean	16	30	Male	Y
14	*Samsung Corby*	Froyo	8	26	Male	N
15	*HUAWEI P6*	Jelly Bean	17	24	Male	Y
16	*HUAWEI P1*	Ice Cream	14	22	Female	Y
17	*OnePlus A0001*	Lollipop	22	27	Male	Y
18	*HUAWEI Honor 6*	KitKat	19	24	Female	Y
19	*HUAWEI P7*	KitKat	19	27	Male	Y
20	*HUAWEI P8 Lite*	KitKat	19	25	Female	Y
21	*HUAWEI Y530*	Jelly Bean	18	21	Male	N

3.1 Descriptive Statistics

The analysis of box plots related to the six features helps to identify whether the features are helpful to discriminate the behavior of users.

Figure 1 shows the box plots related to the *Pitch* feature for each user involved in the evaluation, while Fig. 2 shows the box plots related to the *Roll* feature and Fig. 3 shows the box plots related to the *Azimuth* feature. All these box plots do not exhibit significant differences among the different users. A similar consideration can be done for the features related to the *touch information*, represented in Figs. 4, and 5. The things change when we consider the *LAC* box plots illustrated in Fig. 6. As a matter of fact, users exhibit an evident diversity

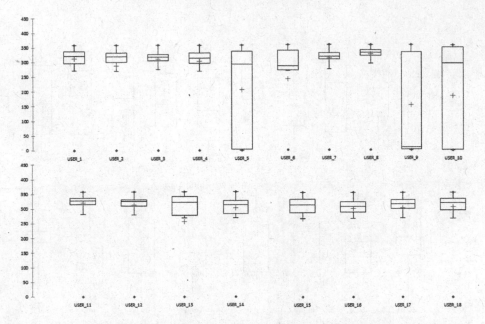

Fig. 1. Box plots related to the pitch feature for each user involved in the experiment.

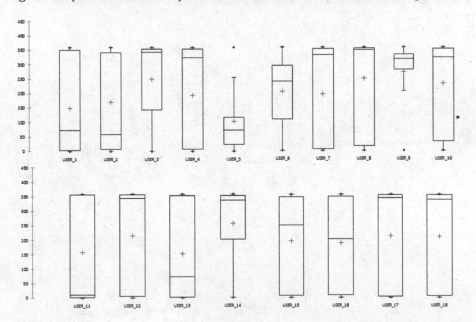

Fig. 2. Box plots related to the roll feature for each user involved in the éxperiment.

among each other, which is represented by the different level of medians for each user and by the variability of the box plots' width. The analysis of descriptive statistics suggests that both *orientation* and *touch information* singularly taken

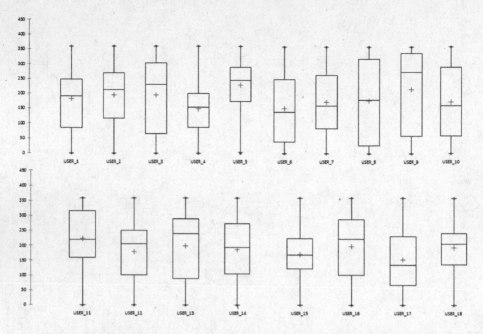

Fig. 3. Box plots related to the azimuth feature for each user involved in the experiment.

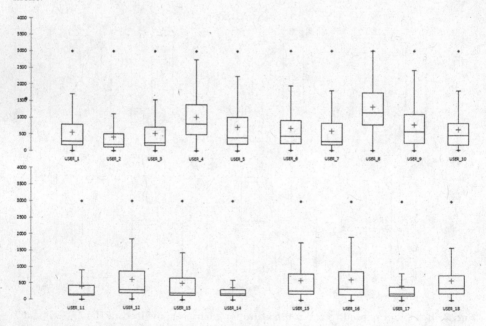

Fig. 4. Box plots related to the touch gap feature for each user involved in the experiment.

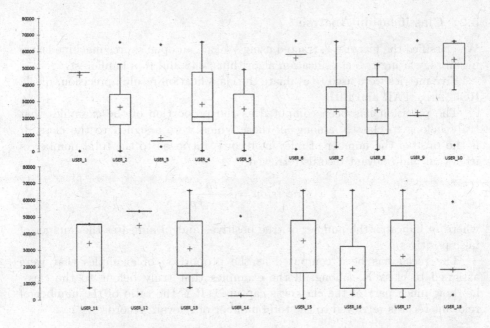

Fig. 5. Box plots related to the CID feature for each user involved in the experiment.

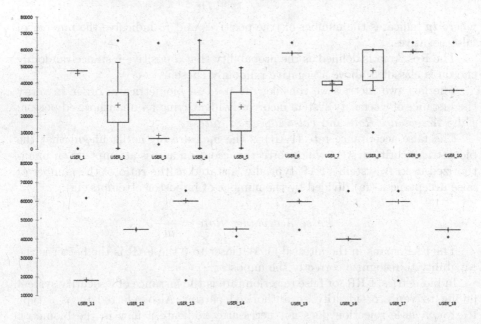

Fig. 6. Box plots related to the LAC feature for each user involved in the experiment.

could be insufficient to discriminate the owner from the impostor. The classification analysis will complete the picture, by indicating that the combination of all the measures can successfully help to identify correctly the impostors.

3.2   Classification Analysis

We classified the features extracted using Weka[2], an open source machine learning library, using two classification algorithms: J48 and RandomForest.

Five metrics were used to evaluate the classification results: precision, recall, ROC Area, FAR and FRR.

The precision has been computed as the proportion of the examples that truly belong to class X among all those which were assigned to the class. It is the ratio of the number of relevant records retrieved to the total number of irrelevant and relevant records retrieved:

$$Precision = \frac{tp}{tp + fp}$$

where tp indicates the number of true positives and fp indicates the number of false positives.

The recall has been computed as the proportion of examples that were assigned to class X, among all the examples that truly belong to the class, i.e. how much part of the class was captured. It is the ratio of the number of relevant records retrieved to the total number of relevant records:

$$Recall = \frac{tp}{tp + fn}$$

where tp indicates the number of true positives and fn indicates the number of false negatives.

The Roc Area is defined as the probability that a positive instance randomly chosen is classified above a negative randomly chosen.

The last two metrics we consider are used in biometrics in order to verify the instance of a security system incorrectly identifying an unauthorized person: *False Acceptance Rate* and *False Rejection Rate*.

The false acceptance rate (FAR) is the measure of the likelihood that the biometric security system will incorrectly accept an access attempt by an unauthorized user. A system's FAR typically is stated as the ratio of the number of false acceptances (fa) divided by the number of impostor attempts (ia):

$$False\ Acceptance\ Rate = \frac{fa}{ia}$$

The FAR spans in the interval [0, 1]: closer to 0 the FAR is the better is the capability to recognize correctly the impostor.

In biometrics, FRR, or false rejection rate is the instance of a security system failing to verify or identify an authorized person. Also referred to as a type I error, a false rejection does not necessarily indicate a flaw in the biometric system; for example, in a fingerprint-based system, an incorrectly aligned finger on the scanner or dirt on the scanner can result in the scanner misreading the fingerprint, causing a false rejection of the authorized user. The false rejection

---

[2] http://www.cs.waikato.ac.nz/ml/weka/.

rate is the measure of the likelihood that the biometric security system will incorrectly reject an access attempt by an authorized user. A system's FRR typically is stated as the ratio of the number of false rejections (fr) divided by the number of owner attempts (oa).

The FRR is defined as:

$$False\ Rejection\ Rate = \frac{fr}{oa}$$

The best FRR has the value of 0, while the worst FRR has the values of 1.

The classification analysis consisted of building classifiers in order to evaluate features accuracy.

For training the classifier, we defined T as a set of labeled behavioral traces (BT, l), where each BT is associated to a label $l \in$ {impostor, owner}. For each BT we built a feature vector $F \in R_y$, where y is the number of the features used in training phase $(1 \le y \le 6)$.

For the learning phase, we use a k-fold cross-validation: the dataset is randomly partitioned into k subsets. A single subset is retained as the validation dataset for testing the model, while the remaining k-1 subsets of the original dataset are used as training data. We repeated the process for k=10 times; each one of the k subsets has been used once as the validation dataset. To obtain a single estimate, we computed the average of the k results from the folds.

We evaluated the effectiveness of the classification method with the following procedure:

1. build a training set $T \subset D$;
2. build a testing set T' = D$\div$T;
3. run the training phase on T;
4. apply the learned classifier to each element of T'.

We performed a 10-fold cross validation: we repeated the four steps 10 times varying the composition of T (and hence of T').

We classify using three different sets of features:

- $S1$: orientation features;
- $S2$: orientation and touch features;
- $S3$: orientation, touch and cell-id features.

The aim of the classification with the $S1$ feature set is to achieve a behavioral pattern in order to succeed in identifying the owner or an impostor considering the device orientation. The $S1$ features set is composed by: *pitch, roll* and *azimuth* that represents an orientation event.

The second feature set, i.e. $S2$, adds to the $S1$ feature set the touch feature, i.e. the touch-gap.

The third features set, i.e. $S3$, adds to $S2$ features set the cell-event characterized by *Cell-Id* and *Location-Area* of a precise cell tower.

Each classification was performed using 20% of the dataset as training dataset and 80% as testing dataset.

We defined $C_{u,s}$ as the set of the classifications we performed, where u identifies the user ($1 \leq u \leq 18$) and s represents the features set used in the classification ($s = \{S1, S2, S3\}$).

For sake of clarity we explain with an example the method we adopted: when we perform $C_{2,1}$ classification, we label the traces related to the user #2 as owner traces, and the traces of the other user as impostor using the S1 features set (i.e., just the orientation features) for classification.

Table 2 shows the results obtained with this procedure using the *S1* features set.

The orientation features are too weak for identifying the owner. As a matter of fact the greatest precision obtained is 0.979, but most values are smaller than 0.96. Additionally, FAR and FRR show very high values, i.e. around 0.1. By considering orientation and touch features together, the performances do not improve significantly, as Table 3 shows.

Performances improve when we accomplish the classification with all the features grouped together, as shown in Table 4. For most users, precision and recall are over 99%.

Table 5 shows the average results obtained using the *S1, S2* and *S3* features set, in order to facilitate the comparison among the different features.

We obtain the following average values when classifying the behavioral traces by using the RandomForest classification algorithm:

- a precision of 0.910 and a recall of 0.859 using the *S1* feature set;
- a precision of 0.896 and a recall of 0.895 using the *S2* feature set;
- a precision of 0.995 and a recall of 0.995 using the *S3* feature set.

We notice that the precision diminishes when moving from *S1* to *S2*, although the latter includes more features than *S1*. The best feature set in discriminating between impostor and owner traces is the *S3* feature set.

In order to measure the performance of our method, we report in Table 6 the average time employed for the classification task. The machine used was an Intel Core i5 desktop with 4 gigabyte RAM, equipped with Linux Mint 15.

The J48 algorithm is faster in classification task than RandomForest, anyway all the classifications employ less than a second.

In order to test whether also a specific mobile application can be used for discriminating between the owner and the impostors we conducted two further experiments.

The aim of the second experiment is to verify if it is possible to use the user events related to a single application to strengthen the performances of *S1, S2* and *S3* features.

We choose two applications installed by all the users involved in the experiment: Telegram[3] and Whatsapp[4].

Telegram and Whatsapp were chosen as they are very widespread among the mobile users community. They are basically free messaging applications,

---

[3] https://play.google.com/store/apps/details?id=org.telegram.messenger&hl=it.
[4] https://play.google.com/store/apps/details?id=com.whatsapp&hl=it.

Table 2. Classification results: precision, recall, ROC Area, FAR and FRR for classifying owner and impostor traces for each user involved in the experiment, computed for *S1* feature set with the J48 and RandomForest (RF) algorithms.

User	Alg.	Precision	Recall	ROC	FAR	FRR
1	J48	0.873	0.892	0.903	0.136	0.117
	RF	0.906	0.910	0.970	0.104	0.084
2	J48	0.776	0.740	0.824	0.230	0.2476
	RF	0.854	0.880	0.935	0.165	0.128
3	J48	0.835	0.820	0.886	0.194	0.139
	RF	0.901	0.910	0.964	0.120	0.079
4	J48	0.835	0.790	0.882	0.154	0.175
	RF	0.879	0.820	0.947	0.130	0.112
5	J48	0.871	0.840	0.908	0.100	0.162
	RF	0.908	0.920	0.964	0.097	0.086
6	J48	0.907	0.910	0.938	0.083	0.104
	RF	0.946	0.930	0.983	0.053	0.056
7	J48	0.774	0.780	0.837	0.284	0.175
	RF	0.872	0.770	0.953	0.154	0.104
8	J48	0.814	0.830	0.856	0.222	0.154
	RF	0.857	0.840	0.938	0.186	0.106
9	J48	0.885	0.880	0.921	0.132	0.097
	RF	0.932	0.950	0.972	0.080	0.056
10	J48	0.939	0.940	0.956	0.073	0.060
	RF	0.961	0.978	0.991	0.0041	0.036
11	J48	0.896	0.880	0.922	0.131	0.079
	RF	0.929	0.916	0.981	0.089	0.055
12	J48	0.823	0.840	0.868	0.224	0.136
	RF	0.979	0.972	0.954	0.152	0.091
13	J48	0.924	0.934	0.946	0.089	0.064
	RF	0.955	0.961	0.989	0.053	0.034
14	J48	0.882	0.800	0.917	0.121	0.115
	RF	0.930	0.918	0.978	0.076	0.0063
15	J48	0.885	0.840	0.926	0.122	0.109
	RF	0.936	0.922	0.982	0.073	0.056
16	J48	0.859	0.870	0.903	0.157	0.126
	RF	0.915	0.900	0.974	0.099	0.070
17	J48	0.862	0.853	0.896	0.161	0.117
	RF	0.915	0.899	0.974	0.099	0.071
18	J48	0.873	0.862	0.917	0.129	0.125
	RF	0.921	0.934	0.973	0.089	0.071

Table 3. Classification results: precision, recall, ROC Area, FAR and FRR for classifying owner and impostor traces for each user involved in the experiment, computed for *S2* features set with the J48 and RandomForest (RF) algorithms.

User	Alg.	Precision	Recall	ROC	FAR	FRR
1	J48	0.876	0.869	0.899	0.134	0.114
	RF	0.902	0.909	0.968	0.111	0.086
2	J48	0.776	0.765	0.832	0.234	0.234
	RF	0.825	0.811	0.911	0.185	0.166
3	J48	0.832	0.839	0.877	0.191	0.146
	RF	0.880	0.842	0.950	0.143	0.098
4	J48	0.840	0.856	0.895	0.180	0.142
	RF	0.877	0.893	0.948	0.140	0.108
5	J48	0.874	0.872	0.911	0.120	0.133
	RF	0.908	0.910	0.970	0.099	0.084
6	J48	0.896	0.905	0.928	0.265	0.111
	RF	0.926	0.938	0.975	0.065	0.084
7	J48	0.785	0.800	0.837	0.265	0.169
	RF	0.850	0.877	0.933	0.195	0.110
8	J48	0.881	0.897	0.917	0.162	0.082
	RF	0.903	0.916	0.956	0.142	0.057
9	J48	0.882	0.891	0.918	0.139	0.098
	RF	0.927	0.919	0.970	0.087	0.060
10	J48	0.925	0.918	0.956	0.091	0.060
	RF	0.949	0.954	0.988	0.059	0.045
11	J48	0.862	0.879	0.896	0.191	0.092
	RF	0.900	0.904	0.964	0.137	0.071
12	J48	0.820	0.841	0.866	0.228	0.138
	RF	0.872	0.889	0.946	0.163	0.093
13	J48	0.917	0.908	0.939	0.106	0.061
	RF	0.942	0.938	0.985	0.070	0.047
14	J48	0.840	0.890	0.890	0.156	0.165
	RF	0.889	0.901	0.957	0.118	0.105
15	J48	0.880	0.897	0.918	0.129	0.112
	RF	0.919	0.924	0.975	0.096	0.067
16	J48	0.850	0.872	0.892	0.167	0.135
	RF	0.897	0.937	0.964	0.124	0.085
17	J48	0.811	0.824	0.873	0.208	0.170
	RF	0.862	0.877	0.941	0.173	0.106
18	J48	0.853	0.849	0.901	0.165	0.129
	RF	0.893	0.927	0.96	0.122	0.093

Table 4. Classification results: precision, recall, ROC Area, FAR and FRR for classifying owner and impostor traces for each user involved in the experiment, computed for *S3* features set with the J48 and RandomForest (RF) algorithms.

User	Alg.	Precision	Recall	ROC	FAR	FRR
1	J48	0.992	0.997	0.994	0.011	0.006
	RF	0.994	0.999	0.999	0.007	0.006
2	J48	0.995	0.992	0.995	0.007	0.002
	RF	0.996	0.997	1.000	0.007	0.001
3	J48	0.999	0.999	0.999	0.001	0.001
	RF	0.999	0.999	0.999	0.001	0.001
4	J48	0.977	0.969	0.983	0.025	0.021
	RF	0.981	0.988	0.998	0.021	0.017
5	J48	0.993	0.996	0.996	0.013	0.001
	RF	0.992	0.995	0.995	0.017	0.001
6	J48	0.995	0.990	0.998	0.005	0.005
	RF	0.996	0.996	1.000	0.004	0.004
7	J48	0.996	0.995	0.997	0.005	0.004
	RF	0.996	0.996	1.000	0.006	0.002
8	J48	0.992	0.994	0.997	0.014	0.002
	RF	0.903	0.909	0.956	0.142	0.057
9	J48	0.997	0.998	0.997	0.005	0.001
	RF	0.999	0.999	1.000	0.082	0.000
10	J48	0.998	0.998	0.999	0.002	0.001
	RF	0.999	0.999	1.000	0.010	0.001
11	J48	0.999	0.999	0.999	0.002	0.001
	RF	0.999	0.999	0.999	0.002	0.001
12	J48	1.000	1.000	1.000	0.000	0.000
	RF	1.000	1.000	1.000	0.000	0.000
13	J48	0.985	0.989	0.990	0.021	0.008
	RF	0.989	0.987	0.999	0.017	0.004
14	J48	0.999	0.999	1.000	0.001	0.001
	RF	0.999	0.999	0.999	0.001	0.001
15	J48	0.987	0.988	0.992	0.016	0.010
	RF	0.992	0.994	1.000	0.013	0.004
16	J48	0.997	0.998	0.999	0.004	0.001
	RF	0.999	0.999	1.000	0.003	0.001
17	J48	0.991	0.990	0.995	0.013	0.06
	RF	0.994	0.993	1.000	0.007	0.004
18	J48	0.997	0.998	0.998	0.030	0.030
	RF	0.997	0.998	1.000	0.003	0.002

Table 5. Classification results: average value for precision, recall, ROC Area, FAR and FRR for classifying owner and impostor traces, computed for *S1*, *S2* and *S3* features set with the J48 and RandomForest (RF) algorithms.

Feat.	Alg.	Precision	Recall	ROC	FAR	FRR
S1	J48	0.861	0.859	0.900	0.152	0.128
	RF	0.910	0.859	0.900	0.098	0.072
S2	J48	0.855	0.854	0.897	0.165	0.127
	RF	0.896	0.895	0.959	0.124	0.087
S3	J48	0.994	0.994	0.996	0.008	0.004
	RF	0.995	0.995	0.999	0.007	0.003

Table 6. The performance evaluation for classifying the *S1*, *S2* and *S3* feature set, with the J48 and RandomForest (RF) algorithms.

Feature set	Algorithm	Time
S1	J48	0.47 s
	RF	0.56 s
S2	J48	0.51 s
	RF	0.72 s
S3	J48	0.68 s
	RF	0.84 s

available for Android but also for Apple and Microsoft devices. Telegram and WhatsApp use smartphone internet connection (provided by mobile network and WiFi) to text other users. In addition they are also able to send and receive photos, videos, documents and vocal messages. The main differences between the two applications is represented by the fact that WhatsApp permits also to make vocal calls, but Telegram at the moment does not exhibit this feature. Considering that both the applications are intensively used by users, we think that they are likely to represent the user behavior.

We selected the users with at least 10000 observations for the two considered applications i.e., users #7, #11, #13, #14, #16 and #17. In order to verify whether the observations discriminate the owner and the impostors, for each user we classify the observation performed by himself with the owner label, while we consider the observations related to the other users with the impostor label. For instance, when considering user #14, the observations related to the user under analysis are labeled as owner, while the observations related to users #7, #11, #13, #16 and #17 are labeled as impostor.

The parameters of the machine learner were the same as the previous experiment.

For the two considered applications, we present the classification results with the *S1*, *S2* and *S3* feature set.

Table 7 shows the results obtained by classifying the S1 feature set while using the Telegram application.

Table 7. Classification results: precision, recall, ROC Area, FAR and FRR for classifying owner and impostor traces related to Telegram application, computed for S1 features set with the J48 and RandomForest (RF) algorithms.

Alg.	User	Precision	Recall	ROC	FAR	FRR
J48	7	0.805	0.833	0.925	0.155	0.068
	11	0.949	0.943	0.979	0.183	0.102
	13	0.906	0.904	0.964	0.096	0.072
	14	0.895	0.899	0.958	0.142	0.052
	16	0.899	0.878	0.947	0.086	0.056
	18	0.904	0.887	0.95	0.098	0.076
RF	7	0.861	0.894	0.987	0.143	0.129
	11	0.974	0.968	0.997	0.201	0.156
	13	0.946	0.938	0.989	0.086	0.054
	14	0.928	0.936	0.991	0.079	0.064
	16	0.929	0.911	0.988	0.105	0.098
	18	0.935	0.923	0.988	0.107	0.097

As in the previous experiment, the features related to orientation are too weak also in considering the observation generated by Telegram application. The greatest precision obtained is 0.974 but in the table very low values appear too, as 0.805. Also FAR and FRR metrics follow this trend.

Table 8 shows the results obtained by classifying the S2 feature set while using the Telegram application.

By considering orientation and touch features together related to Telegram application, the performances do not improve significantly. The best precision value is reached by user #11 (0.97) when using the RandomForest Algorithm, but for the others users the precision value is low, for instance for users #7 and #14 the precision value is under 0.9 for both the classification algorithms.

Table 9 shows the results obtained by classifying the S3 feature set when using the Telegram application.

Considering the S3 feature set, there is an improvement. We obtain precision values ranging from 0.992 to 1 for all the considered users with the J48 algorithm. The FAR and the FRR values are coherent with the precision, as matter of fact the FAR is between 0.016 and 0.002, while the FRR from 0.006 to 0.001.

Table 10 shows the results obtained by classifying the S1 feature set when using the WhatsApp application.

With regards to the S1 feature set classification, when considering only the WhatsApp traces, the precision value ranges between 0.805 and 0.949 with the J48 algorithm and between 0.861 and 0.974 with the RandomForest one.

Table 8. Classification results: precision, recall, ROC Area, FAR and FRR for classifying owner and impostor traces related to Telegram application, computed for S2 features set with the J48 and RandomForest (RF) algorithms.

Alg.	User	Precision	Recall	ROC	FAR	FRR
J48	7	0.803	0.794	0.916	0.105	0.089
	11	0.935	0.983	0.974	0.174	0.079
	13	0.892	0.901	0.957	0.097	0.067
	14	0.874	0.879	0.951	0.246	0.174
	16	0.864	0.864	0.943	0.135	0.084
	17	0.886	0.878	0.945	0.107	0.071
RF	7	0.848	0.851	0.98	0.098	0.082
	11	0.97	0.955	0.996	0.111	0.054
	13	0.927	0.937	0.99	0.091	0.062
	14	0.894	0.92	0.988	0.094	0.061
	16	0.904	0.89	0.985	0.105	0.059
	17	0.904	0.894	0.85	0.113	0.065

Table 9. Classification results: precision, recall, ROC Area, FAR and FRR for classifying owner and impostor traces related to Telegram application, computed for S3 features set with the J48 and RandomForest (RF) algorithms.

Alg.	User	Precision	Recall	ROC	FAR	FRR
J48	7	1	0.998	0.999	0.002	0.001
	11	0.998	0.998	0.999	0.002	0.003
	13	0.993	0.994	0.999	0.016	0.006
	14	0.998	0.997	0.999	0.004	0.002
	16	0.992	0.994	0.999	0.007	0.003
	17	0.999	0.998	1	0.006	0.006
RF	7	1	0.999	0.999	0.001	0.002
	11	0.996	0.997	0.998	0.031	0.029
	13	0.927	0.937	0.99	0.024	0.022
	14	0.894	0.92	0.988	0.031	0.029
	16	0.904	0.89	0.985	0.023	0.021
	17	0.904	0.894	0.85	0.023	0.026

This confirms that the S1 feature set alone is not able to discriminate an user from the impostors, and this happens when considering the full application set running on the smartphone, the Telegram application and the WhatsApp one.

Table 11 shows the results obtained by classifying the S2 feature set when using the WhatsApp application.

Table 10. Classification results: precisiòn, recall, ROC Area, FAR and FRR for classifying owner and impostor traces related to WhatsApp application, computed for S1 features set with the J48 and RandomForest (RF) algorithms.

Alg.	User	Precision	Recall	ROC	FAR	FRR
J48	7	0.805	0.833	0.925	0.154	0.141
	11	0.949	0.943	0.979	0.081	0.061
	13	0.906	0.904	0.964	0.077	0.067
	14	0.895	0.899	0.958	0.081	0.073
	16	0.899	0.878	0.947	0.078	0.075
	17	0.904	0.887	0.95	0.082	0.063
RF	7	0.861	0.894	0.987	0.083	0.075
	11	0.974	0.968	0.997	0.042	0.029
	13	0.946	0.938	0.989	0.046	0.031
	14	0.928	0.936	0.991	0.053	0.048
	16	0.929	0.911	0.988	0.049	0.032
	17	0.935	0.923	0.988	0.050	0.032

Table 11. Classification results: precision, recall, ROC Area, FAR and FRR for classifying owner and impostor traces related to WhatsApp application, computed for S2 features set with the J48 and RandomForest (RF) algorithms.

Alg.	User	Precision	Recall	ROC	FAR	FRR
J48	7	0.846	0.869	0.941	0.181	0.132
	11	0.914	0.899	0.964	0.095	0.077
	13	0.937	0.955	0.984	0.079	0.053
	14	0.941	0.929	0.975	0.068	0.052
	16	0.905	0.896	0.961	0.062	0.066
	17	0.921	0.914	0.973	0.096	0.071
RF	7	0.92	0.913	0.993	0.070	0.046
	11	0.953	0.958	0.995	0.059	0.049
	13	0.962	0.978	0.997	0.048	0.038
	14	0.96	0.956	0.996	0.048	0.036
	16	0.945	0.943	0.995	0.068	0.049
	17	0.959	0.951	0.993	0.049	0.036

The results obtained in the S2 feature set classification related to the WhatsApp traces are closed to the previous one obtained with the S1 feature set classification. As matter of fact, the precision spans from 0.846 to 0.941 with the J48 algorithm while ranges from 0.92 to 0.962 with the RandomForest algorithm.

Table 12 shows the results obtained by classifying the S3 feature set when using the WhatsApp application.

Table 12. Classification results: precision, recall, ROC Area, FAR and FRR for classifying owner and impostor traces related to WhatsApp application, computed for S3 features set with the J48 and RandomForest (RF) algorithms.

Alg.	User	Precision	Recall	ROC	FAR	FRR
J48	7	1	0.998	1	0.003	0.002
	11	0.998	1	1	0.009	0.005
	13	0.998	0.998	1	0.009	0.008
	14	1	1	1	0	0
	16	0.998	1	1	0.009	0.005
	17	0.998	0.997	1	0.011	0.013
RF	7	1	1	1	0	0
	11	0.999	1	1	0.007	0.004
	13	1	0.999	1	0.003	0.004
	14	1	0.999	1	0.003	0.004
	16	1	1	1	0	0
	17	0.999	0.999	1	0.002	0.001

The classification results related to the S3 feature set classification related to WhatsApp application exhibits better results if compared with the previous ones obtained classifying the S1 and S2 feature set.

The precision ranges from 0.998 and 1 with the J48 algorithm, while falls between 0.999 and 1 with the RandomForest one. Consequently the FAR varies between 0.011 and 0, while the FRR spans from 0.013 and 0.

The classification with WhatsApp confirms the expectation: the S3 feature set performs as the best one to authenticate the mobile users.

The best precision is obtained classifying the traces related to the WhatsApp application. As a matter of fact, the precision value is higher than 0.998 for all the considered users.

4   Related Work

There are two categories of biometrics for user identification: physiological (such as fingerprints, facial features) and behavioral biometrics (such as speaking, typing, walking). Physiological biometrics usually requires special recognition devices. Some physiological biometrics, like face and voice can be detected by smartphones, but usually entail expensive computation and energy costs and have a high error rate. For example, in Koreman et al. [15], the (equal error rates) EER for face recognition is around 28% and for voice is around 5%. Keystroke is a popular behavioral biometric: Joyce and Gupta [9] presented a survey on the large body of literature on authentication with keystroke dynamics.

Some researchers proposed authentication token based mechanisms to identify legal users, e.g., wireless token [16]. However, they require additional hardware and are not convenient for daily smartphone usage. On the smart phones with touch screens, PINs, pass-phrases, and secret drawn gestures are the commonly used authentication methods [17].

Recently, there is a growing body of work that uses the features of touch behavior to verify users. Several existing approaches have used the touch behavior biometrics for various security purposes. De Luca et al. [18] propose a password application, by which the user draws a stroke on the touch screen as an input password. Pressure, coordinates, size, speed and time of the stroke are used to identify the valid user. Overall the accuracy of this method is 77% with a 19% FRR and 21% FAR. Zheng et al. [19] use four features (acceleration, pressure, size, and time) to distinguish the true owner and impostor to enhance the security of passcode. Their identification system achieves 3.65% EER. A user enters a password by tapping several times on a touch surface with one or more fingers. PassChord failed to authenticate for 16.3% of the time. There are some other works addressing the user identification issue with touch features, e.g., Seo et al. [20]. With pure touch data, there may be a high error rate.

Riva et al. [21], rather than exploring a new authentication scheme, address the problem of deciding when to surface authentication and for which applications. Their approach combines multiple signals (biometric, continuity, possession) to determine a level of confidence in a users authenticity. They built a prototype running on modern phones to demonstrate progressive authentication and used it in a lab study with nine users. Their system is able to reduce the number of required authentications by 42%.

Kwapisz et al. [22] use accelerometer data to identify or authenticate cell phone users. They aggregate the raw time-series accelerometer data into examples, since most classification algorithms cannot operate directly on time series data. Each of these examples is associated with a specific cell phone user, thus forming labeled training data. For user authentication they build separate models for each user in order to determine whether an example came from that user or from someone else, obtaining an accuracy value equal to 87.6% using the J48 classification algorithm of identification of 10-s examples.

Frank et al. [23] propose a set of 30 behavioral touch features that can be extracted from raw touchscreen logs and demonstrate that different users populate distinct subspaces of this feature space. They collected touch data from users interacting with a smart phone using basic navigation maneuvers, i.e., up-down and left-right scrolling. They propose a classification framework that learns the touch behavior of a user during an enrollment phase and is able to accept or reject the current user by monitoring interaction with the touch screen. Their classifier achieves a median equal error rate of 0% for intra-session authentication, 2–3% for inter-session authentication and below 4% when the authentication test was carried out one week after the enrollment phase.

Killourhy and Maxion [24] collect a keystroke-dynamics data set, in order to measure the performance of a range of detectors so that the results can be compared soundly. They collected data from 51 subjects typing 400 passwords each, evaluating 14 detectors from the keystroke-dynamics and pattern-recognition literature. The three top-performing detectors achieve equal-error rates between 9.6% and 10.2%.

Bo et al. [25] build a touch-based biometrics model of the owner by extracting some principle features, and then verify whether the current user is the owner or guest/attacker. When using the smartphone, some unique operating dynamics of the user are detected and learnt by collecting the sensor data and touch events silently. When users are mobile, the micro-movement of mobile devices caused by touch is suppressed by that due to the large scale user-movement which will render the touch-based biometrics ineffective. To address this, we integrate a movement-based biometrics for each user with previous touch-based biometrics. We conduct extensive evaluations of our approaches on the Android smartphone, showing that the user identification accuracy is over 99%.

Murmuria et al. [26] propose the continuous user monitoring using a machine learning based approach comprising of an ensemble of three distinct modalities: power consumption, touch gestures, and physical movement. They evaluated the method using a dataset retrieved by monitoring 73 volunteer participants using the same device (Google Nexus 5) with Android 4.4.4 version on board. In the evaluation, they obtain an equal error rate between 6.1% and 6.9% for 59 selected users.

Gascon et al. [27] analyze typing motion behavior captured while the user is entering text. The authors developed a software keyboard application for the Android OS that stores all sensor data for further learning and evaluation. In a field study with more than 300 participants, they reached a false positive rate of 1% and a total positive rate of 92%.

Clarke and Mekala [28] discuss the application of biometrics to a mobile device in a transparent and continuous fashion and the subsequent advantages and disadvantages that are in contention with various biometric techniques. In order to facilitate the use of signature recognition transparently, their method must verify users based upon written words and not signatures. From the experiment conducted they were found that current signature recognition systems could indeed perform successful authentication on written words. Based upon 20 participants an average FAR and FRR of 0% and 1.2% respectively were experienced across 8 common words.

Brocardo and Traore [29] introduce a very novel approach for continuous authentication which is based on micro messages, by extracting lexical, syntactic, and application specific features. This technique should guarantee a shorter authentication delay, essential for reducing the vulnerability window of the device. This system obtained an EER of 9.18%, but the main limitation is that it can be applied only to messages, so it cannot be used if the user does not write messages.

Wu et al. [30] propose a method profiling behavioral biometrics from keystrokes and gestures, that also acquires the specific properties of a one-touch motion during the users interaction with the smartphone. The authors demonstrate that the manner by which a user uses the touchscreen that is, the specific location touched on the screen, the drift from when a finger moves up and down, the area touched, and the pressure used reflects unique physical and behavioral biometrics.

Piuri and Scotti [31] presented a set of techniques to extract the fingerprint ridge structure by image processing in images acquired by low-cost cameras and webcams. The approach allows the use of webcams and low-cost cameras as interoperable devices for fingerprint biometrics. Results show that even in normal illumination conditions and by using sensors of about 1 Mpixel (or above), the ridge structure can be effectively extracted. The limited resolution of current CCDs can produces several artifacts in the extracted ridge structure, but experiments have shown that the presence of artifacts can be reduced by using higher image resolutions.

Kotroupolos and Samaras [32] obtain the user's profile from recorded speech signals. They obtained as top accuracy 97.6% which is smaller than the one obtained with our experiment.

The main novelty of our method with respect to the existing literature stands in the set of features selected and in the significant performance obtained.

5   Conclusion and Future Work

Current authentication mechanisms in mobile environment use as mechanisms to identify the device owner pins at login time and textual and graphical passwords. These mechanisms do not offer any protection against access post login. In this paper we propose a method to continuously and silently authenticate the user by extracting a set of features able to characterize the user behavior. The method is silent because it builds the profile of the user's behavior while the user is using the mobile phone, without requiring any further entry by the user, like voice or facial image. Results are significantly better than those reported in literature: we obtain a precision and a recall greater than 0.99 collecting data from 18 volunteer participants in a 10-day time window. Additionally we measured a FAR of 0.7% and a FRR of 0.3%. We further evaluate how the events related to two widespread messaging application, i.e. Telegram and WhatsApp, can be used to strengthen the feature sets in discriminating the owner from the impostors.

We plan to improve our experiment in several ways. With respect to data collection, we intend to increase the number of experimental subjects involved, and to collect further features per user, as well as the frequent patterns of applications used by the user.

References

1. Akula, S., Devisetty, V.: Image based registration and authentication system. In: Proceedings of Midwest Instruction and Computing Symposium, vol. 4 (2004)
2. Davis, D., Monrose, F., Reiter, M.K.: On user choice in graphical password schemes. In: USENIX Security Symposium, vol. 13, p. 11 (2004)
3. Dhamija, R., Perrig, A.: Déjà Vu: a user study using images for authentication (2000)

4. Sae-Bae, N., Memon, N.: A simple and effective method for online signature verification. In: BIOSIG, pp. 1–12. IEEE (2013)
5. Shepherd, S.: Continuous authentication by analysis of keyboard typing characteristics. In: European Convention on Security and Detection, pp. 111–114. IET (1995)
6. Monrose, F., Rubin, A.: Authentication via keystroke dynamics. In: Proceedings of the 4th ACM Conference on Computer and Communications Security, pp. 48–56. ACM (1997)
7. Bhattacharyya, D., Ranjan, R., Farkhod Alisherov, A., Choi, M.: Biometric authentication: a review. Int. J. u- e-Serv. Sci. Technol. **2**(3), 13–28 (2009)
8. Bailey, K.O., Okolica, J.S., Peterson, G.L.: User identification and authentication using multi-modal behavioral biometrics. Comput. Secur. **43**, 77–89 (2014)
9. Joyce, R., Gupta, G.: Identity authentication based on keystroke latencies. Commun. ACM **33**(2), 168–176 (1990)
10. Brown, M., Rogers, S.J.: User identification via keystroke characteristics of typed names using neural networks. Int. J. Man Mach. Stud. **39**(6), 999–1014 (1993)
11. Ahmed, A.A.E., Traore, I.: Anomaly intrusion detection based on biometrics. In: Proceedings from the Sixth Annual IEEE SMC Information Assurance Workshop, IAW 2005, pp. 452–453. IEEE (2005)
12. Shen, C., Cai, Z., Guan, X., Cai, J.: A hypo-optimum feature selection strategy for mouse dynamics in continuous identity authentication and monitoring. In: 2010 IEEE International Conference on Information Theory and Information Security (ICITIS), pp. 349–353. IEEE (2010)
13. Gamboa, H., Fred, A.: A behavioral biometric system based on human-computer interaction. In: Defense and Security, International Society for Optics and Photonics, pp. 381–392 (2004)
14. Canfora, G., Notte, P.D., Mercaldo, F., Visaggio, C.A.: Silent and continuous authentication in mobile environment. In: Proceedings of the 13th International Joint Conference on e-Business and Telecommunications (ICETE 2016) - Volume 4: SECRYPT, pp. 97–108, Lisbon, Portugal, 26–28 July 2016 (2016)
15. Koreman, J., Morris, A., Wu, D., Jassim, S., Sellahewa, H., Ehlers, J., Chollet, G., Aversano, G., Bredin, H., Garcia-Salicetti, S., et al.: Multi-modal biometric authentication on the securephone PDA. In: Proceedings of the MMUA workshop on Multimodal User Authentication (2006)
16. Nicholson, A.J., Corner, M.D., Noble, B.D.: Mobile device security using transient authentication. IEEE Trans. Mob. Comput. **5**(11), 1489–1502 (2006)
17. Dunphy, P., Heiner, A.P., Asokan, N.: A closer look at recognition-based graphical passwords on mobile devices. In: Proceedings of the Sixth Symposium on Usable Privacy and Security, p. 3. ACM (2010)
18. De Luca, A., Hang, A., Brudy, F., Lindner, C., Hussmann, H.: Touch me once and I know it's you!: Implicit authentication based on touch screen patterns. In: Proceedings of the SIGCHI, pp. 987–996. ACM (2012)
19. Zheng, N., Bai, K., Huang, H., Wang, H.: You are how you touch: user verification on smartphones via tapping behaviors. In: ICNP, pp. 221–232. IEEE (2014)
20. Seo, H., Kim, E., Kim, H.K.: A novel biometric identification based on a users input pattern analysis for intelligent mobile devices. Int. J. Adv. Rob. Syst. **9**, 1–10 (2012)
21. Riva, O., Qin, C., Strauss, K., Lymberopoulos, D.: Progressive authentication: deciding when to authenticate on mobile phones. In: Presented as part of the 21st USENIX Security Symposium (USENIX Security 12), pp. 301–316 (2012)

22. Kwapisz, J.R., Weiss, G.M., Moore, S.A.: Cell phone-based biometric identification. In: 2010 Fourth IEEE International Conference on Biometrics: Theory Applications and Systems (BTAS), pp. 1–7. IEEE (2010)

23. Frank, M., Biedert, R., Ma, E.D., Martinovic, I., Song, D.: Touchalytics: on the applicability of touchscreen input as a behavioral biometric for continuous authentication. IEEE Trans. Inf. Forensics Secur. **8**(1), 136–148 (2013)

24. Killourhy, K.S., Maxion, R.A.: Comparing anomaly-detection algorithms for keystroke dynamics. In: IEEE/IFIP International Conference on Dependable Systems and Networks, DSN 2009, pp. 125–134. IEEE (2009)

25. Bo, C., Zhang, L., Jung, T., Han, J., Li, X.Y., Wang, Y.: Continuous user identification via touch and movement behavioral biometrics. In: 2014 IEEE International Performance Computing and Communications Conference (IPCCC), pp. 1–8. IEEE (2014)

26. Murmuria, R., Stavrou, A., Barbará, D., Fleck, D.: Continuous authentication on mobile devices using power consumption, touch gestures and physical movement of users. In: Bos, H., Monrose, F., Blanc, G. (eds.) RAID 2015. LNCS, vol. 9404, pp. 405–424. Springer, Cham (2015). doi:10.1007/978-3-319-26362-5_19

27. Gascon, H., Uellenbeck, S., Wolf, C., Rieck, K.: Continuous authentication on mobile devices by analysis of typing motion behavior. In: Sicherheit, pp. 1–12 (2014)

28. Clarke, N., Mekala, A.: Transparent handwriting verification for mobile devices. In: Proceedings of the Sixth International Network Conference (INC 2006), pp. 11–14, Plymouth, UK. Citeseer (2006)

29. Brocardo, M.L., Traore, I.: Continuous authentication using micro-messages. In: Privacy, Security and Trust (PST), pp. 179–188. IEEE (2014)

30. Wu, J.S., Lin, W.C., Lin, C.T., Wei, T.E.: Smartphone continuous authentication based on keystroke and gesture profiling. In: 2015 International Carnahan Conference on Security Technology (ICCST), pp. 191–197. IEEE (2015)

31. Piuri, V., Scotti, F.: Fingerprint biometrics via low-cost sensors and webcams. In: 2nd IEEE International Conference on Biometrics: Theory, Applications and Systems, BTAS 2008, pp. 1–6. IEEE (2008)

32. Kotropoulos, C., Samaras, S.: Mobile phone identification using recorded speech signals. In: 2014 19th International Conference on Digital Signal Processing (DSP), pp. 586–591. IEEE (2014)

A Javascript Voting Client for Remote Online Voting

Jordi Cucurull[1][✉], Sandra Guasch[1], and David Galindo[2]

[1] Scytl Secure Online Voting, Carrer Enric Granados 84,
08008 Barcelona, Spain
{jordi.cucurull,sandra.guasch}@scytl.com
[2] School of Computer Science, The University of Birmingham,
Edgbaston, Birmingham B15 2TT, UK
d.galindo@cs.bham.ac.uk

Abstract. Remote electronic voting systems enable elections where voters can vote remotely without geographical constraints using their own devices, e.g. smartphones, PCs or other Internet connected devices. Online voting systems have a set of security requirements focused on ensuring at least the same properties of traditional voting scenarios. Specifically, in Scytl's systems we provide end to end security, which guarantees that a vote is protected from the very beginning when it is generated in the voter's device until the end of the election when it is decrypted. This requires a specific software in the voters' devices, referred to as the *voting client*, in charge of performing most of the cryptographic operations required to protect the ballot. Our first voting clients were developed as Java Applets. However, in 2013 Scytl decided it was imperative to develop a voting client purely based on Javascript, due to the better multi-platform user experience that this web technology offers and due to the increasing loss of Java support in the browsers.

This industrial paper describes the initial design challenges of the Javascript voting client, the implementation experience and the lessons learned during its development and deployment for our remote electronic voting systems. The paper is complemented with (1) an analysis of the implemented Pseudo-Random Number Generator, (2) a performance study of the main cryptographic primitives used in our voting clients and (3) a performance study of the voting casting process for a given election setup.

Keywords: Remote electronic voting · Javascript security · Implementation · Performance · Random number generation

1 Introduction

Remote electronic voting systems enable voters to remotely cast votes from their own devices, such as PCs, laptops, smartphones, etc. This is specially suitable for voters who live abroad, who are outside of their region during the election day, and for impaired voters who may have mobility issues.

© Springer International Publishing AG 2017
M.S. Obaidat (Ed): ICETE 2016, CCIS 764, pp. 266–290, 2017.
https://doi.org/10.1007/978-3-319-67876-4_13

In general, remote electronic voting systems have to fulfil a set of security requirements in order to be used in electoral processes, which are focused on ensuring that at least the same properties of traditional voting scenarios are maintained, such as vote authenticity and privacy, result accuracy, secrecy of intermediate results, verifiability and auditability, and uncoercibility and vote selling protection. In order to fulfil such security requirements, remote electronic voting systems use advanced cryptographic protocols (see for example [1–3]) that usually offer end to end protection of the votes. Due to this, the protocols require to perform several cryptographic operations both at the client and server sides. The piece of software which is run in the voter's device, which is in charge of performing the ballot presentation, navigation and most of the cryptographic operations, is referred to as the *voting client*.

The first voting clients implemented in Scytl's products were developed as Java Applets. The usage of Java enabled (1) the possibility to perform complex cryptographic operations on a multiplatform setup and (2) code and expertise reuse of the developers that were already working on the backend. In addition, Java Applets were at that time the only multi-platform technology that enabled the performance of complex cryptographic operations on the browser. However, the use of Java Applets implied a high price to pay in terms of user experience and security. Voters' devices required a Java Runtime Environment (JRE), that was not always present neither updated and that had become a source of security vulnerabilities. In addition, JRE was not supported in most of the mobile devices. Latterly, its support has recently removed from the most popular browsers. Thus, in the recent years, the natural evolution of the World Wide Web standards and the introduction of HTML5 have strengthened the use of Javascript for increasingly complex operations, reaching a point where performing cryptographic operations in Javascript at the browser has become feasible. Due to this feasibility and the advantages the Javascript technology offered in terms of user experience and multi-platform compatibility (specially for mobile devices), in 2013 Scytl decided it was imperative to develop a voting client purely based on this technology to replace the former Java-based versions.

This industrial paper, which is an extension of a former paper [4] presented at SECRYPT 2016, shows the implementation experiences and lessons learned after the development and deployment of several Javascript voting clients that have been used in several real elections. The paper is organised in seven sections: Sect. 2 describes the components of a remote electronic voting system, the main components required by a generic voting client, the interaction of this component with the main system and the cryptographic operations it may require; Sects. 3 and 4 describe the challenges to implement a Javascript-based voting client and the solutions adopted; Sect. 5 explains the testing of a pseudo-random number generator implemented; Sect. 6 does a thorough analysis of the performance of the cryptographic primitives and shows the voting times of the client implemented in Javascript; finally Sect. 7 presents the conclusions and further work.

2   Voting Client

This section introduces the details of generic voting clients used in remote electronic voting systems.

2.1   Remote Electronic Voting Systems

From a high level point of view, a remote electronic voting system can be divided in two main parts, the *voting servers* and the *voting client* (see Fig. 1). During the election, the voting servers provide the back-end services that allow voter authentication, ballot provision, and verification and storage of cast ballots in the ballot box. During the counting phase, the voting servers decrypt and tally the votes providing the election results, while protecting the voter's privacy. A usual approach for this is to perform the processes of cleansing and mixing. The cleansing validates the votes received and removes the voter identity from them, and the mix-net [5] shuffles and transforms the encrypted votes prior to decryption. These two processes break the relation between voters and votes.

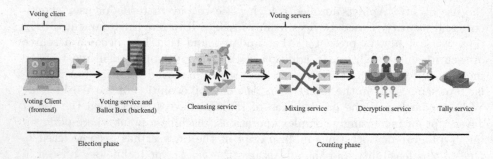

Fig. 1. Remote electronic voting system.

A good practice in remote electronic voting is to cryptographically protect the vote by encrypting and digitally signing it at the voter's device, before it is sent to the remote voting server for being stored. Hence the privacy and the integrity of the vote are protected from the very beginning, right after the vote is generated until it is processed at the counting stage. This is commonly known as end-to-end encryption and it is possible thanks to the voting client application executed at the voter's device.

The voting client is the front-end that allows the voters to authenticate, navigate through the ballot, select their voting options, generate an encrypted and signed ballot and cast it.

2.2   Basic Functionalities

The voting client comprises a graphical user interface and some underlying logics. The following functionalities are implemented by the voting client:

- **Authentication:** The voting client deals with the authentication of the voter in front of the voting system. The authentication subsystem can also be adapted for integration with the customer infrastructure or totally replaced by a third-party authentication system.
- **Key Management:** The voting scenario requires the voters to have their own cryptographic signing keys to sign their votes, e.g. within a smartcard or installed in their computers. However, in many cases this is unfeasible or unpractical. As a consequence the voting system can include a functionality called *key roaming*, which provides the voter with, at least, a pair of cryptographic signing keys. These keys are delivered by the voting server and protected within a password-sealed container such as PKCS#12 [6]. When key roaming is used, the password required to open the keys is usually derived from the voter credentials. In this case, the credentials are never directly sent to the voting system for authentication. Instead another derivation is used for authentication. This prevents the election servers to have access to the voter keys.
- **Vote Generation:** The voting client also generates the ballot to be cast, i.e. it encodes the voting options selected by the voter, encrypts and digitally signs the ballot containing them, and sends the ballot to the remote voting server. Additionally, it may generate mathematical proofs to prove the correctness of the operations performed.
- **Cryptographic Library:** The authentication and ballot generation functionalities require the usage of cryptographic primitives that are not natively provided by the Javascript language. Thus they are included as cryptographic libraries.
- **Pseudo Random Number Generator and Entropy Collector:** A module to generate sequences of secure random numbers, required by some cryptographic primitives, is included for the platforms that do not possess a built-in generator.

2.3   Basic Voting Flow

The flow in the voting client (see Fig. 2) depends on the specific voting protocol implemented each one providing different security properties under different assumptions [7,8]. Despite this, a generic set of steps is common to most of the voting protocols we implement: (1) The voter introduces her credentials to the voting client in order to authenticate; (2) the voting client derives the appropriate identification (Voter ID) and sends it to the server; (3) the server checks the voter is eligible, gathers the voter signing keys and creates an authentication token; (4) then the voting client opens the voter keys and presents the ballot to the voter; (5) then she selects the voting options that represent her voting intent; (6) after the voter confirms her vote, the voting options are encoded and encrypted; (7) mathematical proofs of correct encryption are generated (if required by the protocol); (8) the encrypted voting options and the mathematical proofs are digitally signed; (9) the vote is cast to the remote server; (10) the server computes a vote receipt and its signature; and (11) the voting client validates the receipt signature and presents it to the voter. The receipt allows

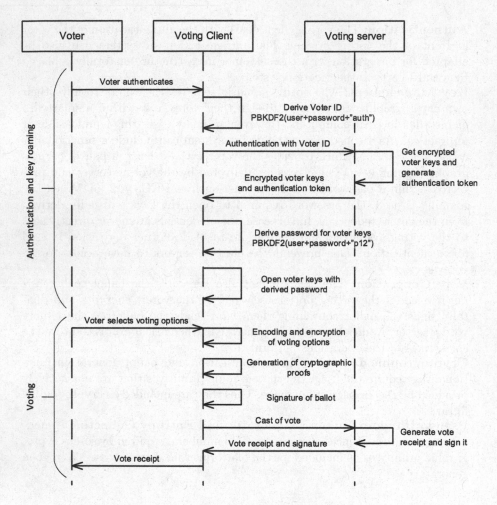

Fig. 2. Authentication and voting flowcharts.

the voter to check her vote has been received and decrypted by the system, since a list of vote receipts is published at the end of the election. The signature of it proofs the authenticity of the receipt, thus it is not possible to create fake random receipts and pretend the system has lost votes.

2.4 Cryptographic Functionalities

The following generic set of cryptographic functionalities and algorithms, depending on the voting protocol implemented, may be required in the voting client:

– **Hash Functions:** they are used for computing certificate fingerprinting and digital signatures. Although the standard for SHA-3 has already been published [9], the previous standard SHA-2 [10] (specifically, SHA-256) has been considered due to compatibility issues.

- **Digital Signature Functions:** they are used for digitally signing the vote and for verifying the digital signatures of the information received from the remote voting server. The RSA-PSS algorithm [11] has been considered.
- **Encryption Algorithms:** they are used for encrypting the voting options. RSA-OAEP [11], RSA-KEM and/or ElGamal encryption algorithms [12], and the AES-GCM encryption algorithm [13,14], are considered for public key and symmetric key cryptography respectively.
- **Zero-Knowledge Proofs of Knowledge (ZKPK):** they [15] are used to prove a certain statement without revealing any other information than the statement is true. For example the Schnorr Signature [16] can prove knowledge of the random ness used for encrypting a message, providing assurance of the originator of an encrypted vote, and preventing vote copying [17].
- **Pseudo-Random Number Generators (PRNG):** these are used for generating the random values required by the cryptographic algorithms.
- **Password-Based Key Derivation Functions:** in the voting client they are used to derive keys for the authentication of the voter and to access private data. The PBKDF2 [18] algorithm is the one selected.
- **Functionalities for Parsing and Opening Keystores:** these are used for providing private signing and encrypting keys to the voters. PKCS#12 [6] or equivalent key containers are used.
- **Reading, Parsing and Validation of Digital Certificates:** these are used to check the validity of the cryptographic keys and X509v3 [19] certificates used in the application.

3 Challenges

The implementation of a voting client in Javascript implied several challenges on cryptography, security and performance.

3.1 Cryptography

Availability of Cryptographic Primitives. A voting client requires to perform cryptographic operations. However, the JavaScript specifications do not include any cryptographic primitives. Instead, some cryptographic functionalities are provided by third party Javascript cryptographic libraries.

Before starting the development of the voting client we performed an analysis of the existing libraries in order to decide which library was more appropriate. The following factors were considered: cryptographic functionalities provided, in order to know what was provided by the library; updates, to know the maintenance level of the code; license, to determine if the license terms were compatible with the ones of the voting client application. In our particular context we preferred BSD, MIT or LGPL licensed libraries.

The results of the analysis, updated on November 2016, are shown on Table 1. This analysis includes an additional library, the asmCrypto, regarding the original one. At the time of developing the solution, in 2013, the conclusion was that

Table 1. Cryptographic functionalities provided by third party libraries.

Name	SJCL	Forge	jsbn	jsrsasign	CryptoJS	asmCrypto
Version	1.0.6	0.6.45	1.4	6.2.0	3.1.8	0.0.10
Hashing	SHA-1, SHA-256, SHA-512	SHA-1, SHA-256, SHA-384, SHA-512	X	SHA-1, SHA-224, SHA-256, SHA-384, SHA-512	SHA-1, SHA-224, SHA-256, SHA-512, SHA-3	SHA-1, SHA-256, SHA-512
RSA signature with SHA-256	X	RSASSA-PKCS1-V1_5, RSASSA-PSS	X	RSASSA-PKCS1-V1_5, RSASSA-PSS	X	RSASSA-PSS
RSA encryption	X	RSAES-PKCS1-v1.5, RSAES-OAEP, RSA-KEM	RSAES-PKCS1-v1.5	X	X	RSAES-OAEP
ElGamal encryption (over Zp)	X	X	X			X
AES encryption	✓	X	X	X	✓	✓
AES cipher modes	GCM, CBC, OCB2, OCB2 progressive, CTR	GCM, CBC, OFB, CFG, CTR	X	X	CFG, OFB, ECB, CTR, CTR Gladman	EBC, CBC, CFB, OFB, CTR, CCM, GCM
Schnor Signature or ZKPKs	X	X	X	X	X	X
BigInteger support	✓	✓	✓	✓	X	✓
PRNG	✓	✓	X	X	X	✓
Parsing PKCS#12 containers	X	✓	X	X	X	X
Parsing X.509 certificates	X	✓	X	✓	X	X
PBKDF2	X	✓	X	X	X	✓
Updates	≃ 2 upd/year	+15 upd/year	No updates	+15 upd/year	≃ 3 upd/year	≃ 2 upd/year
License	BSD 2-Clause, GPL_2.0	BSD 3-Clause, GPL_2.0	BSD	MIT	MIT	MIT

the Forge[1] library was one of the best alternatives to implement a voting client. It provided functions for parsing and opening PKCS#12 containers, as well as managing digital certificates and public key cryptography. Besides this, it had a strong developer support and updates were constantly made. Both SJCL[2] [20] and jsbn[3] were also broadly used in other software. Specifically, jsbn was used in other of the analysed libraries to provide BigInteger support (Forge, jrsasign[4]), and in the Helios voting system [1]. SJCL was a library developed by highly recognised cryptographers. Therefore it was worth to consider it for some of the needed functionalities, such as secure random generation or hash algorithms. jsrsasign and CryptoJS[5] did not seem to provide enough support from the point of view of maintenance and use, as well as functionalities. Considering the analysis performed, the Forge library was selected. The functionalities missing in the library were implemented on top of it (see Sect. 4.1).

The decision to use Forge is still valid considering the updated analysis shown in this article. The only point to consider is the addition of a recent new library, asmCrypto[6], which their authors claim to be faster than the other libraries. However it provides fewer functionalities (some of them required and present in Forge, e.g. RSA-KEM, parsing of PKCS#12 containers and X.509 certificates) and it is updated much less frequently. Another modification to consider, not included in the analysis, is the W3C Candidate Recommendation Web Cryptography API [21] for web browsers. This API includes most of the cryptographic functionalities required by the voting client. However, at the time of writing is still not considered standard, hence it is not guaranteed to be included in all the browsers neither to be included with the same degree of completeness. The advantage of this API is that no external libraries are required and that the computational performance can be better than the Javascript implementations.

Secure Random Numbers and Entropy. Several cryptographic primitives require the use of random values. The quality of the random values (in the sense of their unpredictability) determine the security offered by these primitives (for example, non-random values can lead to weak encryptions). Although Javascript has a native method for random number generation, *Math.random()* [22], its implementation is not considered cryptographically secure [23]. Alternatively, the W3C Candidate Recommendation Web Cryptography API [21], previously mentioned, includes a Pseudo Random Number Generator (PRNG) suitable for cryptographic uses, *window.crypto.getRandomValues()*. This PRNG uses the browser's host system entropy, but is only implemented in recent versions of the desktop and mobile browsers[7].

---

[1] http://digitalbazaar.com/forge.

[2] http://crypto.stanford.edu/sjcl.

[3] http://www-cs-students.stanford.edu/~tjw/jsbn.

[4] http://kjur.github.com/jsrsasign.

[5] http://code.google.com/p/crypto-js.

[6] https://github.com/vibornoff/asmcrypto.js/.

[7] https://developer.mozilla.org/en-US/docs/DOM/window.crypto.getRandomValues.

Some of the cryptographic libraries analysed have their own PRNG implementations. Specifically, SJCL and Forge implement the Fortuna PRNG by Schneier and Ferguson [24]. This PRNG is intended to be used in long-term systems, such as servers, and provides measures for collecting randomness from the system events, and mixing it in order to provide secure random values. However, web sessions in which Javascript cryptography may be used can be very different from a server system, and therefore the same approaches taken in the design of the Fortuna algorithm may not be the best choice. For example, web sessions have a short life time, and the sources of entropy in a browser or in a server are not the same. Current implementations from SJCL and Forge of Fortuna have modifications regarding the original scheme [20]. However, they still have some limitations regarding the entropy sources they use to generate the random numbers. Thus a custom PRNG, based on the Fortuna PRNG, has been implemented (see Sect. 4.2).

3.2 Security

Code Authenticity. One of the challenges to develop a Javascript voting client is to ensure the authenticity of the code to be executed in the voter's device. A modification of this code by an attacker could have severe implications in the security of the solution, for example compromising the integrity and secrecy of the votes.

A classical solution to ensure the authenticity of the code consists of signing it using public key cryptography and enforcing the validation of this signature in the browser. However, as opposed to other technologies such as Java Applets, there is no standard to sign and verify the Javascript code delivered to the browsers. There only exists a proprietary, and deprecated, solution[8], implemented in Mozilla and, formerly, Netscape Communicator 4.x, browsers. This solution was based on packaging the Javascript and HTML code within a signed Jar file, that was verified by the browser when accessed. More promising is the new Candidate Recommendation *W3C Subresource Integrity* [25] that enables the HTML code to include fingerprints of the Javascript code it refers. Despite this ensures the integrity of the included third party code, it does not guarantee the integrity of the HTML files that contain the hashes. Thus, it is not a complete solution for the authenticity of the whole code of the voting client. Finally, there exist proposals ensuring end to end integrity, but they require the installation of browser plugins [26].

Given the current lack of support for guaranteeing the JS code authenticity, the following approaches, to detect code manipulation, have been implemented: (1) TLS communications to guarantee the code transport authenticity (preventing man-in-the-middle attacks); (2) Regular checks of file integrity in the server, including the Javascript voting client code against a baseline, e.g. using software scanning tools such as AIDE[9]; (3) Running a Javascript remote integrity validation service, i.e. an externally executed service to remotely download a selected

---

[8] http://www.mozilla.org/projects/security/components/signed-scripts.html.
[9] http://aide.sourceforge.net.

set of Javascript code from the server as a regular user and check if it matches a previously generated baseline. This service has been implemented and used within the context of an election, but still not to check a voting client code.

Third Party Code. Javascript allows the inclusion of third party code and, more important, the dynamic loading of scripts from different servers. However, embedding third party code dynamically loaded from external servers inside the voting application's website can pose a serious security risk and it is totally unadvised, as this code could access any variable or method of the voting application. A server that does not belong to the election realm may not fulfil the same security policies, potentially becoming a weak point of attack. Any legitimate external server acting as code source must be secured as the main code server is.

An example of this is the vulnerability [27] that a team of researchers discovered in the Javascript voting client that we implemented for the State General Elections 2015 of New South Wales[10]. In this case a third party code owned by Piwik, used by monitoring purposes, was included on behalf of NSW. A manipulation of this code, exploiting the FREAK vulnerability present in the external Piwik server that hosted the code, could potentially allow a sophisticated attacker to alter the voting client code running on the voter's browser and modify the intended voting options. From the point of view of the secrecy and integrity of the vote, the reported vulnerability's potential damage was similar to that of having malware installed in the voter's device. This possibility was already considered in the design of iVote 2015, and the defence against it (regarding the integrity of the vote) was the inclusion of a voice verification mechanism using the DTMF phone input.

Thus, we do not recommend including third party code from external servers. But, this may change if the *W3C Subresource Integrity* [25] candidate recommendation becomes an adopted standard.

3.3   Performance

The computational performance of Javascript is constantly improving, but still below the one obtained by native applications. In addition, the Javascript applications can be executed in a myriad of devices with very different computational capabilities, e.g. smartphones, laptops, etc. Some existing voting client implementations [1] combined Javascript with the usage of Java for certain primitives that required higher performance using a technology called LiveConnect. However, this alternative could not be considered because the aim was to completely eliminate the dependency with the Java Virtual Machine.

As cryptographic operations are computationally expensive, an efficient implementation was required and several optimisations had to be performed at the cryptographic protocol level (see Sects. 4.1 and 4.3) to provide reasonable voting times.

---

[10] http://www.vote.nsw.gov.au.

4   Implementation Experience

During 2013–2015, most of the Scytl voting systems were transitioned to use a Javascript voting client. This section describes the most relevant aspects of the implementation of them considering the challenges previously described.

4.1   Cryptographic Library

Scytl provides different voting systems with different cryptographic protocols, thus several variants of the Javascript voting client were implemented. As a consequence, a cryptographic library containing a large amount of primitives was developed:

Basic Primitives. The basic cryptographic primitives are the most widely used in standard web applications and, therefore, present in some of the libraries studied. For example, SHA-256 hash functions, RSA-PSS digital signature, RSA-KEM encryption, AES-GCM symmetric encryption, key derivation functions such as PBKDF2, and support for X.509 certificates and PKCS#12 containers. These primitives have been wrapped in our library from the Forge library.

ElGamal and ZKPK Primitives. Other primitives such as ElGamal encryption or ZKPKs are more specific to cryptographic protocols such as those for e-voting. Therefore, they are not included in the existing libraries. A custom implementation of these primitives has been built.

ElGamal encryption scheme has homomorphic properties that are essential in electronic voting [1,2,28]. However, the usage of modular exponentiations with large integers is computationally expensive. Therefore, two modifications were performed to the original scheme to improve its efficiency:

- **ElGamal Encryption with Short Exponents:** This is a well-known optimisation [29,30] consisting of using shorter exponents (e.g. of about 256 bits) than those defined by the cyclic group used in the scheme (which may be of about 2048 bits). This reduces the cost of the modular exponentiations without posing at risk the security of the scheme in practice [31].
- **ElGamal Encryption with Multiple Keys:** When the number of plaintexts to be encrypted is higher than one, an optimisation consists of reducing the number of exponentiations to compute by using a different public key for computing each ciphertext, but the same randomness for all them. This does not affect the security of the encryption scheme [2,32], and we show it with an example.

First, we have to introduce the ElGamal encryption scheme: let the encryption scheme be defined over a subgroup $\mathbb{G}$ of prime order q, which has a generator g of elements in $\mathbb{Z}_p^*$. Then, the keypair (h, x) is generated as $x \xleftarrow{\$} \mathbb{Z}_q$, $h = g^x$.

A message m is encrypted as $(g^r, h^r \cdot m)$, where $r \xleftarrow{\$} \mathbb{Z}_q$, and decrypted as $m = (h^r \cdot m)/(g^r)$.

Usually, when more than one message has to be encrypted, the direct approach is to use fresh (different) randomness for each new ciphertext to generate. This means that, when encrypting two different messages m_1 and m_2, the result is: $(g^{r_1}, h^{r_1} \cdot m_1), (g^{r_2}, h^{r_2} \cdot m_2)$. Obviously, given these two ciphertexts an adversary cannot obtain any information about the relation between m_1 and m_2. For example, if it divides one ciphertext by each other, the relation it can observe is $(g^{(r_1/r_2)}, g^{x(r_1/r_2)} \cdot \frac{m_1}{m_2})$, and by the discrete logarithm problem it cannot obtain $\frac{m_1}{m_2}$, given that x, r_1, r_2 are unknown.

On the other side, in the approach we follow by using multiple keys, the result of encrypting m_1 and m_2 is $(g^r, h_1^r \cdot m_1), (g^r, h_2^r \cdot m_2)$, using the keys $h_1 = g^{x_1}$ and $h_2 = g^{x_2}$ respectively. Still, the information that is leaked to an adversary is the same as in the case before: by dividing the ciphertexts, the adversary observes $g^{r(x_1/x_2)} \cdot \frac{m_1}{m_2}$ which, also given that x_1, x_2, r are secret, cannot be used to obtain information about the relation between m_1 and m_2.

In order to maximise the code reuse and reduce the likelihood of errors, we used the Maurer framework [33], which generalises the implementation of ZKPKs for different statements. Thus a unique base code is used for all the ZKPK variants of our voting systems. The Java-like BigInteger functionalities required to operate with the large magnitude integers used in these primitives were reused from the existing libraries.

4.2 Pseudo-Random Number Generator

A pseudo-random number generator (PRNG) is an algorithm that generates a sequence of numbers which is cryptographically indistinguishable from a sequence of true random numbers. PRNGs generate the sequence of numbers in a deterministic manner. The unpredictability of the values generated by a PRNG is given by the unpredictability of the value with which it is initialised, which is called the seed. In order to provide high quality random values for the cryptographic primitives, the PRNG is seeded with entropy (random data) from the system events and information.

We have implemented a custom PRNG to be used in the voting client. Its design has taken into account requirements and particularities of voting clients, specifically a short runtime life and strong unpredictability of the random values produced. The following principles were followed in the design and use: (1) the collection of entropy to seed the PRNG had to start as soon as possible, preferably as soon as the voter started interacting with the system. The implemented PRNG provides methods to start the entropy collection task before the protocol-specific functions have to be called; (2) in order to collect entropy as fast as possible, user-driven events from an extense set of sources were collected; (3) entropy estimation mechanisms were included in order to estimate how much entropy can be attributed to each type of information collected in the browser. These mechanisms ensure that enough entropy is collected for seeding the PRNG and starting generating secure random values.

The PRNG functionality implemented is composed by several parts (see Fig. 3) detailed in the following sections.

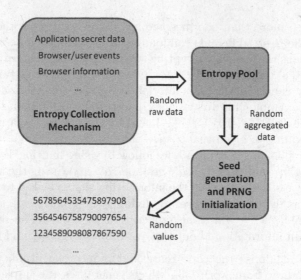

Fig. 3. Diagram of the Pseudo-Random Number Generator.

Entropy Collection Mechanism. Collects information available in the browser, as well as events generated by web navigation and user interaction:

- Sources of information available in the browser or in the voting application.
  - Random numbers from Javascript cryptographic API if available in the used browser
  - Browser information (e.g. User Agent string)
  - Date
  - Regular random numbers from the standard Math library
- Events triggered by JavaScript or Ajax calls, as well as user events.
  - Mouse: *mousemove, mousedown, mouseup, wheel*
  - Keyboard: *keydown, keyup*
  - Touch: *touchstart, touchmove, touchend, gesturestart, gesturechange, gestureend*
  - Device accelerometer/compass: *devicemotion, deviceorientation*
  - Page loads and other AJAX calls

Since the Javascript cryptographic API is a source of cryptographically strong random values, this collector is defined to be the first one to be called. In user events the following information is collected when possible: relative position to the window and to the screen, key/button, date, angle (only for compass) and acceleration components (x, y, z) (only for accelerometer in smartphones, tablets and alike). Each event collected has been assigned with an estimated entropy value, thus it is possible to estimate the amount of entropy gathered by the entropy collector. Most of the estimated entropy values were obtained from existing analysis [20].

Seed Generation and Initialisation. The data gathered by the entropy collection mechanism is accumulated into an entropy pool, and at the same time an entropy counter is increased with the estimated entropy. The entropy collection starts at the very beginning after downloading the voting client. Every time new data is collected, there is the possibility to check if a minimum amount of entropy required by the application has been reached. After collecting enough entropy the collector mechanism is stopped and the PRNG is seeded. An amount of 128 bits of entropy is enough for initialising the PRNG.

Pseudo-Random Values Generation. The PRNG generates sequences of pseudo-random values suitable for cryptographic purposes. Our implementation is based on the Fortuna PRNG [24] and the random values are obtained from an AES cipher in counter mode. The PRNG output has been tested against statistical analysis tools (see Sect. 5) to guarantee its robustness.

4.3 Vote Generator

The Javascript implementation of the voting client has influenced the voting protocols because the computational efficiency is limited and the trust of the underlying platform cannot be guaranteed. An overview of the main considerations is shown below.

Pre-computations. The idea behind this is to pre-compute some cryptographic operations' values while the voter selects the voting options, so that when the voter decides to cast the vote the number of remaining computations is small and the time the voter has to wait for the ballot to be cast is considerably shorter. The amount of operations that can be pre-computed can account up to 95% in certain voting protocols.

An example of pre-computation of ElGamal encryption is the following: considering the ElGamal encryption scheme defined in Sect. 4.1, the most costly operations required to encrypt a message (which are two exponentiations), can be done before the message is available: (g^r, h^r). After that, the remaining operation is a product in order to obtain the encryption of m, $(g^r, h^r \cdot m)$. Since the product is a much more cheaper operation than the exponentiation (moreover given the length of the exponents), there is a significant gain in computation time. Similar adaptations can be done to the ZKPKs, where the exponentiations can be pre-computed and the remaining operations to be done once the values to prove are available consist mainly on hashes (usually fast) and products.

Cast as Intended Validation. Since the voter device cannot be trusted, e.g. it may be infected by malware, some of the voting protocols implemented provide validation mechanisms that allow the voter to check the integrity of the vote cast. For example, in the Norwegian project eValg2013 [2] secret codes received via SMS allowed voters to check that the votes cast contained the voting options they selected. In the Neuchâtel e-voting platform [28], the same approach was followed with the difference that the codes were returned by the same voting client. This option was possible in this case because multiple voting was not allowed, thus the voting client could not learn the codes and vote again with manipulated voting options.

Defence against User Manipulation. Development tools provided by browsers make the manipulation of the code easier for a regular user than in other languages. A non honest voter could take advantage of this by manipulating the processes that happen on her browser to disrupt the election. As a general rule, it is recommended to make at server-side some pre-processing over the data received from the voting client prior to passing it to further layers of the protocol. In addition, voting protocols must be designed to cope with these cases, e.g. including ZKPKs to be verified at the voting server when the vote is received.

5   Test of the PRNG

Since the PRNG is required to produce values with strong randomness, we tested its output against a statistical analysis tool. The tests proved that the implemented PRNG provides random values of the expected quality.

5.1   Testing Tool

Dieharder [34] was the tool selected to perform the statistical analysis, a random number generator testing suite, intended to test generators. It includes tests from the original Diehard Battery of Tests of Randomness [35], as well as tests from the Statistical Test Suite (STS) [36] developed by the National Institute for Standards and Technology (NIST) and tests developed by the author of the Dieharder test suite. Dieharder is well known and highly reputed due to the broad characteristics of random number generators that are evaluated in its tests.

5.2   Test-Bed Setup

In order to test the PRNG, most of the tests available in the Dieharder suite have been performed, except those which need an overwhelming quantity of data (more than 4 GB). Most of the discarded tests overlapped with other tests, thus it was considered not to affect the quality of the testing. Tests which supported different configurations were performed using different input parameters, thus in total an amount of 78 statistical tests were performed.

In order to have a reference of what should be expected from the tests on the implemented ScytlPRNG, two other PRNGs have also been evaluated in the same way: a Flawed PRNG which is known to generate sequences of correlated random numbers, and the AES_OFB generator as the Gold Standard PRNG, which is a commonly known good PRNG.

A set of datasets were generated for each of the PRNGs to test (11 datasets for the ScytlPRNG, 5 datasets for the Gold Standard PRNG and 3 datasets for the Flawed PRNG). Each dataset contained 256 million random unsigned 32-bit integers, which was composed of 400 sets of 640.000 values that were generated with a different PRNG instance and seed. These values composed the input of the Dieharder test suite. Values generated with the PRNG initialised with different seeds have been used in order to test, not only that the values sequentially generated by a PRNG instance have the expected properties (corresponding to a sequence of random numbers), but also to test that different instances of the PRNG (initialised with different seeds) generate uncorrelated random numbers.

5.3   Results

All the tests have been successfully passed by the implemented ScytlPRNG, as well as by the Gold Standard PRNG (see Table 2). On the other hand, the Flawed PRNG has failed most of the tests.

In order to determine the quality of a PRNG, Dieharder tests the *null hypothesis*, which is that the sequence of numbers generated by the random number generator under test is *truly random*. Dieharder computes certain statistics over the random values generated by the PRNG, which ultimately lead to the p-value. This value denotes the probability that a true random number generator would produce a sequence of similar characteristics. That is, it summarises the evidence against the null hypothesis: if the p-value is lower than a certain significance level, the null hypothesis is rejected and the PRNG under test is not accepted as a good one. For other p-values, the null hypothesis is not accepted,

Table 2. Dieharder tests performed.

Dieharder tests performed	Gold PRNG	Scytl PRNG	Flawed PRNG
Diehard Birthdays Test	✓	✓	✓
Diehard 32x32 Binary Rank Test	✓	✓	X
Diehard 6x8 Binary Rank Test	✓	✓	X
Diehard Bitstream Test	✓	✓	✓
Diehard OPSO	✓	✓	X
Diehard OQSO Test	✓	✓	X
Diehard DNA Test	✓	✓	X
Diehard Count the 1s (stream) Test	✓	✓	✓
Diehard Count the 1s Test (byte)	✓	✓	X
Diehard Parking Lot Test	✓	✓	✓
Diehard Min. Dist. (2d Circle) Test	✓	✓	✓
Diehard 3d Sphere (Min. Dist.) Test	✓	✓	✓
Diehard Squeeze Test	✓	✓	X
Diehard Sums Test	✓	✓	✓
Diehard Runs Test	✓	✓	✓
Diehard Craps Test	✓	✓	X
STS Monobit Test	✓	✓	X
STS Runs Test	✓	✓	X
STS Serial Test (Generalized)	✓	✓	X
RGB Bit Distribution Test	✓	✓	X
RGB Generalized Min. Dist. Test	✓	✓	X
RGB Permutations Test	✓	✓	X
RGB Lagged Sum Test	✓	✓	X
RGB Kolmogorov-Smirnov Test Test	✓	✓	X

but it fails to be rejected for this particular test. In fact, for good PRNGs, p-values extracted from different rounds of each test are expected to be uniformly distributed. More information about the null hypothesis and the p-values can be found in [37] and the Dieharder manuals[11].

More explicitly, in order to determine whether a test succeeds or fails, Dieharder internally calculates a set of p-values performing several executions of each test with different data. If the p-values of a given test are smaller than the significance level (usually values in the range of 0.1 to 0.001), then the test fails. In addition, the set of p-values obtained are tested with the Kolmogorov-Smirnov (KS) test to check the null hypothesis is not rejected. The result of this check is a number between 0 and 1.

Since several datasets were generated for each PRNG, each Dieharder test was repeated a few times for each PRNG. In order to test the different runs of each test, we have treated the KS test values output for each test as p-values. Then, we have set a significance level of 0.005 and we have considered the test failed if any of the values were below this threshold. Another issue to be considered is that these values are random variables and, as such, the same test over different datasets should produce noticeably different values. This is why we compared the difference between the maximum and minimum values, and considered the test failed if this difference was smaller than 0.1. Both Scytl's and the Gold Standard PRNG succeed with this test as well, in particular such difference was much bigger than 0.1 for all the tests. On the other hand, the flawed PRNG had many similar values, and as a consequence it failed most of the tests.

6   Performance

A good performance of the voting client application is important to guarantee a smooth user experience. The next sections study the timing associated to the voting client and its cryptographic operations.

6.1   Cryptographic Operations

A benchmarking application was developed to measure the speed of some cryptographic operations provided by our Javascript cryptographic library. Most of the operations tested are used by our voting clients. Others are not used, but they are included as a reference (for example the ElGamal decryption primitives). The benchmarks were performed on a PC with several operating systems and browsers and on two smartphones based on Android and iOS operating systems. The results obtained (see Table 3) are product of one execution of the benchmark application on each of the systems detailed. The time shown for each operation is the average of 1000 executions for the SHA-256, HMACwithSHA256 and AES-128-GCM operations, 100 executions for the RSA ciphers and signers, and 10

---

[11] http://manpages.ubuntu.com/manpages/precise/man1/dieharder.1.html.

Table 3. Cryptographic operations performance (time in ms).

Device	PC 15-3210M CPU 2,50GHz, 8GB RAM						SG S6 Edge	A iPhone 6
OS	Windows 10 Professional				Ubuntu 16.04.1 LTS		Android 6.0.1	iOS 10.0.2
Browser	Chrome 54	Firefox 50	IE 11	Edge 38	Chrome 54	Firefox 50	Chrome 54	Safari 10
SHA-256 1KB	0,116	0,158	0,349	0,322	0,132	0,139	0,388	0,323
SHA-256 10KB	0,521	1,168	3,085	2,832	0,533	0,905	1,743	2,083
HMAC with SHA256 1KB	0,244	0,479	0,809	0,825	0,226	0,199	0,647	0,399
HMAC with SHA256 10KB	1,529	4,547	7,125	6,989	1,387	1,802	3,886	3,258
PBKDF2 with SHA256 20B 32K It	238	593	1606	921	250	520	925	971
AES-GCM-128 1KB Enc / Dec	0,429 / 0,447	0,454 / 0,574	1,141 / 1,178	0,533 / 0,655	0,475 / 0,511	0,504 / 0,684	1,201 / 1,253	0,637 / 0,748
AES-GCM-128 10KB Enc / Dec	2,301 / 2,998	2,298 / 3,845	6,460 / 7,457	2,904 / 3,859	2,558 / 3,214	2,927 / 4,944	6,849 / 8,120	3,781 / 5,888
RSA-OAEP 214B Enc / Dec	2 / 43	3 / 51	2 / 56	2 / 48	2 / 47	3 / 56	4 / 84	3 / 67
RSA-KEM 1KB Enc / Dec	3 / 44	3 / 48	6 / 57	6 / 47	3 / 42	3 / 51	8 / 83	5 / 67
RSA-KEM 10KB Enc / Dec	5 / 46	5 / 51	14 / 72	8 / 57	5 / 45	5 / 55	13 / 90	9 / 73
RSA-PSS 1KB Sign / Verify	43 / 1	48 / 2	71 / 2	52 / 3	42 / 1	50 / 2	82 / 3	67 / 2
RSA-PSS 10KB Sign / Verify	45 / 2	48 / 3	65 / 5	54 / 5	43 / 2	52 / 3	85 / 5	74 / 4
ElGamal Enc / Dec (Normal Exp)	252 / 444	304 / 157	353 / 177	288 / 147	250 / 438	316 / 165	476 / 238	448 / 502
ElGamal Enc / Dec (Short Exp)	115 / 59	40 / 20	46 / 23	34 / 24	113 / 61	42 / 21	62 / 32	131 / 66
ElGamal Enc / Dec (Short Exp + Batch 2e)	173 / 117	59 / 39	68 / 48	63 / 40	170 / 116	63 / 43	93 / 197	193 / 132
ElGamal Precomp / Enc (Short Exp)	115 / 0	40 / 0	52 / 0	36 / 0	113 / 0	42 / 0	108 / 0	130 / 0
Schnorr Proof Gen / Ver (Short Exp)	62 / 112	22 / 38	27 / 52	26 / 40	61 / 111	24 / 45	44 / 67	70 / 138
Schnorr Proof Precomp / Gen (Short Exp)	58 / 3	20 / 1	23 / 2	20 / 2	57 / 3	21 / 1	31 / 4	65 / 4

executions for the PBKDF2, ElGamal cipher and SchnorrProof generator and validators. The PBKDF2 is setup with 32.000 iterations and computes a key of length 128 bits. All the symmetric and asymmetric keys used in the tests are 128 and 2048 bits long, respectively. The ElGamal primitives are tested both with and without the optimisations described in Sect. 4.1. The Schnorr primitive is only tested with the version that uses short exponents, which is the one used in the company's voting clients.

From the performance results obtained we can conclude the following:

- The performance is heavily influenced by the type of device and underlying hardware, e.g. a regular PC is faster than a smartphone. As expected, the regular PC performs faster since it is more powerful than a mobile device. However, we have observed that in the last years the distance between both types of platforms has shortened (see for example the results we presented in [4]).
- There are large differences of performance, for certain primitives, comparing different browsers, e.g. SHA256, HMAC, PBKDF2 and AES are slower in Microsoft Explorer and Microsoft Edge browsers, while the ElGamal and SchnorrProof primitives run slower in Chrome browsers for PC. An extreme example is the PBKDF2, that can present differences of up to 7 times.
- Instead, the operating system does not have a strong impact on the results, e.g. similar results are obtained in Linux and Windows with the same browsers.
- Regarding the operation types, the times obtained for the different types of primitives is the one expected, i.e. the following operations spent more time from left to right: hashes, MACs, symmetric encryption, asymmetric encryption and signature based on RSA, and ElGamal encryption and related ZKPs.
- The results also prove the optimisations of ElGamal encryption explained in Sect. 4.1 are successful. The implementation based on short exponents provides a 5–7 times speedup, the batch encryption spends a 25% less time when two elements are encrypted, and the pre-computations make the final encryption time to be almost negligible.

The results obtained are consistent with the expectations. However, it can be observed that in some cases there are particular primitives that show unexpected timings in a given browser (even in the same browser for a different operating system). For example, the ElGamal decryption without optimisations spends more time decrypting than encrypting in Chrome, when these times should be inverted due to the theoretical complexity of the primitives. This can be related to bugs or faulty optimisations of the Javascript interpreters of the browsers. In some cases, these type of issues can also affect the functionality of the primitives. For example, due to a faulty optimisation of Safari, the Forge library returned incorrect values for certain operations after releasing Safari 10[12]. A workaround had to be implemented by Forge in order to overcome the problem while Apple did not issue a bug fix release of their browser.

---

[12] https://github.com/digitalbazaar/forge/issues/428.

6.2   Voting Client Application

The performance of the voting client may present a high variability depending of:

- **Voting Protocol:** defines the cryptographic primitives and communication handshakes performed with the server.
- **Election and Cryptographic Parameters:** The election parameters define the number of candidates, parties and contests of an election, implying different vote lengths and number of encryptions. The cryptographic parameters define the length of the keys and algorithms used, which influences the timings of the cryptographic primitives.
- **Browser:** Certain browser Javascript engines are much more efficient than others executing the cryptographic operations implemented.
- **Device:** Voter device's processor and memory considerably affect the performance.

The tests performed were focused on measuring the user experience in different browsers and devices for a given voting protocol and set of election parameters. The results reflect the time passed since the voter requests the cast of the vote until the process finishes. Pre-computed operations are not considered since they are executed before the mentioned process.

Neuchâtel e-Voting Protocol. The selected voting protocol is the one used in a recent election in Neuchâtel e-voting platform [28] (March 2015). A test election was setup where the voters had to vote for two contests. In the first contest the voter had to choose one party and 5 candidates, whereas in the second contest the voter had to choose one party and 41 candidates. The operations computed by this voting protocol are summarised here:

1. **Encryption of the Selected Voting Options:** the voting options selected of both contests are multiplied together and the result is encrypted into one ciphertext. The ciphertext is computed using the ElGamal encryption algorithm, which requires 2 exponentiations which have been pre-computed while the voter navigates through the application (see Sect. 4.3).
2. **Computation of Partial Return Codes:** these are codes used to provide cast as intended verifiability (see Sect. 4.3). The computation of partial return codes requires one exponentiation of each voter selection to a voter-specific secret key, which in the test election sums up to 47 exponentiations. Every time the voter selects an option, the corresponding partial return code is computed. Therefore, these operations are already done when the voter pulses the *send* button. Thus this time is not included in the presented test results.
3. **Encryption of Partial Return Codes:** the partial return codes are encrypted using the ElGamal encryption algorithm, under the public key of the server, in order to protect their privacy during their transmission from the voting client to the server. The variant with multiple key encryption, as described in Sect. 4.1, is used. The required exponentiations, which sum up to 47, are also pre-computed while the voter navigates through the application.

4. **Generation of Cryptographic Proofs (ZKPKs):** two ZKPKs are computed. The first, based on the Schnorr [16] identification protocol, proves the encrypted ballot is well-formed. The second, based on the Chaum-Pedersen [5] protocol, prove to the server that the partial return codes match the voting options of the encrypted ballot. For the first proof 1 exponentiation, which can be pre-computed, is required. For the second proof, 7 exponentiations are required, of which 5 can be pre-computed. Thus, in total 8 exponentiations are computed during the proof generation process, from which 6 can be pre-computed.

5. **Signature of the Computed Values:** all the computed values are digitally signed using the RSA digital signature algorithm.

The ElGamal encryption and the RSA signature algorithms use 2048 bit keys. The approach described in Sect. 4.1 for using short exponents (256-bit exponents instead of 2047-bit ones) in ElGamal is used for the encryption of the voting options, for the encryption of partial return codes, and for the Schnorr and plaintext equality proofs.

Table 4. Vote casting and confirmation performance.

Device	OS	Browser	Time
PC i5-3210M CPU 2.50 GHz 8 GB RAM	Windows 10 Professional	Chrome 54	12 s
		Firefox 50	9 s
		IE 11	9.5 s
		Edge 38	8 s
	Ubuntu 16.04.1 LTS	Chrome 54	12 s
		Firefox 50	9.5 s
Samsung Galaxy 6 Edge	Android 6.0.1	Chrome 54	18 s
Apple iPhone 6	iOS 10.0.2	Safari 10	43.5 s

Results Obtained. The results (see Table 4) are aligned with the ones obtained for the cryptographic primitives, although in this case they also include the server and network processing times. The platform is the element that influence the most the results, clearly showing that desktop computers perform much faster. The browser also influences them, being Google Chrome the slowest browser casting a vote in the PC category. But what it is more relevant is that in most of the tested devices the time needed for casting a vote is always below 45 s, and usually much less, clearly demonstrating the Javascript technology is appropriate for implementing a voting client. Notice that, in comparison with the previous paper [4], this results have been updated and they show higher times. The reason is that they currently include the time spent by casting the vote and, also, by confirming it (this last part not included in the former paper).

6.3   Performance Challenges

During the development, one of the first points that arose was that, the execution of cryptographic primitives could be slow on certain browsers and/or platforms. This generated two effects: (a) the browser presented a pop-up indicating the script was not responding and (b) the time to generate the encrypted ballot was too long. Two solutions were applied to the first issue. The HTML5 Web Workers[13] were used if available. This prevented the script from blocking the view of the page and no pop-up was presented to the user. For browsers no compatible with this technology, the solution implemented consisted of dividing the costly operations in smaller operations, thus avoiding exceeding the timeout associated to the pop-up. For the second issue, the overall time taken to generate a ballot, the primitive optimisations described in Sect. 4.1, i.e. ElGamal encryption with short exponents and multiple keys, and the pre-computation of part of the cryptographic operations described in Sect. 4.3 were applied. A second point was related to the generation of random numbers. The amount of entropy we initially required to seed the PRNG was 128 bits. This is recommended, in order to ensure that the random generation is strong enough (i.e. the random values generated are unpredictable). Nevertheless, in order to prevent usability issues due to exceptional cases where the minimum entropy cannot be reached, a minimum amount of entropy collection was not enforced in production. Instead, the entropy estimation mechanism was used only during development time to perform tests that ensured a minimum level of entropy was reached before the first random values were requested.

7   Conclusions

In this paper, a revised version of [4], we have explained our experience and lessons learnt on implementing a Javascript voting client in an industrial environment. The resulting voting client has been extensively used in real elections with a very positive outcome.

The implementation described in this article has allowed us to conclude with several outcomes. First, the implementation of a voting client in Javascript is feasible, both from a security and a performance perspective. The language is powerful enough to implement cryptographic primitives and the current interpreters good enough to support the load, i.e. to perform the tasks in the expected amount of time. Second, the usage of Javascript has provided a much better user experience and larger interoperability than previous implementations of the voting client based on Java applets. The reason is that the Javascript voting clients are much lighter and multi-platform than their Java counterparts. No Java Runtime Environment (JRE) for each specific platform is needed, only a browser with Javascript support. This has dramatically reduced the number calls related to the JRE in the customer support service. At the same time, the number of

---

[13] https://developer.mozilla.org/en-US/docs/Web/API/Web_Workers_API/Using_web _workers.

devices where the client can be run is much larger. On the downside, the usage of Javascript has increased the number of code interoperability issues to consider during development related to each type of browser (Firefox, Google Chrome...). However, this does not impact the final user since it is tackled at development time. Also, as there are multiple browser implementations, the possibility of incorrect functioning due to browsers' bugs is higher. Third, a strong security level is offered, thus the cryptographic primitives used are the same than in the Java voting client implementation. In addition, our client does not suffer from the, increasingly, critical security bugs coming up from the JRE. The only disadvantage of Javascript is that there is no support for signing the code. However, the integrity of the code is guaranteed by the transport layer (SSL/TLS) and by file integrity mechanisms at the server. Additional security measures mitigate this issue, e.g. remote code integrity validation services and use of verifiable voting protocols allowing the voter to verify the vote cast with independence of the voting client logics.

Further work is being performed to deal with the Javascript weaknesses, mostly the lack of code signed support, and performance improvement. On the one hand, an intelligent application for remote code integrity validation service is being implemented. This application issues requests, which should not be distinguishable from regular requests issued by real voters, to retrieve and validate the code served. On the other hand, the cryptographic library implemented is being revised in order to obtain better performance. This is specially important to improve the voting times in resource constrained devices, such as low-end smartphones or smart television platforms. This is endeavoured both by (a) studying the performance of new cryptographic libraries targeted to obtain better performance, such asmCrypto; and (b) studying the adoption of the Web Cryptography API [21] to be used when supported.

Acknowledgements. We would like to thank our colleagues David Salvador, Pol Valletbó, Adrià Rodríguez and Anna Mayola for their help with the performance test environments.

References

1. Adida, B.: Helios: web-based open-audit voting. In: van Oorschot, P.C. (ed.) USENIX Security Symposium, pp. 335–348. USENIX Association, Berkeley (2008)
2. Gjosteen, K.: The Norwegian internet voting protocol. ePrint (2013). eprint.iacr.org/2013/473.pdf
3. Juels, A., Catalano, D., Jakobsson, M.: Coercion-resistant electronic elections. In: Chaum, D., Jakobsson, M., Rivest, R.L., Ryan, P.Y.A., Benaloh, J., Kutylowski, M., Adida, B. (eds.) Towards Trustworthy Elections. LNCS, vol. 6000, pp. 37–63. Springer, Heidelberg (2010). doi:10.1007/978-3-642-12980-3_2
4. Cucurull, J., Guasch, S., Galindo, D.: Transitioning to a Javascript voting client for remote online voting. In: Proceedings of the 13th International Joint Conference on e-Business and Telecommunications - Volume 4: SECRYPT, pp. 121–132 (2016)

5. Chaum, D., Pedersen, T.P.: Wallet databases with observers. In: Brickell, E.F. (ed.) CRYPTO 1992. LNCS, vol. 740, pp. 89–105. Springer, Heidelberg (1993). doi:10.1007/3-540-48071-4_7
6. RSA Laboratories. PKCS #12: Personal Information Exchange Syntax Standard
7. Gharadaghy, R., Volkamer, M.: Verifiability in electronic voting - explanations for non security experts. In: Krimmer, R., Grimm, R. (eds.) Electronic Voting 2010, EVOTE 2010, 4th International Conference, Co-organized by Council of Europe, Gesellschaft für Informatik and E-Voting.CC, 21–24 July 2010, in Castle Hofen, Bregenz, Austria, LNI, GI, vol. 167, pp. 151–162 (2010)
8. Puiggalí, J., Chóliz, J., Guasch, S.: Best practices in internet voting. In: NIST: Workshop on UOCAVA Remote Voting Systems, Washington, D.C., August 2010
9. NIST: Federal Information Processing Standard (FIPS) 202, SHA-3 Standard: Permutation-Based Hash and Extendable-Output Functions. Technical report, U.S. Department Of Commerce (2015)
10. NIST: Federal Information Processing Standard (FIPS 180-4), Secure Hash Standard. Technical report, U.S. Department of Commerce (2012)
11. RFC-3447: Public-Key Cryptography Standards (PKCS) #1: RSA Cryptography Specifications Version 2.1 (2003)
12. Menezes, A.J., Vanstone, S.A., Oorschot, P.C.V.: Handbook of Applied Cryptography, 1st edn. CRC Press Inc., Boca Raton (1996)
13. NIST: Federal Information Processing Standard (FIPS) 197, Advanced Encryption Standard (AES). Technical report, U.S. Department Of Commerce (2001)
14. NIST: Recommendation for Block Cipher Modes of Operation: Galois/Counter Mode (GCM) and GMAC, NIST Special Publication 800-38D. Technical report, U.S. Department Of Commerce (2007)
15. Damgaard, I.: On σ-protocols. Cryptologic Protocol Theory, CPT 2010, v.2 (2010)
16. Schnorr, C.P.: Efficient signature generation by smart cards. J. Cryptol. **4**, 161–174 (1991)
17. Cortier, V., Smyth, B.: Attacking and fixing Helios: an analysis of ballot secrecy. In: Proceedings of the 24th IEEE Computer Security Foundations Symposium, CSF 2011, pp. 297–311. IEEE Computer Society (2011)
18. RSA Laboratories. PKCS #5: Password-Based Cryptography Standard
19. RFC-5280: Internet X.509 Public Key Infrastructure Certificate and Certificate Revocation List Profile (2008)
20. Stark, E., Hamburg, M., Boneh, D.: Symmetric cryptography in JavaScript. In: ACSAC, pp. 373–381. IEEE Computer Society (2009)
21. W3C. (Web Cryptography API) W3C Candidate Recommendation, December 2014
22. ECMAScript. ECMAScript® Language Specification 5.1 Edition (2011)
23. Klein, A.: Temporary user tracking in major browsers and cross-domain information leakage and attacks. Trusteer, September–November 2008
24. Ferguson, N., Schneier, B.: Practical Cryptography, 1st edn. Wiley, New York (2003)
25. W3C. (W3C Subresource Integrity) W3C Candidate Recommendation, November 2015
26. Karapanos, N., Filios, A., Popa, R.A., Capkun, S.: Verena: end-to-end integrity protection for web applications. In: 2016 IEEE Symposium on Security and Privacy, pp. 895–913 (2016, to appear)

27. Halderman, J.A., Teague, V.: The New South Wales iVote system: security failures and verification flaws in a live online election. In: Haenni, R., Koenig, R.E., Wikström, D. (eds.) VOTELID 2015. LNCS, vol. 9269, pp. 35–53. Springer, Cham (2015). doi:10.1007/978-3-319-22270-7_3

28. Galindo, D., Guasch, S., Puiggalí, J.: 2015 Neuchâtel's cast-as-intended verification mechanism. In: Haenni, R., Koenig, R.E., Wikström, D. (eds.) VOTELID 2015. LNCS, vol. 9269, pp. 3–18. Springer, Cham (2015). doi:10.1007/978-3-319-22270-7_1

29. Gennaro, R.: An improved pseudo-random generator based on the discrete logarithm problem. J. Cryptol. **18**, 91–110 (2005)

30. van Oorschot, P.C., Wiener, M.J.: On Diffie-Hellman key agreement with short exponents. In: Maurer, U. (ed.) EUROCRYPT 1996. LNCS, vol. 1070, pp. 332–343. Springer, Heidelberg (1996). doi:10.1007/3-540-68339-9_29

31. Koshiba, T., Kurosawa, K.: Short exponent Diffie-Hellman problems. In: Bao, F., Deng, R., Zhou, J. (eds.) PKC 2004. LNCS, vol. 2947, pp. 173–186. Springer, Heidelberg (2004). doi:10.1007/978-3-540-24632-9_13

32. Kurosawa, K.: Multi-recipient public-key encryption with shortened ciphertext. In: Naccache, D., Paillier, P. (eds.) PKC 2002. LNCS, vol. 2274, pp. 48–63. Springer, Heidelberg (2002). doi:10.1007/3-540-45664-3_4

33. Maurer, U.: Unifying zero-knowledge proofs of knowledge. In: Preneel, B. (ed.) AFRICACRYPT 2009. LNCS, vol. 5580, pp. 272–286. Springer, Heidelberg (2009). doi:10.1007/978-3-642-02384-2_17

34. Brown, R.G., Eddelbuettel, D., Bauer, D.: Dieharder: a random number test suite. Duke University Physics Department (2009)

35. Marsaglia, G.: Diehard: a battery of tests of randomness (1996). The Marsaglia Random Number CDROM, with The Diehard Battery of Tests of Randomness, produced at Florida State University under a grant from The National Science Foundation, 1985. www.stat.fsu.edu/pub/diehard

36. Rukhin, A., Soto, J., Nechvatal, J., Barker, E., Leigh, S., Levenson, M., Banks, D., Heckert, A., Dray, J., Vo, S., Rukhin, A., Soto, J., Smid, M., Leigh, S., Vangel, M., Heckert, A., Dray, J., Iii, L.E.B.: NIST Special Publication 800-22 Rev 1a: Statistical test suite for random and pseudorandom number generators for cryptographic applications (2010)

37. NIST: A Statistical Test Suite for the Validation of Random Number Generators and Pseudo Random Number Generators for Cryptographic Applications, NIST Special Publication 800-22rev1a. Technical report, U.S. Department of Commerce (2010)

Attribute-Based Privacy-Friendly Access Control with Context

Andreas Put$^{(\boxtimes)}$ and Bart De Decker

Department of Computer Science, imec-DistriNet, KU Leuven, Celestijnenlaan 200A,
3001 Heverlee, Belgium
{andreas.put,bart.dedecker}@cs.kuleuven.be

Abstract. In the last decade, the Internet landscape transformed into a service platform. This evolution has brought more importance to security requirements like strong authentication. We propose a secure and privacy-friendly way to augment authentication mechanisms of Online services by taking context into account. Contextual information, such as location, proximity or the current role of a user in a system is useful to help authenticate and authorize users. Context, however, is often of a personal nature and introduces privacy risks. In addition, a source of such contextual information should provide trustworthy information.

In this work, a policy language to express attribute-based and contextual requirements is proposed. In addition, we define a set of protocols to gather, verify and use contextual information and user-attributes originating from third-party systems. The system protects the user's privacy as service providers do not learn precise context information, and avoids linkabilities. Finally, we have implemented this system and our experimental evaluation shows that it is practical to use.

Keywords: Privacy · Context-aware access control · Policy language

1 Introduction

During the last decade, the Internet landscape has changed from an information platform to a service platform. Almost all our daily needs can be satisfied by Internet services. Television, radio, shopping and socializing are just some examples where Internet services have become popular. Furthermore, smartphones have also become commonplace. These devices not only are more prevalent in today's society, they also are being used more and more to access Online services. Now, a surge of other "smart"-devices can be observed. Consumer items like smart-watches, smart-cars or smart-lights are slowly gaining popularity. These items are often described as *Internet of Things* (IoT) appliances.

Security and privacy are requirements that keep gaining importance for Online platforms. Every system or application connected to the Internet has to be sufficiently secured. To use such a service, users have to authenticate themselves to the corresponding service provider, i.e. prove to the service provider that

© Springer International Publishing AG 2017
M.S. Obaidat (Ed): ICETE 2016, CCIS 764, pp. 291–315, 2017.
https://doi.org/10.1007/978-3-319-67876-4_14

they are allowed to use that service. The need for authentication and authorization in Internet applications gave rise to the development of increasingly
advanced systems. Passwords have been an important means of authentication
long before the Internet existed, and they remain an important authentication
tool to this day. However, passwords are an inherently weak form of authentication [1], they can be easily guessed, stolen or shared.

Two-factor authentication, in which typically 'something you know' (a password) is combined with 'something you have' (a mobile phone, a token, an email
account), increases the overall security of password-based authentication. However it does not improve the user experience, as users are required to perform
more actions compared to standard password-based authentication. However,
we now see that service providers and users accept this usability loss in order to
gain added security. This, together with the fact that this penalty has decreased
with the advent of a smartphone, has caused a steady increase in the adoption
of two-factor authentication systems [2].

Other Online systems have moved away from passwords all together. Public-
key cryptography can be used for authentication using digital signatures. These
signatures can be verified through a public-key infrastructure or a decentralised
web-of-trust. However, the problem of key-management that these techniques
introduce compared to the ease of use of password-based authentication explain
why it still is the main authentication mechanism that drives the Internet [1,3].
Context can be defined as followed [4]:

"Any information that can be used to characterize the situation of an
entity. This entity is a person, place, or object considered relevant to the
interaction between a user and an application, including the user and applications themselves"

Contextual information can help to secure transactions without requiring
user-inter-action. For example, credit-card companies use the geolocation of a
transaction to help detect fraud. Furthermore, smartphones and IoT-devices can
capture a wide variety of contextual information. Some of this information, such
as location, proximity, or the user's current activity can be used to assist in
making access control decisions.

However, contextual information is often privacy intrusive. This problem
is made even worse when contextual data from different transactions is compiled into a single profile. A study conducted by Groopman [5] with more than
2000 participants clearly illustrates this problem. The study concludes that
almost 80% of the participants are concerned about the information that service
providers gather and analyse. Furthermore, using context to make authorization
decisions introduces a security risk: context can sometimes be forged or spoofed.

Attribute-Based Access Control (ABAC) is an authorization model that provides dynamic, context-aware and risk-intelligent access control. It helps achieve
efficient regulatory compliance, effective cloud services, reduced time-to-market
for new applications, and a top-down approach to governance through transparency in policy enforcement.

ABAC uses attributes as building blocks in a structured language that defines access control rules and describes access requests. Attributes are sets of labels or properties that can be used to describe all the entities that must be considered for authorization purposes. Each attribute consists of a key-value pair such as "Role = Manager".

In this work, we extend PACCo [6] by adding support for attribute-based access control. PACCo is a system that focusses on the secure and privacy-friendly collection and usage of contextual information that can assist in making access control decisions. To do this, PACCo introduces a new entity, the *Context Verifier* (CV), which will verify, certify, and, if possible, anonymize contextual information. In order to support attributes alongside context, *Identity Providers* (IPs) are introduced in the system, which can provide certified user attributes. Furthermore, our system is privacy-friendly, as multiple transactions with the CV cannot be linked, while the SP and IPs learn the least amount of required information. In addition, we define a policy language that focuses on expressing contextual requirements and also considers the security guarantees that different context sources can offer.

This work makes the following key contributions:

- We have combined existing privacy-enhancing technologies and cryptographic algorithms in PACCo's protocols, to allow a privacy-friendly and secure collection and usage of context. Defining which contextual information types should be used in making access control decisions is not in this paper's scope. What kind of context is used to make access control decisions is not in this paper's scope.
- We define support to this system for attribute-based access control.
- We propose a context-aware policy language that supports the definition of contextual and attribute-based requirements. Furthermore, the specification allows for identity-attributes to be compared to context information.
- We have implemented our system and show our experimental results.

The paper is structured as follows: Sect. 2 presents related work and Sect. 3 illustrates motivational use cases, after which the preliminaries section follows. Next, we define PACCo's policy language. Section 6 shows an overview of PACCo, our threat model and the protocols, after which the security and privacy of PACCo are discussed. Finally, we show the test results of our prototype implementation.

2   Related Work

XACML, eXtensible Access Control Markup Language version 3.0 was ratified by OASIS standard organization [7] in 2005. XACML defines a declarative access-control policy language defined in XML, and a processing model describing how to evaluate access requests according to the rules defined in policies. The XACML specification supports identity-based access control and incorporates some limited contextual information without any formal context-aware access control mode. Furthermore, geoXACML [8] propose a set of extensions to introduce location constraints to the XACML standard.

A fair amount of work has been put into adding support for context into Role Based Access Control (RBAC) models. These models focus mostly on temporal and spacial context [9,10], but also on support for more general context [11,12]. In [13], a context-aware access control model for distributed health-care applications is proposed. Application designers determine which context types are to be used by analysing the system's security requirements. Furthermore, [14] describes a context supporting policy model that focuses to better control "break the glass" attempts in health-care systems.

A general context-aware mandatory access control model is proposed in [15]. This work is capable of dynamic adaptation of policies with context and it offers support for confidentiality and integrity requirements.

PACCo's goal is different from these systems, as PACCo also focuses on minimal information disclosure and secure collection and validation of the actual contextual information.

In Attribute-Based Access Control (ABAC) systems [16–18], subjects are represented by a set of attributes, and access control decisions are made based the current value of these attributes. Context-aware access control is, in essence, similar to ABAC. However, here, the attributes of a subject are often dynamic in nature. Furthermore, contextual information can originate from a wide range of devices that are not necessarily under a verifier's control.

Context-aware authentication between a user and her device is another area that has been thoroughly explored [3,19–21]. However, privacy is of little concern to these systems as the context that is used does not leave the user's device. Furthermore, these papers do analyse how contextual information should be used (e.g. which context types to use or how to combine them to make a decision), whereas PACCo focusses on the secure and privacy-friendly collection and verification of context.

The CSAC system [22] does focus on offering context-aware Online authentication with privacy. However, PACCo targets stricter privacy goals. In CSAC, users obtain location granting tickets from a context broker, which is in contact with different context providers. This ticket is presented to a service provider, which will use it to obtain the user's context at the broker. However, the context broker is able to learn everything about its users (their context, the services that they use, etc.), as it relays all the messages. This problem is avoided by PACCo because service providers do not context the "context broker" directly. Instead, the user collects the necessary proofs from the context broker, which it presents to the service provider.

3   Attribute-Based and Context-Aware Authentication

The following two examples illustrate the benefits and pitfalls of attribute-based and context-aware authentication.

Conference Proceedings. The organizers of a scientific conference want to distribute the proceedings to the participants. To do so, the organizers make the proceedings available on an Online file-server. Password-protected files are made public in such a way that only the registered participants are able to download them. In order to add an extra layer of security, the conference organizers, who do not believe that passwords alone are secure enough, want to only allow access to participants who are present at the conference venue. In addition, access to the proceedings is allowed before the conference starts or after it closes when the participant is in the conference's city.

Contextual access control offers certainly new interesting possibilities. However, it also opens the door for privacy risks. The contextual information can be fine-grained or even unique if the location is determined by e.g. GPS. Furthermore, additional privacy concerns come into play when a third party takes care of the access control. This would require the participants to disclose their location data to a third party.

Consultant Access. An external consultant is assigned to assist an in-house team on a project of the company 'fictionalCo'. Each Monday morning, the team holds a meeting to plan the coming week. Furthermore, certain documents are accessible through an Online portal, which is provided by a cloud service.

The consultant is able to access relevant documents for the meetings, but she is only able to do this during these meetings if she is present in the meeting room. In addition, she is also granted access to those files, but only if she is in the vicinity of the project leader.

However, it is important to note that relying on contextual information alone is often not sufficient. In this case, it would be in the company's interest to verify that this person *actually is a consultant*. Therefore, it could require her to prove that her current *role* attribute is equal to 'consultant' and her *assigned_to_company* attribute is equal to 'fictionalCo'.

Security is essential in this scenario. Attribute-based and contextual information can be extremely useful for making access control decisions. In addition, the information's integrity and authenticity should be verifiable as well and the freshness of the information could also play an important role. Finally, the company can set up trusted devices that provide contextual information, but it might not want this context to leave 'fictionalCo'. Therefore, it is important that the verification of raw context (e.g. by 'fictionalCo'), and making the actual access control decision (e.g. by the cloud service) can be separated. Furthermore, attributes can originate from different (i.e. external but trusted) identity providers.

4   Preliminaries

4.1   Privacy-ABCs

Digital certificates or credentials are essentially a set of attributes signed by a trusted third party, the Credential Issuer. The latter will guarantee that the values in the credential are correct. The X.509 certificates [23] are often used. However, these credentials offer poor privacy properties as a verifier will learn every attribute contained in a credential when the credential's signature is verified. Furthermore, verifiers learn a unique signature and attributes from transactions involving certificates which allows them to link different transactions in which these certificates are used.

Privacy-ABCs, or anonymous credentials, allow for *selective disclosure of attributes*, meaning that a credential owner can hide the attributes that she is not required to disclose to a verifier. Moreover, *multiple transactions with the same credential can be made unlinkable*.

The standard for Privacy-ABC systems has been set by the ABC4Trust project [24], in which the structure of these credentials and their associated protocols have been specified. The most well known and practical privacy-ABC systems are U-Prove [25] and Idemix [26,27]. Idemix is used in our system because of its unlinkability properties. Other than selective disclosure, these credential systems offer interesting capabilities. For example, one can prove statements about attributes in a credentials *without revealing their actual attribute value*. These statements can consist out of inequalities (e.g. age > 18), ranges (e.g. $18 >$ age > 12) or set-membership (e.g. role is in set [approved roles]).

A privacy-ABC owner can be deterred from sharing credentials by including sensitive information in the credential[1] and by linking multiple credentials to the same secret. The person with whom someone shares a credential will learn the sensitive information and will be able to use all her other credentials as well.

An important concept in PACCo are *provable pseudonyms*. Privacy-ABC owners can generate seemingly random pseudonyms of which can be proven in zero knowledge that they were generated with a specific credential [27,28]. Note that if credentials are linked to the same secret (e.g. to prevent sharing), both of these credentials can be used to prove ownership of the same provable pseudonym.

4.2   uCentive

The uCentive [29] system provides an efficient way for an entity to anonymously bind information to a privacy-ABC. A different party is later able to verify the validity of the data together with the fact that this data belongs to the entity with which it is currently interacting. This is done by combining partially-blinded signatures (PBS) [30] and provable pseudonyms. The blinded part of the PBS contains a provable pseudonym, which is only known to the user. The clear part consists out of data which can be verified by the signer (Fig. 1). Once signed, the user can unblind her provable pseudonym, the result of which forms a *uCentive token*. Later, she can show the signed token to another entity together with a zero-knowledge proof of the fact that she owns the pseudonym embedded in the token.

---

[1] Note that these attributes can remain hidden during a credential show.

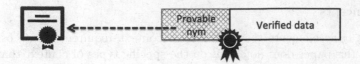

Fig. 1. uCentive token. The provable pseudonym is blinded when the signature is made, while other information is not blinded and can be verified [6].

4.3 Attribute-Based Access Control

ABAC uses attributes as building blocks in a structured language that defines access control rules and describes access requests. Attributes are sets of labels or properties that can be used to describe all the entities that must be considered for authorization purposes. Each attribute consists of a key-value pair such as "Role = Manager".

The XACML policy language specifies four main building blocks:

- a subject
- an action
- a resource
- the environment in which the request is made

Each of these can be described using attributes:

The subject who is demanding access to an information asset. General attributes describing the subject, for instance roles, group memberships, the department/company to which the user belongs, management level, certifications or competencies, user ID, etc., can often be retrieved from an HR system or directory (LDAP).

Common action attributes in authorization requests are 'read' and/or 'write'. In more complex scenarios, the action may be described by a combination of attributes. When one accesses her Online bank account, the action may for instance be described by multiple attributes, such as action 'type = transfer', and 'amount = $500'. The resource identifies the information asset or object impacted by the action.

Common environment attributes are related to the current time and location from where access is requested, to the type of communication channel, such as protocol or encryption strength, or client type (PC, smart phone, etc.). Authentication strength may also be relevant to authorization. Context data can principally be of any type that is relevant to consider to minimize risks or to plan precautions: the number of transactions already made in the last 24 h, normal user behaviour patterns, relations to a third party, availability of related legal contracts etc.

5 PACCo Policy Language

In this section, we introduce the model of PACCo's context-aware access control policy language.

5.1   Concepts

First, the basic elements that make up a context requirement are explained. Although this paper does not focus on the specific types of context that should be used in access control, an example set of these elements is shown in Table 1.

Table 1. Examples of context types and sources with associated operations and arguments [6].

Context type/source	Operation	Argument	Value
Location	inCity	Accuracy	City name
GPS, Wifi	withinMeters	Distance, accuracy	Coordinates
Cell tower	inPolygon	Accuracy	PolygonCoordinates
Time	isBefore	Format	Time (in specified format)
NTP	isAfter	Format	Time (in specified format)
	days	Format	Set of days (in specified format)
Proximity	inRoom	–	Room identifier
Wifi, NFC	nearDevice	MaxDistance	Device identifier
Paired Bluetooth			

Context Source (CS). The Context Source identifies from which kind of device the context originates (e.g. GPS, Cell Tower, Wifi, ...).

Context Type (CT). A Context Type is a collection of Context Sources. For example, the context type *location* contains the sources *GPS, Cell Tower* and *Wifi*. It is assumed that a mapping $CT \rightarrow [CS_1 \ldots CS_n]$ is defined and known to the system.

Operation (OP). Context types support one or more operations. For example, the location type supports the operation *inCity*, while the time type supports *isAfter*. Operations are specified in a function format (i.e. with arguments between parentheses). Furthermore, context sources inherit the operations of their parent type (e.g. GPS supports similar operations as the Location type).

Argument (A). Some operations require one or more arguments to be specified. For example, the inCity operation requires an *Accuracy* argument.

Value (V). A value is used in the evaluation of context requirements. Values are matched to context originating from a CS to which an operation has been applied to. Multiple values are denoted using a comma-separator $(V_1, V_2, \ldots, V_n)$.

Attribute (Att). Attributes are specified by unique identifiers. E.g. the attribute *role* mentioned in Sect. 3 can be specified as "urn:the_consultancy:employee: role". Note that in our policy language, a value (V) can be replaced by an Attribute (Att), meaning that the value related to the specified attribute identifier is used. Similar to context types and sources, different operations can be specified for different attribute types. However, in this work, we will only refer to the *equals* operation on attributes. However, note that this language does not limit itself to one particular operation.

The policy language can be extended by defining new context sources or context types. Note, however, that defining a new CT involve the definition of operations, and, hence, arguments. This extensibility is important as future IoT devices might offer interesting opportunities regarding context-aware access control.

Freshness Property. Freshness of context is of utmost importance. This property, specified in seconds, indicates how old contextual information may be, i.e. a freshness parameter of '3600' indicates that the context should have been collected at most one hour ago in order to be considered as valid.

Security Property. Using context for access-control is not a trivial task as a malicious user could alter and construct information from context sources, or even spoof them. However, context sources can offer varying degrees of security guarantees. Therefore, three security-levels for context sources are defined.

Unchecked information is not guaranteed and, hence, can have been forged, shared as well as spoofed. E.g. originating from a "dumb" device such as a simple sensor.

Certified information is *timestamped and signed*. Hence, it cannot be spoofed or forged. It can, however, be shared. E.g. originating from an IoT device controlled by a trusted entity.

Verified information can be *verified at the context source* by a third party. Not only the authenticity, but also the ownership of the contextual information is verifiable. Hence, it cannot be shared. E.g. originating from an IoT device that can link context to a user.

The security property defines the minimal level of security for a context source (unchecked < certified < verified). GPS, Wifi, NFC and Paired Bluetooth are examples of *unchecked* context sources, as we assume that the sensors providing this information do not offer any authenticity or integrity guarantees. A Cell Tower is assumed to be an *certified* context source[2].

Finally, Time is a *verified* context source as it can be universally verified. IoT devices could also act as context sources. The context type and their associated security parameter which they represent will be determined based on their

---

[2] Although smartphone applications do not have access to cell tower authenticity information, such a feature is technically possible and the source is controlled by a trustworthy entity.

capabilities. Therefore, IoT devices may provide the services of most certified and verified context sources.

Context Requirement (CR). A Context Requirement is the combination of a context type, an operation with its arguments and a value. Instead of a value, an attribute is also allowed. Note that attributes are replaced by the effective value at the time that this requirement is evaluated, and, hence, the actual meaning is similar. Alternatively, the context type (CT) can be replaced by a specific source (CS). Furthermore, the CR can optionally define freshness and security properties. The CR represents a fundamental contextual constraint and has the following form:

$CR := <CT$ or $CS>$
$<OP>(<A_1>, \ldots, <A_n>) <V$ or $Att>$
WITH $freshness =$ '100' $security =$ '$verified$'

Attribute Requirement (AR). Attribute requirements are similar to Context Requirements with the difference that the context type or source is replaced by an attribute identifier. Because attributes are much more static than contextual information, the freshness property can be omitted. Furthermore, the security of attributes is always verified, as they originate from trusted and verifiable sources (see Sect. 6). Hence, both freshness and security can be omitted from an AR.

$AR := <Att> <OP>(<A_1>, \ldots, <A_n>) <V>$

Requirement Set (RS). A requirement set is a conjunction of context requirements and/or attribute requirements. Similar to the context requirement, an RS can optionally define freshness and security. These are inherited by the CRs that did not specify them.

$RS := <CR_1> \wedge <CR_2> \wedge <AR_1> \wedge <AR_2> \wedge \ldots$
WITH $freshness =$ '100' $security =$ '$certified$'

Context Policy. Similar to standard authorization systems, the target of a policy is identified by a Subject, Resource and Action. The condition of a policy is *a disjunction of requirement sets*. It is required to specify a freshness and security properties in the condition, unless the specified requirement sets only contain ARs. The security and freshness properties are inherited by any RS or CR that did not specify properties themselves. If the condition evaluates to 'true', then the policy's effect will be determined (Permit/Deny). When conflicting effects apply for the same target, a conflict resolution strategy such as the assignment of priorities to an effect can be applied.

$P: Target\{Subject = S, Resource = R, Action = Ac\}$
$Effect\{Permit(1)\}$
$Condition$
$\quad \{ <RS_1> \vee < RS_2> \vee \ldots \vee <RS_n> \}$
WITH $freshness =$ '100' $security =$ '$unchecked$'

5.2 PACCo Policy Examples

The first example (Listing 1.1) shows a PACCo Policy related to the first scenario in Sect. 3.

Listing 1.1. Context requirements for the conference proceedings policy.

```
Target{Subject='anySubject',
Resource='anyResource',
Action='fileAccess'}

Effect{Permit(1)}

Condition{
(Location  inCity(Accuracy='250m')  London
AND Time  days(Format='Ddd')  Mon,Tue,Wed
AND Time  isAfter(Format='hh:mm')  19:00)

(Location  inCity(Accuracy='250m')  London
AND Time  days(Format='Ddd')  Mon,Tue,Wed
AND Time  isBefore(Format='hh:mm')  10:00)

(Location  inPolygon(Accuracy='0.001')
50.865389:4.672449,50.862388:4.679377,
50.862759:4.674634
AND Time  days(Format='Ddd')  Mon,Tue,Wed
)
}  WITH  freshness='600'  security='certified'
```

The target of this policy relates to anybody that wants to access any file on the file-server.

The policy condition has three context requirement sets, the first of which specifies that one's location should be in London (within an accuracy of 250 m). Furthermore, the time should after 19h00, and the current day should be Monday, Tuesday or Wednesday. The second set is identical except for the fact that the current time should be before 10h00. Finally, the third set also requires the day to be Monday, Tuesday or Wednesday, while the location should be within a defined area (the conference venue).

The freshness property for the condition is set to 600 s, and the security property is set to *certified*. This will exclude GPS as context source, as it provides unverified context. Cell Tower information is assumed to be certified and it is accurate enough to provide context for the first two requirement set. However, it is not accurate enough for the third RS. Hence, a location service provided by an IoT device at the conference is required.

Listing 1.2 shows a policy related to the second scenario of Sect. 3.

It targets the external consultant who wants to access project resources. The policy condition requires that the meeting currently takes place and that the external consultant is in the meeting room and that the consultant is currently on assignment at this company. Because the proximity requirement has the unchecked security property, any source present in the meeting room could be used. Furthermore, the freshness is set to 100 s to prevent the consultant from accessing the files once the meeting is over. As an alternative, the consultant is allowed access if she is in the vicinity of the project leader. Note that the condition's security property is *verified*, meaning that it should not be possible to share or forge this context. Therefore, the project leader should wear an IoT device that acts as a proximity context source.

Listing 1.2. Context and attribute requirements for the external consultant policy.

```
Target { Subject = 'consultant',
Resource = 'projectResource',
Action = 'anyAction' }

Effect { Permit (2) }

Condition {
(   Time  days (Format = 'ddd')  Mon
AND  Time  isAfter (Format = 'hh:mm')  10:00
AND  Time  isBefore (Format = 'hh:mm')  12:00
AND  Proximity  inRoom ()  meeting_room_A  WITH  security = '
   unchecked'
AND  urn: the_consultancy : employee : role  equals ()  consultant
AND  urn: the_consultancy : employee : assignment_location
   equals ()  fictionalCo )

(   Proximity  nearDevice ()  urn: fictionalCo : project : employee
   : leader : device
AND  urn: the_consultancy : employee : role  equals ()  consultant
AND  urn: the_consultancy : employee : assigned_to_company
   equals ()  fictionalCo )
}  WITH  freshness = '100'   security = 'verified'
```

6   PACCo

6.1   Overview and Threat Model

The five different entities are distinguished in PACCo: the User, the Service Provider (SP), the Context Verifier (CV), the Identity Provider (IP) and the different types of Context Providers (CPs). For simplicity reasons, only one CV and one IP are depicted below. We assume that the SP trusts the CV and the IP.

Users want to make use of the services offered by the service provider. They own a smartphone or another smart-device that is capable of gathering context and authenticating with privacy-ABCs. This device runs a PACCo service that is responsible for managing the user's context.

The *Service Provider* offers an online service to its users. However, in order to improve the strength of its current access-control mechanisms, the SP wants to support context-augmented authentication and context-aware authorization. The SP enforces a set of PACCo policies.

The *Context Verifier* is a third party which will verify the context of the user, after which it gives the user a token that the latter can use to forward to the SP. Separating context verification from the SP not only makes it easier for existing SPs to support PACCo, but also gives this system better privacy properties. In addition, the CV manages the trust in different context providers, keeping track of which CPs are trusted, and which are not.

The *Identity Provider* is a trustworthy third party which has knowledge of a set of user attributes. Users can authenticate to this provider and request a set of attributes from it. These attributes will be certified in anonymous credentials and can later be used to authorize a user by the service provider, or to verify context requirements.

Context Providers are considered as *black-boxes with limited computational capacity*. CPs, however, do have different capabilities. PACCo identifies four types of Context Providers, based on the security guarantees they can provide (cfr. Sect. 5.1).

- *Unchecked* CPs (e.g. smartphone sensors) simply return unchecked context data.
- *Certified* CPs also return a signature on the contextual data, the identifier of the context source, and a timestamp (e.g. cell tower or IoT device).
- *Personal Verifiable* CPs collect contextual information about the users themselves (e.g. IoT activity monitor, proximity sensors). Hence, this information is of a privacy-sensitive nature. Personal context sources offer interfaces to both the user and the CV. Users can request it to gather contextual data. The CP will then collect the requested context and wait for the CV to request it. This is considered a *verified* context source as the CV can verify the authenticity of the context and that this belongs to the user.
- *Global* CPs offer contextual information which can be accessed and verified by anyone (e.g. NTP server). As the CV can gather the (global) context itself, this CP is a *verified* context source

The threat model for this system is organized according to involved entity:

Malicious User. A malicious or compromised user will try to gain access to the service without satisfying the context requirements set by the SP. In order to do this, malicious users can try to share contextual information, steal it, or forge it.

Curious SP. A curious SP will not actively try to corrupt the system. For example, it will not collude with any third party, the CV or CPs. However, it will try to learn as much as possible from the interactions it has with its users.

Compromized SP. A compromised SP could ignore the access control decisions and allow or deny access to users at will.

Curious but Honest CV. The CV will not collude with a third party nor will it fail to correctly verify or certify context of users. Similar to a PKI, the SP will trust this entity to correctly issue certified context. However, the CV will try to identify users based on its transactions so it can build detailed, context-rich profiles of individual users.

Trustworthy IP. An IP is considered to be trusted. It will always provide the correct attributes to users. Furthermore, an IP will not reveal the identity of the user to the SP and/or CV.

Trustworthy CP. A CP is considered to be trusted. It will always provide the correct context to users and CVs. Furthermore, if a CP is able to identify a user, it will *not reveal this information to the CV*.

PACCo assumes that each entity has a copy of the certificate of the CP, CV, IP and SP it communicates with. These certificates are used to set up secure, authenticated channels to prevent man-in-the-middle and network sniffing attacks. Furthermore, network-based attacks on user-anonymity are not considered. However, a brief discussion is given in Sect. 7.2.

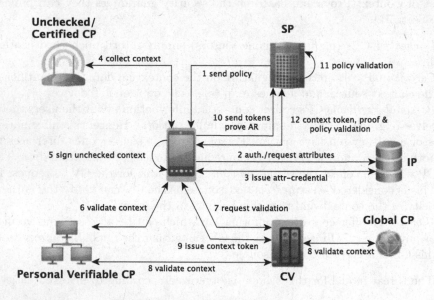

Fig. 2. The high-level PACCo protocol.

6.2   PACCo Protocol

Registration. Before users can use the system, they need to obtain a privacy-ABC, the *PACCo-credential*. This is a one-time step, and can be done at the CV (or at an independent credential issuer that the CV trusts). This credential has at least one attribute, a random value known only to the credential owner, called the PACCo-secret. Furthermore, to prevent users from sharing their credentials, standard privacy-ABC strategies can be applied (cfr. Sect. 4.1).

Users might be required to identify and authenticate themselves towards the CV or credential issuer. However, this does not affect the user's privacy because the issuance of a privacy-ABC is not linkable to its usage [27].

Access Request. The remainder of the protocol is shown in Fig. 2. If the user already knows the access policy, and if she can satisfy it, she can proceed to *step 10*. Otherwise, she will receive the attribute and contextual requirements (AR/CR) in an access policy (1). If the latter should not be publicly accessible, then the SP can require users to authenticate before they are allowed to request the policy.

Attribute Collection. The PACCo service will first extract all attribute identifiers from the access policy. These attributes also identify the specific IP that knows the attribute values. The PACCo service will authenticate to the corresponding IP, after which it requests the required attributes from that IP (2). Next, the IP and user execute the Idemix issuance protocol (3), after which the user obtains a new privacy-ABC. This credential contains all requested attributes and their values. In addition, the IP is allowed to add *meta-data attributes*, such as a version-number, a validity period, etc. Furthermore, this credential is linked to the same secret as the user's PACCo-credential (cfr. Sect. 4.1).

If the user already owns a credential that contains all necessary attributes, steps 2 and 3 can be omitted. If the credential contains only a subset of required attributes, or if the attributes are no longer valid (e.g. expired validity period), the user is required to request an updated credential.

At the end of this interaction, the user owns a privacy-ABC (att^{IP} -*credential*) that contains all necessary attributes and that is linked to the PACCo-credential. This credential will be used for proving attributes or statements to the CV and SP.

Context Collection. The PACCo service running on the user's device is responsible for collecting context from *certified* and *unchecked* context providers (4). The context that needs to be gathered is determined by analysing the access policy. The PACCo service *adds a timestamp and an identifier of the context provider to the information originating from unchecked providers*, after which this data is signed by the service (5). Note that context could be gathered in the background by a smart PACCo service, which could greatly reduce the number of times a user is required to explicitly validate her context.

Context Validation. The context validation (steps 6–9) is shown in detail in Fig. 3.

PACCo allows CVs to validate personal context by accessing the CP directly. Before a user contacts the CV, it will construct a provable pseudonym (nym_1^{CV})

using her credential (cfr. Sect. 4.1). The CP responds with a challenge ($c1$) in which a timestamp is encoded. This is used to create a zero-knowledge proof of ownership of nym_1^{CV} ($p1$), which is sent to CP (6). Due to the computational limitation of a CP, $p1$ is not (immediately) verified. Instead, CP stores $p1$ and nym_1^{CV}.

Next, the user will contact the CV in order to validate her context (7). This request contains the following:

- A collection of contextual requirements, as defined in Sect. 5.1.
- For each unverified or certified requirement, the contextual information and its signature (*data*). This information contains the actual data, the context source and a timestamp.
- An identifier for each personal verified context source that should be accessed (*CP-ID*).
- A provable pseudonym, based on the PACCo-credential (nym_1^{CV}).

Next, the *verifiable* requirements are validated (8). Global context, like the current time, is requested from the CP directly, without a risk to user-privacy. To validate context from a personal verifiable provider, the CV contacts the CP and request $p1$ using nym_1^{CV}. At this point, the CV has gathered all the necessary contextual data to verify whether the provided context requirements are met. However, the CV might still need to know certain attribute-data. In addition, it must first validate $p1$. Using a new challenge ($c2$), the CV asks the user to create a new proof ($p1'$) for nym_1^{CV} in order to be certain that this user is the one that made proof $p1$ (i.e. to be certain that the collected context belongs to this user).

Next, the user convinces the CV of the fact that she satisfies the attribute requirements. Therefore, the user constructs a proof ($p2$) in which she either reveals the necessary attributes, or convinces the CV with a zero-knowledge proof of the fact that an attribute requirement is valid. Whether or not the user discloses an attribute or proves it is entirely dependant on the context requirement. If this requirement has an *equals* operation, or if an operation needs to be performed on/with this attribute, the attribute needs to be disclosed. Otherwise, the attribute can remain hidden for the CV, while the latter is still convinced of the fact that the CR is satisfied.

For clarity purposes, we show two proofs (p1' and p2) being constructed by the client. However, this can be optimized as the user can include a proof of ownership of nym_1^{CV} in p2, while not constructing p1'. This is possible because the PACCo-Credential and Att^{IP}-credential are linked together (cfr. Sect. 4)

Next, the user and CV execute the uCentive protocol in which a partially blinded signature is created on the validated context and attribute requirements, the timestamp of context collection, and on a new provable pseudonym (nym_2^{CV}). CV will not learn this pseudonym, as it is embedded in the blinded part of the signature, however, it will see the context requirements[3]. Note that

---

[3] Details about the cryptographic protocol of uCentive, and how uCentive prevents users from providing someone else's pseudonym can be found in [29].

CV does not actually sign the contextual data itself, it only signs the context-requirements. This makes a large impact on the amount of information that the SP will learn. At the end of context verification, the user unblinds the received uCentive token (9).

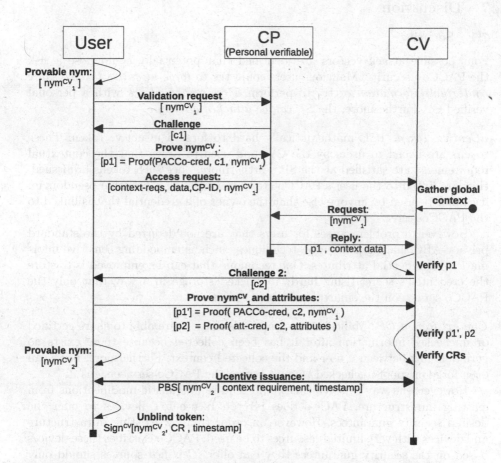

Fig. 3. Context verification protocol (see steps 5 and in Fig. 2). Note that all interactions with the CP are only executed if the system needs to validate personal verifiable context.

Service Provider Access Control. Now, the user sends a new access request to the SP (step 10 in Fig. 2). She first authenticates, after which the SP will validate whether the CRs from the access policy are met (11). Then, the tokens that the user sent to the SP are verified. Furthermore, the user must now convince the SP of the fact that all ARs are satisfied. This is done analogous to the proof that the user created to for the CV (p2). Next, the user proves that she and only she owns those tokens by proving in zero-knowledge that the pseudonyms in these tokens are hers (12). Finally, the user is granted access if the information in the tokens can satisfy the context constraints, if the tokens are valid and if they belong to the user.

7 Discussion

7.1 Security

Four possible attack vectors are identified that potentially could pose a risk the PACCo's security. Malicious users could try to *forge uCentive tokens, share contextual information* or try to perform *a redirection attack* with a personal verified CP. Furthermore, the *SP can be attacked directly*.

uCentive Token. It is mathematically hard to forge a uCentive token. These tokens are issued to users by the CV, and used to prove that the contextual requirements are satisfied at the SP. Furthermore, once such tokens are issued, they are linked to the user's PACCo-credential through a provable pseudonym; it cannot be used by anyone else than the owner of a credential that is linked to the PACCo-secret.

However, a problem arises for users that are not deterred by the standard privacy-ABC sharing prevention techniques, such as embedding sensitive information in credential attributes. One technique that can be employed is to store the credential's secret using hardware-backed storage in a way that only the PACCo service on the smartphone can access it.

Context from a CP. Malicious or compromised users are able to share certified or unchecked information after it has been collected because there exists no verifiable link between a user and the collected context. Furthermore, users can even forge or spoof unchecked context before the PACCo-service signs it.

However, the way to solve this would require unrealistic modifications from existing infrastructure. PACCo does rely on future IoT devices to offer the desired security guarantees. However, in order to allow existing infrastructure and devices with very limited resources to be used, PACCo classifies these devices based on the security guarantees they can offer. *Certified* sources should only be used by an SP if it determines that the probability and impact of context sharing is low. A similar analysis should be done for *unchecked* context sources. *Although the usage of these context sources will never provide an airtight security solution, it will demand more effort from attackers, which might be a sufficient deterrent.*

Request for Verified Context to a CP. Here, two malicious users could execute a redirection attack, where one user will relay the pseudonym, challenge and proof. Normal man-in-the-middle attacks are assumed to be mitigated by setting up secure connections using locally stored certificates. However, it is still possible if the end-user and 'middle-user' work together. This is, however, not an easy attack to execute. Furthermore, the practicality of this attack can be further diminished by distance bounding techniques [31,32].

Compromised SP. Huge problems occur when the entity responsible for enforcing access control decisions is compromised. This can be identified by frequently auditing the system and its logs. This is relatively easy to realize in PACCo as the proofs made in the uCentive protocols can be verified at any time by any third party. In addition, these proofs are unforgeable, making hiding malicious activity by forging the logs a lot harder.

7.2   Privacy

PACCo focuses on three principles. Transactions between user and CV are unlinkable, the SP learns a minimal amount of contextual information and different entities cannot link transactions made by the same user at a different entity to each other (e.g. the IP cannot identity a user at the SP or CV, and vice versa).

Unlinkable Transactions with the CV. The only information that could identify a user to the CV is the contextual data which it needs to validate. This information might in some cases be enough to limit the user's anonymity set with regard to the CV to a few possibilities (e.g. inhabitants of a home). *This is not the case for many other use-cases* (e.g. allow access to information to students on campus). Furthermore, one validation of several contextual requirements that together can identify the user, can be split in multiple, unlinkable validations. Here, a trade-off between privacy and performance should be made.

Network based timing attacks are also not reliable if a large enough set of users access the SP and CV at the same time. Furthermore, the interactions of the user between SP and CV are completely separate. This allows the user to wait a random amount of time between contacting the SP and CV (within freshness limits) in order to make this kind of tracking more difficult. A PACCo service that periodically collects and verifies context in the background would be able to implement these strategies without loss of user experience.

Other network-based attacks, such as IP-tracking could still be used. However, IP-tracking is not always reliable as the PACCo service is running on a mobile phone which has a more frequently changing IP address than a computer. The service could also connect to the CV through an anonymous network.

Other information that a CV could learn originates from the Idemix proof and the issuance of the uCentive token. However, multiple Idemix transactions cannot be linked to each other. In addition, the issuance of uCentive tokens is not linkable to the spending thereof [29].

Finally, if users are required to identify themselves to a CP or IP, PACCo assumes that these CPs will not share these identities with the CV. However, PACCo allows users to choose the CPs that are accessed. Therefore, they should only use CPs that are managed by a trusted organization. Note that in scenario 2 of Sect. 3, the company deploys CPs and the CV. Here, the anonymity of users at the CV could be lost, which is acceptable in a company setting. However, the privacy benefits related to the SP, which is external to the company, remain intact.

Minimal Information Learning by the SP. The SP learns only a small amount from a transaction. It learns (1) that the user satisfies a set of context- and attribute-requirements and (2) the times when the context is collected; the SP does not learn the precise context of the user.

However, whether the SP will be able to identify a user will mostly be determined by the standard authentication mechanism of the SP. In the optimal case, an anonymous authentication system like Idemix, is used, which causes the SP to only learn that the user has a right to access the service, and that she satisfies the context constraints. The SP will be able to link contextual information to specific users in the likely case that it uses a standard authentication mechanism. However, this information is often obvious (e.g. the user is on campus when accessing student material).

Unlinkable Multi-party Transactions. One of the main privacy features of PACCo is the fact that the involved entities can only learn the minimal amount of information required to perform their task. This is in part realized by the fact that entities cannot link a user's transaction made with another entity to a transaction made with the entity itself, even if these entities collude (except for CP and CV).

However, for this property to hold, we assume that *information contained in uCentive tokens and the information revealed during attribute proofs do not uniquely identify users.* Possible information that can pose a risk for user-linkability across different providers are contained in exactly those uCentive tokens and Idemix credential proofs. This is the combination of a timestamp with either a set context requirements, or a set of disclosed attributes and proofs of attribute requirements. In order for this to be possible, the system requires that (1) this information is not unique and (2) enough users are active in the system and are similar (i.e. have to satisfy similar requirements).

In order to achieve the first requirement, PACCo should only allow course-grained timestamps. Hence, instead of a timestamp, a time-frame should be employed. The second requirement is also important for any anonymous system: *there should be enough users in the system in order for the anonymity set to be sufficiently large.*

7.3   Performance

Setup. Our prototype consists out a PACCo service running on a mobile phone, four server components: a CV, an IP and an SP, and three CPs: an NTP server, an NFC chip and a second phone acting as a *personal verifiable* proximity CP. The smartphones are both Samsung Galaxy S3 with a 1.4 GHz processor. A workstation with an Intel Core i7-3770 CPU hosts the IP, CV and SP. The prototype is implemented in Java and uses the PriMan framework [33] to access Idemix and uCentive functionality.

The client owns one PACCo-credential with one attribute, the PACCo-secret (2048 bit modulo and a 1632 bit commitment group modulo). The PACCo service uses 2048 bit RSA signatures in combination with SHA-256. The partially blinded signatures have 1024 bits modulo and 160 bit generator groups[4]. For each test, 100 samples were taken of which the mean value and standard deviation is shown. The core measurements of our tests do not take network time and the time it takes to obtain contextual information (i.e. the time it takes for the sensors to measure the data) into account. As such, we aim to provide a clear view of the overhead that PACCo's security and privacy measures introduce.

Test Case. Our test case will consider the second scenario explained in Sect. 3, as it includes the verification of personal verified context. The policy for this scenario is shown in Listing 1.2. In order to satisfy this policy, one needs to satisfy one of the following two constraints: the current time should be between 10h00 and 12h00 and the user should be in a specific meeting room, or the user should be in the proximity of the project leader. In addition, the user's employee role and assignment location attributes should be verified. The security requirement for the proximity context source in the meeting room can be 'unchecked', while the other sources are 'verified'.

The NTP server is a *global* context provider; the CV can gather and verify its context. The NFC chip is a *unchecked* context provider, as it is scanned using the client's smartphone. The data will be signed by the PACCo service running on the phone. The second phone provides *personal verifiable* context. It will play the role of a CP in the protocol shown in Fig. 3. Table 2 shows an overview.

Attribute Collection. The user contacts an IP in order to get her attributes certified in a privacy-ABC. In doing so, the user and IP execute the Idemix issuance protocol, which is done in under a second on the user's smartphone, while the IP requires 325 ms. The newly created credential has 5 attributes, two of which are required in this scenario. Note that the user is not required to perform this action for every interaction with the SP. Only if the user does not have the required attributes, or the meta-data contained in a credential dictates it must a user execute these steps.

Unchecked Context. Unchecked context is collected through the smartphone sensors after which the PACCo service will add an RSA signature. This operation takes 5 ms on our phone, while the workstation requires 2 ms in order to verify this signature. This signature verification is only performed by the CV.

Certified context is handled similar to unchecked context. However, the PACCo service will not create a digital signature because one is already provided by the CP. Hence, the CV only needs to verify signatures for certified context.

Verifiable Context. Collecting *personal* verifiable context is one of the computationally expensive tasks of PACCo. Creating a zero knowledge proof for one provable nym takes 232 ms on our phone, while the workstation requires almost

---

[4] Note that, due to the limited validity of these signatures, the security parameters can be relaxed compared to certificate signatures.

Table 2. Overview of the performance numbers for PACCo operations. Measurements are depicted in milliseconds, standard deviation is listed between parentheses.

Operation	Client	IP	CV	SP
attCred operations				
Issuance	860 (25)	325 (10)	–	–
Prove/verify	365 (18)	–	143 (11)	143 (11)
Unverified context				
RSA signature	5 (1)	–	2 (0)	
Verifiable context				
Prove nym	232 (9)	–	79 (3)	–
uCent generation				
Earn uCent	226 (8)	–	46 (2)	–
Authentication				
Policy verification	–	–	–	2(0)
Spend 1 uCent	225 (12)	–	–	84 (6)
Spend 2 uCents	236 (12)	–	–	89 (6)
Spend 5 uCents	265 (12)	–	–	98 (5)
Total				
a. NTP & NFC	456	–	48	86
b. Smartphone	920	–	204	86
c. Attributes	1285/2045	–/325	204	229

80 ms to verify it. This proof verification is also a responsibility of the CV. Note that these operations have to be executed twice: one proof is sent to the CP and the second is used to prove that the first one is made by the same person. Whilst our test-scenario does not prescribe it, it is possible that the CV is required to learn about a user's attributes. It will learn this information from a proof made by the user with her attribute-credential.

Collecting *global* verifiable context such as time from an NTP server, is performed by the CV. As explained above, this is not included in our performance measurements as the amount of time it takes to verify is not affected by PACCo.

Generation of uCentive Token. Once the context has been validated, the uCentive protocol is executed, in which a partially blinded signature is created. The creation of one uCentive signature requires 226 ms from the client while the server requires 46 ms. Furthermore, this process scales linearly with the amount of signatures. Generating uCents is a protocol between the user and CV.

Authentication. The user will send uCentive tokens to the SP. Next, the SP validates whether the contextual information in these tokens satisfy the policy. This is a relatively inexpensive step, as it requires on average less than 2 ms.

Furthermore, the client and SP execute the protocol to spend uCentive tokens, in which the client proofs that the pseudonyms in the tokens belong to her. Our smartphone requires on average 225 ms, while our workstation, needs 84 ms to verify.

Spending and verifying additional uCentive tokens is cheap. Spending 5 tokens requires 265 ms on the client and 98 ms on the server. This is interesting as users can spend a set of tokens at once that were collected over time.

Now, the user needs to prove to the service provider that her attribute requirements are satisfied. This is done by creating a proof using her attribute-credential, in which the two necessary attributes are revealed. The user needs 365 ms to do this, while the SP requires 143 ms to verify the proof.

The Big Picture. As shown in Table 2, PACCo needs under half a second on a smartphone if no personal verifiable context or attributes are required (a. NTP & NFC), while a CV requires under 50 ms. The validation of a personal verifiable requirement (b. smartphone) will add about half a second to the client's time and near 150 ms to the CV's time. Finally, adding attributes in this mix (c. attributes) will add 365 ms to the previous time for each proof made (note that it also might be required to make a proof for the CV). However, if the attribute-credential must be re-issued, almost one second is added to the total computing time. For each proof, the SP or CV needs to allocate an additional 143 ms of computing time for verification.

Disregarding network time and the time for the CPs to return contextual information, the whole PACCo protocol takes just over half a second to verify the first requirement set (a.). The verification of information from a personal verifiable context source (b.) takes just over 1.2 s while the protocol takes about half a second more if attributes are also considered and more than 1.5 s more if an attribute-credential needs to be issued(c.).

8   Conclusion

This paper presents PACCo, a privacy-friendly attribute-based access control system with context. By adding support for attributes, which can originate from external (trusted) sources, the PACCo system can be included in complete authentication and authorization systems. We have shown with our policy language how to represent contextual requirements and attribute-based requirements. The PACCo system itself, which focuses on the secure and privacy-friendly validation of attributes and context has been implemented and tested. In addition, our experimental evaluation shows that our system produces an acceptable overhead which can range from about 600 ms to 2.5 s.

However, future work should address not only the security of context, but also the quality of context without sacrificing privacy. Exactly which context should be used in access control and what techniques can be used to improve the decision making are interesting questions, especially with the opportunities provided to us by the Internet of Things. Furthermore, user experience and factors, like power-usage and background-scheduling should be optimized.

A different research opportunity consist out of investigating whether it is possible for techniques like homomorphic encryption or attribute-based encryption to help strengthen PACCo's security and privacy properties. For example, the context verifier could validate context requirements using homomorphically encrypted data.

References

1. Adams, A., Sasse, M.A.: Users are not the enemy. Commun. ACM **42**(12), 40–46 (1999)
2. Stanislav, M.: Two-factor authentication (2015)
3. Riva, O., Qin, C., Strauss, K., Lymberopoulos, D.: Progressive authentication: deciding when to authenticate on mobile phones. In: USENIX Security, pp. 301–316 (2012)
4. Abowd, G.D., Dey, A.K., Brown, P.J., Davies, N., Smith, M., Steggles, P.: Towards a better understanding of context and context-awareness. In: Gellersen, H.-W. (ed.) HUC 1999. LNCS, vol. 1707, pp. 304–307. Springer, Heidelberg (1999). doi:10.1007/3-540-48157-5_29
5. Groopman, J.: Consumer perceptions of privacy in the internet of things. Altimeter Group (2015)
6. Put, A., De Decker, B.: PACCo: privacy-friendly access control with context. In: SECRYPT (2016)
7. Rissanen, E., et al.: eXtensible access control markup language (XACML) version 3.0 (2013)
8. Matheus, A., Herrmann, J.: Geospatial eXtensible access control markup language (GeoXACML). Open Geospatial Consortium Inc., OGC (2008)
9. Ray, I., Toahchoodee, M.: A spatio-temporal role-based access control model. In: Barker, S., Ahn, G.-J. (eds.) DBSec 2007. LNCS, vol. 4602, pp. 211–226. Springer, Heidelberg (2007). doi:10.1007/978-3-540-73538-0_16
10. Atluri, V., Chun, S.A.: A geotemporal role-based authorisation system. Int. J. Inf. Comput. Secur. **1**(1–2), 143–168 (2007)
11. Kulkarni, D., Tripathi, A.: Context-aware role-based access control in pervasive computing systems. In: Proceedings of the 13th ACM Symposium on Access Control Models and Technologies, pp. 113–122. ACM (2008)
12. Bhatti, R., Bertino, E., Ghafoor, A.: A trust-based context-aware access control model for web-services. Distrib. Parallel Databases **18**(1), 83–105 (2005)
13. Hu, J., Weaver, A.C.: A dynamic, context-aware security infrastructure for distributed healthcare applications. In: Proceedings of the First Workshop on Pervasive Privacy Security, Privacy, and Trust, pp. 1–8. Citeseer (2004)
14. Ardagna, C.A., Di Vimercati, S.D.C., Foresti, S., Grandison, T.W., Jajodia, S., Samarati, P.: Access control for smarter healthcare using policy spaces. Comput. Secur. **29**(8), 848–858 (2010)
15. Jafarian, J.H., Amini, M.: CAMAC: a context-aware mandatory access control model. ISC Int. J. Inf. Secur. **1**(1), 35–54 (2009)
16. Yuan, E., Tong, J.: Attributed based access control (ABAC) for web services. In: 2005 IEEE International Conference on Web Services. IEEE (2005)

17. Vimercati, S.D.C.D., Foresti, S., Jajodia, S., Paraboschi, S., Psaila, G., Samarati, P.: Integrating trust management and access control in data-intensive web applications. ACM Trans. Web (TWEB) **6**(2), 6 (2012)
18. Jin, X., Krishnan, R., Sandhu, R.: A unified attribute-based access control model covering DAC, MAC and RBAC. In: Cuppens-Boulahia, N., Cuppens, F., Garcia-Alfaro, J. (eds.) DBSec 2012. LNCS, vol. 7371, pp. 41–55. Springer, Heidelberg (2012). doi:10.1007/978-3-642-31540-4_4
19. Hintze, D., Findling, R.D., Muaaz, M., Koch, E., Mayrhofer, R.: CORMORANT: towards continuous risk-aware multi-modal cross-device authentication. In: Ubi-Comp/ISWC 2015 Adjunct (2015)
20. Shebaro, B., Oluwatimi, O., Bertino, E.: Context-based access control systems for mobile devices. IEEE Trans. Dependable Secure Comput. **12**(2), 150–163 (2015)
21. Hayashi, E., Das, S., Amini, S., Hong, J., Oakley, I.: CASA: context-aware scalable authentication. In: Proceedings of the Ninth Symposium on Usable Privacy and Security. SOUPS 2013, pp. 3:1–3:10. ACM, New York (2013)
22. Hulsebosch, R., Salden, A., Bargh, M., Ebben, P., Reitsma, J.: Context sensitive access control. In: Proceedings of the Tenth ACM Symposium on Access Control Models and Technologies, pp. 111–119. ACM (2005)
23. Housley, R., Polk, W., Ford, W., Solo, D.: Internet x. 509 public key infrastructure certificate and certificate revocation list (CRL) profile (2002)
24. Sabouri, A., Krontiris, I., Rannenberg, K.: Attribute-based credentials for trust (ABC4Trust). In: Fischer-Hübner, S., Katsikas, S., Quirchmayr, G. (eds.) TrustBus 2012. LNCS, vol. 7449, pp. 218–219. Springer, Heidelberg (2012). doi:10.1007/978-3-642-32287-7_21
25. Paquin, C., Zaverucha, G.: U-prove cryptographic specification v1. 1. Technical report, Microsoft Technical Report (2011). http://connect.microsoft.com/site1188
26. Camenisch, J., Lysyanskaya, A.: A signature scheme with efficient protocols. In: Cimato, S., Persiano, G., Galdi, C. (eds.) SCN 2002. LNCS, vol. 2576, pp. 268–289. Springer, Heidelberg (2003). doi:10.1007/3-540-36413-7_20
27. Camenisch, J., Van Herreweghen, E.: Design and implementation of the idemix anonymous credential system. In: Proceedings of the 9th ACM Conference on Computer and Communications Security. ACM (2002)
28. Camenisch, J., Stadler, M., Camenisch, J., Camenisch, J.: Proof systems for general statements about discrete logarithms. Citeseer (1997)
29. Milutinovic, M., Dacosta, I., Put, A., Decker, B.D.: uCentive: an efficient, anonymous and unlinkable incentives scheme. In: Trustcom/BigDataSE/ISPA, 2015 IEEE. vol. 1, pp. 588–595. IEEE (2015)
30. Abe, M., Okamoto, T.: Provably secure partially blind signatures. In: Bellare, M. (ed.) CRYPTO 2000. LNCS, vol. 1880, pp. 271–286. Springer, Heidelberg (2000). doi:10.1007/3-540-44598-6_17
31. Singelee, D., Preneel, B.: Location verification using secure distance bounding protocols. In: IEEE International Conference on Mobile Adhoc and Sensor Systems Conference, p. 7-pp. IEEE (2005)
32. Brands, S., Chaum, D.: Distance-bounding protocols. In: Helleseth, T. (ed.) EURO-CRYPT 1993. LNCS, vol. 765, pp. 344–359. Springer, Heidelberg (1994). doi:10.1007/3-540-48285-7_30
33. Put, A., Dacosta, I., Milutinovic, M., De Decker, B.: PriMan: facilitating the development of secure and privacy-preserving applications. In: Cuppens-Boulahia, N., Cuppens, F., Jajodia, S., Abou El Kalam, A., Sans, T. (eds.) SEC 2014. IAICT, vol. 428, pp. 403–416. Springer, Heidelberg (2014). doi:10.1007/978-3-642-55415-5_34

Protecting Smartphone Users' Private Locations Through Caching

Asma Patel[(⊠)] and Esther Palomar

School of Computing and Digital Technology, Birmingham City University,
Birmingham, UK
{asma.patel,esther.palomar}@bcu.ac.uk
http://www.bcu.ac.uk/

Abstract. Smartphones equipped with advanced positioning technology continuously collect users' location information and make that information easily accessible to third party app and/or library developers. Users are becoming increasingly aware of the resultant privacy threats, and demanding effective privacy preserving solutions that will allow them to securely use location-based services. In addition, academic and industrial communities are paying special attention to the development of more friendly and socially-accepted approaches to location privacy. In this work, we model, design and evaluate LP-Caché, a mobile platform based service that protects locations by modifying the location resource handling process. It applies caching technique to protect users' private locations and establishes personalised location permission controls. We define the design decisions and implementation requirements towards the viability and feasibility of the model deployment. We also evaluate resources and storage requirements in order to minimise the computational and communication overheads. Empirical results of 2 months comparative study show a 2.26% change in the network fingerprints at 34 distinct places that required only 2.07% change in the overall cache storage. Both these results demonstrate feasibility of the model.

Keywords: Location privacy · Location-based services · Smartphones · Caching · Location-based applications

1 Introduction

The explosive growth of context-aware mobile apps has leveraged tremendous opportunities for a whole new class of Location-Based Services (LBS) [1]. Geomarketing and geo-social networking, location-based games, monitoring, assisted eHealth, and energy consumption 3D maps represent a small subset of the third-party apps nowadays available as LBS and can certainly pose a serious threat to the users' privacy [2,3].

Updated and extended version of SECRYPT 2016 conference paper with title "LP-Caché: Privacy-aware Cache Model for Location-based Apps".

© Springer International Publishing AG 2017
M.S. Obaidat (Ed): ICETE 2016, CCIS 764, pp. 316–337, 2017.
https://doi.org/10.1007/978-3-319-67876-4_15

Currently, approaches to privacy settings of user location on smartphones[1] are based on a binary process[2]. Users are forced to rely on third party service providers that in many cases continuously collect, use and share their location data, and in some cases even prompt the user to give away their position on page load [2,3,7,8]. Moreover, both academia and industry agree on the urgent need of adopting a Privacy-by-Design (PbD) approach for the development of more user-friendly and socially-accepted solutions to location privacy preservation on their mobile products and services [9].

To encounter these challenges, in [10] the authors introduced the model called *Location Privacy Caché* (LP-Caché). LP-Caché envisions beyond the simple grant/deny access method and provides the user with advanced mechanisms to decide the extent of disclosing location data with service providers. Several caching based solutions [11–13] have been proposed to minimise the risk of major location privacy threats, but lacking of deployment feasibility. They rely on unrealistic assumptions such as vast cache data storage requirements, or on the app developers modifying the code to incorporate their cached databases. LP-Caché incorporates caching technique to determine users' geographical location in a privacy preserving manner, and with minimum cache storage requirements.

In this paper we overview the main contributions presented in [10] and, further prove LP-Caché's features in an extended experimental setting. In particular, we describe

- A detailed analysis of the current location computation process deployed in smartphones when running location-based apps.
- A detailed definition of the LP-Caché model and architecture as well as its main implementation requirements.
- A complete performance evaluation of LP-Caché, analising the wireless access point data availability and consistency, and the estimated user resource and storage requirements. We will also show that LP-Caché is feasible without modifying installed apps. Estimated storage requirements and monthly datasets of wireless access points have been analysed. Results from the extended experimental setting help us to determine the scalability of LP-Caché.

The rest of the paper is organized as follows. Section 2 outlines the current location computation process and its evaluation. Section 3 reviews the related work. Section 4 presents the design and architecture of LP-Caché, and Sect. 5 fully elaborates on design decisions and implementation requirements. We evaluate the feasibility of WiFi APs availability, resources and storage requirements in Sect. 6. Finally, Sect. 7 concludes and describes current work as well as sets future research plans.

---

[1] Throughout this paper, we use the terms smartphones and mobile interchangeably.

[2] Data protection directives and acts [4,5] across the globe state that personal data should not be disclosed or shared with third parties without consent from subject(s). Such a consent is typically obtained by mandatory acceptance of the conditions mentioned in the End User License Agreement (EULA), or through opt-out possibilities and other regulations [6].

2 Overview of the Current Location Computation Process

In this section, we describe roles and processes involved in the current architecture for computing user's device location.

2.1 Current Architecture

The current location computation architecture to use location-based apps on smartphones comprises four main entities: 1. Smartphones with installed apps, 2. App Provider, 3. Network Infrastructure, and 4. Location Provider. This architecture (Fig. 1) mainly relies on third party location providers, e.g., Google Location Service [14], Skyhook [15], and Navizon [16]. The location provider represents the central database, which maps the received signatures of nearby wireless access points to the geo-coordinates, i.e., latitude and longitude, so handling every geo-location request. Therefore, the location provider has constant access to the user's location as well as to the trajectory data. To respond to any location request, the location provider maintains a database of surrounding network infrastructure, including WiFi Access Points (APs), cellular-towers, and IP addresses, which must be mapped to their exact geographical co-ordinates. Compared to GPS and cell-tower based positioning, WiFi Positioning Systems (WPS) is nowadays considered as a very accurate method for location calculation [15]. Location providers rather use enhanced WPS than GPS, primarily due to current smart-mobile devices benefit from built-in WiFi clients that perform faster than most expensive GPS receivers. This enables the service provider to get user's precise location at all times and, as a result, more effective privacy preservation measures are needed in the current process to mitigate privacy threats.

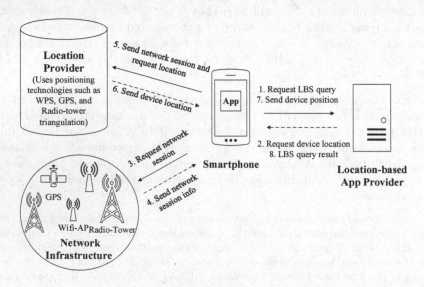

Fig. 1. Current location computation architecture.

WiFi APs continuously announce their existence in the way of network frames/beacons and transmit their Service Set Identifier (SSID) and Basic Service Set Identifier (BSSID)/MAC addresses. Location providers use these WiFi APs identifiers to create network signatures and map them with geo-coordinates, also called geolocation. IEEE 802.11 states two standardised ways to collect beacons from WiFi APs: 1. Active scanning, and 2. Passive scanning. Location providers are capable of deploying systems with either active scanning, passive scanning, or both together. Location providers use three different ways to collect geo-location of WiFi APs:

1. *Statically*- They collect WiFi beacons by the so called *wardiving* process. Basically, they map the equipped vehicle's exact geo-coordinates along with the signal strength of the captured beacons from surrounded APs.
2. *Dynamically*- They can collect data from WiFi APs automatically once the user device uses location services, e.g. Maps and Navigation applications. The user device as configured to be geolocated acquires unique identifiers from the surrounding WiFi APs, even if the network is encrypted, and then sends it over to the location provider in order to perform geolocation calculation. The collected information is utilised to build and update the database autonomously, for example, by applying crowdsourcing [17].
3. *User input*- They encourage users to manually input the WiFi APs' information, i.e., BSSID and the geo-coordinates, into their databases, e.g., Skyhook[3] to register WiFi APs.

2.2 Evaluation of Current Location Computation Process

We conducted a series of experiments on different mobile devices installed with *Android, Windows Phone*, and *iOS* operating systems to categorise the data flow in the current location computation process. With the assistance of sniffers, such as *Wireshark* [18] and *tPacketCapture* [19], we captured and analysed sequence and location data transmission when using location-based apps, e.g., Navigation and Friend Finder.

Observation. These experiments were designed to understand whether there is any difference on the location calculation process on each of these three mobile operating systems. Based on the results, all of them display common patterns of location data retrieval. The user device collects the unique identifiers from the surrounding network along with GPS data, and sends it to the location provider to get the exact device location. Figure 2 shows the structure of the WiFi and Cell-tower objects sent to the location provider. Once calculation is performed, the location provider sends to the device the precise location in the way of a geo-location object containing geo-coordinates. Figure 3 represents the structure of the location object received from the location provider. In short, the app developer over any mobile platform can utilize this location object to get

---

[3] Submit a Wi-Fi Access Point. See http://www.skyhookwireless.com/submit-access-point (last access in March 2016).

the user's geo-location with no need of focusing on the details of the underlying location technology. In the following section, we give the detailed description of the process sequence.

Process Sequence. Figure 4 illustrates the sequence of processes and messages involved in the current location computation architecture. Note that, on a

```
"wifiAccessPoints": [
  {
    "macAddress": "01:23:45:67:89:XY",
    "signalStrength": 10,
    "age": 0,
    "signalToNoiseRatio": -65,
    "channel": 8
  },
  {
    "macAddress": "01:23:45:67:89:YZ",
    "signalStrength": 5,
    "age": 0
  }
]
```
(a)

```
"CellTowers": [
  {
    "cellId": 42,
    "locationAreaCode": 415,
    "mobileCountryCode": 310,
    "mobileNetworkCode": 410,
    "age": 0,
    "signalStrength": -60,
    "timingAdvance": 15
  }
]
```
(b)

Fig. 2. Structure of (a) WiFi AP object and (b) cell-tower object sent to the location provider [10].

```
{
  "location": {
    "lat": 58.0,
    "lng": -0.123
  },
  "accuracy": 1200.4
}
```

Fig. 3. Structure of the location object received from the location provider [10].

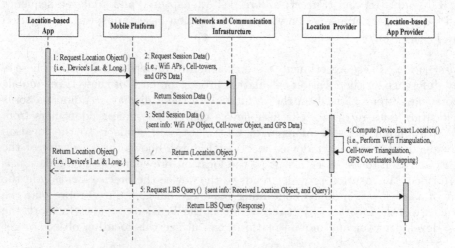

Fig. 4. Sequence diagram of current location computation process [10].

smartphone, location sharing service settings must be 'ON' while using any location-based app. If the location sharing is 'OFF', then the device prompts for changing the setting from 'OFF' to 'ON'; otherwise, user cannot use the service. Once the app obtains the location object from OS, it is then used by the app provider to send the corresponding reply to LBS query via the standard programming interface/API [20].

3   Related Work

Existing approaches to preservation of the location privacy can be classified into three categories: 1. Mobile Platform[4], 2. Location Query, and 3. Privacy-aware Network Communication.

3.1   Mobile Platform

A few studies have proposed static and dynamic methods to detect privacy leaks in mobile platforms. The former method statistically analyses apps by creating permission mapping, generating call graphs and data flow analysis to report privacy leaks for further auditing, e.g., AndroidLeaks [21] and PiOS [22] for Android and Apple iOS, respectively. The application of dynamic methods involves modification of the existing mobile platform. For example, TaintDroid [23] adds taint tracking information to sensitive sources calls from apps, and it tracks location data flow as it generated through applications during execution. MockDroid [24] relies on instrumenting Android's manifest permission mechanism to mock sensitive data from OS resource, including location data, which can affect apps' usability and functionality. LP-Caché not only monitors the location sources but also modifies, if required, the generated location data based on defined user permissions. In another attempt [25], *indistinguishability* technique is applied as location privacy preservation mechanism into the advertising and analytics libraries as well as on installed apps; however, it does not give control on the amount of WiFi and location data that is being shared with the location provider. Moreover, *indistinguishability* technique increases computational overhead on smartphones.

3.2   Location Query

Apps share location information with the provider in the form of LBS queries. The transmission of such queries to the location server may allow attackers to gain access to user location data. Privacy Enhancing Techniques (PET) like k-anonymity, dummy locations, region cloaking, location perturbation and obfuscation, and mix-zone pseudonyms have been applied to different architectures for location query formation and privacy preservation from LBS providers [26–28].

---

[4] Throughout this paper, we use the terms mobile platform and operating system interchangeably.

Most of these techniques rely on theoretical assumptions - like trusted infrastructure to provide the privacy protection, requiring a group of similar app users to be at the same time and same place. The main issue with PETs and cryptographic schemes is that it relies entirely on the data collection servers to comply with location privacy.

Caching. Several authors have used caching scheme along with PETs to build to a database consisting of different contents/datatypes used within location based queries to be re-used in future LBS queries. MobiCaché [11] applies k-anonymity for caching location based queries. Similarly, Niu et al. [13] attempt to improve k-anonymity based caching by adding dummy locations. Both proposals require a trusted infrastructure to maintain privacy. Caché [12] maintains a local cache within the device to reuse the data types available from applications in future location based queries; however, storing entire LBS query data increases the cache storage requirements. Besides, Caché also requires app developer to modify the way app access location data. By contrast, LP-Caché caches the network fingerprints and geo-coordinates, which reduces the storage overhead drastically; it considers installed apps as black box, and therefore, does not require app developer to modify the code, it works as a middleware between the app and the mobile platform. All these cache-based systems either intent to generalise or obfuscate the LBS query or minimise the number of queries sent to the app providers, but they do not provide privacy from WiFi content distributors. Besides, mobile devices not only send vast amounts of location data to app providers but also to location providers creating different location privacy shortcomings [3,7]. In this regard, limited work has been published on privacy preservation from the location provider's perspective [29,30]. Damiani (2011) proposes a theoretical approach for privacy-aware geolocation-based web services to encourage further research to minimise the amount of location data being shared with the location provider. This is mainly due to that the location provider is considered as the only source to get the user location when developing any location-based app. In LP-Caché, we minimise the process of wireless AP data collection by the WiFi content distributors or location providers, and we control information disclosure within the generated LBS query (e.g., points of interests (POIs) and nearest neighbor) since it will be sent to the third-party app provider.

3.3   Privacy-Aware Network Communication

Besides location queries, device's IP address can also reveal user's private locations. To this regard, anonymous communication protocols, e.g., Anonymizer [31] and TOR [32], deal with anonymous service usage at the network layer while communicating over Internet (i.e., the server cannot infer user's location via received device's IP address along with the location query), and they are most prominent and commonly used network layer solutions.

4   LP-Caché Model

In this section, we describe LP-Caché's threat model, design goals, architecture and main processes' sequence diagram.

4.1   Threat Model

Apps deliberately collect user's sensitive data, including location and other sensitive information as part of their operations. User tracking, identification and profiling (i.e. personal habits, movement patterns, etc.) are fundamental threats to location privacy [8,27]. Furthermore, the current direct link of smartphones to the location provider and the continuous flow of LBS queries that include device's exact geo-coordinates over network create a serious risk to the protection of users' sensitive information, even more challenging, in the presence of a malicious location provider and via advanced network sniffing practices.

LP-Caché computes the exact location within user device, without service provider's involvement, and trusts the device on the storage of sensitive data. However, the user has still the option of giving consent for app providers or location provider to access their location. Mobile network providers might, however, collect user location data via cellular clients. It is also excluded from our model the option of manually inserting the location data (e.g., street name, zip code, post code) within LBS query.

4.2   LP-Caché Control Flow Architecture

LP-Caché's three main design goal are: (1) the third-party app provider will not be able to infer the device's exact location without getting uses's consent; (2) the user can set distinct privacy preferences for different apps and private places; and (3) the model works independently without the need of modifying the app's code. Figure 5 depicts the block diagram for LP-Caché architecture; its main components are:

Permission Setter is the user interface (UI), which enables users to set and manage their private places and apply improved personalised permissions when running installed location-based apps. Once received the user inputs, pre-set private locations are sent to the *Private Location Manager* module, and permissions are sent to the *Rule Mapper* Module.

Request Manager is responsible to intercept the event of location access calls, and then lead the app's control flow to the *Private Location Manager* module. Besides, it will also be in control of receiving the processed user location (i.e., could be either anonymised or altered) from *Rule Mapper*, and then delivering it to the app in order to maintain every session's control flow.

Private Location Manager module's main task is to detect unique identifiers of the surrounding WiFi APs and compare them with the stored network fingerprints to determine whether the user is within the set of private places. User inputs from the *Permission Setter* will create network fingerprints for

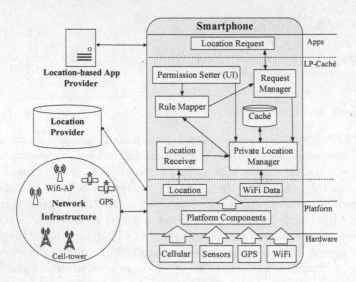

Fig. 5. LP-Caché architecture [10].

known private locations, which are then added or updated in the *Cach* database. Moreover, it maintains a binary flag to detect private places. In the case of a hit the location data is sent to the *Rule Mapper*. Otherwise, the location is received from the *Location Receiver*. Whenever the *Private Location Manager* receives a new private place request, the received location is mapped to the detected network fingerprint and stored in the *Caché* database.

Rule Mapper dynamically collects and checks set permissions from *Permission Setter*. Once the representative location object is received from the *Private Location Manager*, it applies the user permissions on the location co-ordinates, alters them (if required), and outputs the processed location to the *Request Manager* module. If the flag is negative, then it forwards the exact location.

Cache is the established on-device cached database, and it is routinely queried by the *Private Location Manager* module, which can add, update and delete the cached location data. The locations in cach are those which are to be protected, and they can also represent regions of space. Each entry is recorded along with a network fingerprint and geo-location that is acquired from the location provider.

Location Receiver module receives a location object, which includes the user device's geo-coordinates (as in Fig. 3), from location providers and sends it over to the *Private Location Manager* for further processing.

4.3   Process Sequence

LP-Caché modifies the current location resource handling process; however, the involved entities (as in Sect. 2) remain the same. Figure 6 illustrates the sequence of processes and messages involved in LP-Caché:

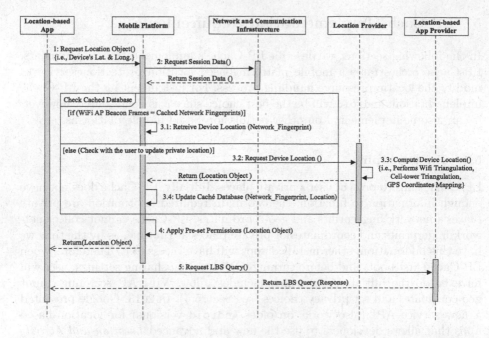

Fig. 6. Sequence diagram of location computation process using proposed model [10].

1. At the event of app requesting the device location, our service will intercept the request to get the location from the cache database instead of sending the request to the location provider.
2. Upon receiving the location request, our service will scan the surrounding network infrastructure.
3. Using observed network frames our service will execute as follows:
   (a) Our service compares the collected beacons with the stored network fingerprints to retrieve corresponding stored representative location coordinates.
   (b) In the case of an unmatched entry on the database, the LP-Caché prompts the user two options either input the location using UI, or allow the query to be sent to location provider that will calculate and send the current location coordinates. Note that this will only occur if the user has set the current location as private but the geo-coordinates are not cached.
   (c) The received location data for the encountered APs will be tracked within the local cache database for future use.
4. User location coordinates can be altered based on the privacy settings. LP-Caché provides three options for controlled information disclosure: (1) Adjust Location Granularity, (2) Obfuscate Location, and (3) No Change. Computed location is populated in the location object and sent to the app.
5. Once the app obtains the location object, it is then used by the app provider to send the corresponding reply to LBS query via the standard programming interface/API [20].

5 LP-Caché Implementation Requirements

In the following sections, we describe LP-Caché's implementation requirements. LP-Caché orchestrates a mobile platform based location protection service to modify the location resource handling process. For instrumenting the LP-Caché implementation, `Android` will be the best choice since it is open source; however, it can also be implemented on other permission-based mobile platforms.

5.1 Bootstrapping

LP-Caché aims to protect user's private places. Initially, LP-Caché does not have enough information to function, the two main required information are private places's network fingerprints and geo-coordinates. LP-Caché cannot collect network fingerprints and coordinatesfor private places at runtime, as by the time we have this information, other installed apps will have access to it. Therefore, when LP-Caché first boots and before turning 'ON' location sharing settings, user will have to do the initial setup, which includes allow WiFi AP scanning, input geo-cordinates and set privacy choices (see Sect. 5.4). In 2013, Google presented a new service API (also works on older `Android` versions) for location-based apps that allows developers to use the new and advanced *Location and Activity API*, i.e., they changed `Location Manager` to `Fused Location Manager`, hence combining sensors, GPS, Wi-Fi, and cellular data into a single API for location-based applications [33]. As a result, separating data from `GPS_PROVIDER` and `NETWORK_PROVIDER` is no longer straight forward. LP-Caché addresses this issue by preventing app's location request to reach the `Fused Location Manager` that collects and sends the network session data to the location provider. Instead, the requested location is retrieved from the on-device cache, and then, it is sent to the requesting app (with privacy rules applied). Besides, geographic tool[5] can be incorporated in the LP-Cache's UI to get the corresponding geo-coordinates. This will allow LP-Caché to achieve effective privacy without affecting location accuracy, at the same time, prevent from the non-authorised sharing of device's exact location and network session data.

5.2 Mobile Platform

For performance evaluation, there are two possible ways of implementing LP-Caché location protection service. The first requires modifying the app's location accessing interfaces and intercepting location updates before they reach the app provider. Whereas, the second option requires modifying the platform and changing the location data before reaching the app.

---

[5] LatLong is a geographic tool. See http://www.latlong.net/ (last access in March 2016).

App Code Modification. This comprises unpacking the app, rewriting the code to work according to the new rules, and then repackaging it again, e.g., [34]. However, app repackaging changes the signature and stops future updates, and therefore, affects its functionality. Another way to modify app's location accessing interfaces is through the creation of an `Android` service and allowing apps to register with it. Then, Apps can use the location data provided by this service. This approach is easy to implement but relies heavily on app developers to modify their app's code, which is highly infeasible and unrealistic. Nonetheless, this approach can be used as simulated testing environment for any developed service.

Platform Modification. For the sake of experimentation, we develop LP-Caché via platform modification. One of the main task is to add a system service, where the class belongs to the location APIs; thus, it is placed in the `android.location package`, which detects private locations via APs and can also be used by other components when calling context. In Android, a context allows an app to interact with the OS resources. Another task is to make LP-Caché communicate with location requesting apps. On `Android` there are two methods to access user's location: (1) Location Manager Service (Old), and (2) Fused Location Manager Service (New) that is a part of Google Play Services. Both methods require the app to request a callback function to get regular updates by registering a location listener. The app receives a new location object when a new location is available, the callback function is invoked. Modifying these two Google services is complicated, but there is a possibility to intercept the the location object before it reaches requesting apps. We will add a static context field to the location class, which will be populated when the app is invoked; this will enable us to know which app is currently requesting the location object, and also communicate with the OS [25]. The created location object will have reference to the requesting app's context, and therefore, it can interact with our external service.

5.3   On-Device Cache Database Creation

LP-Caché requires fixed wireless APs data (i.e., 802.11) to create cached database of private locations. Initially, we decided to focus on WPS since it infers accurate user location. However, we can later include other fixed radio sources (e.g., cell-tower unique identifiers).

Network Fingerprinting. We can distinguish two main types of WPS techniques to determine the position of client devices with respect to APs [35]: (1) Signal trilateration and (2) Fingerprinting. The former undertakes trilateration of Received Signal Strength (RSS), Angle of Arrival (AoA), and Time of Flight (ToF) from observed APs, and the later involves mapping observed APs signatures with a stored database. LP-Caché uses fingerprinting to create cached location database; however, fingerprinting performance is highly related to the number of APs. Therefore, in Sect. 6 we have evaluated WiFi AP availability and consistency. The detected network management frames/beacons are mapped with the device's representative geo-location to create a network fingerprint, which is then stored in the local cached database, an example private location fingerprint is shown in Eq. 1. Moreover, to reduce storage and computation overhead, our model only caches network fingerprints of private places (e.g., home, work, frequently visited places or particular stores), and it relies on user input for initial pre-set up. The user will have to select the option (via LP-Caché UI) to set current location as private place p_i, and then fingerprint will be recorded. Later, the private place will be detected automatically with respect to observed beacons $[n_x]$, such that

$$p_i = [n_1], [n_2], \ldots, [n_x] \rightarrow [l_r] \tag{1}$$

where p_i represent i^{th} private place IDs, n is the scanned beacon, and l_r is a representative location for that private place. WiFi AP beacons $[n_x]$ consists of four attributes $\langle$SSID, BSSID/MAC address, Signal-strength, and Timestamp$\rangle$. The private representative location $[l_r]$ consists of a tuple $\langle Lattitude, Longitude,$ and $Accuracy \rangle$.

In LP-Caché, to set up network fingerprints at every private place, we measure the response rate as the ratio of detection count and the total number of scans for each beacon:

$$R_{l_c,x} = \frac{\sum_{i=1}^{n_{l_c}} b_{x,i}}{n_c}, b_{x,i} = \begin{cases} 1 & \text{if beacon } x \text{ found in } i\text{th scan} \\ 0 & \text{otherwise} \end{cases} \tag{2}$$

where $R_{l_c,x}$ is the response rate of beacon x at the current private location l_c and, n_{l_c} is the total scan count since the private place was entered. The detection count of each beacon is maintained to identify the frequently occurring beacons; and therefore, beacons with higher response rate are used to create the network fingerprint for the current private place $[l_c]$. $R_{l_c,x}$ will be maintained in the LP-Caché database to update the response rate of every detected beacon during a specified time interval spent at private place $[l_c]$.

On-Device Cache-Based Location Calculation Algorithm. The detailed steps of privacy-aware geo-location calculation process are summarised in Algorithm 1. The surrounded beacons $[n_x]$ are scanned and compared to the list of private WiFi fingerprints $[n_i]$ to detect private place $[p_i]$ stored in cached database $[c]$. Further, the representative $[l_r]$ is altered based on set permissions (see Sect. 5.4).

5.4 Personalised Permissions for Location Sharing

A general LBS query consists of different attributes, e.g., LBS query {*POI, Latitude and Longitude, User-Info*}, where included geo-coordinates estimate the device's geo-location. To satisfy one of the privacy property called controlled information disclosure, we designed enhanced permission mechanism to control

---

Algorithm 1. Location Calculation Algorithm [10].

Require: n_x: Network Frames
Ensure: l_r: Representative Location
1:   $n_x = 0$
2:   read n_x
3:   **while** $n_x \neq$ null **do**
4:     **if** $n_x = n_i$, $\forall\, i \in p$ **then**
5:       (step 1) retrieve the corresponding l_r
6:       add flag $f =$ (if private 1, else 0)
7:       send l_r
8:     **else**
9:       (step 2) request l_r from user or location provider
10:      set received l_r to corresponding p_i
11:      update c
12:      send l_r
13:     **end if**
14: **end while**

---

these geo-coordinates before it is sent to app providers. When using LP-Caché, for every installed app and set private place, the UI provides three distinct privacy settings: (1) Adjust Location Granularity, (2) Obfuscate Location and, (3) No Change. In the first option, geo-coordinate truncation method adjusts location precision level; in the second option, geo-coordinate transformation obfuscate user's location; whereas, in the third option, the exact unchanged geo-coordinates are sent to the requesting app.

Enhanced Permissions Algorithm. Once LP-Caché receives an invoked location object $[l_r]$, it alters the location data according to the enhanced permission settings and returns processed location $[l_r']$. The steps involved in enhanced permission mechanism are summarised in Algorithm 2, where u_p is the set permission, g_l is the adjusted location precision level, l is the latitude, and l_g is the longitude.

Geo-Coordinates Truncation. The geographical coordinates are represented by a tuple consisting of {*latitude*: 52°28'59.200"N, *and longitude*: 1°53'37.0001" W}, where the last digits specify more accurate geo-location. Geo-coordinate truncation method will enable us to adjust the location precision level, i.e., by removing last digits and rounding the location accuracy from street to city level or even more general. Generally, for any third party reuse, service providers or data collectors assure in the EULA that this method will be applied on the collected data since the truncated coordinates increase the ambiguity level [36]. On the contrary, LP-Caché applies this method on the user device with user's permission in order to minimise the user's sensitive data collection and privacy concerns.

Algorithm 2. Enhanced Permissions Algorithm [10].

Require: l_r: Representative Location
Ensure: l'_r: Processed Location
1: u_p = User Input
2: read l, l_g, f, u_p
3: **if** u_p = Adjust Granularity **then**
4:      check granularity level g_l
5:      truncate(l, l_g)
6:      replace l to l' and l_g to l'_g
7:      return l'_r
8: **else if** u_p = Obfuscate **then**
9:      randomly generate angle θ
10:     obfuscate(l, l_g, θ)
11:     replace l to l' and l_g to l'_g
12:     return l'_r
13: **else**
14:     unchanged
15:     return l'_r
16: **end if**

Geo-Coordinates Transformation. For privacy preservation, position transformation functions such as scaling, rotation and translation have been used by location data distributors or anonymisers [27,37]. In LP-Caché, we use geo-coordinate transformation on the device to obfuscate user's private locations. Our service represents the geo-coordinate transformation using scaling and rotation, and denotes its parameters as a tuple $\langle s, \theta, (l, l_g) \rangle$, where s is the scaling factor, θ is the rotation angle, and (l, l_g) are the original coordinates. It applies Eq. 3 to generate transformed or obfuscated geo-cordinates (l', l'_g), where angle θ is randomly generated.

$$l' = \theta(s.l)$$
$$l'_g = \theta(s.l_g) \tag{3}$$

6   Feasibility and Usability Analysis

LP-Caché's actual performance evaluation depends on the location-based apps performance. In this section, we analise the WiFi AP data availability and consistency to measure feasibility of WiFi fingerprinting method to be included in LP-Caché's implementation. In [10], we presented a WiFi APs dataset summary for a month; we have extended the sample size for a couple of months and conducted a comparative study of the observations from both, 1st and 2nd month datasets to evaluate the scalability of the WiFi fingerprinting method. For the sake of illustration, we have maintained unique ID and sequence for all the selected 34 private places.

Table 1. WiFi measurement dataset comparative summary.

	1 month	2 months	Total scans
Total number of scans	25480	21140	46620
Distinct private locations selected	34		% change
Total APs detected	486	497	2.26%
Average APs detected	396	393	−0.76%

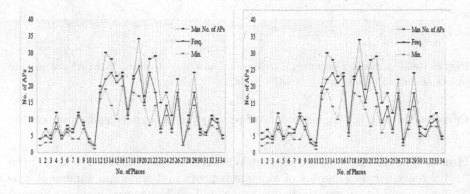

Fig. 7. Measured density of 1 month (left) and 2 months (right) detected WiFi APs at private places.

6.1 WiFi APs Availability and Consistency

Experimental Set-Up. The experimental set-up to measure WiFi AP data availability and consistency consists of the following three steps:

1. *Data Collection.* We collected beacons from fixed WiFi APs using `WiEye` [38] and `Network Info II` [39] apps on `Android` smartphones that have 802.11a/b/g/n radio feature so they can operate in both 2.4 GHz and 5 GHz bands at 34 different private places for a period of two months.
2. *Location Categorisation.* App users are more concern about sharing their private locations [7]; therefore, in our analysis, we selected three distinct categorise of private places: 1. Home (i.e., residential place), 2. Work (i.e., commercial place), and 3. Arbitrary (i.e., any frequently visited place) to determine categorical distribution pattern of WiFi APs.
3. *Data Analysis.* We collected and statistically analysed the scanned WiFi AP data. Table 1 compiles the included sample size and the measured percentage changes; whereas, Fig. 7 shows the relative difference between WiFi APs density, and Fig. 8 depicts the relative average accuracy distribution pattern of detected WiFi APs for each category over the 2 months period.

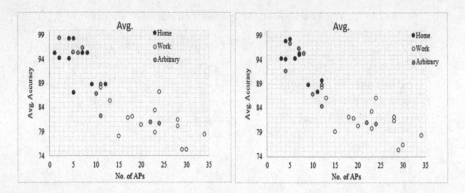

Fig. 8. Relative average accuracy distribution pattern of detected WiFi APs at private places of 1 month (left) and 2 months (right).

Observation 1. For each category of private places, experiments revealed the following:

Home. The results demonstrate that Wifi APs are fixed and frequent and the difference between number of constant beacons and minimum number of similar beacons is comparatively less, and therefore, it achieved highest accuracy rate. Moreover, the ratio of SSID to BSSID is 1:1, i.e., 1 SSID (abc) has 1 BSSID (a0:12:b3:c4:56:78), this makes fingerprints distinct so improving the location detection performance.

Work. This category has many fixed WiFi APs but with fluctuating signal strengths, and therefore, the sequence of available APs changes. However, the observed ratio of SSID to BSSID is many to one, i.e., 1 SSID has many BSSIDs; therefore, in this case, SSIDs along with BSSIDs can be used as unique identifiers to create a fingerprint to detect a private place dynamically.

Arbitrary. In this category, the data collector could select any frequently visited locations, e.g., gym, shop, or friend's home. Figure 8 demonstrates that the outcome of this category is related to the other two categories, it either shows results similar to home or work.

The range of average accuracy for all the three categories of private places falls between 75% to 97%. Hence, it is evident that smartphones regularly detect similar beacons at frequently visited place, for place detection at least one beacon should match with the stored fingerprints. Thus, the result demonstrates that WiFi fingerprinting can be effectively used as private place detection source in LP-Caché. Nonetheless, to achieve efficient capability for place recognition via beacons, a *place discovering algorithm* like [40] can be implemented (in future work).

Observation 2. Table 1 shows comparative analysis of WiFi APs data that has been scanned and collected during both 1st and 2nd month. Considering percentage changes, the number of total detected APs has increased with 2.26% and the number of frequently detected APs remained without change, i.e., with a negligible difference of -0.76%. Equation 2 has been used statistically to identify frequently detected beacons whilst at a particular private place. Pre-set unique IDs and a sequence for all the selected 34 private places allowed us to measure the relative density and distribution pattern of the WiFi APs during both 1st and 2nd month. Figure 7 shows the relative difference between WiFi APs density, and Fig. 8 depicts the relative average accuracy distribution pattern of detected WiFi APs for each category over the period on 2 months.

6.2 Estimated Storage Requirements

Location-based queries that are generated/received from running applications and service providers include several attributes, and their data types require vast amount of storage space. This is the case of some location privacy solutions (e.g., [11,12]) that apply caching techniques on location-based queries as a result of their storage requirement. LP-Caché does not cache location-based queries, instead it stores the WiFi AP data and geo-coordinates of users' private locations. Moreover, the user's pre-set privacy rules are applied to the mapped geo-coordinates at runtime. As a result, comparatively, LP-Caché's on-device cache database does not demand massive storage requirement. By considering the 802.1 Standard and datatypes sizes, Table 2 presents the storage requirements in bytes and database components, where network fingerprint table is a tuple of $\langle no.of beacons, beacon field, counter \rangle$, and permission table is a tuple of $\langle location, placeid, accuracy\ counter, no.of private places \rangle$. Moreover, Table 3 presents the measured changes in the 1st and the 2nd month of WiFi data collected at 34 distinct private places. The results conclude that the average change

Table 2. Estimated storage.

Field storage		Size	Database component	Size
Beacon field	BSSID/MAC	6 bytes	Network fingerprint table	$= (Beacon field + counter) \times no.of beacons$
	SSID	32 bytes		
	Place ID	3 bytes		
	Timestamp/Age	8 bytes		
Location field	Geo-coordinates	32 bytes	Permission table	$= (Location + placeid + accu.counter) \times no.of private places$
	Region	32 bytes		

Table 3. Relative difference of monthly storage.

Storage	1 month	2 months	% change
Network fingerprint	25272 bytes	25844 bytes	2.26% increase
Permissions	2380 bytes	2380 bytes	No change
Total storage	27652 bytes	28224 bytes	2.07% total increase

has increased by 2.07%. cache storage of total 25844 bytes that includes the sum of permissions and network fingerprints for 34 distinct private places. Thus, we can anticipate that the current mobile device internal storage capacity is sufficient for the required storage [41].

6.3   Cache Hits and Cache Misses

In LP-Caché, up-to-date cache database and network fingerprint search result accuracy are main challenges. The three possible outcomes when looking for device's location based on the scanned beacons are:

1. *The location is cached and up-to-date.* This case comes with positive result, and therefore, data can be used effectively.
2. *The location is cached but is out-of-date.* This can occur if the network infrastructure changes, e.g., if router is changed then the cache data needs to be updated. The overall results of Sects. 6.1 and 6.2 prove that this case does not occur frequently. Nonetheless, for data accuracy a method that uses Equation will be incorporated to detect and measure occurrence of such situations of cache misses at runtime. Moreover, the developed method can likewise be deployed to maintain *data freshness* and *data consistency.*
3. *The location is not cached.* This occurs when the observed WiFi AP is not cached and/or mapped to the private locations, then our service will have to interact with user to update the location cache. Besides, the response rate $R_{l_c,x}$ can be further extended to measure runtime occurrences of these outcomes.

6.4   Ongoing Evaluation of Caching Method

Following WiFi data availability and consistency analysis, LP-Caché's feasibility evaluation will be extended to analyse how frequently the cache needs to be updated and what are the trade-offs between the cache update frequency and location privacy and accuracy in order to measure computational and communication overheads. We also intent to conduct a thorough user study to determine usability for the users to accommodate LP-Caché's functionality. Moreover, we plan to extend the fundamental caching-related technical challenges such as cache hits and cache misses, data freshness, data consistency, and estimated bandwidth requirements in an advanced development and implementation of LP-Caché hence paying special attention to storage-efficient caching.

7   Conclusion

Secure gathering and transmission of the location data by mobile apps while preserving users' privacy is a major concern that needs reconsideration. Evaluation of current location handling process confirms that it is vulnerable to location privacy attacks; therefore, we presented a privacy-aware model that provides users with advanced location controls to mitigate major privacy threats. Within a dataset generated in 2 months of experimental setting, we observed a 2.26% change in detected WiFi APs at 34 distinct places and 2.07% change in estimated storage. These results are promising and benefit deployment of LP-Caché's. In this paper, we mainly focused on establishing the design decisions, implementation requirements, and on measuring the feasibility of LP-Caché. Work in progress is on (1) deploying our model on a mobile platform to measure its functionality and efficiency while interacting with different location-based apps; (2) carrying out run-time measurements of the cache storage over an extended period of time, and (3) performing critical analysis of the network fingerprinting and permission mapping methods with dynamic movement patterns. We plan to further assess LP-Caché's scalability in future large scale scenarios and, address end user as well as service providers concerns.

References

1. Pontes, T., Vasconcelos, M., Almeida, J., Kumaraguru, P., Almeida, V.: We know where you live: privacy characterization of foursquare behavior. In: Proceedings of ACM Conference on Ubiquitous Computing, pp. 898–905. ACM (2012)
2. Muslukhov, I., Boshmaf, Y., Kuo, C., Lester, J., Beznosov, K.: Understanding users' requirements for data protection in smartphones. In: ICDE Workshop, IEEE International Conference on Secure Data Management on Smartphones and Mobiles, pp. 228–235. IEEE (2012)
3. Shklovski, I., Mainwaring, S.D., Skúladóttir, H.H., et al.: Leakiness and creepiness in app space: perceptions of privacy and mobile app use. In: Proceedings of ACM Conference on Human factors in computing systems, pp. 2347–2356. ACM (2014)
4. European Commission: Protection of personal data (2016). http://ec.europa.eu/justice/data-protection/
5. IETF: Geographic Location Privacy (2016). http://datatracker.ietf.org/wg/geopriv/charter/
6. Michael, K., Clarke, R.: Location and tracking of mobile devices: Überveillance stalks the streets. Comput. Law Secur. Rev. **29**, 216–228 (2013)
7. Almuhimedi, H., Schaub, F., Sadeh, N., Adjerid, I., Acquisti, A., et al.: Your location has been shared 5,398 times! A field study on mobile app privacy nudging. In: Proceedings of ACM Conference on Human Factors in Computing Systems, pp. 787–796. ACM (2015)
8. Felt, A.P., Egelman, S., Wagner, D.: I've got 99 problems, but vibration ain't one: a survey of smartphone users' concerns. In: Proceedings of ACM Workshop on Security and Privacy in Smartphones and Mobile Devices, pp. 33–44. ACM (2012)
9. Cranor, L.F., Sadeh, N.: A shortage of privacy engineers. IEEE Secur. Priv. **11**, 77–79 (2013)
10. Patel, A., Palomar, E.: LP-Caché: Privacy-aware cache model for location-based apps. In: Proceedings of the 13th International Joint Conference on e-Business and Telecommunications (ICETE 2016) - Volume 4: SECRYPT, pp. 183–194, Lisbon, Portugal, 26–28 July 2016 (2016)
11. Zhu, X., Chi, H., Niu, B., Zhang, W., Li, Z., Li, H.: Mobicache: when k-anonymity meets cache. In: GLOBECOM, pp. 820–825. IEEE (2013)

12. Amini, S., Lindqvist, J., Hong, J., Lin, J., Toch, E., Sadeh, N.: Caché: caching location-enhanced content to improve user privacy. In: Proceedings of ACM International Conference on Mobile Systems, Applications, and Services, pp. 197–210. ACM (2011)
13. Niu, B., Li, Q., Zhu, X., Cao, G., Li, H.: Enhancing privacy through caching in location-based services. In: Proceedings of IEEE INFOCOM (2015)
14. Google Location Service (2016). https://support.google.com/gmm/answer/164614 0?hl=en-GB
15. Skyhook (2016). http://www.skyhookwireless.com/
16. Navizon (2016). http://www.navizon.com
17. Zhuang, Y., Syed, Z., Georgy, J., El-Sheimy, N.: Autonomous smartphone-based WiFi positioning system by using access points localization and crowdsourcing. Pervasive Mob. Comput. **18**, 118–136 (2015)
18. Wireshark (2016). https://www.wireshark.org
19. tPacketcapture (2016). http://play.google.com/
20. Android Developer Reference (2016). http://developer.android.com/reference/
21. Gibler, C., Crussell, J., Erickson, J., Chen, H.: AndroidLeaks: automatically detecting potential privacy leaks in android applications on a large scale. In: Katzenbeisser, S., Weippl, E., Camp, L.J., Volkamer, M., Reiter, M., Zhang, X. (eds.) Trust 2012. LNCS, vol. 7344, pp. 291–307. Springer, Heidelberg (2012). doi:10. 1007/978-3-642-30921-2_17
22. Egele, M., Kruegel, C., Kirda, E., Vigna, G.: PiOS: detecting privacy leaks in iOS applications. In: NDSS (2011)
23. Enck, W., Gilbert, P., Han, S., Tendulkar, V., Chun, B.G., et al.: TaintDroid: an information-flow tracking system for realtime privacy monitoring on smartphones. TOCS **32**, 5 (2014)
24. Beresford, A.R., Rice, A., Skehin, N., Sohan, R.: Mockdroid: trading privacy for application functionality on smartphones. In: Proceedings of ACM Workshop on Mobile Computing Systems and Applications, pp. 49–54. ACM (2011)
25. Fawaz, K., Shin, K.G.: Location privacy protection for smartphone users. In: Proceedings of ACM SIGSAC Conference on Computer and Communications Security, pp. 239–250. ACM (2014)
26. Patel, A., Palomar, E.: Privacy preservation in location-based mobile applications: research directions. In: Proceedings of IEEE International Conference on Availability, Reliability and Security (ARES), pp. 227–233. IEEE (2014)
27. Wernke, M., Skvortsov, P., Dürr, F., Rothermel, K.: A classification of location privacy attacks and approaches. Pers. Ubiquit. Comput. **18**, 163–175 (2014)
28. Khoshgozaran, A., Shahabi, C., Shirani-Mehr, H.: Location privacy: going beyond K-anonymity, cloaking and anonymizers. Knowl. Inf. Syst. **26**, 435–465 (2011)
29. Damiani, M.L.: Third party geolocation services in LBS: privacy requirements and research issues. Trans. Data Priv. **4**, 55–72 (2011)
30. Doty, N., Wilde, E.: Geolocation privacy and application platforms. In: Proceedings of ACM SIGSPATIAL International Workshop on Security and Privacy in GIS and LBS, pp. 65–69. ACM (2010)
31. Anonymizer (2016). http://www.anonymizer.com/
32. TOR (2016). http://www.torproject.org/
33. Hellman, E.: Android Programming: Pushing the Limits. Wiley, Hoboken (2013)
34. Jeon, J., Micinski, K.K., Vaughan, J.A., Fogel, A., Reddy, N.: Dr. Android and Mr. Hide: fine-grained permissions in android applications. In: Proceedings of ACM Workshop on Security and Privacy in Smartphones and Mobile Devices, pp. 3–14. ACM (2012)

35. Bell, S., Jung, W.R., Krishnakumar, V.: WiFi-based enhanced positioning systems: accuracy through mapping, calibration, and classification. In: Proceedings of ACM SIGSPATIAL International Workshop on Indoor Spatial Awareness, pp. 3–9. ACM (2010)
36. Aad, I., Niemi, V.: NRC data collection and the privacy by design principles. In: PhoneSense (2010)
37. Lin, D., Bertino, E., Cheng, R., Prabhakar, S.: Position transformation: a location privacy protection method for moving objects. In: Proceedings of the SIGSPATIAL ACM GIS 2008 International Workshop on Security and Privacy in GIS and LBS, pp. 62–71. ACM (2008)
38. WiEye (2016). http://play.google.com/store/apps/
39. NetworkInfoIi (2016). http://play.google.com/store/apps/
40. Kim, D.H., Hightower, J., Govindan, R., Estrin, D.: Discovering semantically meaningful places from pervasive RF-beacons. In: Proceedings of ACM International Conference on Ubiquitous Computing, pp. 21–30. ACM (2009)
41. Android (2016). http://developer.android.com/guide/topics/data/data-storage.html

Signal Processing and Multimedia Applications

Investigation into the Use of WFSTs and DNNs for Speech Activity Detection in Broadcast Data Transcription

Lukas Mateju[✉], Petr Cerva, and Jindrich Zdansky

Faculty of Mechatronics, Informatics and Interdisciplinary Studies,
Technical University of Liberec, Studentska 2, 461 17 Liberec, Czech Republic
{lukas.mateju,petr.cerva,jindrich.zdansky}@tul.cz

Abstract. This paper deals with the task of Speech Activity Detection (SAD). The main goal is to investigate a new SAD approach suitable for offline as well as online transcription of various radio/TV broadcasts containing a large amount of non-speech segments. For this purpose, Deep Neural Networks (DNNs) with various hyper-parameters are adopted and evaluated. Their training is carried out using artificially created mixtures of speech and non-speech signals. Our SAD scheme also utilizes a decoder based on Weighted Finite State Transducers (WFSTs). The decoder smooths the output from DNN, can operate online and utilizes context-based transduction model, where both speech and non-speech events are modeled using sequences of states. The final evaluation of the developed approach is carried out on standardized QUT-NOISE-TIMIT data set for SAD and in a real broadcast transcription system. The obtained results show that our SAD module yields state-of-the-art results on QUT-NOISE-TIMIT, and, at the same time, it is capable of (a) operating with low latency and (b) reducing the computational demands and error rate of the transcription system.

Keywords: Speech activity detection · Speech transcription · Weighted finite state transducers · Deep neural networks

1 Introduction

The task of speech activity detection focuses on a problem of identifying both speech and non-speech segments in a sound recording. Over the years, various SAD methods have been proposed and an SAD module has usually formed an important and integral component of a signal pre-processing unit in a wide range of applications including, e.g., speech enhancement, speaker/language identification, speaker verification, and, of course, speech transcription. Most of the existing SAD approaches are performed in two subsequent steps, where feature extraction is followed by speech/non-speech classification.

In the former phase, the classic approaches for feature extraction utilize energy [5], zero crossing rate [12] or auto-correlation function [9]. The group

© Springer International Publishing AG 2017
M.S. Obaidat (Ed): ICETE 2016, CCIS 764, pp. 341–358, 2017.
https://doi.org/10.1007/978-3-319-67876-4_16

of more complex parametrization techniques, which have also been successfully employed, include MFCCs [22, 26], multi-resolution cochleagram features [31], multi-band long-term signal variability features [28] or channel bottleneck features [15]. Note that in [32], features based on the use of Deep Belief Networks (DBN) have also been presented. In many practical applications, individual features are usually combined to achieve the best possible results.

In the latter phase, various existing algorithms for classification, such as Support Vector Machines (SVM) [24] or Gaussian Mixture Models (GMMs) [10, 19], can be carried out. In recent years, various DNN architectures started to be employed more and more frequently including fully connected feed-forward DNNs [22], Convolutional Neural Networks (CNNs) [23] or Recurrent Neural Networks (RNNs) [6, 11]. More complex approaches such as boosted DNNs [31] or jointly trained DNNs [29] have also been presented. Moreover, a combination of DNN and CNN is used in [27]. The accuracy of the detection can also be further improved by smoothing the output from the given classifier. For this purpose, various techniques such as the Viterbi decoder [8, 22] or WFSTs [2] have been applied.

Most of the aforementioned works aim primarily at offline applications. The reason is that applying SAD in an online environment brings further restrictions on the system, such as low computational demands and latency. The approaches developed namely for the online task include, for example, conditional random fields [8] or accurate endpointing with expected pause duration [14]. Another approach in [18] utilizes short-term features.

The goal of our efforts was to develop a SAD approach suitable for a speech transcription system that is deployed for online 24/7 monitoring of more than 80 TV and radio stations in Czech, Slovak, Polish and other Slavic languages. This type of input data is specific from a speech transcription point of view by containing a large amount of non-speech parts such as songs or advertisements. For example, broadcasts of some local radio stations may contain only a few percent of speech segments. Here, an utilization of a proper SAD module should allow to reduce the computation demands on the transcription system greatly, because all the segments marked as non-speech may be omitted from the transcription.

An SAD module suitable for our target task should (a) operate at a high level of Real-Time Factor (RTF), (b) have a low latency, and (c) reduce the Word Error Rate (WER) of transcription. To meet all these requirements at once, a new approach is proposed in the present paper. It adopts a DNN classifier that is trained on a data set created by mixing clean speech utterances with non-speech recordings at various desired levels of Signal-to-Noise Ratio (SNR). The output from DNN is then smoothed using a decoder based on WFSTs. To ensure high quality and accuracy of the detection, the employed transduction model is context-based, i.e., both speech and non-speech events are modeled as sequences of three consecutive states.

The work presented in this paper is built on the underlaying research presented in [16], and extends our previous study [17].

The rest of this paper is structured as follows: The evaluation metrics used for the speech activity detection as well as the speech recognition are described in Sect. 2. The process of development of the SAD module is presented in Sect. 3 and in Sect. 4. Section 5 then contains evaluation of the resulting SAD module on standardized QUT-NOISE-TIMIT data set. The results of application of the final SAD approach to a real system for broadcast data transcription are then summarized in Sect. 6. Finally, the paper is concluded in Sect. 7.

2 Metrics Used for Evaluation

This section presents evaluation metrics for speech activity detection (Sect. 2.1) as well as for speech recognition (Sect. 2.2).

2.1 Speech Activity Detection Metrics

Within this work, five different metrics were used for evaluation. The first three focus on the overall accuracy of the speech activity detection while the latter two evaluate the quality of the change-point detection.

The first overall accuracy metric, Frame Error Rate (FER), is defined as:

$$FER[\%] = \frac{M}{N} * 100, \tag{1}$$

where M is the number of non-matching frames in the reference and the decoded outputs, and N is the total number of frames in the reference.

The other two overall accuracy metrics symbolize false negatives and false positives. The remaining relevance measures are not presented here as they are complementary to the presented metrics.

Miss Rate (MR) represents the false negatives and is defined as:

$$MR[\%] = \frac{M_{\text{speech}}}{N_{\text{speech}}} * 100, \tag{2}$$

where M_{speech} is the number of misclassified speech frames, and N_{speech} is the total number of reference speech frames.

Similarly, False Alarm Rate (FAR) represents false positives and is defined as follows:

$$FAR[\%] = \frac{M_{\text{non-speech}}}{N_{\text{non-speech}}} * 100, \tag{3}$$

where $M_{\text{non-speech}}$ is the number of misclassified non-speech frames. $N_{\text{non-speech}}$ is the total number of reference non-speech frames.

To evaluate the quality of the change-point detection between speech/non-speech events, the detected (computed) boundaries and the reference boundaries have to be aligned at first [21]. After that, hits, deletions and insertions can be defined. Given these values, precision (P) and recall (R) can be expressed. The former measure describes the likelihood of how often a correct boundary is determined whenever a boundary is detected. The latter defines the ratio between the number of correct boundaries and the number of reference boundaries. In this paper, the F-value is utilized, which can be expressed using P and R as

$$F-value = \frac{2RP}{R+P}. \tag{4}$$

Given the correctly detected boundaries (hits), it is also possible to calculate an error value for each hit (in seconds) and sort all the hits according to these calculated values in ascending order. In this paper, the measure $\delta_{2/3}$ is utilized, which expresses (in seconds) the maximal error of the alignment for first two-thirds of the sorted (best) hits.

Note that the optimal SAD approach should minimize the miss rate while keeping the false alarm rate reasonably low. The reason is that the desired speech recognition system should transcribe all speech frames with only limited amount of non-speech events added. Additionally, the measure $\delta_{2/3}$ should be as low as possible to provide the speech transcription system with precisely determined speech segments to transcribe.

2.2   Speech Recognition Metrics

To evaluate the performance of the speech recognition, three various metrics are used. The first two focus on the quality of the transcription while the latter one measures the performance of the system.

The first quality measure is Word Error Rate (WER) and is defined as follows:

$$WER[\%] = \frac{I+S+D}{N} * 100, \tag{5}$$

where I is a count of insertions marking words the recognizer added to its output, D stands for the number of deletions (deleted words), S is the number of substitutions, and N is the total number of words in the reference text.

The second one, Correctness (Corr), is defined followingly:

$$Corr[\%] = 100 - \frac{S+D}{N} * 100, \tag{6}$$

where D stands for the number of deletions (deleted words), S is the number of substitutions, and N is the total number of words in the reference text.

The speed of the decoding is measured using the metric Real-Time Factor (RTF), which can be expressed as:

$$RTF = \frac{T}{PT}, \tag{7}$$

where T is the duration of the recording and PT is the processing time of the decoding. Higher RTF values mean speeding up the decoding.

The use of the SAD module should ideally lead to significant increase in RTF while keeping the other metrics at least at the same level as before.

3   The Proposed SAD Approach

Within this section, the gradual development of the proposed SAD approach is described.

3.1   Data Used for Development

A total amount of 6 h of recordings were gathered into a data set for development and evaluation of SAD modules. This data set originated in TV and radio shows from several Slavic countries. It consisted not only of clean speech of Czech, Slovak, Polish and Russian languages but also of segments with music, advertisements and jingles.

The data set was at first annotated by the baseline DNN-based SAD approach (Sect. 3.2). During the subsequent stage, these annotations were fine-tuned by hand. Note that approximately 70% of the data set was labeled as speech while the remaining 30% as non-speech events.

3.2   Baseline DNN-Based Approach

A feed-forward deep neural network with a binary output was employed for the baseline approach. Note that no output smoothing was applied for this experiment. In total, 67 h of recordings were used for training. 30 h of clean speech of several Slavic languages and English were used as the speech part. The non-speech part was composed of 30 h of various musical genres and 7 h of diverse non-speech events/noises. The sampling frequency used was 16 kHz.

The designed hyper-parameters and settings of the DNN were following:

- 5 hidden layers;
- 128 neurons per hidden layer;
- ReLU activation function;
- 0.08 learning rate;
- mini-batches of size 1024;
- 10 epochs;
- features: 39-dimensional log filter banks;
- input vector: concatenation of 25 previous frames, the current frame, and 25 following frames;
- local normalization within 1 s window.

The DNN was trained using the torch framework[1] on GPU.

The results for the baseline approach are summarized in the first row of Table 1. They show that approximately 4% of speech segments were misclassified and thus omitted from the transcription. This negatively influences the accuracy of the speech transcription system. Another issue was caused by a large amount of false non-speech segments with a duration of 1 or 2 frames. This is the partial reason for the extremely low value of F-value metric.

---

[1] http://torch.ch.

Table 1. Summarized results of individual SAD approaches described in Sect. 3.

Approach	FER [%]	MR [%]	FAR [%]	F-value [%]	$\delta_{2/3}$ [s]
Baseline DNN-based	4.7	3.7	7.1	0.3	0.42
+ Basic smoothing	2.9	2.2	4.7	28.5	0.27
+ Artificial training data with noise	3.1	0.3	10.1	41.3	0.34
Modified artificial training data + Context-based smoothing	2.4	0.5	7.2	52.7	0.26

3.3   Smoothing the Output from DNN

As previous section stated, each frame was classified by the detector independently. However, the speech/non-speech events usually last longer (at least several frames). Therefore, a smoothing of the output from the DNN is necessary. For this purpose, weighted finite state transducers with the use of OpenFst library[2] were utilized.

Two transducers form the final decoding scheme. The first one models the input signal (see in detail in Fig. 1). The other transducer, the transduction model, represents the smoothing algorithm (depicted in Fig. 2). The transduction model is composed of three states; the initial state is denoted by 0. The speech/non-speech labels are emitted by transitions between states 1 and 2. These transitions are penalized by penalty factors P1 and P2. Their values (500 and 500) were experimentally tuned on a different data set in several experiments not presented in this paper.

Given the two above described transducers, the decoding process is performed using on-the-fly composition of the transduction and the input model of an unknown size. This is feasible since the input is considered to be a linear-topology, un-weighted, epsilon-free acceptor. After each composition step, the shortest-path (considering tropical semiring) determined in the resulting model is compared with all other alternative hypotheses. When a common path is found among these hypotheses (i.e., with the same output label), the corresponding concatenated output labels are marked as the final fixed output. Since the rest of the best path is not certain, it is denoted as a temporary output (i.e., it can still be altered later in the process).

The effect of the smoothing is shown in the second row of Table 1. An overall improvement in all metrics was achieved. As an example, the improvement in FER was from 4.7% to 2.9%, in MR from 3.7% to 2.2% and in F-value from 0.3% to 28.5%.

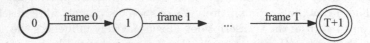

Fig. 1. The transducer modeling the input signal.

---

[2] http://www.openfst.org/twiki/bin/view/FST/WebHome.

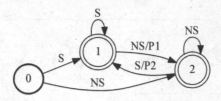

Fig. 2. The transducer representing the basic smoothing model without any context.

3.4   Using Artificial Training Data

Even though the achieved value of MR (around 2%) is fairly low, it still leads to worse performance of the speech transcription system (approximately 1% difference). So far the training data only consisted of clean speech (data for training of acoustic models for speech recognizer) and clean non-speech recordings with no recordings with background non-speech. The majority of the mistakes the SAD module does is thus on segments with background noises.

To resolve this issue, we wanted to employ speech recordings with various non-speech events (e.g. background music, background noise or jingles). Because of the lack of such annotated data, we created a 30 h set by combining 30 h of clean speech recordings with various non-speech recordings. For this purpose, a larger set of non-speech recordings of a total length of 100 h was prepared first. After that, every speech recording was mixed with a randomly selected non-speech recording from the prepared set. Note that every non-speech recording used for mixing had to have the same or longer duration than the given input speech recording (the selected non-speech recording was trimmed to match the length of the speech recording) and its volume was increased or decreased to match the desired level of SNR (which was also selected randomly from an interval between −30 dB and 50 dB).

The annotations were created automatically. If the SNR of a recording was lower than a defined threshold (0 dB), the recording was labeled as non-speech. Otherwise the frames of the recordings were marked as speech.

The third row of Table 1 contains the results of this experiment. It is evident that a significant improvements in F-value and mainly in MR were achieved. The downside of this approach was an increase in FAR and more importantly in $\delta_{2/3}$ from 0.27 s to 0.34 s. Due to this issue, a further refinement of the smoothing algorithm was investigated.

3.5   Improved Context-Based Smoothing

The proposed refinement to the smoothing scheme is depicted in Fig. 3. Here, the speech and non-speech events are represented by sequences of 3 states. The outer states model the context (e.g. the beginning and ending of the speech or non-speech event). In analogy to the model of smoothing without context, the transition penalties are only defined for transitions from speech and non-speech events.

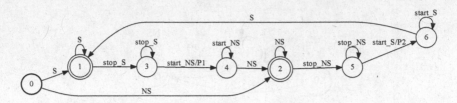

Fig. 3. The transducer representing the context-based smoothing model.

To train the DNN for this experiment, the training data from Sect. 3.4 had to be modified first. At each time, two recordings were randomly selected from the artificial training data, one speech and one non-speech. They were then concatenated in a random order to form a final recording which contained either a transition from speech to non-speech or from non-speech to speech. Again, the annotations of final recordings were done automatically. All frames except for the last 25 frames from the first recording and for the first 25 frames from the second recording were labeled as either speech or non-speech. The remaining 50 frames were marked as transitional and labeled in following manner; 25 labels *stop_NS* followed by 25 labels *start_S* (for non-speech to speech transition) or 25 labels *stop_S* followed by 25 labels *start_NS* (for speech to non-speech transition). Note that the number of transition frames was derived from the size of the context window of the input features. A total amount of 30 h of training data was compiled.

The obtained results show (see the fourth row of Table 1) that the approach with the context-based smoothing resolved the issue of an increase in $\delta_{2/3}$. In addition to reduction in $\delta_{2/3}$ from 0.34 s to 0.27 s, a significant decrease in FER, FAR and increase in F-value was achieved. The negligible disadvantage was a slight deterioration in MR by 0.2%.

4   Hyper-Parameters of DNNs

Within the next experiments, we revised our initial settings of DNN hyper-parameters that were utilized within the baseline experiment (see Sect. 3.2) for the SAD module as presented in Sect. 3.5.

4.1   Width of Layers

The first tunable hyper-parameter of the deep neural networks we focused on was the width of the hidden layers. The reason is that the number of neurons per hidden layer can significantly influence the performance and computational demands of the SAD module.

Within this experiment, 7 various networks were trained and tested. The number of neurons per hidden layer varied from 64 to 256 with a step of 32 neurons. The other hyper-parameters of the DNN remained the same as described in Sect. 3.2. The obtained results are summarized in Table 2. Although the deep

Table 2. Results of experiments with the width of layers of DNN.

Width of layers	FER [%]	MR [%]	FAR [%]	F-value [%]	$\delta_{2/3}$ [s]
64	2.2	0.8	5.8	56.4	0.28
96	2.3	0.7	6.3	56.5	0.28
128	2.4	0.5	7.2	52.7	0.26
160	2.6	0.4	8.1	54.3	0.30
192	2.9	0.3	9.5	49.5	0.32
224	3.0	0.3	10.0	48.6	0.34
256	2.8	0.4	9.1	49.8	0.30

neural networks with more neurons per hidden layer (192, 224 and also 256) yielded the best value of MR, their results were accompanied by an increase in FER, FAR and $\delta_{2/3}$ and also by a decrease in F-value. The slight decrease in MR was not worth the trade-off. The only advantage for the network with 160 neurons per layer over the bigger networks was an increase in F-value. However, the other metrics still made this network a worse option. The smaller networks (64 and 96 neurons per hidden layer) yielded better results in FER, FAR and F-value over the network architecture with 128 neurons per layer. However, the increase in MR and more importantly in $\delta_{2/3}$ forced us to choose the network with 128 neurons per layer as a compromise to better support the final application of the SAD module; speech transcription.

4.2   Number of Layers

Another tunable hyper-parameter of the DNN that we explored, was the number of hidden layers. The reason was the same as for the previous investigation with width of the layers.

As a part of this experiment, 3 deep neural networks with different number of hidden layers (4, 5 and 6) were trained and evaluated. The other hyper-parameters of the DNN remained untouched. The results are summarized in Table 3. They show that the network with 5 hidden layers performed as the best. Additional layer worsened all of the metrics with only the exception of a slight decrease in MR. Although the model with 4 hidden layers yielded an increase in F-value, it's unfortunately accompanied by an increase in FAR and $\delta_{2/3}$. The model with 5 hidden layers was thus used in all following experiments.

Table 3. Results of experiments with DNNs of various depth.

Hidden layers	FER [%]	MR [%]	FAR [%]	F-value [%]	$\delta_{2/3}$ [s]
4	2.4	0.5	7.5	55.3	0.27
5	2.4	0.5	7.2	52.7	0.26
6	2.7	0.4	8.3	52.1	0.31

4.3   Activation Function of Neurons

The activation function used is an another parameter of DNN that can influence the performance of the SAD module. Within the scope of this experiment, we evaluated 3 different activation functions; sigmoid function, hyperbolic tangent function and ReLU function.

The results are depicted in the Table 4. They show that sigmoid activation function performed worse than the other two. The experiments using hyperbolic tangent and ReLU activation functions yielded fairly comparable results. However, the slightly lower MR and $\delta_{2/3}$ were in favor of the ReLU activation function which was thus used in the final model.

Table 4. Results using different types of activation function.

Activation function	FER [%]	MR [%]	FAR [%]	F-value [%]	$\delta_{2/3}$ [s]
Sigmoid	2.8	0.4	8.9	47.2	0.27
Tanh	2.4	0.6	7.2	55.7	0.28
ReLU	2.4	0.5	7.2	52.7	0.26

4.4   Size of the Input Feature Vector

Within this experiment, we evaluated 5 SAD modules with different context window sizes. In all cases, the input feature vector was created as a concatenation of n previous frames, the current frame and n following frames. The rest of the DNN settings remained the same. The results are shown in Table 5. The models based on feature vectors of sizes 5-1-5 and 80-1-80 missed more speech (higher MR) and thus were not used. The metric $\delta_{2/3}$ was significantly worse for context window size of 35-1-35. The remaining models performed similarly. The model with input feature vector of 25-1-25 was selected for our final SAD module as it yielded lower values of FAR and also $\delta_{2/3}$.

It should also be noted that important factor of choosing the size of the feature vector is the computational time needed for decoding. This time was 2 and 1.7 times lower for 5-1-5 and 25-1-25 window sizes, respectively, than for long feature vector (80-1-80).

Table 5. Results for various sizes of the input feature vector.

Feature vector size	FER [%]	MR [%]	FAR [%]	F-value [%]	$\delta_{2/3}$ [s]
5-1-5	2.5	0.6	7.2	52.9	0.22
15-1-15	2.4	0.4	7.5	53.3	0.28
25-1-25	2.4	0.5	7.2	52.7	0.26
35-1-35	2.6	0.4	8.2	52.3	0.34
80-1-80	2.7	0.9	7.3	55.6	0.48

4.5   The Importance of Local Normalization

All of the previously concluded experiments utilized local mean normalization within 1 s long window. In order of saving the computational demands during the training and evaluation phases, we experimented with DNN models with no local normalization applied. The rest of the DNN parameters remained unchanged.

Table 6 contains the obtained results. They show that the local normalization is necessary for better performance of the SAD module. Without local normalization, all of the metrics were noticeably worse. The final SAD module thus employs the local normalization of inputs within 1 s long window.

Table 6. Results of the experiment with local normalization.

Normalized	FER [%]	MR [%]	FAR [%]	F-value [%]	$\delta_{2/3}$ [s]
No	3.4	0.8	10.0	35.6	0.29
Yes	2.4	0.5	7.2	52.7	0.26

5   Evaluation of the Proposed SAD Approach on QUT-NOISE-TIMIT Corpus

To compare the proposed SAD approach with other systems, a standardized corpus QUT-NOISE-TIMIT [4] for speech activity detection was utilized. This corpus allows training and evaluation of SAD systems in various conditions. The comparison was done with five approaches already presented in [4] and two newer approaches with even better, state-of-the-art, results [10, 30].

The five original SAD systems were: standardized VAD system ITU-T G.729 Annex B [1], standardized advanced front-end ETSI [13], Sohn's likelihood ratio test [25], Ramirez's long-term spectral divergence (LTSD) [20] and GMM based approach with use of MFCC features [4]. The other two approaches were (a) voice activity detection using subband noncircularity (SNC) [30] and (b) complete-linkage clustering (CLC) for VAD [10].

5.1   QUT-NOISE-TIMIT Corpus

The idea behind the QUT-NOISE-TIMIT was a creation of a standardized corpus for training and evaluation of numerous SAD systems in various target environments and SNR levels. For this purpose, 600 h of recordings were created by combining clean speech from TIMIT corpus [7] with background noise recordings from QUT-NOISE data set [4]. The background noises from the QUT-NOISE database origin in five different scenarios (cafe, home, street, car and reverb). Each scenario also contains two different source locations for the background noises. For example, the reverb scenario locations were indoor swimming pool and partially enclosed carpark. The final QUT-NOISE-TIMIT corpus was divided into two groups; group A and group B. Each group contains recordings from each scenario in various SNR levels. The ratio of speech and non-speech events is also changing through the recordings of the corpus.

5.2   Evaluation Protocol

The evaluation protocol recommended for QUT-NOISE-TIMIT corpus presented in [4] was followed. That means that no information of the target scenario was utilized during the training phase. The only prior knowledge available for training of DNNs was the level of target environment SNR; low noise (10, 15 dB), medium noise (0, 5 dB) or high noise (−10, −5 dB). For each of the three target environments, group A was utilized for training and group B for testing and vice-versa. Additionally for each target SNR, we also evaluated the performance of the system in different scenarios.

The output segments were compared with QUT-NOISE-TIMIT ground truth labels. The results are presented in a form of miss rate and false alarm rate. In addition to MR and FAR, Half-Total Error Rate (HTER) is also computed. It's defined as an average of MR and FAR.

Note that the proposed SAD approach was trained as described in Sect. 3. The artificial training data was not used.

5.3   Low Noise Conditions

For the experiment in low noise conditions, recordings with SNR level of 10 and 15 dB were utilized. The comparison of the proposed approach with other systems can be seen in Fig. 4 (left part). The absolute reduction in HTER was more than 2% over the formerly best complete-linkage clustering. The proposed solution thus yields state-of-the-art performance in low noise conditions.

The right part of Fig. 4 shows the performance of our proposed approach in all scenarios. The easiest scenarios turned out to be car and street while the

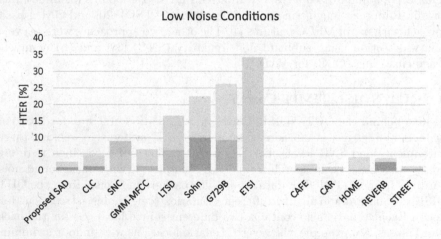

Fig. 4. Low noise conditions. The left part of the figure shows comparison of various SAD systems across QUT-NOISE-TIMIT corpus, the right part performance of the proposed SAD approach in various scenarios. The contribution of MR and FAR to HTER bars is displayed by darker and lighter shades, respectively.

algorithm struggled more with scenarios home and reverb. Also in the reverb scenario, the SAD module missed more speech (higher MR) making this scenario harder to transcribe.

5.4   Medium Noise Conditions

In this experiment, recordings with SNR level of 0 and 5 dB were used. The obtained results can be seen in the left section of Fig. 5. Similarly to the experiments in low noise conditions, the proposed SAD approach outperformed other systems and it yielded state-of-the-art results in medium noise conditions. The absolute reduction in HTER was over 2%.

The performance in various scenarios is in the right part of Fig. 5. As in low noise condition, the car and street scenarios were the least problematic. The HTER was the worst in cafe and reverb scenarios. Also the reverb scenario remained the hardest for the speech transcription.

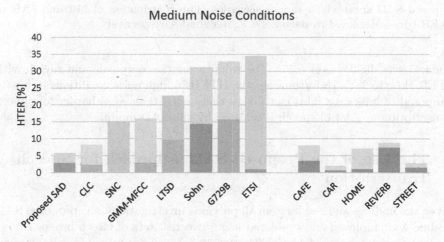

Fig. 5. Medium noise conditions. The left part of the figure shows comparison of various SAD systems across QUT-NOISE-TIMIT corpus, the right part performance of the proposed SAD approach in various scenarios. The contribution of MR and FAR to HTER bars is displayed by darker and lighter shades, respectively.

5.5   High Noise Conditions

The high noise conditions included recordings with SNR level of −10 and −5 dB. Figure 6 (left section) shows the comparison of various approaches. In these conditions, the complete linkage clustering approach performed the best. The HTER of our approach was approximately 2% worse. However the other approaches were still outperformed by a fair margin.

The performance in various scenarios is in Fig. 6 (right section). The scenario car remained the easiest to segment by our approach. The HTER in this

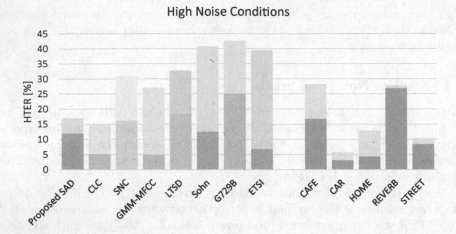

Fig. 6. High noise conditions. The left part of the figure shows comparison of various SAD systems across QUT-NOISE-TIMIT corpus, the right part performance of the proposed SAD approach in various scenarios. The contribution of MR and FAR to HTER bars is displayed by darker and lighter shades, respectively.

scenario was slightly over 5.5%. The worst scenarios were cafe and reverb with HTER close to 28%. Unfortunately, the HTER in high noise conditions is mostly composed of miss rate. This fact makes these conditions even harder for speech transcription as a lot of speech is omitted by the SAD module.

6   The Use of the Proposed SAD Approach for Speech Transcription

Given the findings and results from all previous investigations, the proposed SAD module was employed and evaluated using two test sets of Czech broadcasts.

The first set contained 4 h (22204 words) of recordings from a Czech live news TV channel. Approximately 60% of its content consisted of speech segments. The other set represents broadcast of a Czech local radio station. Its length was 8 h, it contained 7212 words, and speech frames formed only 10% of its content.

The transcription system employed an acoustic model based on a Hidden Markov Model - Deep Neural Network (HMM-DNN) hybrid architecture [3], where the baseline Gaussian Mixture Model (GMM) is trained as context dependent, speaker independent and contains 3886 physical states. The training data for this model contained 270 h of speech recordings. The parameters utilized for the DNN training were as follows: 5 hidden layers with a decreasing number of neurons per hidden layer (1024-1024-768-768-512), ReLU activation function, mini-batches of size 1024, 35 training epochs, learning rate 0.08. For input signal parameterization, log filter banks were employed with context windows of 5-1-5 and local normalization was performed within one-second windows.

The linguistic part of the system was composed of a lexicon and a language model. The lexicon contained 550k entries with multiple pronunciation variants and the language model was based on N-grams. For practical reasons (mainly with respect to the very large vocabulary size), the system used bigrams. However, 20% of all "word-pairs" actually include sequences containing three or more words, as the lexicon contains 4k multi-word collocations. The unseen bigrams are backed-off by Kneser-Ney smoothing.

6.1   Experimental Results

Results obtained after transcription of test sets (a) with and (b) without the use of the SAD module are presented in Table 7. This table contains values of WER and Corr. Moreover, also values of RTF are presented to show computational demands with and without SAD.

Table 7. Evaluation of the proposed SAD approach for speech transcription.

Test set	Live news TV channel		Local radio station	
SAD module	Yes	No	Yes	No
WER [%]	12.4	12.7	14.0	17.9
Corr [%]	89.7	89.7	88.5	88.4
RTF	2.4	1.3	13.3	1.2

The reached results show that the utilization of the proposed SAD approach was advantageous on both test sets. The number of insertions coming from the non-speech parts was limited and hardly any speech parts were omitted.

With SAD module employed, the transcription system operated with improved accuracy and, at the same time, with RTF almost two times, and more than eleven times higher for the first and second test set, respectively. Of course, the reason for this difference is that the data in the second set contained fewer speech segments. Note that RTF of the SAD module itself is around 80 and all presented RTF values were measured using processor Intel Core i7-3770K @ 3.50GHz.

The transcription system complemented with SAD can also be utilized for online transcription without any major delay, because its latency is around 2 s.

7   Conclusions

In this paper, various approaches to SAD were investigated and evaluated. The resulting developed SAD module is suitable in offline as well as online speech transcription systems. The module employs a DNN-based speech/ non-speech classifier and training data created artificially by mixing speech and non-speech recordings at various levels of SNR. The core of the module is formed by a WFST-based decoder that smooths the output from DNN using a context-based model in which both the speech and non-speech events are represented as sequences of states.

It has been shown that the module yields state-of-the-art results on QUT-NOISE-TIMIT data set in low and medium noise conditions. Its utilization to a speech transcription leads to (a) significant increase in RTF of the whole transcription process, and (b) a slight decrease in WER. The former advantage is namely important for 24/7 monitoring of streams containing a large proportion of music (e.g., local radio stations), where the computational demands on the transcription system can be reduced greatly.

There are two possible ways of the future development of our SAD module. The first focuses on the SAD module itself, various deep neural networks architectures, such as RNNs, and different feature extraction techniques could be investigated. The latter option lies in application of QUT-NOISE-TIMIT corpus in combination with our artificial data to create even more robust detector.

Acknowledgements. This work was supported by the Technology Agency of the Czech Republic (Project No. TA04010199) and partly by the Student Grant Scheme 2017 of the Technical University in Liberec.

References

1. Benyassine, A., Shlomot, E., Su, H.Y., Massaloux, D., Lamblin, C., Petit, J.P.: ITU-T recommendation G.729 annex B: a silence compression scheme for use with G.729 optimized for V.70 digital simultaneous voice and data applications. IEEE Commun. Mag. **35**(9), 64–73 (1997)
2. Chung, H., Lee, S.J., Lee, Y.: Endpoint detection using weighted finite state transducer. In: INTERSPEECH, pp. 700–703. ISCA (2013)
3. Dahl, G., Yu, D., Deng, L., Acero, A.: Context-dependent pre-trained deep neural networks for large-vocabulary speech recognition. IEEE Trans. Audio Speech Lang. Process. **20**(1), 30–42 (2012)
4. Dean, D., Sridharan, S., Vogt, R., Mason, M.: The QUT-NOISE-TIMIT corpus for the evaluation of voice activity detection algorithms. In: INTERSPEECH, pp. 3110–3113. ISCA (2010)
5. Evangelopoulos, G., Maragos, P.: Speech event detection using multiband modulation energy. In: INTERSPEECH, pp. 685–688. ISCA (2005)
6. Eyben, F., Weninger, F., Squartini, S., Schuller, B.: Real-life voice activity detection with LSTM recurrent neural networks and an application to hollywood movies. In: ICASSP, pp. 483–487, May 2013
7. Fisher, W.M., Doddington, G.R., Goudie-Marshall, K.M.: The DARPA speech recognition research database: specifications and status. In: Proceedings of DARPA Workshop on Speech Recognition, pp. 93–99 (1986)
8. Gao, C., Saikumar, G., Khanwalkar, S., Herscovici, A., Kumar, A., Srivastava, A., Natarajan, P.: Online speech activity detection in broadcast news. In: INTERSPEECH, pp. 2637–2640. ISCA (2011)
9. Ghaemmaghami, H., Baker, B., Vogt, R., Sridharan, S.: Noise robust voice activity detection using features extracted from the time-domain autocorrelation function. In: INTERSPEECH, pp. 3118–3121. ISCA (2010)

10. Ghaemmaghami, H., Dean, D., Kalantari, S., Sridharan, S., Fookes, C.: Complete-linkage clustering for voice activity detection in audio and visual speech. In: INTERSPEECH, pp. 2292–2296 (2015)
11. Hughes, T., Mierle, K.: Recurrent neural networks for voice activity detection. In: ICASSP, pp. 7378–7382. IEEE (2013)
12. Kotnik, B., Kacic, Z., Horvat, B.: A multiconditional robust front-end feature extraction with a noise reduction procedure based on improved spectral subtraction algorithm. In: INTERSPEECH, pp. 197–200. ISCA (2001)
13. Li, J.Y., Liu, B., Wang, R.H., Dai, L.R.: A complexity reduction of ETSI advanced front-end for DSR. In: ICASSP, vol. 1, pp. I-61–4, May 2004
14. Liu, B., Hoffmeister, B., Rastrow, A.: Accurate endpointing with expected pause duration. In: INTERSPEECH, pp. 2912–2916. ISCA (2015)
15. Ma, J.: Improving the speech activity detection for the DARPA RATS phase-3 evaluation. In: INTERSPEECH, pp. 1558–1562. ISCA (2014)
16. Mateju, L., Cerva, P., Zdansky, J.: Study on the use of deep neural networks for speech activity detection in broadcast recordings. In: Proceedings of the 13th International Joint Conference on e-Business and Telecommunications - Volume 5: SIGMAP, pp. 45–51 (2016)
17. Mateju, L., Cerva, P., Zdansky, J., Malek, J.: Speech activity detection in online broadcast transcription using deep neural networks and weighted finite state transducers. In: Submitted to ICASSP (2017)
18. Moattar, M.H., Homayounpour, M.M.: A simple but efficient real-time voice activity detection algorithm. In: 2009 17th European Signal Processing Conference, pp. 2549–2553, August 2009
19. Ng, T., Zhang, B., Nguyen, L., Matsoukas, S., Zhou, X., Mesgarani, N., Vesely, K., Matejka, P.: Developing a speech activity detection system for the DARPA RATS program. In: INTERSPEECH, pp. 1969–1972. ISCA (2012)
20. Ramırez, J., Segura, J.C., Benıtez, C., Torre, A.D.L., Rubio, A.: Efficient voice activity detection algorithms using long-term speech information. Speech Commun. **42**, 3–4 (2004)
21. Räsänen, O.J., Laine, U.K., Altosaar, T.: An improved speech segmentation quality measure: the R-value. In: INTERSPEECH, pp. 1851–1854 (2009)
22. Ryant, N., Liberman, M., Yuan, J.: Speech activity detection on Youtube using deep neural networks. In: INTERSPEECH, pp. 728–731. ISCA (2013)
23. Saon, G., Thomas, S., Soltau, H., Ganapathy, S., Kingsbury, B.: The IBM speech activity detection system for the DARPA RATS program. In: INTERSPEECH, pp. 3497–3501. ISCA (2013)
24. Shin, J.W., Chang, J.H., Kim, N.S.: Voice activity detection based on statistical models and machine learning approaches. Comput. Speech Lang. **24**(3), 515–530 (2010). doi:10.1016/j.csl.2009.02.003
25. Sohn, J., Kim, N.S., Sung, W.: A statistical model-based voice activity detection. IEEE Signal Process. Lett. **6**(1), 1–3 (1999)
26. Sriskandaraja, K., Sethu, V., Le, P.N., Ambikairajah, E.: A model based voice activity detector for noisy environments. In: INTERSPEECH, pp. 2297–2301 (2015)
27. Thomas, S., Saon, G., Segbroeck, M.V., Narayanan, S.S.: Improvements to the IBM speech activity detection system for the DARPA RATS program. In: ICASSP, pp. 4500–4504. IEEE (2015)
28. Tsiartas, A., Chaspari, T., Katsamanis, N., Ghosh, P.K., Li, M., Segbroeck, M.V., Potamianos, A., Narayanan, S.: Multi-band long-term signal variability features for robust voice activity detection. In: INTERSPEECH, pp. 718–722 (2013)

29. Wang, Q., Du, J., Bao, X., Wang, Z.R., Dai, L.R., Lee, C.H.: A universal VAD based on jointly trained deep neural networks. In: INTERSPEECH, pp. 2282–2286. ISCA (2015)
30. Wisdom, S., Okopal, G., Atlas, L., Pitton, J.: Voice activity detection using subband noncircularity. In: ICASSP, pp. 4505–4509, April 2015
31. Zhang, X.L., Wang, D.: Boosted deep neural networks and multi-resolution cochleagram features for voice activity detection. In: INTERSPEECH, pp. 1534–1538. ISCA (2014)
32. Zhang, X.L., Wu, J.: Deep belief networks based voice activity detection. IEEE Trans. Audio Speech Lang. Process. **21**(4), 697–710 (2013)

Boundless Reconstruction Using Regularized 3D Fusion

M.A.A. Rajput[1(✉)], E. Funk[1], A. Börner[1], and O. Hellwich[2]

[1] Department of Information Processing for Optical Systems,
Institute of Optical Sensor Systems, German Aerospace Center, Berlin, Germany
{muhammad.rajput,eugen.funk,anko.boerner}@dlr.de
[2] Computer Vision and Remote Sensing, Technical University Berlin,
Berlin, Germany
olaf.hellwich@tu-berlin.de

Abstract. 3D reconstruction from image based depth sensor is essential part of many offline or online robotic applications. Numerous techniques have been developed to integrate multiple depth maps to create 3D model of environment, however accuracy of the reconstructed 3D model exclusively depends upon the precision of depth sensing. Economical depth sensors such as Kinect and stereo camera sensors provide imprecise depth data which affect the integration process and produce unwanted noisy surfaces in 3D model. There exist several approaches which use image filtering based depth map denoising, however applying filtering directly on depth data can result in inconsistent and deformed 3D model. In this paper we investigate and extend a recursive variant of total variation based filtering to incorporate multi-view based depth images while applying implicit depth smoothing. Proposed framework uses sparse voxel representation to aid large scale 3D model reconstruction and is shown to reduce absolute surface error of final reconstructed 3D model by up to 77% in comparison with state of the art 3D fusion techniques.

Keywords: Large scale automated 3D modelling · Mobile robotics · Efficient data structures · 3D database

1 Introduction

Robotic applications equipped with visual depth sensors gained strong developmental momentum in recent years. Almost all robots are designed to utilize some degree of depth sensing for self localization and map generation, such maps play a vital role in terms of re-usability by other robots or human inspection. Guided or unguided robots equipped with economical visual depth scanning equipments (such as Kinect, Stereo camera based depth sensor and Kinect2) can be deployed to inspect areas which are inaccessible for human interaction. It is possible to reconstruct a 3D model of robot's journey using recorded stream of depth images by the process of incremental reconstruction. Various factors such as low or high

© Springer International Publishing AG 2017
M.S. Obaidat (Ed): ICETE 2016, CCIS 764, pp. 359–378, 2017.
https://doi.org/10.1007/978-3-319-67876-4_17

lighting, distance of perceived object and cost of sensor determines the suitability and selection of depth sensor and hence affect the overall 3D reconstructed model.

For similar reasons mobile robotic community focuses its research and development towards implementing frameworks for 3D reconstruction and modeling. Unfortunately, 3D reconstruction is notoriously complicated research problem which suffers prominently on quality of acquired depth data, process of incremental reconstruction (fusion) and trajectory of sensor movement (localization). Improving the localization of sensor movement and increasing the quality of depth data are independent research fields and there exist numerous techniques to improve both aspects, but process of fusion is somehow primeval to accommodate and remove unwanted noise at the time of fusion. Reconstruction of such models can take hours or even weeks depending upon the scale of environment, and models are highly affected if the system is expected to produce real-time fusion. However, a system capable of incremental real-time updates on large-scale reconstruction is vital for applications such as robot navigation [1,2], area inspection [3], virtual and/or augmented reality [4,5] and change detection [6]. In recent years few methods have been proposed to produce 3D models of observable geometry through RGB-D measurements [7–9].

These however, do not cater the issue of acquired noise in depth data and hence the resulting model is directly dependant on the quality of the captured RGB-D measurements. Sensor measurements inform of RGB-D images are highly affected by depth sensing mechanism and surroundings. For example RGB-D measurements from active depth sensors such as Kinect and ASUS Xtion pro are affected directly by the distance of observed object from sensor, while Time of flight (ToF) sensors based sensor such as Kinect2 are shown to misjudge depth of dark surfaces. Similarly passive depth sensors such as stereo camera based depth sensors are prone to produce unwanted noise with textured planar surfaces.

Image based depth smoothing schemes as used in KinectFusion [10] are shown to produce stair-case effect in reconstruction. This motivated the research on the noise suppression with the use of Total Variation (TV) filtering embedded at the core of RFusion [11]. The main contribution of this paper is the extension of RFusion to work with depth maps from multi-view image stream and to improve the underlying processing to increase the processing speed.

RFusion is an incremental 3D fusion fusion framework with sparse voxel data structure which enables it to process and store large scale 3D models. Section 2 introduces state of art volumetric 3D fusion frameworks aligned with the presented approach. In Sect. 4 core principal of RFusion is presented which elucidates the novelty of underlying principal. We demonstrate applications, quantitative comparison and evaluation of presented approach with two selected state of art techniques Sect. 5. Final remarks and future aspects are described in Sect. 6.

2   Literature Overview

2.1   Reconstruction

Early real-time dense approaches [12,13] were able to estimate the image depth from monocular input, but their use of a dense voxel grid limited reconstruction to small volumes and to powerful GPU devices due to high memory and computation requirements. Also suffering from the scalability issue, KinectFusion [7,10] directly sensed depth using active sensors and fused the high quality depth measurements over time to surfaces. The scalability issue has been resolved by voxel hierarchy approaches [14] or direct voxel block hashing [8] to avoid storing unnecessary data for free space allowing scaling to unbounded scenes. At the core, the mentioned approaches rely on the volumetric fusion arithmetic from [15], which expects accurate depth measurements. Thus, the issues with error prone data remains uncovered.

2.2   Noise Suppression and Fusion

Regarding the noise suppression of error prone depth measurements, direct depth image filtering became state of the art and has been applied in several projects [12,13]. Basically, the TVL_1 technique from [16] is applied enforcing the photo consistency and depth smoothness between multiple images observing the same object. This approach delivers high quality results given depth measurements of low quality. However, the TVL_1 fusion computation is performed every time a new depth image is added to the scene leading to slow frame rates.

3   Research Objectives

This work addresses the extension of application domain and implementation improvements of RFusion to achieve further processing speed. Furthermore, we address both critical challenges identified from the literature in upcoming text, which are: (i) The reconstruction of unbounded environments. This is addressed by the method of [7]. (ii) The 3D fusion of error prone depth data into a volumetric 3D space, which is the main aspect of this work. The goal of this research was to perform TV fusion directly on the 3D voxel space while replacing the L_1 cost by a recursive L_2 optimization.

4   Methodology

In state of art 3D fusion frameworks whether they are of online or offline nature, orientation of sensor (generally referred as sensor pose) is extremely significant information and is calculated for each image instance using a variety of Visual-SLAM techniques [17–20], the problem of estimating camera pose is generally

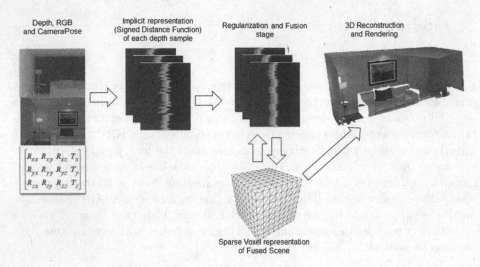

Fig. 1. Simplified fusion process with RFusion.

referred to as tracking problem. Pure Visual-SLAM techniques use visual camera tracking from frame to frame or globally consistant model to estimate sensor orientation [17–19], while others [20] fuse ego-motion of the sensor calculated by variety of sensors with visual odometry to further enhance the estimate and produce better tracking results. Extensive research has been conducted on various traits of the tracking problem and since the main focus of this work is to enhance the fusion process, we postulate that camera poses for each depth image are calculated prior to fusion process. Simplified diagram of the proposed framework is shown in Fig. 1. At first, RGB and Depth images from depth sensor along with respective camera pose are represented using implicit surfaces (in 3D) followed by regularization and fusion (RFusion) stage which process implicit surfaces and reduces the depth noise while respecting 3D geometry. Finaly sparse voxels and mesh generated.

4.1 Camera Model and World Representation

In order to align our framework with existing fusion techniques while maintaining generalization, we designed our proposed framework to handle a sequence of depth and color images captured with standard depth and color cameras. In the special case of stereo cameras we assume that disparity maps are converted into above mentioned depth maps and aligned color images are pre-calculated. We further assume that standard intrinsic properties such as central point $c = (c_x, c_y)$ and focal lengths (f_x, f_y) of both color and depth cameras are known. In case of offline processing our framework accepts input stream of depth and color images with time stamp $[0, 1, ..., n]$. At time instance t, we employ depth image $\mathbf{Z}_t$ and color image $\mathbf{I}_t$ from input stream, however respective camera pose at t consisting of rotation $R_t \in SO(3)$ and translation $T_t \in \mathbb{R}^3$ can be computed from SLAM techniques. Every $pixel(row, col)$ on depth image plane can be mapped to a global 3D point in world space $P_w \in \mathbb{R}^3$ by

$$P_w = R_t \cdot \begin{bmatrix} (row - c_x)\frac{Zt(row,col)}{f_x} \\ (col - c_y)\frac{Zt(row,col)}{f_y} \\ \mathbf{Z}t(row, col) \end{bmatrix} + T_t. \tag{1}$$

Additional desired scaling can be applied to P_w to incorporate multi-scale representation. In some situations where voxel space and model have different scales, the model can be re-sampled in 3D voxel space. Each voxel $V_{(x,y,z)} \in \mathbb{R}^3$ contains a signed distance function value to the corresponding projective iso-surface.

In traditional volumetric depth integration based 3D fusion Levoy et al. suggested to use a truncated signed distance function (TSDF) which is computed for all voxels. Such dense computation of TSDF is only viable when the model is relatively small. State of the art volumetric approaches [8,9] adopted the use of voxel integration using weighted addition of TSDF values.

For reasonably small objects or environments TSDF can be calculated for the whole observable environment, however such dense calculation does not works when dealing with large scale environments such as a room. For large scale reconstruction, existing state of the art techniques (such as InfiniTAM and Fast-Fusion) use voxel blocks which are only initialized along the expected surface and hence the calculation is reduced drastically. In contrast to the either dense or voxel block SDF we lean towards the use of the idea proposed by Funk et al. [7] in which fusion framework access and manipulate voxels which lie along-the-ray from camera origin Cam_w to all 3D samples in world space P_w, we denote such voxels collection as SDF-signal and an example of such selection is illustrated in Fig. 2.

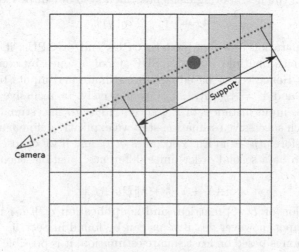

Fig. 2. SDF signal and selected voxels [11].

This particular selection of voxels provides reasonable surface estimation while using very low amount of read/write access to implicit representation. We use the Truncated Signed Distance Function (TSDF) in our implementation in which each voxel's TSDF value can range between $[+1, ..., -1]$, such truncation of values based on number of voxels in SDF signal (referred compactly as *support* in further description) ensures that the zero-crossing (also known as iso-surface) lies at center element of SDF-signal. Usability of SDF-signal in the recursive fusion framework is explained in Sect. 6.

In order to avoid localization estimation error which can affect the fusion process, we incorporate ground truth camera poses to obtain high quality 3D reconstruction. This assumption plays vital role in experimentation process and ensures that every aspect of proposed framework is evaluated.

4.2 Regularized 3D Fusion

In contrast with existing techniques which work on the principle of convergence based estimation and noise suppression, our system solves a system of linear equations to estimate depth and fuse multiple depth samples in a recursive manner. The proposed system treats the surface estimation from depth samples as linear least squares estima-tion problem and hence fusion system can be expressed using standard notation

$$\|Ax + y\|_2^2 \tag{2}$$

where x is the estimated TSDF value for a particular voxel in world space derived from input TSDF value y. We further presume that transformation between y and x is linear in nature. To introduce total variation based regularization effects in Eq. 2 we introduce a regularization term consisting of regularization parameter λ combined with penalization function $g(y)$ which penalizes every element depending upon the neighboring elements. Such system can be expressed as

$$\|Ax + y\|_2^2 + \lambda \|g(y)\|_2^2 \tag{3}$$

To utilize computation power of modern CPUs and/or GPUs, it is possible to access and update multiple values of SDF-signal at once by containing them in vector form. Hence vector based system estimate and inputs becomes, $X = \{x_0, x_1, ..., x_n\}$ and $Y = \{y_0, y_1, ..., y_n\}$ respectively. In recursive least squares systems, various input instances of Y can contribute to the estimation of system X hence for each successive estimation step we explicitly define v as latest input instance. Therefore $g(y)$ from Eq. 3 becomes $g(v)$, and if we choose the penalization function to be a second order finite difference function, then Eq. 3 can be re-written as

$$\|AX + Y\|_2^2 + \lambda \|Dv + C\|_2^2 \tag{4}$$

Actual derivation of D, C matrices and simplification of Eq. 4 is beyond the scope of this paper, however detail steps can be found in Sect. 6.

Since RFusion is based on least square estimation, it is possible to implement various variants of least square estimation. For our implementation we derived a recursive variant of RFusion which allows incremental updates while performing the regularization at each stage of depth fusion on TSDF values.

Fig. 3. (left) Representation of implicit surface with noise (right) effects of regularization parameter [11].

A 2D implementation of RFusion is used to highlight noise suppression and optimized depth estimation effects of regularization. To highlight the inherent regularization of RFusion while avoiding the smoothness by fusion of multiple depth data, we use a single synthetic implicit surface as shown in Fig. 3 (left) and applied RFusion. The effectiveness of TV filtering can be observed from Fig. 3 (right) in which only a single implicit surface was processed; this behavior can play vital role in smoothing surfaces when a portion of the observed surface has limited instances of depth samples.

4.3   Multi-view to Depth Maps

Various open-source libraries (such as OpenMVG[1], MVE[2] etc.) provide functionality to convert multi-view images to depth images and color images, however this type of direct conversion is highly affected by localization estimation error. It is possible to obtain high quality depth maps after using bundle adjustments and loop closure techniques on multi-view images. We used the system pipeline proposed by Strackenbrock et al. [21] to convert multi-view images to high quality depth maps.

4.4   Update Algorithm

It is possible to update and fuse the complete SDF-signal in a single instance as suggested by Eq. 4. A simplified Algorithm 1 briefly explains estimation of SDF-signal, however in actual implementation RFusion uses multi-threads to utilize latest CPU computation power. At first we instantiate a sparse voxel data structure proposed by [7] in line 1 followed by the series of steps depending upon the locality of a particular depth sample. These steps are:

- calculation of 3D world coordinate P_w at (*row, col*), line 10
- getting RGB value at (*row, col*), line 11

---

[1] http://imagine.enpc.fr/~moulonp/openMVG/.
[2] http://www.gcc.tu-darmstadt.de/home/proj/mve/.

- generating linear TSDF values (i.e. $[+1, ..., -1]$) depending upon the *support*, line 12
- reading current SDF value from voxels and creating SDF signal from W, line 13
- getting value of d and c matrices using method described in Sect. 6
- compute the new SDF signal x_t from previous estimate $\hat{x}_{t-1}$, line 15
- updating W with latest estimate for a particular depth sample in line 16.

Algorithm 1. Simplified RFusion algorithm [11].

1: let $W \leftarrow$ DataStructure (from [7])
2: **procedure** FUSE
3:     $t \leftarrow$ currentFrame
4:     $\mathbf{I}_t \leftarrow$ RGB image and $\mathbf{Z}_t \leftarrow$ Depth image
5:     $T_t \leftarrow$ Translation
6:     $R_t \leftarrow$ Rotation
7:     support $\leftarrow 5$
8:     **for** $i = 0$ to $rows$-1 **do**
9:         **for** $j = 0$ to $cols$-1 **do**
10:         $P_w \leftarrow R_t \cdot \begin{bmatrix} (x - c_x)\frac{\mathbf{Z}t(x,y)}{f_x} \\ (y - c_y)\frac{\mathbf{Z}t(x,y)}{f_y} \\ \mathbf{Z}t(x,y) \end{bmatrix} + T_t.$
11:             color $\leftarrow \mathbf{I}_t$.getColor(i,j)
12:             $y_t \leftarrow$ getTSDF()
13:             $\hat{x}_{t-1} \leftarrow W$.readVoxels($P_w$,$T_t$,support)
14:             $[d,c] \leftarrow W$.getDC(x)   ▷ from Equation. (20)
15:             estimate $\hat{x}_t$ ▷ from Equation (21)
16:             W.updateSystem($\hat{x}_t$,color)
17:         **end for**
18:     **end for**
19: $t \leftarrow t + 1$
20: **end procedure**

---

5   Experiments

In order to examine the working of RFusion and test the regularization aspect, we did experiments on both synthetic and realistic datasets. A synthetic dataset by ICL-NUIM was chosen to gather quantitative evaluation results since ground truth surface as well as trajectory were known while use of realistic dataset highlights the application of RFusion with existing sensor systems.

5.1   Synthetic Dataset

RGB-D benchmark dataset [22] by ICL-NUIM consists of the four trajectories of virtual camera movement inside a textured living room environment while capturing depth and color images along the way. The dataset contains combination of sharp and planar objects which allows it to be highly effective for evaluation of depth fusion and 3D reconstruction frameworks. Moreover there exists a variant

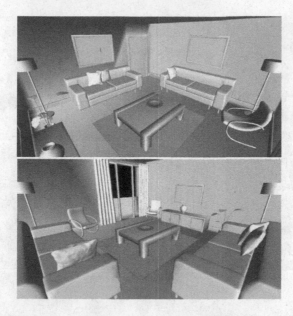

Fig. 4. The interior of our synthetic living room scene (color removed to highlight geometry). The scene is composed of various common objects e.g. vase, table, lamp, chairs, sofa etc. [22].

of all trajectories with noisy depth samples which is targeted to mimic the noise in real sensor depth perception. In our experimentation we used both clean as well as noisy datasets to evaluate the 3D reconstruction by RFusion. Figure 4 shows a screenshot of the living room RGB-D dataset.

5.2 Evaluation of Synthetic Dataset

After mandatory scaling and alignment of reconstructed models from synthetic dataset, we evaluated the reconstructed models by comparing them with the ground truth model. For each vertex in the reconstructed model a closest triangle is registered and perpendicular distance is recorded. Five standard statistics (Mean, Median, Standard Deviation, Min and Max etc.) were computed from the recorded distance as suggested by [22]. For the sake of simplicity, the quality of reconstruction is evaluated with the help of absolute surface error, Tables 1 and 2 show mean absolute surface error in meters for clean and noisy datasets respectively. Figure 6 shows color coded error maps generated by re-projecting absolute surface error onto reconstructed model.

Candidates for quantitative comparison are following fusion frameworks:

1. Fast Fusion [9]
2. InfiniTAM[3] [8]
3. RFusion

---

[3] We were unable to modify the working of InfiniTAM to use ground truth camera poses from ICL-NUIM dataset we are using the Mean values published in [8] for this dataset.

Fig. 5. Screenshots from reconstructed model with RFusion (left column) and FastFusion (right column) [11].

Table 1. Comparision of absolute surface error (in meters) [11].

Dataset	Method		
	RFusion	FastFusion	InfiniTAM
LR0	**0.003045**	0.011895	0.008900
LR1	0.002947	0.011204	**0.002900**
LR2	**0.003183**	0.006634	0.008800
LR3	**0.002978**	0.018180	0.041000

To maintain coherence and avoid biased analysis we used ground truth camera poses in both FastFusion and RFusion which ensures that reconstruction is only evaluated on the basis of depth fusion instead of camera pose estimation error. Figure 5 shows the reconstruction with RFusion vs FastFusion. On close inspection it was found that RFusion was able to successfully produce consistent surfaces for miniscule details of model (such as lamp pole, leaves of plants and planar patches of wall).

Table 2. Comparision of absolute surface error on noisy dataset (in meters) [11].

Dataset	Method	
	RFusion ($\lambda = 0.3$)	FastFusion
LR0	**0.01336**	0.05672
LR1	**0.01416**	0.07523
LR2	**0.01979**	0.07082
LR3	**0.02090**	0.06643

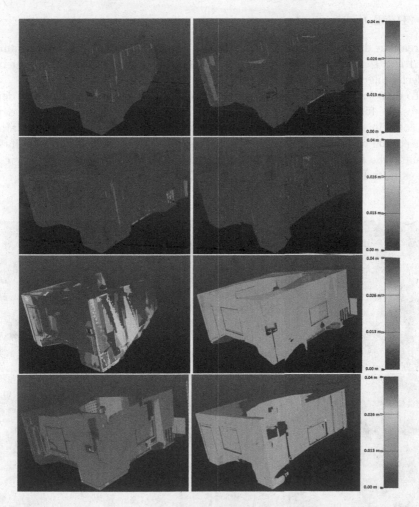

Fig. 6. Color coded errormaps from RFusion (Upper 2 rows) vs FastFusion (Bottom 2 rows) along with absolute color scale used to generate errormaps [11] (Color figure online).

Due to vectorized based implementation of RFusion which optimized the use of memory accesses, processing performance of RFusion has been improved from 4–5 frames per second to ˜10 frames per second. In our experimentation we found that although FastFusion outperforms RFusion in terms of processing speed but quality of reconstructed models suggest that RFusion outperforms both InfiniTAM and FastFusion.

System used for experimentation has the following specifications: Intel Core i7-4790, 8 GB RAM with Windows 7 (64-bit) OS.

5.3   Realistic Dataset

For realistic dataset, we use depth and color images captured from stereo camera based IPS sensor [23] and multi-view images captured with quadrocopter over Andechs pilgrimage.

To demonstrate the effectiveness of RFusion with limited instances of depth images, we fused 40 instances of depth and color images. Some arbitrary depth and color images from IPS dataset are shown in Fig. 8. For multi-view dataset we used 400 high resolution color images captured from multiple view points to evaluate the large scale depth fusion aspect of RFusion. Some arbitrary color images from IPS dataset are shown in Fig. 7.

Fig. 7. Arbitrary images from quadrocopter flight.

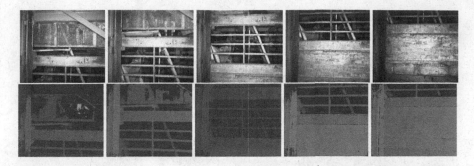

Fig. 8. Arbitrary instances of color and depth images captured from IPS sensor.

Camera poses for IPS dataset ware calculated by fusing camera poses from visual-SLAM and IMU while for multi-view dataset camera poses were estimated with structure from motion estimation combined with bundle adjustment algorithms.

5.4 Evaluation of Realistic Dataset

Due to the realistic nature of data only visual inspection of the reconstructed surface can be examined. Screenshots from reconstructed models are shown in Figs. 9 and 10 for IPS and multi-view dataset, respectively.

Fig. 9. Reconstructed model with IPS dataset.

Fig. 10. Large-Scale reconstruction with multi-view dataset.

6   Conclusion and Outlook

In this paper we presented an extension of RFusion which is shown to produce high quality 3D models from depth images from multi-view datasets by the use of L2 regularization based TV filtering. We demonstrated that RFusion can be extended to handle generic depth maps, and large scale environments can be modeled with RFusion. We also demonstrated that with the targeted implementation of RFusion (i.e. vectorized implementation), it is possible to enhance the processing capability while retaining the inherent noise suppression aspect. Furthermore, it would be interesting to investigate the online and real-time application of RFusion in future research exploration.

Appendix

Derivation of RFusion

In this section we derive the equations of RFusion, for the sake of better readability we will simplify the equations for 2D fusion system rather than 3D fusion system. Assuming n = support of SDF signal, $\hat{x}$ is the estimated state of system for a particular 3D voxel and y = new TSDF signal. Then such system can easily be described by the following equation;

$$y = \phi\hat{x}$$
$$\hat{x} = (\phi^T\phi)\phi^T y \qquad (5)$$

In order to integrate the true aspect of second order finite difference it is assumed that

$$\hat{Y} = Y - \lambda D^T C \qquad (6)$$

Since Eq. 5 is only valid if we have single input SDF signal, we assume that we have multiple SDF signals, Then we can extend Eq. 5 for batch based least square system as follows

$$\begin{bmatrix} y_{0*1} \\ y_{0*2} \\ \\ ... \\ \\ y_{0*n} \\ y_{1*1} \\ \\ ... \\ \\ y_{m*n} \end{bmatrix} = \begin{bmatrix} 1\ 0\ 0\ 0\ 0 \\ 0\ 1\ 0\ 0\ 0 \\ \\ ... \\ \\ 0\ 0\ 0\ 0\ 1 \\ 1\ 0\ 0\ 0\ 0 \\ \\ ... \\ \\ 0\ 0\ 0\ 0\ 1 \end{bmatrix} \hat{x}$$

where m is the number of SDF signals about to be merged

$$\hat{Y} = \Phi x$$
$$x = (\Phi^T\Phi)\Phi^T\hat{Y}$$

The regularized variant of the batch-based system can be re-written as

$$\hat{x} = \left(\Phi^T\Phi + \lambda D^T D\right)\Phi^T\hat{Y} \qquad (7)$$

where λ is a regularization parameter. In order to convert batch based to recursive system we assume that Φ, Y and D follow recursive succession

$$\Phi_{k+1} = \begin{bmatrix} \Phi_k \\ \phi \end{bmatrix} \quad \hat{Y}_{k+1} = \begin{bmatrix} \hat{Y}_k \\ \hat{y} \end{bmatrix} \quad and D_{k+1} = \begin{bmatrix} D_k \\ d \end{bmatrix}$$

Equation (7) for $k + 1$ instance can be written as

$$\hat{x_{k+1}} = \left(\Phi_{k+1}^T\Phi_{k+1} + \lambda D_{k+1}^T D_{k+1}\right)^{-1}\phi_{k+1}^T\hat{Y}_{k+1} \qquad (8)$$

For better readability we use substitution of P_{k+1}^{-1} from Equation (15), and using the recursive versions of Φ and Y we get

$$\hat{x_{k+1}} = P_{k+1}\Phi_{k+1}^T\hat{Y}_{k+1}$$
$$P_{k+1}^{-1}\hat{x_{k+1}} = \Phi_{k+1}^T\hat{Y}_{k+1} \qquad (9)$$

Similarly for k^{th} instance

$$\Phi_k^T \hat{Y}_k = P_k^{-1} \hat{x}_k \qquad (10)$$

Resuming from Eq. (9) we get

$$\hat{x_{k+1}} = P_{k+1}\left[\Phi_k^T \hat{Y}_k + \phi^T \hat{y}_{k+1}\right]$$

By using the value of $\Phi_k^T Y_k$ from Eq. (10) we get

$$\hat{x_{k+1}} = P_{k+1}\left[P_k^{-1} \hat{x}_k + \phi^T \hat{y}_{k+1}\right]$$

By using the value of P_k^{-1} from Eq. (16) we get

$$\hat{x}_{k+1} = P_{k+1}\left[\left(P_{k+1}^{-1} - (\phi^T\phi + \lambda d^T d)\right)\hat{x}_k + \phi^T \hat{y}_{k+1}\right]$$

$$= \left(P_{k+1}P_{k+1}^{-1} - P_{k+1}(\phi^T\phi + \lambda d^T d)\right)\hat{x}_k + P_{k+1}\phi^T \hat{y}_{k+1}$$

$$= P_{k+1}P_{k+1}^{-1}\hat{x}_k - P_{k+1}(\phi^T\phi + \lambda d^T d)\hat{x}_k + P_{k+1}\phi^T \hat{y}_{k+1}$$

$$= \hat{x}_k - P_{k+1}\left(\phi^T\phi + \lambda d^T d\right)\hat{x}_k + P_{k+1}\phi^T \hat{y}_{k+1}$$

$$\hat{x}_{k+1} = \hat{x}_k + P_{k+1}\left[\phi\hat{y}_{k+1} - (\phi^T\phi + \lambda d^T d)\hat{x}_k\right] \qquad (11)$$

by using the assumption of Eq. (6) we can further assume that

$$\hat{y}_{k+1} = y_{k+1} - \lambda d^T c$$

Hence the final Eq. (11) for RFusion will become

$$\hat{x}_{k+1} = \hat{x}_k + P_{k+1}\left[\phi(y_{k+1} - \lambda d^T c) - (\phi^T\phi + \lambda d^T d)\hat{x}_k\right] \qquad (12)$$

From the fundamental regularized LSE Equation

$$\hat{x_{k+1}} = \left(\Phi^T\Phi + \lambda D^T D\right)^{-1}\Phi^T y$$

where $P_k = \left(\Phi^T\Phi + \lambda D^T D\right)^{-1}$ $\qquad (13)$

$$P_k^{-1} = \left(\Phi^T\Phi + \lambda D^T D\right) \qquad (14)$$

For the recursive part we can extend the Φ and D matrices as

$$\Phi_{k+1} = \begin{bmatrix} \Phi_k \\ \phi \end{bmatrix} \quad \text{and} \quad D_{k+1} = \begin{bmatrix} D_k \\ d \end{bmatrix}$$

Then Eq. (14) will become

$$P_{k+1} = \left(\begin{bmatrix} \Phi_k \\ \phi \end{bmatrix} \begin{bmatrix} \Phi_k & \phi \end{bmatrix} + \lambda \begin{bmatrix} D_k \\ d \end{bmatrix} \begin{bmatrix} D_k & d \end{bmatrix} \right)^{-1}$$

$$P_{k+1} = \left(\Phi_k^T \Phi + \phi^T \phi + \lambda D_k^T D + \lambda d^T d \right)^{-1}$$

$$P_{k+1} = \left((\Phi_k^T \Phi + \lambda D_k^T D) + \phi^T \phi + \lambda d^T d \right)^{-1}$$

$$P_{k+1} = \left(P_k^{-1} + (\phi^T \phi + \lambda d^T d) \right)^{-1} \tag{15}$$

$$P_{k+1}^{-1} = P_k^{-1} + (\phi^T \phi + \lambda d^T d)$$

$$P_k^{-1} = P_{k+1}^{-1} - (\phi^T \phi + \lambda d^T d) \tag{16}$$

$$P_{k+1} = \left(P_k^{-1} + \begin{bmatrix} \phi^T \phi & I \end{bmatrix} \begin{bmatrix} I \\ \lambda d^T d \end{bmatrix} \right)^{-1}$$

For simplicity assuming
$B = \begin{bmatrix} \phi^T \phi & I \end{bmatrix}$ and $C = \begin{bmatrix} I \\ \lambda d^T d \end{bmatrix}$ we get

$$P_{k+1} = \left(P_k^{-1} + BC \right)^{-1}$$

Using matrix inversion lemma

$$(A + BC)^{-1} = A^{-1} - A^{-1} B (I + C A^{-1} B)^{-1} C A^{-1}$$

$$P_{k+1} = P_k - P_k B (I + C P_k B)^{-1} C P_k \tag{17}$$

Formulation of D Matrix

Since we are dealing with elements in a 2D matrix each cell and respective neighboring cells can be accessed by their respective spatial information (i.e. row and column values in case of 2D). However the actual implementation of the proposed technique is carried out to handle 3D depth fusion. For each voxel value a_k (where $0 \le k \le support$) in the vector SDF signal v, assuming that i and j are index values of row and column respectively for accessing a_k in Eq. (18), finite difference in vector form can be written as

$$\nabla a_k = \begin{bmatrix} \nabla_{xx} \\ \nabla_{yy} \\ \nabla_{xy} \\ \nabla_{yx} \end{bmatrix}$$

$$\begin{bmatrix} \nabla_{xx} \\ \nabla_{yy} \\ \nabla_{xy} \\ \nabla_{yx} \end{bmatrix} = \begin{bmatrix} a(i-1,j) - 2a(i,j) + a(i+1,j) \\ a(i,j-1) - 2a(i,j) + a(i,j+1) \\ \frac{a(i+1,j+1)-a(i+1,j)-a(i,j+1)+2a(i,j)-a(i-1,j)-a(i,j-1)+a(i-1,j-1)}{2} \\ \frac{a(i+1,j+1)-a(i+1,j)-a(i,j+1)+2a(i,j)-a(i-1,j)-a(i,j-1)+a(i-1,j-1)}{2} \end{bmatrix}$$

(18)

Elements of Eq.(18) can be separated depending upon whether elements are in the incident ray which is currently being fused or in neighboring cell. The separated elements can then be written using multiple matrix form as

$$\nabla a_k = D_k v + C_k \tag{19}$$

where

$$D_k = \begin{bmatrix} -2 & 1 & 0 \dots 0 \\ -2 & 0 & 0 \dots 0 \\ 1 & 0.5 & 0 \dots 0 \\ 1 & 0.5 & 0 \dots 0 \end{bmatrix}$$

$$C_k = \begin{bmatrix} a(i-1,j) \\ a(i,j-1) + a(i,j+1) \\ \frac{a(i+1,j+1)-a(i+1,j)-a(i-1,j)-a(i,j-1)+a(i+1,j+1)}{2} \\ \frac{a(i+1,j+1)-a(i+1,j)-a(i-1,j)-a(i,j-1)+a(i+1,j+1)}{2} \end{bmatrix}$$

D_k and C_k matrix in Eq. (19) are only valid[4] for a_k (where $k = 1$). However by using the same method, composite D and C matrices can be formulated and written as

$$\nabla v = \begin{bmatrix} \nabla a_1 \\ \nabla a_2 \\ \dots \\ \nabla a_n \end{bmatrix} = \begin{bmatrix} D_1 \\ D_2 \\ \dots \\ D_n \end{bmatrix} v + \begin{bmatrix} C_1 \\ C_2 \\ \dots \\ C_n \end{bmatrix}$$

$$\nabla v = Dv + C \tag{20}$$

Matrix C from Eq. (20) is used in the later stages of RFusion to incorporate the integrated smoothing.

References

1. Dahlkamp, H., Kaehler, A., Stavens, D., Thrun, S., Bradski, G.: Self-supervised monocular road detection in desert terrain. In: Proceedings of Robotics: Science and Systems, Philadelphia, USA (2006)
2. Urmson, C., et al.: Autonomous driving in urban environments: boss and the urban challenge. J. Field Robot. Spec. Issue 2007 DARPA Urban Challenge Part I **25**, 425–466 (2008)

---

[4] Values of D and C matrices are calculated at run time. Elements depend upon the angle of ray, size of SDF-signal etc.

3. Mahmoudzadeh, A., Yeganeh, S.F., Golroo, A.: Kinect a novel cutting edge tool in pavement data collection. Int. Arch. Photogrammetry Remote Sens. Spat. Inf. Sci. **40**, 425 (2015)
4. ATAP Project Tango Googl (2014). http://www.google.com/atap/projecttango/. Accessed 22 Nov 2015
5. Hicks, S.L., Wilson, I., Muhammed, L., Worsfold, J., Downes, S.M., Kennard, C.: A depth-based head-mounted visual display to aid navigation in partially sighted individuals. PLoS ONE **8**, e67695 (2013)
6. Taneja, A., Ballan, L., Pollefeys, M.: City-scale change detection in cadastral 3D models using images. In: Computer Vision and Pattern Recognition (CVPR), Portland (2013)
7. Funk, E., Börner, A.: Infinite, sparse 3D modelling volumes. In: Braz, J., et al. (eds.) Computer Vision, Imaging and Computer Graphics Theory and Applications. Communications in Computer and Information Science. Springer, Cham (2017)
8. Kähler, O., Prisacariu, V.A., Ren, C.Y., Sun, X., Torr, P.H.S., Murray, D.W.: Very high frame rate volumetric integration of depth images on mobile device. IEEE Trans. Vis. Comput. Graph. **22**, 1241–1250 (2015). Proceedings International Symposium on Mixed and Augmented Reality 2015
9. Steinbruecker, F., Sturm, J., Cremers, D.: Volumetric 3D mapping in real-time on a CPU. In: International Conference on Robotics and Automation, Hongkong, China (2014)
10. Izadi, S., Kim, D., Hilliges, O., Molyneaux, D., Newcombe, R., Kohli, P., Shotton, J., Hodges, S., Freeman, D., Davison, A., Fitzgibbon, A.: Kinectfusion: Real-time 3D reconstruction and interaction using a moving depth camera. In: ACM Symposium on User Interface Software and Technology. ACM (2011)
11. Rajput, M.A.A., Funk, E., Börner, A., Hellwich, O.: Recursive total variation filtering based 3D fusion. In: Proceedings of the 13th International Joint Conference on e-Business and Telecommunications - vol. 5: SIGMAP, pp. 72–80 (2016)
12. Stühmer, J., Gumhold, S., Cremers, D.: Real-time dense geometry from a handheld camera. In: Goesele, M., Roth, S., Kuijper, A., Schiele, B., Schindler, K. (eds.) DAGM 2010. LNCS, vol. 6376, pp. 11–20. Springer, Heidelberg (2010). doi:10.1007/978-3-642-15986-2_2
13. Newcombe, R.A., Lovegrove, S.J., Davison, A.J.: DTAM: dense tracking and mapping in real-time. In: Proceedings of the 2011 International Conference on Computer Vision, ICCV 2011, pp. 2320–2327. IEEE Computer Society, Washington, DC (2011)
14. Chen, J., Bautembach, D., Izadi, S.: Scalable real-time volumetric surface reconstruction. ACM Trans. Graph. **32**, 113:1–113:16 (2013)
15. Curless, B., Levoy, M.: A volumetric method for building complex models from range images. In: Proceedings of the 23rd Annual Conference on Computer Graphics and Interactive Techniques, SIGGRAPH 1996, pp. 303–312. ACM, New York (1996)
16. Rudin, L.I., Osher, S., Fatemi, E.: Nonlinear total variation based noise removal algorithms. Phys. D **60**, 259–268 (1992)
17. Endres, F., Hess, J., Sturm, J., Cremers, D., Burgard, W.: 3D mapping with an RGB-D camera. IEEE Trans. Rob. **30**, 177–187 (2014)
18. Kerl, C., Sturm, J., Cremers, D.: Dense visual slam for RGB-D cameras. In: Proceedings of the International Conference on Intelligent Robot Systems (IROS) (2013)

19. Whelan, T., Kaess, M., Fallon, M., Johannsson, H., Leonard, J., McDonald, J.: Kintinuous: spatially extended KinectFusion. In: RSS Workshop on RGB-D: Advanced Reasoning with Depth Cameras, Sydney, Australia (2012)
20. Zhang, H., Wohlfeil, J., Grießbach, D.: Extension and evaluation of the agast feature detector. ISPRS Ann. Photogrammetry Remote Sens. Spat. Inf. Sci. **III–4**, 133–137 (2016)
21. Strackenbrock, B., Hirzinger, G., Wohlfeil, J.: Multi-scale/multi-sensor 3D-dokumentation und 3D visualisierung höfischer prunkräume. KONFERENZBAND EVA BERLIN: Elektronische Medien & Kunst. Kultur und Historie **2014**, 110–117 (2014)
22. Handa, A., Whelan, T., McDonald, J., Davison, A.J.: A benchmark for RGB-D visual odometry, 3D reconstruction and slam. In: 2014 IEEE International Conference on Robotics and Automation (ICRA), pp. 1524–1531. IEEE (2014)
23. Baumbach, D.G.D., Zuev, S.: Stereo-vision-aided inertial navigation for unknown indoor and outdoor environments. In: Proceedings of the International Conference on Indoor Positioning and Indoor Navigation (IPIN). IEEE (2014)

Wireless Networks and Mobile Systems

Social-DBSCAN: A Presence Analytics Approach for Mobile Users' Social Clustering

Muawya Habib Sarnoub Eldaw[✉], Mark Levene, and George Roussos

Department of Computer Science and Information Systems, Birkbeck,
University of London, Malet Street, London WC1E 7HX, UK
{eldaw,mark,g.roussos}@dcs.bbk.ac.uk
http://www.dcs.bbk.ac.uk

Abstract. The ability to discover social groups that can be attributed to the learning activities taking place at target locations, provides an invaluable opportunity to understand the presence and movement of people within a university campus. Utilising density-based clustering of WLAN traces, we illustrate how granular social groups of mobile users can be detected within such an environment. The proposed density-based clustering algorithm, which we name Social-DBSCAN, has real potential to support human mobility studies such as the optimisation of strategies of space usage. It can automatically discover the duration of the academic term, the classes, and the attendance data. For the evaluation of our proposed method, we utilised a large Eduroam log of an academic site. We chose, as a proof concept, selected locations with known capacity. We successfully detected the regular learning activities that took place at those locations and provided accurate estimates about the attendance levels over the academic term period.

Keywords: Density-based clustering · Social-DBSCAN · Wireless Network(WLAN) Traces · Eduroam · Social groups · Class attendance · Human presence · Presence analytics · Learning activity · Mobile data · Mobile users

1 Introduction

Eduroam [10] and other pervasive wireless technologies, generate vast amounts of detailed information, which provides an invaluable opportunity to study different aspects of people's presence and movement behaviours within work, study or leisure environments. These pervasive technologies increase people's ability to access information, which undoubtedly affects the way the target environment operates. It is therefore essential that we build real-time monitoring systems as well as theoretical frameworks to understand how people's presence and its dynamics reshape the structures of such environments. With these measurements put in place, we can potentially discover hidden patterns of behaviour at both the collective and at the individual user levels, thus increase our understanding about

© Springer International Publishing AG 2017
M.S. Obaidat (Ed): ICETE 2016, CCIS 764, pp. 381–400, 2017.
https://doi.org/10.1007/978-3-319-67876-4_18

human presence, and in turn, enhance our ability to make informed decisions when we plan for our environments.

We place special emphasis on investigating the social dimension of the human presence within an academic environment, with the objective of discovering meaningful social clusters of users. In particular, we apply our proposed data mining algorithm using the WLAN imprints that visitors leave behind as they move about from one location to another across the different sites at Birkbeck College. Our intuition is that we should be able discover clusters that match the users groups formed on the basis of attending lectures of individual modules. Gaining knowledge about the social group that regularly attends a target class such as the size of the group, allows us to make accurate estimate about the attendance level of the learning activity. Furthermore, by clustering learning activities (e.g. modules) together we can discover a higher level of grouping that matches the clustering formed with respect to the membership in the study programmes that the students are enrolled in.

The raw WLAN traces used in this research were collected at Birkbeck, University of London during the period from the 1st of October 2013 to the 10th of April 2015. In comparison to most data sets used in previous Eduroam based studies [5,16], the data set containing these traces is larger in size with respect to its number of users as well as the number of days it spans.

The paper makes the following contributions to presence analytics:

1. It presents a social density-based clustering method that uses WLAN traces in order to detect granular social groups of mobile users within a university campus. The proposed clustering method, which we call Social-DBSCAN, relies on the underpinning semantic context for parameterisation, i.e. utilising information from the semantic context to determine the values of the clustering algorithm parameters such as the minimum class size value, which we use to ensure that the number of individual students in any discovered social group remains within a certain range values.
2. Make accurate estimates about the actual level of attendance of learning activities. Linking the discovered social group that regularly visits a target location and the learning activity that takes place within the same context, will allow us to estimate the attendance level of these learning activities.

The remainder of the paper is organised as follows. In Sect. 2, we present the motivation for this work. In Sect. 3, we review the related work. In Sect. 4, we describe the social clustering of mobile users, and provide the definitions of the concepts used in this work. In the same section, we provide the description of the details of our clustering approach such as the formulation of the clustering problem, distance computation, the detection of regular learning activities and the discovering of the arbitrary-shaped clusters of users. In Sect. 5, we give a description of the data set we used for the evaluation of our proposed approach, followed by the evaluation of the discovered clusters. We provide a comprehensive discussion of the results in Sect. 6. Finally, in Sect. 7, we give our concluding remarks and a brief description of future work.

2   Motivation

In [11], we investigate the human presence within an academic environment and examine four types of behavioural patterns that correspond to the four different aspects of the data: social, spatial, temporal and semantic. Motivated by our findings, we set out to study more closely the social aspect of presence analytics, with the aim of gaining better understanding of the human presence within the case-study environment - the Bloomsbury campus of Birkbeck University of London. Based on the analysis carried out in [11] there is high temporal regularity in the human presence (see the evident seasonality pattern in Fig. 3), which can be interpreted as the visitors having preferences with respect to the visited locations. Moreover, our analysis reveals that the distribution of revisiting users across the various affiliations is approximately a power-law [7]. The various patterns investigated: daytime, evening, weekdays and weekend, show that most users belong to a small number of affiliations as can be implied from the analysis of the distribution, shown in Fig. 1. It is not surprising that these affiliations, which include Birkbeck College, are the ones that hold the most regular teaching and research activities across Birkbeck's sites. Furthermore, as shown in Fig. 2, we discovered that the users' revisits are distributed as an exponential mixture across locations. The combination of these findings gives very strong indications of an underlying semantic users/visitors grouping on the basis of the learning activities that take place at Birkbeck's Bloomsbury campus in central London.

2.1   The Intuition of the Proposed Density-Based Clustering Approach

Social relationships are an integral part of every community and there is no doubt that numerous social communities exist between the people of the same university. The people at Birkbeck College are no exception to this. Based on the day-to-day social activities such as lectures, seminars and other regular meetings, we have strong evidence about the existence of finer-grained relationships as opposed to the high-level social grouping by the user's academic affiliation. In this paper we utilise a density-based clustering approach to discover the social groups formed on the basis of these learning activities. Our choice of a density-based clustering over other types of clustering methods is motivated by the semantic underpinning of the visits made to the various locations in the College. In most cases, when a location is visited, the visit is normally motivated by the desire to attend the learning activity taking place at the target location. For instance, when a student makes a visit to one of the lecture-rooms he or she is most probably doing this because they are attending a class taking place at that location.

It is important to note here that with exception to the minimum class size and the minimum attendance threshold, which we discussed in Sect. 4.4, we do not make any specific assumptions about the level of attendance of any given regular learning activity. Moreover, we do not make assumptions about the density or the variance of attendance or the shapes for the clusters that we would like to

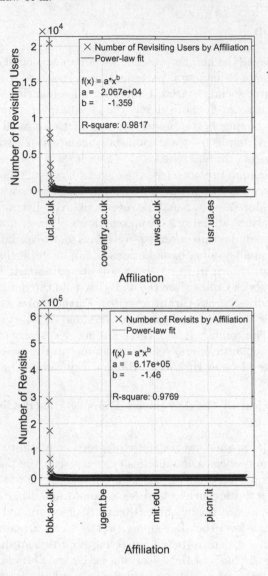

Fig. 1. Distribution of number of revisits by affiliation. In this figure, the affiliations are ranked by number of revisits. The top plot shows the distribution of number of revisiting users by affiliation and the bottom plot shows the distribution of number of revisits. The distributions in these figures were computed over the 11 week period covering the Spring term of 2015 (From the 5th Jan to 20th March 2015) [2].

discover. The reason is that these measurements about the attendance, i.e. the density and the shapes of the social clusters of users, are partly the kind of information that we set out to discover in this research, and consequently we take into consideration an unbiased prior view about them.

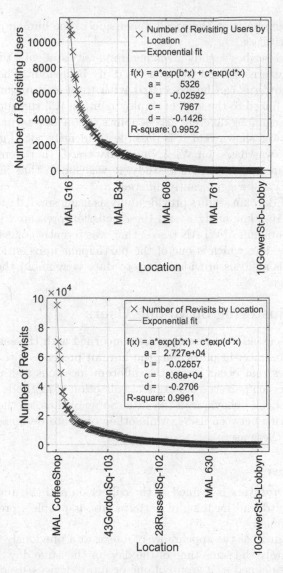

Fig. 2. Distribution of number of revisits by location. In this figure, the locations are ranked by number of revisits. The top plot shows the distribution of number of revisiting users by location and the bottom plot shows the distribution of number of revisits. The distributions in these figures were computed over the 11 week period covering the Spring term of 2015 (From the 5th Jan to 20th March 2015) [2].

3 Related Work

Numerous studies investigated the usage of WLAN traces in order to understand the human dynamics within a target institution. We review some of these studies and lay special emphasis on the social dimension of the human presence within an academic institution.

In [9], which describes a study involving university students, the authors identified activity patterns related to the users daily behaviour. The study showed that the daily patterns can be associated with the user's major of study and, consequently be linked to the level of employment. In [15] the authors estimated the network usage among different access points over a long-term. In a study discussed in [14] it was shown that it is possible to identify social groups amongst users. The study was based on WLAN mobility traces that were collected over a period of one month. In the same study, it was shown that male and female session duration can be significantly different.

Most recent Eduroam studies provide analysis using small data sets of WLAN traffic traces [5,16]. The analysis and the discussion presented in this paper is based on a large amount of WLAN traces, that was recently collected at Birkbeck University of London, which is one of the participant universities in Eduroam. Furthermore, this analysis provides an up-to-date view about the current trend in Eduroam usage.

4 Social Clustering of Mobile Users

The patterns discussed in this section are concerned with the social perspective of the human presence, in particular, the human presence with the respect to learning activities that occur across the different locations at a university campus. To examine such patterns, we utilise a collection of methods to measure the influence of the social behaviour in the data. Some of these methods capture the degree of similarity between users, while other ones are designed to detect the social groups of these users.

4.1 Definitions

1. *Presence Analytics* is defined as the collection and the analysis of mobile data in order to find meaningful patterns about people's presence within a given environment.
2. *Revisit* is defined as the appearance of a user at a previously visited location at approximately the same time of the day on the same day of the week.
3. *An Event* is defined as a group of one or more devices/users connecting to the network from a particular location within a given time interval.
4. *Pattern of Events* is defined as a time series of occurrences of a given event, associated with a given time. For example, the attendance of a module with a regular weekly class delivered for a number of consecutive weeks at the same given location is a *Pattern of events*.
5. *Noise* is defined as the presence of mobile users within a given spatio-temporal context but this presence is not linked to the attendance of the regular weekly class session that takes place within the same context. For example, the presence of an individual in a classroom at the time when a regular weekly class session takes place, while he or she is not a member of the group of students, who usually attend the session.

4.2 Problem Formulation

Suppose that we have the individual users' records of revisits, of a group of users U, to a target location L. Moreover, suppose that all these revisits were made within a fixed time interval of a given weekday D for k consecutive weeks. We would like to automatically discover whether this collection of revisits represent a *pattern of events* of a learning activity that was taking place at the location L over the k consecutive weeks.

In the remainder of this paper we use the terms *learning activity*, *class* and *pattern of events* interchangeably to refer to the same concept. Similarly, we sometimes mention users, people, students and visitors all to mean the same thing.

4.3 Distance Measure

An important question that automatically arises when we want to decide whether an observed user can be associated with a particular group of users, is how to compute the distance between the observed user and the members of a group. An equally important question to address here is how much information is required to determine a realistic value for such a distance. To answer these questions we utilise information extracted from the semantic context to inform our model about the kind of distance measure to use and the amount of information needed to compute the distance between two users' records of attendance.

Jaccard Distance. We choose Jaccard Distance, which we argue is a natural measure, based on the application and the data. Intuitively, the Jaccard Distance, substantially captures the difference between two records of attendance. It is defined as 1 minus the Jaccard similarity, which we compute as the ratio between the intersection and the union of the two compared records of attendance [1]. The formal definition of this metric, as a function $d(p_a, p_b)$ that takes two arguments, can be given as follows:

$$d(p_a, p_b) = 1 - \frac{|p_a \cap p_b|}{|p_a \cup p_b|}. \tag{1}$$

where p_a and p_b represent the records of revisits of user a and user b respectively.

Term-Based Distance Computation. One of the key challenges that we needed to address when computing the distance is how much information is required to determine a realistic value. In the context of this work, the presence and movement of people can be highly dictated by the learning activities that takes place across the College. For example, the regular presence of students and the teaching staff in lecture-rooms is highly dictated by the modules taught in these rooms. Similar to other academic institutions, these learning activities such as lectures and lab sessions are highly dictated by the timetable, which gives the location and time allocation for the different learning activities across the

Analysis of Revisits to Malet Street Site

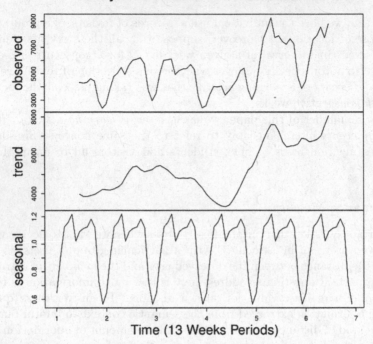

Time (13 Weeks Periods)

Fig. 3. Time series analysis of number of revisits to Malet Street site. In this figure, the top plot shows the original time series in which the data is divided into 13 week periods (Each 13 week period covering an 11 week academic term plus an extra week on either sides of the term). The plot second from top shows the estimated trend, and the bottom plot shows the estimated seasonal constituent.

academic year. Here at Birkbeck College, this allocation is usually different for the different academic terms, with exception to a selection of core modules that continue to run for more than one term. Nonetheless, within the term period many people are likely to be present at the same location at the same time at least once a week. This observation was confirmed by the regularity found in the temporal patterns as shown in Fig. 3. Based on this finding, we decided to compute the distance over the 11 week periods - each 11 week period corresponds to one of the academic terms contained in the data set described in Sect. 5.2.

Example: Suppose that we have three students s_1, s_2 and s_3, who attended a class c that ran every Monday for 11 weeks. We can denote the attendance of each of these students as a set representing the student's individual session attendance. In Table 1, which shows the Jaccard distance between the attendance of the three students, s_1 and s_2 have similar attendance while the pair s_1 and s_3 and the pair s_2 and s_3 have dissimilar attendance records. In this example, two records of attendance are considered similar to one another if they have a Jaccard distance value lower than 0.5.

Table 1. An example for the term-based distance computation. The numbers given in the sets representing the attendance records, correspond to the IDs of the sessions attended by the students. The sets do not feature the sessions that the student did not attend.

Student ID.	Attendance record	Jacc distance		
		s_1	s_2	s_3
s_1	$\{1,2,3,6,7,8,9,10,11\}$	0	0.11	0.73
s_2	$\{1,2,3,6,7,8,9,10\}$	0.11	0	0.82
s_3	$\{4,5,6,7,11\}$	0.73	0.82	0

4.4   Discovering Regular Classes

To explain how our proposed method successfully detects the occurrence of a class, we rely on the intuition that the visitors to a target location, where the regular sessions of a module are delivered, naturally form a social group that most likely meet on a regular basis over the number of weeks that the module covers. The experiments we conducted, as shown in the analysis presented in Sect. 6, were designed to discover such groups by performing a two stage process, which addresses the following challenges.

Noise Reduction. With the kind of WLAN data utilised in this work, it is not guaranteed that all the individuals who visited a particular location were there, merely to attend the learning activity taking place at that location. In order to successfully detect a regular class that takes place at a target location, we discard from our processing the data of any individual whose total number of visits to the target location was less than a *minimum attendance* threshold.

Another concept that is closely related to level of attendance is the *minimum class size*, which is the smallest percentage of the total number of students registered for the class that must be present for a learning session to hold. Note here that the *minimum attendance* and the *minimum class size* vary between the different schools and departments within the case study university. For the proposed method evaluation, we experiment with a range of values, for those two parameters, which we discuss in more detail in Sect. 6.

Attendance Coherence. Even with the noise being eliminated, we still cannot guarantee that those individuals who visited a particular location were there merely to attend the learning activity that was taking place there. Therefore, it is imperative to verify that those students that attended the potential class are *coherent* in attending the individual sessions of that class, over the 11 week academic term. A *coherent* cluster here is defined as a group of individual users that have *similar* attendance. For example, if two or more students consistently attended the same sessions of a class then they are members of a coherent cluster. In the distance computation example given earlier (See Table 1), assigning the students s_1 and s_2 to the same group is likely to result in a coherent cluster, whereas grouping the students s_1 and s_3 or s_2 and s_3 together is likely to create an incoherent group.

To verify the coherence of attendance, we apply our proposed clustering method to find out whether those individuals, whose attendance satisfy the minimum requirement, form a single cohesive group with respect to their attendance of individual sessions across the different weeks of the academic term period.

We emphasise here that due to the pair comparison of records used in the proposed clustering method, the students do not have to attend exactly the same sessions in order to be clustered together in one group. As discussed in Sect. 4.4, the method recursively searches for all density connected data points to assign to the same cluster.

Discovering Coherent Clusters. The clustering approach we are proposing is based on the DBSCAN algorithm, the density-based spatial clustering of applications with noise [12], which scales well for large amount of data [13]. The original DBSCAN takes two parameters, namely epsilon (a distance threshold) and minPts (a minimum number of points which is used as a density threshold). Given some data points for clustering, DBSCAN relies on these two parameters to identify density connected points in the data. It uses the concepts of direct and density connectivity to group points together forming transitive hull of density-connected points, which yields density-based clusters of arbitrary shapes. In DBSCAN, two points are said to be *directly connected* if they are at distance less than the threshold epsilon and a point is said to be a *core point* if it has more directly connected neighbouring points than the threshold minPts. Furthermore, two points is said to be *density connected* if they are connected to core points that are themselves density connected to one another [13].

In our proposed social variant of DBSCAN, which we refer to as Social-DBSCAN, we use information from the semantic context of the human presence to inform the DBSCAN algorithm about the distance and the density threshold values, which the algorithm utilises to discover the social clusters present in the data. In particular, there are two main differences between our version of DBSCAN and the original version published in [12]:

1. The distance measure we utilise is based on the Jaccard coefficient, which as discussed earlier in Sects. 4.3 and 4.4, plays an important role in capturing the degree of coherence between the records of attendance of two individuals, i.e. it compares the total of shared attended sessions to the sum of sessions attended by either of the two users.
2. A further important difference, which is closely related to the data set being clustered and also related to how the clustering is performed, is that the points representing the individuals who attended the learning activity, are ordered in descending order based on the individual's level of attendance, i.e. ordered by the individual's total number of attended sessions. The ordering of the points in descending order captures the idea that the higher the level of attendance the more likely that the individual is part of the social group that

attended the learning activity. This is a key concept of how the clustering is performed in our proposed version of the DBSCAN algorithm.

The proposed clustering algorithm, which we call Social-DBSCAN, can be described in pseudo code following the original version of DBSCAN described in [12]:

```
Social-DBSCAN(Dataset, CohCoff, MinClassSize):
  # The Data set is ordered in descending order of attendance level.
  SGroup = getNewSGroup()
  for(point P in Dataset):
    if VisitedPts.contains(P) == True:
      continue
    VisitedPts.add(P)
    # findSimilarPts() returns all points similar to P, i.e. points
    # with Jaccard distance < CohCoff. The returned set of points is
    # presented in descending order according to attendance level.
    pSimilarPts = findSimilarPts(P, CohCoff)
    if pSimilarPts.size() < MinClassSize:
      NOISE.add(P)
    else:
      SGroup = getNewSGroup()
      SGroup = expandSocialGroup(P, SGroup,
      pSimilarPts, CohCoff, MinClassSize)
      if SGroup.size() > 0:
        DiscoveredSocialGroups.add(SGroup)
```

In the pseudo code shown above, the parameters $CohCoff$ and $MinClassSize$ represent the *coherence coefficient* and the *minimum class size* threshold values respectively. Note here that the value of the $CohCoff$ is computed as a Jaccard distance, i.e. $1 - Jaccard$. From a practical perspective, the values of these parameters are heavily influenced by the context in which Social-DBSCAN is being applied. In the pseudo code shown below, we illustrate how a discovered group is expanded, where the code only differs from the $regionQuery()$ in DBSCAN, in that the neighbourhood of a given point is returned as ordered list, based on the number of sessions the user attended over the term period. In DBSCAN the neighbourhood list is not returned in any particular order.

```
expandSocialGroup(P, SGroup, pSimilarPts,
CohCoff, MinClassSize):
  SGroup.add(P)
  for(point Q in pSimilarPts):
    if VisitedPts.contains(Q) == False:
      VisitedPts.add(Q)
      qSimilarPts = findSimilarPts(Q, CohCoff)
      if qSimilarPts.size() >= MinClassSize:
        # add all points in qSimilarPts to pSimilarPts.
        pSimilarPts = pSimilarPts.add(qSimilarPts)

    if DiscoveredSocialGroups.contains(Q) == False:
      SGroup.add(Q)
```

5   Data Analysis

5.1   Birkbeck University of London

Birkbeck is one of the member colleges of University of London and a major provider of evening higher education. Based on the most recent available statistics, there are approximately 16,500 students attending Birkbeck. Most of Birkbeck students are part-time, with approximately 88% of them enrolled on part-time programmes [3].

Birkbeck's Bloomsbury Campus in central London, is located very close to campuses of other colleges of University of London, such as UCL and SOAS. This proximity to these other campuses was naturally translated in a large amount of collaboration between these universities. As a result, Birkbeck's Bloomsbury campus is shared by thousands of academics, researchers and students from these universities on a daily basis.

Birkbeck, is also one of the participant of Eduroam, a WLAN service developed for the international education and research community that gives secure, world-wide roaming access to the Internet [4].

5.2   Data Set

The evaluation of the proposed clustering method, Social-DBSCAN, is based on recent WLAN traces collected at Birkbeck. This data set of WLAN traces is a snapshot of the College's Eduroam access data for the period, from the 1st of October 2013 to 10th of April 2015. It contains 223 locations and 167,272 users, who come from 2,462 institutions and departments. The 223 locations given in this data set are divided between 11 of the 17 sites of the Bloomsbury campus.

There are four types of data in this data set: *authentication details*, *pre-proxy details*, *post-proxy details* and *reply details*. User-ID, access location, timestamp and affiliation are the basic information for each processed record. Based on these records, we designed new types of data representing the four aspects of the human presence: social, spatial, temporal and semantic aspects. In order to detect the attendance of classes, we create spatio-temporal vectors, where each vector denotes the visits made, by one of the users, at a given spatio-temporal context (i.e. a specific target location, within a fixed time interval of day, on a target weekday and over a period of 11 weeks). The data division into 11 weeks periods is motivated by the temporal regularity found in the data as shown in Fig. 3, where each 11 week period corresponds to a single academic term.

In this work we also make use of the room capacity information, which is available independently through the College's website. All of the 15 locations we chose for the evaluation of the proposed clustering approach are rooms with known capacities.

Data Privacy. All sensitive information that we do not use in this work, such as the users email address, has been removed from the data set. Every other data item of personally identifiable information has been anonymised notably the device MAC address. Eduroam access point BSSIDs have not been anonymised during processing, however access information is aggregated by BSSID but not per user, and specifically no attempt has been made to create individual user fingerprints or reveal the locations of access points on a map. These data processing and related security and data management provisions have been approved by the Colleges ethics committee.

5.3   Evaluation of Discovered Clusters

Our evaluation methodology is designed to verify whether the presence of a discovered group of individuals represents regular attendance of a learning activity that has taken place at the target location. It verifies the results obtained from the two stage process, which addresses the noise reduction and the coherence of attendance, against the initial intuition that the regular visitors of a given location on a given day of the week naturally form a single coherent social group (see the discussion in Sect. 4.4 for more details). From a practical point of view, there are two criteria that the clustering result must fulfil in order to justify the occurrence of a regular class at the target location:

1. There must be a dominant *coherent* discovered group with the majority of the students (e.g. 50% or more) being members of such group.
2. Following the reduction of noise, the average number of students per session must be within the capacity of the target location, where the detected class was taking place.

6   Discussion of Results

In our experiments, we examined the visiting patterns from 15 randomly chosen locations with known capacity. These chosen locations are usually used for learning activities such as lectures and lab-based classes. As shown in Table 2, the number of unique visitors greatly varies between these chosen locations. For a few of them, the number of visitors exceeds the location capacity, which is a clear indication that those visitors were not all regular class attendees at these locations. Therefore, it is important that we remove the noise from the data and only preserve the records of those visitors who most likely visited those locations in order to attend the learning activities that were taking place there.

We restricted our investigation to the data covering the Spring of 2015 (i.e. the period from 5th Jan–20th March 2015). The results shown are for the time interval from 18:00–21:00 of every Monday of this period. As a proof of concept we only report on two sets of experiments. These two sets correspond to two values of the *minimum attendance* threshold, which is used in detecting the regular learning activities that took place at those selected locations. We now summarise the results of the experiments in these two categories.

Table 2. Location information.

Location ID.	Location name	Number of unique visitors	Capacity
#1	MaletSt-402	239	35
#2	MaletSt-G16	194	60
#3	Clore-102	135	33
#4	MaletSt-b35	72	125
#5	MaletSt-153	66	66
#6	MaletSt-b34	43	222
#7	MaletSt-b29	48	30
#8	MaletSt-417	49	60
#9	MaletSt-423	42	39
#10	Clore-204	32	33
#11	MaletSt-352	21	20
#12	43GordonSq-g02	24	28
#13	MaletSt-314	32	36
#14	MaletSt-b20	16	99
#15	43GordonSq-b04	17	127

6.1 Clustering with 30% Minimum Attendance

To ensure that only individual with consistent attendance appear in the data set being clustered, we filter out the records of those individuals with attendance lower than 30%. The intuition here is that the group of those individuals with regular attendance of 30% or more will include all those who attend the actual class and possibly include some noise as well, i.e. individuals who are not regular attendees of the class such as those who happened to be in the vicinity of the target location when the class was taking place.

Although 30%, from a practical perspective, is a low threshold value for minimum attendance, we nonetheless utilised such a value to assess the performance of the proposed clustering method at this level of attendance. The results of the experiments can be summarised as follows:

1. As shown in Table 3, we had more than one discovered group for many of the locations, which is a sign of incoherent attendance of the regular sessions of the target class. This is totally consistent with the intuition that setting the minimum attendance threshold to such a low percentage, i.e. 30%, will allow the presence of noise in the data. As a result, it is more likely that more than one group of individuals with different level of attendance can be discovered.
2. In some cases, as shown in Table 3, the average number of students per session is larger than twice the capacity of the target location, which is another sign of existence of remaining noise in the data.

Table 3. Social-DBSCAN clustering result for 15 unique locations. The student's minimum attendance threshold was 30% and the coherence coefficient was 0.6. This result was computed for the time interval from 18:00–21:00 every Monday of the Spring term of 2015 (11 weeks period).

Location ID.	Number of students	Number of discovered groups	Group no.	Group size	Group attendance			Standard deviation	Avg number of students per session
					Min	Max	Avg		
#1	217	2	1	211	4	10	5.08	1.25	98.09
	217	2	2	2	4	4	4	0	
#2	171	3	1	163	4	9	5.23	1.32	79
	171	3	2	2	4	4	4	0	
	171	3	3	2	4	5	4.5	0.5	
#3	126	3	1	104	4	10	5.17	1.35	50.91
	126	3	2	2	4	6	5	1	
	126	3	3	3	4	4	4	0	
#4	71	1	1	64	4	10	5.91	1.56	34.36
#5	60	2	1	40	4	10	5.5	1.53	21.27
	60	2	2	3	4	6	4.67	0.94	
#6	43	1	1	31	5	9	6.87	1.29	19.36
#7	47	3	1	27	4	9	6.3	1.67	17.18
	47	3	2	2	4	6	5	1	
	47	3	3	2	4	5	4.5	0.5	
#8	47	1	1	35	4	9	6.43	1.57	20.45
#9	41	2	1	33	4	8	5.58	1.44	17.55
	41	2	2	2	4	5	4.5	0.5	
#10	31	2	1	18	4	9	5.89	1.56	10.36
	31	2	2	2	4	4	4	0	
#11	21	2	1	8	5	10	6.75	1.71	6.27
	21	2	2	3	5	5	5	0	
#12	24	1	1	14	4	9	6.29	1.44	8
#13	30	3	1	13	4	9	6.23	1.37	9
	30	3	2	2	4	4	4	0	
	30	3	3	2	4	6	5	1	
#14	16	1	1	11	4	8	5.18	1.27	5.18
#15	17	4	1	2	9	10	9.5	0.5	7.82
	17	4	2	8	4	7	5.63	1.11	
	17	4	3	2	4	4	4	0	
	17	4	4	3	4	6	4.67	0.94	

It is evident from this result that performing the 30% filtering was not sufficient to remove all the noise and thus 30% is rather a small value for the minimum attendance threshold.

6.2 Clustering with 40% Minimum Attendance

Following the result shown in Table 3 and the discussion given in Sect. 6.1 above, we argue that using a higher minimum attendance threshold value will filter out more noise and thus increase the coherence in the discovered groups. For the set of experiments discussed in this section, we raised the minimum attendance

Table 4. Social-DBSCAN clustering result for 15 unique locations. The student's minimum attendance threshold was 40% and the coherence coefficient was 0.6. This result was computed for the time interval from 18:00–21:00 every Monday of the Spring term of 2015 (11 weeks period).

Location ID.	Number of students	Number of discovered groups	Group no.	Group size	Group attendance			Standard deviation	Avg number of students per session
					Min	Max	Avg		
#1	118	1	1	116	5	10	5.94	1.08	62.64
#2	102	1	1	99	5	9	6.00	1.15	54.00
#3	62	3	1	47	5	10	6.28	1.22	31.91
	62	3	2	8	5	6	5.13	0.33	
	62	3	3	3	5	5	5.00	0.00	
#4	53	1	1	50	5	10	6.40	1.40	29.09
#5	34	1	1	28	5	10	6.07	1.46	15.45
#6	32	1	1	30	5	9	6.93	1.26	18.91
#7	27	3	1	13	5	9	7.62	1.21	12.18
	27	3	2	4	6	7	6.25	0.43	
	27	3	3	2	5	5	5.00	0.00	
#8	32	2	1	27	5	9	7.04	1.23	18.18
	32	2	2	2	5	5	5.00	0.00	
#9	26	3	1	15	5	8	6.87	1.02	11.18
	26	3	2	2	5	5	5.00	0.00	
	26	3	3	2	5	5	5.00	0.00	
#10	17	3	1	9	5	9	7.11	1.20	7.64
	17	3	2	2	5	5	5.00	0.00	
	17	3	3	2	5	5	5.00	0.00	
#11	17	2	1	8	5	10	6.75	1.71	6.27
	17	2	2	3	5	5	5.00	0.00	
#12	15	1	1	13	5	9	6.46	1.34	7.64
#13	16	2	1	9	5	9	6.67	1.33	6.55
	16	2	2	2	6	6	6.00	0.00	
#14	10	1	1	6	5	8	6.00	1.15	3.27
#15	11	2	1	2	9	10	9.50	0.50	5.45
	11	2	2	7	5	7	5.86	0.99	

threshold to 40% in order to obtained a more accurate and consistent result, which we summarised as follows:

1. With exception to locations #9 and #10, for every location (see the result in Table 4), we detected a smaller number of groups as opposed to the result shown in Table 3. This is an indication that the visitors of the target location were more likely attending a regular learning activity that was taking place there, over the 11 weeks period.
2. With exception to location #1, for every location, the average number of students per session was always smaller than the capacity of the target location. After the verification against the timetable, it appears that location #1 hosted two classes on Monday evening; one class running from 18:00–19:30 and the other from 19:30–21:00. The fact that the average number of students

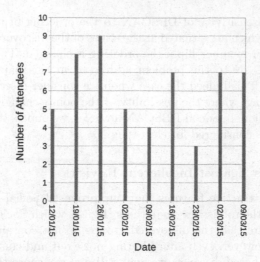

Fig. 4. Attendance of the XML class as seen through Eduroam activity traces. The small attendance value recorded on 23/02/2015 was for the module reading week, in which the regular class session did not run.

per session for the location was only 11% lower than twice the capacity, confirms that the clustering result is consistent with the finding that the location hosted two session on Monday evening.

3. As shown in both Tables 3 and 4, the average number of students per session for some of the locations was far too small in comparison to the capacity of the target location (e.g. locations #14 and #15). Such situation can be attributed to the possibility that a substantiated number of students in those classes might not have been active Eduroam users.

6.3 Removing Noise Due to Irregular Attendance

When discovering a class, it is very usual to have noise due to the Wifi detecting all movement within the vicinity of a target location. One way to ensure that such noise is filtered out from the data is to approximate the time spent at the target location and discount those individuals who spent a short time in the vicinity of the location. However, an individual who is present in the vicinity with no intention to attend the class at the target location is very unlikely to consistently appear at the same location at the same time of the day over the 11 week period. Thus, the noise due to such inconsistent appearance at the target location, can be removed by raising the minimum attendance threshold, which ensures that only individuals with consistent attendance remain in the data.

6.4 Sensitivity to Ordering of Points in the Dataset Being Clustered

A key advantage of our proposed Social-DBSCAN, over DBSCAN is that the latter is insensitive to how the points are ordered in the data set considered for clustering. This insensitivity of DBSCAN to the ordering of the points means that those points which are situated at the edges of the discovered clusters might change their cluster membership if the ordering is changed. Therefore, applying the original DBSCAN to the problem addressed in this paper may not give the correct result. This indeed the case when we consider discovering the social grouping in a setting, where the possibility of the points changing their ordering is a common situation. In Social-DBSCAN however, we impose a specific ordering for the data points considered for clustering.

6.5   Robustness Against Incoherent Revisits

One of the very attractive features that our proposed Social-DBSCAN shares with DBSCAN is the robustness to outliers [12,13], which Social-DBSCAN capitalises on to ensure that the discovered groups do not contain any incoherent member points. However, even after filtering noise out and clustering the points using the Jaccard-based distance, we may still discover more than one coherent group. In the context of class detection, the occurrence of such scenario can be attributed to the possibility that there may be two classes sharing the period from 18:00–21:00, e.g. one class running from 18:00–19:30 and another running from 19:30–21:00.

Another explanation for discovering more than one group is based on the fact that some students may have irregular attendance patterns. The dataset used for the evaluation contains records of attendance of many mature students, who have daytime jobs and may occasionally miss classes due to some special circumstances such as unexpected additional work commitment. In such case, the majority of the students are usually clustered together in one single large group while those students with irregular attendance form a small-sized group or groups (see the result for location #3 in Table 4). In any case, Social-DBSCAN ensures that incoherent behaviour is separated from the dominant coherent pattern extracted from the data.

6.6   Measuring Class Attendance

By combining external data from the teaching timetable with the social, spatial and temporal information extracted from the dataset, we can identify groups of users whose presence at a given spatio-temporal context can be linked with the learning activity taking place within the same context. Moreover, the size of the discovered group of students can potentially gives an accurate estimate of the class attendance. As a proof of concept, we conducted an experiment in which we analysed the socio-spatio-temporal patterns for one of the computer labs at Malet Street site. From the teaching timetable, we selected the XML module, which had regular teaching sessions that took place every Monday from 18:00 to 21:00 in the period from the 12th of Jan to the 9th of March 2015. From those students registered for the module, a total of 14 students had traces recorded within our data set. In Fig. 4, which shows the attendance records of the selected group, a total of 13 students regularly attended the class sessions.

Our analysis showed that one of the selected students had no recorded traces within the spatio-temporal context in which the class took place. Interestingly, this student was present at other locations just before or after the time interval in which the XML session ran. The failure to detect the sessions attendance of this student can be attributed to the possibility that the student's mobile device might have been switched off just before the student attended the class and was only switched back on after the end of the session. Despite the failure to detect this student, by accurately tracking the attendance of 13 out of a group of 14 students, this experiment demonstrates the potential of using Wifi traces to measure class attendance. We acknowledge here that a substantial proportion of the students who attended the class were not active users of Eduroam. However, Eduroam is increasingly becoming more pervasive and more popular amongst the regular and non-regular visitors of the College. The analysis of more recently recorded traces shows that there is a steady increase in the number of Eduroam users across the university's main site.

7 Conclusion and Future Work

7.1 Conclusion

We showed how by clustering WLAN activity traces we can detect granular social groups of mobile users within a target academic environment. Moreover, we showed how by being able to detect social groups at target locations, we provide an invaluable opportunity to understand the presence and movement of people within such an environment. Using the proposed Social-DBSCAN, we demonstrated how we can automatically detect the regular classes taking place at target locations, and provide accurate estimates about the levels of attendance.

7.2 Future Work

Some of the interesting directions that we would like to pursue can be summarised as follows:

1. The next step for the work discussed in this article is to cluster or group learning activities (e.g. modules) together in order to discover a higher level of grouping. The intuition here is that these higher level groups will directly correspond to the clusters formed with respect to the membership in the study programmes that the students are enrolled in.
2. A key research that we are currently focusing on is how students spend their time during breaks. We are particularly interested in finding out where students spend their time during breaks and whether they maintain any social grouping during this time and how often such social groups meet.
3. Given the capacity of a target location, we would like to estimate the actual space usage over the term period as well as the aggregate usage over the whole academic year. Unfortunately, a substantial proportion of the students are not active users of Eduroam within the current data set, and thus we do

not have fully accurate statistics in order to provide accurate estimates about the usage of space.

Acknowledgements. We thank the members of the Birkbeck IT Services who extracted the data set for us for the purpose of this research.

References

1. Charikar, M.S.: Similarity estimation techniques from rounding algorithms. In: Proceedings of the Thirty-Fourth Annual ACM Symposium on Theory of Computing, pp. 380–388. ACM (2002)
2. Eldaw, M.H.S., Levene, M., Roussos, G.: Density-based social clustering for mobile users. In: Proceedings of The 13th International Joint Conference on e-Business and Telecommunications, WINSYS, vol. 6, pp. 52–62 (2016)
3. Birkbeck in numbers. http://www.bbk.ac.uk/about-us/bbk/downloads/2014-artic les/bbk33-53-numbers.pdf
4. Eduroam at Birkbeck. http://www.bbk.ac.uk/its/services/wam/Eduroam
5. Allahdadi, A., Morla, R., Aguiar, A., Cardoso, J.S.: Predicting short 802.11 sessions from radius usage data. In: 9th IEEE International Workshop on Performance and Management of Wireless and Mobile Networks, pp. 1–8. IEEE (2013)
6. Cheetham, A.H., Hazel, J.E.: Binary (presence-absence) similarity coefficients. J. Paleontol. pp. 1130–1136 (1969)
7. Clauset, A., Shalizi, C.R., Newman, M.E.: Power-law distributions in empirical data. SIAM Rev. **51**(4), 661–703 (2009)
8. Späth, H.: Cluster Analysis Algorithms for Data Reduction and Classification of Objects. Ellis Horwood Limited, Chichester (1980)
9. Eagle, N., Pentland, A.: Reality mining: sensing complex social systems. Pers. Ubiquitous Comput. **10**(4), 255–268 (2006)
10. Eduroam. https://www.Eduroam.org/
11. Eldaw, M.H.S., Levene, M., Roussos, G.: Presence analytics: discovering meaningful patterns about human presence using WLAN digital imprints. In: Proceedings of the International Conference on Internet of Things and Cloud Computing, p. 53. ACM (2016)
12. Ester, M., Kriegel, H.-P., Sander, J., Xu, X.: A density-based algorithm for discovering clusters in large spatial databases with noise. In: KDD, vol. 96, pp. 226–231 (1996)
13. Kriegel, H.-P., Kröger, P., Sander, J., Zimek, A.: Density-based clustering. Wiley Interdisc. Rev. Data Min. Knowl. Discov. **1**(3), 231–240 (2011)
14. Kumar, U., Yadav, N., Helmy, A.: Gender-based feature analysis in campus-wide wlans. ACM SIGMOBILE Mob. Comput. Commun. Rev. **12**(1), 40–42 (2008)
15. Lee, J.-K., Hou, J.C.: Modeling steady-state and transient behaviors of user mobility: formulation, analysis, and application. In: Proceedings of the 7th ACM International Symposium on Mobile ad hoc Networking and Computing, pp. 85–96. ACM (2006)
16. Mulhanga, M.M., Lima, S.R., Carvalho, P.: Characterising university WLANs within Eduroam context. In: Balandin, S., Koucheryavy, Y., Hu, H. (eds.) NEW2AN/ruSMART -2011. LNCS, vol. 6869, pp. 382–394. Springer, Heidelberg (2011). doi:10.1007/978-3-642-22875-9_35
17. Sneath, P.H.: The application of computers to taxonomy. J. Gen. Microbiol. **17**(1), 201–226 (1957)

Tracking Down High Interference and Low Coverage in 3G/4G Radio Networks Using Automatic RF Measurement Extraction

Marco Sousa[1,2]($\boxtimes$), André Martins[1,3], and Pedro Vieira[2,3]

[1] CELFINET, Consultoria em Telecomunicações Lda., Lisbon, Portugal
{marco.sousa,andre.martins}@celfinet.com
[2] Instituto Superior de Engenharia de Lisboa (ISEL), ADEETC, Lisbon, Portugal
pvieira@deetc.isel.pt
[3] Instituto de Telecomunicações (IT), Lisbon, Portugal

Abstract. This paper presents an automatic approach for the detection of high interference and low coverage scenarios (overshooting and pilot pollution) in Universal Mobile Telecommunications System (UMTS) /Long Term Evolution (LTE) networks. These algorithms, based on periodically extracted Drive Test (DT) measurements (or network trace information), identify the problematic cluster locations for each evaluated cell and compute harshness metrics, at cluster and cell level, quantifying the extent of the problem. The cluster based detection associated with an auto-correlation distance for shadow fading, enables to detect prevailing under performance areas and mitigate detections caused by the radio channel variability. Future work is in motion by adding self-optimization capabilities to the algorithms, which will automatically suggest physical and parameter optimization actions. The proposed algorithms were validated for a live network in both rural and urban scenarios. A total of 173 4th Generation (4G) cells were self-diagnosed and performance metrics were computed. The most negative sub-performance scenarios concern high interference control in urban environment and low coverage in rural environment.

Keywords: Wireless communications · SON · Self-diagnosis · Coverage detection · Interference control

1 Introduction

The increasing network complexity, in terms of number of monitored parameters and parallel operation of 2nd Generation (2G), 3rd Generation (3G) and 4G, is increasing dramatically, besides the ever growing traffic volume and service diversity. In the first quarter of 2016, an average monthly data traffic of almost 6 ExaBytes was registered, with an increase of 60% compared with the first quarter of 2015 [1]. This increases the network Operating Expense (OpEx), forcing mobile operators to pursue strategies for reducing it. Self-Organizing Network

© Springer International Publishing AG 2017
M.S. Obaidat (Ed): ICETE 2016, CCIS 764, pp. 401–425, 2017.
https://doi.org/10.1007/978-3-319-67876-4_19

(SON) algorithms have been seen as the solution, and a way to automatically operate the current and beyond mobile networks.

This paper is an extended version of [8] with results focused in 4G technology instead of 3G as the original work. It focus on the automatic-diagnosing algorithms of low coverage and high interference scenarios, used to trigger optimization processes in self-optimizing functions (within SON). Problem detection is based on periodically extracted DT measurements or geo-positioned network traces [2]. The DT data provides measurements of received signal strength and quality for the different pilot or reference signals that reach a certain location. Moreover, specific filtering is applied to identify the data that denotes either, coverage issues or interference problems, such as overshooting or pilot pollution.

SON and self-diagnosing is a hot research topic and recent work has been done leading to the current research stage [3–5]. The paper contribution is incremental to previous works. Firstly, the used cells service area approximation based on propagation modelling is more accurate when compared with existent research. Secondly, a new cluster partition approach using the auto-correlation distances for shadow fading [6], to limit cluster size, results in a more coherent data analysis. Finally, this work addresses the DT minimization target of 3rd Generation Partnership Project (3GPP) by allowing trace based inputs.

The aim of the present work is to be the cornerstone in a fully self-optimization algorithm. This work corresponds to the network data analysis phase, which will report the detected areas with low performance issues and all relevant data for the further optimization algorithm. Additionally, harshness metrics are already computed, accessing the cells detected problems.

This paper is organized as follows: Sect. 2 defines the scope embedding the present work. In Sect. 3 the concept of DT reliability is presented. Section 4 presents the detailed self-diagnosing process for each algorithm. The results are shown in Sect. 5 and finally, in Sect. 6, conclusions are drawn.

2   Self-optimization

Self-Optimization, aims to maintain network quality and performance with a minimum of manual intervention. It monitors and analyses, either Key Performance Indicator (KPI)s, DT measurements, traces [2] or other sources of information, triggering automated actions in the considered network elements.

Mobile operators have always made extensive DT campaigns to gather RF data. This data is used since a new site is initiated, to assure it's been well deployed, as well with the purpose of optimizing any given area.

By performing a DT campaign, both power and quality of the incoming signals are being continuously measured (might measure different cells signals at the same location and time) and incorporating the Global Positioning System (GPS) locations. This data source provides the support for this work results.

DT data entails considerable operational costs. In alternative, research work has been done to geographically locate an user using the signaling messages exchanged between the terminal equipment and the network. In [2], based on

Measurement Report Messages (MRM), a User Equipment (UE) was positioned. Moreover, the MRM contains Radio Frequency (RF) measurements, as DT data has. In this way, the algorithms presented in this work, can use either DT data or trace based data.

The self-optimization diagram for a network is shown in Fig. 1.

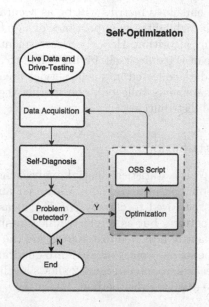

Fig. 1. Self-optimization diagram [8].

The first block, Data Acquisition, should extract automatically the available performance data, either DT or trace data and network topology. Moreover, it should introduce a reliability index R for the input data, which asserts the quality of the data, thus introducing a control mechanism for the self-optimization process. Only when the available data, is significant to access the cells performance, reflected by a value of R higher than a certain threshold, min_value, the self-diagnosis is executed. Otherwise, the available information is not sufficient to retain any strong conclusion.

The valid data should be analyzed by the Self-Diagnosis block, which should detect coverage holes, overshooting and pilot pollution scenarios. When one of this problems is detected more information is added to the detection result, namely, a harshness index H_{cell} is calculated accessing the problem severity in the cell.

In case of being detect any problem by de Self-Diagnosis block, the Optimization block will provide a new antenna configuration to solve or minimize the detected problem. The Operational Support System (OSS) script block is not implemented and remains as future work. It should create the necessary scripts and support files in order to upload the new configurations into the live network.

3   Drive Test Data Classification

There is an undeniable correlation in the assertiveness of the DT based algorithm results and the completeness of a DT campaign. In this sense, it should be guarantied that any algorithm result is based on DT data which is representative of the cell being evaluated, by using DT data above a certain quality threshold. As well, the harshness metrics will be as accurate as the DT is complete or significant. This highlights the importance of a quality metric associated with the DT used in any algorithm. Hence, an assessment of the DT quality is executed before the use of DT data itself, giving origin to a DT reliability index R [4]. It evaluates the data collected in a cells service area, taking into account the percentage of measurements collected, considering the existent road/street network, and its spatial distribution.

3.1   DT Spatial Distribution

The quadrant method [7] is a statistical spatial analysis method used as a mean to test a population point pattern (random, clustered and dispersed). In this context, the method is not used to classify the DT measurements on its geographical distribution pattern, but as a relative measurement of the dispersion level. This allows to quantify how well distributed are the DT measurements.

For that purpose, the service area is divided into quadrants and the number of DT measurements on each accounted. Figure 2 shows a cells service area divided into equal areas, before applying the method.

Fig. 2. Cells geographical area.

Considering the quadrant method data,

$$[Y(A_m)]_P = [x_1, \ldots, x_m] \tag{1}$$

where x_m is the number of measurements in the m quadrant, for all A_m quadrants covering the service area P. Using this data set, the Variance to Mean Ratio (VMR) parameter, that quantifies the DT data pattern, is calculated. It allows to identify the distribution pattern of a data set and it is given by,

$$VRM = \frac{s^2}{\bar{x}} \tag{2}$$

where s^2 is the variance of the number of measurements and $\bar{x}$ the average measurements number in each quadrant. For VMR values higher than one, the pattern is clustered. Below the unit is dispersed and if it's equal to one, the pattern is considered random.

Due to the direct correlation between DT measurements and the own existence of roads, the pattern can't be random and hardly will ever be dispersed. So, the relevant information is how much clustered might be. This knowledge is reflected in the Dispersion Index D_i for a cell i. Using (2), over the data set given by (1) the DT data VRM is calculated. The Dispersion Index D_i, results from the normalization of the DT data VMR, given by,

$$D_i = 1 - \frac{VRM}{VRM_{max}} \tag{3}$$

where VRM_{max} is calculated using (2) in the case of all measurements being in one single area A, the worst dispersion case, thus resulting in a relative value of the data distribution.

3.2 Road Filling Ratio for DT Measurements

The aim is to calculate the road filling ratio, P_i, which represents the percentage of road/street covered in cell i service area, by the DT. In order to proceed, the road network information is fetched using an Application Programming Interface (API). The obtained data is linearly interpolated, for resolution purposes, resulting as shown in Fig. 3.

Regarding, the raw DT data, collected by a DT campaign, it suffers a restructuring before being used by the algorithms. All cells signal measurements are grouped to constitute a bin. A bin represents a geographic area of 10 by 10 m. Moreover all measurements belonging to the same cell whiting a bin area are turned into one, either by averaging the RF values or other statistical approach. In addiction, one bin could contain more than one cell. The bottom line is that the maximum frequency of the binned DT data, is one bin by each ten meters.

From the DT data it's extrapolated the binning grid used to bin the DT raw data. Combining this with all the road/street network points it can be retrieved the theoretical maximum number of DT bins, that a DT campaign would gather if it covered all roads whiting the service area. Only then P_i is calculates as,

Fig. 3. Street data information.

$$P_i = \frac{M}{Max_m} \tag{4}$$

where M is the number of collected bins and Max_m the equivalent of bins for all the road/street extension in the service area of a cell i.

3.3 DT Reliability Index

The DT Reliability Index R_i, gets values in the zero to one range, and it merges the previous two metrics, in the following way,

$$R_i = \alpha_d D_i + \alpha_p P_i \tag{5}$$

where α_d is the weight of the dispersion index D_i, for cell i and α_p is the weight of the percentage of road covered P_i, in cell i. Regarding the weights of both factors (α_d and α_p) they resulted from empirical knowledge, through a statistical analyze of fifty DT classification inquiries, performed to Celfinet's experienced radio engineers [4].

4 The Self-diagnosis Process

The underlying process for the identification of either coverage holes, overshooting or pilot pollution scenarios has a common ground. The goal is always, regarding the specific algorithm, to diagnose prevalent under performance situations in the form of clusters. Furthermore, to attribute a harshness metric based on a statistical analysis to each cluster, and a harshness level of the cell, including all clusters, as presented in Fig. 4.

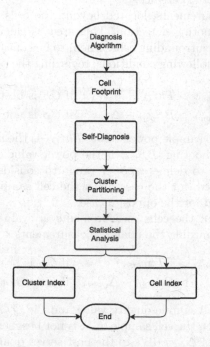

Fig. 4. General detection flowchart [8].

Detecting Coverage Holes. A coverage hole is defined as an area where the pilot (or reference) signal power is in between the lowest network access threshold and the lowest value required for assigning full coverage. Users in this area tend to suffer poor voice or data user experience and possibly dropped calls or high latency.

From the cells footprint, a coverage hole sample must accomplish two conditions. Firstly, it must be best server or within a small power interval to the best server of the respective bin. To these, we will refer as serving samples. Note that best server is the measurement that corresponds to the best cell, and that should serve the mobiles at that point. Secondly, the best server measurement from the respective serving sample bin, must be below the coverage threshold,

$$BS_{power} < Thr_{CH} \qquad (6)$$

where BS_{power} is the best server value and Thr_{CH} is the minimum serving power value, which is technology (3G/4G) and use case dependent.

Detecting Overshooting. An overshooting situation occurs when the cells coverage reaches beyond what is planned. Generally, occurs as an "island" of coverage in another cells service area. Overshooted areas may also induce dropped calls and bad quality of experience.

Only the DT measurements, located beyond the cells service area are considered for the overshooting detection. This area, is calculated using the first interference tier of the surrounding cells. Then, to be considered overshooting, it must comply with the following conditions, regarding the power value measured,

$$\begin{cases} CS_{pwr} > Thr_{OS}, & \text{if } CS \text{ is best} \\ CS_{pwr} > BS_{pwr} - \Delta_{pwr}, & \text{if } CS \text{ is not best} \end{cases} \tag{7}$$

where CS_{pwr} is the cell sample power value, Thr_{OS} is the minimum power value to be considered overshooting, BS_{pwr} is the power value of the bin best server cell and Δ_{pwr} is used to define a power range to consider overshooting. Two conditions are presented, for the case when the cell sample, CS, in analysis is the best server cell and for the opposite case.

Also, the quality of the cells measurements is evaluated, using the same conditions as 7 but regarding the quality measurements,

$$\begin{cases} CS_{qual} > QThr_{OS}, & \text{if } CS \text{ is best} \\ CS_{qual} > BS_{qual} - \Delta_{qual}, & \text{if } CS \text{ is not best} \end{cases} \tag{8}$$

where CS_{qual} is the cell sample quality value and the $QThr_{OS}$ is the minimum quality threshold. When the cell sample, CS, is not best server it must be within a quality value range of Δ_{qual} dB's to the best server quality value, BS_{qual}.

Not all overshooting situations are harmful to the network or non-intended. Even though effectively being far from the normal service area, it might happen that, due to terrain profile, it still might be the cell in best condition to serve in that area. In that sense, when the overshooting cells measurements are above the second best server cell by at least a power warning threshold, it indicates the above-mentioned situation. They will still be identified as an overshooting and continue the process, but containing an observation that optimizing this overshooting area might reduce the overall network performance.

Detecting Pilot Pollution. Pilot pollution remarks a scenario where too many pilots (or reference signals in the case of LTE) are received in one area. Besides the excess of pilots, it lacks a dominant one. These areas are usually highly interfered, resulting in a poorer user experience.

The cells measurements inducing pilot pollution, are in a serving ranking bellow the ideal maximum number of cells serving in that area. To the cells footprint where the previous is verified, the following conditions must be complied to be in a pilot pollution situation,

$$\begin{cases} CS_{pwr} > BS_{pwr} - \Delta_{pwr} \\ CS_{qual} > BS_{qual} - \Delta_{qual} \end{cases} \tag{9}$$

where CS_{pwr} is the cell sample power value, BS_{pwr} is the power value of the bin best server cell and Δ_{pwr} is used to define a pilot pollution power range. The second condition is equal to the previous, but regarding quality measurements.

4.1 Cluster Partitioning

The radio mobile channel is uncertain due mainly to the effects of fading and multipath. So, the values caught on DT measurements, which are reported at one single instance of time, may not correspond to the average behavior of the radio channel in that point. In order to mitigate this variability, the detection process is executed at the cluster level and not at bin level. This enables to detect prevailing under performance areas and not simply variations, normal and non-correlated with network issues. Therefore, using the auto-correlation distance for shadow fading [6], to limit cluster size, this gives more assertiveness in the detected results.

Regarding the cluster division process itself, it is accomplished using a dendrogram structure [9]. It is a tree diagram that, in this application, translates the distance relation between all DT measurements detected, as in Fig. 5.

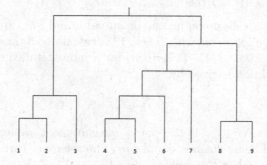

Fig. 5. Dendrogram structure [8].

The tree diagram building process, aggregates successively the closest bin/cluster pair until all the bins form a unique cluster. At each aggregation, a different cluster division possibility is built.

The next step is to define which cluster arrangement is the best. Several algorithms accomplish this purpose, and throw different metrics and approaches. Overall what they evaluate is how well concentrated are the points in clusters, when the distance similarity [11] is high. The used approach was the silhouette method [12]. It provides a metric $s(i)$,

$$s_i = \frac{b(i) - a(i)}{max\{a(i), b(i)\}} \tag{10}$$

where $a(i)$ is the average dissimilarity to the other points of the cluster, $b(i)$ the lowest average dissimilarity of i to any other cluster. It evaluates how well any given point lies within its cluster. Thus, an $s(i)$ close to one means that the bin is appropriately clustered. This approach is only applied to the cluster division possibilities that respect the maximum cluster size.

4.2   Cluster Statistical Analysis

A statistical analysis is conducted to each detected cluster. The purpose is to classify the harshness (severity of the problem) and rank it. The result is a harshness index, $H_{cluster}$, per cluster, given by,

$$H_{cluster} = \frac{\sum_{i=1}^{N} \beta_i U(c(i))}{\sum_{i=1}^{N} \beta_i}, 0 \leq H_{cluster} \leq 1 \tag{11}$$

where β_i is the weight for condition i and the $U(c(i))$ is the percentage of bins, from all bins aggregated in one cluster, that verify condition $c(i)$. Once again, these conditions are dependent on the behavior that is being analyzed.

The coverage hole algorithm calculates its $H_{cluster}$ index (11) using the following conditions,

$$C(i) = Prob(CS_{power} \leq Thr_i) \quad i \in [1,3], \tag{12}$$

where CS_{power} is the cells power measurement value and Thr_i are different coverage thresholds to be compared with. Then, 12 is calculated 3 times using different thresholds (e.g. $\{-105, -111, -117\}\, dBm$) for a more detailed assessment.

The forth condition is given by,

$$C(4) = Prob(NS_{power} \leq Thr_4) \tag{13}$$

where the variable NS_{power} is the power measurement value of the best cell other than the cell being diagnosed and Thr_4 the reference threshold, which has an equal value to the last threshold used in 12.

These conditions allow to classify the harshness of a coverage hole in two forms. The condition (12) only concerns to the power value of the source cell. Using different Thr_i values, a cluster will be classified more or less harsh. The forth condition (13), evaluates the existence of other fallback cell in the cluster. These thresholds are defined using as reference the power detection threshold.

The coverage hole harshness index H_{cell} represents a percentage of clusters in coverage hole vs the clusters of the cell footprint. This metric might be devious, especially if the DT data is low in number. In that case, the metric will exceed the true percentage value. That's why the DT reliability index R is so important in terms of interpreting the results.

The overshooting cluster harshness evaluation proceeds with the conditions,

$$C(i) = Prob(CS_{power} \geq Thr_i) \quad i \in [1,3], \tag{14}$$

where CS_{power} is the cells power value and Thr_i are power thresholds to be compared with. Once again, 14 is evaluated three times, with different thresholds (e.g. $\{-95, -85, -75\}\, dBm$), allowing more resolution in distinguishing overshooting clusters in severe terms.

The last evaluated condition, aims to quantify the quality degradation caused by the overshooting cell,

$$C(4) = Prob(Degradation_{qual} \geq Thr_{deg}), \qquad (15)$$

where $Degradation_{qual}$ is calculated based on [10], where an equation was deduced, based on DT data to estimate the quality degradation caused by a given cell. Thr_{deg} is the reference threshold to be compared [10].

The overshooting harshness index H_{cell} represents the average percentage of overshooting clusters against the victim cells footprint, divided also in clusters. Once again, the importance of the DT reliability index must be highlighted.

Concerning the pilot pollution algorithm, the conditions to evaluate the harshness level are the following,

$$C(i) = Prob(BS_{qual} \leq Thr_i) \quad i \in [1, 3], \qquad (16)$$

where BS_{qual} is the signals quality of the best server and Thr_i are the reference values to be compared with (e.g. $\{-10, -14, -18\}\, dB$). The higher the percentage of bins that satisfy 16 the more interfered is that area.

Furthermore, the last condition evaluates the best server power values,

$$C(4) = Prob(BS_{power} \leq Thr_4) \qquad (17)$$

where BS_{power} is the signal power of the best server measurement and Thr_4 is power threshold to serve as reference (e.g. $-90\, dBm$).

In the pilot pollution case, being a scenario where cells affect another cell performance, the approach for the pilot pollution harshness index H_{cell} is the same as described in the overshooting module.

5   Applying the Algorithm to a Live Network

The developed algorithms were applied in a 4G live network using real DT data, for both an urban and a rural scenarios. 84 4G cells operating at different bands, for rural environment, and 89 cells for urban scenario, were self-diagnosed and performance metrics were computed.

Regarding the algorithm's thresholds used to identify the under performance behaviors, they are extremely dependent on mobile operator policies, requirements, type of service, etc., so a set of default parameters was used, as detailed in Table 1. The columns "CH", "OS" and "PP" refer to coverage holes, overshooting and pilot pollution algorithms, respectively.

5.1   Rural Environment

In this section it is presented one detection example, obtained in the rural environment. Some figures representative of the diagnosed cell are presented with the clusters detailed information.

Table 1. Algorithms thresholds.

	CH	OS	PP
Min. RSRP threshold [dBm]	−115	−110	−110
RSRP delta [dB]	3	6	10
Min. RSRQ threshold [dB]	N/A	−10	N/A
RSRQ delta [dB]	N/A	6	6
Min. bins/cluster [#]	5	5	5
Max. cluster radius [m]	57,5	57,5	57,5
Max. serving cells [#]	N/A	N/A	3

Coverage Holes. Figure 6 exhibits on the right the diagnosed cell and on the left side four clusters in coverage hole condition.

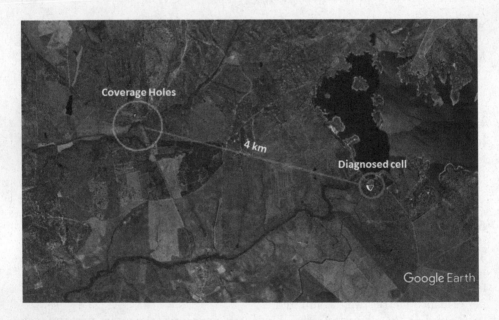

Fig. 6. Rural coverage hole scenario.

It can be observed, that a co-site cell is differently highlighted as in the coverage holes cluster areas, both cells (including the diagnosed cell) exhibit cell dominance. The dominance is evaluated taking into account the serving cell measurements (see Sect. 4). In this case, the algorithm (based solely on the DT data) could not identify with some degree on certainty, which cell should primarily provide coverage in that area. In such a scenario, the optimization of either cells could provide the coverage requirements for that area. Concerning the H_{cell} index, it was obtained 10%. This reveals that 10% of the diagnosed cell footprint has coverage issues.

In relation to the detected clusters, they were four and their detailed information is shown in Table 2, including the number of detected bins, the average values of RSRP and RSRQ and the average bin distance to the diagnosed cell.

Table 2. Rural coverage holes measurement details.

	Bins [#]	Average RSRP [dBm]	Average RSRQ [dB]	Distance [m]
Cluster 1	9	−117	−13	4046
Cluster 2	11	−124	−16	4123
Cluster 3	7	−118	−14	4490
Cluster 4	12	−118	−14	4328

The cluster detailed information, shows approximated RF values for all clusters except one, as the clusters are located next to each other. In terms of coverage, the average RSRP is very low, as the average value per cluster has a maximum of −117 dBm, which is not enough to provide QoS to the 4G services.

In Fig. 7 the terrain profile between the diagnosed cell and the coverage holes clusters is shown.

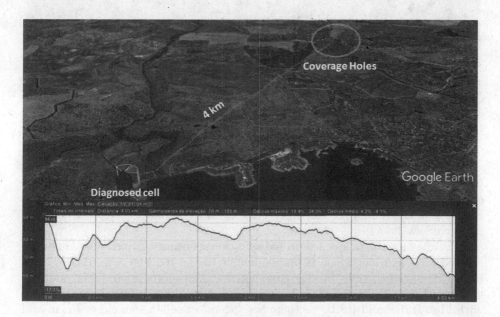

Fig. 7. Rural coverage hole terrain profile.

The diagnosed cell is located on the left side of the terrain profile view and the clusters on the right side. It can be seen that there is Non-Line-of-Sight (NLOS) due to the highly irregular terrain altitudes. Furthermore, the diagnosed cell is not oriented directly to the affected area which admits less power to that area. Finally, the diagnosed cell was parametrized with 5° of Electrical Downtilt (EDT), lowering the emitted power to the cluster areas. A possible optimization could be the decrease of the applied downtilt.

Overshooting. One example of rural overshooting is displayed in Fig. 8, where the diagnosed cell is on the left side and the overshooting clusters on the right.

Fig. 8. Rural overshooting scenario. (Color figure online)

It was added a red line between the diagnosed cell (left side) and the detected cluster (right side) in order to facilitate the image interpretation as the detected cluster is at 28000 m of the diagnosed cell. These clusters were diagnosed accordingly to Sect. 4.

The diagnose of this cell detected one overshooting cluster. This cluster is located on a highway which is perpendicular to the red line (Fig. 8). In addiction, there are two cells directly covering that highway stretch. This validates this overshooting scenario. The diagnosed cell should not be reaching that area with high RSRP and RSRQ as there are two other cells much closer (5 km and 4 km) with good coverage conditions. Respecting the cell harshness index, it was obtained 2%. This indicates that the overshooting cell is affecting 2% of victim cell DT data that constitutes its cell service area.

Table 3. Rural overshooting measurement details.

	Bins [#]	Average RSRP [dBm]	Average RSRQ [dB]	Distance [m]
Cluster 1	5	−103	−14	28148

In Table 3 the overshooting measurements details, in terms of number of bins, average RSRP and RSRQ and the distance to the diagnosed cell are displayed.

In this case, the overshooting cluster was constituted by 5 bins with a considerable power, average RSRP of −103 dBm, given the high distance of around 28 km.

To further complete the analysis of this scenario, Fig. 9 exihbits the terrain profile between the diagnosed cell (left side) and the detected cluster (right side).

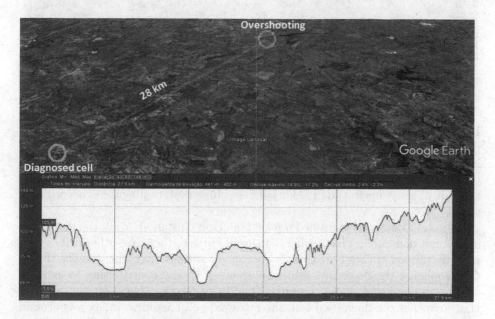

Fig. 9. Rural overshooting terrain profile.

It can been seen that there is Line-of-Sight (LOS) even though the high distance separating the cell and the overshooting cluster. In addiction, this cell is emitting on the 800 MHz band which is know to have lower path loss. Regarding the cell parametrization, the 2° of EDT are not sufficient to avoid this overshooting scenario taking into account that also the cell is oriented to the overshooting area. This conjunction of situations and parametrization enables the non intended overshooting scenario which could be diminished by adding downtilt to the antenna or reducing the transmitted power.

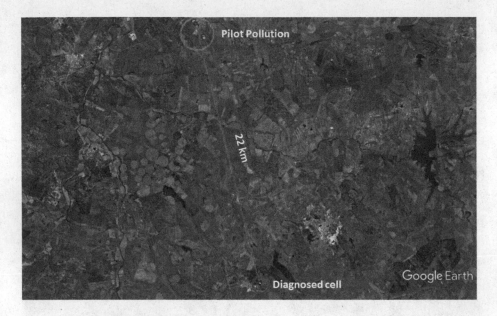

Fig. 10. Rural pilot pollution scenario. (Color figure online)

Pilot Pollution. Completing the rural diagnosed examples, in Fig. 10, is displayed a rural pilot pollution example. The diagnosed cell (bottom of the image) is connected with a red line to the detected pilot pollution clusters (upper side). Once again the red line was added to help the analysis, as the involved distance is of great magnitude (22 km). These clusters were diagnosed accordingly to Sect. 4.

The cells diagnosis identified 6 pilot pollution clusters. For all, the diagnosed cell is non dominant. This means that in all clusters there are other cells which provide service in those areas in far better conditions than the diagnosed cell. Consequently, the diagnosed cell in those areas is only contributing to increase the interference and diminishing the Quality of Service (QoS) for the users in that area. For the diagnosed cell, the retrieved cell harshness index was around 9%. It denotes, that on average, there is more than one victim cell, meaning that the victim's footprint affected percentage was 9%.

In Table 4 is showed the measurement details of the identified pilot pollution clusters. It contemplates the average RF metrics as well as the number of detected bins and its distance to the diagnosed cell.

The measurement data indicates approximately constant values between each cluster as they are all located on the same area. The interference on that area might be evaluated by the low values of RSRQ exhibited, which are around −20 dB.

In Fig. 11, and to complete the analysis, it is displayed the terrain profile between the diagnosed cell (left side) and the pilot pollution clusters (right side).

Table 4. Rural pilot pollution measurement details.

	Bins [#]	Average RSRP [dBm]	Average RSRQ [dB]	Distance [m]
Cluster 1	5	−114	−19	21517
Cluster 2	6	−114	−19	21669
Cluster 3	12	−110	−19	22662
Cluster 4	5	−111	−20	22742
Cluster 5	11	−110	−21	22898
Cluster 6	5	−109	−18	23146

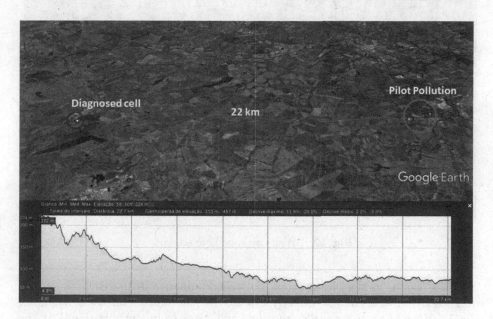

Fig. 11. Rural pilot pollution terrain profile.

The diagnosed cell is on a location significantly higher than the clusters location heights, enabling LOS for a wide area. In addiction, it operates on the 800 MHz band which provides even more coverage. With this setup, the diagnosed cell footprint will be wide spread overlapping other cells service areas, such as the above mentioned pilot pollution scenario. The diagnosed cell parametrization indicates that neither Mechanical Downtilt (MDT) or EDT is applied, which could be a possible optimization to minimize the interference issues.

5.2   Urban Environment

In this section is presented some examples of diagnosed cells in a 4G urban scenario, supported by representative figures of the detected scenarios.

Coverage Holes. The first example is a coverage holes scenario, which is represented in Fig. 12. The diagnosed cell is highlighted in the upper side of the image and the detected coverage hole is on the bottom side. This cluster was diagnosed accordingly to Sect. 4.

Fig. 12. Urban coverage hole scenario.

Once again, in the cluster area, the cell dominance is shared between the diagnosed cell and the cell directly oriented to the cluster on the left side of Fig. 12. Each of these two cells are valid candidates to be optimized and fix the low coverage situation. Regarding the diagnosed cell, its cell harshness index is 8%, indicating the extend of the cell low coverage.

The detailed information of the coverage hole cluster is presented in Table 5.

Table 5. Urban coverage holes measurement details.

	Bins [#]	Average RSRP [dBm]	Average RSRQ [dB]	Distance [m]
Cluster 1	8	−120	−20	755

In this case, the average RSRP is very low (−120 dBm) even though the distance to the cell is of 755 m. Moreover, this cluster is composed by 8 different bins, where the diagnosed cell is in coverage hole condition.

To complement the analysis of the diagnosed cell, Fig. 13 exhibits the elevation profile between the diagnosed cell (left side) and the coverage cluster on the right side of the figure.

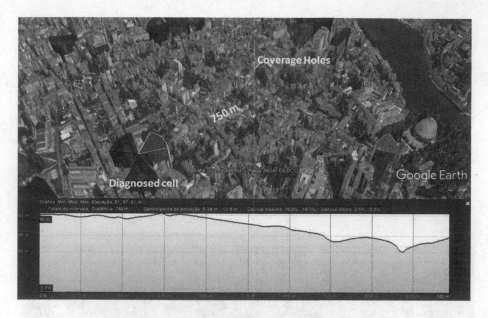

Fig. 13. Urban coverage hole terrain profile.

From Fig. 13, it can be ascertained that in one hand the cluster is on a lower height that the diagnosed cell and in another hand, due to the existing buildings the LOS is probably obstructed. In addiction, the cell operates on the 1800 MHz band which is more vulnerable to the radio channel attenuation. The other dominant cell in the cluster area is highlighted on the right side of the Fig. 13 an is directly oriented to the cluster area. Besides building obstruction the terrain elevation does not grant LOS. Furthermore, both cell antennas are downtilted. The conjunction of these aspects leads to the coverage hole existence.

Overshooting. Moving to the urban overshooting example, it is represented in Fig. 14, where the diagnosed cell is on the bottom side of the figure and the detected overshooting clusters on the upper side, separated by a distance of 5000 m.

The diagnosed cell is in overshooting situation as is providing coverage on an area far beyond the diagnosed cell service area. Moreover, there is an highlighted cell in the upper side of Fig. 14 which is identified as the cell that should provide service in the cluster area, thus constituting the victim cell. It can be ascertained that the victim cell should cover the cluster areas taking into account solely the DT data and topology information.

More detailed information on the detected overshooting clusters is presented in Table 6, containing the RSRP and RSRQ averages values for each detected cluster as well as the number of bins and the average distance to the diagnosed cell.

Table 6. Urban overshooting measurement details.

	Bins [#]	Average RSRP [dBm]	Average RSRQ [dB]	Distance [m]
Cluster 1	12	−97	−9	5218
Cluster 2	5	−96	−9	5402

Firstly, the average bin distance to the diagnosed cell of more than 5000 m, in a urban scenario is evidence of a possible overshooting. Moreover, associated high values of RSRP and RSRQ characterizes an overshooting situation. Likewise, the number of detected bins is representative of a repetitive radio channel behavior which enforces the classification of this scenario as an overshooting situation.

Fig. 14. Urban overshooting scenario.

The terrain height information, between the diagnosed cell and the overshooting clusters, is displayed in Fig. 15. The diagnosed cell is on the left side and the detected clusters on the right side.

The diagnosed cell is in a higher ground than the overshooting cluster as it can be seen in Fig. 15, providing LOS between the diagnosed cell and its overshooting clusters. Even with 6° of EDT the received power is still high enough for this overshooting case be detected. A possible optimization for this scenario could be a reduction of the transmitted power.

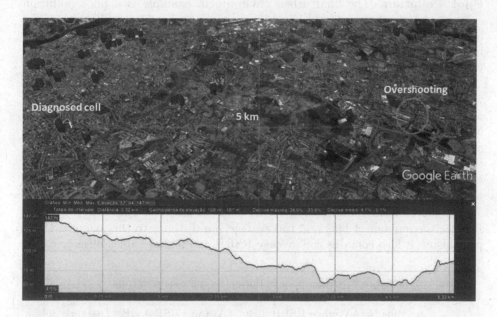

Fig. 15. Urban overshooting terrain profile.

Fig. 16. Urban pilot pollution scenario.

Pilot Pollution. The final urban environment example is a pilot pollution example, which is presented in Fig. 16. The diagnosed cell is highlighted on the bottom of the figure. 2 clusters were diagnosed, where the diagnosed cell is inducing pilot pollution, in the middle of the figure. The other highlighted cells, were best server in at least one of the bins with pilot pollution.

As stated, 2 different clusters were noticed, where the diagnosed complies with the pilot pollution conditions (Sect. 4) and the diagnosed is not dominant, which confirms the clusters areas do not belong to the diagnosed service area. Nonetheless, in this particular case, the number of different reference signals in the cluster areas is in such amount, that based on the DT data the algorithm could not identify with a minimum of certainty which cells were being affected by the diagnosed cell. In such a scenario, it is not possible to calculate the cell harshness index.

For more detailed information on the detected clusters, Table 7 is presented. Besides the number of bins and the average bin distance to the diagnosed cell, per cluster, it also contains the average RSRP and RSRQ values measured.

Table 7. Urban pilot pollution measurement details.

	Bins [#]	Average RSRP [dBm]	Average RSRQ [dB]	Distance [m]
Cluster 1	6	−90	−17	731
Cluster 2	5	−92	−20	1073

The data presented in Table 7 is evidence of a more severe case of pilot pollution comparing with the rural example. The average quality of the reference signal is still low, but in this case the average RSRP is significantly higher. With higher values of power, the reference signal quality is expected to be higher as well.

Finally, to understand the influence of the terrain profile in this pilot pollution scenario, Fig. 17 presents the elevation profile between the diagnosed cell and the pilot pollution clusters.

It can be confirmed the existence of LOS between the diagnosed cell and the detected clusters and the non existence of major obstacles. Moreover, the distance between them is small given the radio channel propagation characteristics and the 800 MHz band. Regarding the antenna parametrization, both the MDT and the EDT are set to zero degrees which is favorable for the diagnosed cell overlap excessively the surrounding cells service areas. A possible optimization could be applied (a downtilt to the antenna) to restrain the propagation of the diagnosed cell reference signal to areas that it should not provide service.

5.3   Overview

The overall results are shown in Table 8. It can ascertained that in rural environment the main RF issues regard low coverage opposite to the main interference

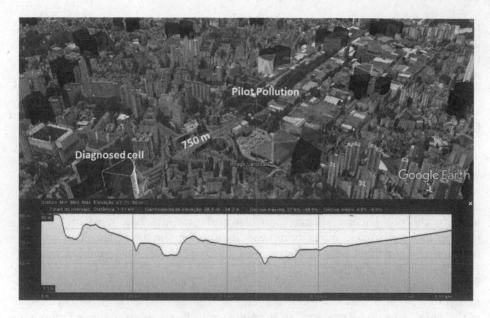

Fig. 17. Urban pilot pollution terrain profile.

issues in urban environment. It is an expected result, as the site density on urban environments it much higher than in rural environments.

Table 8. Self-diagnosis detected scenarios

	Rural			Urban		
Radio environment	CH	OS	PP	CH	OS	PP
Analyzed cells	84			89		
Detected cells	15	3	9	19	9	34
Average bins [#]	21	10	13	29	11	9
Average index H_{cell}	39	3	17	14	2	18
Average index R	35	47	41	52	57	59

Concerning to the number of detected bins in coverage holes, overshooting and pilot pollution, it does not reveal a significant difference between radio environments, which suggests that the extend of each problem does not depend on the radio environment. Nonetheless, comparing the extent of the problem between the algorithms, it can be established that the coverage holes scenarios tend to be in greater dimension than the interference problems (overshooting and pilot pollution).

Respecting the index H_{cell}, the values between rural and urban are discrepant only for the coverage hole situation. The H_{cell} corresponds to the percentage of the cells footprint in coverage hole, and the footprint depends on the completeness of the DT. In rural environments, as the cell service area is much higher than urban environments, it is less likely that the DT retrieves data for all the service area. So, the H_{cell} is calculated based on incomplete data leading to an overestimated index.

6   Conclusions

This research work presents a RF self-diagnosis module to be used in a network self-optimization feature. The self-diagnosis module detects low coverage and high interference scenarios (overshooting and pilot pollution) in UMTS/LTE networks. These algorithms, based on periodically extracted DT measurements, identify the problematic cluster locations and compute harshness metrics, at cluster and cell level, quantifying the extent of the problem. The above-mentioned algorithms were validated for a 4G live network with real DT data in rural and urban scenarios.

The result section was based on the analysis of 84 cells for rural environment and 89 cells ins urban environment. The results showed that in urban areas, with a high site density, the main optimization efforts rely on the interference mitigation and not coverage optimization. Oppositely, in rural areas the coverage optimization is priority to interference control.

The cluster division, with a RF correlation distance limitation, revealed it self as a more accurate approach to detected prevalent, non intended behaviours of the mobile radio channel. Moreover, the cluster division could provide a valid simplification for the optimization module, in the sense that, the optimization process could be reduced to the optimization of clusters, and not the DT data itself.

Future work is in motion by adding self-optimization capabilities to the algorithms, which will automatically suggest physical and parameter optimization actions, based on the already developed harshness metrics.

References

1. Ericsson: Ericsson mobility report, Technical report, ERiCSSON (2016)
2. Vieira, P., Silva, N., Fernandes, N., Rodrigues, A.J., Varela, L.: Improving accuracy for OTD based 3G geolocation in real urban/suburban environments. In: Wireless Personal Multimedia Communications Symposium - WPMC (2014)
3. Duarte, D., Vieira, P., Rodrigues, A.J., Silva, N.: A new approach for crossed sector detection in live mobile networks based on radio measurements. In: Wireless Personal Multimedia Communications Symposium - WPMC (2015)
4. Sousa, M., Martins, A., Vieira, P., Oliveira, N., Rodrigues, A.: Caracterizacao da Fiabilidade de Medidas Rádio em Larga Escala para Redes Auto-Otimizadas. In: 9th Congresso do Comité Português da URSI - "5G e a Internet do futuro" (2015)
5. Sallent, O., Perez-Romero, J., Sanchez-Gonzalez, J., Agusti, R., Diaz-Guerra, M.A., Henche, D., Paul, D.: Automatic detection of sub-optimal performance in UMTS networks based on drive-test measurements. In: 2011 7th International Conference on Network and Service Management (CNSM) (2011)

6. Kysti, P., Meinil, J., Hentil, L., Zhao, X., Jms, T., Schneider, C., Narandzi, M., Milojevi, M., Hong, A., Ylitalo, J., Holappa, V., Alatossava, M., Bultitude, R., Jong, Y., Rautiainen, T.: IST-4-027756 WINNER II D1.1.2 V1.2. Technical report, EBITG, TUI, UOULU, CU/CRC, NOKIA (2007)
7. Kalkhan, M.A.: Spatial Statistics: Geospatial Information Modeling and Thematic Mapping. CRC Press, Boca Raton (2011)
8. Sousa, M., Martins, A., Vieira, P.: Self-diagnosing low coverage and high interference in 3G/4G radio access networks based on automatic RF measurement extraction. In: Proceedings of the 13th International Joint Conference on e-Business and Telecommunications (2016)
9. Izenman, A.J.: Modern Multivariate Statistical Techniques: Regression, Classification, and Manifold Learning. Springer, Heidelberg (2008)
10. Sanchez-Gonzalez, J., Sallent, O., Prez-Romero, J., Agust, R.: A multi-cell multi-objective self-optimisation methodology based on genetic algorithms for wireless cellular networks. Int. J. Netw. Manag. **23**, 287–307 (2013)
11. Zheng, N., Xue, J.: Statistical Learning and Pattern Analysis for Image and Video Processing. Springer, Heidelberg (2009)
12. Witten, I.H., Frank, E.: Data Mining: Practical Machine Learning Tools and Techniques. Morgan Kaufmann Publishers Inc., Burlington (2005)

On the Use of Load Balancing for Saving Capacity in Dual Layer 3G Radio Access Networks

Tiago Pedro[1,2], André Martins[1,3(✉)], António Rodrigues[1,2], and Pedro Vieira[1,4]

[1] Instituto de Telecomunicações (IT), Lisbon, Portugal
andre.martins@celfinet.com
[2] Instituto Superior Técnico (IST), Lisbon, Portugal
[3] Celfinet, Consultoria Em Telecomunicações, Lisbon, Portugal
[4] Instituto Superior de Engenharia de Lisboa (ISEL), Lisbon, Portugal

Abstract. In order to progress in a highly competitive and complex market, Mobile Network Operators (MNOs) have to be efficient in managing their resources. This is definitely important in what concerns the available network capacity. This work presents a method to improve the longevity of the installed capacity for the MNO's Base Stations. This was achieved using a Load Balancing algorithm, which takes into account the channel element usage of 3rd Generation (3G) sites, and sets a Received Signal Code Power (RSCP) threshold value for each one. Its evaluation is done by using a Traffic Forecast algorithm, based on a fitting method, in order to obtain an estimate of when the sites' capacity limit is reached, before and after applying Load Balancing. The utilised input data consists of real traffic statistics, including geo-located indicators. During the course of this research work it was possible to develop a semi-automatic method for network optimisation using geo-located data, thus contributing to the development of research on Self-Organizing Networks. This project was developed in collaboration with a Portuguese telecommunications consulting company, Celfinet, which provided valuable supervision and guidance. Using the proposed method, and considering a year of observation and implementation, savings of about 70% in capacity expansions in the network were achievable.

Keywords: 3G Wireless Access Networks · Traffic Forecasting · Load Balancing · Capacity management · Geo-positioned indicators

1 Introduction

The Telecommunications industry is subjected to many expenses, coming either from day-to-day operation costs, usually called Operational Expenditure (OpEx), or from investments that need to be made in order to improve the network, Capital Expenditure (CapEx). Technological progress in the field, namely the appearance of more powerful user devices such as smartphones that allow higher bit rates, demands an increase in network capacity. Just last year, the

© Springer International Publishing AG 2017
M.S. Obaidat (Ed): ICETE 2016, CCIS 764, pp. 426–449, 2017.
https://doi.org/10.1007/978-3-319-67876-4_20

total mobile data traffic grew 69% [1]. Additionally, it is expected that by the end of 2021 data traffic will have increased ten-fold [2].

In order to keep CapEx, and also OpEx, to a minimum, operators should make the most out of the available resources. Mobile operators need to be able to define network capacity in terms of useful costumer-centric Key Performance Indicators (KPIs), install capacity in the several network elements on a just-in-time basis and exploit soft capacity properties of modern network technologies [3].

Densification of the networks in order to meet these traffic demands causes a greater level of complexity when optimizing the network parameters. The only way this optimization can be cost-efficient is to have more automated and autonomous systems such as Self-Organizing Networks (SON) [4]. Implementing a SON allows savings in expenditure for operators, for example by delaying the need to upgrade the capacity of a site that otherwise would be considered at its limit.

1.1 Objectives

In order to present a solution for the problems previously mentioned, it was decided to develop two algorithms: a Traffic Forecasting algorithm, which will allow the operator to know when to perform a capacity upgrade, adding radio equipment hardware in base stations in order to increase the traffic throughput of a site; and a Load Balancing (LB) algorithm that will allow this moment to be delayed as most as possible.

This work was developed for Third-generation (3G) Wireless Access Networks, which operate in two different frequency bands, 900 and 2100 MHz. Operators usually don't distribute traffic equally between these two bands, creating an overload in the 2100 MHz band. This band is usually given a higher priority for connections, since the 900 MHz band is used mostly to assure site coverage. The developed Load Balancing algorithm will try to correct this issue.

In order to develop a meaningful, realistic and technically accurate solution, a collaboration with a Portuguese telecommunications consulting company, Celfinet, was established. Celfinet provided the necessary input data for the development of this research work as well as guidance and supervision throughout the project. This allowed designing a semi-automatic algorithm for network optimization, thus contributing for the development of SONs in Portugal.

The first results of this ongoing research work were previously published in [5]. This paper presents the more recent and extensive results around saving capacity in real 3G radio access networks.

1.2 Related Work

Extensive work is being developed in both Traffic Forecasting and Load Balancing algorithms in both academia and industry environments. The work developed in [6–10] present several solutions for Traffic Forecasting which were already tested, employing different methods such as fitting functions, entropy theory and Auto-Regressive Integrated Moving Average (ARIMA). In [4] several theoretical methods and driving factors for Load Balancing are detailed and in [11], a practical example of an algorithm using adaptive thresholds is presented.

1.3   Structure

This article is organized in five sections. The first introduces the problem at hand and inserts it in the current network situation. The second presents the solution developed for Traffic Forecasting, along with the corresponding prediction error analysis. The third section presents the Load Balancing solution used to solve the issue presented in the first section. In the fourth section, an analysis is made combining the two algorithms in order to know the obtained gained from the Load Balancing algorithm. The final section sums up the conclusions taken from this work and presents some possible future improvements that can be made.

2   Traffic Forecast

As previously mentioned, the Traffic Forecast algorithm was developed with the objective of providing a tool for predicting when a site's capacity limit is reached. The chosen approach was to design a forecast algorithm based on a fitting model. In order to validate the algorithm, real traffic statistics and KPIs were provided by a Portuguese telecommunications operator. The data is from a total of 43 sites with dual frequency band deployment and spans of the course of 192 days with a daily sample frequency.

In order to obtain more significant results, since the data is highly periodical over each week, it was decided to also apply the algorithm to three different compressed data sets. These compressed sets make use of the data periodicity by grouping each 7 consecutive samples and creating a new array with a weekly sample frequency. The three methods used for compressing the data are defined in Eqs. 1 to 3:

- **Weekly Average:**

$$W_{t_{avg}} = \frac{1}{7} \sum_{k=7t}^{7t+6} D_k \tag{1}$$

- **Weekly Peak Value:**

$$W_{t_{pk}} = \max_{k=[7t,7t+6]}(D_k) \tag{2}$$

- **Weekly 90th Percentile:**

$$W_{t_{90}} = D'_i, \quad i = \left\lceil N\frac{P}{100} \right\rceil \tag{3}$$

In the equations above, W_t is the weekly value obtained, where t indicates the corresponding week number (beginning in 0) and $\mathbf{D}$ is the original daily vector, where k represents the corresponding day number. In Eq. 3, $\mathbf{D'}$ is a sorted vector of daily values for each week t, from least to greatest value, N is its size, which is 7 since it is a weekly vector with values for each day, and P is the order of the percentile desired, which in this case is 90. In practice, since i equals 6, the 90th Percentile will choose the second biggest value of the week.

2.1 Weekly Site Characterization

In order to understand how each site's usage is distributed along each week, a function was developed to differentiate sites in three separate categories: working-days sites, weekend sites and sites with no weekly trend. This was achieved by comparing the average traffic, over the 192 day sample period, during weekends and week-days and considering a threshold of 10%, i.e. if the average usage in working-days is 10% greater than the average usage in weekends then the site is considered to be a working-days site.

Since most of the sites are located in the city centre the results are not very significant, however this function can be used to characterize a sample of sites with a larger disparity in weekly usage. The obtained results for the available sample of sites is detailed in Table 1. In Fig. 1 the sites are portrayed in their actual geographic locations using Google Earth^{TM}. The sites marked in red are working-day sites and the ones marked in yellow present no weekly usage trend.

It can be observed that the sites marked in yellow are essentially located in touristic locations. Another relevant case to be mentioned is a site which covers one of the football stadiums. These sites do not have a defined weekly trend since the aforementioned situations are independent of the week day. The obvious exception is the football stadium, which has a high usage during certain weekends, usually every two weeks, and also on some working days when there are European competitions.

These results can be used in forecasting traffic by selecting the more relevant set of data to predict. For example, if a site is considered a weekend site, then the forecasting algorithm can be adapted to predict only the weekend usage of the site, which will be the capacity limiting period. This can allow better prediction errors as well as more significant results for the operator, who needs to decide when and how to expand the capacity of the sites.

Table 1. Site characterization according to weekly usage [5].

Site type	Number of sites
Working-days site	35
Weekend site	0
No trend	8

Fig. 1. Mapping of sites according to their weekly usage [5]. (Color figure online)

2.2   Forecast Methodology

In order to be able to validate the algorithm, the full length of the data set was divided into three equal sub-sets, as detailed in Fig. 2. The first two are used as the input for the algorithm whereas the last will be used to compare with the obtained forecast for validation.

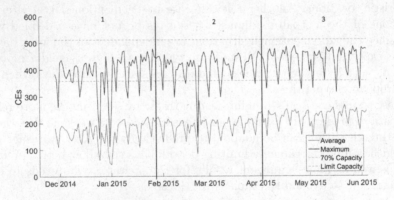

Fig. 2. Splitting of input data into the 3 sets [5].

2.3   Stages

A fitting algorithm tries to fit the input data to a set of functions and chooses the best fit to make a forecast. The set of chosen functions should reflect typical traffic behaviour in mobile networks. Taking into account this consideration, five different functions were chosen to find the best fit, these are detailed in Eqs. (4) to (8), where x represents the time variable, in either days or weeks, a,

b and c are the function parameters to be obtained in the fitting process, and y will be the resulting forecast obtained through the fitting process:

- **Linear Function:**
$$y = ax + b \tag{4}$$

- **Quadratic Function:**
$$y = ax^2 + bx + c \tag{5}$$

- **Power Function:**
$$y = ax^b + c \tag{6}$$

- **Gaussian Function:**
$$y = ae^{-\left(\frac{x-b}{c}\right)^2} \tag{7}$$

- **Logarithmic Function:**
$$y = a + b\log(x) \tag{8}$$

This particular algorithm has three stages: fitting, decision and validation. The overall view of the algorithm is detailed in the flowchart of Fig. 3. On the first two stages, the algorithm takes as input data the two first sub-sets mentioned earlier. In the fitting stage, it fits the first sub-set to each of the five fitting functions. Afterwards, in the decision stage, the algorithm makes a forecast spanning over the duration of the second sub-set. Then, it compares the obtained forecast with the real data and finds the best fitting function for it, minimizing the prediction error.

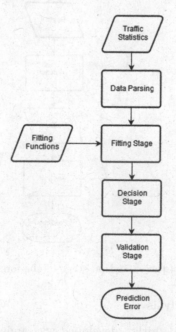

Fig. 3. Overall flowchart of the Traffic Forecast algorithm.

After obtaining the best fitting function for the data and its parameters it is possible to make a prediction using the `predint` or `polyval` functions, in a process similar to the decision stage of the algorithm. These functions calculate the fitting function's values with the given parameters for a given future time span. Their output is a vector containing a prediction of the future value of the data for a certain number of given periods, where in this case each period is a single day or a whole week depending on the input data format.

By comparing the actual values of the data with its prediction it was possible to obtain a quantitative measure of the algorithm's accuracy. This comparison was made using a Mean Absolute Percentage Error (MAPE) and a Normalized Root Mean Squared Error (NRMSE), as in Eqs. 9 and 10, where n is the total number of samples, Y_i is the actual data value at time i and F_i is the forecast value at time i. In Eq. 10, $\bar{Y}$ represents the mean value of vector $\mathbf{Y}$.

$$MAPE = \frac{1}{n} \sum_{i=1}^{n} \left| \frac{Y_i - F_i}{Y_i} \right| \tag{9}$$

$$NRMSE = \frac{\sqrt{\frac{1}{n} \sum_{i=1}^{n} (Y_i - F_i)^2}}{\bar{Y}} \tag{10}$$

The flowchart that illustrates this stage of the algorithm is presented in Fig. 4.

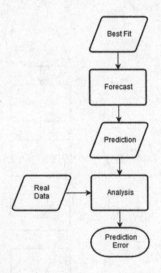

Fig. 4. Flowchart of the validation stage of the forecast algorithm [5].

2.4   Results and Analysis

The developed forecast algorithm developed was applied to several Quality of Service (QoS) metrics and statistics, including traffic volume, number of users and Channel Element (CE) usage in both Uplink (UL) and Downlink (DL). An example of the obtained prediction can be seen in Fig. 5. The input data used in the example was the daily maximum UL CE usage in Site 2. In Fig. 6 is illustrated an example for the same site but now with a weekly input data using the 90th percentile. From Figs. 7, 8, 9 and 10 are examples of the forecast algorithm's output when using the remaining metrics as input data.

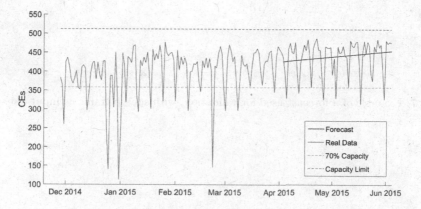

Fig. 5. Example of a forecast used for validation [5].

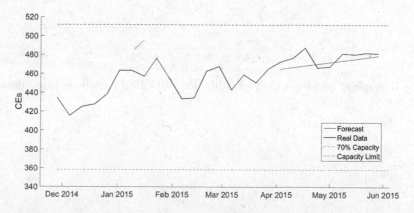

Fig. 6. Example of a forecast used for validation, with weekly input data [5].

The detailed prediction error results obtained for each case are presented in Tables 2 and 3, using MAPE and NRMSE, respectively.

From the obtained results it is easily concluded that the weekly compressed data sets provide much better prediction errors, meaning it is easier to predict the weekly behaviour of the sites than its daily behaviour. Moreover, for most cases of input data, the 90th Percentile is the better aggregation method, minimizing the prediction error. However, in the Maximum DL CE usage, EUL and R99 DL

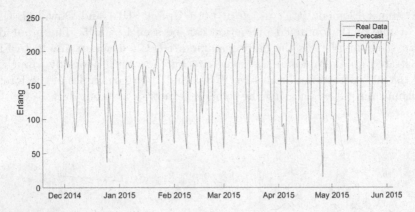

Fig. 7. Example of a forecast used for validation, with speech traffic as input data [5].

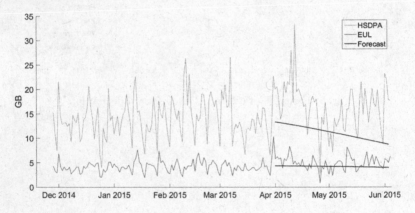

Fig. 8. Example of a forecast used for validation, with HSPA traffic as input data [5].

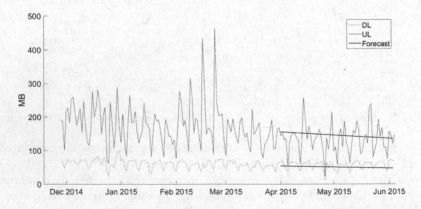

Fig. 9. Example of a forecast used for validation, with R99 data traffic as input data [5].

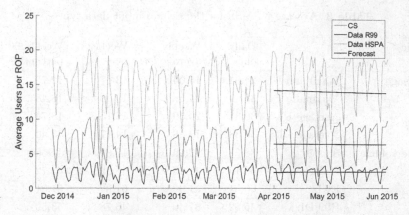

Fig. 10. Example of a forecast used for validation, with user number as input data [5].

Table 2. Average MAPE for the several input data types.

	Metric	Daily data [%]	Weekly average [%]	Weekly peak [%]	Weekly 90th percentile [%]
CE usage	Maximum UL	24.46	13.52	11.69	10.92
	Maximum DL	42.66	12.70	15.88	15.09
	Average UL	32.80	18.93	16.88	17.57
	Average DL	47.04	12.27	12.43	11.66
Traffic volume	Speech	58.98	18.11	15.29	15.87
	HSDPA	57.22	39.48	43.72	41.82
	EUL	71.37	39.72	57.65	56.97
	R99 DL	48.29	34.58	43.25	40.21
	R99 UL	98.70	54.90	90.59	83.20
Number of users	Speech	49.86	18.22	16.79	16.52
	HSPA	36.05	24.83	23.88	23.99
	R99	69.62	24.71	25.93	24.20

Traffic Volumes present a slightly different trend, not having the 90th Percentile as the best method for aggregation of the input data. This may be due to the fact that these metrics present low usage, such as R99 DL Traffic, or highly irregular behaviour resulting in high prediction errors, as can be seen in Figs. 7, 8, 9 and 10. In fact, for these three metrics the best aggregation method is a weekly average, since this is more stable for irregular data than the 90th Percentile.

It is also possible to verify that the CE usage data is the easiest to predict, mainly because it is the most stable indicator. After that, the most reliable indicator is the number of users statistics. Where it comes to traffic volume, the algorithm finds more difficulties due to its highly irregular behaviour along

Table 3. Average NRMSE for the several input data types.

Metric		Daily data [%]	Weekly average [%]	Weekly peak [%]	Weekly 90th percentile [%]
CE usage	Maximum UL	24.94	15.04	13.67	12.75
	Maximum DL	35.59	14.58	19.63	18.48
	Average UL	30.35	20.59	18.15	18.74
	Average DL	36.88	13.88	14.17	13.40
Traffic volume	Speech	38.77	19.66	17.09	17.56
	HSDPA	50.19	41.13	45.62	43.72
	EUL	65.51	41.96	61.92	61.01
	R99 DL	45.62	37.40	46.78	43.59
	R99 UL	80.64	52.86	79.85	74.91
Number of users	Speech	38.16	19.62	18.48	18.08
	HSPA	34.12	26.59	25.51	25.73
	R99	45.87	25.77	27.56	25.64

the sampling window. However, the speech traffic and number of users statistics reveals itself as a good indicator, having a considerably lower prediction error.

In order to evaluate the chosen functions' usage and performance, a statistical test was performed. In Table 4, the usage of each function is presented, grouped by data type as well as a global view, which is an average of all input data cases. In Table 5, the same analysis is presented for the prediction errors (MAPE) obtained for each function.

Table 4. Usage of each function in the forecast algorithm.

Function	Daily [%]	Weekly average [%]	Weekly peak [%]	Weekly 90th percentile [%]	Global view [%]
Linear	23.49	14.53	13.84	12.56	16.10
Quadratic	6.16	3.37	8.84	8.95	6.83
Power	10.12	12.56	13.14	13.37	12.30
Gaussian	22.67	28.26	23.02	24.30	24.56
Logarithmic	37.56	41.28	41.16	40.81	40.20

From the previous tables it is possible to conclude that the logarithmic function is the most common choice of the forecast algorithm, whereas the Quadratic is the least chosen function. In terms of prediction error, the Quadratic function presents the worst performance, opposed to the Gaussian function that presents the best performance. There is a certain consistency between usage and performance, since the worst performing function is the least chosen and the best performing is the second most chosen function.

Table 5. Prediction error associated with each function chosen by the forecast algorithm.

Function	Daily [%]	Weekly average [%]	Weekly peak [%]	Weekly 90th percentile [%]	Global view [%]
Linear	48.41	24.00	26.00	25.88	33.70
Quadratic	85.63	52.37	64.31	58.80	65.84
Power	53.70	30.98	30.27	29.77	35.13
Gaussian	44.58	22.09	25.15	22.31	28.05
Logarithmic	62.66	30.74	37.45	36.66	41.42

Note that the most chosen function does not always provide the lower prediction error. This is due to the fact that the fitting function is chosen in a way that minimizes the error in Sect. 2 of Fig. 2, and thus does not assure that it is the best choice for the third section.

3 Load Balancing Algorithm

There are several factors that may be used as triggers for a Load Balancing mechanism. In this work, the used indicator will be the maximum UL CE usage, since the CE resource availability in the UL baseband pool is the restraining capacity factor.

For this algorithm, the input data will also be provided by the same Portuguese mobile operator, and it consists of user traces, geo-located reports of Received Signal Code Power (RSCP) with the corresponding timestamps. These traces were positioned through an algorithm developed by Celfinet [12,13]. The measurements were made in a set of 40 sites, all belonging to the same set as the one used in the previous section, and spans over the course of one hour, from 10:00 to 11:00 AM on April 27th, 2015. The samples were collected every second. However, the available data only includes one carrier in the 2100 MHz band, so the statistics for the 900 MHz band will have to be estimated.

3.1 Imbalance Analysis

Before applying the load balancing algorithm to a site, it is beneficial to know the degree of imbalance between the 900 MHz and 2100 MHz frequency bands present in the site, which will be referred to as U900 and U2100 from here onwards. For this purpose, a small routine was designed.

Firstly, it evaluates two factors: the percentage of capacity used by each band and the ratio between the allocated capacity in each band. Then, it checks how far from perfect balance the site is. This is done by comparing the imbalance factor of used capacity (I_{usage}) and the imbalance factor of the allocated capacity ($I_{capacity}$), originating the imbalance differential (ΔI). Ideally, this differential should be equal to zero, but most times it is bigger since the U2100 band is usually overloaded.

The 3 factors are detailed in Eqs. (11), (12) and (13), where $n_{CE_{U900}}$ and $n_{CE_{U2100}}$ represent the average CE usage reported on the corresponding day for both frequency bands and $n_{CE,lim_{U900}}$ and $n_{CE,lim_{U2100}}$ represent the allocated capacity in both frequency bands. These values were taken from the traffic statistics file used in the previous section, for the forecasting algorithm.

$$I_{usage} = \frac{n_{CE_{U900}}}{n_{CE_{U2100}} + n_{CE_{U900}}} \times 100[\%] \tag{11}$$

$$I_{capacity} = \frac{n_{CE,lim_{U900}}}{n_{CE,lim_{U2100}} + n_{CE,lim_{U900}}} \times 100[\%] \tag{12}$$

$$\Delta I = I_{capacity} - I_{usage} \tag{13}$$

It was decided that a site must have an imbalance differential larger than 10% to be a candidate for improvement. This means that a site is overloaded in the U2100 band while there is still considerable capacity available on the U900 band. From the 43 initial sites 23 were selected. There are a few sites with negative imbalance differential, only one with a factor greater than 10%, but these sites will not be considered since the objective of this research work is to offload the U2100 band.

3.2 U900 Band Parameter Estimation

Before the Load Balancing algorithm can be applied it is necessary to estimate the traces of this band. Since its objective will be to offload the U2100 band, it is not necessary to know exactly where the trace data is generated but only the number of events that are expected to occur in the U900 band.

To estimate this value we take the usage imbalance factor obtained earlier and calculate the expected number of events considering that it is proportional to CE usage. This is, of course, assuming that the used capacity depends only on the number of events recorded in each band and that each event has the same weight in the total CE usage of the site. The estimate for this parameter is then given by Eq. (14), where N_{events} represents the number of reported events in each band [5].

$$N_{events_{U900}} = N_{events_{U2100}} \frac{I_{usage}}{100 - I_{usage}} \tag{14}$$

3.3 Strategy

In the following sections, the strategy taken to perform the load balancing for the selected sites will be detailed. Firstly, the site is analysed to check if it is a viable candidate, which was already done in Sect. 3.1. Afterwards, a target for the number of events in both bands is calculated based on the imbalance factors. Finally, the required threshold to achieve the target load distribution is calculated.

After having a threshold estimate, the new distribution of the load can be made. This stage will be important to obtain an objective evaluation of the effectiveness of the Load Balancing algorithm.

Target Number of Events. The target number of events is calculated based on the capacity imbalance factor, since this value is the optimal load distribution for each site. Taking the total CE usage and multiplying by the imbalance factor we obtain the target usage for the U900 band. The target number of events for the U900 band is rounded down to the closest integer in order to eliminate fractions of events from the calculations. Afterwards, the U2100 band usage is simply the remaining from the total usage. This process is detailed in Eqs. (15), (16) and (17) [5].

$$N_{events_{total}} = N_{events_{U2100}} + N_{events_{U900}} \tag{15}$$

$$N_{target_{U900}} = \left\lfloor N_{events_{total}} \frac{I_{capacity}}{100} \right\rfloor \tag{16}$$

$$N_{target_{U2100}} = N_{events_{total}} - N_{target_{U900}} \tag{17}$$

RSCP Threshold. Originally, all cells have an admission threshold of -115 dBm. This means that only UEs with a higher or equal RSCP value may connect to the cell. The output of this Load Balancing algorithm will be a suggested RSCP threshold value in order to achieve a better load distribution between the two frequency bands. This is illustrated by Eq. (18). Note that $n = N_{events_{U2100}}$, which means it is the number of events in the U2100 band before the Load Balancing is applied [5].

$$T_{RSCP} = RSCP_i \,, \quad i = n - N_{target_{U2100}} \tag{18}$$

New Load Distribution. After having a suggested threshold, the number of events in each band (N_{result}) is calculated, as well as the new imbalance factor (I_{result}) obtained in order to understand what is the impact of the algorithm in the site capacity.

To calculate these parameters we have to check how many events have a reported RSCP value equal or superior to the obtained threshold for the U2100 band ($RSCP_{event} \geq T_{RSCP}$). These events will remain in the U2100 band, whereas the rest will now switch to the U900 band. The new number of U2100 events will be designated as $N_{result_{2100}}$. Eq. (19) [5] shows the taken approach to find the number of U900 events.

$$N_{result_{U900}} = N_{events_{total}} - N_{result_{U2100}} \tag{19}$$

Having the resulting number of events for both bands, it is possible to calculate the new imbalance factor. The new imbalance differential (ΔI_{result}) is also relevant to understand the effectiveness of the algorithm. Eqs. (20) and (21) detail how these factors are calculated [5].

$$I_{result} = \frac{N_{result_{U900}}}{N_{result_{U900}} + N_{result_{U2100}}} \times 100[\%] \tag{20}$$

$$\Delta I_{result} = I_{capacity} - I_{result} \tag{21}$$

If the algorithm is to be considered effective, then the new imbalance factor should be close to the capacity imbalance factor, thus obtaining the perfect balance. This means that the imbalance differential should be close to zero. The analysis of the factor ΔI_{result} will then be the validation method for the Load Balancing algorithm. In Fig. 11 the whole process is illustrated through a flowchart.

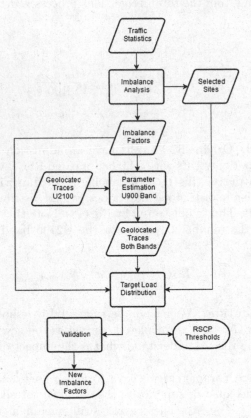

Fig. 11. Flowchart of the Load Balancing algorithm [5].

3.4   Results and Analysis

In Table 6, the obtained values for the imbalance differential before (ΔI) and after (ΔI_{result}) Load Balancing are presented, as well as the RSCP threshold values obtained in dBm for each selected site.

The results show a significant change in the ΔI parameter, which had values greater than 10% for the selected sites and now have an average value of 1.78%. This value demonstrates a good effectiveness for the Load Balancing algorithm since it comes close to the specified target of zero for the perfect balancing of each site.

Table 6. Summary of Load Balancing results.

Site	I_{result} [%]	ΔI_{result} [%]	T_{RSCP} [dBm]
1	41.42	0.05	-98
4	32.65	0.11	-100
5	22.84	0.97	-104
7	37.90	0.56	-96
9	30.95	2.38	-103
10	21.39	0.04	-109
18	34.47	0.01	-104
19	36.68	1.15	-103
20	56.95	0.19	-96
21	30.93	0.99	-103
23	42.84	1.02	-100
24	48.48	1.52	-99
25	13.48	16.52	-115
26	45.41	0.01	-100
27	36.78	0.36	-99
28	41.93	0.93	-93
34	40.65	0.38	-105
36	37.50	0.96	-91
37	32.14	1.19	-102
39	29.63	6.73	-114
40	42.26	0.60	-105
42	40.00	2.86	-108
43	51.16	0.84	-96

However, Site 25 presents a value much higher than desired. This is due to a huge number of events with a low RSCP value, more specifically -115 dBm. This fact makes it very hard for the algorithm to decide on a suitable threshold for the site, since a higher value than the original -115 dBm will cause a capacity overload situation in the U900 band. Because of this, it decides to keep the original value unchanged.

In Fig. 12 these results are illustrated next to the old imbalance values.

In order to better understand how the Load Balancing algorithm affects the load distribution the before and after Cumulative Distribution Function (CDF) of the imbalance differentials (ΔI) is presented in Fig. 13. It can easily be concluded that after the Load Balancing about 95% of the sites show a good load distribution, opposing to the previous 45%.

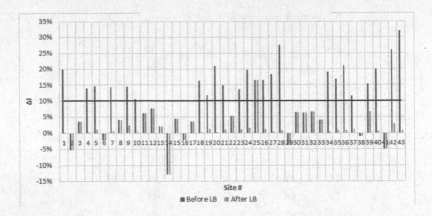

Fig. 12. Imbalance factors for all sites, before and after Load Balancing [5].

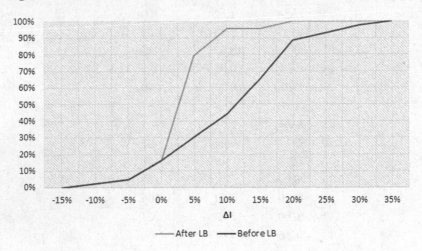

Fig. 13. Imbalance differential CDF before and after Load Balancing [5].

3.5   Coverage Impact

Reducing the RSCP thresholds of the sites has an impact on their coverage area, more specifically the coverage of the U2100 band. Theoretically, increasing the threshold will cause a reduction on the coverage area while decreasing it will cause the opposite effect, since the users further away from the site should have a lower RSCP due to the higher path loss they are subjected to.

In Fig. 14 the coverage of Site 24 is illustrated, after the Load Balancing algorithm is applied. The blue dots represent events in the U2100 band and the red dots events that switched to the U900 band after changing the admission threshold. Despite what was predicted, the results do not show a strong correlation between switched events and their distance to the site. This happens because the reported RSCP value of a UE depends on other factors such as being indoor or outdoor. Indoor events tend to have lower RSCP values, due to penetration

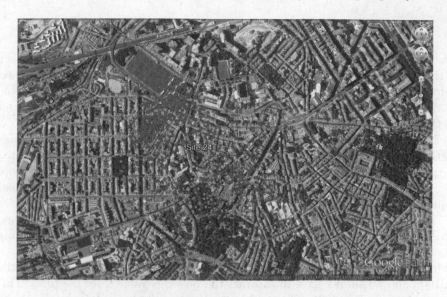

Fig. 14. Coverage of Site 24 after Load Balancing, in blue are represented events which remained in the U2100 band and in red are represented events which switched to the U900 band [5]. (Color figure online)

Fig. 15. Coverage of Site 20 after Load Balancing, in blue are represented events which remained in the U2100 band and in red are represented events which switched to the U900 band [5]. (Color figure online)

losses, when compared with outdoor events at the same distance to the site. This causes the appearance of red dots closer to the sites and an overall homogeneous looking coverage map. The coverage of Site 20 is illustrated in Fig. 15. In this case, the reduction of coverage of the U2100 band is more perceptible.

4   Capacity Limit Estimation

The objective of this part of the work is to quantitatively determine the effect of the Load Balancing algorithm. Estimating when the capacity limit is reached before and after the Load Balancing and comparing the results it will be possible to determine the real gain. This gain can be presented according to several methods, such as site longevity or overall CE and economic savings.

In this part of the work, the necessary input data will be the CE usage statistics, more specifically the UL usage since this will be the limiting factor for the capacity of the sites [6]. However, since this data is only available before the use of Load Balancing, an estimate of the CE usage statistics after Load Balancing must be calculated.

The post Load Balancing estimate is based on the obtained imbalance factors, which are presented in Table 6. Taking the total CE usage in a site, *i.e.* summing the two frequency bands' usage, and multiplying it by the imbalance factor an estimate of the U900 band, CE usage is obtained. To get the same data for the U2100 band we simply have to subtract the previous value from the total. This process is set in Eqs. (22), (23) and (24), where n_{CE} is the vector containing the CE usage statistics before Load Balancing and $n_{CE,LB}$ is the vector containing the estimates for CE usages after Load Balancing [5].

$$n_{CE,total} = n_{CE_{U900}} + n_{CE_{U2100}} \tag{22}$$

$$n_{CE,LB_{U900}} = n_{CE,total} \Delta I_{result} \tag{23}$$

$$n_{CE,LB_{U2100}} = n_{CE,total} - n_{CE,LB_{U900}} \tag{24}$$

In order to find an estimate of the capacity limit, the full set of available data was used, spanning from November 28th of 2014 to June 4th of 2015. Moreover, since it produced lower prediction errors, a weekly conversion of the data was made, more specifically using the weekly 90th Percentile. In this case, the Forecast algorithm skips the validation stage, and only executes the fitting and decision stages.

4.1   Improved Forecasting

Since the input data for the Forecast algorithm is known in detail, it is possible to improve the algorithm in order to increase its accuracy. This improvement is done by dismissing one or several fitting functions, since they produce greater prediction errors.

In order to decide which functions are to be removed, the Forecast algorithm is ran for all U2100 Nodes and for the designated input data, *i.e.*, weekly 90th percentile of the maximum UL CE. In Table 7 the results are grouped by fitting function chosen by the algorithm. It is evident that the Quadratic function produces the worse results in terms of prediction error. Due to this fact, this function will be removed from the analysis.

Table 7. Prediction error grouped by the chosen fitting function.

Function	Average error
Linear	2.45%
Quadratic	15.79%
Power	7.75%
Gaussian	4.01%
Logarithmic	7.19%
All	7.69%

Afterwards, the Forecast algorithm is ran again only with the designated input data and it is validated by using the same method described in Sect. 2. The output is once again the prediction error, calculated with MAPE, for each site. Moreover, a sequential analysis is done by splitting the validation window into three equal parcels (28 days each) and calculating the prediction error for each section. This allows a better perception of how the error behaves with time. In Table 8 the prediction error averaged over all the analysed sites is presented. It is easy to conclude this approach lowered the obtained prediction error in about 2%.

Table 8. Prediction error for improved Forecasting algorithm.

	Parcel 1	Parcel 2	Parcel 3	Total
Average	4.56%	6.51%	9.05%	6.22%

Based on the results obtained in Table 8 it is possible to extrapolate the error obtained in predictions made farther in the future. In Fig. 16 this is detailed. Day 0 is considered to be the first day of available data, so between Day 0 and 56

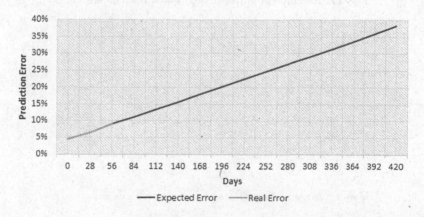

Fig. 16. Prediction error distribution for selected data input.

the values presented are the values obtained in Table 8, and from there on is illustrated an expectation of the prediction error for the next 390 days using a linear regression. At the end of these 390 days, expected error is almost 40%, and this progression will be considered when calculating the longevity of the sites in the following section.

4.2   Results and Analysis

Using both cases, before and after Load Balancing, as input for the Forecast algorithm it is possible to obtain an estimate of when the capacity limit will be reached in a site. In Figs. 17 and 18 an example of how the Load Balancing algorithm affects the capacity limit of sites is presented. In Fig. 17 the forecast obtained for the U2100 band of Site 21 before the Load Balancing process was applied, whereas in Fig. 18 the forecast obtained after the Load Balancing is considered. It is clear that on the first case, the site is on the verge of reaching its capacity limit, but after the Load Balancing algorithm is applied, this instant is delayed for a considerable amount of time.

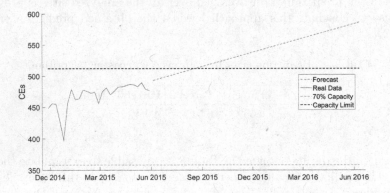

Fig. 17. Example of Forecast before Load Balancing [5].

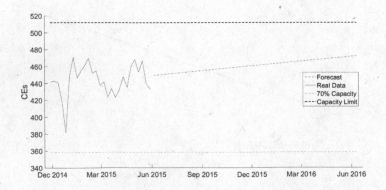

Fig. 18. Example of Forecast after Load Balancing [5].

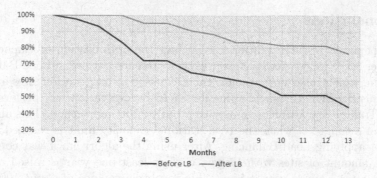

Fig. 19. Capacity Limit complementary CDF [5].

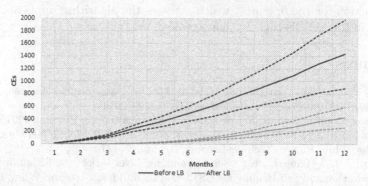

Fig. 20. CEs needed for expansion of all sites over one year [5].

The output of the algorithm is presented using the corresponding complementary CDF, in terms of site longevity, see Fig. 19. The graph shows that, before Load Balancing, 80% of the sites analysed had a predicted longevity of more than 3 months, whereas after the Load Balancing process the predicted longevity is greater than 1 year for the same amount of sites. Another way of interpreting is realizing that, before load balancing, only about 50% of the sites had a longevity greater than one year. After Load Balancing, this figure rises to 80%.

However, a more practical approach is to estimate the amount of CEs that the Load Balancing process allows to save after a certain amount of time. Figure 20 illustrates the amount of CEs needed for expansion in all sites for a time duration of up to one year. It also includes a confidence interval for the forecast, obtained by considering the mean value of the expected prediction error for each month. The dotted lines represent this interval for both cases.

In one year, before Load Balancing, the operator would need to expand the sites in about 1400 CEs. After Load Balancing this value drops to around 400 CEs, representing a gain of about 1000 CEs. In terms of time this would save the operator between 6 and 7 months before having to make an expansion of just 400 CEs.

5   Conclusions

In this paper, a research platform regarding the optimisation of Capacity for dual-layer 3G Wireless Access Networks was presented. It uses a Load Balancing algorithm, which takes into account the CE usage of base-station sites and sets an optimised RSCP threshold value for each. Its evaluation was performed by using a Traffic Forecast algorithm, with a built in fitting method. This allows to obtain an estimate of when the base-stations' capacity limit is reached, before and after applying Load Balancing. After using the algorithm it was concluded that the amount of sites with longevity of at least one year is raised in 30%, and that after a single year it is possible to obtain savings of about 1000 CEs, meaning a 70% saving in capacity expansions of sites. This result means a true cost reduction for the operator, which stresses the algorithm applicability and usability in the MNO's capacity management field.

References

1. Cisco Visual Networking Index: Global Mobile Data Traffic Forecast Update, 20142019 [White Paper]. Technical report, Cisco (2014)
2. Ericsson Mobility Report [White Paper]. Technical report, Ericsson (2015)
3. Northcote, B.: TEMS Capacity Manager: Cost-Efficient Mobile Network Dimensioning [White Paper]. Technical report, Ascom (2014)
4. Ramiro, J., Hamied, K.: Self-Organizing Networks: Self-Planning, Self-Optimization and Self-Healing for GSM, UMTS and LTE, 1st edn. Wiley, Hoboken (2012)
5. Pedro, T., Vieira, P., Martins, A., Rodrigues, A.J.: An efficient approach for capacity savings using load balancing in dual layer 3G wireless networks. In: International Conference on Wireless Information Networks and Systems - Winsys, Lisbon, Portugal (2016)
6. Cunha, T., Martins, A., Vieira, P., Rodrigues, A., Silva, N., Varela, L.: Energy savings in 3G using dynamic spectrum access and base station sleep modes. In: URSI Atlantic Radio Science Conference (URSI AT-RASC), Maspalomas, Spain (2015)
7. Li, R., Zhao, Z., Zhou, X., Palicot, J.: The prediction analysis of cellular radio access network traffic: from entropy theory to networking practice. IEEE Commun. Mag. 52, 234–240 (2014)
8. Yu, Y., Song, M., Fu, Y., Song, J.: Traffic prediction in 3G mobile networks based on multifractal exploration. Tsinghua Sci. Technol. 18, 398–405 (2013)
9. Yu, Y., Wang, J., Song, M., Song, J.: Network traffic prediction and result analysis based on seasonal ARIMA and correlation coefficient. In: International Conference on Intelligent System Design and Engineering Application (ISDEA), Changsha, China, pp. 980–983 (2010)
10. Dawoud, S., Uzun, A., Gondor, S., Kupper, A.: Optimizing the power consumption of mobile networks based on traffic prediction. In: 38th Annual International Computers, Software and Applications Conference, Västerås, Sweden, pp. 279–288 (2014)
11. Li, J., Fan, C., Yang, D., Gu, J.: UMTS soft handover algorithm with adaptive thresholds for load balancing. In: IEEE 62nd Vehicular Technology Conference, vol. 4, pp. 2508–2512 (2005)

12. Vieira, P., Varela, N., Fernandes, N., Guedes, N., Varela, L., Ribeiro, N.: A SON enhanced algorithm for observed time differences based geolocation in real 3G networks. In: 16th International Symposium on Wireless Personal Multimedia Communications (WPMC), Atlantic City, USA, pp. 1–5 (2013)

13. Vieira, P., Silva, N., Fernandes, N., Rodrigues, A., Varela, L.: Improving accuracy for OTD based 3G geolocation in real urban, suburban environments. In: International Symposium on Wireless Personal Multimedia Communications (WPMC), Sydney, Australia, pp. 362–366 (2014)

Coverage Range Analysis and Performance Evaluation of Wireless Technologies in Industrial Channel Conditions

Armin Wulf[✉], Lisa Underberg, Ramona Croonenbroeck, and Rüdiger Kays

Communication Technology Institute, TU Dortmund University,
Otto-Hahn-Str. 4, 44221 Dortmund, Germany
{armin.wulf,lisa.underberg,ramona.croonenbroeck,
ruediger.kays}@tu-dortmund.de
http://www.kt.e-technik.tu-dortmund.de/cms/en/

Abstract. While current reliable and ultra low latency industrial communication is based on wired fieldbus systems, wireless communication is the key to enable future industrial applications. However, the reliability of state-of-the-art wireless technologies is not sufficient for many industrial application scenarios. Thus, novel wireless approaches are being investigated at the moment, from which three promising physical layer (PHY) technologies are depicted for detailed evaluation in this paper: Ultra Wide Band (UWB), Frequency Hopping Spread Spectrum (FHSS) and Parallel Sequence Spread Spectrum (PSSS). In order to assess each system's performance, Key Performance Indicators (KPI) are derived from industrial application constraints. In this paper, industrial applications are therefore categorized by vital requirements such as spatial extent, number of nodes, cycle time, PER and user data length. The depicted technologies are evaluated regarding the KPIs error rate and coverage range in AWGN and industrial fading channel conditions.

Keywords: Coverage range · Error rates · FHSS · Industrial communication · Industrial channel · PSSS · UWB

1 Introduction

Wireless technologies are desirable to be employed in industrial applications. Currently installed wired fieldbus systems entail high installation and maintenance efforts, which are mitigated by usage of wireless systems, since they offer advantages regarding flexibility, mobility and retrofitting. However, most wireless communication systems are not yet able to compete with wired fieldbus systems, because their performance is not deterministic. Due to this, they also are not able to satisfy ultra low latency requirements with minimal jitter tolerance, which is mandatory in industrial applications.

As a result, novel wireless solutions are a topic of recent research and development. In order to meet industrial application requirements, especially physical

© Springer International Publishing AG 2017
M.S. Obaidat (Ed): ICETE 2016, CCIS 764, pp. 450–473, 2017.
https://doi.org/10.1007/978-3-319-67876-4_21

layer choice and medium access strategy are of vital significance. Often the physical layer technology is chosen first based on the applications' demand of coverage range and data rate. Then, the medium access is planned and optimized with regard to the very application requirements.

Since industrial applications serve various purposes, they show greatly diverse demands. Thus, to facilitate the communication system design, they are often categorized by their field of operation and their major requirements like number of nodes, cycle time, Packet Error Rate (PER) and user data length. Based on the resulting categories, wireless systems can be designed for each field of application. Although the exact definition of application categories is crucial to a successful system design, currently no de facto standard is established.

Thus, industrial requirements are investigated and aggregated in Sect. 2. UWB, FHSS and PSSS are shortly introduced as promising wireless approaches in Sect. 3 and discussed regarding their suitability in terms of error rates and coverage range in Sect. 4. In addition to [1], where this analysis is performed based on an AWGN channel for the three physical layer approaches, industrial channel conditions are investigated in this paper. Summary and prospect on further work are given in Sect. 5.

2 Industrial Environment

A survey on industrial application categories and their respective requirements is given in this section. These requirements include network size, environment, topology and safety as well as timing limitations. Moreover, suitable frequency ranges are presented and reviewed regarding regulatory aspects.

The survey reveals challenging requirements for wireless industrial communication in all application categories. As a consequence, physical layer concepts must be chosen carefully, especially concerning reliability and coexistence aspects.

2.1 Application Requirements

The requirements of industrial applications are very diverse and commonly classified into three categories to facilitate considerations: Factory Automation (FA), Process Automation (PA) and Condition Monitoring (CM).

In a typical factory environment the number of nodes as well as the spatial extent are evidently small, whereas the safety and reliability requirements are very strong. A typical FA scenario is a production cell, in which sensors and actuators both interact on a soft or hard real time basis. In FA, a star topology as shown in Fig. 1 (a) is often chosen to enable shortest cycle times covering the small spatial extent.

Contrary to FA, CM has a wide spatial extent combined with lower safety and timing requirements in its sensor network, which has no control but only monitoring purposes. The monitoring data need to be transmitted over long

Table 1. Application requirements overview [1–7].

Property	FA	PA	CM
Maximum spatial extent	10 m × 10 m × 3 m	100 m × 100 m × 10 m	1000 m × 1000 m × 50 m
Nodes per system	30	100	1000
Nodes per m^2	0.3	0.01	0.001
Number of co-existent systems	10	5	5
Number of locally parallel nodes	300	500	250
Network topology	Star	Star/mesh	Mesh
Cycle time	<1 ms	>10 ms	>100 ms
PER	$<10^{-9}$	$<10^{-4}$	$<10^{-3}$
Battery lifetime	<1 year	5–10 years	>10 years
User data length	<30 Byte	30–1500 Byte	<1500 Byte
System data rate	>7.2 Mb/s	<2.4–<120 Mb/s	<120 Mb/s

distances, whereas timing requirements are low. Thus, here a mesh topology with multi-hop transmissions as depicted in Fig. 1 (b) is usually employed.

PA is often associated with chemical processing plants, which have an intermediate spatial dimension and also intermediate safety and timing requirements. Often PA comprises monitoring tasks with few and slow control processes. Depending on the very deployment, the topology is either a star or a mesh network.

In case of a star topology, the coexistence of multiple communication structures is required. In large factories with more than one production cell this means both the coexistence of different systems (inter-system-coexistence) and the coexistence of different star topologies employing the same technology (intra-system-coexistence). Table 1 shows major properties of these three categories compiled from various publications. [2] lists requirements of communication in production cells, factory halls and on plant level. Typically, FA is employed in production cells, whereas communication on factory hall scale is congruent with PA properties. Communication on plant level is a subset of CM, but is generally matching CM requirements. Spatial extent, nodes per system, number of coexistent systems, number of locally parallel nodes and the network topologies are taken from this report. Nodes per m^2 is calculated based on these values.

Cycle time and user data lengths values are taken from [4], where similar categories are investigated. Moreover, they are congruent with requirements specified in [6], where three closed-loop applications (machine tools, printing and packaging machines) are listed with their requirements in number of nodes, packet size, cycle time and jitter. Limits for packet error rates are defined in [3], which discusses primarily coexistence issues regarding wireless industrial communication. The system data rate is calculated based on the number of nodes and user data lengths.

Nowadays, wired fieldbus systems based on Ethernet are employed in FA and PA applications due to their strict deterministic performance. In contrast to that, CM comprises recently in terms of machine-to-machine communication

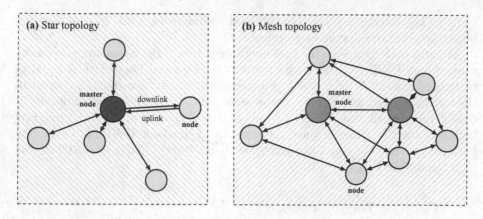

Fig. 1. Typical topologies in industrial environments and link description.

and the Internet of Things (IoT) emerged use cases. These use cases are rather new, since up to now they could not be handled with wired systems due to their minor flexibility.

In summary, wireless communication is desirable in all three categories of industrial applications and promises a raise of efficiency while reducing installation and maintenance efforts.

2.2   Frequency Ranges for Industrial Communication

Currently Industrial, Scientific and Medical (ISM) bands are used for wireless industrial communication, since there is no dedicated frequency range available. The ISM bands offer three worldwide relevant frequency ranges: Sub-1 GHz (868 MHz in Europe and Africa and 900 MHz in America respectively), 2.4 GHz and 5.8 GHz [8,9]. Unfortunately, the 2.4 GHz band in particular is broadly employed posing a challenge to each technology's coexistence techniques. As a consequence of the need of heavy employment and wide usability, each ISM band is strictly regulated regarding several usage indicators such as transmission power and duty cycle. Based on this regulation, inter-system-coexistence of different technologies is enabled. The regulation renders the ISM bands unfavorable for many industrial communication systems, especially regarding FA and PA. With higher transmission power, a "listen before talk" (LBT) algorithm has to be implemented, which impedes the guarantee of a particular transmission delay. Mostly, low transmission powers are allowed without LBT, but hence the coverage range is significantly reduced.

Obviously the interest in defining a dedicated frequency band is increasing. This interest is met by ETSI initiative TG41, that aims at a regulation guaranteeing exclusive use of 5.725 GHz to 5.875 GHz for wireless industrial communication systems. Here the transmit power is planned to be increased from 14 dBm to 26 dBm EIRP [8]. However, an exclusive use of a dedicated frequency band leads to less interference between different technologies, while it reinforces the importance of intra-system-coexistence.

An approach bypassing the ISM band regulation is the use of large frequency ranges as in UWB [10] technologies. Here the employed bandwidth is equal to or larger than 499.2 MHz, which provides high interference resistance owed to the applied spreading concept. At the same time, the power spectral density is considerably small, thus UWB does not impede primary users in their operating bands. Currently three frequency ranges are defined for UWB: sub-gigahertz band from 249.6 MHz to 749.6 MHz, low band from 3.1 GHz to 4.8 GHz, and high band from 5.8 GHz to 10.6 GHz.

3   Wireless Technologies

The PHY layer technology vigorously affects the overall system performance. Thus, it has to be chosen carefully for a certain field of operation. The range of available technologies from wireless standards and recent research projects is wide. It reaches from UWB technologies promissing coexistence with established wireless systems to 5G cellular machine to machine (M2M) solutions, that can cover large areas and huge numbers of devices. With its Single Carrier Frequency Division Multiple Access (SC-FDMA) and Orthogonal Frequency Division Multiple Access (OFDMA) schemes for uplink and downlink and the enhancements from LTE Rel-11, 5G seems to be a promising approach for PA and CM. However, its latencies are not capable of meeting the FA requirements. Another promising technology for PA applications is Sub- 1 GHz-WLAN in IEEE 802.11ah, which shall achieve low-cost long range connectivity [11]. Technologies like ZigBee [12] with its star, mesh and cluster tree topologies suit rather good for CM purposes. Wireless Sensor Actuator Network for Factory Automation (WSAN) is designed for FA and coexistence with common technologies in the 2.4 GHz ISM band and based on the IEEE 802.15.1 standard [13]. WirelessHART is a recent approach that is also based on the IEEE 802.15.4 standard. It covers industrial applications in the fields of FA and PA [14].

Nevertheless, these standards cover the FA requirements insufficiently, so that wireless communication technologies, which meet the FA requirements, are current research topics. Among others, UWB, FHSS and PSSS are PHYs of relevant communication standards for FA and subject of recent research projects. These three promising wireless technologies are depicted for further analysis.

3.1   UWB Overview

In order to realize short-haul links for data communication for low power and low rate devices in a Wireless Personal Area Network (WPAN), the IEEE 802.15.4a standard offers several PHY transmission modes [10]. The investigated Impulse Radio (IR)-UWB PHY specification supports data rates from 0.11 Mb/s to 27.24 Mb/s with different Modulation and Coding Schemes (MCS). The IR-UWB impulses are modulated using burst position modulation (BPM) and binary phase shift keying (BPSK). In the BPM-BPSK modulation scheme two bits of information are carried in each UWB symbol. The first bit is determined by the burst's temporal position and the burst's polarity indicates the second bit. A complete burst is specified by a spreading sequence defining the polarity of it's impulses [10]. Figure 2 shows the structure of an IR-UWB PHY symbol. T_{dsym} corresponds to the total symbol duration. T_c is referred to as chip duration and N_{cpb} as number of chips per burst. T_{burst} is the burst duration and T_{BPM} corresponds to the duration of a BPM interval.

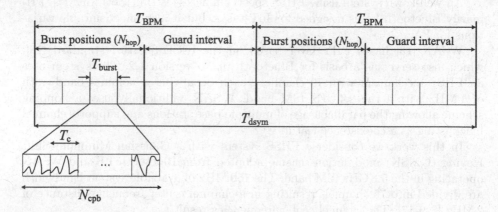

Fig. 2. IEEE 802.15.4a IR-UWB PHY symbol structure [10].

The significant parameters of selected IR-UWB MCSs, including the FEC rates of convolutional coding (CC) and Reed-Solomon (RS) coding, are listed in Table 2 [15]. With the large number of scalable parameters, the IR-UWB PHY is adaptable to different communication scenarios from FA, PA and CM. With a symbol duration T_{dsym} of 64.10 ns MCS 4 reaches a data rate of 27.24 Mb/s with coherent reception [16]. In order to suit best for FA scenarios, delay requirements have to be met, and therefore MCS 4 is investigated in this paper.

Table 2. IR-UWB PHY parameters.

MCS	CC rate	RS rate	N_{cpb}	T_{dsym} [ns]	Data rate [Mb/s]
1	0.5	0.87	128	8205.13	0.11
2	0.5	0.87	16	1025.64	0.85
3	0.5	0.87	2	128.21	6.81
4	1	0.87	1	64.10	27.24

For the performance evaluation in Sect. 4.3 the 7.9872 GHz mandatory channel is depicted due to regulatory aspects such as duty cycle and power restrictions.

3.2 FHSS Overview

For automation and sensor networks, FHSS is one of the most common transmission techniques. The transmission channel has a relatively small bandwidth is changed frequently in order to achieve coexistence between multiple connections and to enhance the transmissions' robustness. Thereby, the hopping frequency can vary from static channel usage up to 1600 Hz, depending on the technology. For most frequency bands this type of frequency usage is covered by regulations [9].

An well-kown system using FHSS spectrum access is Bluetooth LE [17]. Primarily Bluetooth LE is designed for IoT tasks, but it also offers suitable variations for FA.

WSAN [13] has a PHY layer based on the IEEE 802.15.1 standard [18], which also serves as a basis for Bluetooth up to version 1.2. The system uses an FHSS mechanism with 79 channels, each occupying a nominal bandwidth of 1 MHz within the 2.4 GHz ISM band. WSAN additionally uses a hopping scheme allowing the parallel usage of multiple base stations and supports channel blacklisting as a coexistence feature.

In this work we consider a FHSS system with a Gaussian Minimum Shift Keying (GMSK) modulation scheme adopted from Bluetooth LE and WSAN operating in the 5.8 GHz ISM band. The 150 MHz of available system bandwidth are divided into 75 channels resulting in a channel center frequency distance of 2 MHz [8,9,17]. The channel center frequencies result as

$$f_c = 5726\,\text{MHz} + (i-1) \cdot 2\,\text{MHz}, \quad i = 1 \ldots 75 \tag{1}$$

with the channel number i.

The 2.4 GHz ISM band is not taken into consideration for neither FHSS nor PSSS due to interference with existing wireless systems. Example are the company's own WLAN networks or the factory worker's smart phone devices with WLAN or Bluetooth applications.

3.3 PSSS Overview

In order to reduce communication latencies, the parallel access enabled by spread spectrum techniques offers promising properties. Direct Sequence Spread Spectrum (DSSS)-techniques spread each bit with an appropriate pseudo noise (PN)-sequence. The usage of multiple PN-sequences allows simultaneous access of multiple users. In contrast to that, PSSS is an approach based on spreading with a single sequence. PSSS was firstly presented in [19,20] and is, based on a base sequence length of 31 chips, part of IEEE 802.15.4-2011 [10]. In general, m-sequences of any length are applicable and also other types of sequences are conceivable. In this paper, a short overview of PSSS en- and decoding is given. A detailed description can be found in [21].

The bits of the data vector **d** are spread each with the same, but cyclically shifted, m-sequence of length n as shown in Fig. 3. $m_{\to 0}$ denotes the basic m-sequence, whereas correspondingly $m_{\to i}$ refers to the same sequence, but cyclically shifted by i chips. Thus, in one PSSS symbol up to n bit can be transferred

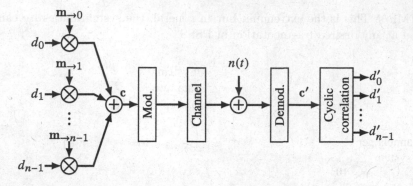

Fig. 3. PSSS downlink coding and decoding process.

in parallel. The spread bits of $\mathbf{d}$ are added chipwise, yielding a multivalent PSSS symbol $\mathbf{c}$, which is then transmitted. Therefore, an arbitrary modulation scheme can be used. For the analysis in Sect. 4.3 an Amplitude Shift Keying (ASK) is utilized.

The PSSS decoding is performed by cyclic correlation of the received multivalent PSSS sequence $\mathbf{c}'$ with the basic m-sequence. As shown in Sect. 4.3, a longer m-sequence leads to a more reliable result of the cyclic correlation, assuming a uniform distribution of data bits.

3.4   Technology Comparison

Though all three described technologies are promising in terms of wireless industrial communication, their properties are divergent. Figure 4 shows an overview of relevant properties based on the assumptions made in Table 3 in Sect. 4.3. Using a bandwidth of 499.2 MHz with one channel per system, UWB achieves a total data rate of 31.2 Mb/s.

FHSS employs 75 channels with 1 Mb/s data rate each, resulting in a system data rate of 75 Mb/s. The depicted configuration utilizes all available channels for a single communication system. For cellular coverage of the factory floor, the system can also be rescaled by reducing the number of utilized channels, making a coexistence of parallel systems possible. For a 3×3 pattern eight channels can be utilized per system in average, when inter-system interference is avoided.

PSSS is exemplarily assumed to be employed based on an m-sequence with a length of 255 chips, which is further denoted as PSSS 255. With a Frequency Division Duplex (FDD) system, up- and downlink provide a number of 255 channels, occupying a bandwidth of 20 MHz each. This results in a total system bandwidth of 40 MHz. With a link data rate of 78 kb/s the total system data rate is 40 Mb/s. If the link data rate for one node of a single link is too small, multiple links can be grouped to achieve a lager data rate, but concomitantly the number of simultaneous nodes in service is reduced. In this example one node utilizes all links at the same time, yielding the maximum possible link data rate of 40 Mb/s. This is the extremum, but in general, the system data rate can be shared at any desired fragmentation in PSSS.

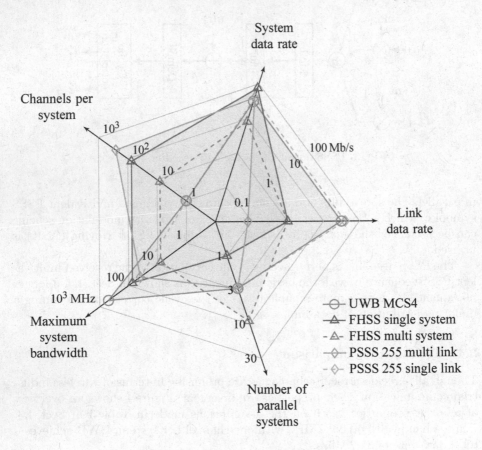

Fig. 4. System capacities.

4   System Evaluation

The proposed PHY technologies are investigated in the subsequent sections regarding their applicability for FA. Based on the Bit Error Rate (BER) analysis, the coverage ranges are considered for typical packet sizes based on an AWGN channel model. The technologies' feasibility is validated as given in Table 1.

4.1   Theoretical Analysis

In this section, the performance of the three proposed systems in AWGN is analyzed for the purpose of the subsequent error rate and coverage range analysis. For simplicity reasons, we assume that the systems are perfectly synchronized and have the correct symbol clock and phase.

UWB Analysis. In order to evaluate the system's performance, typical receivers have to be analyzed. Coherent UWB receivers are often implemented as correlation receivers. Here the detection is performed by cross-correlation between the received signal and a local reference signal. Assuming pulse-position modulation (PPM), perfect synchronization and binary symbols with AWGN, the mean value u_{b_k} of the received signal results as derived from [22] in two separable cases:

1. for a transmitted bit $b_k = 0$

$$
\begin{aligned}
u_0 &= \mathrm{E}\{g_k | b_k = 0\} \\
&= E_b \cdot [\mathrm{AKF}(\tau_0) - \mathrm{AKF}(\tau_0 - \Delta)]
\end{aligned}
\tag{2}
$$

2. for a transmitted bit $b_k = 1$

$$
\begin{aligned}
u_1 &= \mathrm{E}\{g_k | b_k = 1\} \\
&= E_b \cdot [\mathrm{AKF}(\tau_0 + \Delta) - \mathrm{AKF}(\tau_0)]
\end{aligned}
\tag{3}
$$

where g_k is the decision variable resulting from correlation of received signal $r(t)$ and local reference template as given in 4.

$$
g_k = \int_0^{T_{dsym}} r(t) \cdot \underbrace{[\nu(t) - \nu(t - \Delta)]}_{\text{template}} \, dt.
\tag{4}
$$

With AWGN, the BER results as

$$
\begin{aligned}
\mathrm{BER} &= \frac{1}{2} \cdot [\Pr(\mathrm{err}|0) + \Pr(\mathrm{err}|1)] \\
&= \frac{1}{4} \cdot \left[\mathrm{erfc}\left(\frac{u_0}{\sqrt{2}\sigma}\right) + \mathrm{erfc}\left(\frac{u_1}{\sqrt{2}\sigma}\right) \right],
\end{aligned}
\tag{5}
$$

with σ^2 being the two-sided noise density [16]. Equation 5 can be simplified for MCS 4 assuming equal transmission probabilities for each of the binary symbols to

$$
\mathrm{BER} = \frac{1}{2} \mathrm{erfc}\left(\sqrt{\frac{E_b}{N_0}}\right),
\tag{6}
$$

which is equivalent to BER of antipodal signaling [1].

When the fading channel is taken into consideration, u_0 and u_1 change to

$$
\begin{aligned}
u_0 &= E_b \cdot \sum_{l=1}^{L} \alpha_l \left[\mathrm{AKF}(\tau_l - \tau_0) - \mathrm{AKF}(\tau_l - \tau_0 - \Delta) \right] \\
u_1 &= E_b \cdot \sum_{l=1}^{L} \alpha_l \left[\mathrm{AKF}(\tau_l - \tau_0 + \Delta) - \mathrm{AKF}(\tau_l - \tau_0) \right],
\end{aligned}
\tag{7}
$$

with the channel tap index l, the number of channel taps L, the tap factor α_l and the tap delay τ_l. The decision variable changes to

$$g_k = \int_0^{T_{\text{dsym}}} r(t) \cdot \underbrace{[\nu(t - \tau_0) - \nu(t - \tau_0 - \Delta)]}_{\text{template}} \, dt. \tag{8}$$

FHSS Analysis. While a FHSS system with Frequency Shift Keying (FSK) was selected for analysis in [23], a more realistic approach is chosen in this paper. For the later analysis GFSK with modulation index $\eta = 0.5$ and a bandwidth time product $BT = 0.5$ is assumed.

For the coverage analysis, we consider limiter-discriminator reception (LD), which is incoherent and thus does not need phase recovery to operate. This makes it suitable for fast FHSS systems and allows packet communication without syncwords [17]. The receiver filter h_r is chosen to be a Gaussian filter and is given by its impulse response in 9. For the following investigations this filter's bandwidth time product $BT = 1$ is assumed.

$$h_r(t) = \sqrt{2} \cdot BT \cdot \exp\left(-2\pi(BT)^2 \cdot t^2\right) \tag{9}$$

The performance of the limiter-discriminator depends on the width of the receiver filters frequency response and the modulation index. The authors in [24–26] have evaluated its performance for FSK in AWGN. The bit error probability sums up from two components.

$$\text{BER} = P_{\text{cont}} + P_{\text{click}} \tag{10}$$

The error probability resulting from clicks P_{click} dominates for low SNR figures, whereas the continuous error probability P_{cont} dominates for high SNR. Since the receiver's filter leads to inter symbol interference, the error probabilities must be averaged over all possible bit sequences $\mathbf{d}$. When the receiver filter's BT is larger than or equal to one, a bit sequence length of three is sufficient. Assuming that every click leads to an error, the error probability resulting from clicks P_{click} is equal to the average number of clicks $\bar{N}$ averaged over all possible bit sequences $\mathbf{d}$ [25]. When Gaussian impulse shaping is applied with a $BT = 0.5$, the length of the sequences $\mathbf{d}$ has to be increased. For the investigated filter chain, an overall sequence length of six symbols is sufficient.

$$P_{\text{click}} = \overline{\bar{N}}^{\mathbf{d}} \tag{11}$$

P_{cont} can be calculated semi-analytically with 12, where $\Delta\varphi$ is the phase difference between two symbols and Ψ is the modulo 2π phase difference between the two symbols that are superposed with correlated complex Gaussian noise [27].

$$P_{\text{cont}} = \overline{\Pr\{\Delta\varphi - \pi \leqslant \Psi \leqslant 0\}}^{\mathbf{d}} \tag{12}$$

Equation 12 can be solved with the help of (20) in [27].

For extended comparison in the system evaluation in Sect. 4.3 we also take FSK with coherent reception (CR) into consideration. As given in [28] in this case the BER is calculated as

$$\mathrm{BER} = \frac{1}{2}\,\mathrm{erfc}\left(\sqrt{\frac{E_b\,(1 - \Re\{\rho\})}{2N_0}}\right),\tag{13}$$

where ρ is the correlation coefficient. For orthogonal signaling, which is given in case of MSK, the correlation coefficient qualifies as $\rho = 0$ [1].

$$\mathrm{BER} = \frac{1}{2}\,\mathrm{erfc}\left(\sqrt{\frac{E_b}{2N_0}}\right)\tag{14}$$

PSSS Analysis. The simulative base band evaluation given in [20] for 31 chips is calculated semi-analytically in this work and extended to a general description for arbitrary m-sequences, on which this paper's evaluation is based. In the following, the derivation is explained shortly. Employing a spreading technique with orthogonal PN-sequences, the BER is calculated by 6, which is equivalent to the BER of a BPSK [28]. Since m-sequences are not orthogonal, a penalty coefficient $\gamma(n, p)$ is defined to adapt the BPSK calculation for PSSS. The cyclic autocorrelation φ of an arbitrary m-sequence is given by

$$\varphi(\tau) = \mathbf{m}_{\to 0}\,\tilde{\otimes}\,\mathbf{m}_{\to 0} = \begin{cases} n, & \tau \bmod n = 0 \\ -1, & \text{otherwise} \end{cases},\ \tau \in \mathbb{Z}\tag{15}$$

The cross correlation yields the maximum at $\tau = i$ respectively, where i denotes the cyclic shift. Thus, superposed cyclically shifted m-sequences influence each other in their maximum value depending on the bit values carried. The effective correlation amplitude in the relevant shift after superposition is further defined as

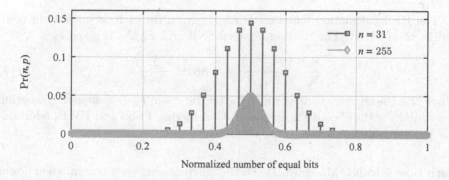

Fig. 5. Distribution of equal data bits in **d** [1].

$$\varphi(\tau = i) = \epsilon(p) \tag{16}$$

and can be calculated with respect to the number of used sequences and the value of all other values in $\mathbf{d}$. Especially the superposition of equal bits in $\mathbf{d}$ is critical, since the correlations' result is degraded due to lacking orthogonality. Assuming a uniform distribution of the bit values in $\mathbf{d}$, a binomial distribution of the number of equal bits p results as shown in Fig. 5. Taking this into account the penalty coefficient can be calculated as

$$\gamma(n,p) = \frac{\epsilon^2(p)}{\overline{\Pr(n,p) \cdot \epsilon^2(p)}^p}. \tag{17}$$

The effective correlation amplitude $\epsilon(p)$ is squared since it influences E_b/N_0 and is normalized by the probability of p equal bits since E_b/N_0 is defined as mean over all bit combinations in $\mathbf{d}$. The BER of PSSS is thus calculated as a function of n as

$$\mathrm{BER} = \overline{\Pr(n,p) \cdot \frac{1}{2} \, \mathrm{erfc} \left(\sqrt{\gamma(n,p) \cdot \frac{E_b}{N_0}} \right)}^p. \tag{18}$$

Caused by the averaging, the slope of the BER curve is not falling monotonically [1].

The BER calculation with multi-tap channels is non-trivial, because due to the non-orthogonality of shifted versions of the m-sequence, the channel taps do not only influence a single sequence, but also all other sequences, depending on their delay and the impulse shaping [29, 30].

4.2   Evaluation Methodology

The presented technologies UWB, FHSS and PSSS are further compared in BER, coverage range and PLR. In this section the evaluation principles are explained shortly.

The BER calculation based on E_b/N_0 is given for each technology in 6, 10 and 18 respectively. The relation between SNR and E_b/N_0 is given as

$$\frac{E_b}{N_0} = \frac{P_{\mathrm{RX}}}{P_{\mathrm{N}}} \frac{1}{B \cdot T} = \mathrm{SNR} \cdot \frac{1}{B \cdot T}, \tag{19}$$

where B is the effective bandwidth, T the bit duration, P_{RX} denotes the reception power and P_{N} the effective noise power. Considering PSSS and UWB, additionally the spreading gain has to be taken into account.

Path Loss Model. Moreover, P_{RX} is the difference between transmission power P_{TX} and path loss a_{dB}:

$$P_{\mathrm{RX}} = P_{\mathrm{TX}} - a_{\mathrm{dB}} = P_{\mathrm{N}} + \mathrm{SNR}_{\mathrm{dB}} \tag{20}$$

Assuming free-space propagation, a_{dB} results as

$$a_{\mathrm{dB}} = -G_{\mathrm{TX}} - G_{\mathrm{RX}} + F + I + 20\log_{10}\left(\frac{4\pi \cdot d \cdot f_c}{c_0}\right), \tag{21}$$

where G_{TX} and G_{TX} denote the antenna gains of transmitter and receiver respectively. F defines the noise figure, and I describes implementation losses. f_c is the carrier frequency and d the distance between transmitter and receiver, which is equivalent to the coverage range.

Finally, 21 can be solved for d, and a_{dB} can be substituted with 20. The coverage range $d_{\mathrm{dB}} = 10\log_{10}\left(\frac{d}{1\mathrm{m}}\right)$ results as

$$d_{\mathrm{dB}} = \frac{1}{2}\left[G_{\mathrm{TX}} + G_{\mathrm{RX}} - F - I + P_{\mathrm{TX}} - \mathrm{SNR}_{\mathrm{dB}} - P_{\mathrm{N}} - 20\log_{10}\left(\frac{f_c}{1\mathrm{GHz}}\right) - 32.44\right]. \tag{22}$$

Industrial Fading Channel. The commonly approved IEEE 802.15.4a UWB channel model is chosen to ensure a realistic model of channel conditions in factory environment [31]. For our analysis we assume all transmissions to have a direct path, as we focus on FA and PA applications. Therefore the CM 7 LOS model is adopted. For a reasonable comparison between AWGN and fading channel, free space propagation model is assumed when the CM 7 model is used.

The fading for the three diverse types of spectrum usage are basically generated in the same matter:

1. Cutting out the 150 MHz wide 5 GHz ISM band or the 499.2 MHz wide UWB channel from the IEEE 802.15.4a UWB model, respectively.
2. Normalizing the cut out transmission function to a mean power of 0 dB.

For UWB we have the desired channel. For PSSS and FHSS the procedure continues with:

3. Cutting out the transmission channels using the receiver filters. For PSSS a raised-cosine window with roll-off factor $r = 0.2$ is used and for FHSS the filter is given in 9.

In our PSSS fading channel simulations we use the resulting transmission channel. For FHSS we assume the FHSS channels to be flat, since the equivalent receiver bandwidth of 1 MHz is small in comparison to the coherence bandwidth of IEEE 802.15.4a CM 7 scenarios. Therefore, the fading is modelled by:

4. *SNR* calculation by using the transmission channel results in an offset for the AWGN model [32].

As suggested, only the best performing 90% of the generated CM 7 realizations are used for evaluation of mean BER and PLR, in order to match reality at best [16].

Packet Loss Rates. For a reasonable system comparison in terms of Packet Loss Rate (PLR), Forward Error Correction (FEC) and physical layer overhead have been neglected for this analysis. The PLR thus is calculated by

$$PLR = 1 - (1 - BER)^{N_{bit}}. \tag{23}$$

where N_{bit} denotes the number of bits per packet.

Since we expect the fading channel to be constant during a packet transmission, 23 is only valid for AWGN. When PLR analysis with the CM 7 channel 24 is applied, where reali corresponds to the number of channel realizations used for the simulation and is set to reali = 100 for all simulation result presented in this paper.

$$PLR = \overline{1 - (1 - BER_{reali})^{N_{bit}}}^{reali} \tag{24}$$

4.3   Evaluation Results and Discussion

In the subsequent section the three suggested systems are compared with each other considering the key requirements for FA resulting from Sect. 2.1. Based on Sect. 4.1, a bit error evaluation is performed for both AWGN and industrial channel. Afterwards the systems are collated in a coverage range comparison for the AWGN channel model, before the results are discussed regarding their suitability for FA.

BER versus SNR. Figure 6 illustrates the BER performance versus E_b/N_0 of the described PHY layer technologies in AWGN. Under the preliminaries described in Sect. 3, the IR-UWB performance is congruent with the performance of binary antipodal signaling. Comparing the considered FHSS reception techniques, we observe the expected performance difference between MSK with coherent reception (CR) and GMSK with limiter discriminator reception (LD). The performance of the FSK reference with CR is congruent with binary orthogonal signaling. In contrast to that, the LD reception loses about 4 dB in the range of practically relevant BERs.

Regarding PSSS demodulation, we observe the influence of the length of the utilized PN-sequence, which is explained in Sect. 4.1. The PSSS 31 system loses about 5 dB compared to antipodal signaling. By increasing the sequence length by a factor of approximately 8 to PSSS 255, this performance loss is reduced to less than 0.5 dB.

In Fig. 7, the abscissa scale is changed to BER versus SNR in order to clarify the effect of the different concepts of frequency spreading. While FHSS spectrum spread effect arises from frequency changes, UWB and PSSS originate their wideband characteristics from impulse or sequential spreading. In order to illustrate the effects of sequential spreading, in Figs. 7 and 8 we assume a user data transmission utilizing only one sequence, while all sequences are in use. This can only occur in PSSS uplink scenarios, where it is possible that more than one transmitter transmits simultaneously. In all other considerations we

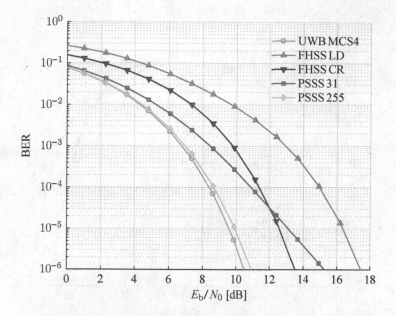

Fig. 6. Bit error rate versus E_b/N_0 for AWGN channel [1].

assume a fully utilized downlink scenario. In Fig. 8 the bit error performance of the suggested technologies in AWGN and industrial channels is compared. 100 realizations of the IEEE 802.15.4 CM 7 LOS model are taken for the baseband simulation for each technology. As mentioned in Sect. 4.2, only the best performing 90% are taken into account for the analysis. The resulting BER curves are averaged in order to get one significant curve for each technology. Due to the chosen evaluation methodology, the individual FHSS channels are flat. The other technologies use Zero Forcing (ZF) for channel distortion correction. Due to better comparison between the technologies, the distortion correction is not chosen optimal and also the FHSS hopping scheme has room for improvement [23]. Due to the influence of the different spectrum usage techniques, the impact of the industrial fading channel varies among the technologies. While UWB suffers from a virtually constant SNR offset of about 10 dB compared to the AWGN performance, the offset to AWGN conditions for FHSS performance is dependent on the desired BER. For very low error rates the performance degradation is basically dependent on the worst performing channel, which corresponds to the deepest fade of the channel. The PSSS spreading concept achieves a kind of averaging of the channel SNR what reduces the impact of the channel fading. Nevertheless, the channel echos lead to interference between the cyclically shifted sequences, resulting in a flatter slope of the averaged BER curve [29,30].

Coverage Range Analysis. In order to determine realistic coverage ranges, a set of reasonable values describing the transmission characteristics has to be

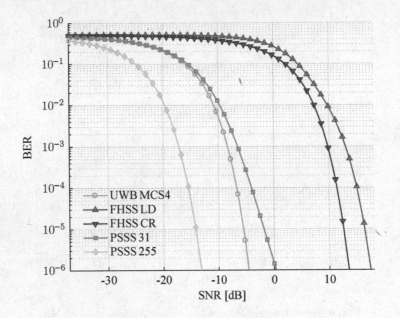

Fig. 7. Bit error rate versus SNR for AWGN channel [1].

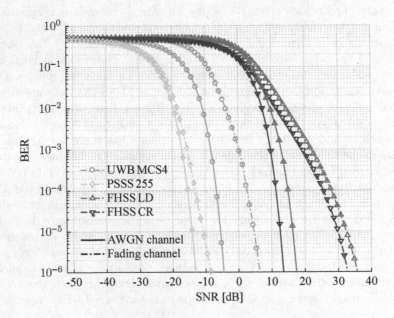

Fig. 8. Bit error rate versus SNR for AWGN and industrial fading conditions in comparison.

chosen. For the three depicted technologies, Table 3 summarizes the parameters used in 20 for reasonable coverage range estimation.

Table 3. Parameters for range calculation.

Parameter	UWB	FHSS	PSSS
f_c	7.9872 GHz	5.825 GHz	5.825 GHz
B	499.2 MHz	1 MHz	20 MHz
P_{TX}	10 dBm	14 dBm	14 dBm
P_N	−86.99 dBm	−113.98 dBm	−100.97 dBm
N_{bit}	60 Byte = 480 Bit		
G_{TX}	0 dBi		
G_{RX}	0 dBi		
F	5 dB		
I	10 dB		

To ensure interoperability with existing communication systems in the 2.4 GHz ISM band, for the FHSS and the PSSS system the 5.8 GHz ISM band is chosen for coverage range analysis, whereas the 7.9872 GHz channel is selected for UWB as defined in Sect. 3.1. For a reasonable system comparison, the system parameters including antenna gains G_{TX} and G_{RX}, noise figure F and implementation losses I, are chosen identically. Nevertheless, the parameters f_c, B and P_{TX} differ among the three technologies.

As a result, Fig. 9 is obtained from 22. As depicted in Fig. 7, the sequential spreading concepts are able to stand harsher SNRs, but certainly suffer from higher P_N (see Table 3). The absolute EIRP transmission power is equal for FHSS and PSSS, but IR-UWB is subject to a regulatory limitation of 0 dBm per 50 MHz bandwidth in the 6 GHz to 8.5 GHz range [33].

In Fig. 10 the BER results from the fading channel simulation are plotted over the distance d, again assuming free space propagation, what is a good approximation for industrial FA fading environments. We observe, that the average BER of the FHSS systems drops below 1% for large distances up to 300 m. This can be explained with the probability of good channels in the hopping sequence. The desired BERs for FA use cases are only reached when the impact of bad channels can be covered by the link margin. The PSSS BERs start to decrease from distances <200 m, but the BER curve stays relatively flat, compared to the AWGN curve, because of interference between the cyclically shifted sequences.

Figure 11 shows the evaluation results for AWGN in terms of PER versus coverage range. The PLR considerations are calculated with 23 and a packet size of 60 Byte, which includes user data, which is up to 30 Byte for FA (see Table 3), packet overhead and FEC overhead. In order to attain a reasonable system comparison without MAC layer evaluation, the packet size is kept the same for all three PHY technologies. Despite that we reserve packet data for

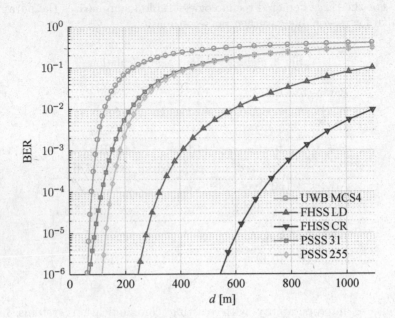

Fig. 9. Bit error rate versus coverage range for AWGN channel [1].

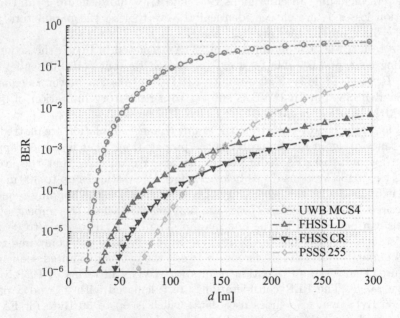

Fig. 10. Bit error rate versus coverage range for industrial fading channel.

FEC, we do not perform any type of FEC in order to retain good comparability in the PLR evaluation.

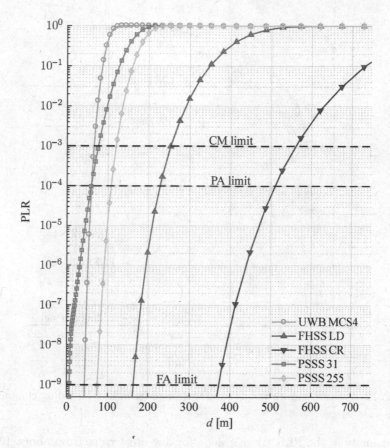

Fig. 11. Packet loss rate versus coverage range for AWGN channel [1].

The PLR results considering the industrial fading channel are presented in Fig. 12. The displayed averaged error rates result from 24, assuming that the fading channel has a constant transfer function for the duration of at least one 60 Byte packet. Since the abscissa scale is changed, the results from Fig. 11 are included as a reference.

In comparison to the AWGN result, the achieved coverage ranges drop dramatically for all probed technologies, when the FA requirements are applied.

Discussion. As displayed in Fig. 11, even under AWGN conditions and assumed free space propagation, the PSSS 31 system does not meet the FA coverage range requirement and turns out as impractical for this application field. Therefore, this system is not considered for analysis with a fading channel environment. The

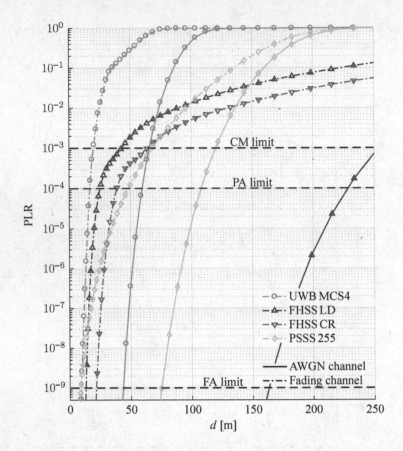

Fig. 12. Packet loss rate versus coverage range for industrial fading channel.

inhomogeneity in the PLR curve's slope for low error rates from about 10^{-7} to 10^{-8} results from the averaging over binomially distributed bits per PSSS symbol as indicated in Sect. 4.1. The PSSS 255 system as well as the UWB system are comparatively low range, but both match the range requirements for FA under ideal free-space conditions. Only with FHSS other communication scenarios are applicable, leading to its higher flexibility.

While the UWB PHY reaches a coverage range of 43 m for a PLR of 10^{-9}, the PSSS 255 system covers up to 75 m and the FHSS LD system up to 156 m. For the determination of the PSSS coverage range it is assumed that all codes are utilized, thus the maximum data rate is available. When the number of utilized codes is reduced, the coverage range for the remaining codes is increased depending on the coding gain factor, which is up to 255 for PSSS 255. Furthermore, the BER degradation coefficient γ is influenced by less concurrent codes (see Sect. 4.1).

Figure 12 shows that all three systems have different capabilities in industrial fading conditions, but when the FA requirements are applied, the systems' performances are close together and none of the systems achieves coverage ranges of more than 25 m. Considering these coverage ranges we have to factor in that no FEC was applied and neither the used hopping scheme, nor the distortion correction were chosen optimal.

As depicted in Sect. 3.4 the considered systems vary in their parameters and so does the link data rate. Regarding the latency requirements, the achieved data rate is vital. FHSS and UWB have a fixed channel data rate, which is equal to the link data rate. In contrast to that, the PSSS system can adapt the channel data rate dependent on the specific application data rate. For FHSS the fixed channel data rate can only be adapted in restricted limits by parallel reception on multiple FHSS frequencies as realized for WSAN [13]. In case of UWB, cycle times for scenarios with large numbers of connected nodes are high, since the UWB system is dependent on Time Division Multiple Access (TDMA) for serving multiple clients in a star topology [16]. For media access in a FHSS system, besides TDMA, a Frequency Division Multiple Access (FDMA) channel access scheme with advanced transceiver concepts is possible. But on the other hand, this abrogates the advantage of simple transceivers. With PSSS, a combination with Code Division Multiple Access (CDMA) is possible, allowing very low latencies and novel and flexible resource management strategies, which are currently being investigated.

5   Conclusion

In this paper, constraints of industrial applications have been discussed. Focusing on deriving KPIs for evaluation of wireless technologies, these constraints were categorized by vital requirements and applications were sorted by their field of application into FA, PA and CM. Focusing on FA, the performances of IR-UWB, FHSS and PSSS physical layers were analyzed. Regulatory aspects were introduced and taken into consideration for the systems' analysis and comparison with realistic reception concepts in AWGN and IEEE 802.15.4 CM 7 industrial fading channels [31]. The systems were discussed considering delay and reliability requirements and their potential with respect to appropriate medium access strategies was outlined.

The system analysis includes evaluation results for AWGN, that have already been discussed in [1], and industrial fading channel conditions. Since we made non-optimal assumptions regarding channel distortion in favor of a good comparability, advanced analyses regarding FEC and receiver concepts including delay models have to be performed separately for each technology. In this paper we neglected the aspect of both inter- and intra-system-coexistence. But with rising numbers of nodes and non proprietary frequency bands, a coexistence analysis will contribute a vital piece on the feasibility of the presented PHY concepts.

Acknowledgements. Part of the research leading to these results has received funding from the German Federal Ministry of Education and Research under grant agreement no. 16KIS0223 also referred to as ParSec, as well as under grant agreement no. 16BU1222 also referred to as KUSZ.

References

1. Wulf, A., Underberg, L., Kays, R.: Coverage range analysis of wireless technologies for industrial automation - system overview and performance evaluation. In: Proceedings of the 13th International Joint Conference on e-Business and Telecommunications, vol. 6, pp. 74–83. WINSYS (2016)
2. ETSI: TR 102 889-2 V1.1.1, Electromagnetic compatibility and Radio spectrum Matters (ERM); System Reference Document; Short Range Devices (SRD); Part 2: Technical characteristics for SRD equipment for wireless industrial applications using technologies different from Ultra-Wide Band (UWB). Technical report, European Telecommunications Standards Institute (2011)
3. ZVEI: Coexistence of Wireless Systems in Automation Technology - Explanations on reliable parallel operation of wireless radio solutions. Technical report, ZVEI - German Electrical and Electronics Manufacturers' Association, Automation Division (2009)
4. VDI/VDE: VDI/VDE Guideline 2185: Radio Based Communication in Industrial Automation. Technical report, VDI Association of German Engineers, VDE Association for Electrical, Electronic & Information Technologies (2007)
5. Güngör, V.Ç., Hancke, G.P.: Industrial Wireless Sensor Networks: Applications Protocols and Standards. CRC Press, Boca Raton (2013)
6. Frotzscher, A., Wetzker, U., Bauer, M., Rentschler, M., Beyer, M., Elspass, S., Klessig, H.: Requirements and current solutions of wireless communication in industrial automation. In: 2014 IEEE International Conference on Communications Workshops (ICC), pp. 67–72 (2014)
7. Holfeld, B., Wieruch, D., Wirth, T., Thiele, L., Ashraf, S.A., Huschke, J., Aktas, I., Ansari, J.: Wireless communication for factory automation: an opportunity for LTE and 5G systems. IEEE Commun. Mag. 54, 36–43 (2016)
8. ETSI: EN 300 440-1 V1.6.1, Electromagnetic compatibility and Radio spectrum Matters (ERM); Short range devices; Radio equipment to be used in the 1 GHz to 40 GHz frequency range; Part 1: Technical characteristics and test methods (2010)
9. FCC: CFR Title 47: Telecommunication, Part 15, Subpart C - Intentional Radiators (2016)
10. IEEE: IEEE Std 802.15.4-2011, IEEE Standard for Local and metropolitan area networks, Part 15.4: Low-Rate Wireless Personal Area Networks (2011)
11. Aust, S., Prasad, R.V., Niemegeers, I.G.M.M.: Outdoor long-range WLANs: a lesson for IEEE 802.11ah. IEEE Commun. Surv. Tutor. 17, 1761–1775 (2015)
12. ZigBee Alliance: ZigBee Specification, Document 053474r20 (2012)
13. PNO: WSAN air interface specification technical specification, version 1.0 (2012)
14. IEC: 62591 Ed. 1.0: Industrial communication networks - wireless communication network and communication profiles - WirelessHART (2010)
15. Reinhold, R., Underberg, L., Wulf, A., Kays, R.: Industrial WSN based on IR-UWB and a low-latency MAC protocol. Frequenz 70, 339–352 (2016)
16. Reinhold, R.: Concepts for Reliable and Time-Critical Industrial Communication Based on IR-UWB Systems. Prof. Dr.-Ing. Rüdiger Kays, Dortmund, Dortmunder Beiträge zur Kommunikationstechnik (2016)
17. Bluetooth SIG: Bluetooth specification version 4.2 (2014)
18. IEEE: IEEE Std 802.15.1-2005, IEEE Standard for Information technolog - Local and metropolitan area networks - Specific requirements - Part 15.1a: Wireless Medium Access Control (MAC) and Physical Layer (PHY) specifications for Wireless Personal Area Networks (WPA) (2005)

19. Wolf, A.: Verfahren zum Übertragen eines Datenworts, document DE 103 01 250 A1 (2004)
20. Schwetlick, H., Wolf, A.: PSSS - parallel sequence spread spectrum a physical layer for RF communication. In: 2004 IEEE International Symposium on Consumer Electronics, pp. 262–265 (2004)
21. KrishneGowda, K., Messinger, T., Wolf, A.C., Kraemer, R., Kallfass, I., Scheytt, J.C.: Towards 100 Gbps wireless communication in THz band with PSSS modulation: a promising hardware in the loop experiment. In: 2015 IEEE International Conference on Ubiquitous Wireless Broadband (ICUWB), pp. 1–5 (2015)
22. Ge, L., Yue, G., Affes, S.: On the BER performance of pulse-position-modulation UWB radio in multipath channels. In: 2002 IEEE Conference on Ultra Wideband Systems and Technologies, UWBST 2002 - Digest of Papers, pp. 231–234 (2002)
23. Reinhold, R., Schaefer, F., Kays, R.: Performance evaluation of an enhanced frequency hopping transceiver in 5 GHz band for wireless sensor networks. In: 2013 Tenth International Symposium on Wireless Communication Systems, pp. 823–827 (2013)
24. Cartier, D.E.: Limiter-discriminator detection performance of manchester and NRZ coded FSK. IEEE Trans. Aerosp. Electron. Syst. **AES–13**, 62–70 (1977)
25. Simon, M.K., Wang, C.C.: Differential versus limiter-discriminator detection of narrow-band FM. IEEE Trans. Commun. **31**, 1227–1234 (1983)
26. Pawula, R.F.: Refinements to the theory of error rates for narrow-band digital FM. IEEE Trans. Commun. **36**, 509–513 (1988)
27. Pawula, R.F.: Distribution of the phase angle between two vectors perturbed by Gaussian noise II. IEEE Trans. Veh. Technol. **50**, 576–583 (2001)
28. Proakis, J.G., Salehi, M.: Digital Communications, 5th edn. McGraw-Hill, New York (2008)
29. Croonenbroeck, R., Wulf, A., Underberg, L., Endemann, W., Kays, R.: Parallel sequence spread spectrum : bit error performance under industrial channel conditions. In: Proceedings of 19th International Conference on OFDM and Frequency Domain Techniques, ICOF 2016, pp. 70–76 (2016)
30. Underberg, L., Wulf, A., Croonenbroeck, R., Endemann, W., Kays, R.: Parallel sequence spread spectrum : analytical and simulative approach for determination of bit error probability. In: 2016 IEEE 21st International Conference on Emerging Technologies and Factory Automation (ETFA), pp. 1–8 (2016)
31. Molisch, A.F., Balakrishnan, K., Cassioli, D., Chong, C.C., Emami, S., Fort, A., Karedal, J., Kunisch, J., Schantz, H., Schuster, U., Siwiak, K.: IEEE 802.15.4a Channel Model - Final Report. IEEE P802 15, pp. 1–40 (2004)
32. Wulf, A., Underberg, L., Kays, R.: Adaptive frequency hopping communication for factory automation. In: Proceedings of 19th International Conference on OFDM and Frequency Domain Techniques, ICOF 2016, pp. 1–8 (2016)
33. ETSI: EN 302 065-1 V1.3.1, Electromagnetic compatibility and Radio spectrum Matters (ERM); Short Range Devices (SRD) using Ultra Wide Band technology (UWB) for communications purposes; Harmonized EN covering the essential requirements of article 3.2 of the R&TT directive; part 1: Common technical requirements (2013)

Author Index

Printed in the United States
by Bookmasters

Printed in the United States
By Bookmasters